THE EVER-FLOWING STREAM

THE EVER-FLOWING STREAM

The National Library of Poetry

Melisa S. Mitchell, Editor

The Ever-Flowing Stream

Library of Congress
Cataloging in Publication Data

ISBN 1-57553-571-8

Proudly manufactured in The United States of America by
Watermark Press
One Poetry Plaza
Owings Mills, MD 21117

FOREWORD

Throughout life, we store information collected from experiences and try in some way to make sense of it. When we are not able to fully understand the things which occur in our lives, we often externalize the information. By doing this, we are afforded a different perspective, thus allowing us to think more clearly about difficult or perplexing events and emotions. Art is one of the ways in which people choose to externalize their thoughts.

Within the arts, modes of expression differ, but poetry is a very powerful tool by which people can share sometimes confusing, sometimes perfectly clear concepts and feelings with others. Intentions can run the gamut as well: the artists may simply want to share something that has touched their lives in some way, or they may want to get help to allay anxiety or uncertainty. The poetry within *The Ever-Flowing Stream* is from every point on the spectrum: every topic, every intention, every event or emotion imaginable. Some poems will speak to certain readers more than others, but it is always important to keep in mind that each verse is the voice of a poet, of a mind which needs to make sense of this world, of a heart which feels the effects of every moment in this life, and perhaps of a memory which is striving to surface. Nonetheless, recalling our yesterdays gives birth to our many forms of expression.

Melisa S. Mitchell
Editor

Editor's Note

Traditionally, lying has its place. In taverns, in pubs, and in other public gathering places, groups called "liar's clubs" meet, exchanging tall tales, weaving yarns, boasting about whatever seems boast-worthy. It is in these situations that "fish tales" often begin: One member of the group mentions a particularly remarkable achievement, then another member will share a story, exaggerating the details to impress his or her companions. These stories have often carried over from an oral, folk tradition into literature. Washington Irving and Mark Twain are among the most well-known authors who made literary use of the tall tale.

It is a common stereotype that the Irish are merry drinkers, oftentimes willingly embellishing the truth, telling their tall tales to their friends in bars over a pint of beer. This stereotype perhaps comes from the penchant for people to boast about having done what is taboo. Possibly one of the most common sins about which to boast is one that might be considered severe according to one's religion. For many Christians, sexual intercourse out of wedlock is among the most dire transgressions; it is regarded as a mortal sin, resulting in severe punishment in the afterlife. Unfortunately, the establishment of any taboo makes the wrongdoing more tempting for some. Because of a lasting double-standard, this particular sin is looked upon with more scorn when committed by a woman than by a man. For this reason, though many might not submit to temptation, men tell exaggerated tales in public meeting places, especially in bars, to impress their friends. This lying about having committed an egregious sin and the struggle against temptation has been dealt with in literature for ages. For example, twentieth-century Irish poet Patrick Kavanagh, in his poem "The Great Hunger," alludes precisely to this situation:

> *And there would be girls siting on the grass banks of lanes.*
> *Stretch-legged and lingering staring—*
> *A man might take one of them if he had the courage.*
> *But 'No' was in every sentence of their story*
> *Except when the public-house came in and shouted its piece.*

The temptation exists, though to try would do no good—the girls are bound by what they've been taught: to say "No." When the men enter bars, however, their stories tend to be embellished with half-truths and whole lies. Because of this inclination to brag, as in L. Giannico's poem "(One Night) In Shannon's Bed," the reputation of an innocent girl can become unnecessarily tarnished.

> *"You made me stray from venial, Shannon lass,"*
> *I said the night your laugh like legs in strut*
> *marched me to cliffs of green and back.*

In this first stanza, Giannico presents the embodiment of the persona's temptation—Shannon— whose mere presence entices him to overstep pardonable, or venial, sin into something more severe. Even her laugh is provocation: It is almost parading playfully before him, a reminder of something that he cannot possess. She seems to indulge him to a certain point, taking him to the edge of sin and back. This return from the edge of the "cliffs of green," though, implies that no actual, *mortal* sin occurred; he merely "stray[ed]."

The mention later in the poem of "Catholic boys who dressed / in anxious wait for Catholic girls" spells out the religious influence in the poem. The girls "lie / in knee-socked truth"; they are innocent, but they flirt superficially with the boys, teasing them with harmless lies. They know that the boys will not attempt to cross the religion-established boundaries, nor would they allow the boys to do so, because of the ramifications.

Still, despite the unbridgeable physical breach between Shannon and the persona, he is haunted by her presence, finding "ticket stubs in relic vests / from four-starred movie, eastered past." He finds signs of her from their happy times together, and each fragment symbolically resurrects their relationship, his "lost cinema."

Finally, seeming to be frustrated by the innocence of his relationship with Shannon, the persona brags the contrary to his friends in the bar:

> . . . *Our irished boasts ran fast*
> *with cold-draught toasts, then rushed along to catechismed*
> *pride. You clash with canons massed*
> *these long, goodfriday years. . . .*

Despite his boasting, the persona is still aware of the truth, and that being with Shannon tempts him to sin. These feelings run counter to what for his whole life he has been taught is good and proper. Perhaps because of this conflict within himself, he decides to tell Shannon about his lies:

> . . . *Cut glass*
> *you splintered, rapture likened to a sin, but*
> . . . .
> . . . *Eyes mute in that*
> *Last-rite, you went, sham rocked and rent . . .*

The lie, or "sham," destroys both her reputation and her feelings. The words "sham rocked" also create a pun on the word "shamrock," an allusion to Ireland. This is perhaps used to reinforce the religious influence, as Ireland is predominantly Catholic. In the end, the persona is duly remorseful for the effect his lies have upon Shannon: ". . . I retreat confessed and locked in lent." He has confessed his lying to her, and he is still penitent for his actual sin, though he clearly does not repent his imagined one.

Throughout his poem, Giannico uses unique treatment of a universal experience, colorful language, and remarkable images to create a nearly flawless sonnet. This traditional form is quite difficult to execute, particularly with the admirable creativity seen in this poem. For these reasons, L. Giannico has been awarded the Grand Prize for the contest held in conjunction with **The Ever-Flowing Stream.**

Another poem that illustrates the interpersonal conflict that can be caused by thoughtless words is Alexander Pepple's "Restless Tongue." Pepple depicts a dumb-struck persona who is frustrated by a conflict with a woman and her "fast and lettered tongue."

Because of the woman's sharp tongue darting out toward his "handsome quiet ear," his own thoughts are "[s]tuck in flicker, in this throttling cove / (Under the sluggard grips of ebbing vows)." The word "vows" indicates that this argument results from the breakup of a marriage, or at least of a committed relationship. Under the weight of the crumbling relationship, the persona's hopes of a fruitful and long-lasting connection—"the rumble of man and woman towards time"—are also destroyed. Instead, he is left with "Yesterday's dreams . . . / Of a coasting, ever-chosen, cherished past."

In the end, nothing is resolved. The persona still helplessly listens to the woman's verbal attacks: "To her, the rippling, laid-back ear must cock." He is left feeling perpetually restless and uneasy; he is "[a]wash in the waves tugging on to action / In the swelling tides of recursion."

Stephen Koehler depicts another restless situation in his poem "Cherry Street." In this instance, instead of being a moment of personal inquietude, the persona describes the daily tumult of the activity on the street and sidewalk in this snapshot of city life.

The poet creates a series of very specific images, each describing a portion of the whole scene. Each image is full of motion, creating a backdrop for the persona's "people watching" that is both dynamic and ever-changing. The whole cityscape is described as a "painted maelstrom," evoking images of swirling and disordered graffiti, full of sounds that are both separate and combined in a city-symphony. The persona pays careful attention to each group of people: those in suits on their way to work ("pinstriped arrogance"), those who are homeless or dressed in an eye-catching way ("a brazen motif"), those who are deep in discussion ("conversations walking by / with tension in their eyes"), and those quietly sitting in their cars watching the others ("serene, not needing to impress / content to observe"). All of these very different groups combine to create "strides complementing complete difference."

The motion of each element of the scene is also discussed in unique detail: The people walking down the sidewalks are a "river moan[ing] in abrasive motion"; the steel of the cars is "mak[ing] friction with its face"; the trash on the curb is "paper performing circus humor." Despite the complementary nature of the elements, they are also discordant; "they never connect." Each part of the scene exists singly, despite its being surrounded by all of the other elements; the elements combine like an emulsion, each discrete element remaining separate from the next. "Cherry Street" is an excellent illustration of separation and alienation within a crowded city.

In "Bardless Wonders," Stephen Elder discusses another type of alienation within our busy, technologically-advanced society. Television, the prevalent medium of news dissemination in the latter part of the twentieth century, has eliminated the roles of historians in the modern world. In the past there were bards, musicians who memorized the historical events of their villages and traveled around recounting them to other villages. Later, this oral story-telling tradition was written down. Now, these latter-day historians who spent their lives recording the events of the day and of the times before have been rendered obsolete by the advent of visual media:

> . . . *unsouled entities*
> *unembodied photons at six with film to follow at eleven*
> . . . .
> *numbers, numbers, numbers, digits, ciphers*
> *who can sing of quality when quantity is what we are*

Instead of a bard, touting the greatness of the acts of men, visual media present story after story of the everyday. What once was unique, powerful, special, is now commonplace and unremarkable due to sheer overexposure to events and ideas:

> *the peaks of our accomplishments*
> *ground down*
> *to plains of mediocrity by our weight*
>
> *glorious lays of valor and derring-do cannot be heard*
> *above the susurrus of billions*

Later in the poem, Elder appropriately refers to Malthus, an early nineteenth-century economist, who argued that if neither nature nor destructive human means (such as war) intervene, the human population will continue to increase beyond its means. The persona suggests, then, that each person is one member of such a large group that the individual is no longer significant. There are so many people now that not only have we outgrown the ability to note the tiny details that render each of us unique, but we will soon outgrow our planet and its resources altogether and will no longer be able to survive as a species. Though providing nothing specific, Elder notes that "we need a swift solution to us," to all that we've done, "lest that peerless / prognosticating possum / be proven right." Our general reaction to our collective actions is summed up well by one particular line from the poem: "what's the difference?" Our individual deeds, no matter how good or bad, are preserved solely by television and other such media; our personal contributions will most likely not be seen in history books, nor heard in narratives sung by bards. We are the "Bardless Wonders," fumbling through time, each of us an insignificant member of the whispering billions.

These are just a few of the many remarkable works contained within *The Ever-Flowing Stream*. Among the many others there are certain unique works that deserve careful attention. Share in Jason Grimste's cynical look at "The American Dream" (p. 10). Indulge in your memories of growing up with Phyllis A. Leach in her "Reflections of Childhood" (p. 13) and with Amanda Price in "Plumeria Kingdom" (p. 9). Experience David A. Townsend's disturbing account of the loss of someone close to him in his untitled poem (p. 4). Feel the strong emotions expressed by Emily Stone in "Picker" (p. 10). Watch in quiet awe with Daniel Calamuci in his poem, "For the Old Man at ABC No Rio" (p. 11). Finally, "seize the day" with Francis S. Smith in "Auld Lang Syne" (p. 9). Congratulations to all of the poets appearing in this anthology.

I would like to thank the staff members of The National Library of Poetry, without whom this book would not have been possible. Judges, editors, associate editors, customer service representatives, data entry personnel, graphic artists, office administrators and administrative services staff have all made invaluable contributions to this effort. I am *grateful* to them for their contributions and support.

Melisa S. Mitchell
Editor

Cover Art: Carolynn Redwine Geer

Grand Prize Winner

L. Giannico / New Smyrna Beach FL

Second Prize Winners

Daniel Calamuci / Brooklyn NY
Stephen Elder / Pittsboro NC
Jason Grimste / Sarastoa FL
Stephen Koehler / Green Bay WI
Phyllis Leach / Ft. Worth TX

Alexander Pepple / San Jose CA
Amanda Price / Bethany OK
Francis Smith / Emmitsburg MD
Emily Stone / Decatur GA
David Townsend / Ocean Grove NJ

Third Prize Winners

Eliza Anderson / Paris MI
Bruce Antrim / Pacific MO
Caroline Bassett / Minneapolis MN
Yseult Bayard / New York NY
Lee Berkson / Wilmette IL
Sidney Blake / Indianapolis IN
Ellen Bowers / Kansas MO
Lanre A. Brown / Detroit MI
Charlie Burnett / Carolina Beach NC
Barbara Burwell / Perkasie PA
Marti Buscaglia / Costa Mesa CA
Robert Chancellor / Phoenix AZ
George Chidester / Kent WA
Wilbur Childs / West Falls NY
Marianne Connor / Willow Grove PA
Russ Couch / Scottsdale AZ
Renee Coville / Scotia NY
Mary Crudup / Covington GA
Mark Decker / Lakewood CO
Ted Donaldson / Los Angeles CA
John Ennis / Evanston IL
Desmond Fairbairn / Laconia NH
Amber Fields / Miami FL
Jean Grau / New Orleans LA
Drew Griffiths / Cranbury NJ
J. René Guerrero / Dallas TX
Harry Haigh / Queensbury NY
Mark Heisey / Lexington OK
Michael Igoe / Boston MA
Eric Jackson / Carmel IN

Laura Jarrett / Anchorage AK
Judith Kalinowski / South Milwaukee WI
Aroon Karunamurthy / Roselle IL
Van Der Aa Keeffe / Albuquerque NM
Anne Venables Kyrke / New York NY
D. Lottes / Monticello IN
Jody Martinson / Gig Harbor WA
Hesse McGraw / Olathe KS
David McMillen / Chicago IL
Victor Murphy / San Francisco CA
Moira Pascale / New Haven CT
Liz Peyser / Wichita KS
John Pole / Gainesville FL
Elizabeth Richardson / Albuquerque NM
Margaret Rinkel / Mahomet IL
Robert / Rohnert Park CA
Raymond Rossi / Frankfort IL
Pepper Sbarbaro / Berkeley CA
Robby Schlayer / Santee CA
Olivia Seaton / Rapid City SD
David Sobel / Berkeley CA
Thomas Staley-Trull / Greensboro NC
H. James Stewart / Salt Lake City UT
Jack Tootell / Santa Rosa CA
Edward Turner / Newport Beach CA
Karen Villesvik / Charlotte VIRGIN ISLANDS
Catherine Waddle / Kailua-Kona HI
Craig Watson / Cardiff CA
Sophia Zimmerman / Georgetown TX

Congratulations also to all semi-finalists.

Grand Prize Winner

(One Night) In Shannon's Bed

"You made me stray from venial, Shannon lass,"
I said the night your laugh like legs in strut
marched me to the cliffs of green and back. Cut glass,
you splintered, rapture likened to a sin, but

You haunt like ticket stubs in relic vests
from four-starred movie, eastered past. My
lost cinema. We Catholic boys who dressed
in anxious wait for Catholic girls who'd lie

In knee-socked truth. Our irished boasts ran fast
with cold-draught toasts, then rushed along to catechismed
pride. You clash with canons massed
these long, goodfriday years. Eyes mute in that

Last-rite, you went, sham rocked and rent,
as I retreat confessed and locked in lent.

L. Giannico

Pumpkin Patch

It plumped a pumpkin for October
during August
whose nights were slashed
by invisible shafts of sin
that ricocheted
off the pious waters of the symbiotic pond
on whose granite shore
a transfiguration gown
melted in cold sweat
on the fevered corpulence of Halloween.

Some frosty April equation
for the power of impotence
which on detonation
mushroomed
to philosophical heights
in whose turbulent dimensions
nuggets of acid
bulged the pockets of converts
who washed dust from their skulls
in the muddy water of the pernicious valley.

Wilbur J. Childs

On an Elegy for the Flute

for Robert Taylor

How am I to praise this music
Fevered into time of a three-day passion?

I listen, but I cannot praise.

For me, you said, yet as much for you:
Eight years lay of silence from your father's death to mine,
The numbed unthinking stare out into the garden,
To the eyes that cannot see as the notes leap unwombed:
All comes outward now in the tribute doubly paid.

And yet, I cannot praise
This gift neither mine nor yours,
The flute's ancient cry that seized
With the quickness of a father's death,
But praise only (with all I have for speech)
The obsessed hands and the anguished heart.

I listen
                and hear
                                your self
                                                impaled   by the crossing
                sounds

Ted Donaldson

Damselfly

Your skin bursts wide upon the dock-post's side,
While blood-filled wings and abdomen extend,
Creating your new form, as you perform
These steps to which, instinctively, you tend.
Your lace-veined wings must dry before you fly.
This last, miraculous phase before you leave,
To mate, lay eggs, then quickly die . . . I grieve.
Too brief a life, my beautiful damselfly !

Unlike the transformation of damselfly,
Occurring in the evening of her life,
My metamorphosis was in the womb.
Unmindful of this miracle did I lie,
Protected from life's ravages and strife,
In physical birth I left this bodily tomb.
And if, from birth to death, I nourish my soul,
Its metamorphosis enriched by me,
As damselfly escapes her shell-like hearse,
So I, my final transformation whole,
From physical constraints shall ever be free,
To fly the endless boundaries of the universe.

Harry Haigh

Wedding of Jasmine and Wool

Thin threads so few and far almost bound my mind to earth.
Tenuously abandoned worries vanish as if a self-smoked screen.
Spun wool simplifies concepts for one too carefree, as me.
Planting myself before my loom then proceeding to weave,
I grasp at elusive rainbowed weft, wend it round taut warp,
Encircling the woof of life to claim my brain's redoubt.

In and out, back and forth, telescoping time to deliver
Absolution from errant thoughts now resolved, now sublimed.
Jasmine fragrance borne on sea-breeze blankets wool and me,
Blowing in blessings twixt every woven pixel of colored fuzziness.
Now bestow a dowry for the yarns slipping between flying fingers
Softly, wedding the wools in my tapestry, forever there we linger.

Craig Watson

Papyri

Why sacrifice the victim virgin tree,
The lame log idol of the idle thought,
To sanctify a simpered sophistry
That lisps its ethos through thin dash and jot?

Why offer up some black of dark blue blood
In mystic rites of writhing rights and wrongs,
Asperging reams and rabble with a flood
That dubs dead relics "living hymns and songs,"

While thuribles and censors fume and stink
In wisps which join the greater synergy
Of throngs that wait beyond tomorrow's brink,

Who may, one day, have cause to pause and think,
Not of our fossil angst and energy,
But of our wasted paper's wounds of ink?

Robert Chancellor

Montmartre by Morning

At the morning edge of Montmartre,
Scintillating peace. No traffic
Flows, just starched and nodding neighbors
Knee deep in summer, wending their ways
to mass, to market, to morning tea
Past fresh stucco dwellings, open
Wrought-iron gates, and sentinel trees
Leaning tall against the gold-tipped
Day. Vibrant as plucked harp strings
They blend and thrum in the morning mist,
These artless players attuned to life.
No hint of discord, want to design
In this pale-gold pastoral setting
At the morning edge of Montmartre.

Margaret Rinkel

The Hush Between Us

She was dozing in the chair beside me,
Resting easy, sure of me,
Sharing veneration, even unaware—
Always, there had been a hush between us,
Silent, sparking awe of potent presence.

She was much too tired to notice
When I went to gather in the garden tools.
Light rain had started.

When I came back,
I couldn't feel her presence
And the hush had drowned in thunder.
My throat was dry and hard.
I went to get some water and I couldn't drink.

I always thought we'd go together,
Lying together some cold night,
Arms around each other.

Jean E. Grau

The Wedding Waltz

Seconds as round as lustrous pearls
Descend into the scented air
Moments before a sweep of swirls
Ensnarl them in a winding flare.

As streams of feeling chart their course
In the ribbons of their circles
They glide towards a mystic force
Vaulted over skies of dazzles.

Their word-guests in full libation
Send waves of expression
For prompting sense and abstraction
To crest into infinity.

From a new angle of vision
They enter into the spirit
Of a sacred destination
Higher than their bounded orbit.

All conspire in time to align
In pure poetic unity
As pen and page at an incline
Waltz instinct 'round creativity.

       Yseult Bayard

Discipline

The skeptic distances himself from reality
At least two arms length or his teeth will fall out,
deeming him restless, unable to complain or express his dismay
at home he domineers his dark room
piloting a table,
burning beady bullet holes in his checkbook
with his magnifying mind,
browsed in a stray dream,
concerned only in the flower grass happenings of the sky
This meditating is liability,
beset holy upon a masked man he denies
with casual "we told you's" and
quick to please answering machine replies
He's been hammering down needs with stone birds
and he lives behind the weeds among the herd,
in the cardboard tribe

       Robby Schlayer

The Past Is Never Far Away

They say you can't go home again.
Well, at least I know I've tried.
Only papered walls bear witness
to old secrets locked inside.

I pause 'neath antique photographs
peering down through gilded frames.
The eyes show age and wrinkle,
yet I still recall their names.

I climb the creaking staircase
now facing barren rooms above.
Old memories linger in shadows there,
like the after-shave of a long lost love.

The past is never far away
from the complex life you lead.
All the falling down and dusting off
lend experiences you'll need.

So, tap the wealth of childhood schemes
weighing carefully the paths you pick.
Use the past and present as your guide
building new dreams brick by brick.

       Judith A. Kalinowski

Contrasts

celebrate 50 years, d-day 1994,
armadas from the past, steel shadows prowling ancient waters,
kissing beaches lined by ocean mist,
the Savior arrives, Hitler roars in protest
a chorus falling upon deaf ears,
tell me, do floating bodies remember?

and, oh, Vietnam, emerald rice paddies and
whirling blades, phantoms darting through the night as
trails of orange death drift across a sickened land,
our souls lost in the process,
tell me, who will save us?

too late we honor the women,
nurses who held us through darkest of memories,
memories repeating, repeating,
tell me, who is the Savior, and who is Hitler?

finally, a nation's conscience visible, naked against
the stark, black, ebony wall, above, the red white and blue
waves "glory be" . . . to the stillness of taps,
silent as the names etched in stone,
tell me, we remember our dead, don't we?

       Pepper Sbarbaro

Restless Tongue

She wears a tangled halo of tempered gold
In her breezy, telling wake from cold.
Then, flashing by the handsome quiet ear,

A fast and lettered tongue darts out quick,
Rising to a crescendo, it's growing thick.
Stuck in flicker, in this throttling cove

(Under the sluggard grips of ebbing vows)
Is the rumble of man and woman towards time,
Yesterday's dreams echoed on shrunken dime,

The stow-away journey from the embers
Of a coasting, ever-chosen, cherished past
As tomorrow's yet unspoken fears loom fast.

It is the pounding of the labored hearts—
Drenched in a barren dream garden of rocks
Just riding restless alien shores run amok.

To her, the rippling, laid-back ear must cock
(Awash in waves tugging on to action
In the swelling tides of recursion).

       Alexander Pepple

Untitled

Waiting, pensive for the sun
Sunday paper ink, not yet dry
I have the red bandana you borrowed
still smelling of Mexico,
of Heaven and now,
Scented for death
Crystal wrists of yours:
smashed against the Chicago skyline

Waiting, pensive for the ambulance
I have tasted the strychnine on your lips;
mixed masterfully with peyote and Maybelline
Walked the desert behind your eyes
Parched and burned, emerging into this lightless dawn
Gently pressing a bandana to my face

       David A. Townsend

Bardless Wonders

who sings of these our deeds save unsouled entities
unembodied photons at six with film to follow at eleven
providing our ennui will freeze us
to our couches like tubers
or tumors
what's the difference

numbers, numbers, numbers, digits, ciphers
who can sing of quality when quantity is what we are
the peaks of our accomplishments
ground down
to plains of mediocrity by our weight

glorious lays of valor and derring-do cannot be heard
above the susurrus of billions
and were it possible
who would voice them to us
malthus maybe

we need a swift solution to us
lest that peerless
prognosticating possum
be proven right

Stephen Elder

Complaints From the Vatican

Its umbilical cord severed, cut by
a snap of wind
The helpless disciple fluttering
about the cruel earth scraping
its tender yellow flesh against
the stiff and coarse concrete
The stem sparks red flames of
flustered anger at the base of
its spine while its brethren shake
like preachers precariously hung
by a stalk of wavering
faith.

Drew Griffiths

Vacation Memoir

My father always sang as he drove,
and I would echo after out of tune.
My mother held the map and wove
the road from printed lines and runes.
My elder sister, clever, like a tailored glove
invented "auto sports" which we all strove to win,
except my brother who dove like a buffoon in
and out of windows to catch out-of-state tags and flies of
rare beauty which dutifully he displayed to his 4 sisters for free.
Barbara and Sandy, weighed 80 pounds together, made wise
wondrous eyes at those flies.
That past now shattered haunts my dreams in code:
the songs, the games, the map, the flies, the road.

Sophia Zimmerman

My Mother Was a Whore

the roads were flat and
straight out of there
she took a greyhound then a maverick
and left her clothes in colorado springs

the pup-n-taco sign spins and
shines beneath the western moon mountains
she gets tired of the same burrito night
after night

kansas is part tense and
the rent is due

Karen Villesvik

Muse II

I know a great ship of a woman
sloop-shouldered and spume-white
tossed hair crested to the waves
tundra of her inferno longitude,
not far enough too far, she hoists
buccaneer flag, sails secret sea garden,
drifts through glass, through sunspots,
thin hands tinged pink as flamingos, stretching
vast canvas, the incredible paint she steers.
Her castaway smile shifts an imaginary Marlboro,
the blue smoke she would blow circling my soul.
What does she say? I slam my word processor,
hunch over a cheap cigar, let the gray smoke
reek and billow, and the great white wings of her armada
fold me in. Oh—she fades, she fades,
redraws her boundary eyes flashing crimson
flesh fiercer than I eat for breakfast
and I sip my chamomile tea, nibble
at my millet toast, my lip not enough to bite.
"I know," she would echo.

Lee Berkson

Memorial River

Large smooth stones bake on the river's edge,
While mossy tongued shore puckers soft mud lips,
To lap at our bare ankles and canvas feet,
Damp nylon vests cool and cling,
As the dented metal sends humid rays,
Bouncing and playing through lazy camp smoke,
Water and sand hush and berate,
Beer-filled keels and voices,
While unseen cicadas electrify treetops,
Of deep green waving over spring fed blue,

Passing through pockets of stranded canoes,
Smells of grilling food, sun block and sweat
Bob and float on sounds of laughing children,
Like so many Styrofoam pieces, we drift,
And occasionally splash along in the current,
Ahead lies the pullout, a concrete bridge,
And the tired yellow school bus,
Faces glow in embarrassed pink as we sit
In still-sodden clothes, she kisses my shoulder
As I nod against the window and the outside

Russ Couch

Second Row Balcony

And so he stayed away beyond the footlights,
the mass of population gazes away,
from those who entertain the thoughts and dreams,
as their voices penetrate their hearts,
up there.

The swishing flow of fabric is photographed,
his mind shutters with the backflash of a blackout,
enveloping his home, his world and escape,
to join the lucky chosen few is an impossibility,
up there.

The story had unfolded before his innocent eyes,
he too had wanted to be narrated;
his senses tingled to reach out, touch this world,
where the fellowship's attention could embrace him,
up there.

He drowns in the clapping sea of hands,
without the veil of fantasy and the poise of magic;
he flees as soon as possible before the urge burns through
before he could replay the warm pictures of the ones,
up there.

E. D. Jackson

King of the Maple Leaves

Yellow paper on the ground, frayed
pieces here and there and their destroyer sitting
on the throne of maple leaves—shredding, picking, splitting
every scrap that did him wrong
bearing truthful words—black and white—
what happened to the child who never listened—
the voices told him not to,
told him to go away
let the wind be his only friend (it has no heart or mind)
two souls running, drifting between
white, unconscious worlds and
nightmare memories
he didn't want to hurt anyone—
the leaves found him
held him up in brittle arms
red and green and yellow and orange—
held the vibrant, lively dead
man with fingers moving
quickly and mindlessly
tearing the life apart that had him buried long before.

Amber Fields

Impermanence

An unheard fallen oak echoes more loudly than the sound of
one hand clapping, cragly snagly elbows and fingers bent in
tired arthritic knots crushing cedarlings and small hickory trees
beneath a hollow, yet still-sturdy trunk.

You hollow trunk, once a seedling, how long have you felt ill?
Seeing and hearing the changes of the ages, winged creatures
of the north and south, perhaps creatures which no longer rest
in cedar-sweetened air of these rocky hills.

You listened to bright trills of cardinals red, salamander
slithering sounds through leaves like light water lapping
perhaps, to the sensitive ears of an oak on a quiet evening,
like the roan-spotted white dog's tongue slapping water.

Saliva drips from the dog's mouth, old oak, slippery
like the mossed rocks, rain-soaked and the muddy roots which
once anchored age to space, life to earth and back again.

Under the watchful eyes of the stars this oak predicted
changes in the heavens. This oak loved the red rocky clay
soil it ate from and dropped its red yellow green leaves,
feeding green leaves, arthritic arms, fingers, and feeding
other cragly snagly trees some years off.

Bruce Charles Antrim

Spring in Fairview Cemetery

I glimpse forsythia bushes first.
Their desert thirst assuaged
by last week's splattering rain,
they leap alive
and, just as plain as fire,
fling yellow sparks up every twig.

The park lies still.
Three lesser finches dip
and chase
and flash their feathered flame
across green graves.

No loss so big this Spring
that living color cannot quell.
I kneel
and smell the yellow sweetness everywhere,
until, with Sun inside, I cross all time
to grasp the Void
where Lightning dwells.

Elizabeth Richardson

Wild Horses Chariot my Dreams, Bits Flecked with Foam

I strain the reins, awaken far from home.
Come sleep again, let me the night mare ride
Until the white sweat shows on her dark side.
Ride, where cold deserts stretch, and chasms yawn
Far from the sun and rosy-bosomed dawn—
Far from that lethal light when mortals rise
Begrudgingly, and put on their disguise.
To puppet dance, and listen through the day
With ovine ears to what the few will say.
No freedom lies for them, in day or night
That darkened horse, for them, a sign of fright.
Maned beauty, fleet of foot, just let me stay
Upon your back and gallop far from day.

Ann Venables Kyrke

Sonnet #2

Two days ago I asked the wizened sage
To weave a spell to cure all of my pain:
"My Treasure is now gone, I am not sane;
Her leaving marks the passing of an age;
She sails across a storming sea of rage;
Her ship is torn apart like pounding rain
Like dragon's breath that leaves a barren plain.
I beg you, work your magics master mage!"
To this, with great composure, he replied:
"For me to do my work would be a waste;
This is no mystery of ancient lore.
You sought and failed where many also tried:
A honey pot has much that's sweet to taste,
But deadly is the poison which it pours!"

Sidney Blake

Tyndale's Bibles

The world is safe enough and rational in the streets of New York:
Rectilinear, with sidewalks and traffic lights,
In Bryant Park full of daffodils lining the walks
and brown baggers eating at tables,
In the Public Library, grand and old.

The world is safe and rational in this dim room
within the thick walls of the library,
The exhibit telling of Tyndale,
His Bibles safe behind glass,
His life laid out for us on square white panels on the red wall.

The world is not safe or rational at all.
Tyndale said, "Even a ploughman should know God directly."
The Church said, "Only we speak for God"
And strangled and burned him and kept God Latin, for a while,
Until the snake of change slid inexorably out of cracks.

Caroline Bassett

Raison d'être

La mort ne surprend point le sage, il est toujours prêt à partir . . .
                                        —La Fontaine

In the mottled wood an old man sits upon a stump,
Elbows on knees, back burdened by years,
Brow furrowed in intense consideration.
A limp, black fish—glistening with a reluctant light—
Hangs in his gnarled hands, like a sad refrain,
On a heavy summer's night in the December of his life.

He ponders the fading coruscation, the drying skin.
Will I lie limply as this, eyes parched and sightless?
Is this death? Is this the shedding of the mortal coil?
As the last breath rattles will everything just stop?
Does this fish know it has ended? Does this fish care?
As my eyes dim and my flesh begins to decay, will I care?
Do I need to know a god, or create one to deal with this?
The fecund smells fill his nostrils; the flies buzz. Well, do I?

George A. Chidester

November 22

Purposefully northward in the arrow shape
rowing against heaven, on that cloudy journey
that is instinct triumphing over the world's amplitude—
a thousand miles and a thousand on the cold winds,
answering a voice in the marrow of hollow bones,

over hills that remember and wide watered places,
river and pond and cedar-scented lake,
the chinook gale fresh-rising from a far ocean
to fling rain lavishly over blue mountains.

Suddenly out of ambush the alien crack
of a gun, and the leader who had been breaking the trail
of air into conformable waves for us
is gone, descended broken from the pattern.
Pity us, Instinct, for our grief now, pity us.
We will continue, yes, but we continue empty,
doubtless again we will nest on the summer tundra
where the sun hangs circularly, never setting—
we, always survivors of savagery and of this, too—
and before November again beat upward and southward
through the ancient inclemencies, the dangerous skies.

Jack Tootell

The Topic of Disease

Her mercury-belly protrudes itself against my aluminum chest,
however we both are seated . . .
amidst these middle-back contusions
A prolonged breath—performance of sadness
to encounter our next victim?
No longer is the orange-softness of your neck as innocent,
the merciless nape, so abrasive
space becomes the sum-total of her sex-appeal
aplomb, aplomb
Forsooth, the pardoned interference
and so much train of thought
What can she profess? What can you display?
Other than the three-fifths of your [public flesh]
Late-afternoon seduction and indeed
She is the sole-proponent of phallic injustice.
She holds a mock-marriage in her beak.

Hesse McGraw

Ghost-Making

She wakes this morning and puts the Talking Heads
in the tape deck, dancing madly to Psycho Killer and then
going to the bathroom to throw up. The doorbell bing-bongs
right on time, and she opens to a fist full of flowers,
For today she is making a ghost.

He cannot stay for the whole procedure, so he drops her
at the door, driving away to play golf, as if this were
an ordinary day. No big deal, he has told her, but she knows
That today she is making a ghost.

The beautiful, black nurse holds her hand hard
and tells her to breathe. Afterwards, she toughs her out of bed
and gets her walking. "It hurts less, if you keep moving."
For now the ghost-making is done.

Months later, at her mother's house a summer picnic
runs wild with children. Her sister desperate for relief
shoves a newborn into her arms and points her toward inside.
There, the silence falls like eternity upon the echoes
of an empty house. She looks down on the tiny, sleeping face
speckled in sunlight. A perfect little hand reaches out into space
lost to grab hold of her pinkie. The haunting has begun.

Marianne Connor

Tabula Rosa, In the Garden

Me? I walk alone.
The unnamed shadow,
Sitting isolated in the cold dark,
Learning to love the light.
I was born dead to this—
The flawed and faded garden.
In my haunted sleep I gather them,
My dream memories of you,
Of times, places, that never were,
They follow me like deep-throated orchids,
Beautiful, but cruel past bearing,
And crying aloud over vilification.
The dark man of my imagination hunts me down;
One day I'll have my death of him.
Is this what your love is then?
This viscous and slippery red.
If this is the truth you'd feed to me,
Then why is it dulled with blood?
All I want back is what I was before,
Before the fall and my wintering.

Renee A. Coville

Once More

Winter's icy edge begins its thaw,
as the warmth of the sun shows its face.
The hasty cold, unforgiving wind,
bows down reluctantly to take its place . . .
and let the earth receive its full embrace.

New growth embarks its journey upwards,
facing the light to contest the cold.
Painfully breaking through the mire,
she reaches for the freedom to unfold . . .
and speak of her captivity untold.

The fragrance of this new, small blossom,
caresses the womb of broken hearts.
It reached out with every ounce,
of purpose and vitality is starts . . .
The gradual ascent towards life's fine arts.

But his strong hand precludes springs coming
as the wintry claw appears once more,
to herald the hold on his empire,
in fond memory of its ugly sore . . .
and chill from the inside her pale decor.

Catherine Waddle

I Met a Phone Booth in an Antique Land

There's a phone booth that stands just outside of Karachi:
The door's hanging loose and the paint job is patchy.
The natives say it never ever rings:
Its name is Ozymandias, king of kings.

It's a splash of the new on the face of the old
And the Hindus and Moslems agree, so I'm told,
That the phone is as fine as you'll find on Broadway;
Yet the lone and level sands stretch far away.

They say, once American soldiers were here
In barracks of wood, drinking bottles of beer;
But the desert is cruel and will have its own way.
The booth stands alone in colossal decay.

A Parsi spake thus as he looked at the sky,
"The desert lives on and all other things die."
Still I'd like to call that phone booth from Canarsie
And make liars out of Shelley and the Parsi.

Desmond Fairbairn

Crossing Pulaski

I drop you off at Lawrence and Pulaski
among the Korean shops, corner cleaners
Mayfield's food and liquor
and the fantasy adult bar
And the car reeks of smoke and coffee
as parking lot dust blows through the cracked window
the sun glares into my eyes
and my hangover pulses harder
And I'm startled by the tinkle of a rolling forty
the crinkle of garbage bag
and the blast of a Toyota all at once
And everyone's trying to get somewhere
three small Asian boys running for the light
that bag lady pulling her cart into the alley
the bus driver bearing down on a slow Cadillac
But I just want to sit here a little while and smoke
watch you cross Pulaski with that heel n' toe walk
see the wind catch up your blazer and flip your hair back
and breathe in the exhaust the dust the sun the smoke the you

David McMillen

Sulla and the demon-god spring

Each day, the same question:
who is this child?
This bare-chested boy of ten,
dark-skinned and silent,
fire-brown eyes and a tuft of hair.
Who is this child that plays in the vineyard
among the houses of the older spirits?
Each day he comes a little closer to the pile
of aged equipment behind the shed.
I offer him cinnamon sticks, confectioner's sugar.
He will not touch me, though.
Occasionally, my children find him, throw rocks
and pebbles . . . and it snows.

I hear you Metrobius. I hear your constant exclamations,
know well your pale skin and ripe body. Once a year,
I force myself to see you, out in the open,
under God and the heavens. I am too easily teased.

It is the one night I do not sleep
in that bed of pomegranates and rust.

David Sobel

Dust Bowl Childhood (Remembering)

From her eyes shines
　　　　　blue Kansas sky
years ago,
when little girls
in patched, pink dresses
picked wild daisies
and pale, purple clover.
When sprightly breezes
stirred dust devils,
where once it danced with corn.

Hard work,
empty bellies, cold feet,
　　　　　laughter, and music
around a dying fire.

The sky clouds,
　　　　　her eyes shut,
and tears of memories missed,
slide down her wrinkled cheek;
a benediction
after prayer.

Olivia N. Seaton

Raining in New York 2

Livid yarns streaming from her throat
cracked, tarnished from the years of clean living,
melodious eyes
blue crescents
just past the new moon of believing.
She easily could have told the truth
and let me make the wrong decision
for the right reason
but that would have been too easy.
The pop songs swagger through the sweet room
standards for the moment,
things we swear we'll never forget
we remember,
the familiar beat
so comforting
and as deadly as a clandestine shagging in the rain.
And about as fascinating.
What were we talking about?
Oh, yes, the death of innocence.

J. René Guerrero

Drunkard's Dream No. 44

Beyond the hissing lampost, on the ground floor of a haze,
I watched while Paddy Nunzio polished up his blade,
At the corner of Tenth and Torment,
in the early seeds of morning,
he smiled while he stroked the edge and
reached down for more bourbon.

In an alleyway of brick and mortar,
where our shadows scraped the wall,
and the rats crawl with impunity while
a cat lurks down the hall,
Paddy plunged his spruced up shiv through
a murky swath of darkness,
carving a sliver of night from there, clean,
and passing me the carcass.

I snatched it up with sheer aplomb,
gazed down into the hole
Paddy made with his well groomed blade,
and saw a raging rum river of gold.

Charlie Burnett

The Election

Set us free!
of encrusted banality
Ezra and William lament
popularity like a pox infects

. . . is just another word
like battle hymn of bramble
your support is unbearable
providing witness to dry rot

Volunteers of Kafka
Savoir tinsel signs
sunk with arms from the grave to envelope
polls that close in thoughtless pores

Exchanging glances is so trying
less is more taxing
to beat the cheat drums beat
or press on for favors revered

Punch 1 for suicidal deceit
Punch 2 for bloody gumwrappers
Punch 3 to carpet Bob
Care for punch? them out.

Raymond E. Rossi

The Breakfast Table

Gritty fresh strawberries
remind me of my waif-like grandmother
who made me let me pick strawberries
every summer.
She let me eat as many as I wanted
sitting on little girl haunches
amid rows and rows of strawberries
alternating with rows of gladiolas
each a different variety and name
reds, exotic purples
lush abundant open beauties
with no purpose
but to grace my grandmother's breakfast table
where she gave me whatever I wanted for breakfast
7-Up, ice cream and crescents of juicy cantaloupe.

Ellen Bowers

The Forum (Rome)

Our future lies here in these ruins' shade
Where wiry stray cats tread on temples' chips.
A spring drips over cracked torsos of jade
Like the sad virtue that falls from your lips.
You pull back toward a soul undiscovered
Under marble ghosts' gaze, frozen in wince.
I sprint up ancient stairs to recover,
My steps dull echoes of what I've lost since.
Our feline familiars prowl night's landscape,
Homeless survivors, desperately free.
I loosen my sweaty grip from your shape,
Since your own is all I want you to be.

Kiss me gently, to know, to inspire,
To grace the fall of another empire.

John Wellington Ennis

For the Lucky Irishman

Your poem lies throttled deep inside,
Close to where I live, you
Secreted scraps of rough drafts
Unsanded by callous red pens of editors,
Equating my adoring words with the sentimental entertainment
Of a clown tutored in juggling redundancies,
Phrases sans meaning, sentences sans thoughts.
Inadequate lines groan under a tonnage of driveling connotations,
And I want you tumbles loose from the scratchings
Of the imperfect rhythms.
Here comes the dreaded public humiliation:
Cut, cut, delete, do away with excess romanticism, now. Now!
But I cannot touch an irregular beat of it.
To us untrained and simple bards,
there is nothing more than to be tossed up.
The verse: I love you.
Et cetera.

Laura Jarrett

To the Cemetery

I went back to where
I thought you might mock me
by taunting me there
From behind a tree
Or from our hide-out on that hill,
But you only seemed to be near;
And I guess, because it was so still,
My mourning was all that I could hear.

Nevertheless, tarrying there that day,
Once again I remembered how you,
Smothered in flowers, had been put away
Into a place I had wanted to go, too;
And, trying to terminate that time's grief,
I forfeited a fondness for my belief.

D. Lottes

Plumeria Kingdom

In Pearl City, when I was young,
I would walk barefoot everywhere, down
the dirt road to my Auntie's, where ceiling nook
geckoes chirped, sunlight peeked through walls
which Uncle never mended. It never got cold,
insulation wasn't needed.

I would suck on dried squid and pickled plums,
walk the tracks to eighteen bridge
where Grandpa wrestled hammerheads
when he was young. Past the graveyard
where Baban saw fireballs, phosphorous ghosts
that would follow her home.

I would weigh fallen mangoes in my palms,
scoop green coconut meat with my fingers,
and string plumeria into crowns, so by night
I would be nectar sticky, pollen dusted,
and my Aunties would be queens
who would carry me to bed.

Amanda Price

Auld Lang Syne

Time will not wait for me
I snatch at life in little
pieces
precious moments because
I have no endless hours
to wile my boring days—
I cram each hungry moment
with measured morsels
snatched from
the hungry jaws of time
whose dozen faces
double-feed mortalities
gnawing appetites for
growing boys to
grab piecemeal
the little things (non-trivia)
infinite mosaics of eternal life
I cannot grasp
en masse

Francis S. Smith

Untitled

The stones laid before you
Are not made of clay and horse hair,
Nor cotton fibers weaved by sand slugs,
Nor zinnia petals nor good things.
Stones—color of morning fog
rapping at my bedroom window.
Tied on bedposts
Voice like boots dragging
Along white lined tar,
Under the bed; praying moon
of the mantis, erected by
Hurricane-withered bones.
The stones laid before you
lick at your heart
raging hills,
and roll back out with the tide,
seaweed stones.
Black eyes weeping
for stones
that never left.

Jody A. Martinson

Arbol

sunny sidewalks with magnetic gait
over corduroy shoulder
a monster companion awaits
stretching one motionless,
horrible thumb
over hot-to-the-touch concrete aisles
blue green gray wizard cripple handshake
stretching perpendiculars
over railroad ties:
subsonic perfect motorized.

On behalf of the workday,
let me apologize to you,
the gnarled fruit of a tangled earth:
I could stop and extract your
beauty for instant analysis
I really should
Blame it on the heat
and blame it on the short distance
between here and home.

Thomas Staley-Trull

Picker

she is small and breaking up all over
and she spills like rain onto the table where we sit,
smoldering after torment
she moves timidly out of a stare and picks up
her pieces to store them in the box
where her life is slowly building, transformed, and
here is where it disintegrates, in front of me,
splinters prickly and cold fragments,
where she is broken.
patterns develop and are played out at the table,
in the living room, at the kitchen sink where I keep my post.
she creeps into the room already clutching herself, oh, to hold
herself together just once she thinks, but the pieces of her face
already slip off at the meeting glance.
her fingers and pre-determined thoughts, rebuttals, flicker and at
once are shaken to dust by my cool expertise. she will never win.
so back to her room, to spill more of herself into a box that looms
larger as we advance in our years.
I tiptoe in at night, open the box with my key,
and spit on her parts.

Emily Stone

The American Dream

Shooting stars fall
into empty beer glasses
lined with dried foam,
resting on rotting bars
stained with the American Dream.
I stand tall,
and read the real religions
scrawled on the bathroom walls,
and I cry on my dead brother's shoulder.
Another day older
I thank god for the nothing he granted me
when he planted me here
knowing I could only wilt
if I didn't stand on my own two feet
and make the best of my abilities.
Tranquility enters my eyes in the purple hues of dusk,
and I'm put to rest
the best of my days behind me
shining like falling stars.

Jason Grimste

Thinking of You

as rats dance in the felt of venus,
and the sun and moon collide,
as smoke fills the holes in the ugly,
and chemical sisters ride,

the sitar robot army manhunt
ties the noose of empty shade,
making hell for jello-mold girl
and the disco razor blade.

this wonder led gulls' dead pink hot pants
and the sun to moon-collide.
the gas of 2-timed leak-brain good deeds
un-did gunman homicide

until the force of maddened plastic
dictionary leather urge
led the path to nightmare no place,
forcing flip-book serpent surge.

Robert

The Air Is Blue in Chartres

The air is blue in Chartres,
like baccarat; palest
chroma perfectly diffused.
A blueness that invades
a body's pores as well as senses.

Look at me: I was a child there.
Now I am old, still within that
blue and idle interval:
blue sun, blue snow, like a
Picassoesque blue period.

Think about it.

There is no need to go back,
nor rest for the weary of it,
nor sane remedy nor conclusion.
We've bonded, as they say,
that stirring blue and I.

And when I break
it isn't unlike crystal.

Mary C. Crudup

Cherry Street

Sounds within this painted maelstrom, so content to go by
genuflect for gracious separation
fairies, punks, bums
a brazen motif alongside a pinstriped arrogance
strides complimenting complete difference
in this car—serene, not needing to impress
content to observe the conversations walking by
with tension in their eyes, and
the river moans in abrasive motion
where the steel of stealing ships makes friction with its face
as all the innocence is leaving (me—here)
the intersections feed from their crossing
they never connect
I grow with the same careless moments of the tarnished mall clock
aging towards the glass of noon
across the way is my age in a cigar shop
teething at seventeen and seething at everything
will the paper performing circus humor break on the curb . . .?
before the rains take the opportunity from the tread of wheels
spinning like those clockhands

Stephen Robert Koehler

Reality vs. Life

What does my dog dream?
Do you still sell cockroaches cheap?
Every time I bend over I dream of another shot
Faced with a corrupt group of lives trying desperately to take
It all with them
Carving my initials in a hollow pane door
Using my hair to mop the vomit off the floor
Filled with tears we still hang on to the toilet for safety
Our limits are challenged at times
But you always have a sandwich artist to talk you down
Though we question our spirituality
We all still find ourselves in sin
We try to find our inner strength to say hi to Betty Lou
And to come to peace with the thought that love for our ideas
Is never found
I plant my body underground in hope to bloom into a bouquet
Of wilted flowers

   Van Der Aa Keeffe

Wailing Peace

As we grind our daily life away,
To file in the recess of our memory,
We realise that war's raw,
That when we love we vo'w'el;
Thus we syntax, which taxes our tenses.
So we growl, but did not grow
Neither learn while we grow,
Thus rave, which drive us to drivel
And we hail peace without pace so we wail,
On the Wailing Wall.
Now the cloud shifts by sifting thus lifts
As the slim Muslim thundered, so the jew
In jewelry, nailed by the weeping rain
As he wails at the Wailing Wall,
As he paces through the pieces of the peace
In his thought, thus by making peace we ought to pace
As our heart pounds away, so we hope, hoping to
Hop to next wishywashy hope
To realize that we're not dope.

   Lanre A. Brown

A May Day—San Francisco

The open window leaves a black gash
On the brightly painted wall of the house next door,
A hole of dark foreboding in this bright summer morning.
Wispy, white clouds hang limply in the blue heavens
And the birds chirp warily, calling to each
Other to warn of the cats lithely
Edging their ways through the blanketing
Bushes and flowers. I stroll about
My garden, taking stock of the tight
Rosebuds accumulating in the mottled
Leaves, anticipating the galaxy of
Color to greet us in the coming weeks.
But from all this heady bounty
My eyes wander back to the window
Looking dankly down upon the
Serenity of my summer garden,
Casting its shadow of gloom and
Sadness on this oasis of nature's glory.

   Victor C. Murphy

The Color of Grief

I press my body toward him, chair hiccupping
on the rucked-up Cancer Center carpeting;
his bolts back, into itself.

I've come to talk about a death, let him know
the way his blood's betrayed him: words to
arc the cold wide space between

him, fourteen, silent boy of color, and
me, fifty, articulate white professor,
divided by disparity.

His mother waits her vigil out beyond
the fettering hoop that binds us in
service to each other.

I speak. And the pupils start their dart,
schooled in black-white deference, can't
rest their fear upon me.

At last, subjugate, the head drops. Tongue
licks furtively away a boulder tear
rolled on this young man's cheek.

   John Graham Pole

For the Old Man at ABC No Rio

Creeping slowly, inching through the desolate streets
of late-night winter in Brooklyn,
Drowning in the ocean of the midnight sky, buried under
layers of synthetic fiber molded together to form sweaters
of magnificent color, the old man curses his life
and mutters obscenities under his breath.
The old brick apartment houses of Ocean Parkway
loom ominously over him, surrounding him in shadows,
blocking out the sliver of light illuminating from
the street lamps. Taking a drag off his cigarette,
the flaming embers on the tip providing little warmth,
he curses himself for starting smoking.
The clouds of smoke circle 'round and 'round his head,
enveloping his frost-bitten ears and choking him in a
world of carcinogens. Thinking of childhood,
when his mother read him "Goodnight Moon,"
he bids goodnight to everything in sight and
trudges onward through the angry streets looking
for the catharsis that will let him breathe freely
in this confining, stifling world.

   Daniel Calamuci

Penitence

A special box, locked away,
with sundry mementos
preserved in a cardboard coffin
laid to rest
two stories above ground.

Dry, picked bones remain to tell their various tales:
photos of a vain relationship
replace emptiness in albums to be unoccupied once more;
a distanced transition revealed again
in dusted death.

Exceptional no more,
its extraordinary purpose
worn away through time
like engravings on a head stone.
Memories rekindle the past
like an urn following the burn.
Ribbons untie letters that fuel and kindle;
its smoke rising to the heavens at last.

   Eliza J. Anderson

Riverrun

Riverrun, a glade of glistening soft puddles
coagulating like veins throughout a human body
Softens and stretches infinitely through a vast expanse of data and
Drains me of colour and contrast
Due back by midnight, a winter agape with the fortune of spring
Loosens its tendrils to overwhelm me with the arches of blood
flowing with a thick Thump
Against my windowpane, and to chase away the demons
of another fortnight without rest or Belief in anything
Crescendo of noise drowns out all pain and Riverrun gasps and births another galaxy
Adam and Eve close in around each other and feed the pain of an innocent century
Through their chapped lips
and all is Quiet with a soft ringing in my ears, the aftermath of a Lost Paradise
a Paradigm of guilt and confession and sin, it will all boil over into the Suns,
another loose tendril around the Corner of my Glade
        Aroon Karunamurthy

When I'm Ninety

When I'm ninety I'll hie myself to Tom's
To fix that little extra house he has
With white sides and a porch to sit and rock
Unfettered so, I'll count this venture as
My chance to rest.

I'll plant a dozen herbs against the back
A larch tree somewhere in a spot that's wild
I'll set aside each fretful useless care
And treasure being near at least one child
In such a nest.

I'll walk the paths among his giant trees
And sing old hymns and long forgotten lays
I'll fish whene'er the stream and I are fit
And ponder how considering all my days
These were the best.
        Barbara Burwell

Ndoki, the Last Place On Earth

On his couch you feel the dark educating flame.
The Ndoki sorcerer begins to teach the elephant vision,
So you will know how nomads count the full and gibbous moons.

There is rain for a few days of paradise.
A sweet African Bagombe for steamy existentialists.

The magic Man will teach the elephant hearing,
So you will hear and find
That macabre compass between the eyes.

Only the sun and shadows can follow them
To their kitchens, to the place of sleep, to where the children play.

And he will teach the Tsetse's wind song,
So you will know of the long slumber, of the silence of many tongues,
And of the Dry God's Disappointment.

The Malaria has left some places unpeopled,
But the sickle-cell is ice on the fire of life and death.

And before you go, a final lesson,
So you will know that there are more names for life than there are for death,
In Ndoki, the Last Place on Earth.
        H. James Stewart

The Bird's Nest

It has always been easier to destroy than to allow to propagate—Life!
Inconvenience seems so significant; five minutes of discomfort daily,
Compared to the life of another creature.
Make your home somewhere else, sir Swallow—Your mess clouds
And fouls my step.
Such a small inconsequential act, that of destruction of a nest.

Yet, think of that spring morning when, upon rising, you are first aware
Of Spring's arrival—sweet sounds of singing, piping, whistling beyond the window.
Your heart leaps with the song—Spring is here!
Move on, be gone, get along to somewhere else!
We do not wish the chance to watch you flutter and fly, and teach your young the art of
Winged dance; we do not want the mess!

Precious minutes mindlessly wasted gaping at reruns on TV . . .
Worrying, waiting, watching, and wasting . . .

And I, I am the villain. I am the Nazi damned.
I am the profiteer. I am the one who looked away.
I am the traitor, I am Judas, I am Brutus, and I am you.
I am anyone who watched, who knew, or even thought, and did not intervene.
I am the silent Onlooker.
I allowed this to happen.
        Mark Decker

Sea She Painting

a mind's creative hands, caught up in water-nature, reaching over,
will show great endless and even sharp divisions, without losing
connections, span into wondered-of places between here and there so you
always have the right bridge
to go to another side of what you are, you never knew you needed . . . to see.

there is a way to have currency with infinite differences, and
still remark the one web of it; and still love all parts of an old story without
having to tread upon any of its flowers

the waterwind spawns exhilarance, suggests
odd postures where vision discovers a last lost world's venturers,
as they were, then long after their folly glory became a memory,
way beyond, after where you and I are now living as
spirit matter woven over, within a muted still-brilliant Gilded City,
sunk to the bottom of the sea, that bore Her, to keep.
now cradled in perpetual embrace, that very captured place, where wishings
never die, coming before, inhabiting within, beckoning beyond
Venice, however illicit, and masked, child of dreams.

Beauty tells such things; wears old rags, salt washes, tolls troubles,
laughed away, sighs, misted, richly pretended forgotten utterance,
  a pulse.
    Edward D. Turner

Venus Of Simple Miracles

Circumstance: as there were seven restless veils
There were ten stars and ten candles before the dance
I watched as signal, outside the window, as if you rent me
I will not die but submit, others sought the cars parked
Sauntering on the pavement, with different human urges
A living lie, taut and constricted like the hand that
Holds a foreign coin.

Where she lived and why she danced is unknown,
She danced for cigarettes from the underworld
In the science of seduction, hanging on tight,
Scratching the constellatory roof with rhythms of the zodiac.
Penultimate, before crawling into the abyss, she showed all
A sirocco in the trade winds that brought a sudden streak of recovery.
Penultimate: where the stickman bounces in beggar's slang,
Where the cusp in rags is defined as something in me
That life was not denied in the dance that is the flag and ticket.
    Michael Igoe

Reflections on Childhood

Sheets flapping like white specters riding the wind
A dust cloud billowing on the horizon
  where the tractor meets the turn row
Picking summer squash from sticky vines
  while wiggling toes into the black earth
The hum of the water cooler and snapping green peas
  in front of the 6 o'clock news
The Fourth of July at the Baptist church
  where horseshoes chinked against rusted metal stakes,
  and wasps droned in dizzy circles around a ceramic jug
Splashing in a claw-foot tub on hot summer nights
  and games of Forty-two
The smell of tobacco and sweat and dinner rolls
A man and a woman
  willing slaves to the land
    rich in heart
      and faith
Leaving a legacy of love.
    Phyllis A. Leach

Afternoon In Honduras

In the sweaty, sultry hours
Between one and three
When life is too hot
To endure any longer,
We women gather
On the big beds in the adobe room
To lazily fan ourselves and
Talk of men, the price of onions, mango jam
And the unbearable heat.
The absolute stillness of
The smoke-filled sky and orange-colored world
Surrounds our heads and invades our dreams
Of men and mangoes
As we slip into the siesta, hoping
That sounds of rain will saunter in
And awaken us.
    Liz Peyser

killer nocturnals

When someone in Madagascar dreams us,
  his precarious ability to poison veins,
  bag man's last breath sealed for mother
    (in time
      /he thinks/
        we'll find
          IT IS that
            last
              wind
            that holds
          the eternal),
we'll stand (you a
  nd I, lovers) effective
  in dissecting time
  as knifed technicians.
    Mark Heisey

Wooden Child

You arch your bow like a great hunter
until golden light embraces the emptiness.
And the answers that you sought lie
hidden in dampness, a red dew
upon the city.
Wooden child, unbending in recompense
of a tortured soul
the darkness in your eyes embraces,
detaches, and dances through
the crowd unbridled, unheard
and undisturbed.
A mother's heart lies swollen
with unshed tears, sculpting, chiseling
until the marble scatters like so many pieces
of a broken mirror.
Wooden child, you have no way
to soak away the fear.
    Marti Buscaglia

Nash Street

April breeze tosses junk food bags
empty with rain water into my daffodils.
Reaching for garden gloves
I hum Gershwin on the turntable,
copper fish outside my window knocking
out of time to Rhapsody in Blue.

Opening the front door,
I imagine myself tan in a white cotton dress
legs swinging out of birch bed
feet dashing across oak floor
and plunging into warm sand, salty ocean.

Cold water spits from the plastic bag
wetting the fingers of my blue gloves.
A Datsun pushes 50 down this one-way street.
Holding the bag at arm's length,
I close the gate behind me.
    Moira Pascale

The Mystic Land

I wandered one day to a Mystic Land,
The beauty alarmed me—everything seemed so grand.
What does this Mystic Land mean to me?
I feel my very being and my soul seem so free.
The bright light that permeates the scene,
Was something emanating from the unseen.
The flowers were of a brighter hue, that captured the scene.
The gurgling stream went on its way, enchanted by the aura of light.
A tree stood by, the branches keeping track of a thousand leaves.
Then came birds of every hue and size, in flight.
What a scene!
A thousand leaves began to move; the birds increased in the
Mystery of the breeze.
Then the vision of one who stood beside all those years,
The touch of whose hand calmed my fears.
This is what the Mystic Land brought to me—
                    Remembrance

Sheila Brolsma

The Life of the Elderly

The life of the elderly is important to everyone,
They are special to all generation.
To all of us, mother, father, daughter and son,
No matter where you go, you will hear their conversation.

The life of the elderly both women and men,
Some of them are sick, while others are well.
We want to hear their stories of way back when
In their loving hearts they want to tell.

All about the times when they were young,
I remember mother told me one day.
It was great hearing the song they sung,
I wouldn't want to take care of children today.

It doesn't matter if the elderly are black or white,
They know Jesus will love them with all his heart,
Wherever they go they will be all right.
Life of the elderly is special, from the start.

Margaret L. Rodkey

I Have No Worries

I don't have to worry, I have everything I need.
I don't have to worry, for needs I never plead.
I have a home, though plain it is, 'tis filled with lots of love.
I have a home eternal, home with God in heaven above.
I always have good food to eat, though steak not everyday.
I have clean clothes and shoes to wear,
        though names they may not say.
I don't have to worry about anything you see—
Because I know Christ Jesus and I know that He loves me!!

Richard Brian Hayner

Graduation 1997

Tears run down my face
As I think of one of the hardest words
Ever spoken in the English language.
It's the one I never wanted to say to you—
Good-bye.
Friend just isn't the right word for me to use,
Because you were so much more to me than that.
Growing up and moving on
Is a big part of life,
But with you as my friend in Christ,
One day we will meet again.
Whether it is here on earth
Or meeting our Father face to face,
I look forward to it.
Since I don't like good-byes too much,
Until then, my friend, see you later.

Kristen Kiddy

Three Little Poems

1. Today, I did not step into my art,
   Because poetry filled my heart.
   And so I stepped inside myself
   And felt a world apart.

2. I will not shirk my work
   Until each job is done.
   For only then will I be free
   To share this joy, quite clear to see, in hospitality.

3. Too many voices tell me what to do.
   I'm not a cow, a soft moo
   Swishing along this trail of life,
   Following each spoken word with the herd.
   Sure, life's a game full of strife.
   But there's lots to learn while you earn.
   In quiet moment I discover
   There's no need to roll the dice
   My own judgement offers sound advice.
   I'm not a cow, a soft moo
   Plodding after the herd
   As they heed each spoken word.

Cathy Babcock

The Dandelion

They say I'm a nuisance, and I don't know why;
There is no one around as pure yellow as I .

I travel the world on the breath of the wind
And settle wherever it's pleasing to him.

I try to avoid missing anyone's home;
I'm very impartial, so I just roam.

Sharp knives and mowers do cut me down,
But I strive to jump up as fast as a clown.

I know I'm a weed, but I shine in the sun;
And I multiply and add quicker than anyone.

I flatter myself as I bask in my beauty;
Nestled in green grass—it's the dandelion's duty.

Yellow and green are beautiful together,
And they're specially lovely in any weather.

Children delight in making a ring
Of my head and stem and everything.

I'm luscious, I'm told , as a potent drink,
And I need acceptance, too, don't you think?

Shouldn't I have a place in this world of ours
That's reserved for especially beautiful flowers?

Marguerite Popovich

Tomorrow

Tomorrow never knows what tomorrow brings
Tomorrow never knows what's tomorrow
And I cry all day and I cry in my sleep
It's so hard to deal with these days of mine
And my eyes are tired of crying
And I have to stop worrying
About this love that has nothing to do with you
Crossing your hands you play for me
And I sit in the chair like I'm not even there
But I'm here in Dreamworld
With the blue mountain men
It's so hard to understand me
It's so hard again
The TV is phony and the Nazis are here
Within my dreamland
Shoot them down with my mind's eye
Start with peace within yourself
This poem ain't making sense

Beth Blinebury

Happily Ever After

once upon a time, a long time ago,
a mother tried to strangle her daughter on a public street.
the woman accompanying them saw nothing strange in this
and hid them with her jacket.
a public educator was arrested for driving under the influence,
townsfolk were more concerned that he was wearing lipstick
and panties at the time.
somebody threw a newborn baby into a dumpster after
beating it to death; just another pickup for the garbage trucks.
sleeping in coffins and drinking blood are quite the rage,
just as well to drink your cup of AIDS and live forever.
some people thought they'd catch a space ship to
heaven and figured drugs, booze and plastic bags
tied over their heads would get them there even faster;
they missed the ship, and nobody had a return ticket.
but always in the springtime, flowers come up between the cracks
in the streets, lovers meet to kiss and touch under a sparkling
blue sky, and everywhere, you can hear the delightful sound
of children running and playing in the sun.

denise duncan

Is It Spring Yet?

Patches of snow sill linger on the ground.
Three crows sit in a tree, that is still
dormant, having a long serious conversation.
In the distance two pair of hawks circle
round and round, hoping their breakfast
will soon be found. Two pair of geese fly
over head noisily honking their loud
conversation, as a pair if robins hunt for
worms in the unplowed ground. A red-headed
woodpecker is drilling a hole in the old
apple tree that grows at the edge of the
garden. I'm sure his breakfast will soon
be found. Winter should be almost over.
Spring should soon come to our town.

Alyce M. Nielson

Twilight in May

Twilight in May wears a velvet cloak,
Touched by the whispers of night to portray,
Muted sounds as their murmuring evoke,
Secrets of love which were lost through the day.
The crickets, promise in symphony sing,
Of life in its offering rich joy to fulfill,
As the fragrance of roses, enchantment bring,
When twilight enfolds hushed valley and hill.
This is the time to pause a while,
To savor life's happenings with quiet grace,
To put aside the day's constant trial,
To cherish the moments of peace to embrace.
For twilight in May is too soon gone,
Yet this is the prelude of June at dawn.

Josephine Cordero

Whiteness

The whiteness penetrates my barriers,
as I watch its solidness,
merge and grow,
pushing tension back to blissfulness.

It's plain, yet untouched, beauty,
bleeds into my soul,
the glowing truth pulsates in me,
filling all my empty holes.

Slowly, my mind expands reaching, grasping,
to touch that gentle white flow,
finding I have my own sanitary,
within the peaceful silence I've longed to know.

Denise A. Massaglia

"Red" and the Ruby

Where is Mia May?
She used to smile, she used to dance,
She believed in life,
And always shared life's precious gifts.

She saw the sun, when most viewed the moon,
And leaped with the Angels in the pouring rain.
Yet lately, the sun fails to dance in her eyes,
The moon sleeps in the sky
And her smile is swept away by the wind.

Near the rocks by the trembling sea,
Mia seeks peace and tranquility.
She sits close within her body
And wonders if she will ever escape,
From the "Red," nightmare!
It shattered her life beyond repair.
The assault bruised her soul,
and enraged her beloved's mind
In the end nothing was spared.
For he had snatched her prized possession; The Ruby
Her Mind, Body and Soul.

Melissa M. Ferrari

Wonderful Peace

Peace, wonderful peace is what we need.
As, without peace, the world is crumbling
And so full of death and pain.

War will never help us in any way
Without peace our souls are full of trouble
And our lives draw nigh unto the grave.

As we see so many fall around us and in pain
Why is the world so far from peace, it is due
To greed and hatred in the heart of man.

If righteousness and peace would kiss each other
And leave the whole world in wonderful peace,
If all would hear what God speaks, peace, peace,

To his people, if mercy and truth are mete,
Together and will leave the world in peace.
If all over the world would dwell on peace

Jesus who died for all would be satisfied
If all the world would dwell on peace,
There would be peace, and heaven and earth be one.

Nellie M. Brand

Marking Time

Worn paths survive in Forest Park
Where trees keep memories growing—
Still drawn toward paper birch, I carve my mark.

Comparing such with tougher bark
Seen while my pen's fast-flowing,
Worn paths survive in Forest Park.
Now later as a bough turns stark,
With wind's old wolfish blowing . . .
Still drawn toward paper birch, I carve my mark.

Although aware of skylark
Whose note of sundown's glowing . . .
Worn paths survive in Forest Park.

And warned again of coming dark
By black bird's bold scare-crowing,
Still drawn toward paper birch, I carve my mark.

Though but one star set loose her spark
To light the way to knowing
Worn paths survive in Forest Park,
Still drawn toward paper birch, I carve my mark.

Jane R. Harwood

Two Shiny Eyes

I climbed into bed and turned off the light,
kissed my family, said good night.
The room was dark except for the lines
made by the moon shining through the blinds.

Suddenly something leaped on my bed.
Scared out of my wits, I turned my head
Just in time to see it jump on the floor with a thump.

I pulled the sheet up over my head
and moved down deeper into my bed.
Quietly I lay listening and waiting, listening and waiting and
waiting.
Not a sound could I hear—did it disappear?
Slowly I lowered the sheet, moved to the edge to get a peek.

Staring at me were two shiny eyes, with a body of an enormous size.
Quickly I pulled the covers back, listening and waiting for the attack.

The next thing I heard was my mother moving about.
My name, she called out,
"It's a school day, can't be late, I'll put your breakfast on the plate."

I crawled out of bed, stumbling over a soft furry head.
Then I remembered the night before,
two shiny eyes and the thump on the floor.

Jeanne Wood

The Hush Between Us

She was dozing in the chair beside me,
Resting easy, sure of me,
Sharing veneration, even unaware—
Always, there had been a hush between us,
Silent, sparking awe of potent presence.

She was much too tired to notice
When I went to gather in the garden tools.
Light rain had started.

When I came back,
I couldn't feel her presence
And the hush had drowned in thunder.
My throat was dry and hard.
I went to get some water and I couldn't drink.

I always thought we'd go together,
Lying together some cold night,
Arms around each other.

Jean E. Grau

Euphoria

inspired by Jenny Ansama
Every morning I see you standing there
Your golden-brown hair shining brilliant as saffron
Your sun-soaked skin so beautiful, so rare—
I am in instant intoxication.

Every ultraviolet ray reflects your face
I desire you more than you will ever know.
Every curve of your body is without disgrace
Disappearing from sight, you leave me in your afterglow

Your breasts are so perfectly shaped
Like two mounds of golden sand
My senses within have escaped
For you walk, so nimble, to where I stand.

Your voice carries the dulcet tones of an angel
I want to grab you, press your body against mine
And take you with me, close to the flaming sun we travel,
Caressing you, kissing you, your lips sweet as wine.

Let us spend our time in euphoria, precious one
For I know not even of your inner being;
Which is what quest I hope will be won.
Let us be one, together, both in the presence of healing.

John Patrick Hanssen

I Remember

Memorial Day, the last Monday in May,
Is a holiday of remembrance
To honor our Guys and Dolls who served,
Would it be their last chance for romance?

To see your buddies do their very best,
Never forget those who gave their lives.
This War was Hell, never a day of fun,
Our Guys and Dolls all rated High Fives.

I remember that day of celebration,
We marched in my hometown
Up Broad Street, to the strains of Stars and Stripes,
Smiling faces, not a sign of a frown.

My five years of Army service,
Was not wasted one bit
I did my duty, came home alive,
My poetry proved a hit.

Whenever I had some time to spare,
With pen and paper in hand
My buddies requested I write them poems,
My poetry was in great demand.

Marty Rollin

It Can Begin With You

Do you see life as it Is,
or as you'd like it to be?
Our ideals often cloud
reality
Sometimes life is just so harsh
we can't accept the truth!
I'd like to disbelieve the world has those who are
cruel, insensitive, uncouth.
Yes, I'd Like to think that everyone
is gentle, loving, and kind
but, a person who has only virtues,
is impossible to find!
All of us have our share of faults,
and we can only endeavor
to minimize our bad points,
and exercise them never.
Find within you what is good
and in others too;
for improvement in the world,
can bring with You.

Betty D. Mason

Reeds and Stars

Ask for a sign of truth and love;
You are handed a reed of height and breath.

In a day, the reed was broad and tall.
It grew from a singular depth in the river.

A child was found hidden there,
In a hopeful basket in the rushes.

With a reed they measured the city, the temple,
The length, the breadth, depth, and height.

Holding a reed, he measured the hours,
The days, but three, in the depths of earth.

On rising, under the brightest sun,
No longer was the reed in his hand;

Instead, he held seven stars,
Seven stars, angels immortal,

Seven stars in his right hand,
Messengers to bring the Lord's Word.

He held them that they measure the breadth,
The length, depth, and height of the Kingdom.

Carolyn T. Abbot

Agony of DeFeet

Calluses and corns, splinters and thorns,
    blue-black stone bruises.
Socks with holes, tacks in the soles
    of too-tight shoeses.
Tormenting itch of athlete's foot.
Edema from constrictive knee-high boot.
Felon, gout, frostbite, chilblains.
Ankylosis, arthritic aches and pains.
Fallen arches, ingrown nails.
Bunions, blisters—groans and wails—
Congenital malformations, digital amputations,
    podiatrists' bills!!!
Numerous options in malodorous concoctions
    and resting pills.

The heartbreak of psoriasis would beat a
    hasty retreat.
In a confrontation with the agony of de feet.

Willette Caudle McGuire

The Judas Chair

In a church in a southern city
There is a quiet-time chapel
Unlike any that I'd ever seen before.
Comprising the entire front wall
Of the small windowless room
Is a floor-to-ceiling, stained glass
Depiction of Jesus the Christ.
Soft lights behind the imposing figure
Lend it a soft, translucent glow.
On each side of a narrow center aisle
Are six comfortable easy chairs.
Each chair bears a small brass plate
Inscribed with the name of an Apostle.
The upholstery of the chairs shows signs of wear,
Except for the Judas chair, that is.
Its upholstery is factory-fresh,
As though the chair had just been installed.

Robert K. Moorhead

A Poem Born

In twilight a living cloud of words take flight.
The wind blows high throughout the night,
Emerging from mind's dark cave.
Light comes in mysterious waves,
It flutters cold then breaks with dawn's gold.
Dipping and sipping air's night,
Black ink turns white.
The ghost dance has been won,
The poem is done.

Doris Denton Carr

Arthritis

Arthritis is a painful disease,
It most commonly starts in
your hands and feet.

Learn how to take control
of your pain,
Or else, by it, you will be beat.

Some of your days will be good.
And others will be bad.

Sometimes the simple things are hard to do,
And it makes you mad.

Just know that when you hurt so bad,
others will feel it to.

When you start to feel alone,
God is there for you.

Paula J. Heath

The Other Side of Mourning

"Got a right to sing the blues," the lyricist wrote.
But why swallow the quote? Grief shackles.
A catalogue of "why we cry" stands on every self.
Fate's buffets include one for every self.
Jim aches over a storm-wrecked house,
Shards of unreturnable joys and smashed kid's toys.
Jill for an adored garden that dies
By drought or hairy white flies.
The Reaper's call is the stinger that lingers.
We don't leave the cemetery alone,
Ghosts steal a ride, beat you to the door.
Inside, the house is as bereft as you are.
Yet. Call forth your stalwart gene
To resurrect your highs.
Try this idea on for sighs:
What you mourn is not gone.
Recall: "What wonder years those were!"
Demand from Heaven and end to sadness.
Relish your remembered gladness,
And sorrow will skip tomorrow.

Auren Uris

My Grandma's Apron

Versatile bib aprons—uses are many
Indispensable and saved many a penny
Each morning donning a fresh one so neat
In winter and in summer's heat.

Made on Singer sewing machine—and of many different designs
Provided uses of many kinds
From flour sacks or worn-out dresses
A hundred uses—including cleaning up messes.

Serving as a basket for freshly picked veggies and fruits
Egg-gathering, holding chicken feed, or whatever suits
Carrying newly-hatched chicks to a warm house
Helping hold tools etc. for her spouse.

The apron was a real catch-all
On cool evenings—acting as a shawl
On tough duties like opening a tight mason jar
Or a swipe on dining room table to prevent a mar.

Children benefited with the wiping of a tear
Or hiding under when a stranger was near
An apron served better than a basket or pail
Memories for always—and remember I shall.

Shirley M. Pannell

American?

All but the Native Americans are strangers to the land
European prison refuse, greedy invaders
Religiously persecuted who persecute in turn
Africans enslaved by Africans, sold to white traders
Poverty stricken peasants desperate to survive
A people of mixed blood and origin call this home
Pluralistic country embracing so many cultures
Melting pot, none and all belonging, America's own

Vickie L. Vanderhoof

Just Slip Away

Dying is something we all must go through.
It is the end of life, not the end of you.
Your spirit will soar through that now open door.
Sustenance, you will never need.
No voices to answer, no vices to heed.
Free at last, you're at your best,
All because you've been laid to rest.
It seems so hard while you're alive.
You have to give all just to survive.
In the end, it's best not to stay.
Life now eludes us, we just slip away.

H. H. Hunter

The Wind

Colorful leaves drop from the tree one by one,
Swaying back and forth,
They land on the soft, fertile ground
Winds whistle by, pick up the leaves in caring hands,
Taking them off to a world
Familiar, yet, so far away.
Walking to the trunk of the willow,
Resting its long limbs on the edges of the pond.
Caressing the water, the tree moves back and
    forth over the surface.
Close The eyes and cross the legs.
Now, sitting next to the loving tree,
Envisioning wind . . . into spiraling breezes.
Experiencing, touching, beauty surrounds.
Feeling the leaf within.
The reddish, greenish, yellow leaf glides through
Layers of the sky,
Passing through clouds and flying over mountains.
The wind dies down and the leaf softly floats
    to the ground.

Christina Martin

Grief

A child dies, a child is killed,
And suddenly Life is a shattered shell;
You say "I am strong, and I have willed
That I will survive through this tragedy.

But the days and weeks pass and there is no sun
And you become a giant aching void;
You go through the motions of what must be done,
And the Black Hole within you screams in Sadness.

People around you pursue their duties,
And you wonder how they can go on as before
While your world will never be the same,
Since the child that was your life is no more.

You trudge through your duties, mostly by rote;
Friends tell you they know how you feel. They don't.
Unless they have stood by their child's grave
They cannot fathom the depth of your grief.

The years pass by and the tears flow less,
And in time you learn to laugh once more;
But if you live to one hundred, the hurt will remain
Beneath the thin veneer of Life as before.

Ralph B. Johnson

Slave on the Nile

I was my Lords right arm
To do His will exactly.
His word was Law absolutely,
His power total, his reign eternal.
But all around him men fell dead.

I was there in the kingdom on the Nile,
Forever watching my Lord and Master,
Seeing first what must come after,
Killed as a significant nothing,
Yet too young to die—I learned.

I learned so exactly, I became his will,
I knew before he spoke, what I must do—
But knew someday there would be still,
The man who would replace me as on cue,
So I lived the life of health and Love.

As time went on I could feel the change,
That doing my Lords will imposed—
His will, my strength, my thought so strange,
Secret rebellion from heart arose,
I planned the last fight, my Lords demise.

Clara Demmer

Summer's Blessing

Through time immortal,
Does the figure pace,
A moving gem is her form,
A tranquil peace after a summer storm.

The grace of heart is with light,
A bright vision to guide the soul,
So her pose greets the eye,
A pleasant sight beneath the starry sky.

Come she may to any door,
Her life alone is the cure,
With her love the seasons glow,
Causing the cup of hope to overflow.

Hold fast to her hand,
For no other shall be once more,
Now is time to take the hour,
The moment the fields eternal begin to flower.

Frank K. Kovac

Gift of Spring

Mist laden hills surround me,
Steam rises slowly from the ground.
Gray squirrels scamper up the trees,
Mouths filled with corn they have found.

Tree buds swollen with new life,
Waiting the right moment to burst.
Raccoons heading for the rushing creek,
Where deer come to slake their thirst.

The pasture dotted with daffodils,
Faces lifted to greet the suns rays.
Wild flowers rising from winters sleep,
Take their places in springs new play.

Country roads gray against verdant meadows,
Blending so many shades of green.
Pink blossoms, white blossoms and pine trees,
All preened and waiting to be seen.

The beauty is not only breathtaking,
But so peaceful and serene and still.
Only the Master with His paintbrush,
Could give us a foretaste of His will.

Rose A. Benavente

For the Love of the Wind

To me the wind will always be
the friend of excitement and curiosity

Childhood dreams that never let go
still draw me close when I hear the wind blow

This love affair that forever brings
me closest to soaring as on eagles' wings

Together we'd skip over meadows of green
touching the sky but never be seen

Kissing all flowers and ruffling the grass
while the trees bough down and let us pass

In winter we'd romp and tease the snow
into all kinds of patterns and shapes we'd blow

In the heat of summer we'd cool the brow
tickle the leaves on every branch and bough

And when it's time to stop the play
we'd wait again for another day

The wind has a special place of rest
turns into fog the place it loves best

And so it's there for you to see
for the love of the wind will always be

Marilyn Harberts

Little Jill's Lullaby

Go to sleep, go to sleep, my little Jill
Go to sleep, go to sleep, my little sweet
You, my little Jill, must try and go to sleep
The sky is aglow with tiny, twinkling golden stars

Go to sleep, go to sleep, my little Jill
Go to sleep, go to sleep, my little sweet
Together, let us row to the world of dreams
In the sky, the crescent moon will be our golden skiff

Go to sleep, go to sleep, my little Jill
Go to sleep, go to sleep, my little sweet
You are truly a darling, you must not cry
In the sky, rocking, are your cradle and golden dreams

Yoshiyuki Otoshi

Forever in Our Hearts

To the memory of Anthony Michael Martinez
Though you are gone, you're not forgotten,
You're ever in our hearts,
Though only ten and full of love,
Upon us you left your mark.

You taught us how to love each other,
You taught us how to care,
You taught us how precious life can be,
But we learned these in despair.

Though we'll never hear your laugh again,
Or see your beautiful smile,
We'll hold these memories in our hearts,
Till we meet at heavens' aisle.

A mother mourns, a father too,
A brother, a sister, they mourn too,
A neighbor, a friend, others unknown,
The town of Beaumont, California mourns for you.

You're forever in our hearts
Rest in peace Anthony

James G. Greenfield

The Oak in the Meadow

There's a big oak tree that stands alone
In the middle of a meadow.
It calls out to me, and I go to it,
And sit beneath its shadow.
I sit silently protected from the sun,
And think of all the songs the birds in
This tree must have sung.
Oh, the stories this old tree could tell,
Stories of loves that succeeded and loves that failed.
I'm sure it could tell us of hearts about to break,
And advise us on chances we're afraid to take.
I wonder what secrets to this tree have been told,
Or is it limited to only the secrets I know?
The branches of this tree are like arms
Keeping me safe,
Within its shadow I find a comfortable place.

Tobie Leigh Sims

Life's Song

Once when I was very young,
Life held only sweet songs to be sung.
But I found that the melody of life out-poured,
Is not always composed on a major chord;
That each day has a minor strain
Written in sorrow, trouble and pain.
I know now that the song to treasure
Is the one that holds a bittersweet measure.

Grethe Bichel

Foreclosure

Oh, little house of my dreams
Each day you grow dearer to me
I know I must leave and depart
There is an ache in my heart.

I wander dejected from room to room.
Nothing can cheer me or dispel the gloom
The radio plays softly, the moon shines above
Bringing close reality of the things I love

Grief overwhelms me, no one can share
In secret alone I must bear,
My sun has stopped shining
My moon has gone out
Nothing but sadness and stillness about,

Yesterday nor tomorrow mean nothing to me,
A feeling of rebellion at my coming doom,
It will all be over for too soon
My life will end and I'll be free,

Frances Knupp

The Thunderstorm

It moves in with the ferocity of a wounded tiger—
This thunderstorm of steamy summer;
The rain-heavy beads of prismatic jewels
Fall from the pregnant clouds to the thirsty Earth.

Jagged streaks of electricity shoot across the sky
Followed by deafening claps of thunder—
Giant-sized children playing with colossal blocks
High above humanity in the firmament
Bedlam reigning in kindergarten.

The gusty wind bends the tree limbs—
Immense exhalations of the Creator's breath;
While furry squirrels scamper for shelter
And mere mortals run for safety.
Suddenly, the downpour ceases,
And the thunder becomes a faint echo.

The birds flit atop the screened porch—
Rejoicing lightheartedly in Nature's gifts—
Their sweet songs a paean to divinity;
The tree branches still with somnolence
As the storm moves ponderously into infinity.

Susan J. Friedman

Abandoned Outcast

The shadow of crippling effect, about to be cast
How long can I survive, and continue to last

A dream now tainted, by a loved ones illness
Forever separated, by an apart stillness

Communication, has now been ceased
Level of life, has just decreased

The warm embrace, you once knew
Now engulf, by a darkness view

You cannot see the reason of fate
But you can feel, the desolation of, the abandoned gate

An outcast of not being a family part
Do to your loved ones, past life start

The chill of being kept a haunting distance
Your heart and soul, calling for assistance

It was to be a new beginning, of home and life
A dream coming together, now stricken with strife

An emotional upset, each day to face
Tears and a longing, for things to be back in place

May the power of loves connection, be the winning force
To rid the lonely, abandonment road of course

Dee Brady

Doors

Many swing both ways . . . others spin around
and remain opened while some are kept locked
Through seen everywhere, yet some can't be found
to buzz ring or chime, much less to be knocked

They open to freedom . . . these same confine
at someone's control who will push or pull
These are forbidding but some are just fine
that open for us to our jobs or school

Of steel and of glass, and many of wood
which we slide on tracks while some are drawn up
You'll never use some, while others you should
and are built to last, or briefly setup

They're opened with keys, some even scan cards
which come in all shapes, the old and the new
While most are left vacant, some require guards
who watch us walk through, then . . . one is in you

Among all the doors, and there are countless
this one we're to guard most diligently
Is our hearts wherein spirits seek access
where, even the Lord respects your own key

Bob G. Martinez

Untitled

God created a beautiful view.
When he made the trees, the grass,
The sky so blue.
And God knew what he had in mind.
When God decided to lay down the line.
All rules were made for everyone.
No one is left behind.
And God will judge us one and all.
Not with cruelty,
But being kind.
He knows we all have fallen before.
He knows if your heart is true.
He knows your faith is strong enough.
If only you follow through.
Let God guide you.
He will show you the way.
Follow his rules faithfully.
In heaven you shall stay

Lillian Brink

Two in One

Her Surname or even First
One needs to know least
For, she is sure known best
By her prototype name—"Church Lady";
For a glimpse or a catch
Or some sort of a clue
Of her spontaneous character,
If to search for a possible automatch
In a Super Computer
Like "The Deep Blue"
And if one match shows up, God willing or blessing
That can only be a mysterious blending
Of her lip-loud-flat theory: "Praise The Lord"
And of her own life—deep practice: "Curse the neighbor"—
A master blending of her two poles in close harmony;
Her Daily Communion at each Eucharistic ceremony
And its application on her neighbors seem to be never-ending;
Neighbors or parishioners, however, seem to die to love her
To meet Jesus' most challenging Commandment:
"Love your enemy"—no further comment or amendment.

John Thanickal

A Reflection

To be needed is important, in every lifetime plan,
A sense of being wanted, and giving all you can,
To know that someone needs you simply just to have you near,
Fills that empty place and makes your roads ahead so clear.

The time and space you occupy can only stretch so far,
Its limber elasticity can tell you where you are,
Diminishing, as people do, is seen in any mirror,
An image of reflection, soon becomes so very clear.

You've one more crease to count you didn't notice yesterday,
Perhaps you have miscounted? Or will it go away?
Is this your age progressing as time is passing through?
Does it reflect true likeness, as mirrors so often do?

Recall the face you used to view and gaze upon with glee?
You tell yourself "there is no change" so little do you see!
The same full hair you had before, without a sign of gray.
It says "you are distinctive" "that's so very true" you say!

Are you the one whose fooling you? You look just like a kid!
Observers must be nuts! Or else they've simply flipped their lid!
The truth is right before you—Yes, it's right before your eyes,
You finally found a mirror that simply fits your image size!

Herb Walsh

A True Story

Mother, as a teenage bride, you sailed the
unknown waters from southern China to U.S.A.

Father and you settled in a small California
agricultural town with unpredictable days.

Sacrifices were made during unstable times.
Raising six children left no moments to unwind.

You encouraged us to excel.
Unbeknownst to us, God blesses as He wills.

I shiver at the memory of one wintry flu
epidemic, fears of will we die or live.

As the virus attack weakened our family,
the survival lesson was to "pitch in" and give.

Mother, years of healthy living hurried by.
You later became ill and went into a coma,
without our knowing why?

Family members prayed, you amazingly recovered
briefly, calling out to God.

At the funeral service, your incandescent face
was beautiful and unbelievably peaceful.

Without emotional panic, closure was a final nod.

Dora Low Fung

How to Stay Young at 92

Pick up your heels,
And don't forget to pay your bills.

Don't get sad and blue,
Keep warm, don't get the flu.

Eat right,
Digest plenty of carrots to improve your sight.

Hug a puppy,
And tuck in that protruding tummy.

Wear a smile on your face,
But at 92, don't go on a 3 legged race.

Put on your hearing aid,
Don't let your lovely memories fade.

Make phone calls like you did as a teen,
And don't forget to keep your dentures clean.

Terry Lee Pieszchala

Friend

A friend is a companion, pal, or mate,
someone to understand, realize and appreciate.
A friend will listen to what you have to say
whose continuous love is like a golden ray.

When you are in pain and fear,
they care enough to linger near.
A true friend will not leave you alone
though it tears their heart to hear your moan.

And when you are happy and full of glee,
a friend will be with you. He will not flee.
And when you have finally achieved fame,
a friend will be happy you fulfilled your aim.

A friend will be with you night or day,
if not in body, in spirit anyway.
Your happiness is important but also your fear,
That's when the word friend is especially dear.

June Wiley

Grampy

As I know you
Wearily
You get out of your magical sleep
You put on your usual smile
Happy to breathe the morning air
Your freckled smile grows and grows
As I know you
You put on the socks that are as white fluffy as the clouds
Smiling with delight
Humming a special old tune
As you make your delicious morning coffee
As I know you
You sit down in a chair
You sip your coffee and you are overjoyed
You have as much freedom as a butterfly
And feel as marvelous as a peacock
After you take your final sip
You go out the blushing red door
Knowing the excitement will come again tomorrow
As I know you Grampy

John Hoysgaard

Mother Dear

To you, my dear, there was no other,
Like you, my own kind, loving Mother!
For me, you labored since I was born;
Your hands and face were wrinkle and worn.
Your great big heart was overflowing with Love,
Inheriting your love from God above!
Doing things for me, to you, was Pleasure
And Everything about you I'll always Treasure!

Annie D. Beard

God's Plan

God created man in His own image
Then He breathed His own breath of life into him
And he became a living being.
He did not create any one nationality
To be superior to any other
In God's eyes we are all sisters and brothers.
If you see a sister or brother who is in need
You are compelled in God's word to offer a helping hand
For that's the way it was intended to be in God's plan.
If we could become as little children
And lay all our prejudices aside
There would be no more wars or crime
If together in God's love we would learn to abide.

Wynona Kuntz

A Good-Bye to an Actress

Inspired by Pegasus she bursts forth
    from mount Helicon
To wield her power as did Thespis with his
    poems.
With a blow of her hoof she struck her roles
And brought all to savor heights of glory
    upon the boards.
Oh, regal lady, where now do you turn your
    queenly eye?
Look you back to scores of people you depicted?
Look you back to moments of joy and sadness
    expressed?
And end with the mighty solo of the cane!

Margaret V. Harold

Spring Awakening

In the far distance a faint rumbling becomes closer
and louder turning into whispering roars, which yells fully,
shaking the solid foundation of calm security;
unnerving the staunchest confidence to be found!

Enveloped by a shroud of electrifying lightning;
leaping, skipping, prancing across the stormy night sky,
striking with tremendous explosive power, lighting up the
immediate surroundings, in hues of splendid dancing colors!

A whipping clap smacking sane senses to dust,
awakens trembling fear in all living creatures, to stand at alert;
listening, watching the midnight cry of redemption coming near;
protecting the hopeful humble faithful Christians!

Disrupting storms do eventually sputter to an end,
giving way to the dawning of the morning star rising
brilliantly, smiling warming rays upon wounded hurting hearts;
tenderly healing torn scared emotions with rejuvenating
ambitious energy, that restores physical strength and beauty!

Patrick A. Moats

God's Canvas

Nature is a wondrous scene
From her majestic mountains
To the trickling water droplets of a life giving spring
I gaze upon God's canvas
Everything—so full of life
Breathing, growing, changing
Brilliant colors, dark and light
Each and every living thing was strategically placed by deity
Intelligence and energy coexisting in perfect harmony
My appreciation of these intricate creations
Are sufficient gratitude for Jesus
For that is why he placed them here
For our own joy and happiness.

Manderie Simper

May

The grass is green, the sky is blue,
The foothills have a bluish cast,

Snow peaked mountains, the snow won't last.
A foretime scene.

Waterfalls, water in the springs, pure, pristine,
Wild flowers in mounds, beauty abounds.
A drop of water in a water glass.

Wild life is living a high life, abundance of food. No askance,
A triple crown race conformity that time cannot erase.

Graduation, proms, a new endeavor, sounds of joy,
for an achievement, interpretation.
Maypoles, with ribbons, dancers, weave in and out,
Special delivery of May baskets, that is what beauty is all about.
Preparation, invocation, precaution, for come what May.

Florence G. Axton

Different

We are all born beautiful in God's sight,
and, no, we don't all look alike.

How boring life would be, if we all looked
alike, you and me.

If we all talked and dressed the same,
What a bore, what a shame,

Being different, makes life interesting.
Different colored eyes, different colored hair,
different colored skin,
Is just the package we came wrapped in.

It's what's in the package and what's in that soul,
that really counts,
For deep down in all of us, we have love to give,

So give that love to others, no matter how
different that they be,
For God filled us all up with love inside,
to give away and not to hide.

Ruth E. Steepy

Summer Summer

With warm sunshine and rain
That blesses and kisses the earth
Again and again
Beautiful flowers every where
The setting is sweet and fair
With rich red cherries as red as can be
Hanging on a bough
Lovely you know
How it glows
Dwelling in beauty
The blue berry blue as can be
The black berry black as can be
All in great delectable delightful summer day.

Morton Cohen

Yesterday's Thieves

Aubergine shadows flung down the hillside,
Sound webs spun out by the loon's liquid call,
Glove the horizon in shimmer and silence—
Cover for lovers,
Yesterday's thieves—

Thieves who wander barefooted in thickening twilight,
Threading through whispers and rushes,
Old footfalls of pain—
Thieves who tread so softly, so surely
They step over the threshold
Into the Loom's all shuddering
Now.

Nancy M. Midwood

Success

To walk across the desert dry,
And stumble on the painful cacti.
To see a mirage of water before you,
Seems to be God's way of telling us,
Look to the future, for our salvation.
Ahead of us is a new beginning
Seek it out, and stop the sinning.
Pray for guidance, instead of winning.
Success is yours to earn; at the top
Of your ladder of steps you turned.
Whatever those steps, represent in your life
You've overcome them, in all the strife.
In all the sorrow, in all the ways,
You made a better tomorrow.

Rose E. Snyder

President Roosevelt

His eyes were sunken and tired
His face exhausted and worn
His hair gray and thin
His body frail and flabby
The wars in Europe and Russia
And America and Japan
And the war in North Africa
Have made the President an old man
But his soul is on fire
When the lying, bashing Republican Party
Attacked the President he responded
Even though in a sitting position he spoke
He met the crowds through rain and snow
He still had that touch of a master politician
His speeches of his progress and the United Nations
And America's progress and the quick end to WWII
That his great mission must be completed
And the American people returned President Roosevelt
For a historical 4th term in the White House
He still had the touch

Norman J. Sadler

Old and Lost River

Old and Lost River, the small sign read
I crossed it on a high green bridge one day.
I parked at the end and walked back to the span
and looked down the chasm to where the stream lay.

It looked deep and dark, unhurried and still.
Who named it, who lost it long, long ago?
Was it sad to be lost, did it hurt to be old?
Or had it flowed past the pain to turn peaceful and slow?

Did the fish leap high when the summers came?
And did little boys swing on vines from the shore?
Did it splash and sing on its way to the sea?
Was there a falls filled with spray and a roar?

I feel a deep kinship with that old stream,
With its memories of splendid days so free.
Still survival is sweet and the peaceful and slow
carry the Old River Lost and me.

Shirley Scholl

Dreams of the Past

If only we could capture our dreams of the past
We would never cry or weep as nothing lasts
Voices call out from the grave trying to be heard
Telling us stories we never knew
In a dream state of mind we can realize
we participated in a dream
Our feelings are confused leaving us with deep thoughts
Can our dreams tell us what is ahead
or prepare us for future happenings?
Frustrated though it may be
Our dreams are with us always
It is matter how we handle our dreams.

Charlotte Burke

Epictetus' Forty-Third (A Free Will)

Two images that confuse,
two actions, two thoughts.
Only one can be chosen,
the other may not.

Hard choices between extremes,
woefully, only one within my means.
One given power and, therefore, free,
with the other, unsatisfied, still haunting me.

Allen E. Brogan

My Special Garden

Come to the garden of prayer—
It's so easy a path; strewn with Roses;
and there within the gate—Is the Lord so fair
Waiting and eager to hear; and within His
arms He will gently hold you
O! Come to the Garden of prayer

There He is within the Gate; He backs you
where no other has been and gently He'll talk
to you there.
He will love you and teach you and comfort
you there—
O! Come to the Garden of prayer.

The birds within O! So gently do sing
He will counsel you there and bring you
great joy; as you share in the spirit with Him
He His life He has given; these joys
to bestow so come to the garden of Prayer.
His blessings He bestows to those who
are there—Waiting and Watching for Him
Within these Gates Heaven opens

Ethel Marshall

The Look of Christmas

White snowy streets aglow with wreaths and candles
Stores full of smiling faces and scurrying people
Christmas bazaars, company parties, dinners and dances
This is the look of Christmas.

Houses lighting up for weeks at a time
Everyone sending the message of peace in
Each separate act preparing for the twenty-fifth
This is the look of Christmas.

Shining faces with bright twinkling eyes
Fancy foods and sugar plum dreams
Special treats saved for all year
This is the look of Christmas.

Loving prayers and candle light services
Choirs praising the birth of Christ
Sharing, giving, laughing and crying
This is the look of Christmas.

What is so special about a tree in your home
All covered with lights, trinkets and garlands
That it fills you with wonder, joy and peace?
This is the look of Christmas.

Patricia Wylie Gilbert

The Defector

It was nice to have a steady, more than just my friend,
To share some precious moments, and not have to pretend.

We like to go on picnics and lay out in the park.
We used to spend all day and end up in the dark.

He told me I was different and not like all the rest.
Of the many he had known he like me the best.

Often we went dancing, on his feet he was so light,
But sometimes we'd just park, and make love through the night.

I confessed my love for him, this guy with the blue-grey eyes.
He said he loved me also, but I know now he lies.

Last week he took me boating on one that had a sail,
I thought the time was right to tell my little tale.

I told him I was pregnant and the child would need a father.
He said he could not be one, it would be to much bother.

I blinked as he told his story, his eyes a cold blue blend,
"Fact is I don't love you, but you'll always be my friend."

The moral of this story is not hard to detect.
It's better to be married than to have a friend defect!

Albert Patchin

Schizophrenia

Laying in a padded room,
the stray jacket is your doom.
You often have to break a sweat,
from running away from the monsters in your head.
You hear the voices screaming at you,
always telling you what to do.
All it is, is an internal fight,
at your mind the enemy bites,
You try to grip your sanity,
but this disease won't let you be.
So tonight you fight once again,
and just maybe it will be the end.

Nick Walton

"My Treasure"

Today I watched a sunbeam as it danced across the room;
I touch the velvet petal of a rose;
And a most delicious odor—I cannot give it a name—
Sent tantalizing sweetness to my nose.

I heard a haunting melody—I was humble, I was proud;
It filled my heart, it made me glad that I am me!
I tasted milk and honey and it satisfied my soul
And I thought: "This is life as it should be!"

The sunbeam that I watched was a pair of happy feet;
The rose—the fresh smooth skin of tender youth;
The tantalizing odor, mixed with jam and soap and paste,
Was an all-revealing childlike love and truth.

The song that stirred heart with emotions that were mixed
Changed words and tune as children's often do;
But to me a mighty chorus filled the air with perfect song
And each time I heard, it lifted me anew.

The sweetness of honey mixed with milk was just a kiss,
But it had the precious value of a pearl;
No gem that earth can yield ever be so pure
As that precious gift from God—my little girl!

Kathyrine Benedict

These Things I Love

Discovering a book that takes me away
To places I've never been
Learning something new about someone
That gives me joy within.
Searching the scriptures and traveling far
To lands unknown
Being a mother and the joy it brings
When a child is born.
The blessed assurance that trouble don't last
Forever and a day
And life with Jesus will be much better
And is just a breath away.
Studying his word from day to day
And trying to do his will
Having friends who know my faults
But love me still.

Laura B. Overton

An Ode to Lebanon

While the little green marker on the uncharted course
    Sits patiently to watch a handful of fools
Destroy what means so much to many
    A country, beautiful indeed
A people that want to live in peace
    I'm an American Lebanese never seeing
The beauty of my fathers country,
    But seeing the beauty in him
All Lebanese must rise
    Recognizing that they are one
So the children can live and love in peace

Jimmie Abraham Shamon Jr.

The Shadow of Retirement

I am longing for the good old days, when I felt so free,
And I didn't have a "Shadow" always watching over me!

There used to be days, I could come and go as I pleased,
But now I have a "Shadow," he's here even if I sneeze!

I can't dust the furniture, or even sweep the floor,
Without my "Shadow" peeking around the corner of the door!

I can't do the laundry, or go alone now to the grocery store,
My "Shadow" even laughs, and says he listens to me snore!

When I am in the kitchen, and I try to do the cooking,
My "shadow" is always there, and it's just a looking!

But I think what I hate the most, is the bathroom scene,
Because I like to take my time, and scrub, until I am clean!

And when I use the toilet, oh privacy is my dream,
But my "shadow" is usually there, I could really scream!

Perhaps I could lock the door, but would that keep it out,
Or would the dreadful "shadow" come, from within the waterspout!

So if you know what I can do, will you tell me please,
Or one day soon, I may give my "shadow's" neck a squeeze!!

Ruth J. Braun

The Shell

I am a turtle, snug, hard on the top; procrastinating before reason
I walk along the border and watch the botchery that is going on.

As I sit on the table mixed with broth and pepper all around me,
society slups me with a spoon.

I snap as the contaminate weeds grow around my four scaly limbs,
tries to change the diet of the inner mass.

But my bones are covered with an everlasting shield of God.

Lonna Traynor

Wanting

Gasping for air, watching life go by,
walking the treads to keep alive.
Pushing on, keeping the faith
never looking back, always grasping for the ring.
Surrounding oneself constantly with others,
alone within oneself, pushing away reality.
Wanting what is not attainable, denying
what one has, as if never really there.
The possessions and trappings are the
substitute for what is important.
Single, solitary, hollow, always wanting.

Michael Lefkoe

The Whips and Scorns of Time

The once strong, surging force
That easily haphazardly
Rolled over life's hills and valleys,
Through its placid glades and sheltered forests,
Around troublesome barriers, rocks and boulders,
Down glistening, spraying waterfalls,
A clear, rippling, flowing, vibrant stream.

Burdened by the impedimenta
Of life and nature
Their excrement and offal
Slowly very slowly,
Unwillingly but inexorably succumbs:

A still, unrippled, stagnant pool
Oozing into a muddy morass
Drying out slowly imperceptibly
Into dust
Whence it came.

Isaac C. Donner

My Mother Always Had a Light

My mother always had a light.
To keep away the dark of night.
She slept in fear without a light.
She thought God could not see her soul if it was not bright.
He came for her in the middle of the night.
Guided by her light.
Now she rest where it is never night.
But always warm and bright.

Rose A. Buck

Summer Parting

A gentle breeze stirs the humid air
She walks into the amber sunlight
She stands there like a sunlit goddess
Chestnut hair cascading down her shoulders

She stands in a gown of the finest green silk
Her alluring curves so gently highlighted
Flowing together in her perfect form
As a gentle summer rain begins to fall

He longs to scoop her into his arms
To feel her delicate body
Nestled so close to his heart
As he holds her until the end of time

Her tender red lips kiss his cheek
Stirring the fires of his soul to new heights
As a tear glides down her porcelain cheek
And walks into the golden horizon

But this is not the end for them
For her sweet rose will never wither
In his eyes she is most beautiful
And he will never forget her sweet laugh

Brian Ganninger

Prison

The bars, the fence, the 6 by 9 cell.
The solitude the anguish, the inmates living hell.
Prison isn't the rules the walls or even the time.
Prison is the sanity of one man's mind,
Leaving family and loved ones behind.
Oh, how the heart regrets the crime of the mind.
The mind is the soul, and the soul is you.
The conscience is the judge of the evil you do.
The conscience soothes your mind, and protects your soul.
Your mind is the prison your conscience controls.
The spirit is the breath that the conscience mind left.
The wickedness that you do brings the soul death.
So clear your mind, and free your soul,
And the evil in your heart will forever be let go.
You can lie to yourself but never to me,
Because I am your soul, and I beg to be free.

Willie Walker

For Sale

Shiny black, leather, upholstery staring back from the display
Case of vehicles, outside the windowpane,
Of an empty minded fool of shameless compromise.
The menarche of freedom expelled upon youthful expectation
Of independence and individuality.
Sharpness of mind dulled by the senses of conformity
And steal from the pocket book of childlike wonder,
Igniting a field of dreamlike trances
From which one can not be called to return.
Sold upon the scripted promissory note of time and taxes;
One arm and one leg left behind.
Driving the force of wisdom into the futuristic mind.

Kim Boshears

What Are We Fighting For!

Rage, Hate, this is just the start,
Bombs, shooting is everyday's part.
Nobody really cares, in my days we did not look the other way.
What are we fighting for, we sang in the days of Vietnam.
Nutty people they called us, till they saw what came!
Unity, Protest for Violence and Hate.
Most People today doing just the same,
They take the Politician's bait.
What does it take to stop the Hate!
I ask myself again, look around
"What are we fighting for," this is not Nam.
Everyday people Die, ask yourself why?
Do you still care?
Or is your heart empty and bare
From greed for wealth, disregarding Love,
Which is Unity, Peace and Health!

Marika H. Austin

Look for "Yellow Pods" Dotting

"No butter? 'n you're servin' sweet corn?
Or, because the doctor sez "No butter?"
Why, people were eatin' it before we were born
Well, there's a way for the problem to solve!
This moratorium doesn't have to last long.
For this denial may well be dissolved
"Butter the seed corn" will be our song!
As we plant our "specimen" in the ground
And with our "guests," 'n others will await our gong!

"In a row, by itself, this experiment, will plant
and keep "our eyes" watchful, less other people
will trespass 'n say "we can't!"
"We will, also, watch for any new signs
Husk it carefully 'n hopefully, for nature's new design
And set "our specimen" on this dish
Look for "yellow-pods" dotting every two kernels
Look, look! look! There's rows of "butter-pods"
In the midst of kernels of corn!"

Herbert Moorhouse

Waterford Express

I remember standing next to her
Dropping pennies into water—
Crystal-clear in my mind
I remember watching her clean the crystal
She was very proud of its shine
I remember when she passed away
Still, crystal clear in my mind
And, I remember standing on the Golden Gate Bridge
To bid her a farewell
As she disappeared over the horizon
Aboard the "shiny" Waterford Express
I'll remember you, always, Mom.

Dee Dee Brinkman

My Mother, Mary

My Mother's all love . . . it overflows from her heart,
You see it extending to everyone, right from the start!

Many's the time, she has herself done without,
Obtaining our needs instead, of this I've no doubt!
Teaching us by example, her patience just so evincing,
How tender her hugs, even my bros do no wincing!
Evident to all, her love for God and the Blessed Mary,
Really razzed 'bout her name, she is NOT "quite contrary"!

My Mother's my role model, which she makes look so easy,
A Saint, my dad calls her, (I'm speaking quite Frank-ly)!
Rarely, a halo and wings, in the flesh, will you see,
Yet, that's what my Mother is . . . an ANGEL to me!

Peg Mitchell

Stardust Serenade

Ivory white,
silver light,
sparkling like crystal of Morn's dew.
Nature of fragile sensitivity.
Sweet as the newborn lamb of God.
Purely innocent.
Sweetest Shetland Sheepdog.
White lullaby
of
blue Skylight . . .
Twilight in her eye.
Melody glittering
with
Love, Hope, and Faith.
A Serenade
embraced in glittering paw prints of Angel Dust . . .
My precious little darling.
My little lamb.
My Star.

Michelle J. Murphy

The Historical Jesus

The Historical Jesus, the promised of the ages,
born by a mother undefiled.
Reared by her and His foster father, Joseph.
Both descendants of King David. Loving, kind,
dedicated and qualified to care for this child.

Worshipped by three Kings from afar,
who were guided to the cave of his birth
in Bethlehem by a brilliant star.

Grown to manhood graceful to behold.
By Him ten lepers were made whole.
The sick healed in body and soul.

Raised the daughter of Jairus, and Lazarus
back to life. Power without equal, His right.

Destroy this temple and in three days,
I will rebuild it. After His death, the meaning
of His words, were made evident in the
Resurrection.

His ascension into Heaven has taken place
where He awaits, the forgiven and the purified
of the human race.

Sarah A. Gracie

Cause and Effect

Be responsible for your own behavior.
Make a decision—what then will be the consequences?
Were you taught right from wrong?
How does it make you feel when you do something bad?
Bad for you, bad for someone else.

You may justify your behavior, anyway you want:
You were mistreated as a child.
You are not loved. (God loves you, you are his child.)
You're not beautiful, rich, or smart.
Whatever!

You are probably mind sick.
You may suffer from "Cognitive Dissonance."
When you believe one thing (Cognitive = knowledge)
Then behave differently from those beliefs (Dissonance = discord)
You make yourself sick.

If you have money you can hire a Psychiatrist.
If you change your behavior and live according to your beliefs
You may get well—if you haven't become too corrupt.

It's up to you.

Merilyn Alexander

Alone

You start out a pain. You love and have such a
friendship. You are always together in heart and soul.
   Your life grows in such wonderful ways. Children
come, join your love. They make life more complete. You
watch them grow and make their own life of love.
   Through out your life, friends come and go, but there
are some that are always there to the end. They make your life
have such pleasure. You share many things together.
   Then things change. You are alone, one has gone to
God. And things change for good.
   Your friends rally around you. Your family stays
close by. Then it hits, your alone
   They all go their way, you no longer fit in you
fill like you are left out in the cold. No longer,
will life be the same, you no longer fit in, they
don't come to visit, they just let you alone.
   Now you are really alone.
        Alma Jean Massey

A Church on a Hill

A church in a field looks just right
For it was called by God to be that light.

A hill to stand out among the rest
That means God has called us to do our best.

A road that leads us to a door
We open it and look for more.

What we find is a God so beautiful and bright
And a heart of love that will be just right.

So be a light on a hill to shine
A church that knows God will do just fine.
        Frank Pfitzenmeyer

The Journey

They came gushing forth as a liquid torrent
Through tiny fissures in the mountain cleft
Down, down they descended low;
Their mighty rush roared with vibrant force.

The flowing mass thundered past my ear
Crashing, splashing near my feet.
They looked like tiny crystal beads that danced
And bounced from rock to rock.
Then they disappeared.

Now, at last, the little splashing beads will rest
In quiet arms that soothe their torrential past.
Joined with others, they flow rhythmically
Toward the sea, gently lapping the earthen nest.

Will I ever see those little crystal beads again?
If I run to the sea and look intently
Through the sun's sparkling prismed hue,
I'll find them ascending where the rainbows have no end.
        Carrie Inman

Poetry Is Born

Poetry is born
Along the feathery edges of the world
Where light meets dark
Where known and unknown mate
Where consciousness is forming and unformed.

Poetry is built
Of tiny pebbles, gathered on the shores
Of Newtons' mighty ocean—
Too small to build a house, and yet
Too loved to throw away.
        Marion Perkus

How I Love Thee

I love thee more than the vastness of the sea
I love thee more than the freshness of air we breath
I love thee more than the tallest of redwood tree
I love thee more than the sun does shine free
I love thee more than the gatherings of honeybee
I love thee more than the greatest of symphony
I love thee more than the day and night that be
I love thee more than the most beautiful of sites to see
I love thee more than anything, so this I plea
Love me for at least half as much as I love thee
        Francine Yenner

Stray Dog

Whining, tail drooping, begging to be owned.
Guardian of life with no master.
Kicked, scorned, chased away.
He thinks back to better days.
No one cares, he ambles along the road.
Car too fast—now broken and dying.
Who notices that a stray dog sleeps here?
Now, he's lonely no more—new home, new master.
        Mildred Hyatt McLoud

Don't Weep for Me

Don't weep for me when am gone,
For I will be up in heaven rejoicing in a Marathon.
You see, I was called home by my Heavenly Father.
He said, "Dear child, come on in; you have led a
good life after turning from sin.
You have grown and blossomed into a beautiful flower.
Now I can prune you to use in my heavenly garden.

Your life on earth was not always a joy,
But now you will be compensated as my angel,
like every humble girl and boy.
Don't look back, come on in; rejoice with
me and all your friends,
Earth is just a learning field
Where all my angels are sent to be fulfilled.
You have had your share of trails and tribulations,
Although it was a growth process for your rejuvenation.
Therefore to enter into my heavenly gate,
you had to be refined into an angelic state."
So friends and loved ones, don't weep for me,
For I am up in heaven, with God and all His glory.
        Nola Grace Holder

Death as a Person

I see His shadow
Hovering over me as
He comes towards me
His shadows seems like Black Dark blankets

I sense His eyes staring at Me
Dark and Deep as the Depth of an Endless hole

I hear His footsteps
a rhythm that seems like He is hesitating
as He comes towards Me

I feel His Desire
to wrap Me around His Black shadow
that seems to swallow Me whole
falling into a Deep Sleep

I smell His Escape CK fragrance for Men
that seems to warn Me
the smell takes me
into a Deep Trance

I taste the tears flowing from His Dark eyes
His teary eyes shows me that
I must follow Him to the place of Darkness
        Elaine Kwong

Sonnet for Love Rediscovered

You are far away now,
but never really far.
You are as close as the smell of autumn on a cool day in October.
Chrysanthemums are everywhere this fall,
Filling my sight with their gay color.
Like curly towheads they brighten every place.
Who can forget a chrysanthemum?
It is a chunk of sun to keep you warm all winter.
I'll never forget them, or your face!
Now winter has covered everything with snow
And I have put my heart away 'til spring.
Some morning the south wind will burst into my room
With April in his arms!
Then I will uncover my heart and find you.

Nadine Lewis

The Time We Love Is Drawing Near

The time we love is drawing near
    all the children delight to hear
Of old Saint Nicholas whom we love
Who comes down the chimney from above
    The stockings all hang in a row
To see them Santa says ho, ho, ho.
    Then each stocking one by one
Santa keeps filling 'til he's done
    after all the stocking have been well-filled
Santa never thinks of having them billed
    He picks up his pack and mittens too
And away he goes up the chimney flue.

    He's now making his way across the plain
To cheer all the children once again
    Then Santa and his reindeer disappear
And will not be seen 'til another year.

Grace M. Glover

Heart Gauge

Been ridin' around this town for hours
and the gauge is gettin' kinda low.
I see your car behind every set of headlights
Your arm around every girl.
Drivin' past your house
My eyes are brimmin' with tears.
You're not there.
Should I try to find you?
Or should I listen to my gauge,
tellin' me I'm out of time?
We started on a full tank
Now I'm drivin' all alone on empty.
We just need a spark
and the feeling will explode again.
Please don't let the gauge get too low.

Lori Beth Hudson

Unset Amethyst

I never dreamed that I should hold
Effects of cataclysmic chaos of the world.
But here before my eyes, devoid of earth,
The precious story lies, perfection tempered
By the run of years untold.
Unmeasured skies saw nature's alchemy unfold
Amid the pressures of events, in earthquakes
And volcanic heat, a crucible to test the elements,
The passing hours only marked
By shifting banks of mist.
No secret of the unseen Chemist's skill
This earth can claim
But must instead yield all the good
The years have told,
Embodied in the limpid clarity of this unset amethyst.

Ella May Frazer

The Salt Runs Down My Face

I hesitate by the vast ocean
Weighing her wonder and my fear
She is awesome and I tremble
And the salt runs down my face
My toes wiggle in the warm soft sand
I stand content then promenade along the crashing beach
A sharp barnacle kisses my toe
My knees buckle and the warm sticky blood marries the sea
I drop backward and my eyes burn.
The wave crashes over my head and my tears touch the sea
And the salt runs down my face

Alexis Wood

Individual Soul Salvation

No one can live your life for you
No one can get your reward that is due
So save yourself from this untoward generation
For this is an individual soul salvation
Some will dispute the need to be saved
some have fought holiness all the way to their grave
But if you are open minded, humble and aware
You would say "it's me oh Lord, standing in the need of prayer"
Judging first yourself, to avoid the greater condemnation
Ignoring hypocrites knowing it's an individual soul salvation
I find that you have everything to gain with Christ
and without Him everything to lose.
Still the way you live is up to you
But it shouldn't be hard to choose
In brief, God set before us good and evil—life and death
And said choose ye this day sin or righteousness
In these last days we find—
Men are living God's word by their own interpretation
But I'm here to tell you
There is one Lord, one faith and one plan of salvation.

Joel B. Parker

The Cycle

One life ends,
Another one begins.
When one begins it brings joy to all,
The joyful tears start to fall.
When one ends it brings tears too,
The ending of life makes them blue.
They're both different, yet both the same,
For they both involve a name.
It goes on day after day, and year after year,
The beginning is marvelous, but the ending is feared.

Rose Bucklew

A Small Child

A child is so precious and dear,
you have to be very quiet for the things
they might hear.

You give them a bath,
the bubbles pop, float around and they don't last.

When their stomach ache,
they had too much on their plate.

A little shy, a little fear,
but don't worry mommy, daddy is near.

Sugar and spice everything nice,
I don't want to tell you more than twice.

You go to the doctors for a shot,
they told you that you were a great little tot.

It's great being a child,
when I can slip and fall, keep a smile.

Tina M. Poole

Me and My Ocean

Me, who will swim at your full body of water,
Who names you ocean.
Ocean, who will make waves from the wind,
That the atmosphere has, will hit me
With all his power back to my land.
Ocean, who has fish, whales, sharks, treasure
For so many years, will stay rich.
And I who always swim and dive will be poor.
With the hope of getting.
With the hope of success.
While you don't have any hope
But to stay with everything you have.

Jose L. Funes

I Am Who I Am

I am a child. I play, I eat and I have fun.
I am who I am and that's who I'll be for all eternity.

I am a teen. I talk, I love and I joke around.
I am who I am and that's who I'll be for all eternity.

I am a mother. I cook, I clean, and I work.
I am who I am who I am and that's who I'll be for all eternity.

These people are all dreamers, lovers and hopers,
And they all love being just that for all eternity.

Valynn Lee

I Don't Want to Die

With roses in my hand I'm as sad as can be,
As I walk along through the cold cemetery.
Looking for the gravestone that might be hers,
Having painful memories and flashback blurs.

We drove to a party that wasn't too far,
Only to be hit by a drunk driven car.
I ask myself "Why did I live and she have to die?"
As I stand over her gravestone and begin to cry.

I wish I was dead instead of her,
I wish it were her that would go on and endure.
I lay down the roses and begin to walk away,
Thinking of the price that she had to pay.

The tears I weep could fill buckets and pails,
When I think of the idiot that killed her, thankfully he's in jail.
It was one year ago today in which she died,
The day when the whole world wept and cried.

And I remember her face as a tear filled her eye,
As she spoke to me her last words
"I don't want to die."

Jason Morales

Society's Child

Small child with wondering, large, innocent eyes.
So sensitive and bewildered,
Unable to accuse or despise.

A child that's caught in between
A whirlwind unpredictable society
Battles a cold fast future world,
That exists in endless poverty.

He never questions or complains his part
In this hard life.
He just learns to be strong
As he learns to survive.

When he grows older
There's a stand he'll take.
With reason, fight, and determination,
A better world someday he'll make.

Cherylann Gray

Killer

Unstoppable we feel,
Sometimes invincible and unreal.
Like a nine year old boy
Aiming his first blue steel.
His target captured in the scope of his eye
Giving him the feel of a true-to-life spy.
His breath has now ceased
But the killer in him yet not released.
He wipes off the sweat of his hands
And cocks back his gun for this final stand.
He whispers to himself, "I want to see the white of your eyes,"
Like his idol, Clint Eastwood, in the flick, Hang 'Em High.
Feeling the blood rush to his head,
He feels no remorse; he just wants him dead.
His first shot echoes in the air.
His target hit with five shots to spare.

Alida J. Gonzales

The Magic of Love!

Love is like magic, it always will be,
For love shall remain a sweet mystery.

Love works in ways that are wondrous and strange.
There's nothing in life love can not change.

Love can transform in the most common places,
Into beauty, or splendor, or sweetness and grace.

Love is unselfish, understanding and kind,
For it sees with its heart, and not with its mind.

Love is the answer that everyone seeks.
Love is the language that every heart speaks.

Love can't be bought, it's priceless and free.
Love, like a pure magic, it's life's sweet mystery.

Mike D. Ogden

Gratefulness

The urge to strive for more
To work at first and then work harder
Laziness one must abhor
In order for one to become smarter.

The greatness of one human being
To be a guide and help others out
To answer questions in every little thing
Till one destroys every single doubt.

They are both equal in importance
For one could not exist without the other
To which is better there is no preference
In the way one would love both, a son or daughter.

But the teacher is the one you respect the most
For they not only know, but take the time to be your host.

Fernando Recalde

Though You Slay Me

My sky is falling . . . down all around me.
My world is crumbling . . . coming to an end.
All hope abandoned . . . except that in your name.
You're still here . . . you are my only friend.
The devil fighting . . . hard to make me stumble.
All out attacks . . . come from every side.
Lord, I am weak . . . down on my knees I'm crawling.
Father, in your strength . . . is where I must abide.
Tears not just trickling . . . but streaming down my cheeks.
I cry our in terror . . . and then you comfort me.
Because you know why this is happening . . . what I'm going through.
And you must have a plan . . . even though I don't know what to do.
Even when I'm weak . . . and on my own not standing.
Father, though you slay me . . . I will always trust in you.

Alex Dooley

I'll Meet You There

Today's the day, or maybe the next,
At the sound of the trump, our Lord shall return.
This great day is coming, just wait and see
Just think what rejoicing there will be.

The Dead in Christ shall rise first,
And those that are left that's His, will join them.
In just the twinkling of an eye,
Our Lord we shall meet in the sky.

Steve Roberts, my brother and dearest friend,
Has cancer we're told, but not from sin.
Lives are touched in miraculous ways,
Our Lord will receive all the Glory, all the Praise.

What's my sickness? What is yours?
Sin's the greatest sickness of this world.
Christ has paid the price for all sin,
We must not give up, nor give in.

The Gift of Life is what we need.
For by Grace are we saved, through Faith.
Christ Blood was shed to set us free,
So overcomers we must, we shall, we will be!

Dr. Larry A. Wiley

The Crash

I thought of you, Mom, before the crash.
Four friends in the car; two beers on the dash.
The driver was drunk and reeking of booze,
and his friend right beside him started to snooze.
The driver laughed and awoke his friend,
And with the wet slippery road around the bend.
The car spun around and hit a tree,
then I awoke and saw blood on me.
Then I got scared, Mom, when I saw the blood.
We never should have been in this car with Bud.
Crying and screaming from this bloody mess,
please, dear Mom, don't think anything less.
He seemed able to drive, he said "I'm fine,"
no beer in the system, the fault is not mine.
But it is my fault for getting in the car.
I saw the two beers on the dash from the bar.
My head's getting cold, Mom, my hands I can't feel,
this isn't a dream, I know it's for real.
I'm sorry to leave you, to not say good-bye,
but with my four friends, I'm waiting to die.

Tom Carter

My City

If the ocean could shelter life
From melancholy or endless strife,
And keep the spirit in its harmony,
From wandering and from insanity;

If the sun could shelter the light
From the widening shadow of the grave in sight,
And give a touch of warmth to the coldness near
To halt silent the runaway stream of tears;

If the night could shelter the stars
Before the perplexing dawn reveals our scars,
And let the mind ponder over the awesome vision
Of an eternal realm or the strings of fiction;

If the wind could shelter the breath
Of the tormented soul before the approaching death,
And hold in its vast whirlwind to the brink
The longing man, searching for the missing link,

My City will be the hollow and sacred Temple
Where the faithful come to pray and no longer tremble,
Away from the shattering roar of gods and prophets,
Where humanity waits as the ultimate conquest.

Michael J. Kassouf

V

Once i crossed the Alps
i didn't have a hundred African elephants
i didn't have a thousand Carthaginian soldiers
i didn't have Hannibal's mighty heart
but with me i had a friend.

Once i sailed the turbulent seas and oceans
i didn't have a schooner as hardy as a battleship
i didn't have a fleet as fit as the English navy
i didn't have the courage and knowledge of Captain James Cook
but with me i had a friend.

Once i trekked the Sahara under the scorching desert heat
i didn't have a camel to carry me over the sand
i didn't have any water to quench my thirst
i didn't have any nomadic blood or perspicacity to help me
persevere
but with me i had a friend.

Once i just used to think of these feelings of mine
but today, i sit and write this ode
for you my friend
only for you.

Asna A. Matin

A Question in the Night

When he was born
He stepped in not knowing a thing
Covered in bliss
Do no wrong
They told him that's how to live
But he stabbed it down
Never thinking of the future and no regrets
It soaks his skin
And fills his veins
I am lost he told himself
Never scared because he had it right by his
As he lays on a wet ground
He looks up at the stars
And asks himself
How can one of my enemies be my best friend

Donald Gomez

We Ship Our Love, Our Precious Pearls

It starts with mother and father,
then it goes to sister and brother.
Our plants and flowers
have a place in our vase,
and that puts a smile on our face but:
The love between moms and babies
sail around the world,
Like a boomerang our love comes back to us
in our little boys and little girls.
They are like pearls that were shipped from the orient
to the other side of the world and:
Circle back to our hearts like ship from the start;
Our little circle of pearls.
And the circle goes on and on and on . . .

Brenda Joan Henderson

Dreaming of Snow

Leaping, reeling children play
within the snow upon this day.
In the snow the children roll
as they think of the North Pole.
As I tread on the snow, my footprints are aglow.
As snow falls lightly in the night,
I look out my bedroom window.
What a sight! I pull over my covers tight,
When I dream of snow tonight.

Blair Áine Riddell

On Mothers' Day

Mother is a word I know so sweet and gentle,
Whose only heart holds memories so close;
In her care a child's confidence is not so little,
For the word "Mother" is strong and composed.

The voices of wisdom encompass her way,
Agility accompanies her love and encouragement;
Her forbearing nature heals wounds of dismay,
Strength she will provide in time of disparagement.

A mother's smile will give a sufficient assurance,
When coyness and uncertain feelings will occur;
Her patience available to extend a faraway distance,
A mother's love as clear as crystal will not deter.

When insecurity and confusion lead to destruction,
A mother's arms provide a strong and solid fortress;
Her sensitivity will give sufficient instruction,
A child finds safety haven in her sweet caress.

Her children may go places so faraway,
Only to find out that "There is no place like home."
A mother's incomparable love will lead the way,
Home, into an open arms and to a familiar tone.

Virginia E. Sigley

Strutting in the Rain

Umbrellas bloom along streets of the city,
Bumbershoot color on a ra"-ainy' day;
Everyone's ears love to hear what they hear,
As the pitter/patter rain drips from cocky display!

Splish/splash sloshes of galoshes,
Ladies in a rhythmic strut say, "Hey!"
Drippy weather doesn't ruffle any feathers,
It's the city and another, colorful day!

[Chorus:] I am strutting in the rain;
Rhythm in showers sublime!
I am strutting in the rain;
Spirits are smooth as a fine aged wine!

Frontwards/backwards through the puddles,
At the windy city it's a time to play
Wise-quack wobble with a duck-like waddle,
Umbrellas twirling, it's a ha"-ap'-py day!

Stiff breeze blows across the sidewalk,
Face getting wet from a misty spray;
Fresh air zipping, smiles are dripping,
But the spirits aren't wet in the city today!

Gary Bitson

Fallen Angel

They called you an angel.
You must have fallen.
They called you a princess.
Someone must have stolen your diadem.
Your angelic grace is gone.
Your princess-like innocence has disappeared.
You look out at the misery you caused,
Yet you don't seem to care.
Pain was brought to all those who loved you.
Sorrow surrounds you,
Yet you remain untouched.
Are you immune to any emotion?
Do you feel the pain you cause?
You look down and see the grey land below you,
Yet still you smile.
You feel nothing.
Nothing has an effect on you.
Your heart is empty.
Your soul is cold.

Teresa Dinkins

Looking Inside

Who I am,
I don't quite know.
I've been raised a certain way,
But I feel it's not the real me.
On the out side my life is wonderful,
All though the inside is different.
The feeling of not pleasing anyone,
Or being not as pretty as the girl next door.
I feel alone,
But maybe not.
Living in the place I do,
Everyone is happy—
Except me.
I don't quite know,
Who I am.

Melissa L. Shaw

My Dear Friend

I've thought of you lately remember knowing you once,
Somehow we lost touch, days, weeks, then months.
I doubt very seriously you'd recognize me now,
At first so slight—I've changed and how.
I miss the expressions, the thoughts, your song,
"Take a break—it's okay" but Lord was I wrong.
To know you again what a pleasure it would be,
The whole picture—oh yes. Again I would see.
But how do I find such a long lost friend?
One within my own soul, together till the end?
Where to look, I don't know, who to ask, I can't see,
This challenge—most clever—because my dear friend is me.

Holly C. Connolly

Celebrate Life

Let's celebrate life today, as if it were
Our last day on earth
Let's cling to each other with the memories
Of yesterday smiling along the way
Tides of water from the beach—our eyes yearning to meet
Let's celebrate our youth even when
It's in our old age, life at its own pace
Remember it's only the turning of another page
Each with its own story full of vigor and roaring glory
Let's celebrate our song that we keep close to our heart
With the stirring thought it might bring us apart
Only to meet again in years to come
Laughing with joy at how we've grown
Let's celebrate life today
It's not far away it's here forever and ever to stay.

Joyce E. Lee

The Clock

The clock strikes 12 midnight,
A baby is born.
What a cute baby!
The baby is full of curiosity.
The years pass by.
The clock strikes 2 o'clock,
The child is in the 6th grade.
The child is full of imagination.
The clock clicks to 3,
The teen graduates from high school.
The teen is full of excitement.
The adult is full of happiness.
The adult has a child of her own.
This child will be a nice and loving child.
The adult dies.
The family knows that the adult has lived a
full, healthy, happy life.
The clock strikes 12 midnight,
A baby is born.

Michelle Andoniello

Cloud Nine

When I think about you, and how we were,
And knowing you were mine,
I remember thinking to myself
"You know, I like the atmosphere up here on Cloud Nine."

When I think of how we used to be,
It only makes me cry.
But I used to always turn to you to share my grief,
So I'll just let my tears dry.

Because I realize now, that when I turn
You'll only be farther away;
But it pains me to think thoughts like that
So I open my eyes to the day.

Your shoulder was always there for me
Whenever I needed to shed a tear.
I felt so safe in your arms like that
Knowing you had no fear.

So here I am, alone in the dark,
Wishing you were mine.
And I'm still thinking about the happy atmosphere
Up there on Cloud Nine.

Shamita Trivedi

Daily Preservation Checklist for Peace of Mind

Awaken, love yourself, and the day . . .
Look in the mirror, like what you see . . .
Your beautiful, special, essential to thee . . .
Feed thy desires, with fruits, and grains . . .
Energize destiny to carry thy plans . . .
Love who you are, and teach who you can . . .
Absorb true expressions of your fellow man . . .
Ponder the day as it falls into night . . .
Capture the specialties of true delight . . .
Listen for pieces of thy days plight . . .
For it will begin again at day light . . .

Elizabeth A. Heintz

Our Love of Trees

To Sarah, my first granddaughter
If you could see a little tree a standing all alone,
would you put your hands around it and say "Hi tree"?

If you could see a bigger tree a standing all alone,
would you put your arms around it and say " Hi tree"?

If you could see a great big tree a standing alone,
would you put your arms as far as you could reach
and say "Hi tree"?

If your grandma put her arms as far as she could reach
and take your hands in hers, would you squeeze your
arms around the tree so we could say "Hi tree . . . we Love you."

Sandra E. Nelson

My Love

I walk into the room and there you are.
From across the room I see you over the sea of faces.
My, how I've missed you.
You have no idea how long I've wanted to be with you again.
Pushing and shoving I slowly make my way.
The closer I get the more anxious I become.
I begin to think of all the good times we had.
At long last we are finally together.
I reach deep into my pocket
I grab what I have been longing to give you.
As I insert the quarter you begin to beep
As if to ask where have you been.
Finally we are one again.
I grasp your controller
We pick up were we left off so many years ago.

William Miller

Untitled

I rise with you
Hoping to feel your warmth
Seeking your glow

Yearning to feel your soft touch upon my body
I search for you, long to feel you near
All around . . .
All the time

Follow your movement across my room
Excited by the shadows you cast
When you leave I am spent from begging, chasing
Wanting wishing you to stay a minute more

I wait as a lover for your return

M. L. King

My Friend and My Love

I'm so happy to be able to call you My Friend and My Love
Our hearts were placed together at a time in our lives
When we both needed someone.
There will be moments when I will need
My Friend and My Love shoulders to lean on,
There will be moments when you will need
My love and My shoulders to be there.
That's when we realize that My Friend and My Love
Will never let you down.
My Friend and My Love reach out for my hand to hold.

Tasya Michellena Arrington

Beyond the Graveyard

There is a place beyond a graveyard,
My dreams have taken me.
A place so beautiful, I wish all could see!
There was a man sitting upon a stair,
It looked as though the sun shined throughout his hair!
His face was so bright, with absolutely no flaw.
Never will I forget this man I saw!
As I looked into his eyes, visions of my past appeared.
Accompanied by a beautiful voice only I could hear!
The message was clear as I heard it say;
"Your sins have been forgiven this very day."
Soon it was time, I had to go.
But before I did, my feelings he'd know.
For he said ; "Just say my name, and I'll be there."
I know he's waiting upon that stair!
Never will I forget, and always I long to see
The man "Beyond The Graveyard," who waits for me!

Therese "Leitch" Qasir

A Memory This Olde House

For many years I looked around
Then one day—I found
This olde house
It was big and old—with memories inside
Children, wealth—then sorrow but still pride
A lifetime of memories—they had to leave
Now it was my time to add to a dream
I cleaned and painted—but left the olde lore
We would make our memories to store
Though our children were older—there still was time
For our lives to blend here and bind
The years sped by as they always do
Graduations, weddings and babies too
Alas—now we are older—this house is too
Time for us to move on—and let someone new
Add to this olde house—their dreams—many or few
For me—I always cherish this Olde House
But I have a nice picture—and that will suffice

Kathryn R. Myer

The Rainfall

From Zion Jah sendeth the rain
And the earth is satisfied once again
Jah loves us in many ways
who feels it knows.

Every time at this time I get in a trance
listening to the rain drops
I praise Jah some more.

Oh Jah, I feel so comforted as if I am the rainbow,
because when the rain falls
that's when it shows.

I'll give thanks for a refreshing atmosphere
I'll give thanks for the abundance of water
The vegetation is contented by its bounty
With trees standing in their confinement
Preserving the earth from a deteriorated ozone.

It is raining, and all rivers get high
It is raining, only gray clouds in the sky.
Does your world grow dark? Well not mine,
Because whenever the rain falls
I feel like I am the sunshine.

Peter Seraphine

Joanne

Golden brown eyes that shine a light so fair
a sweet voice like music born upon the fresh spring air.

A beauty so deep within but clear for all to see,
lady how you do enchant me.

If I placed thee upon pedestal
Thou would place me on one higher,
Therefore thou have become the object of my eternal desire.

If I were thine thee I'd walk behind
If thou were mine I thou would walk behind
Thou art thine and I am mine
May we walk together side by side to the end of time.

In the season of our love we grow stronger together,
yet we be not bound by promised words, rings, or fetters.

In the seasons of our lives
We live in our spring,
We are young and strong with flowers in our hair
We walk along and ancient love songs our hearts do sing.

Our summer sun may one day change to winters rain,
We may grow old and gray, but our love shall never wane.

Each and every day I pray, that our paths should never go astray.

James LeClaire

One Lost Star

One lost star in a world of many.
Not one thing is equal.
Nothing in this world is the same.
In a world of plenty;
So lonely to a sequel;
No one to blame, but one lost star.

One lost star where others see
So beautiful to visualize;
So glossy and shiny;
Ready to rise!
Who will realize? Only me.
The best surprise it will be, for one lost star.

One lost star no one will understand.
What is the purpose of it all?
No one knows.
Reach out with your hand
So the star will not fall
Then your love shows, to one lost star.

Jacqueline Marrero

Silent Cries

Hear the silent cries of the children
The children of the street, hear them?
We meet but, never greet children of the street
I repeat never greet, never greet.

Hear their silent cries of a life so bleak
See them in the dark sleeping in the park
Lost in the night, how can this be right?
It makes my heart go weak, weak, weak.

Hear the silent cries of the children
Don't let their cries fall on deaf ears
Out of sight out of mind, it's just not right
Must they fight this fight alone?

Hear their silent cries of hunger, feel their pain
They are the children of the street, hear them?
They are our children and this is not right
They are in a place where they do not belong.

Hear their silent cries, hear them, help them
They think of abuse and wonder what's the use
How did things go so wrong, wrong, wrong
We can right this wrong, only if we see the light.

Lou Nied

My Southern Man

I'm roaring since you're gone my southern man.
My scream such a yield but endless quiet.
If they shoot me, there is no blood
I'm filled full with hate
Now I can't sleep with the huge loneliness
In my ear your voice scream yield.

But empty look, deaf silent
I can't find to result to complete solution
to solve if I want to cry
I can't cry. Oh! youth years so I left
to tavern now good-bye
What a strange wind blowing
Like a September night

Little later I'm going for a walk
If I have enough power I will screaming
to Santa Monica to you.

Now faraway from this city
this time a middle of the night
happiness to you, happiness, southern man.

Nuray Mulka

Happiness Is . . .

Happiness is . . . the first day of Spring.
Happiness is . . . Summer vacation.
Happiness is . . . the first blooming flower.
Happiness is . . . a baby kitten or puppy.

Happiness is . . . winning the lottery.
Happiness is . . . a warm day.
Happiness is . . . is a new pet.

Happiness is . . . being loved by someone.
Happiness is . . . writing a poem.
Happiness is . . . peace and quiet.
Happiness is . . . reading a book,
Happiness is . . . learning something new.

Happiness is . . . peace.

Happiness is . . . my little sister (sometimes).
Happiness is . . . ice cream.
Happiness is . . . love.
Happiness is . . . climbing a tree.
Happiness is . . . drawing a picture.

Happiness is . . . having someone to look up too.
Happiness is . . . friends who act like friends.

Cassie Cupper

A Feeling

I feel so strange. What could it be?
I don't understand why I can't see.
I can't see the harsh things that I know are there.
Why do I feel asleep? Why am I not aware?

Is it because of him? I don't know.
And are these feelings a friend or foe?
What do some people call it? What's that word?
I'm absolutely positive that it's one I've heard.
Love! That's it! Is that what this is?

Or is it just puppy love that goes out with a fizz?
Whatever it is, this feeling is great.
Another thing is that it's impossible to hate.
It's like being in a storm, but not feeling the rain.
Or getting cut and not feeling the pain.
Hey, I could live with this. Of me, it's a part.
And I hope very soon it's in everyone's heart.

Rebecca Dawn Parker

Heartwarming Friendship

You are the one who makes each day fun,
You are the one who gives me your kind love,
You seem to be the perfect friend,
So I know we'll be together till the end.
For no matter what,
You're always there,
And no matter what,
You always care.
A part of you has grown in me,
And so you see,
It's you and me.
Together for always and never apart,
Maybe in distance but never in heart.

Jennifer Wilkin

To Live For

My sky is blue when you shine on me
The cold is warmed when you spare me a smile
Nightfall gives way to the light of your soul
Angels sing with a whisper of your mouth
Your vision of beauty intoxicates me so
A touch of you heals all of my doubts
The mention of your name brings me to sing
A thought of you cleanses the mind
Reality melts into dream
A dream is now upon me
Your breathe life into my lifeless self
Your eyes reflect the purity of your soul
A maiden of truth in the depths of doubt
Refreshing is the thought of you
An oasis in the storm
You are

Paul L. Cross

Small Wonder

Your baby is beautiful
So precious and small
She doesn't know she has Down Syndrome at all.

So love her and cherish her
Talk and play with her each day.
She will take you through life
In her own special way,
And the beauty and wonder
You see each day
Will almost take your breath away.

How do I know?
Well, take it from me,
God has given to us a special angel you see
And I'm happy to say, she is a beautiful part of our family

Jody Raloff

Beyond

The rodent voiced one agonizing scream
Before the eagle's talons closed upon
His frail flesh to terminate his dream,
And in one awful moment life was gone.

On strongly beating pinions swiftly rose
The conqueror as Heavenward he bore
His prize to stem the hunger pangs of those
High in a nest above the valley floor.

This life would not be wasted, for the shell
Of flesh with which the spirit had been clothed
Would bone and sinew be for those who dwell
Above the world—to wind and sun betrothed.

No longer landlocked and by Nature told
To spend a life imprisoned by the weeds
And stones he now may be more bold,
And go perform more elevated deeds.

So with my mortal body—finished now
The deeds expected of me here on earth;
Oh, spirit, travel upward—leave the plow
And reap the harvest of a noble birth.

Ira W. Hoff

Missing You

As I lay here at night on my bed,
Memories of you come into my head;
Your warm smile that set the pace,
And your gentle touch that made my heart race.

Recalling times we've spent together,
Wishing our love could last forever;
Knowing that our love was true,
I realize now that I'm still missing you.

The love and happiness we shared back then,
That burnt so deep in our heart's den;
How I wish we could renew this love,
It shines so brightly like the heavens above.

If there could be but just one wish for me,
I would keep you in my arms for eternity;
But if this wish doesn't ever come true,
I hope you realize that I'll still be missing you.

Joey E. Bihlear

Entwined

Dedicated to my mother-in-law, Meredith Haskett
Blessed I am to have heard your words
Dropping on my ears like the songs of birds,
Perhaps together we are bound,
By rhymes of blue morning glories twisting round.
Across chasms of strife and pain,
Your poet's words have kept me sane.

Susan Milligan Haskett

Yet Far Away

We are in the same room,
But we are two countries
On the opposite sides of the globe.
We are five inches into each other's personal space,
but still we are five miles away.
Your hand shake is so intimate,
It is like foreplay prior to making love.
Your hello is vibrant,
It sounds as if you said, I love you to me.
Your absence brings out a feeling of wistfulness
Similar to waiting for spring to arrive.
When I see you,
I feel as if I walked into a surprise party.
So close, yet far away.

Marie Audene Tse

A Tribute to My Grandpa

Oh Grandpa, Oh Grandpa, how dear you are to me.
When I was little, you sat me on your knee.
When I was older, you were a friend to me.
With a lighted pipe, and a twinkle in your eye
You would have a story for you and me.
My first pair of ice skates, my first cooked Christmas goose.
Striped suckers for Mary Ann and me,
Red striped one for me, green striped one for her.
Why Jamie wasn't James, why Jeremy wasn't Albert.
Coffee was always on, have a cup with me.
When the cold wind blew, you were the mailman of the neighborhood.
And as time grew on, you would write to tell me you were all right.
You are my best friend,
A Dad,
And of course, a Grandpa to me.
I just want to say Thank you,
For being you to me.
Your Granddaughter,
Rita

  Rita Huschka

Bedtime

When supper time is over,
When your toys are put away,
When you've played with your boats in the bathtub,
When you can't go out and play,
When you're wearing your pajamas,
When you're neatly tucked in bed,
When you've had your milk and cookies,
When your last "good night" is said,
When someone's turned your light out,
When no one else is there,
That's exactly when I'll visit,
My name is Teddy Bear.

  Katie Weisenburger

My Special Friend

No moving parts, no batteries
No monthly payments and no fees;
Inflation proof, non-taxable,
In fact, it's quite relaxable.

It can't be stolen, won't pollute,
One size fits all, do not dilute,
It uses little energy,
But yields results enormously.

Relieves your tension and your stress,
Invigorate your happiness;
Combats depression, makes you beam,
And elevates your self esteem!

Your circulation it corrects
Without unpleasant side effects
It is, I think, the perfect drug:
May I prescribe, my friend . . . the hug!

  Diana Sum

A Tree

A tree start out a frailing thing
But soon learns to spread its wings and sing.
Up against a sky dark and gray
It perseveres knowing there will be a better day
Where skies are blue and clouds float by
The sun shines bright
To show the twinkle of its eyes,
The tree grows strong against all demise
And with each day becomes wise.
The rivers flow and birds fly
But the tree stands tall against all time
Knowing how to rhyme and sing its song
One day at a time.

  Jeff Connors

The End

The day comes to an end
The sun hides behind the trees.
Birds stop singing
As the crickets line up in harmony.

Day turns to night
The moon rises in the sky
Nothing is more beautiful
Than what is outside.

Grass is whispering a gentle word
As trees are singing a heavenly song.
Nature by itself, that's what it ought to be.
Hasn't been like this in so very, very long

Day turns to night
The moon takes command.

  Jessica Avery

Little Children at Play

The sun just rising out of the east,
Darkness turns into day once again.
Two young children play in a meadow near their house.
They run among the flowers.
The young boy catches a frog in the creek,
He has been hunting him for a week.
The girl seeks out to find a butterfly,
One that has all the colors of the rainbow.
The children are free here,
Here is where they become their true selves.
Their mother calls to them,
"Matt, Shannon, dinner is ready."
Soon after dinner the children scamper off to their beds.
Their father reads "Goldilocks and the Three Bears" to them.
The sun sets in the west.
Day turns into night, but not for long.
The sun will rise again.
So little children can play again.

  Michael Hinkle

Mothers' Day

I think of my mother quite a bit,
Mothers' Day and other times during the year.
I loved her very much.
I miss her very much,
Especially since she passed away in January 1984.

  Helen Felice McGill

Love and Hate

Can it be that our world is at war?
Will the hate ever cease?
What is all this fighting for?
Will it bring us peace?

Is our world in danger;
of coming to an end?
Why is hate and not love;
becoming our only friend?

He looks at the world through our eyes;
and it hurt for Him to see.
Just how He made the world with love;
and what it came to be.

Why does He take our loved ones away from us?
I do not understand.
Why can't people of different races;
walk hand in hand?

Will He put a stop to this?
Or will it stay the same?
When will the world go back to love?
And hate go down the drain?

  Mindy Brunn

Before Rain

Clouds scurry across the sky,
Taking bites of the sunshine.
Winds bluster across the grass,
Turning leaves on trees upside down.
The smell of rain rides on the wind.
Curtains of drizzle march across the fields.
Single raindrops make small puddles on the porch.
Thunder rumbles and rolls,
Daring earth to refuse the rain.
Lightning snakes across the sky,
Accentuating the threat of thunder.
Curtains swirl at windows and doors slam
As wind rushes through the house ahead of the rain.
Music ripples through the air
As wind chimes sway with the breeze.
Rain suddenly pours down,
Beating a tattoo on the roof.
The rain gentles into a soft splish-splash
And lulls us with a peaceful patter upon the roof.

Louise Norman

Changing Times

Being a senior citizen qualifies me
To compare today's times, with the times of yore

It is true that today we have many luxuries,
That we didn't have before,

But in the world of sports,
I will opt for yesteryear,

As taking a family to a ball game
Today is far too dear.

Major league baseball today is far
Too expanding,

Next thing you know,
There will be a team in Mays landing.

I liked the days
When the networks televised the game for free

When it was televised
For the impoverished to see
Is it any wonder the fans do not endeavor,

When the double headers
Are gone forever.

William Bosworth

Worlds Apart

Sounds surrounding us
So quietly echoing around one
Sweet melodies formed in silence
Just before the morning hue we greet
Scampering worlds apart brushing the light of day.

Responding intricacies of life
Surviving creatures all are we
Capturing moments in our crossroads shared.
Omniscient worlds apart reflecting nature's bond of mind?

One finds gesturing trails defined
Inscribed in worlds apart unknown to few.

One hears chirping, chattering, scurrying along
Awakening to Intelligence's presence
Eclipsing not with harmony at hand.
Linking our gap of man.

Is it possible we are one?

I think one is.

For in worlds apart we are free
Discovering Mind
Conceived in the hush of Creator's touch.

Suzanne McMillen

Ode to a Poem

How many paintings may a poem inspire?
If a picture is worth a thousand words,
With an endless use of adjectives and verbs.
For these are the colors of a poet's desire.

A paper for canvas, the stanza's a frame.
Behold the magic of the poet's dream.
The stroke of each line creates a new scene,
Of love or beauty even sadness and pain.

For a poem comes from feelings within.
The emotions are chosen and then thrown about,
All over the composition out.
It can be still life or a fantastic whim.

The reader beholds the wonder and awe.
Visual pattern come to the mind.
Each can explore and seek a new find,
Trying to discover the meaning the poet saw.

So if a picture is worth a thousand words,
A poem is worth a thousand pictures observe!

Danny Bourcier

Illusions

I close my eyes, Swirls of smoke follow me into shady serenity.
The music, sweeter than before, sings a melancholy song.
As I embrace the candle lit warmth of my room,
the fields of flowers and grassy knolls swim in illusion.
The bear across the room smiles an ebony grin.
Rain, I hear rain, there are clear skies, grey happy moon.
The dragon's tongue looks embracing.
The wizards gift never ceasing.
Caress me gently, into my youth.

Kelli Marchman

Heaven's Door

You have gone away to knock on heavens door
We're so lost without you
And we will be forever more

Sometimes the pain is just too much to bare
We feel nothing but loneliness and deep despair

We don't know how our lives will go on
With our precious Grandmother gone to her life beyond.

She is sadly missed and always will be
But at least we all have our own special memories

Dreana Merrill

Curiosity

There never was a spirit so brave and so frail
as the kitten with the question mark tail.

The kitten is sittin' with his little white paws,
wishing he can grow some bigger claws.

Right next to Spike, he jumps upon a stump.
He appears to be no bigger than a bump.

With the quickness of a flea he is leaping off the log.
The kitten thinks he's beating up the dog.

Then away in a flash, you can hear the dog yell
as he's snapping at the question mark tail.

He jumped out of the bushes and ran under the house.
He saw the shadow of a scurrying mouse.

Mice run fast but cats are sleek.
Soon the mouse will have no squeak.

There never was a spirit so brave and so frail
as the kitten with the question mark tail.

Lucas Panetto

Mother's Passing

Oh God, walk with me through this Weary day.
Let the sun shine upon me to light my way.
Draw my cares and my
Worries to your bosom strong
And let not my grief be suffered long.
When I'm overcome by the storms of life
Give me a rainbow to lessen my strife.
With your love I can suffer any loss.
Oh God, may I live in the shadow of the Cross.

Doris Sue Lineberry

Tasks

When I was a very young girl
One of the words I recall so well is "tasks"
Most frequently mentioned and seriously undertaken
At their proper times!
Not to be taken lightly!

And now, as I grow old and as I am somewhat reflective
I think of all the "tasks" that were done—ho hum.
Could it be that we placed these tasks before us as reminders—
To assure ourselves that we could keep order in a place of chaos?
This world seems more to me as an illusion,
Since unlike truth it cannot remain the same.
It is constantly changing before our eyes.
What if the only task before us
Were forgiveness and love each to the other?
Not to be taken lightly!
And now I ask—could this be the answer
To our plight our way out of darkness into the light?

Beverly Casey Uzanas

Carpe Diem

How fragile is our life on Earth
We travel towards death from the moment of birth
Each breath you take could be your last
It could happen to you that fast

Don't take for granted that you'll have another day
To rectify any mistakes you've made
Because eventually the time must come
When God will feel your work here is done

Always be the best person you can possibly be
Treat others with the respect you'd like to receive
Most importantly always make your feelings clear
To those around you whom you hold dear

If you live a good life you have nothing to fear
When the appointed hour finally draws near
You can let go of this world knowing for sure
That what awaits you is so much more

Maria Balestrieri

Smile

Smile, when things are hardest around you.
Smile, when it seems everyone is against you.
Smile, for when these things befall you.
Smile, for they happened to the Lord also, just like you!

I know that is hard to smile, when everything seems so hard.
I know that is difficult to smile, when everyone makes it so hard.
I know that it may be hard to smile, while it is yet so hard.
But, just keep looking up, and things won't be so hard.

For the Lord, will brighten your day.
He will keep you out of all harms way.
If you but keep Him in your heart all the day.
He will bless you and keep you all the day.

He "Will remember you" when He comes that great day.
When He comes to claim His own on that glorious day.
So Mike LaBuda, remember what has been told you this day.
The Lord God almighty loves you each and every day!

Michael Stephen Arnold

Words of Wisdom

In the early years, remember:
Live your dreams to their fullest, taking nothing for granted
Reach for the impossible and make it happen
Never abandon your beliefs, your values, your convictions
Let your visions become reality with no limits or restrictions.

As the years pass, remember:
When things go wrong, as they sometimes do,
Believe in yourself to carry you through.
Listen to your heart, but obey your mind
Help those around you, always being respectful, sincere, and kind.

In reflection of your life, remember:
Let your regrets be few, your memories hold dear
For this is what you reflect on from year to year.
All that you have learned from the time of your birth,
Pass this knowledge on before you leave this earth.

When all is said and done,
These are the words of wisdom I leave to you, my son.

Dale Ann Sylva

The Search

From the very depth of its soul
Comes the mournful cry of a child.
Nightly I am awakened by the sobbing.
The sounds are so close, so clear.

I run to each window, anxiously hoping.
Only my reflection looks back at me.
Each night I search, always in vain.
Each night a pattern of the last.

Days I'm haunted by memories of night.
Echoes of abandoned cries possess my thoughts.
I'm weary, but dread night to come.
Tormented night, with unending wails of sorrow.

Finally, blessedly, I sleep through the sounds.
Still, even then, I am drawn, beckoned,
To a place only revealed in dreams.
I see myself there, following the sounds.

Suddenly, there, deep within my own soul,
Where only God and dreams can see,
I found and held the grieving child.
The child in my arms was me.

Janet L. Gabbard

Routine

Routine, routine, oh will it ever end?
Another day, another chore, repeated once again.

Do the things you've done before.
Excitement? This is not.
Backwards, eyes closed, with a twist,
You act without a thought.

The cycle starts and stops on cue.
The path—it never strays, you look for variation
In a life of xeroxed days.

No room for change, nor hope-filled dreams.
No one has scheduled these!
They'll interrupt the flow of things,
The diem may be seized!

Safety, come in sameness,
New ideas are best unheard,
Just duplicate the day before
And dare not say a word.

To risk? It sounds to risky!
(And there could be pain involved.)
Avoid the unknown at all costs for fear you may evolve!

Linda Coffey Wojcuich

In Memory of Tara Padula, Who Is Gone, But Not Forgotten

It was the morning I woke up with sad news,
I was crying frustrated and didn't know what to do.

I went to a memorial service that night for you,
I was wondering why God had taken you so soon,.

All my memories of you went through my head,
As I lay that night, crying in bed.

I wondered how my brother would feel,
When he heard the sad new, would his broken heart ever heal?

After months of you being passed away,
I think of you everyday.

There has not been one day that's gone by,
That I don't think of you and cry.

I hope and pray in every way
That we will reunite in Heaven someday.

Noelle Gartside

Getting Started

I have just sat down intending to write.
But my thoughts are jumbled. My brain is still tight.
Like alphabet letters mixed in a container,
Waiting to sift through my mental strainer,
Ideas are abounding, though haphazard and fleeting.
Reacting like atoms under violent heating.
Yet as bees in a hive making ready to swarm,
They are many at first but as one when they form.

So too I believe, as the tempo decreases,
When drifting and daydreaming finally ceases,
An energy builds and may lift the haze
To see me through this unending maze.
Then a peace may be felt to slowly subdue me.
Allowing one message to flow and come through me.
And finally quiet will envelop my mind,
Then a theme will emerge and the thread unwind.

Richard Woods Sr.

My Little Wagon

My little wagon follows me with a big red bow.
I pull and pull up to the hill top I go.
I push it and push it down to the stream below,
To my Daddy's work shop and to Mommy's garden hose.
I carry my purse, teddy bear, and tea set
In the wagon sitting neatly in a row.
I try to move our dog, big Ben.
He must weigh 1, 5, or maybe 10.
We sure have a lazy pet.
I pull my wagon to my hiding place that no one knows.

Patricia Schmidt

You

My heart is heavy with the pain of your love,
as I smile, and eagerly ask for more.
My heart is filled with a sweet torment,
as your love entangles me, as we passionately kiss.
When we are apart, I feel your loving embrace
penetrating my body like broken glass as I
scream out your name in silence while pretending not to care.
You are my breath of life,
as I whisper I love you, and cheerfully hand
you my heart, gift-wrapped like a present.
My eyes joyfully shed a tear from the sweet
sound of your voice, as I sit and watch
flowers bloom in your name.
I have a shattered soul that makes me cry with laughter,
in my never-ending thoughts of you.
Wherever you go, I am with you.

W. Edward Poole Jr.

Mr. Smiley Face

Mr. Smiley Face you're always happy, you don't know
what it's like to be sad, neither do you know how to feel mad.
Life must be so perfect for you, never sad never blue,
You always know just what to do.
Mr. Smiley Face, I envy you.
You see I too can act the same, while burying my deepest pain.
But are you the same as me, do you hide your pain so they can't see?
Were you hurt like me so long ago?
Did you swear your feelings would never show.
Have you held them back all these years,
while fighting back those painful tears.
You see, I swear I'm fine but they can't see,
that there is something wrong with me.
If they don't know I won't tell,
promise to bring no one to our personal hell.

Jennifer Olson

Shore Etchings

Red sun ball—waking the sea gull to his raucous call
Silhouetting fishing boats, already at their labors
Spotlighting the ever-searching beachcomber
Capping the waves rough edges with sea diamonds.

Beach prints—small ones, of running childish feet
Deep, climbing prints, on high sand mounds
Delicate spray prints of the sandpipers,
As they endlessly race with the incoming tide.

Wind-wafted laughter—of midday family fun
The bright sound of youth at play,
Reveling in its respite from desks and books.

Sunset—God's inimitable artistry
Stirring to reverence.
Lullaby of the quieted sea—soothing—renewing.
Benediction—His Peace.

Marguerite D. Kennedy

Mama Nature

I'm not a force of calamity
I'm a force of integrity
I'm not the light that strikes upon the night
I'm the light that strengthens with all might
I'm not a soul of destruction
I'm a soul to give instruction
I'm like paper in the wind,
Spreading my wings, and soaring around the bend
I'm the magnetic field that pulls you in deep,
massages your mind to keep you at ease
My eyes are flowing with misery,
But it's up to us to overcome diversities
The concern of emotions is my conviction,
And as I rise to the top
It's my universal intention

Adrian Taft

Memories of Grandpa

My Grandpa was the best of them all—he had a scroll saw!
He made a humming bird in a heart.
Me and Grandpa ran into the trailer with the golf cart!
My Grandpa liked Fig Newtons and coffee with cream
and my Grandpa was a cookie eater!
He played a lot of golf.
He worked hard in the basement.
My Grandpa could make anything.
He would look from the window and see the deer
And we saw a lot of turkeys, geese and foxes!
My Grandpa was the best of them all
he had a scroll saw!

Brittney Taylor

How Can People Be So Cruel

There are people killed all the time,
Every few seconds there's a crime,
Sometimes they kill just for kicks,
They rob people and shoot them, it makes me sick.
How can people be so cruel

Sometimes these people are sick or take pills.
It drives them crazy, then they kill.
I don't know why they do it, I don't understand
I couldn't kill anybody, not one single man.
How can people be so cruel.

Then there's the war, where people fight and die.
It's so crazy I never know why.
Why can't they stop, have peace and be free.
Everyone could share the land and the sea's.
But they won't stop for any reason.
They fight all the time and all the seasons.
How can people be so cruel.

Yes, how can people be so cruel
        Sheila Wigington

Circle of Color

Help!
I'm trapped in a place where colors count!
People fight and even kill over a color!
What happened to "all men are created equal"?
Why can't that be everyone's motto in life?
I'm trapped in a circle of pain, war, and death!
Is the color all that matters?
If it is, it's destroying us all!
A simple color difference will be the death of us all!
Don't our feelings count?
Why can't everyone care?
Why do we look only skin deep?
Why can't we look further?
So what if there's a slight color variation!
Don't you understand that I'm crying out to you?
I can't take it anymore!
Help me end this plague of death!
Because we're all in this together.
Help me!
Before it kills us all!
        Francheska Glasz

I Saw a Tree

I saw a tree as old as old,
Standing in the winter cold.
Standing on high and high,
Watching winter months go by.

I housed a wren, a robin, a lark,
Standing so cold in the park.
I used to sit under, its shady limb,
And doze off, on a whim.

It used to be tall and proud,
But its leaves and branches, no longer a shroud.
I loved that tree when I was young,
I played in its branches, and just had fun.

Now the tree will be cut down,
I am sad, and I do frown.
But a new tree is being planted,
And a little wishes will be granted.

A new life will be started,
Little wishes, never parted.
The tree will grow, strong and tall,
And be the greatest, of them all.
        Andrew Hagen

The Money Tree

The money tree now standing tall on the hill
Its leaves once glittered as gold,
It brought forth fruit that filled the till
But now it's growing old.
The limbs are drooping low and its branches
Are becoming bare,
Now when you go to gather fruit you will
Find nothing there.
The money has blown away by the swirling
Winds of time,
Swept away to unknown places far beyond our
Searching mind.
When it's hewn down and hauled away
To the mill,
Will soon be forgotten where it once stood
High on the hill.
No longer to be seen swaying in the breeze
With its limbs like dancing fingers,
As time goes by as it always will,
Perhaps some faint memories will linger.
        John A. Brown

Melancholy

On silken wings my love flies to you
like a monarch butterfly
to land on a wild flower
softly its nectar to try.
On damp sands I write your name,
the birds call out loud
I look at the sky and see your face
in the passing clouds.
Where are you now and what do you think?
Do you know about me at all?
These questions hang in emptiness
and rain continues to fall.
The sweet sound of your voice
echoes in the night
as I contemplate the moon
and speak to it of my plight.
Where did it come from? . . . Where is it going?
This bittersweet dream of mine
in the wind may come an answer
someday, somehow, in time.
        Virgilia Baldo

My Love

As I lay here thinking of you, my heart grows warm and tender.
For being with you ignites the flame in my soul.

I need to feel your warm body next to mine.
I need to gently kiss your mouth.

Only then does my body come alive. Alive with passion,
Alive with joy and happiness.

When you touch me, my body melts,
It melts so deep beyond the surface of reality.
I feel the flames of fire.
All I want is you, my love.

When I awake from my sleep,
And you are not next to me.
My eyes begin to water.

Why does this loneliness hurt so much my love?

How do I know how you feel, my love?
I can feel love when I stare into your eyes.
God knows how lost into your eyes I become.
I need to feel your soft skin, I need to kiss your body.
I need to be held by you, my love.
Until we can be together again, I Love You.
        James P. Laieta Jr.

Ode to My Son Darwin on His 39th Birthday

It was very late in the month of June
And you kept saying, "I'll be arriving real soon."
As I didn't want to be caught in some undesirable spot
(Especially when it was getting so darn hot)
So a couple hours early to the hospital I hurried
When your daddy said; "I'd rather go fishing then be hurried."
But I'd been there before and they waited silently by the door.
The first pain came I pulled the light (no exam).
They rushed me to the delivery room full flight
Then I said, "This will take a cramp or two."
They reminded me this is "nothing new."
The rest is vague and pretty mixed up
And I was really wishing they would "shut up."
But when Dr. M said "boy" I came to life
But I really felt like I had been cut with a knife (and I had.)
That's your arrival story—not that it matter.
We are still here and not really in tatters.
39 years is about half way through.
And about all I've got to say is, "What else is new?"

Cheryl T. Horton

It's Tax Time

It's tax time—Yes the time we dread
As numbers clutter up our head.
Why do we fret—we cannot win
We paid our bills—is this a sin.

Afraid to earn more every year
But interest high—and debt we fear.
The bottom line looks like we have
more than we do—Our Uncle's glad.

Shall we see a CPA,
or clutter up our minds and pray.
Take out our bills—and check the date
Will sick calls help deter our fate.

Percentage of that ghastly debt
May help to save us—do not fret.
The charges that we use each day
give finance we must throw away.

Deductions are less every year
We must earn more, but earn we fear.
Our Uncle will think we have more
Our Hundred thousand—and still we're poor.

Dorothy Rettberg

Another Mother

As you curl up warm beside me,
sleeping baby—oh, what joy!
Did she feel the same,
I wonder, that other mother for her boy?

Did she marvel at His features,
little hands and nose and feet?
Did she press her face against Him
to smell His hair and skin so sweet?

Did she kiss His tiny forehead
and plant still more upon His cheeks?
Did she lay with one ear open
for baby cries and sighs and squeaks?

Did He spread his arms across her
and nuzzle tight beneath her chin?
Did her gaze melt as He cuddled
and her heart grow soft within?

Did she squeeze His chubby fists and flex His fingers one by one?
Did she dream about His future and pray God's blessings for her son?

She surely must have felt the same—that other mother long ago—
And surely, then, her heart was broken when she had to let Him go.

Tammy Adamson-McMullen

My Mom

The days grew long and weary as she worked upon the farm
And my mom was always there with her everlasting charm

She worked with Dad from sun up till sunset
Sometimes it seemed she would never get to rest

But when the days work in the field had all been done
It was back to the house where her other job had begun

It was cook, sew, clean and raise the kids
But rarely a complaint from my mom who always did

With everything else she had to do
Mom always found time for kids' activities too

As the years passed and her children left her nest
She was left alone with Dad, who was always at his best

Too short a time was theirs to be alone
Til Dad had passed on, and it seemed everything was gone

But Mom was strong and knew she must go on
Cause she had six kids who put her on a throne

Many years have passed since Dad has passed away
So it's time to get together, and respect to you we'll pay

This poem was written for you to carry with you on
For I will always love you, my kind and gentle Mom

Charles A. Strong

Entermost Ascending

Through the setting off of the day,
I knock on the door of my vision room.

As I knock, the door opens and
There awaiting ready to greet me is my mind.

Showing all hospitality,
She introduced me to her soul.

Then we began our journey
and met with the depths of the spirit,
For it was there
That the light of the Holy Ghost brightened the room.

Enchanting us with the array of power
Presented by the guest of honor,
Our Father in Heaven.

Now, being brought to completeness
In thought, we have formed
A house of Glory
Built from the stones
Of thy room of vision.

Tawanna Jackson

To My Beloved Evening Star

Tell me where you are.
Please me not far.
You are my heart's desire.
You are my greatest delight.
I wish that you would ravish me on a bed of
white satin trimmed in purple, silver and gold.
In your arms, your eyes I want to behold.
A great love my dreams have foretold.
Never, I pray, let me go.
I drink from the cup of love.
A bittersweet white wine,
to last until the end of time.
I dance beneath the stars and the moon.
I love forward to the sun
My beloved evening star cover me
like an eclipse now.
I can wait no more.
I am before your door.

Peggy J. Meeks-King

Night Noise

She weeps and wails and curses her man
screams echoing across the halls
scrabbling of rats in the wall
sirens screaming rushing for the demented and dead
a gun at her head, the dogs bark, night noise

And she thinks of another a long time ago
are you searching for why? She has all your answers
they come at night with the noise and to this day she wonders
have you had such nice toys

He told her tales of Vietnam and the dead
of opium dens and the screams in his head
and when he was gone she still called his name
and the night noise roared

A hard rain falls as a holiday dawns
but no one feels festive and she's so far from home
the moon is in Cancer and she's in her own madness
and the noise within goes on in the night

    Ursula M. Wall

A Mother's Child

A mother's love is her child.
   A mother's child is her heart.
My heart beats for you every day.
   Even though you're far away.
Sometimes I find myself at night
   Just hoping and praying I could hold you real tight.
I can't see or hug, or give you a touch
   But you need to know I love you very much.
I think about you all the time.
   If not you're always on my mind.
I think about you every single day.
   I thank God you're only just a dream away.

    Mary Cole

Love

Love is a mixed up feeling,
You never know if you're coming or going.
Love seems to bring out our jealousies of our own
guilt and uncertainties.

It shows our feelings of insecurity and of our fears.
Why can't real love be our happiness and our giving times?
Where we glow with an abundance of love,
That everyone can see just by looking at us.
Love is just a confusing and difficult feeling to
accomplish and understand in any means of today's world.
Why?

    Deborah Cameron

Falling Leaves

Falling leaves are such interesting things.
They twist and turn in descent.
Each has a path that is only its own,
But you never have to guess where each went.

Gravity takes over as each one's released,
And they start their trip to the ground,
Where all will be raked into one monstrous heap,
A playground in the form of a mound.

Wind and the children will re-scatter these leaves,
Neither having purpose in mind.
The children do it for sheer joy and fun,
While the wind simply joins them in kind.

When they're re-raked they'll be set on fire,
A practice that's followed each fall,
And smoke rising through the bare limbs of the trees,
Will be noticed and enjoyed by all.

    E. R. Case

Love Sees No Color

"Love sees no color," she said to me.
"But how," I replied, "could this possibly be?"

Green is the envy with which I see.
Traits, found in others, that are missing in me.

Yellow is the shame of which I have felt.
For what I have done, with what I've been dealt.

Red is the anger I sometimes let go.
Just where it comes from, God only knows.

Blue is the sadness and loneliness too.
Each I'd felt often, until I met you.

For your love is blind to the color I see.
Your eyes probe deeper to see the real me.

    Douglas J. D'Heilly

Will I

All I seek is a little happiness,
With love and caring for the rest of my life,
Finding it is so terribly complicated,
I feel so trapped without a life.
I try not to look back so I won't have any regrets,
Is the rest of my life just a dream,
It sometimes seems like a hopeless dream,
As I go down this road of life.
I look for a cross road, a right turn or a left turn.
Not even a fork in the road do I see ahead,
They must all be behind me.
Not even a reduce speed, slow curve ahead,
Or a stop sign have I seen.
The last rest stop It was such a long time ago.
Life does not seem to offer me many choices anymore.
I hope I do not run out of gas before I find out
The meaning of my life, if it has one.
I hope I am not driving so fast,
That I could have passed it by.

    Phillip Hilbert

Untitled

A cool breeze gently caressing the beach
Each turn of the tide reveals a new greeting.
Elegant birds singing to an internal rhythm,
Pure sand glittering in the moonlight.
A crystal reflection of us—together,
While upon pure sand we fall.
Imprints of a whole remain,
As two sets of footprints are patterned.
And the breeze loves no longer.
The tide has turned to say good-bye.
The birds have lost their rhythm to the morning.
The sand now shines toward the sun.
Yet, the impression remains—
And so do we.

    Amy R. Schneider

He Is With You

He is with You all the time
He is with You when the sun don't shine
He is with You when you are asleep
He is with You for your soul He'll keep
He is with You when you're doing wrong
He is with You when the road is too long
He is with You on your bad days and sad nights
He is with You to tell you that it will be all right
He is with You when life is unfair
He is with You to show you he cares
He is with You when you are afraid
He is with You in many ways.

    Francine Gallegos

King of the Maple Leaves

Yellow paper on the ground, frayed
pieces here and there and their destroyer sitting
on the throne of maple leaves—shredding, picking, splitting
every scrap that did him wrong
bearing truthful words—black and white—
what happened to the child who never listened—
the voices told him not to,
told him to go away
let the wind be his only friend (it has no heart or mind)
two souls running, drifting between
white, unconscious worlds and
nightmare memories
he didn't want to hurt anyone—
the leaves found him
held him up in brittle arms
red and green and yellow and orange—
held the vibrant, lively dead
man with fingers moving
quickly and mindlessly
tearing the life apart that had him buried long before.

Amber Fields

As We Parted

As we parted today
To return to our separate lives for a while,
I left with you
My heart,
The light in my eyes,
The joy in being alive,
The peace in my soul.

I took with me
Fear of the unknown,
Anticipation of sad things to come,
An inevitable ending
To something begun in hope.

As we parted today,
You gave me
Your heart,
Your strength and courage,
And the certainty that while each moment apart
Will seem to last an eternity,
You and I will at last be one,
For all time.

Rebecca J. Trantham

When I Think of You

When I think of you,
I am relieved of the pressures of this world.
Your eyes are like magnificent jewels.
Radiating a glorious shimmer of love and caring;
Like glistening diamonds amid a body of pearls.

When I think of you,
My heart sighs . . .
Your long flowing hair tossed lightly by the wind,
Like a field of wheat in a midsummer's breeze.
The brilliance of your countenance warms my heart,
Like the early morning sun warms my soul.

When I think of you,
I am at a loss for words.
Your soft, tender voice constantly reverberates in the far reaches
of my mind,
Giving me the aura of your presence at all times.
When I think of you,
All of these thoughts converge in my mind.
When I think of you, I think I've fallen for you.
When I Think Of You

Justin M. Murray

A Flower

I am a flower in March who is ready to bloom.
I am not sure when to bloom, so can you help me?

I cannot wait to bloom.
The yellow and black honeybees will suck my nectar.
I will look so pretty in the front of the house.
The soil will be nice, cool and healthy for my roots.

In April and the beginning of May it will rain, I shall drink.
I will grow some more.
A few days before mother's day a boy or girl will pick me
and put me in a vase.

I can do it stretch, stretch and stretch . . .
My petals will glitter when it rains then shines.

I can do it stretch, stretch and . . . Stretch!

I did it! Now I have to wait.
I am just letting the breeze blow right through me.

Maybe you will pick me!

Jacqueline Elizabeth Rocle

My Father's Dream

He was taken from me long ago, as a child,
My happy, gentle, loving father.
He left me with a determination to pursue his dream
Because he couldn't;
His short, fragile life was full of hopes and dreams
For his daughters whom he loved with all his heart.
Today, after more than half a century,
I still feel my father's presence:
On the day I was married;
At the birth of my children;
When I became a grandmother.
He has been my guardian angel.
These have also been his dreams.
I see his face, and feel his gentle hands guiding me.
His sense of humor still sustains me.
Everyday of my life, however long.
I know that he will always be near.
He is there, saying to me:
"Be happy, and you will have fulfilled my dream."

Shirley Moroney Davis

Illusion

Mad as a huntress, charged with insanity . . .
An intoxicating mind of self destruction.
Drunk with passion at the midnight hour,
Filled with the desire to touch paradise.

Inebriating entities numb the pain,
Leaving behind an empty smile . . .
The inner truth hides.

These artificial trips won't last forever.

Reality hits . . . burning like an arrow
Piercing the poisoned heart.

The broken spirit bleeds with despair,
Crawling through a bed of thorns . . .
Chained to the shadow of fear.

Barefoot in hell . . .
Looking for freedom in your version of heaven.

Illusion it is called.

Anna Karin Kristensson

The News Dark Age

The worth of human life was dropping . . .
We held out for a bargain.
Around the block,
Around the planet
We stood in a line
A generation long
To shop what was left upon the shelves—
Perhaps a scrap of food for thought,
Some dressing for our wounded spirits,
A can of something saccharine,
To falsely quench our thirst for knowledge
And leave us parched and seeking more
Of the lukewarm draft.

And now at home we gorge ourselves
Dark before the blinking sets
An hour later hungry—but we got to wait until 11!
For the latest moving cave drawings.

Marcus Wolf

Age and Youth

Life is ebbing,
The room is dark.
The windows are shut
And gone is the lark.

The book lies open, old and worn.
Some phrases are missing, and the pages are torn.

She passes her days, in the rocker alone.
She opens the Bible
And the page is gone.

Laughter is ringing, outside of this room.
The sun must be shining
For the bride and the groom.

She is hoping that someone, would knock at her door.
She would be happy to say
Good morning once more.

The knock did not come,
Disappointment was great.
The youth passed by, the creaking old gate.

Her eyes grew weary, her hands grew cold.
It is so good to be young, and so sad to be old.

Rose Feyer

Ode to Billy Jeff

Billy Jeff who's from Arkansas
Thought he was exempted from the law.
Once he told the truth. Surprise! Surprise!
It seemed to us a bunch of lies.

He asked his friends to give much cash
To be invited to a coffee klatsch.
The door prize was a night in Lincoln's bed
That Abe didn't sleep in, so it's said.

His honored guests were gangsters 'n' thugs,
Dealers in guns and illegal drugs,
People who wanted shady deals,
And things that most crooks cannot steal.

The G O P did not hesitate,
They were ready to investigate.
Said Billy Jeff, "I did no wrong,
Let's quit bickering and get along."

The G O P crawled in a hole
and Billy Jeff's still standing in control.
The G O P sings this song,
"Mea Culpa. Let's just get along."

Lawrence E. Hamilton

Urgent

What is your future after you die
Can you tell me for certain and look me in the eye
Think about it hard right now please
I will pray for you down upon my knees
Tomorrows not promised to anyone here
If you are lost than your life you must fear.
After your spirit leaves its body than it is too late
For you have sealed your eternal fate.
Hell is the place of eternal pain
But there is one person in your life you must gain.
He is the only savior we have in this place
It is not our home we are still running the race.
Heaven is the place you must choose to be
But before you can enter you must have the key.
He holds it so gently in his nail scarred hand
Ask him to show you, I know that he can.
As he stretches his arms out and looks in your face
You find that no key has fallen from its case.
Then you discover that the key is within him
Just fall down and pray, Jesus I want to come in.

Sandy Davis

Empty Nest

"Empty Nest"
a cute phrase designed to mask
change, loss, loneliness, less.

You gave your best
love, home, encouragement, hope.
They'll figure out the rest.

It's hard to believe they're gone
Graduated, independent, employed,
But sweet memories linger on.
Listen, you can still hear the sounds,
scraped knees, tears, questions of "why?" and "why not?"
The decibels of family life all around.

You done good, truth be told
passing on your true inheritance
a legacy and blessing before your old.

You've given the better part,
Your imprint of flesh and spirit
on your own Trinity . . . a great start.

David Johnson Rowe

Butterfly (Requiem)

5:30 in the graveyard
and each seem content
yet I hear my name breathed . . .
requiem, butterfly, requiem
where have you fluttered?

The elderly gather to reclaim their dignity
uniform in uniform, propped up by the younger
no longer seen, but faintly heard
as the breeze taps weed against stone

Requiem, butterfly, requiem
where have you fluttered?
Did you lay in peace?
The little child doesn't understand,
doesn't comprehend where I have fluttered.
Don't forget.

6:01 in the graveyard
the child looks away
I fly out the gate sideways

Daniel E. Lasiter

To My Bride

Just as the morning sun shatters the darkness of night
Or the howling wolf cries to a lonely moon
A ray of delight filled the room, the day I saw you.

Just as a parent who sees their child's first step
Or a climber who reaches the ultimate peak
A ray of happiness filled my soul, the day I befriended you.

Just as the athlete who trains for the gold
Or the young entrepreneur who dreams of success
A ray of hope filled my heart, the day I loved you.

And just as the rose whose smell is so sweet
Or the ring that shows my commitment to you
A ray of love has filled my life, this day I married you.

Brian J. Strader

Like Mother, Like (Foster) Daughter

To my foster mother: Cherie Byant
The innocent, but victimized child.
Abandoned and isolated from everyone.

She has no place to turn to next,
and nobody to turn to besides the saints.

Until one day a kind soul and her met,
the hearts of the two souls joined as one.

Leaving all trace of the abandonment behind,
courageous and fearless love was there between the two.

Only the beholders of the intellectual moments together,
know the outstanding and spontaneous feelings
as two tender hearts combine.

Jessica Baillargeon

A Sports Couplet Poem

There are many sports in the world today,
Which can be played in any way.

Some sports are baseball, hockey, football,
Tennis, soccer, and basketball.

The sports can be played by anyone,
Especially if you think they're fun.

In tennis with a racket you make a hit,
When in baseball you catch a ball with a mitt.

In soccer you kick a ball into a net.
In basketball you shoot a ball into a basket.

In hockey with a stick you hit a puck
into a net to make a goal,
And in football you run with a ball
to score a field goal.

Swimming's another that's fine,
When you swim in a pool to the finish line.

Sohil M. Shah

A Mother

A Mother is someone you need all your life
From the time you're an infant 'til you're a husband or wife.
She cares for your needs from the day you were born,
She watches your progress—gives advice and not scorn.
She loves you no matter what you have done,
Helps smother your sorrows, basks in your fun.
She takes care of your diet, your manners, your clothes
And, when you need her, she's there—for she knows.
For all that she does to make your life good
She expects not a "thank you"—but to be understood.
So tell her you love her and give her a kiss
Because when you're older she's the one you will miss.
Mother's Day—it's Her day—so let's hear a cheer
For the one whom you love—your own Mother dear.

Loraine A. Phelan

Always With Me

Dedicated to P.J.
Your warm embrace through the shadows of the night
Keep me safe and content till the morning light

Your gentle touch like the suns early glare
Say when I need you, you'll always be there

Your sweet smile brightens up even my darkest day
Like a beam of light being shown my way

Your feelings for me show through your eyes
What is not always said, can easily be read

Your heart and soul run deep as the sea
You'll find to be secure with me

Robbin A. d'Arcy

My Pain

My pain is deep and great.
It's when I'm sad but happy at the same time.
It's when I feel like I died inside,
Just to realize the day has just begun.
It's thinking about how much I don't have,
But realizing how much I do have.
It's extreme prejudice.
Revenge.
Love, and great sadness.
It's plotting a way to get your enemy back,
but knowing all the while
that you're not going do anything.
Everyone's pain is different.
My pain is called life.

Shenise Marie Turman

So That Love Can Find Its Way

There's a dark chasm in my empty soul.
One filled with anger, no where to go.
I can't tell the difference
between my friends and my foes.
What's wrong with me and my empty soul?

There's a dark, dark sentence
that is born on our souls.
No place to hide it, no place to go.
But we look to find the good inside
of everyone that we see and know.

I look around and who do I see?
Society's soldiers in my panoramic view.
The citizens of this deep, dark world
are confused beyond their own recognition
and still looking for an answer.

We have to speak, speak aloud
in a deep strong voice, spread our hopes
to the highest mountain peak,
so that love can find its way.

Craig Firsdon

You're Everything to Me

In dedication to my beautiful sister's wedding day
Pamela Meyer Scirri & Frank Scirri, July 28, 1995
You're everything to me and my eternal vision that I see.
How did I exist before you,
but now how can I exist without you.
You are the radiance that surrounds me.
You are the flame that burns beneath me.
The love you give me guides me
through every move I make and every breath I took.
I may have love before you,
but never have I loved as I love you
with all of my existence captivated by you.
Love is forever and you are forever love.

J. R. DuMond

We Were Always Exposed to Poetry

How strange to think that our family tree
Would not mention a certain ability
To always remember a verse of a line
From a poem that one of us thought sublime.
And how many times when we gathered would
We hear a grandfather or uncle or aunt who could
Recite a ditty that fit the occasion
And catch us all in hysterical summation.

Between the toils of our daily lives
We occasionally can show our surprise
That a relative has penned a word or two
That rimes and, perhaps, keeps us from the blue.
A surprise it really should not be
For it is a legacy in our family.

So we say some words, or pick up a pen
And let our thoughts and feelings begin
To appear on paper or be heard 'cross the air.
We all should be proud, we all should care
That one more thing besides heredity
Is blessing us yet and through eternity.

Barbara Mote

In My Heart

Night and day
you seem so far away
My dreams and hopes
are to be with you, to teach and play
The tears in my eyes
the pain in my heart
I'm sorry for all the trouble
that has kept us apart
It's these days that are full of weary
that my heart is full of fury
Until this ice has melted beneath our feet
It's the thump of your hearts, I long to hear beat
Someday you'll understand
as you grow up to be men
Right now you are boys
something I'd like to share from within
I've missed you so much especially your touch
It's this time we've been apart
that someday you'll understand
that you've always been in my heart.

Mark L. Jankowski

The Girl at the End of the World

Come weary travelers, rest in my domain
Eat and drink from happiness
And worry not of silly rain.
Let my radiant love warm you for you've come so far
And the sun has now set
So rest my sleepy friend
You've worked and battled since the beginning of the world
And now you've reached the end.
You've reached my home your most final goal,
So for you, my most valued crown.
Your tears and sweat will now pay off
As you gracefully lie down.
Oh dear comrade, don't be silly!
You're no bother at all!
For I'll place you in a noble grave
When the nightingale sings her call.
If nothing else, remember me,
The one with whom you danced and twirled,
If nothing else, remember me,
The girl at the end of the world.

Jennifer R. Noles

Life's Pathway

As we travel down life's narrow and dusty road
We often wonder what the future holds
Trouble will surely invite itself in
Stand close to Jesus, He is your true friend
Problems will come and bright with it doubt
Jesus knows the answers, He will work things out
Anger has a place, but not in the home
Stand firm in what you believe, you will never go wrong
Patience is a virtue, so we have been told
It has its rewards when you're young, even when you're old
Life can be fulfilling to those who want to achieve
If God is your guide, you will definitely succeed
Give thanks and praise to Him who watches from above
He gave us a gift and that gift is Love

Bridgette B. Riddle

Words

"You may have something there is no cure for," the doctor said,
as I left his office,

My seeds of anger have overtaken me
For two days ago
I appreciated a flower, baby Robert's smile
I knew how to love
I knew peace
I enjoyed the presence of the moment.

This RAGE, the hurricane
The ice pellets upon my window
The size of snowballs
Torrents of rain—
Water—
Adrift with the tide
My anger, demons tearing me out of my bed.

What am I empty of—
SELF
This pain.

Joan Ann Kulla

I Remember . . .

I still remember, the first time we held hands.
Palms sweating with anxious anticipation,
Hand longing to be held,
Mind wandering what you were thinking
Acceptance or denial?

I still remember, the first time we danced.
Legs trembling—no sense of direction,
Arms wandering blindly in the dark,
Bodies pressed together as one
The perfect union.

I still remember, the first time we kissed.
Lips dancing—hit or miss?
Eyes closed—in each other we trust,
Souls bonding for the first time
Now and forever!

I'll always remember, the first time you told me.
Heart singing your name,
Ears never heard such a beautiful thing.
Voice aching to also be heard—
Simply put, "I love you too!"

James Taylor Barnard

The Other Day

The other day I thought to myself what will become of me,
The other day I was scared and frightened,
The other day I loved and worshiped,
But at last it is today and I think nothing of it,
For I have no control of what might happen.

Kathryn Marcinak

This Poet

This poet writes of pain.
This poet writes of provoked wars
And needless bloodshed.

This poet writes for the youths who die young.
And the young wives,
Who are made widows.

This poet feels the pain of the motherless child,
Crying on empty bellies.

This poet sees rejection, famine,
Starvation, unemployment.

This poet cries with the afflicted,
The persecuted and the innocent.

When this poet sees, this poet writes.
When this poet feels, this poet cries.

Judith P. Hudson

When My Father Became Ill

No one was able to warn me
Not a single soul could relate
There is no lesson you can take to help you cope the change

When My Father Became Ill

I have trouble accepting the fact
I can't believe even though I see him everyday
In the morning I wake up and hope it is all a bad dream

When My Father Became Ill

He was so strong, he was so tough
He was the one with all the answers for me
How our relationship changed

When My Father Became Ill

I'm unsure if I am doing the right thing
I feel as if at time I have no strength to go on
I pray to God for guidance

When My Father Became Ill

I wonder if I will look back to this point of my life and realize
there was a purpose and a reason and if I will understand it
completely as a person, a care giver, and a daughter.

When My Father Became Ill

Linda Good

Vanishing Beauty

The golden lake dances in the evening sun
Huge green trees cover the ground
What will happen to the earth's wondrous beauty?

Ocean waves crash against the shore
Green pastures cover the ground like blankets
The golden lake dances in the evening sun

Oil spills pollute the crystal waters
Smog fills the once clean air
What will happen to the earth's wondrous beauty?

Snow covered mountains wait for the skiers
Steep, rocky hills are anxious for the hikers
The golden lake dances in the evening sun

Litter thrown along side the road
Acid rain pouring down on the healthy plains
What will happen to the earth's wondrous beauty?

Hills, mountains, forests, the ocean, lakes, and streams
Smog, littered streets, polluted waters, suffering plants
The golden lake dances in the evening sun
What will happen to the earth's wondrous beauty?

Lori Bulow

The Motion of Poetry

Poetry is like watching the ocean;
It has beautiful lines and a lot of motion.
For one to write poetry it is to learn;
For the one who doesn't it is to yearn.
Poetry is written in many styles;
So write that book and forget that pile.
To write poetry, it takes a lot of time;
You don't need rhythm as long as you got rhyme.
Poetry is sometimes funny in a way;
It's like the morning fog over looking the bay.
Poetry has feeling and a lot more;
All you have to do is open the door.

Thomas M. Fortune

Two Little Girls

Two little girls as cute as can be
Sat reading a book under a tree
Their eyes never left the book to wonder
First one turned a page, then the other
Pictures appeared in the book to see
Cheryl turned to Amy, said that's funny
Words were read and pages turned
Until the book came to an end
They closed the book and smiled at each other
And said, one down, tomorrow another.

Martha Rockhill

The Journey

It was a long and frustrating journey
Its road which was once smooth
Became rough and rocky

It was a journey that seemed to have no end . . .

I traveled through rain and sometimes thunder

I thought the sun would never shine

The sky was black,
there were no stars to guide the way

I was alone on this journey
Scared and at time's lost

There were no traffic lights,
to me it seemed that I was the only driver on the road

I thought all that traveled this way,
either got to their destination
or made a u-turn and started again . . .

But I knew I had come to far
on this journey to turn around.

Shawn Singh

Awareness

This heart is full—it cannot speak at times
Like these—although it tries.
A gesture and a tearful eye—but it cannot speak
It only cries.
What misery has made this heart so numbed
By pain it feels apart
From all old feelings deep inside—the laughter
Once that used to start.
So quickly, how it bubbled up and lit the face and made it glow
And all around were touched by joy
Contagious happiness would make it so.
Now see them quickly move away—this solemn mood
Embarrasses each one
Bitter pain is not for them—these people searching just for fun.
I must go away, oh! far away—from all those who do not understand
And find my joy and offer it to all the lonely
With their outstretched hands.

Helen Simek

Beyond the Barrier and Beyond the Bliss Lies Me . . .

Beyond the barrier and beyond the bliss lies me, the person
who is afraid to allow myself to be free.
Free from the fear that lies so deep within my heart.
A denial that takes me away from the reality of life
and all that is related to it.
For you that reality will diminish from all of the disbelief
and come to see that along with life comes the beauty of love.
A love that up until now I only knew as a remark.
I have solely been responsible for my doubtful way of thinking.
Now, afar from the false appearance is a recurring passage
where only lovers will come to enter.
My passage has concealed itself with a permanent fasten
that only you have the power to make accessible.

Dina M. Perriello

Venus

There's a celestial Butterfly who decorates heaven
bringing color to life with the planets of 7.
A special diadem in the Crown of Creation
who has a fierce Angel to protect with dedication,
the honor of Purity it collects from flowers
in the brightest of days and most mystical of showers.
Untouchable at times but how wonderful to behold,
oh Angel of destruction may you continue to bestow
thy service of fury to guard a faith
in the Power of Thunder and the Lightning of fate.
So that it may fly in the aura of realms
always and forever above man-made hells.
Praise be the one who created by far
this creature Butterfly who overwhelms the stars.
With the Glow of a beauty that was made so ethereal
it is a profound constellation called The Venus Imperial.

ELancelot

Can You Hear Me?

There was a time when I was like you,
I was a young child, whose worries were few.
I became an adult with many burdens to bear,
My lifetime experiences you cannot compare.
The people around me, they gave me respect,
But now I am old and there's a different effect.
I am still human, with desires and dreams,
Why won't you listen? I'm a burden it seems.
I don't ask for much, just let me be me,
Listen to me, for that is the key.
For those of you who cannot hear,
Remember that your time is near.

Karen E. Zappa, RN

Preacher

In everyday life he's quite ordinary
Just like you and me.
But come Sunday morning,
He stands there in the pulpit
So tall and straight with that special look
That only one who proclaims Gods' word can have.

As he closes and gives the invitation,
Only the spiritually sighted
Can realize the agony in his soul
As he waits for the lost to come into the fold.
The love and compassion felt for his flock
Can almost be reached out and touched.

Come Monday morning there he is
Bright and shiny ready to study and visit
Those who could not come.
Another week has begun
And plans he must make
To comfort his flock and teach the Word.

Sue O. Mangum

Tuff Love

With the innocence of an angel a sweet kiss fresh as the morning dew,
Young song's sung from their heart like the sound of a harp,
Tells you true is this child's love for you.

Life's innocence born at birth existing only in a child's life and time,
Nurtured with love, peace and serenity even then it won't survive
Through the showers of time.

For their life they must live and go forward, blessed even with love
They are destined to stumble and fall,
From which strength and endurance and knowledge will grow
Yet from our love they will gain most of all.

Tuff love is always the hardest to give for it comes from a broken heart,
Which will heal when your child returns to his roots
Renewed and remembering your love where he first got his start.

Your love though it's been tested and tattered as a strange path
Your child chose to go, has grown stronger and deeper with more love
For this child than others will ever know.

Because of your life long convictions and morals, as well as your love
For this child born from your soul, you must not relax
Your life's standards just remain to encourage the ones you love most
To reach for a higher goal.

Darlene Joyce Guy

Amanda

Called up a friend today, whom has had a very serious illness
for quite some time. She's been on my mind

Most of the time her voice is bright, cheerful and strong.
She's been knowing the LORD all along. She's been on my mind.

We've talked about things big and small. Oh! We've talked
about it all. She's been on my mind.

Have you ever met someone who instantly you know
they're special. She just has to be a passenger on God's vessel.
She's been on my mind

You see, I think we are all travelling on our own individuals paths,
hopefully doing work for HIM. It's up to us to make it bright or dim.

When Amanda sought out the LORD, she made a great find
She's been on my mind.

And at time now you can tell maybe the time to call on her may
be getting shorter, but that's OK! She's still been on my mind.

The Lord has her tucked close to HIS bosom.
There isn't a thing I can do, even if I had all the wisdom,
. . . except . . . pray . . . and keep HER on my mind!

Lorraine Walker Vincent

Broken in Two

Today you said, that we were through. I thought our love, was forever
true, but you tossed me away like a worn out shoe. I'm tired at all
the games you play. This makes the third time, you've strayed away.
What can I do to make you stay? My heart has been broke in two,
I wanted to spend my life with you.
Oh how I'm feeling so blue, I wanted so much to say I do.

All I do is sit and cry, I can't hide my feelings inside. All you did
was say Good-Bye, you really didn't want to try. Give our love
another chance, you have me in such a trance. Oh how I love to
be romanced. The problem here, is you and your friends, you
stay with them to the very end. Why not treat me like a friend,
then our love would never end.

I've watched you come, I've watched you go, but in my heart
the love still flows. How has our love, gotten so out of control?
Within my heart is still a glow. I'll never forget the love we had, I
never wanted our love to go bad. Now I will live forever sad, until I
find the love we had. You're young and wild, and live a carefree
style. Let's play the music oh so loud, and quit acting like juveniles.

Ruth Slyfield

A Day of Sense

Is there an essence registered by at least one sense
that may go unheard of during the absorption of a day?
A day so unforgettably beautiful it is sinful, if not evil.

A day that warmly licks itself off the human skin,
through pores bleeding rivulets of salt.
Turning thoughts held by a mind.
Locked inside a skull that cooks and pounds against a bone-hard anvil,
into an unheard shape of belief.

While the day,
a beauty of soundless light and colorful discord, rips and tears
the tender skin.
Hiding away the true essence inside itself,
beyond the physical, the sinful, the evil, the decay.

A day such as this is worth remembering.
In the right sense of course.

Ernest Serna

Pain

There are so many different kinds. Sometimes it starts with the little toe,
The one you dropped the butter dish on.
The doctor didn't think it was broken,
But you've got the bump to prove it was!

"You're not going to be a ballet dancer!"
Was his comment when saw it. What does anyone care?
It seems we are so alone with our sea of thoughts.

You can have your knees replaced, but your heart may not
withstand the trauma. Since the quality of your life is so poor,
What have you got to lose, try it!

It's all in the attitude, some will say.
Damned right—how do you think I've existed this long?
We are born in pain and we go out the same.
"What's it all about, Alfie?" we ask.

It's bad enough having a broken body.
Thank God the mind is still active and alert!
To have the mind stop functioning is the worst dilemma of all.

Not to know loved ones and friends,
The glossy eyed stare of non-recognition—
Thank you, "No." I'll not trade it for how I am!

Nancy B. Ott

The Urchart Castle

It stands proudly upon the rocky terrain of Loch Ness.
Cold winds ice it's stone, now weather-beaten through time.
Remnants strew its base, many carted away by tourists.
Shrieking gulls fly circles overhead as if to crown its glory.
In the early Scottish morn a vanishing mist uncovers its awe,
Like one would remove a blanket after a night's slumber.
The chill is bone deep, the same frigidity Celtic warriors
Felt centuries ago, when many battles were fought.
Tales of the castle's history could be told for hours.
God chose it to protect one of the world's most bewitching lochs.
From the rise of the morning sun, till darkness,
Through rain or highland fog.
The curious line up along the dew soaked banks and eagerly
Walk down the many steps engaging its domain.
Then up the winding castle stairs they trod to its cloistered tower,
Overlooking a mystical paradise.
Is it to encounter Urchart's breathtaking beauty
And historical past they make this pilgrimage?
No! It's to hopefully catch a glimpse of "Nessie."
The Loch Ness Monster.

Edward A. Nicholson

Mothers

Mothers are precious things, we cannot do without one.
They imprisoned us for nine months, thank God that's done!
We ripened in their tummies until we were golden tan.
Then they were there in tears as we moved our feet and ran.
Soon they left us at the dreaded place known as preschool.
But later we realized being in the eight grade just wasn't as cool.
Then it happened, and they will complain until they are dead,
They sent us to a place where professors were paid to pound our head!
Soon years went by and college was kind of, in an odd way, fun.
And sure enough the summer came and school was finally done.
So the wedding day came too slowly for the ones at play,
But for mother she was losing her precious baby that day.
And one day the same might happen to us, the kid.
So be smart and mature, don't do what mother did!

Angela R. Gilligan

Plato's Lament

For awhile we stood, and for a moment lasting,
our souls blended into one,

But heaven rebelled and turned away,
jealous of what was between us,

No love lived and none died, it floated around touched and fled,

But holiness of sanctity and virtue of what was will linger
in the atmosphere above,

And Angels will have known, and pass on the pollen of our love,
though lost in space and gone from our hearts, the effects linger on,

Until, again two souls will meet and stand, and then again
heaven and earth will meet and blend.

Theresa K. Uglow

Ol' Ted

I met a man. His name was Ted.
    He was so kind, but his heart was dead.

We talked for days, and he spent all his money.
    Now it's all gone, but ol' Ted's still my honey.

Let it be known ol' Ted has his grumpy moments, too;
    but in my eyes he's one of the chosen few.

He sometimes becomes angry, and I get angry back.
    I wonder, is this all worth it? Or will ol' Ted die of a heart attack?

Each day I wake and feel I've made so many mistakes.
    It's hard to find such a special man.
If anything happened to dear ol' Ted,
    Poet heart would surely break.

Georgiann Kirt

For the Lucky Irishman

Your poem lies throttled deep inside,
Close to where I live, you
Secreted scraps of rough drafts
Unsanded by callous red pens of editors,
Equating my adoring words with the sentimental entertainment
Of a clown tutored in juggling redundancies,
Phrases sans meaning, sentences sans thoughts.
Inadequate lines groan under a tonnage of driveling connotations,
And I want you tumbles loose from the scratchings
Of the imperfect rhythms.
Here comes the dreaded public humiliation:
Cut, cut, delete, do away with excess romanticism, now. Now!
But I cannot touch an irregular beat of it.
To us untrained and simple bards,
there is nothing more than to be tossed up.
The verse: I love you.
Et cetera.

Laura Jarrett

Life in Strife

I have never written a poem, but I feel like reflecting on life
Goods and gadgets have consumed me so immensely
I have no time for my wife

I have never written a poem, but I feel like reflecting on my spouse
Work has occupied her day and night
We are longing to find time for our kids to relax and browse

I have never written a poem, but I feel like reflecting on my kids
They do their thing and we do ours
While we do our work related bids

I have written a poem, but I feel like reflecting on my social life
I amaze myself watching TV and play with my PC
That is my tragic personal digital strife

I have never written a poem,
but I feel like reflecting on my personal strife
Consuming and fixing goods I consume,
I feel, is consuming my life

I have never written a poem,
but I feel like reflecting on life in strife
God take away all the goods and gadgets
So I could spend time with my kids and my wife

    J. S. Duggal

Untitled

I am truly blessed.

I am Jewish. I was taught to learn about and appreciate my Judaism.
I was raised in a loving home. I am truly blessed.

I have three lovely children. They are healthy, bright and beautiful.
I am truly blessed.

I have a wonderful husband who supports and loves me.
I don't mind when he wants more "yard toys,"
and he doesn't mind when I want a new "toy."
I am truly blessed.

I have family and friends who love and care about me.
I am truly blessed.

I have a roof over my head, food on my table and God is with me.
I am truly blessed.

So when an organization, or a friend, calls and asks if I can help
with my time or energies or support of any kind I answer, yes,
Because, I am truly blessed.

    Carol Ann Schwartz

Love Hurts

I feel like a part of me has died.
When I lost you, I lost my heart and my soul.
There is many a time when I have asked myself,
"How could I lose the one thing that meant so much to me?"
I told myself that I would not fall for you
when we first started dating one another.
But, when I looked into your eyes, so blue,
that first night, all that I had said I wouldn't do
began to fade for all eternity.
Never to be known about again.
Now, our love has failed and I feel as if I am to blame for the failure.
My heart cries out to me constantly, but there is nothing I can do for it.
I feel helpless and unwanted while my heart
continuously closes down on me with slow and painful deception.
I shall never love another,
'cause I have lost the ability to love anyone else,
except for the one that my heart and soul continue to cry out for
every minute of my undecided life.
Why can't I just forget about us and our times together?
It haunts me with every breath I begin to take.
I wish I could stop the ache,
but that will be too complicated to pursue!

    Amanda A. Allen

A Birthday Rainbow

Oh rainbow, rainbow
What a glow
How did you know
I needed your glow
High, high in the beautiful blue sky
Like streams of bright ribbons sitting high
How did God know, I'd never seen a rainbow
The Lord did bestow a magnificent show for all of us to behold
I wanted to tell everyone I know, I've seen a double rainbow
Never have I felt such a wonderful glow
As birthdays come and birthdays go
I will always feel the warmth of its glow
What an exciting birthday surprise
A double rainbow, before my very eyes!

    Vivian A. Cardwell

At First Flight

Earthbound since birth
Held prisoner by mother earth
Always longing to fly
Like the birds—Wanting to touch the sky
At first just leaping effortlessly into the air
But at first flight wishing to remain forever there

A bird, yes, that's what he wanted to be
An eagle maybe a hawk
Would rather fly than walk
But his earthly bonds wouldn't set him free

In an airplane or a fast car
Going a little too fast
Going a little too far
Searching for a feeling that would last
Trying to touch the nearest star
But too soon back down on the ground
And that feeling so short lived when found
Refused to believe he would always be earthbound

    Mark A. Crosbie

I Dreamt of Heaven

Come with me to a place that dwells deep in our souls.
Feel the essence of peace that we wish we could ream of forever.
Touch the river of life that flows on into Eternity.
Gaze upon the shimmering golden gates that lead to Heaven.
Listen to the beautiful hymns the angels are singing.
Rejoice in the reunion of loved ones from days past.
Play in the lovely garden that echoes the laughter of children's souls.
    Come, let's dance freely in the lush green fields of Heaven.
    For I can no longer wait till the angels call my name!
    I would gladly trade all my days and nights for just one glimpse.
    Oh, what a wondrous place to dream of.

    Michelle Jessup

Been Here

To my Teeny from her Henny, where love does exist after all
    Been Here
The tide washes in carrying its sweet scent . . . the ocean sprays me
A mist of sensitivity that brings to mind a refreshing memory a memory
Where I've been . . . a déjà vu
A ghostly holograph . . . a fading spirit
Alas I touch you does that image turn real
I know . . . I know . . . we had been here
Surrendered souls to the night and its tranquil light, how serene
How my heart has missed thee
The star shone bright to show us the way . . . our guide! . . . our love!
To stay
The moon, the night, the surf prepares for tomorrow's brighter day
A smile overwhelms me, then a stare
Our eyes connect, frozen lids need not fret, we dare not blink
Our lips magnetized, drawn together our bodies wet and again I think
I know . . . I know . . . we had been here

    Haniff Espada

Morning

Have you ever seen the sky just as the moon leaves?
Its grey loneliness harmonizes with the morning lark.
After the evening's dance, they shy lover retires to her home
In fear of what the day may bring. For one brief moment the sky is alone,
with no one's rays to wrap it safely in time.

Gnomes say this is the time when dreams become real and Hope is born.
"This is when kings are born," says Archimedes.

From the sky's tears come man's link to the eternities.
His epiphany now knows it's time. For only in one's pain can beauty
or patience come. For only through suffering's fire can truth be forged.

Have you ever seen the sky just as the moon leaves?
Its grey loneliness melody is with the morning lark
After the evenings dance the sky lover retires to her home,
In fear of what the day may bring.
For on brief moment the sky is alone, alone like the morning lark,
Alone like the truth, alone like every love, alone like me.
Not bitter or painfully said, alone like virtue,
Alone like purpose for to find one with the same creed is a jewel
on a river or mercy on a throne. Yet, mine is the lesser.

For one brief moment the sky is alone,
With one rays to wrap it safely in time.

Elizabeth J. Long

The Mountains

A phrase I heard not long ago.
Appointed to me by someone I know.
He replied . . . "If the mountains don't block your view."
Said to mean one thing; but so many others I knew.
The mountains where I was born and raised.
Those mountains where all my memories were made.
The secrets these ol'' mountains keep.
Are hidden where no one can ever peep.
For me they blocked out the cruelties of life,
Temptations soon to face, toil, and strife.

These beautiful mountains are here to stay.
That only God, himself can take away.
A tear comes to my eye when I think of leaving,
Maybe for life, it's hard believing.
If someday I leave, it will be to soon.
But, I'll come back and lie under the moon.
Then I'll thank the Lord for making them here.
These mountains and memories I hold so dear.
When that day comes and I'm laid down to rest.
Bury me here . . . in the place I love best.

Karen Parrish Woodard

Untitled

As the sun rises,
The bright orange and yellow distracts me.
It slowly ascends from its hiding place.
The sky is getting lighter,
And the sun is getting brighter.
As soon as it turns evening,
The sun is bright yellow.
Its rays beat on our backs.
Suddenly the sun is setting.
It again turns bright orange and yellow.
The sky turns light and dark blue, green, and yellow.
After the sun has set,
A purplish red color starts to blend in.
Then it suddenly grows dark.
And in the sky,
There's a bright glow.
Ah, yes.
It's the serene moon that glows overhead.
The moon is accompanied by twinkling stars.
And once again the sun starts to rise.

Sylvia Gomez

Time and Life

There is time in life,
And there is life in time,
In the first,
Time rushes,
In the latter,
Time stands still.

In the time in your life,
There is birth, graduation, marriage, work,
Tears, joy, companionship,
Loneliness, ecstasy and death.

In the life in your time,
There is the rhythm of the universe,
The echo of eternity; the pulse of love,
The feeling of oneness with music, flowers, birds, tides, mountains, and
Falling leaves in Fall.

We live in,
Two different worlds—
In this moment of time,
And where time,
Doesn't matter at all.

Robert Ellis

Unknown

I look in the distance.
A bright blue and green ball is there.
It is small.
I can cover it with my finger.
It looks so alone.
Alone in the vast black empty nothingness.
I want to return.
It takes me days to reach it.
As I look down, I see a light gray dirt.
Lifeless and dull, boring and still.
I wonder if there was ever life on it.
Maybe.
Lots of craters in the surface. Big and small.
It is cold here and I feel light on my feet.
I must return.
As I get closer, the big blue and green ball becomes larger and larger.
Days pass, seems like months. I am very close.
It's getting hot and bumpy. This lasts for a minute.
Then I fall.
Hit the water. I am home, safe from the unknown.

Cody Macartney

Little Angels

When Father God calls little children home to live with Him above,
We parents sometimes doubt the wisdom of His love,
For no heartache or grief can compare with the death of one small child.
They do so much to make our lives seem wonderful and mild.

Perhaps, at times, the Lord tires of calling the older ones to His fold,
So He picks a rosebud before it can grow old.
Only God knows how much we need them—so He takes just a few
To make heaven more beautiful to view.

To understand this is difficult but somehow we must try.
The saddest word we have heard is good-bye.
So when a child dies, we who are left behind must trust in God,
Little Angels are hard to find.

And because I trust in God, I know someday I'll hold my child's hand,
And we'll walk together on golden streets all over that heavenly land.
I know my son's safe now in arms of Jesus.
There's just assurance in that name, that wonderful name of Jesus.

And Jesus let me see one night in a dream
How God wanted my child for a sunbeam.
He went home to be with the Lord at seven.
He's a Little Angel now, with Jesus up in heaven.

Johnny Dakota

Untitled

My love of life, the time has come for me to confess;
To pour my heart out, and do not hold back, I profess.

Remember, "live for today and let the future take care of itself";
Shout out your sorrows, cry out your troubles, worry not and shelf.

The ambiguities and unknowns that are not here yet;
The things that have not come and you have not met.

Tomorrow you grief on my grave and shed some tear;
Embrace the precious happy thoughts that you endear.

How long can you carry on in your state of mind?;
How much can you put yourself, in a daily grind?.

You wake up one day, and see the reflection of gone times;
Your youth and beauty vanished, for no reasons no rhymes.

No matter what, no reason why, I cannot bear to see you so sad;
My life is at end, to watch you suffer, to see you never glad.

When you recite "live for today and let the future take care of itself";
Bundle all your troubles and toss them on an unreachable shelf.

You are so precious as the temple of God, yes you smirk and nod;
You will not believe, as humans we are the pea of the same pod.

Alas you forgot, to smile today, and praise the Lord;
You are well and sane, you worry in vain, so, I behold.

Ray Vazin

Yellowstone's Shame, Winter of '96/'97

I am the Buffalo and I held these lands,
from the winding Snake River through Tetons Grand Range
A century past the white man he came,
For the sake of his cows, he murdered our clans.

My children are numbered, but slowly we grow.
For a time we were happy, but then came the snows.
Ice harder than granite buried our food,
We were left with the choice to die here or move.

I am the Buffalo, the park ranger's friend,
we thought man had changed, that we could trust again.
At Yellowstone's gates we were met with their guns,
those park ranger Judases slaughtered my sons.

The soulless cattle ranchers finished the job, the snow ran with bison
blood and nary a sob. In fear for their livestock, two thousand
they waste, for disease transmission without a documented case.

I am the Buffalo and sad is my song, my children lie dying,
I won't be here long. When we are gone, who'll remember our name?
Who'll guard these mountains; will man know his shame?
When tourists come gawking, what will they show now—
Buffalo bones and a picture of a cow?

Rosemary Callahan

We All Have a Part

God uses the weak things of the world to shame the strong
It is the intent of the heart He looks upon
There is a man in the church who to walk must roll
Still, the desire to serve burns in his soul

When will the veil of fear be torn?
When will we realize that we all have a part in accomplishing God's will?
It's time a footprint is made with the tread of a wheel
For what God delights in most is His child

There is a woman sitting in the pew without her sight
Yet, she finds great joy in leading the children to the Light
For she knows a star shines the brightest in a dark place
And The Truth is more important than the Braille her fingers trace

When will the veil of fear be torn?
When will we realize that we all have a part in accomplishing God's will?
It's time we make God's vision real
For what God delights in most is His child

Gloria Caballero

Life Goes On

To work to hard for your money is to know not.
For no one puts a price on extra effort.

And respect is earned not always given as a gift.

So as we grow, we let our instincts guide our way,
For no two people think the same.

And no rules or notes for life the perfect way, no class in
School could we take to obtain, or gain knowledge on how to
Survive and succeed as adults today.

But we learn.
And we learn, not always the right way,
But the hard way.

And as we grow, we have come to understand
The road to success is never traveled just paved.

Dana Hoover

My Father

My father has a brain of wisdom like a wise owl who's lived many years.
His eyes are like the fire that the Comanches once danced around.
His hair is like that of a young male bear in search of adventure.
My father's body is like a power plant pumping raw electricity
into machines and substations.
My father has the strength like an earth cat.
My father's hands are made of raw steel.
My father's legs are made of treads challenging the barren land.
My father's feet are made of thunder booms all through the night.
His head is made of all the warriors of the Karankawa.
When my father speaks the world trembles at his feet.
I am wealthy because of my father.
Before me I am prideful.
Behind me prideful.
Under me prideful.
Over me prideful.
Around me prideful.
I am overjoyed and prideful.

Daniel Jared Gillit

Lake Watery Grass

A sigh of deep relief as I perch myself upon a Stone older than I am.
I respect that Stone, for that Stone has seen more than I ever will,
yet less than I could ever hope to. That Stone and I have been
through a lot together. But to the Stone, I am just another
passerby. Something that has no relevance in the stone's
existence. But to the watery grass, I mean so much more!

Could it be possible that I could "walk" on the most important thing
in my life and never even realize it? Yes, and it has happened. To
stop and smell the grass was never taught in literature class.
Beautiful green grass does not need any fancy colors to define
it. So what have I seen my entire life when gazing upon the
enchanting creature? Green.

Today when I sit in my favorite pasture with the Stone, I think that I
shall reach down and touch the green and see if I can feel it. I have
never seen one single piece of green before. Alas I know that to
see the green and touch the green will never be enough. Forever
will I seek the infinite wisdom and the countless stories that the
green has to tell.

Mario Efrain Berrios

The Lesson

The lesson began the day of birth, several years ago,
It was taught with a tenderness only a parent could show,
The classroom was a space created by wide held open arms
That sheltered, cradled and protected us, keeping us from harm.
The teachers, perhaps to some, were a simple and common pair,
But what was so uncommon was the love they were willing to share.
Their lesson taught the importance of honesty and trust,
They challenged us to stand on principals and do whatever we must . . .
To respect each life we are blessed to touch, as if it were our own . . .
To be a faithful companion to those who are alone . . .
To be a positive image in creating a better life . . .
To be a light, a beacon, directing away from strife . . .
To seek wealth and prosperity in treasures of the heart . . .
To plant the seed of forgiveness, when anger drives us apart . . .
To remember and to cherish the Spirit that allowed us to be. . .
But the important part of the lesson was learning,
the lesson continues with me!
Marilyn Beale Leverson

Time

Time is the moment we emerge from our Mother's womb,
Time is the tunnel which destiny travels us through the years of school.
Time is the catalyst that ignites development with growth.
Time, the source which creates boys and girls,
As men and women develops forth.
Time a mere memory; once future, past.
Time, a speeding bullet that refuses to let good times last.
Time, a theater that eventually costumes her youth.
Time, a meandering hour glass, which slowly falls when we toil by need,
We do not choose.
Time is all there is, there was, and ever shall be.
Time, were it not for this stranger, we would live infinitely.
Time, the glorious years of man's invention,
Intelligence and computer age;
Yet, no man can capture.
Only to God and His Infinite wisdom, constant love and undying spirit,
Can time be, but a chapter.
Joann Bass

That's Over Now

On a stool in a bar, not very far from his house, where he'd wanted to go
He sat there remembering the untimely ending of the
Only love that he'd known

But that's over now and though he doesn't know how
It all happened so fast, 'cause it was supposed to last
Love once seemed so sure he never thought it would hurt
But that's over now

He found he strength to survive when true love had died
Inside a bottle of lies to sort out if he dries
He'll try to stop without knowing where to start
A tall glass of whisky to drown out the memory
 of her and the pain she put in his heart
With his hand on the bottle, and his foot on the throttle
He didn't know what to do with his life
But that's over now
Chris Boyington

Bedtime in My Room

In my room all safe and sound
With all my stuffed animals all around
And milk and cookies for my bedtime treat
My pillows fluffed, I'm all tucked in between my soft warm sheets
With crickets chirping outside my window
And whippoorwills serenading in the distant meadows
Mom and Dad come in to hear my prayers and thanks for all my blessings
And to tell a real cool story with a happy, peaceful ending
So as I fall asleep and dream in wondrous colors of the rainbow
From my room I bid thee all good night, sweet dreams until tomorrow
Robert Charles Steinmeyer

An Ode to Grandma

Dear Helen, a grandmother so sweet
that your presence truly made life a treat.

You always made it a priority
to be fair and treat others with equality.

Full of spunk was your life
as you lead each day without an ounce of strife.

Remembering the twinkle in your eye
it is now time to say good-bye.

Our Father has called on you this day
and that is why you could not stay.

Your love is with us until we begin
the journey that allows us to see you again.

Peace and serenity are with us
because we know that you are with Jesus.

We love you Grandma—Danielle Marie
Danielle Marie Russell

Nature's Song

Life is like a placid stream,
Flowing gentle along.
Through meadows and lanes
Joining in nature's song.
The melody heard,
Lingers in the air.
Giving rise to the lark,
To join in nature's song.

My days do pass
And like the stream,
My journey cascades
Over rocks and ridges,
Thrashing and crashing, thundering to the sea,
To join in nature's song.

All is still, all is quiet,
Peace and rest is here at last,
As all God's creation,
Joins in nature's song.
Ralph F. Kirst E A

Someone Else's Pony

everyone is brought into the world longing
to leap onto the constant merry-go-round of life
simply living is not enough
everyone longs to be the best
each wanting the merry-go-round to slow down
one day it stops
everyone is not on the highest pony
each longs to sit on the highest horse
this will not happen
though nothing is forever
the highest horse cracks
its rider falls
scattered pieces
never picked up
the merry-go-round starts again
everyone scrambles to get on
one's success rides on the fall
of someone else's pony.
Korey Jaben

Dads

A ship without a rudder is like a home without a dad who with
help of God and mate steers to keep his family straight.

Dads come in all shapes and sizes, some are short and some are
tall, some are big and some are small, some are gray and some are
not, while others are just bald. No matter what the size or shape
we love them just the same as truth to tell, we couldn't do without
them as none could take their place or name.

Dad always comforts us if we get hurt and mothers not around,
he cleans our wounds and soothes us
with his great big gentle bear hugs that do abound.

Dad works hard to meet our needs, to work each day he goes in
fair weather, rain or show and never complains
when he's too tired or too sick to go.

To those of us older we remember our dear Dads with memories
we have of Sunday rides, laughing and singing to our hearts' content,
going on picnics or weekend retreats, games of sports and family
to meet after Sunday School and church. Tears of sadness
fill our eyes as flashes passe' conjure up memories in our minds
and hearts that within do abide.

I can't imagine a family without a Dad whose half the center of our hearts.

Marolyn E. Baker

The Lost World

Since the world's filled with prodigious bores,
I'd prefer to live with dinosaurs.
To feel the earth rumble and quake,
As a three story T-Rex gives his tail a shake.
Life with these creatures would be sublime, merely avoid them at meal time!
Imagine, flying birds, the size of whales,
And placid Sauropods with 40 feet tails!

To wake with the sun to incredible choruses,
Of bat-wing lizards and Brontosauruses.
At the river, for the day's first drink,
Apatosaurs and parasaurs, at the brink.
Perfect cohabitation, without mayhem,
At least, at water's edge, in the A.M.
Living where time stands still, millenniums ago . . . if you will.

No thoughts about today's quandary,
No rushing to work, or getting the laundry.
Residing in the land of fruit and flowers,
Warming sunshine, and occasional showers.
The earth . . . as it used to be, to support, to amuse and amaze just me;
Sort of like living in Eden's Garden, without having to beg Adam's pardon!

Marshall Kline

Carpe Diem

Death is like a black blanket—curl yourself up in it, and let it embrace you.
Let it cloud your mind, blocking out all hopes and dreams.
See nothing good in life, see only bad; nothing is good, and all is bad.
Let the darkness sweep you away Be a walking automation of hate—
and sorrow—and feed on your own internal fears and superstitions.
Everything in this old dying world is by nature corrupt and depraved.
So why should it matter what one person's happiness is?

Life is like an unopened gift—you never know what is within it
until you tear away the outer layer ad take a look inside.
Let it sweep into your very soul, and appreciate every last minute,
because it will never come again.
Let a sunset inspire you by its beauty. Be a lover of life, and let it
embrace you with all of its goodness and passion.
Time is a never-ending beacon, a companion helping you along the way.
Look at all the beauty before you, all of life in cadence as one,
flowing like a river to the sea. So why should hate command your life?

Either live with a cloud of hate and fear hanging over your head
for all time, or accept existence for all that it is.
For only then will happiness be with and within your soul.

Martin M. Wasserman

A Team and a Coach

There once was a team . . .
For which much training was needed.
Each and everyone's personalities varied.
Most naive, almost no experience, fragile;
Just a bunch of kids placed together.

There was a coach . . .
Who was very talented strict and clever,
Also a dreamer, a fighter, a believer,
With the right attitude, a free minder.
By all means a teacher, a coach, a trainer.

They put the team and the coach together . . .
The coach loved then, and he was appreciated.
These kids were taught skills in the art of living,
They were too, trained in all the games rules,
And he built their minds as well as their bodies.

And they say that at the end of this story . . .
The team could not even have one single victory.
But these kids were a team, for they were united,
Everyone got the best games spirit and character.
What other victories did they need to achieve?

Elba I. Delgado

The Storm That Pours From the Eyes

Tears
The culprits
That scar my cheeks
Leave me shaken
For days upon weeks
Cause me to ache and moan and throw a fit
Leave me to fear
That death is near

Tears
A clue
Evidence number one
Of unhappiness
Tears
Shed by the victims of life's brutal attacks

Tears
Are worn by those who have looked in the face
Of disappointment and hatred
And lived to tell about it
Tears dry
But scars never die

Karolyn Patterson

Conspiracy to Destroy Me Mentally

My raggedy ripped clothes fitting loose on my body
My shoes are all torn, I've had them for years
I step out the front door into society
This poor world, it's plotting against itself
We just can't face the fear

It's a conspiracy, my mom wants me to clean my room
It's a conspiracy, my dad wants me to get a job soon
It's a conspiracy, my teachers won't let me out of school
It's a conspiracy can't you see
To destroy me mentally

I'm afraid to open my eyes
I fear the person I see
I never ever want to tell a lie
Because everyone will believe me
But then again when I plea for my life
I'm the girl who cried suicide but never gave it a thought

It's a conspiracy, my house has nothing to eat
It's a conspiracy that I have to live by the rules
It's a conspiracy can't you see
To destroy me mentally

Erin Lee Snow Spinney

He Will Bear Your Burden

Seniors I salute you, for you have reached the goal you sought.
From kindergarten through twelve grades, so much you have been taught.
You're now tall and strong in stature, your mind crammed with knowledge.
Now you must go forward, to a job, or off to college.
'Tis the moment you have longed for, with anticipation
To hold your diploma, yes, it is your graduation!
You'll say good-bye to classmates, as you go separate ways.
In the future, you will look back, on these your carefree days.

May Jesus be close beside you, as you face the future,
If the Lord is walking with you, you'll feel safe and secure.
For He will bear your burdens, day and night He will be there.
May God bless each of your lives, that is my earnest prayer.
Amen.

Sarah L. Shaw

Visitors of Time

Milestones by the road side.
Rough edges worn smooth by the river of time.
Faded distant memories of my mind.
Fresh cut grass in fields of green.
Smell days of years gone by.
Outspread rows of corn stalks are yearning to reach the sky.
Windswept Poplar trees sing their song of autumns breeze that won't be long.
August crickets fill the air.
A red tail hawk circles his field to stare.
How I watch as the years go by like the cars of a freight train in minds' eye.
Earth is our passage as we know.
A brief stop in time before we go.
Time is a gift that's given to us.
As we enjoy all the seasons,
To be thankful we must.

Kevin Kavanagh

My Quiet One

Girl, you are as quiet as the stillness of moonlight on a darkroom.
You possess an honest and sincere manner which is very thoughtful of others.
You are to me what honey is to bees and flowers to nature.
You add love to what you touch and life to what you do.
What I feel about you is an extraordinary thrill.
Were we made for each other or are we playing with one another?
I always want and need to be close to you.
I am with you in spirit everyday even for the short time I have known you.
It has been a wonderful pleasure.
You have stayed on my mind for a long time.
You are the apple of my eyes and as humble as pie.
You are also as sweet as sugar, spice and everything nice.
Your love is something I can't measure,
but in my heart it's a very special treasure.

Gregory Andrews

The Setting Sun

I sit writing at my small wooden desk looking out the window
The afternoon winds have started to bellow through the valley below me
As I watch birds take flight
I yearn to fly away above the treetops into the setting sun
Away and into your arms
Tears smear the ink of the pages that I write
Crumbled, they are left piled high on the floor below
The words that I write are useless chatter
I keep writing knowing the pages will never be sent
Days are long and lonely, night seems like day
Sadness abounds me as I look around my room
Going through the motions, my daily routine without you is meaningless
Knowing that you will never return
Wishing you were here by my side
Unfamiliar voices beckon me to join life
But, my desire is only of you, my love
Oh, to be back with you, I yearn to fly away
I yearn to fly away high above the treetops into the setting sun
Away and into your loving arms.

Patricia Payan-Prizio

In the Dark

In the darkness I sit alone,
In the darkness I've made my home
In the darkness which gave no token,
The shallow darkness made me broken.
It made me look, it made me see
It made me blind, it made me be.
The light is my enchanter, my last dark dream,
I sit here alone or so does it seem.
I hear and listen but no one speaks,
I hear a drip from the darkness
From which my mind leaks.
Surrounded by no one, I speak to myself,
In the darkness I am someone else.
Darkness encloses my mind and soul,
Into its own dark hole.

Allison Word

The Flame of Love

At the light of a match
The Flame engulfs
Dancing in the spring's breeze
Free as a bird flying high
Set to burn The Flame does grow
The Fire burns from with in
Involving all it comes to know
Looking past differences and becoming Love
Love dancing in the spring's breeze
Larger and more immense The Flames does grow
Burning, yearning to touch another
A kiss ignites the Flame in the heart
A single kiss
The beginning of a bellowing Fire
A passion
Love

Charlotte M. Williams

Barely Alive

Stretched out on the floor, barely breathing at all
The silence like screaming, and the black closing in

Rain falls outside, water seeping in through the wall
Involuted by the weight of me, failing to realize my wretchedness

I'm crushed and broken and hurting inside
I'm floating, I'm drowning in a sea of despair
But I'm living and breathing with hope in there (somewhere)

Waiting on the edge, tomorrow so far away
Not able to contain it all, today is too much to handle

Every ache oozing at the seams, bleeding with the thorns
Flying too high I forgot how to land

Recoil at the thought of me, I'm not really what you see

Ashley Lassiter

How Will I Know You

When I die and leave this place, it's said;
we will go to this never before seen; glorious heaven,
and in time we'll all be together again.
How will I know you?
Will you have the same face?
They say it is so wonderful there, so grand;
possible I'll know by touching your hand.
It's a mystery,
one I try hard to understand
You must have faith they tell me;
I do! I think; and it consoles me
With all my heart and soul so deep, I pray;
if not all that at least my memory; I'll keep.

Joseph Barreiro

She Couldn't

She couldn't go out at night—her parents thought she would get killed.
She couldn't wear high heels—her parents thought she would get a bad back.
She couldn't read mysteries—her parents thought she would have nightmares.
She couldn't have posters—her parents thought she would become a freak.
She couldn't travel—her parents thought there was too much pollution.
She couldn't listen to the radio—her parents though she would become a hippie.
She couldn't talk about boys—her parents thought she was too young.
She couldn't talk about living alone—her parents thought she shouldn't be alone at twenty-one.
She couldn't go to school—her parents though she was too fragile.
She couldn't associate with other people—her parents thought she would get ideas.
She couldn't go out with her friends—her parents thought they would take her away from them.
She couldn't wear pants—her parents thought she would become a tomboy.
She couldn't take horseback riding lessons—her parents thought she should take ballet.
She couldn't have animals—her parents thought she was allergic to them.
She couldn't play with her younger brother—her parents thought it would be too much.
She killed herself. Her parents thought she was happy.

Faith L. Abramowitz

The Greatest Love Affair

My pen, the lover of my life, make love that only the two of us can understand.
As I hold Mr. Pen, he trusts me and believes that I would never steer him wrong.
As I push, he never inserts a stop or caution sign and as he glides across Mrs. Paper
to gently soothe her waiting emptiness, she never goes away feeling unsatisfied.

But, the bet part of this relationship is my Sister Imagination.
Sister Imagination loves Mr. Pen and adores Mrs. Paper.
As Mr. Pen allows Imagination to leave the confinement of her thoughts,
she eagerly explores those mysteries far beyond the stratosphere of comprehension.

When Sister Imagination takes flight, Mr. Pen dashes past unforgiveness and whispers mercy,
He dances pass confusion and replaces it with peace,
He cruises pass insecurity and showers it with strength,
He circles about pleasure and graciously lands in love—
a love which surpasses all human understanding.

As Mr. Pen gently penetrates Mrs. Papers existence, he bleeds joyfully in her presence.
Only then does Mrs. Paper sigh with relief, knowing that once again,
she has experienced a small taste of Heaven here on Earth!

Kecia A. Hill

Midnight Walks

Around the inlet's murky edge, seashells cling to the sand;
As I walk along an oyster bed I think about us holding hands;
Waiting to find a special place, where we can share a common space,
but midnight walks lead me back home, yet to find I'm still alone;
As moonlight falls on shadowed waves, where I'd like us both to stay,
and as the tide's endless race toward the shore, holds an embrace;
Could silver beams of starlit nights bless us more in amber lights,
I've learned these paths so very well, from river runs to ocean swells;
Inside my heart your love I crave, like mighty ships upon the waves,
I know your heart is always true, as morning comes marching in robes of blue;
Upon our first enchanted kiss, love broke through columns of ocean mist.
Your eyes right from the very start, made flames of love jump from my heart,
oh, I was flattered to be there, in your arms so debonair;
soft passion from your loving face welcomed me to your warm embrace,
while looks of love unveiled the night, when you so lovingly held me tight,
now midnight walks on golden beams, where joyous thoughts from my heart streams.

Betty Jean Taylor

Paris

I wish you could come to Paris with me.
I would show you the Eiffel Tower in Paris.
I would show you the most beautiful statues and paintings in the rural city.
I would show you the Notre Dame Cathedral
And pick the most beautiful flowers from the Luxembourg Gardens.
And when we meet again I will show my love for you.
And you will be mystified by France's beauty.
You will be beautiful in everyone's eye.
And I will always be by your side.
Till then my love, goodbye.

Jennifer O'Leary

Momma's Hem and Spit

I started up the steps that seemed to reach the sky
Oh my! Oh my! I never knew a slide could be so high

Down the slide I flew, wind whistling past my ears
How fun this is, then suddenly, a mass of mud appears

Clutching to the sides, grinding in my feet
Nothing seems to slow me down, the mud I'm soon to meet

Speeding down the slide, I splash into this pit
Like lightening from the sky, comes momma's hem and spit

Now on display, for all to see
So why must she, start cleaning me

She cleans my face, she cleans my ears
But never does she see, those onlooking peers

Not catsup, nor mustard, nor even open pit
Could ever stand a chance, with momma's hem and spit

Fighting and twisting, I was losing all the way
But cagey are my thoughts, when a bath can wait, another day

So many are my thoughts of her, when I stop and think a bit
But nothing comes to mind of her, like momma's hem and spit
        Michael D. Case

Untitled

As women and young girls
We travelled the same roads
We come from the same people
Am I not your sister?

My hair may not be as tight
My skin much more light
Am I not your sister?

I am not better, you are not less
Let no society dictate who is best
Am I not your sister

I feel as you feel
I am strong as you are strong
Am I not your sister?

There are things that keep us apart
Things that WE did not start
Am I not your sista?

I am your sister through and through
You want to be like me, I want to be like you
I am your sista

It is time to unite, my sistas
Welcome me, as I welcome you!
        Kelly D. Haithcox

The Last Day of August

The Lord is my shepherd, He's given to me;
A fine home and pond, lazy frogs and a bee.

I sit by my pond, this warm August day;
Watching as summer, is passing away.

The air is so quiet, a fly buzzes by;
The willows swing gently, and move with a sigh.

My lazy dog flops, in the shade of a tree;
Unwilling to move, too far off from me.

A dragonfly swoops, the turtle swims by;
The afternoon's quiet, and now so am I.

I wonder if heaven, has frogs and a bee;
A pond with a turtle, and a great willow tree.

If not I'll be sad, but I'll bet you this day;
The bees there don't sting, and we'll all want to stay.
        Lori Joan Brashear

A Minute of Rain

I awoke this morning to the sound of rain
I must have known it was the sound of pain.
Tears softly falling from the darkened sky
We seldom stop and wonder why.

I looked around to see what was wrong,
All I could find was life's mournful song.
If we look to nature we will see
For all the mysteries of life we hold the key
A babe's wail from the beginning of time
Wars of tribulations for all earthly kind.

Falsehoods and trickery will lead us astray
Pestilence and death will take us away.
As life continues every day
We must remember to hope and pray.

A child's laughter causes a pause.
It helps us to remember what once was.
We cherish the old days and rejoice at the new.
I couldn't help but wonder if the drops were too few.
        Delores Strauser

Naked America

I smell the essence of a women.
I was never taught how to respond.
I've been raised to mute tones.
My virgin hands would paralyze—
if my nerve pads felt ancient skin.
My religion forbids me, to think such thoughts,
of picking apples from her tree.

Her eye twitch-tease sets my mind—
to the swing of heaven's pendulum's.

Behind these iron bars, the walls of sexual frustration—
turn Caucasian, and the scent seeps through.
Not even the walls of science, could keep her out.

Naked America has us hiding, red, white, and blue, on a flag.
Naked America has us seeing yellow.

Our fantasy's have been sold, to the Devil himself.
We let the government censor our lives,
and we get lost somewhere between naked, and appropriate.

It's time to cut the meat down, and stop market square torture.
It's time to shed our winter coats, and flush the mint blood—
that has numbed our bodies.
        Seth Grant

The Tale of Two Tides

Down beside the shore I walked one day,
Enjoying the sand and the ocean's spray.
As I walked, I turned and looked back.
There on the sand were imprinted my tracks,
Deeply etched for all to see
That the one who passed that way was me.

As I returned later that day,
I found my steps had been washed away.
For the tide had rolled in—armed for a war,
Waves with white helmets bombarding the shore.
Then slowly and calmly it had retreated—
Marching out to where it was needed.

Then the thought came to me, "How sad it would be,
When my tide rolled out there'd be nothing to see.
No accomplishments recorded, no victories won,
Nothing to show for the work I'd done.
If I am just a name on a very long list
Or a face in a thronging crowd,
And no one was better because of me, I'd count my life a tragedy."
        Mary Lou Keller

Red Is the Color of Good Deeds

I saw my chance to go to Heaven
and latched onto it with both hands,
The Uebergruppfuehrer, may he hang in peace,
said killing Jews was a barefaced mitzvah,
(as the darting desperates would wild-eyedly say
if they had any breath left to speak),
And anyway, he went on to wheedle,
somebody's got to do it—it—you know;
And I thought, the Crusades are back, by God,
and here's my shot at the infidels
whether Saracen, Yahweh or Jew,
and I shot and shot until red in the brain
and ended up in this Heaven, Canada,
Where Redcoats guard my every right,
today's, tomorrow's—yesterday's.

William Greenhill

The Dream

Once upon a winter's day,
I dreamt to run away.
Run from the dark, and hark;
Let us be free, free from the hands of Evil.
But then there was a light so bright,
That Satan couldn't stand the sight.
But then a man stepped from the glow and said:
Satan please, let them go.
I'll say it once, I'll say it twice,
If I say it once more you'll pay the price!
Satan gave in to the good Lord's plea.
Then the people hailed:
Now we're free, for all eternity!
Then I awoke as the good Lord spoke,
"Don't worry it's just as it seems."

Stephanie Weller

Silence of the Night

The silence of the night brings many feelings down upon you.
Will you seize the light, or will you let its glare
obscure your view?
And endless stream of miracles exists there for all to hold.
Yet blinding darkness brings confusion and leaves
you hanging in the cold.
Peering through its misting haze nights reality becomes clear.
The night is there to be controlled, not something there to fear.
Quiet thoughts remain hidden, building in their toll.

The silence of the night will reflect ones inner soul.

Gerard M. Libutti

Native American History of Colonial Times

We helped the white man through the winters . . .

They paid us back by killing us;
They took the land that we were willing to share,
and cut down our home, the forest.
They killed many animals, and we slowly began to starve.

All this time we were quiet . . .

We spoke up once and they called us ungrateful
for all the things they did to help us.
We tried to explain that they were hurting us,
and they called us savages.

Finally we took up arms and started to fight back . . .

They told other people how evil we were,
and said shameful things about the Great Spirit.
They soon began to hunt us,
as they once did the wild turkey.

And now we are almost all gone . . .

Jeffrey Parker

Being Held to a Perfect Day

I'm like a thunderstorm.
Smooth and controlling,
Throwing caution into the wind,
With love and hate clouded thoughts,
Falling rain goes drop by drop,
A moment of silence rushes in,
Thoughts clash, anger strikes,
Unresolved feelings uprooted,
Emotions fall down in sheets of guilt,
Love clashes with hate,
Causing a whirl of a feeling of loneliness,
Lying down rushing into a sewer of forbidden trust,
Raining, raining into buckets of lost memories,
Left behind one day later,
Sucked dry from all feelings,
As the pain is washed away,
Breaking free with hope for another day,
For I'd rather be a cold cloudily day,
Some good, some bad,
Then being held to a perfect day.

Kristine Cohn

Pendulum

A playground bakes, its gritty, worn sand
clumping at the foot of the seesaw, congregating in the tire swing.
One empty swing bounces, deserted by some thankless boy
that ran off from the precious seat to greater and better things.
It sways, lingers—then stops. I see it tilt its head at me,
and smiling curiously to myself, I sit down and begin to swing.
The cool-whipped, golden air trickles down my face and
dances through my hair, and I close my eyes . . .
back and forth and back and forth
Behind me all the youthful sounds blend together
and become a huge, floating marshmallow . . .
back and forth and back and forth

But I know something is staring at me.
An aged oak stands solemnly behind my straightened legs,
holding lifted crowns of ripe leaves.
Its muscular trunk of motionless stature is wide and noble;
It is near and heavy.
I let my legs drag, but suddenly I feel the small, sticky hands
of the playful breeze tug at my t-shirt . . . just once more.
The sun heightens, and I swing back and forth.

Deepa Ramachandran

Prayer for My Angel Dear

Lord above, please stay close his first night.
In his best outfit he is dressed.
The color of his eyes, baby blue and white.
To you I give my son, as I lay him down to rest.

Promise that he will miss me none.
I'll love him always, from year to year.
How dearly missed he'll be; my sweet son.
My heart will forever ache to have him here.

I loved his smile, the dimple on his cheek,
And the way he smelled so sweet after his bath.
He left me way to soon, before he learned to speak.
If he could talk, his love he'd say I hath.

For his first morning, Lord I pray,
Hold him close, that was how he fed,
So I could see his sweet smile each day,
And when he's through, gently kiss his sweet head.

So please dear Lord, I plead,
Give him special care his first day,
If you could; your comfort he will need.
Give him all he needs, and love him in my way.

Sandra Lee LaVelle

Brothers

Sometimes when I'm feeling down, they always seem to come around;
To cheer me up, make me laugh, they seem to have a knack for that.

Now we've gone our separate ways and I feel sad on lonely days;
Then I recall the fun we've shared and different times
They showed they cared.

Laughing down hills of snow and ice, their wedding day, throwing rice;
Their newborn child who will call me aunt;
Their life we'll share if God will grant.

At family dinners when we hold hands and gather 'round to say Amens;
Our eyes are misty as we recall four more hands we used to hold.
The number is doubled with their wives and also with two wee lives.

We pray for peace; we pray for health; we pray for wisdom, not for wealth.
We pray our love will keep us strong until the day we've all come home.

Jenny Czarnecki

Past Perfect

If they knew then what they know now, the things they could have done
How foolishly they spent their time debating who had won . . .

They look upon themselves this day to see that they have grown
Into two young men who have it all, family, friends and home.
The love they feel, the bond they share these two are best of friends
Through the years these two realized that each must sometimes bend.
The world is at their feet, it seems, they've learned what makes a man
It took some time, nay, far too long but now they understand.
It has to do with many things they learned along the way
Courage, temperance, ambition, drive have led them to this day.
The most important key they found which led to now from then:
A single word called "family" and what was learned from them.
These two owe much to that one word it helped them start their quest
To grow together, not apart and always do their best . . .

If I knew then what I know now how different it would be
We started late but made amends it just came naturally.
We now walk together side by side, our journey has begun
We two are one for all our days, my father's other son

T. A. Scarafoni

Love, Still Ours

The days of our youth, which we thought were well spent.
No worldly acclaim, no less flair—sometimes a few tears,
A few harsh words, but mostly forgiveness was meant.
Nevertheless, we were together, in hand, through the years.

Time, seeming to pass more quickly, now—as our pace grows slow.
Busy, with things of the day and not dwelling on spoils of the past.
We'll conjure up thoughts of less taxing times, the mood of years ago.
We won't worry wasting precious time, and will it all last.

There's not a doubt, this love of ours has brought us through.
We've shared an adventure, in all of those years . . .
Though, now, we're bespeckled and get out of bed with a grimace or two,
Defying the odds, weathering storms, and overcoming fears.

We'll stop to look at each other, and see more charm in our smiles—
Or laugh, while we help each other get out of our car.
But never had we been sorry that we walked down that isle.
Through trial and error, neither of us had strayed too far.

The vows we made—our own to each other, til we see no more dawn,
Nor the rainbows of the sunset, that eventually grow dim—
We'll not regret, or have need of yesterdays that are gone . . .
For God waits for us both, to spend eternity with Him.

Nessie Gray

"M"

I watch Him.
He dances with an intense ferocity,
And his body glistening with sweat
is a siren call to me;

And I am obsessed.

But he is just an image on the screen,
And I can no longer face the reality of knowing
I shall never feel his touch
I shall never have his eyes stare into mine;

For I am obsessed.

Instead I welcome the oblivion of insanity
For within it I have found peace.
Now I can light up the screen and bring his image
to dance for me again, and again, and again;

For I am obsessed.

Christine E. Maylath

So I Gave

I needed peace in my life,
so I gave peace.
I needed truth in my life,
so I gave truth.
I needed to see a smiling face,
so I smiled at everyone I saw.
I needed to feel love in this world,
so I gave a compliment.
I needed to change some of my ways,
so I gave myself the courage to change them.
I needed a friend,
so I gave friendship,
I needed health in my life,
so I gave blood, sweat, and tears.
I needed a lasting relationship in my life,
so I gave my heart.
I needed God in my life,
then I received everything I had given, times ten.

Scot Schreiber

A Mother's Love

A mother and daughter is a special bred.
A mother provides for her daughters needs.
Together they go hand in hand,
Learning what is Gods command.
Mother teaching from a tender age.
Gods word! Yes every page.
Her child to know for herself Gods Will.
'Cause life is sometimes a battle up hill.
So knowing what's right from the very start
God is not God unless He dwells in your heart.

Betty Allnutt

Dorito

You are my poker game
My dusty evening sun
The florescent rust of sand and cross-country uniforms.
Without you the fiesta is over
The chicken is hairless
The pumpkin without mold.
I yearn to hear your voice again
The crunch of dry leaves under my feet
The cheering of the crowds.
I miss your sandy dunes
Your roaring campfire sparks.
Oh my cave of wonders
Return to me and again we will slide down the mountain
Ranges of your childhood parties
And bury ourselves in the sun.

Sara Shansky

Frozen

Inside of my heart, deep within my soul,
was a place that was frozen.
As this deep-freeze slowly destroyed me, while I was waiting to die,
I met someone.
I met a woman, with hair down to there and eyes that don't match,
and she was frozen, too.

At the very same time, in the very same place,
for she was the same as I.
I talked, and she listened, and we learned from each other,
and she told me I needed to smile.
This woman, with her hair down to there and eyes that don't match,
was slowly melting, just like me.

As I sat there that night, with slender ribbons of blood
dripping down my wrist,
I looked into her green and brown eyes and saw tears shimmering,
gently rolling down her cheeks.
She sat by my side, with her hair down to there and eyes that don't match,
and I cried with her, for I realized what I'd done.

   Rachel Bennet

Television

If in the mood for entertainment, whether serious or fun
The selection is for you to choose, something there for everyone

Talk shows, sitcoms, soap operas, too; to pass the time away
Documentaries, concerts, movies, and shopping twenty-four hours a day

The morning shows are filled with guests and various information
The weather is reported on all the country's key locations

Some people turn the TV on at night to hear the news
And some people turn it on because they've nothing else to do

The little ones don't really care since they're busy with play-dough
But older kids just love to watch the games and cartoon shows

The men like to watch the sports with drinks and lots of food
When games are through it sure does help improve the women's moods

While some just never have the time because they're always on the go
Others are glued to their seat and are considered couch potatoes

All in all, it isn't bad if you control how much you see
But some could never give it up, they just love to watch TV!

   G. M. Terlecki

If Only

If only the sun would shine for more hours each day
I would be able to live to enjoy the world around
The nature, the fields, the flowers, the sky, the tranquility.
A serene life—
To wake up and spend time looking out the icy glass that flames
The beautiful yard, the grass, the crystal pool, the yellow buds.
Time to hear that "chirp," the one that stays inside me the rest of the day,
Reminding me of nature's beauty.
Time to sit on a meadow and watch animals scurry past me.
But even more important, time to think,
Think about my life, my soul, my inner feelings.
Time to understand, to search inside
To comprehend what is going on,
To discover exactly who and what I am,
Time to establish myself in peace, and after all that time,
To watch the eternal sun finally go to bed,
Watch if finally turn off its light, and terminate its illumination,
Knowing it would wake up again tomorrow
And renew its everlasting shine.

   Monica A. Manginello

Winning

Sometimes people say: "Winning isn't everything."
However people get mad when you lose.
Sometimes they can't choose to be mad if you lose,
Or be glad that you tried until you cried.
In this life in spite of what we've learned about Winning,
Or losing we still blame others for our mistakes.
Not knowing or caring about what we do to them.
In their minds in their hearts, making them feel Horrible
Taunting them and hating them until the day they Die.

This is a warning to all of you, Winning isn't everything
Sometimes Losing can be good, because it Teaches you
All of the lessons that it should, I do know for sure,
It teaches more than Winning ever could.

   Michelle Benson

Springtime and Love

Springtime and love go hand in hand
Hearts racing wild and free,
Oh, how wonderful to have had a dear one
Who thought the world of me.

Springtime and love go hand in hand
That's the way God meant it to be.
Flowers and rings and all those things
When he and I became We.

Springtime and love go hand in hand
I think I ought to know.
To remember the sweetness of springtime and love
And the loss when a dear one must go.

   Elwanda R. Sewell

The Breakfast Table

Gritty fresh strawberries
remind me of my waif-like grandmother
who made me let me pick strawberries
every summer.
She let me eat as many as I wanted
sitting on little girl haunches
amid rows and rows of strawberries
alternating with rows of gladiolas
each a different variety and name
reds, exotic purples
lush abundant open beauties
with no purpose
but to grace my grandmother's breakfast table
where she gave me whatever I wanted
for breakfast
7-Up, ice cream and crescents of juicy cantaloupe.

   Ellen Bowers

Off the Pedestal

Who are we now to each other?
Now that we've lost our reverance and glitter,
Now that our hearts have been exposed and sliced open,
their black linings shining like the stars we reached for,
having fallen from the navy sky . . .
Who are we now that some limbs are gone,
and others ravaged beyond recognition?
Now that I must carry part of you with me always?
When we walk,
fleeing to our separate destinies,
will your memory turn heavy and pain-tinted?
Or will it fade and drift away on the breeze?
Will I offer your lessons at a gathering of friends?
Or hide my wounds in a leather-bound diary?
Wherever I go,
I will remember that you molded me and warped me,
sanctified me and saw through me,
took me down off my pedestal and looked at what was underneath.

   Kaitlin Willihnganz

Middle Change

Smoking atop the furnace with asbestos overhead globally connected
wired to the world with that dusty history of books powdering with age
wondering at the next generation smoking and fluid in mechanics of digital light
pulsing with the flow of neurons cross branching I feel old and jackal-like
stiff and with hand to paper, blood to loins, bit to byte serial communication
and the steady chomping coming to some conclusions of my prey
without a lot of options and alternatives judgement valued youth
expended in my prime yet outpaced by the flashing colored lights
on cathode ray tubes Jet fuel moves my atoms to go East to people
nation building Asia with concrete the Pacific century the nation in decline
at the end of the millennia my home a second world view in decline too of time passing again.

Craig Purcell

Killer Bees on the Go!

Killer bees, hear them humming the creatures are coming. I saw it on TV.
The plot will unfold and the truth will be told about your killer Bee.
This persistent winger, with poisonous stinger is ready for the fray.
This insect unwanted is marching undaunted, it seems he's here to stay.
This dreaded assassin soon will be passing into our native land.
His coming was quoted, his progress was noted, this Bee we would have banned
This arrogant beast keeps coming by leaps, we cannot change his mind.
G-men will attest that his forward progress leaves plots and traps behind.
A biology teacher said this violent creature can main and sting and kill.
Your Bee that's a-buzzing and this deadly cousin can mate and sometimes will.
The wise men and Bee-men, and farmers and G-men are all busy fighting this foe.
By just keeping moving our villain is proving the killer Bee's still on the go!

Carl W. Davidson

The Depot

The desolate depot slumps quietly outside the bustling activity of its creator . . .
Forgotten and alone, yet remembering its once arrogant existence . . .
It waits pleading for a place in the future.

Now quieted, its once pulsing limbs longingly extend to the horizon,
Awaiting the return of the black whore charged with need for a needless existence.
Speed by sweet whore there's no one here to see or care.

Windows stained and broken now gaze remorsefully upon their life sustaining artery
Not unlike an old man awaiting recognition for accomplishments past,
Yet realizing that progress has no time for reminiscing.

The junk train blows proudly in the distance, seeking recognition from its once
Powerful forefather, the protector of its existence,
But in hurtful shame, it rushes by the silent depot.

Stand there massive fortress . . . Yesterday your lobby throbbed with throngs of life.
Powerful locomotives raced through your veins removing the excess,
making room for the new . . .
Rushing, grasping—needing.
Little did you know or care that the enemy, disguised awaited . . .
Knowing you too would succumb to transient progress.
Continue to watch proud fortress. The signal will soon fall, for time is in the block.
Her disguise gone . . . her glamor rusted into age.
But with steam enough, we think, to go the mile.

George Larkin

Long Lizard Tongues

Down a narrow hallway, tripping over heavy rugs and long lizard tongues.
Tongues that continue to talk and saying untrue thoughts, deep and dark.
I can dance like a cat over the floor on my toes, because you are too tall to kiss.
I lean back, my lips parted. My breath escapes out the window
like a bird free of the cage and on its way across tree tops.
Where soft the green touches my feet. Where all life began and ends,
like the wind through the chimes outside my window.
But who's listening now?

Tonya Willis

Beware My Certain Ways

I am the good earth
The place where humans berth
With natures wonders and treasures
Contributing to their pleasures
I am happy nature birthed
These pleasures pristinely earthed

Don't make me betray my creed
To supply and meet your need
When you tamper with me
I will not salute thee
When pollution is your do
You harshly drive nature askew
I am then inclined to brute you
As you brew earthly disasters anew

Treat me gentle and kind
Then you will easily find
I bring the horn of plenty
Filled with nature's bounty
But beware my certain ways
To counter human reckless forays

Louis T. Tocci

My Kind of Mother

You are a beautiful kind of mother
Wonderful just as any other mother
Very glad for you to be my mother
I compare you to love my mother

Had I choose you would be my mother
Truly a blessing you being my mother
I compare you with stars my mother
Because you shine being as my mother

Glad to be from your life my nice mother
You express beauty just being my mother
Emotional rainbows of colors my mother
Golden as sunshine just being my mother

Good thoughts of love for my nice mother
Heart rhythms of love for my nice mother
For the life to me you gave, my mother
Caring love being in poetry for my mother

I love you mother for giving me your best
Born from your life you made me my nest
As just to prepare me as for life's quest
After being an adult I could manage the rest

Larry Curtiss Davis

Pumpkin Patch

It plumped a pumpkin for October
during August
whose nights were slashed
by invisible shafts of sin
that ricocheted
off the pious waters of the symbiotic pond
on whose granite shore
a transfiguration gown
melted in cold sweat
on the fevered corpulence of Halloween.

Some frosty April equation
for the power of impotence
which on detonation
mushroomed
to philosophical heights
in whose turbulent dimensions
nuggets of acid
bulged the pockets of converts
who washed dust from their skulls
in the muddy water of the pernicious valley.

Wilbur J. Childs

Who Knows the Feelings of Someone Else?

Who knows the feelings of someone else,
In one twenty-four hours of a life?
Is a smile covering a big tear?
Is laughter a dressing over fear?
Much lasting pain dwells within each life.
Havoc wanders and combines its strife.

Who knows the feelings of someone else,
Within any time span of a life?
Who's to say a life is good or bad,
Judging any part of life one's had?
One's needs are unfit for another.
May kind love be shown to each other!
How many kinds of thorns have one felt,
Tasting of life where venom has dwelt?

One's life hours, you never know.
Envy's faulty for one's worldly show.
Envy not laughter or a smile.
Think on these things as a living style.
In each life, roses bloom—fade—and go.
Someone else's feelings—who could know?

Ruth Bay

Conception

At the moment of conception,
An immortal soul is born.
In an instant of inception,
A lightening bolt is torn.
In a flash from east to west,
As heavens roar with thunder,
A new born soul is blest,
As a predetermined wonder.
The holy spirit breathes
A destiny divine,
While the creator weaves
A masterful design.
The miracle repeats,
Into infinity,
As providence completes,
It's planned divinity.
The earth is being seeded
With immortal souls.
The harvest has succeeded,
God's optimistic Goals.

William R. Davis

They Do Not See As I Do See

That golden dawn that I do see
Ere it fades o'er far off seas
Others pass by so very blithely
Seeming head in clouds, now be gone.

Gone to face another dawn
One, again, I do hope to see
To be ever there each dawn to see
Before, once more, it too be gone.

And yes to see it go to rest
In that golden sunset in the west
A golden twilight on high
That none ever do appear to see but I.

As I stand in awe to see, and wonder "why"
When all others do fail to see.
Beauty so high, each evening, every morn
Every morning and night sky.

So when I be gone to eternity
I ever hope, out yonder, ever I to see
Those golden sunsets . . . golden dawn
Guiding through new life to be.

Edwin P. Spivey

Reverie

Amorphous veils mid reverie
Regale the poignant tides of yore.
Dry leaves in blustered moments,
But vistas remain to adore.

One teaches, I remember.
No triviality there.
Imbued with a zest for knowledge
And empathy to spare.

Each child viewed as a treasure,
And honored as a friend.
She delved their hopes and homilies.
Young habits that propend.

I woke with fondest memories
Four score till that day and hour.
More than ripples in a whirlpool
The soul needs dreams to flower.

Rejoice and savor life's dessert.
Her entry served and trays long gone.
The honeyed sweetness that she served
Were precious morsels in life's song.

John Adams

I Am Somebody

I am somebody with a lot to give
Makes me happy and want to live
If I can give a helping hand
I can be happy on this land
Extend your hand out
Because that's what life is all about
Self-esteem and the words I am
Give assurance that I know I can
So being somebody is an important word
Everyone near me I hope has heard.

Theresa Glogowski

April Snow Before the Crocus

White feathers of snow
on a soft spring breeze
dusted the up-reaching
arms of the trees,
hung in the air
like an eerie mist
brushing the earth
with a farewell kiss
before wafting away
in the wake of the sun
. . . thus, is the hour
of the crocus begun.

Sara Hewitt Riola

The Sun

As morning dawns, the sun comes up
And peeks beneath my shade,
It enters my unconscious mind
And answers prayers I've prayed.

I awaken to its soothing light
Preparing me for what's ahead,
It reveals to me that all is well,
And the day has naught to dread.

Its warmth embraces me in love
Its light encompasses my soul,
This wondrous sphere of energy
Doth make my body whole.

So when worries plague my psyche
And my thoughts all come undone,
I know my frazzled mind will mend
If I can find the sun.

Diane L. Hall

You Are

Come lie with me let's sleep on it
Until the morning sun is lit
And shines so brightly in our eyes,
Come my love, lay by my side.

Hear my heartbeat, feel my touch
That will show you just how much
My love for you grows everyday
In each and every lasting way.

For all the years we've been together
This is something I have never
Felt before or known existed
Without you, I'm only twisted.

The years to come are precious dreams
Of you and me and all the things
That make our family strong within
Our hearts, where we let love begin.

You are my love, you are my life
You are forever my lovely wife,
Within my heart you'll always be
The only one that's loved by me.

Edie Newman

No Time for Life

In this world of stress and strife
It seems we have no time for life;
To enjoy life's treasures——
A glorious sunrise or a serene sunset.

The fast-paced daily life's struggle
Just to supply each day's bread
For all those who on us depend
To provide them a place to lay their head.

Days pass quickly into weeks
And, soon the weeks become months;
Before we know it another year is gone
And, oh how swiftly time fades.

All too soon our life's work is done
With little time to prepare
To curtail our life's toils
And enjoy our rewards before our final rest.

Rebecca Rhoden

Ever Since That Wonderful Day

Ever since that wonderful day,
That I first laid eyes on you.
You've inspired my thoughts,
On things I hope to come true.

I toss and turn at night,
While laying in my bed.
Thinking thoughts about you,
That keep going through my head.

My mind keeps wondering,
About all kinds of things.
About true love and life,
And what happiness brings.

There's so much that I don't know,
And so much I'd like to say.
About the feelings I have for you,
Ever since that wonderful day.

I'll keep thinking these thoughts,
That I hope will come true.
Because I know you're very special,
And I can't take my mind off you.

Steven R. Williams

On Listening

A tumult of music
Tumbles over me.
The sound envelopes,
It engrosses,
It passes as water
Over a dam.
It cascades in beauty,
Falling in notes,
Dotted and quartered,
Until it lands in a pool
At the bottom of my soul.
And I listen—
In loneliness.

Philip A. Eckerle

The Worst Event?

They tell me this is my child.
Is it really a part of me?
This puling lollipop, how wild,
doubtful, it cannot be!

My life has been of pleasure bent
the sea has been my home
A child would be the worst event.
Me, give up waves and breaking foam?

Sometime—was it last year?—
we had a fling or two.
Would it not be rather queer
if "this babe be yours" is true?

And yet it looks a bit like me
it breaths, it coos, it lives!
May hap extends my family tree
new meaning that it gives.

How strange! A quickened beat of heart;
the infant tot has won.
This babe, in minutes, becomes a part
of my life. My World! My Son!

Elizabeth R. P. Shaw

To Be

I rise to view our fertile sphere
From a nebula atoll
Then fall softly as a petal
Into this hortensial bowl.
I glide into depths of mighty oceans
To surface on a moonbeam lighted shoal
Then float above the breath of angels
Free from within hate and anger's
Destructive and immoral hold.

I stride the earth discovering
The ancient's footprints in the sands
As one by one they stepped to be
Entered on humanity's roll,
From before the beginning
To beyond the end
Linking past and future
With every unbounded soul.

Joseph Binder

Magna Cum Laude

High within their subterranean towers,
Reaching for surface and light,
The scholars are probing
With a steady instinct
Honorific of gravity
And those true dead centers
Of hidden, vital worlds.

David L. Hyde

Wherever You Walk

Wherever you walk
There will I walk too.
Deep within is the feeling
of Sunlight and Joy . . .
of Life and its Mystery
I felt, as I now still feel
When I saw you that day
Not too long ago.

And I heard myself say,
"What a treasure
To have beside me!
To be able to walk
With such Beauty
Would be a Gift
Of meaning and of Life."

We have walked
Together wherever.
Wherever you walk, we walk
For there
Will I ever walk too.

David Glaser

Gracious God Above

The Maker, our Creator
My most wonderful Helper
Who gave me knowledge and
Wisdom to decipher
All the things I encounter.

He enabled my achievement
Encouraged me when I was unstable
Gracious God above, how reliable
Is your love.

Golden Images I do not craze
Your love is my only praise
To consider all my burden
And pick me up when heavy-laden.

Who is my Savior
The Almighty Creator.

Donna Baker

A Deep Blue Farewell

With arms outstretched
I reach towards the sun
And I am drawn upwards through the sky
Until the Earth is but a speck of dust
And drifting through space and time
I feel great joy as I go ever higher
Into the deep blue vastness
On a peaceful journey home

Holly Mock Kadota

You Lie, You Cheat, You Steal

The way you treat
me is unreal,
You expect me to sit
around and wait, when I could
be out with another
date,
I always thought you
where the one,
but now I've deceived were
over and done.
Sure I'll always love
you,
But not until you
can love me too.

Samara Anthony

Old Age

When we get old
And can't shake our fears

We have aches
And pains and so
Many tears

Oh to be young
Once, more in time

I would be happy
And church bells
Would chime

Angela Piccinni

Drowning

Woman in lake
Drowning.
No help in sight.
Flailing,
Flailing,
Flailing.

Man rows by
"Help!" she cries.
He keeps rowing
Lost in sea of fear.
Drowning.

Diane R. Simon

Orchid Was Her Name

In a forest beyond the waterfall
A fairy castle lay hidden.
Moon shines through shifting leaves
Against the stone gray wall.

Captured from a cradle one night,
The changeling longs for home
Her sighing soft as gentle breeze,
Her tears shining so bright.

To return again to her flowered land
A gentle love must come.
Give a secret, special gift
Like nothing ever so grand.

Many a knight came on a dare,
But sadly failed once more.
Then a beggar came one day
And found this beauty in his care.

A delicate, waxy plant he saw
Along the misty path.
For a drink of water he gave the flower
When he knocked upon the door.

Carol Pfankuchen

Time's Value

"Time is money" is only half true
for it can be much more than that.
It may mean someone cares for you
And that his very love you had.

For the most precious gift to make
is to bestow one's time and skill—
whatever hours it may take you,
never discourage you it will.

Thus, it means more than getting paid,
although this may be needed too,
for, when all is thought out and said,
the priceless things are best for you!

Maria K. Gerstman

Wheat Circles

The circles etched in the wheat fields
Are messages of peace and love.
Sent by God thru His angels
Telling us of life in heaven above.

Each drawing is a message
Telling us to love—not hate,
Leaving messages of the future
Warning us of mankind's fate.

We need to heed their message
Not worry if they're false or true.
Learn to follow God's word
And change the things we do.

The circles are drawn to give us hope
That man can live in peace.
We can love our neighbor,
Hate and war need to cease.

Sandra Fleming

A Gift From God

A smile from you
Was all it took
To be under your spell,
And when I looked
Into your eyes
Deep in love I fell.
You're like a gift
That God has sent
From heaven high above,
You've given me
The best of you
And filled my life with love.

Susanna Coronel

The Cynthia

Is a very special and unique
Flower, that only blossoms
Once in every twenty-four hours.

It unfolds the twelve pink petals,
By the moonlights dew. The sweet
Wet nectar aroma, fills the
Air with life and beauty.

Only the purest of hearts may
Touch it. Without her consent,
For the prickly thorns can be
Very deadly. Indeed, she is one
Of a kind. Unique in every way.

Fred M. Lundy

Sea of Hope

Beyond our dreams and fantasies
there lies a sea of hope,
filled with expectations
of a life which we can cope.

Brought on by excitement
is a glisten we emit.
Current too strong with determination
to ever let us forget.

On this sea sails a ship,
its passengers, our emotions.
Diving into sporadic waves,
giving us outrageous notions.

Threat of sinking is constant,
caused by unknown destiny,
but with a quest of happiness,
our trip should prove tranquility.

Tia Smith

Whilst I Sleep

As shadows reach to cuddle me
To hold me whilst I sleep
I bid good night the waning light
And warmly greet the deep

I shall not fear the creatures here
That live beneath my bed
I'll dream instead of breakfast morn
And belch my belly fed

My quilt enwraps my body warm
And walls enclose my room
Secure me from the nighttime storm
So dark yet void of gloom

I sleep in peace for I've been reached
And held most tenderly
A kiss of words has touched my heart
Daddy said he loves me!

Rob Rook

A Vision of Loveliness,
A Dream of a Dreamer

If all the world only knew
The greatest thing ever known,
Its loveliness is nicely shown,
Love has loveliness of its own.

If one could only see the unseen
Diamond that had never been
Sighted, even with sight so keen,
The unseen is often forsaken.

If the heart is made for loving
Without the contrast of hating,
The world would rejoice with cheering,
Happiness is the aim of living.

If one only knew that someone
Has a loving and caring heart,
A heart that suits the heart of one,
Always true, warm, will not depart.

Merlin Archivilla

Flag of Our America

Flag of our America . . .
Whose colors bright and true
Hold a special meaning . . .
Within red, white and blue.

Soldiers proud and brave
Died when duty called.
Folded flag rests on the grave . . .
Pays tribute to them all.

Salute and pledge allegiance
For centuries to come . . .
Cause, Pilgrims proudly founded
Our wonderful nation!

Robyn Murray

The Dreamer's Thoughts

The dreamer thinks of many things,
Sometimes they're imaginary
    and have wings!
Sometimes they are very hairy,
And that makes them very scary!
Some of them dance with lace
With a beautiful amount of grace.
Other want to make you cry,
And there is no reason why.
These are the dreamer's thoughts.

Ashlie Wicker

Esther's Birth

December night
Streets of Dallas,
Christmas bright
Grandeur palace.

Hospital halls
Sterile white,
Shadowy walls,
Glaring light.

Nurses flying
Birth unfurl,
Pink and crying
Baby girl.

Smile puddles
Baby charms,
Snugly cuddles
Mommy's arms.

Hearts cleave
Maternal wand,
Threads weave
Eternal bond.

Wanda Atkins Almodova

Wedding Day Reflection

My day, she said, this is my day
    I've dreamed of for so long
and now it's here I'll pray away
    those things that could go wrong.

My day, he said, this is my day
    I've found true love at last
to share my life forever
    now I'll store away the past.

Their day, we say, this is their day
    on which we wish them love
with prayers and many blessings
    reigning from above.
And in those prayers we humbly ask
    Pray, their love will always last
and lessen things unpleasant
    as together their future is cast.

Our day, they say, this is our day
    from whence our lives entwine
as we vow to love each other
    through Eternity and time.

Dorothy Mollo

Castle

Caught in a spell never ending
Lingering on insanity
Life's fantasy, reality unbearable
Sometimes to get away
She rebuilds the wall
The silence, takes over
As she begins to fall
Over the edge
Wake up in a pool of sweat
Just another bad dream, or was it?

Another day to get away
Another day to fall
Another day locked inside
The fortress she'd built so tall
And the days turn to years
As the wax of the candle melts away
Chosen to stay
This way all alone
Caught in a spell never ending
Lingering on insanity

John Stanley

Fear

Fear is within my mind
Fear is within my soul
Fear is what comes to me
When I feel all alone . . .

It starts within my head
and works down to my toes
Though, at other times
I don't know where it goes
To me it's a feeling
I know I can't explain, but
I'll just say it's like a chill you get
When you're out in pouring rain.

Stephanie Cappadona

Lament for My Friend

My friend has gone away from me
Her face I never again shall see
Her memory's all that remains with me
Beneath our dear old willow tree
Under this tree we used to play
Upon each sunny summer's day
And here it was we always came
To play our special little game
But now my friend has gone away
And here it is that I must stay
Never to see my friend again
On whom I always did depend

Alexis Black

The Little Lord

    The little Lord,
became a man.
    As a man,
he was a saint.
    As a saint,
this man was in God.
    With God on his side,
he was one of and with the Earth.

    The little Lord,
as a man
    Was great and wise,
he took for us, our sins.
    He put them on himself,
and forever he will be
    in our hearts;
    For this great sacrifice.

Stephanie Beck

See the Bright World

See the bright world dripping honey,
Drenched in sunshine's golden glow,
Or the silverwork of moonlight
Shedding radiance below.

Hear the melodious tones of silence.
Thrill to nature's euphonies—
The babbling, buzzing, singing, roaring
Or the whispering of the trees.

Feel the ecstasy of hilltops
With the endless sky above.
Feel the earth and wind and sunshine
Like the warmth of heavenly love.

See the bright world dripping honey—
Oozing sweetness at the seams,
Vibrant, breathing, pulsing, churning,
Echoing life's fondest dreams.

Esther Ferrell Seadeek

Untitled

With every rain and through the flood
You give me reason
    to shed my blood
With every beat
    and every breath
You bring me closer
    to my death
I've lost myself
    to all temptation
But with every rain
    there comes the Spring
The life you give
    the joy you bring
You save me from
    my hate I behold
You bring me in
    from the winter cold
I crawl inside
    you keep me warm
but I sit here waiting for next year's storm

Cheri Thompson

Pluto Monkey

They make me feel guilty
For liking the things I like
And I make myself feel guilty
For liking the thing they like
They think they're better than me
Or maybe I think they're better than me
I agree and disagree
Or maybe I agree to disagree
Am I angry because I can't have you
Or am I angry because I don't want you
The answers will come in time
Or time will be the answer

Cyrus Kai

The Promise

"I love you," he whispered
As he held out his hand
"No matter what—I'll understand."

"I'm there for you . . .
I'll never let you down
Please, my love, let there
Never be another man."

"I love you," he whispered
As he wiped away her tears
"Please let me be enough," he said,
As he shared his fears.

With a radiant smile
And a sparkle in her eye
She whispered, "I love you too
And I will until I die."

Beverley Riley

Sleep Tight

The dark of night
Stands out alone.
The stars are hidden,
Low and behold.
The dreams are dreamt,
And wishes sought out,
The prayers are whispered,
Eyes closed and heartfelt.
And now we lay
Down to sleep,
A new day is dawning,
Just wait and see.

Teresa J. Iacovangelo

Dreaming of You

Dedicated to the slain Tex-Mex singer, Selena

Today I saw you in my dreams
And your light touched my life.
I might never know the reason
That your memories touched my life,
Every time I hear the songs you left
In short, and brief life,
My heart breaks inside.
And even if we never meet in life.
For some unknown reason,
Your memories are locked within my heart
And this poem is a tribute to
The memories you left in this life,
Today I saw you in my dreams,
And your light touched my life,
Memories of you for the rest of my life.
And when I listen to your songs,
My heart cries inside,
And your light shines my path,
Dreams of you and the legacy you left
Deep within my heart.

Miriam Sanchez

Lest We Forget

How long does man remember
The body being a temporary thing
The mind even lesser?

Paul urges us to lift up
The brothers, the sisters.
What man recognizes in you
Is uplifting at the moment
And encouraging to the ego,
The spirit.

This is temporary
This, man soon forgets!

On the other hand,
There is another
Who watches you with his all seeing eye
Who's counting up your works on earth
For that great judgement day.

And the seed will multiply,
And yield a hundred fold
As you go along life's way.

Fannie B. Smith

My Love for You

My love for you is bigger than life,
To not have you, would cut like a knife.
My love for you is never put in vain,
To not have you, would fill me with pain.

My love for you, is like a shooting star,
It can express itself, even from afar.
My love for you will last forever,
To give you up, I would dearly never!

Eddie Berg

Untitled

If but one flower,
Would stand between your knowing
And not knowing
If I loved you,

I would walk to the farthest point
Of the earth,
And pluck it,
And bring it to you!

All my love
All my life.

Tom Stosberg

Mia Celle

May you walk in beauty
And always with the light
Facing life's pure duty
And making all things bright.
It's for this we honor
Your sojourn here on earth
Ours would seem much longer
Devoid of your dear worth.
Thankful for your kindness
We're blest with your sweet love
You reflect the goodness
Of great spirit above.

Dianna Drinkard

Love

Will you look upon my face?
Touch my cheek and caress my lips?
Brand your name upon my heart—
An "ever-fixed mark" on my soul.
Words flee from your presence,
For they have no power there.
Though they hang on every man's lips,
Their strength lies not in their numbers.
You have form, but no face.
Substance, yet you answer to no name.
Tell me truly, Love,
Will you hold out unto the end?
A glance, and my heart is ablaze.
A smile, and I soar amongst the heavens.
A touch, and I find my resting place.
A kiss, and I am home.

Robert Weible

Music

An unspoken language,
found in the heart and soul
of everything imaginable.
A rhythm as true as a heartbeat,
yet not held only in the heart.
A melody that lusts for freedom,
and a beat that rings true to man.
Harmony sweeter than peace,
yet you find it in life and death.
It has a power to move mountains
and the ability to ease pain.
Today tomorrow and forever
Music will be with us.

Kimberly Ann Eason

The Baby Bluebird

The baby bluebird fell out of its nest,
the first time his mother wanted him
to test his wings.

The little blue bird did not cry.
But his cheeks grew bright,
for he wanted to fly.
He wanted to prove to the world
who he really was.

He will grow soon and go on his own,
and that is the only tear you will see.
It's from the mother blue bird
crying at night,
wanting her baby blue bird
not to know flight.
Thus the tear comes from love,
she has to let go.

Some day he will return,
and she will then know that
she raised him the right way.

Antonio Rupert

He Is Gone

He was tall and handsome the day we met
A good looking guy you can bet
Kind and loving he was too
He worked so hard to achieve
What I wanted for us
Let me tell you he was great
With a plus
And then a disease took over his body
And then he couldn't work
Not even on a hobby
If there is a heaven
He should be there I guess
And I hope the answer to my poem
He is at rest.

Sara Romeo

The Pressure Is On

The pressure within me
  is seeking to escape.
My heart is pounding faster
  as I reach an exploding state.
But, powers that obsess me
  hold the steam inside,
Making me boil
  till there are tears in my eyes.
When the pressure bursts
  my mind is in a fury.
And, once this confusion is past me
  I can see things clearly,
Now that the pressure is gone
  and there is no turmoil,
My heart can finally start
  to beat like normal.

Peter Gennardo

Friendship

10 cups of friendship
75 cups of love
25 ounces of handshakes
50 lbs. of faith
30 cups of thoughtfulness
40 oz. of joy
100 lbs. of kindness
1 barrel of prayer.

Mix friendship and love
Stir in with handshakes
Work in faith
Continue to stir,
Blend with thoughtfulness.
Prepare the full pan of joy
Icing with kindness
Pour one barrel of prayer
Forever mix well.
Heat oven 350 degrees
This will last a lifetime,
Serve to All . . .

Ollie Bryson

Hate

Hostility toward someone who is not
  the same is where hate gets its name

Another hateful thing is when

The people who hurt to defend,
  but for

Either one to make a change
  we have to learn we are all
  the same.

Lazette Hall

Ah-Yes! Soap Operas

"As the World Turns"
"The Guiding Light" reveals
"Another World" where
"The Young and the Restless" become,
"The Bold and the Beautiful"
A tour of "General Hospital"
Shows us that "All My Children"
are "Loving" and
"Days of Our Lives"
Reminds us that we have but
"One Life to Live"
Meanwhile:
"Stella Dallas," "Ma Perkins"
"Lorenzo Jones," "Mary Hartman"
and the others, along with
"My Gal Sal"
all continue to
"Search for Tomorrow"

Alice Marshall

My Master for Eternity-Closure

Submit to my silence,
I wish we were pure
I long for sweet innocence
Not your love to endure
Take me, use me,
Torture my soul,
Love me, or hate me,
Your words are so cold
Submit to my silence,
Hold me, and break me
Cherish my name,
And I'll lay still while you rape me
I'll give you my body,
But never my essence
I'll confess to my master
I'll do your penance
So, take what you need,
And leave me alone,
I submit to a silence,
No longer my own.

Leah Marsh

Trouble

Why does trouble follow me
everywhere I go?
I ask this question often
And no one really knows.
I live my life quietly,
I try not to complain.
But as soon as the sun begins to shine
It suddenly starts to rain.
I wish I could find the answers
I'm so confused
About this terrible trouble
That makes me feel so blue.

Ruthy Cyrus

Untitled

Surpass expectations,
That's what peace and love can do.
Put you on a natural high,
Higher than any drug can do.
Put a smile on your face,
Chase your blues away,
It can start with a kind word.
It can start with a simple how do?
It can start with one.
It can start with two.
It can start with me.
It can start with you.

Timothy J. James

All Over Again

Relationships are things
   that come and go
Some real strong
   some so-so

When one breaks your heart
   and says good-bye
You feel as if
   you want to die

As time goes on
   you meet someone new
Then you fall in love
   out of the blue

You feel as if
   your love's so strong
You feel as if it
   could never go wrong

Then your heart gets broke
   all over again
You've learned, and know
   the pain will end

Danielle Sulzer

Humble Majesty

The tree that in the morning burns
'Twixt me and snow capped peaks
Heralds both the grandeur
And the knowledge man still seeks
Of where within the wonder
And awe of majesty
Does rest the hope for humankind
To one with Glory be.

Where midst those snow capped mountain
And the sunrise all aflame
Is there a place where man may dwell
And does it have a name?
Is it above the suffering
And doubt the fills the day?
Is there a way to find it
And who shall show the way?

Will it be the wind that tells me
Or the flaming light above,
Or will it be a hand perhaps?
A simple act of love.

Robert B. Aukerman

Man of Contradictions

We share the same space. We talk.
He seems to be in the North . . .

He extends a hand to bring you up.
He exudes the want to nurture;
to lead to roads to self-fulfillment.
To enjoy the mind and heart to heights in
dreams attain. But the
Pole is moved as by a slide.
The ego fed, the guard down, then,
contrary to thought, the hand a ghost
precludes the path conversely seen.
The road strewn with pebbles and
branches, broken, obscure objectives.
Clouds descend to cloak the issues
in colors dark and yet with opal fires.
But hopes are dashed as night dims
the light. The fires, abused, fade.
Dreams are forever more a fluff.

And integrity—of truth and honesty
. . . is about buried in the South.

Irene M. Gaza

Kali Ma

You are all,
And nothing—
Even the time between.

White as a virgin,
Red as the blood of life,
Black as the death to come.

In all of you—
We embrace,
For we must
Pass through all stages.

You are loved,
And hated—
But never understood.

Judy Beschoner

In Process

Far away and far between
the skies have parted
as if by hands of touch.
Pulling like the tug of a child
hoping to find the cure
for the heart has become
distorted or twisted
like the strands of the rope,
fraying at one end.
At some point, it will break
stopped before enables the reprieve.
Binding the strength
making it stronger
adding some, willing to let some
go away, stray or not be captured
constructing the new
as if a brilliant design.
Architects working together
to build the forever foundation.
Glass added later.

Carrie Hodge

Love

Evening sighs
embracing in
the fragrance
of the sphere—
I tremble
from your
soft touches—
eternal flame
embraced—
burying our
daily worries
with kisses . . .

Edith B. Molnar

A Smile Or a Frown— What's Your Crown?

A smile or a frown what's your crown?
A smile says, "Hello,
I'm someone you want to know."
When a frown brings everyone down.
While a smile says, "Hi, come
and talk for awhile."
So remember to smile, it will
make everything worthwhile.
Because if you frown, no one will
want you around.
So the next time you feel down,
Ask yourself what's your crown?

Chandra Troxclair

Blue Boy

There's a Blue Boy by my window,
That's a spin wheel I see all day;
Whenever the whirly winds blow,
O making blue plates fly one way!

Blue Boy is a friend of the wind,
You see it spinning on a post;
From left to right or right to left—
Like turtles running to the coast!

The winds do take time for a pause,
Like a comma after a clause;
From dawn of day to setting sun,
Like mother's work is never done!

All praise be to God for the wind
That makes lives on earth like the spin;
All praises be to God on high,
Who made the winds and birds that fly!

Jean VS Calder

Dottie

She walks in violets of Pleasure
and swims in the morning dew.
She keeps the promises of her treasure
Her icons and rubicons are few.

She is a lady of pink stars
In her struggle of circumvention.
Her mind has no bolts or bars,
As she processes her intentions.

She is kissed by promises of tomorrow.
Asleep to the dreams of yesteryear.
She closed the door on pain and sorrow,
Hid away delusions and fear.

She walks proudly to that good night,
That has followed her deciduous adventure.
Her pearls and rubies shine bright
As she delays her Rosemary departure.

Norma V. Finney

A Promise

As time goes swiftly fleeting by
and life's so very fragile
For those we love both laugh and cry
and slowly become less agile
The strength and courage they display
no matter what confronts them
gives us the hope that is some way
that we may always touch them
but now they're gone away from us
and though we miss them dearly
the promise of eternal life
we all can see more clearly

Bob Johnson

I Am

I am blind, yet I see.
I am lost, I walked away from me.
I am here, but I'm gone.
I have friends, yet I am alone.
I can hear, but yet I'm deaf.
I want to live, but wait for death,
I want to be heard, but I won't speak.
I am strong, but I am weak.
I am warm, yet I'm cold.
I am quiet, but I'm bold.
I am dark and I'm mad.
I am happy, but I'm sad,
I am blind, yet I see.
I am you, but I'm me.

Faith Finholm

Trees

Trees' roots into the ground have dug,
making home for the bug.
The bug is food for the bird,
for this is the chain that I have heard.

Trees green and lush
are homes for the thrush.
Thrush weightless and small,
Thrush with a call,
into his tree house home does fall.

Trees are soon gone.
Don't believe the con,
They'll be gone for all time;
A tree for a dime.

Animals will lose;
Is this what humans choose?
The chain will break,
It must stop for nature's sake.

Matthew Schafer

Child of Time

When darkness sits
On the window still
The quiet of night
Soon crawls in at will
But this child of time
She cannot sleep
For she knows the loneliness
Of the day soon starts to creep
Oh child of time
People call and they say
What is on your mind
Will you not say today
But this child of time
She cannot speak
For her will has been broken
And the secrets she keeps

Colleen W. Case

Glory Time

I hear the roar and thunder
Of tens of thousands wings.
The shouts and yells of glory
Through the ages they ring.

The rush of warring peoples
The pounding of their feet.
All saints from throughout all time
They can't wait till we meet.

The fight is on, evil loses
All over, battles rage.
Together saints and Jesus
Destroy the ruler of this age.

Then the glory time is here
Saints and Angels singing.
Forevermore to His throne
Glory we are bringing.

Carol Beneux

Touching

Touching is the answer
Touching is the key
A burst of loving energy
A gift to you from me
A sweet kiss on the cheek
A gentle hug, oh so sweet
A feeling of warmth that
Makes your day complete

Victoria Best

Sojourn

Woman oh Woman
I owe you so much
How do I repay you
I owe you my life

I . . . conceived in a womb
Nurtured by the breast
Loved by a woman
In love with a woman

I . . . know a man
But still a son
Will return to the womb
Earth oh mother earth

Stephen Allistair Yearwood

People—People

People—people everywhere
Very few to care
Busy—busy everyone
Little time to share.

Many may be sick-a-bed
Aged shut-ins all alone
Someone in the nursing home
Or layed up with broken bone.

Someone—someone
Close by too
Needs some time
To spend with you.

People—people everywhere
People need to care
Everyone can find some way
A little time to share!

Nancy R. Nichols

Poetry and Me

So many words and thoughts to choose from,
Heady with imagination.
Where the dull and ordinary dare not roam,
Freeing me from earthbound camouflage.
My love affair with poems
Leaves me breathless with emotion
Compensating all the losses I have known.
A flight from boredom
Into realms of spirit.
This is what I search for
Beyond the mundane crowds,
With more to reach humanity
Up there above the clouds.
In my mind I seek release
So I can soar completely free
Toward the greatest love affair of all,
My poetry and me.

Bonnie Loveuc

The Dawn

Bring us strength, oh light of day,
To warm our hearts so deep inside
And face each challenge, come what may
To leave us feeling full with pride.

Then on the misty, cloudy morn
Let our inner light arise
And show the peace and love reborn
Reflected in our very eyes.

A day of hope surrounds each one
With whispers on the gentle wind
That speak of quiet hours of dawn
To wake a new day to begin.

Nancy Geist

Untitled

Within the wall
there is a secret,
A steady whisper
that haunts the night

Within the walls
a fire is burning,
Another soul
is filled with fright

Within the walls
there is a master,
that watches every move

Within the walls
there is a politician,
that has a point to prove

Within the walls
there is a storm,
a cold winter freeze

Within the walls
there is silence,
another heart brought to its knees

Lisa Thompson

Romance With a Rebel

Insolent October,
 Summery, yet fall,
The glinting sky, your crown,
 The blazoned trees, your shawl.

You dance, you leap,
 In blues and golds,
Embrace the warmth,
 Ignore the cold.

With sunshine, you caress me,
 Blow me kisses in the breeze,
Tossing leaves that tickle
 And scuffle 'round my knees.

You charm me with your changing,
 November gray, defy.
Kaleidoscope, you promise,
 December white, deny.

In weak instants, I believe you,
 When you pledge the harvest moon.
I cherish our moments together,
 For I know you'll leave me . . . soon.

Debbie Taber

The Desert Sands

The sands of the desert with its
multi-colors and as the sun
appears and the air begins to fill
with heart and God brings forth
a new day.

The sun and sands are here forever
time stands still as we turn to
God for relief and pray.

And the murders of the desolate
land stand alone with God
creation of a flower called a
cactus that its prickly leaves
gives us the liquid of life
a true blessing from above

Many people that have taken
the pathway through these
desert sands thanks God for
bringing us closer to him
and his spiritual love

Elaine Loveday

Wanting Someone

I only wanted someone to love me
Wanted someone to care
Can't you feel my heart ache.
Don't you see the tears.

This didn't happen yesterday
It's been going on for years.
You used me, and abused me
took everything in sight
From my pride down to my money
you made a fool of me.

Don't say you loved me or
that you ever cared
When I really needed someone
you weren't even there

The heartache pain and suffering
is now all in the past
I'm with those who really loved me
I'm home at last
I have paid
I'm in my grave.

Joan Monat

Moving On

Kiss me good-bye,
Hold back your tears.
Wish me well
Don't voice your fears.
This is it
I'm on my way.
Today is gone.
Tomorrow's a new day.
I can't stay here to wait
For my ship to come in.
I know it's coming,
I'm not sure when.
I'm running to meet it
My arms open wide!
This is life, it's for living.
I'm not going to hide.
So wish me good luck
Please try to see,
I don't love you less
I just have to be free.

Rhonda J. Tuttle

A Soldier's Memory

When we were young and in our youth,
We laughed and sang in the sun.
Then we were changed from boys to men,
Just to feel the hurt within.

We were sent so far away,
Just to be the enemy's pray.
Then we were stripped of all our pride,
Just to watch the young men die.

We were trusted to go and play,
But not enough to have our say.
Now we reach for some help,
From those who stayed and gave us hell.

We're good enough to bleed and die,
But still not able to live a lie,
For this we're still condemned and
blamed,
Just to see our flag in flame.

I am a Vet who still believes,
They could not give us peace.
Now we have the wall of pain,
Which none of us can explain.

James W. Johnson

Miss You

Miss you, why?
Because I loved you.
Need you, why?
You were my mother.
Cry for you, why?
A piece of my life is gone.
Someday when I think of you,
I'll remember the joy
Because you were such fun.
For now, tears fill my eyes
When I remember your love.
Sadness slips in my heart.
Anguish decorates my empty soul.
You were there for me,
Holding me at birth.
You wept when I cried,
Smiled when I laughed.
You comforted me as you died slowly.
That's why I miss you,
My most treasured friend.

Rose Martin

A Dummy's Message

Cars, trains. Airplanes and even tempers
Just as well does this wooden dummy
Have their own specific factor in common
A controlling person by their side.

A person that always needs to control
King of the hill is his way of survival
Self-esteem is definitely a requirement
He lacks this wonderful word assurance

"A brain is what I like to have.
I'm tired of sitting on knees,
Saying only what is programmed,
Being manipulated by my master."

"I live in this dark box forever
Never seeing the light of day,
Unable to think, talk or play,
Along life's rivers and highways."

"In watching it came by no surprise
You may be the dummy in disguise,
If you try using control as a tool
Oh! How easily you could be a fool!"

Sally Pierson

Santa Can You . . .?

Amidst the ruthless truth of life,
 the child stood alone;
Encountering her sentiments,
 her diverse minded done.
It is mamma or papa,
 she is made to choose;
The de June of law,
 yet made ties loose.
Drowning in fathomless, agony
 she hunts;
Mamma's care and papa's love
 is what she demands.
"Why love so quickly ebb?"
 —her little mind delve;
"Can't love be returned,
 with the nice law's helve?"
It is Christmas now, and
 the child tries further;
"Can you gift me Santa
 my parents together?"

Aparna Chowdhury

Remember

Remember not what I shall miss
remember what I had,
Remember that my life was full
and for this you should be glad.

Remember not the pain and sorrow
in time this to shall fade,
Remember all the happiness
the memories I made.

Remember all the beauty
I was able to see,
Most of all remember
you will always be with me.

Remember what I took from life
and all the things I did,
Remember not that I have died
remember that I lived.

Francine Rosen

The Rainbow

Look at the rainbow there in the sky,
Colorful, unending to the eye
So much beauty for one to see,
It's like Gods saying "Behold, see Me!"

Rich and vibrant the colors appear,
Sometimes hazy, yet more often, clear,
They're marbled, blended, yet reveal
Separate blessings to those who will kneel.

A rainbow can't be compared to me,
For there's far too much missing—beauty;
But like the love deep in my heart,
There's just no ending, only a start.

Heavenly Father, show me the way
As the rainbow on a rainy day,
Give me some beauty, love the key
When people look, they'll see God in me!

Shirley L. Jennett

Death

Lighting whips across the sky
As I drop down to one knee
More lightning pieces the sky
As I drop down on both knees
I look heavenward and feel the rain
As it mixes with my tears
I cry aloud, "Oh, God, help me"
As my head drops between my knees
My body slowly falls forward
As I feel my head sink into a puddle
I never knew love could be so strong
As a gasp for air fills my lungs with water.

Jennifer Schroeder

Endorphins

Endorphins, flowers of the mind
Open to reveal the pleasures
Of mankind.
Release the essence like a fine
Mist and calm the nerves like
A Hypnotist.
Every cell is bathed and renewed
Taking on a new
Attitude.
A long walk brings about the feeling
That soothes the soul and promotes
Healing.

Martha Helene Gauthier

Summer Dreams

It's winter now
so I can't do much
riding and swimming
and catching and such.

Can not lay in the sun
or run through the park,
because those black clouds
make the whole world dark.

But I can still dream
dream summer dreams
about friends and sun and
fun it seems.

Dream that I'm swimming,
not standing in snow.
Summer games are much more
fun you know.

Christen Wynn

For Brendan:

You are the gardener
we are the buds
that blossom into roses
with your tender care
You nurture us
and guide us
weeding our path
and feeding our souls

We come to you
as seedlings
unsure of our way
growing wild and unchecked

With a stern hand
and loving eye
you teach us to bloom
each becoming a wondrous rose

Robert Ray

Canopy

Big green trees fill the canopy
way up high, real hard to see.
The forest floor is filled with things
like baby birds with just two wings.

As I look up above to see
the beautiful trees that flow so free,
a little bunny hops to and fro
as the tree tops rustle, move, and blow.

Clouds fill the air and the
rain goes drip, drop.
The puddles, they flow
as they go flip, flop.

The perfect place is like a fantasy
the birds, the trees, the canopy.

Jeni Grochala

Grampy

My Grampy made me so happy.
If I was bad he would slap me.
My Grampy made me so glad.
For when we went away,
I knew he would never be back,
Someday, he said he would be back.
Someday. He went so far away that day.
I always prey and say,
see you someday. My Grampy I prey!

I love my Grampy so,
I just want to go.

Anita Moulton

Thank You

Thank you
for everything you've given me
for pointing out things I never see.

Thank you
for sharing all you have and know
for helping when my spirits are low.

Thank you
for being there while I cry
for bringing my moods back up high.

Thank you
Is what I'd like to say
Just for being there everyday.

Veronica Torres

Untitled

She awaits,
driven by a conspiracy of thoughts
to a place much higher
than the bottoms floor.
Her eyes form wrinkled slits
as she shelters from a blazing fire
burning from within a place
she thought forgotten.
A life is all she lived,
and a life is all she sought.
She remembers nothing
but that which she exhaled.
She whispers into the night,
as the stale air rustles trees overhead,
and stars flicker there codes.
And all who is mortal
listens to her sighs.

Johnathon Lowther

We'll See Her Again

Just remember the smiles
And all the good times
She's gone to a better place
A place where she'll do just fine

Although it may hurt
Because she's gone away
Now she's at peace
And there will be brighter days

There will be a day
When we will see her again
A day full of joy
When we all will hold hands

So, as the pain comes to an ease
We will all be there for you
Because we will see her again
Holding hands, joyfully too

Jewel White

The Song That Changed Time

Oh beautiful for spacious skies,
A story of the past.
It tells us how glory came,
Though sometimes at half-mast.
How many people gave their lives,
For this undying dream.
How Liberty's torch forever flames,
Like gold—without a gleam.
This is the song that changed all time,
Won't let us look back with glee.
To our kin that long ago died,
To set our country free.

Kate Marchewka

Brave Faced Lady

I know I've been a short time gone
from where we sit it seems so long.
I see the pain there in your eyes
They've played mean games
Made my lady cry.

Hang on my lady, I'll be home soon
My brave faced lady, see our misty moon

Some folks don't know
How deep love goes
They poke and prod at what they don't know

Hang on my lady, I'll be home soon
My brave faced lady
    See our misty moon

I don't believe the lies some may say
Hang on dear lady
And kiss our misty moon
My brave faced lady
    I'll be home soon

J. Frederick Lloyd

Agony Within

She's been gone
almost three years
And with her the family died
Broken by her passing

Torn apart by her husband
Thinking he was hurt the worst
but he hurt his family even more
The day he took another

And now the ties are broken
Time heals no wounds
Hurt lasts forever
Only the memories survive

All that's sacred is shattered
Nothing changes what's happened
And in the end we all lose
Our hearts have been torn apart
And we'll never be the same
We hope and pray
This won't happen to our children
Time Heals No Wounds

Brad Still

My Friend

I'd like to thank you for all you've done,
for me these past few years.
You've been there for me through it all,
the laughter and the tears.

You always know just what to say,
to me when I'm feeling blue,
I can't imagine how I'd get along,
without the support from you.

You haven't tried to change me,
into someone I am not.
You respected me for who I am,
and to me that means a lot.

I never thought two very different people,
could be so close 'til the end.
I guess that's probably because,
I never had such a great friend.

As life moves on for both of us,
no matter how far we go,
You'll always be my best friend.
I just thought I'd let you know.

Erica J. Therrien

No Sale!

My bathing suit is faded,
My bathing suit is thin,
It fits my aging body,
Just like a second skin.

I went to buy a new one,
The suits are made for youth,
They barely cover anything,
And that's the honest truth!

I took a suit up to the clerk,
The best of those I'd tried,
When she told me the cost of it,
I very nearly cried!

I'm not impressing anyone,
The sea gulls do not care,
My children are so used to me,
They don't know what I wear.

Never mind, I tell the clerk,
(I put away my charge).
She hung the suit back on the rack,
Where it said, "Extra Large."

Marge Shelden

Death of a Troubled Man

And so I look down,
Down at my instrument of death:
The ground.
I close my eyes and imagine
What it will feel like to die.
The rush of the sky and
The pull of gravity.
The sharp pain of bones crackling
And limbs snapping
As I crash into the earth below.
Shall I flail like a mad man
Or glide like a bird?
The tears slide down my cheek
As an old lullaby twists through my mind.
It'll be over soon,
And I shall see what looms beyond.
I shall feel death's tight grip,
As icy and cold as it is.
And I shall finally be at rest.
I shall be at peace. . . .

Todd A. Brownlie

Perfect Peace

O Lord you see what's in my heart.
You know me through and through.

You said you'll give us peace of mind,
whose minds are stayed on you.

So help me through this day, O Lord,
and help me find the way.

That I can keep my mind on you
and not on yesterday.
    Thank You Jesus

Pauline E. Abron

Lost Words

Wasted phrases lost
in morbid slums
Listless hatred pressed
through my gums
Words stir but fall
to silent ground
Kept from passion
by broken tongue

Christian David Gennerman

Love Images

I dreamed of far off places,
And I thought of you.
The gentle breezes touch my face.
I long to be with you.
I heard the melody of a songbird,
And I knew you were close by.
There is peace as I search the night sky.
I feel your love reach out to me.
I hear the rippling water.
In my heart I embrace you.
Walking through life's turmoil,
You are my strength.

Dona Walton

Life

Life has meaning.
Going, doing, and helping.
Living are for the making.

Life is being alive.
Keep your dreams.
The heart, body, and mind.

Life is having a good mind.
Happiness, dreams that like gives.
Alive is being able.

Joseph J. R. Boisvert

Who Am I

In times of uncertainty and doubt
The question still arises
Who am I

Once I was a young man
Of dignity and pride
But I found my sword to be dull
Too heavy to lift instantly in defense
My self-respect my esteem
The discipline of my knowledge
Was absent of cohesiveness

Now I am an older man
My sword sharper and light
My worth is motivated by my heart
Not yet bold nor overwhelming
Scared and slightly stained
But honest is all I wish to emerge

Who am I
The question still arises
In times of uncertainty and doubt

Anthony C. House

The Picture

An old, worn picture in a wallet,
many times he had taken it out,
and looked at it for hours.
Each time he did, he cried,
Each tear for the times he missed.
He didn't intend for it to be like this,
but the weeks had turned into months,
and the months into years.
She was no longer the baby in his picture,
she was a young woman.
He wanted to tell her he loved her,
to be a part of her life,
but it was too late.
So, as he did so many times before,
he brought out the old, worn picture,
and cried.

Sarah Wilbur

A Thought

The snow comes down I ragged sheets
And through the storm a wether bleats
Yon formless hill is cold and bare
And wants the forage for a hare.

And cross the fields in drifts so deep
The swirling snow comes with a sweep.
The babbling brook which once I heard,
Her frozen mouth says not a word.

Beneath the trees the cattle stand
And shiver in this frozen land.
Let others tread the frozen wastes
There find their joy if that's their taste

Content am I beside the fire
And let the flames my pen inspire.
At peace with all the world am I
And let the winter cold go by.

John W. Roach

Summer Romance

Seashore-girl,
Boy-whirl.
Moonlight kiss
Domestic bliss?
Return city,
Oh, pity,
Vanished lover
Under cover!
Relax, dear.
Next year!

John A. Wheeler Jr.

Let Him In

What a humbling adventure
This walk I'm on
My last thought at dusk
My first thought at dawn
In prayer I say,
"Father open my heart, fill the space
That once was dark."
He continues to do this
And not let me down
He'll do it for you
Once you come around
So open your heart, and let Him in.
Come join the journey
That will never end.

Lisa G. Gibson

It All

Playing in the sunshine
Dancing in the rain
Singing for the joy of it all
And not feeling any pain.

Thoughts go fleeting, fleeting
Across the screen of mind
Oh, but to feel more happiness
In this life of mine.

Giving, willingly, happily
Is never cause of sorrow.
Being tricked, deceived,
Catches up with the doer's tomorrow.

Oh, but for a way to know
How to survive it all.
Sadness come in the night
But dawn's sun erases it all.

Lauretta Jane Lowell

Mistakes of a Relationship

When I met you
I had no idea how to be
I thought I did,
But I would soon see,
But not soon enough.
You told me
I did nothing wrong
And in my mind
I seemed to agree
But knowing me
I wouldn't buy it.
As I started to heal
I started to feel
To see it from your side.
I reasoned that I failed,
I became too emotional
Not from the start
But from the heart.

Garry FitzGerald II

Laughter Gone Home

Her name was Bernice
And she was born in December of '46.
She was truly a darling woman
With outstanding wits.

When she left her son and daughter
To go up to see God.
They never dreamed or imagined
That life without her could be so hard.

If you wish to talk to Bernice
Or write a note to just say Hi.
Do it now, say it now . . .
Don't let the moment pass you by.

You don't have to shout it out,
You can whisper or say it low.
There's no doubt that she will hear you,
Because she's with you wherever you go.

Bernice and God are watching over,
She's walking with Him.
Looking down on her daughter Denise,
And her son named Tim.

Tabitha Taylor

The Second

The second baby is the last
To really bring you joy,
To know there's not another one
I'm glad she's not a boy.

My baby is my longing
Of everything that's real,
I hope my darling baby
Has a soft heart that can feel.

You know she is your last one
She's even special so,
You anxiously survey her
As you watch her learn and grow.

You're softer with your baby
Because her sister went ahead,
You learn by trial and error
By deeds and words you've said.

You'll always love your baby
It'll always be that way,
You'll always love your baby
More than words can ever say.

Debra J. Bingham

Reincarnation

Did you see me when I died?
I saw you looking down,
My heart was heavy—sad, it's true but—
There was nothing I could do.

To solace and comfort I was no use
My eyes were closed for all to see,
And yet within my temple's soul
I saw you looking down at me.

Weep no more, for I am here
Not in a body strong for sure
Weep not darling, for I see you
And cannot more of hurt endure—

So joyful be—think of me
As once you recalled our love,
My heart was light—and yours was too
Rejoice—lift your eyes above.

Don't look down—there's nothing there
Naught remains but ashes, dust.
Remember me in heart, and life
Goes on. You must—you must—you must.

Arlene Schlang

Father on Earth

I think of you often,
I miss you so much.
Your big strong arms,
Your soft gentle touch.
So many times
I wish you were here.
Just to hear your voice
So deep, yet so dear.
Our time was so short
Only twenty-four years,
Of laughing, talking
And drying my tears.
You taught me to love
An unconditional way.
To teach, to forgive
And never turn away.
Our quality time together is gone
For heaven was calling you to part.
You were my father here on earth,
The memories are always in my heart.

Sheryl L. Peterson

Broken Wings

O' Lord mend my broken wings,
So that I might fly true and straight.
For if I am whole, I can reach the heavens,
And soar through your pearly gates

I can't seem to get off the ground,
I wander hopelessly about the land.
I know you can mend my broken wings O'
Lord,
By the touch of your holy hand.

So lift me up high O' Lord,
The highest I can be,
But please don't let me go,
Until you've made an eagle out of me.

I want to fly with the others O' Lord,
I'm so tired of flying alone,
I want to soar with the righteous one's
I just can't make it on my own.

So mend my broken wings O' Lord,
So that I might spread them far apart.
And soar into the heights of heaven,
To build my nest inside your heart.

Kevin McGarrahan

Dr. Martin Luther King, Jr.

What happens to a dream when the dreamer
is destroyed by hate?
Does it die with the dreamer?
Sealed in his heart because of the
ignorance and hatred of men who would
not allow themselves to dream?
Or does it live with other dreamers?
People who saw the dream as a beautiful,
fragile piece of the dreamer
that must be shared with their children.
Whatever happens to the dreamer,
the dream will live on.
And despite the hate of other men
the dream can change the world.

Kelly W. Dyer

Spiritual Honesty

Falling dreams
This mountain
proclaims.
In blood I claw,
Emerging from this moment
Atop dead angels and demons
That have my face,
And weep the sum of all
In one tear
At the dawn that banishes the cold.

Brandon Murphy

Knowing Him

When no one can understand me

You reach out and hold me
In the palm of your hand.

I feel the warmth
of your spirit all around.

As I reach out the more,
I understand.

Many, many, many, others,
will understand.

To feel the spirit within
Is the gift
to gifts you've given man

The Angels, now all around me
Are all around now,
"your spirit"
The gift you've given man.

Nancy Rutkowski

Sea of Tears

I am a young whale in the sea.
I swim. I jump. I play.
My mommy stays close by my side.
We swim. We frolic all day.

Along comes the flying monster,
To wound, to pierce, to kill.
My mommy leaves her big blue home.
Her spirit the heavens now fill.

Her earthly case is used and sold.
To feed man's greedy wants.
While I go on without mommy,
Her soul will always haunt.

As I grow in size and in mind,
I watch, I learn, I grieve
Through all the many horrid deaths,
That one day I too will leave.

Keely A. Crippen

Lamb of God

Behold the lamb of God
Who died for you and me
God sent His son to die for us
So we could be set free

He took upon Himself
All our sins alone to hear
And all He wanted for Himself
Was our love with Him to share

Behold the lamb of God
Who came willing to Calvary
Oh! the suffering He endured
As He hung from that ole tree

You see that man was Jesus Christ
Gods one and only Son
Just think how much He loved us
For this is what He done

Billie R. Madding

St. Christopher

Sainted Christopher,
Christ-bearer; Reprobus.
One of God's chosen,
Inspirit us through prayer.
A desired wish,
Complete belief in miracles.
Blessed with angelic heartening assurance,
One's hopes attained by faith.
Under the aegis, heaven-sent,
Divine messenger unto God.

Kimberly J. Vandetta

My Love for You

If I could give you riches, dear,
'Twould make me happy too,
I'd turn this old world inside out,
To see what I could do.

If I could give you health, sweetheart,
'Tis all that I can say,
I'd ask of this for you each day,
When to my Lord I pray.

If I could give you fame, my love,
With all my strength and might
I'd hold you up and keep you there
Until your name was bright.

Far greater than the riches, health,
Far greater than the fame,
My love for you and only you,
Will always be the same.

Arthur E. Thom

Twilight

The sun is cut,
by the blurred horizon.
There is no boundary;
The sun and horizon become one.

Not quite night,
The sun holding on
to any light it still has.
Innocence turns to experience.

Some stars appear,
The moon shines bright,
The stars shine bright,
The sun fades away.

The child disappears,
And a man emerges.

Ross Mullican

The Special Day

Today, oh God, is a special day
sent from Heaven above.
On the wings of an angel
the light appears
just to start day once more.

I think of the precious butterfly
that flies so very high.
It twitters in the morning light
flying kissing the daisy high.

I praise the God of above for
allowing me to know. He sent His
love from Heaven above.

Thank you Lord for not forgetting me.
Just like the butterfly. I too will soar so
very high, to touch some other lives.
So I accept the challenge to soar on
high with thee. So thank you
now as I abide—I carry out my
task to lift up others who too
will see the light.

Chalotte Simpkins

Ties That Bind

The journey of our hearts and souls
Will travel for all eternity.
Yet day by day, as time goes by
the bonds that hold us
are ties that bind.
Frustrations at what will never be
will bond us unconditionally.
This life only gave us dreams
of what really couldn't be
but may the next one
make these dreams
Actually become reality.
As this life leads us where it may
together forever we'll always stay.
Together our love will see us through . . .
Heart to Heart
And Soul . . . to Soul . . .

Charlotte R. Daddona

Baby Child

*An inspiration from William Blake's
"Cradle Song"*
Baby child so slight of form,
Sweet words I send to one unborn.

Call I now an image searched,
From head and heart, your picture perched.

I speak to you as I light,
And pray to Him for the might,
To protect you now and through the night.

Stealing looks as through a gauze untorn,
Showering kisses on your sleeping form,
I gaze upon a face unborn.

Lying down so soft and fair,
Only once, I stroke your hair.

Lashes lie upon thine cheek,
My baby child.
So mild! So meek!

Fairest child, sleep the night,
Play amongst the stars so bright.

And nestled 'gainst my breast so warm,
Sleep the night, safe from harm.

Robert J. Klemyk

Untitled

For years we traveled different roads,
With many downfalls all the way.
Then we found one another,
With love so strong, it's here to stay.

Today we took those special vows,
That opened up a whole new life.
No longer are we just a couple,
Now and forever we are "Husband and Wife."

I love you more than words can say,
And I give it to only you.
My love is strong and very deep,
And I meant it when I said "I Do"

Madeline Jean Rager

The Dark Life

Watch your life pass you by,
For you don't get a second try.
Dwell upon your wicked past,
And wake unto a furious blast.

Pain will swell into your head.
Fall asleep and join the dead
Blink awake and see the light
Shouts and screams of pain and fright.

Don't look ahead with wondering eyes,
For all you'll see is blackened skies.
Slice the skin and feel the pain
And watch the clouds drop acid rain.

Burrow deep into your mind.
There's nothing evil, yet nothing kind.
Take your dreams and make them real.
And you might live for your next meal.

The web of your heart starts to swell,
Welcome to your living hell.
Live for the moment and exhale each breath,
For at the end it's always death.

Scott E. Wheaton

Unity

You don't have to go.
You can stay forever.
You can help me finish the life
we've started together.
Fate brought us together
and fate can tear us apart.
We have to be stronger now
and listen to our hearts.
You have mine and I have yours.
That's all we need.
You and me. Just you and me.

Adrienne Repsher

Until

Until we're together again,
Let the warmth of your covers
Give you the warmth of my arms around you.
Until we're together again,
Let the rain upon your face
Be the kisses of time I can't replace.
Until we're together again,
Let the rays of sunshine
Be my love shining down on the two of you.
Until we're together again,
Let the whispers of the wind
Be the secrets we would have shared.
Until we're together again,
Do know that I love you both and I do care.
Until.

Rena Henson

Rust

On the grayest
of days
in December,
a bit of
translucent water
ran down
the sturdy, gray
and sophisticated
steal
that held up our
strong and beloved
skyscraper.
It left a
path of
barely visible
rust
that could
and would
never be
washed away.

Amy Piskorowski

The Thin Wire

The thin wire
spindling on
from me to you . . .

So dances, prances,
propped-up images of seconds past.

And what remains forever now
(As if I could catch it bare-handed)
is the current.

Patricia A. Berkshire

Extraordinary Circumstances Brought Us Here

Bigger events
than any headline
poured us into
the arms of the
world.

With not a stitch
on our backs
and not a cent for
some milk

We had only our Charm
and the compassion and
care of some big person . . .
To secure the ocean
of life, light, moving
forms, smells, tastes.

Hold me please

While I ponder those
Extraordinary
Circumstances.

Marguerite L. Carney

Brief Time

A lonely sigh
Awaiting
Yearning for the thrust of life
to penetrate my soul
A flower wilts
Precious time
Fragile flower
Brief time
When fruit will bear

Karen Lee

It's Simply Called Nature

It's beautiful, it's awesome, it's powerful
and it's tranquil;
It comes in all sizes and colors and
the sight of it is an eyeful.

From the smallest blade of grass to
the highest mountain peak,
It encompasses a vast area, yet sometimes
to find it we have to seek.

To look upon it and be lost in it gives
us such a peace of mind;
A happy, carefree serenity comes from
nothing else you will find.

The hopes and the dreams and the
aspirations it inspires,
May give us strength and abilities
beyond our ultimate desires.

Its name is nothing fancy or even clever
but one thing is for sure;
There's nothing more amazing and wonderful
and it's simply called nature.

Karen L. Davis

I'll Never Walk Alone

The beauty of your hair.
The softness of your voice
The smoothness of your walk and
the way you say I love you.
This is why I'll always walk
behind you, so everyone can see,
the loveliness of a person
who means so much to me.
I love you so, you'll never know
the thrill you bring to me,
And now, you're only mine alone.
I hope I'll always walk
behind you and never walk alone.

Michael Provenzano

Flowers

Flowers, flowers, all around,
They are like colors of the
Rainbow that touches the ground
They don't talk but whisper
I don't want them to be
Picked by my greedy sister,
But just sit there with delight,
And sparkle in the sun
With colors nice and bright,
I open my blind and there they are,
They glisten like a lonely star.
They make me happy and
I feel good inside,
And I hold them tight
With my greatest pride.

Christine Hall

The Wishes of Stumblers

Riders of the dawn,
Have no friends or enemies,
They have no home,
They just ride.
The others hide themselves,
With masks and other material things.
We watch in pursuit of the rider,
We wish to steal his horse,
And travel into endless sunsets,
That greet him at the end of his ride.

Stephen Rea

Who Took the Sparkle

Who took the sparkle from your eyes
And the smile upon your face
Did I hurt you so very much
That someone else took my place

They took away the smile I loved
And the eyes that shined so bright
I wonder just what I could do
To make them shine tonight

To put the smile back on your face
And the eyes that used to shine
If I'd hold you in my arms
Once again would you be mine

I still loved you when I went away
I didn't know your eyes would dim
Or that beautiful smile would disappear
When I left you there for him

I guess I knew that you still loved me
I took the sparkle from your eyes
And the smile you had for me
When I left and said good-bye.

Ruth Shelton

Just Forever

Forever in a million years
will a heart be easy to break.

Every minute love is shattered
by not giving it what it takes.

Still, we wish for any moment
that true love would take our hearts.

Forever could have us searching
for a magic that makes a wish start.

Forever seems like every day
as my love sits on a shelf.

If yesterdays could be tomorrows,
I would still have you,
not just myself.

Not just forever.

Raymond A. De Leon

Rich Man's Life

He had everything,
But who was he?
He knew many people,
But did any know him?
He lived in a mansion,
He shared with no one.
Sometimes he was grumpy,
And others he was fun.
He cared a lot for other,
Did anyone care for him?
For now this kind old man is gone,
Does anyone remember him?

Dan Brock

Love is Confusion

Love is confusion
And sometimes illusion
Not knowing who
Is right for you
But when it is real
You will feel
Deep in your heart
Right from the start

Kim Baran

Your Real Self

Take me in your arms
And never let me go
Show me all your charms
Let your emotions show

You always try to act like a mack
Just to show off to your friends
I want the guy I met back
So tell me when your act ends

You know I love my boo
Everyone knows that's true
You'd be stupid to ask me who
Baby you know it's you

Why can't you be the same
Tell them it's me
And stop this foolish game
Cause I'm the 1 whom
With you want to be

Valerie Cruz

Circles

Bare branches, curled up
Under a blanket of snow

Morning

Tiny buds peek out
Leaves stretch
To meet the warm sun

Noon

Full green trees
Fruit, seeds, nuts
Feast for the animals

Dusk

Sunset hues of
Yellow
Orange
Red
Purple

Evening

Trees remove
Their clothing of leaves
Bed down under a blanket of snow

Nicole Hulet

The Void

Chaos.
Time whirls by.
No time for thought,
No time for cry.
Fear and agony,
Pain and tears.
No one knows how to rid me of my fears.
You try not to cry,
You try not to scream.
Things fly by,
Too fast to see.
Dizzying pictures,
Frightening sights.
People, afraid . . .
To live their lives.

Cathy Dodge

Tortellini

Almost too
Slippery and oily
To hold

Tortellinis
Slip from my fingertips
Into your mouth

As you do the same

Gently biting
Tortellinis
And fingertips
And lips
Indiscriminately

Appealing to
Taste and touch

Our eyes and
Our mouths
Moist with sensation

Absorb
The human delicacies
Of life

Maria daVenza Tillmanns

The Dandelion

I saw a lovely dandelion
growing in the grass,
I carefully sneaked upon him
and kicked his little ass.

Ona Foster

A Stormy Night in Paradise

The palm trees shudder in the wind,
Lightning flashes, thunder crashes,
Mother Nature sings.
Fine sand, wind-swept from the beach,
on nearby houses within reach,
strips the paint from off the boards,
Sounds harmonious, sea-scape chords.
The ocean jarred from self rocked sleep.
Its waves are high, its currents deep.
No gentle rain, a waterfall,
From heaven to earth a solid wall.
The boat shocked,
rocks and slips from sight,
into the breakers, foamy, white.
Debris on the shoreline lies,
A stormy night in paradise.

Barbara Devereau

The Willows

The swaying willows
Gracefully wisping about.
They wonder lonely
Only speaking to the sun
As the earth holds them staring.

Matthew John Riddle

The Sound of Her . . .

The sound of her
    "I love you, daddy."
I could touch, taste, hear and see.

Now, the sound of her
    "I love you, daddy."
Will never slide,
        fade or disappear from me.

Walter L. Mitchell

My Mother

This poem is dedicated in loving memory of my mother.

The meaning of my mother
Can you really see?
How she has affected,
The lives of you and me.

From her gentle loving smile
To her tender loving touch.
The cards she sent
The love she gave so unselfishly . . .

There is no greater woman
My mom, your friend, you see
She loved life and gave so much
To all of you and me.

And now that she is gone
Her memory will still live on.
And when you think of her
Reach deep inside and beyond.

And turn your life around, give the gift of love.
And I know she will be smiling, from that heaven up above.

Dawn Jolin Shireman Watson

One of a Kind

Dedicated to Kelly

My friend Kelly, one of a kind
No one can equal, not in my mind

A little rough around the edges, but crystal inside
She tells it like it is, nothin' to hide

A son with medical problems, a father now gone
Not wavering in hard times, just marchin' on

As she focuses on the good things, and makes the most
Of friends, good times, a fishing hole on the coast

Life doesn't always turn out the way we had planned
And the answers can't be found in castles in the sand

Some people go on day by day, complaint at every turn
Others enjoy what God gives, and from hard times they learn

They say it's adversity that makes us what we are
After all, new tissue is what makes up a scar

Each disappointment, each heartache is a feather one more
Without which we would never have the wings to soar

What we are dealt in life is beyond our control
But how we choose to handle it, comes from the soul

Eileen Stewart

Visions

In the quiet darkness of the late night hours, I lie awake.
I am helpless to control the images racing through my mind.
Bits and pieces, fragments of thought, spirits of the past,
All are reflection of memories and time.

Alas, the shadows I see in the mirror of my mind,
Are not the woman, but images of a child.
A child with lonely eyes,
A sad smile.

In the mirrors of my mind,
Through the darkness of the night,
A sad and lonely soul cries out to me,
The woman.

Touch the broken spirit and the lonely soul that you see,
For the child, the soul, the spirit, the woman,
They are all one.
They are me.

Susan McCarthy

Midnight

I walk alone . . . through the eyes of the night I see
Only here can one truly be free

The secret whisper of the wind in my hair
I travel in places no other would dare

The moon is full . . . silent and round
Tis' midnight' sun looking down upon the frozen ground

The still black waters of the icy lake
This kingdom is mine . . . mine to take

Secluded here . . . free from pain
Only in this darkness can sanity remain

A place unchanged . . . no need for death
The falling snow is the nights cold breath

Here I'll stay . . . and so remain strong
Unable to hear the hearts twisted song

Never to be found . . . in this world I'm lost
The torment fades like winter frost

Here is forever . . . time has no meaning
Have I escaped the pain? Or am I only dreaming

Michael G. Hauptly

Susie

Hearts are filled with sadness,
Eyes are filled with tears,
Beautiful memories collected,
Remembered throughout the years.

Never forget those memories,
Those held so close and dear,
Those memories will keep you going,
Shielding all your fear.

She would want us to laugh,
Remembering the times,
Look down and see our smiles,
Not our tear filled eyes.

She is always with us, gliding up above,
The sun shining with her smile, the clouds raining all her love.

When sadness overwhelms your heart, do not be afraid to cry,
For she will always be with you, floating by your side.

Laugh—don't cry—don't say good-bye,
Her beautiful spirit next to you,
Will—always fly . . .

Shannon L. Modugno

The State of All Life

Sin bombard incessantly on all life,
Yet, life must go on nonstop,
Weary and unmindful of the burdens it carries already.
Then an unforeseen turmoil unequalled in ages past,
Causes it to heave in pain, faltering, gasping for breath,
At best sustaining life within its fold, as it must,
With every possible measures taken as just,
Restoring a semblance of order but for a time,
And suddenly, like tornadoes, turmoils reign again,
Forsaking man's ingenuity and toil of many years.
"Shame!" It cries, "For shame!"
Errs of yesteryears go unheeded, laden only to be turned
Into power struggles and strife.
What horrendous power man wields for wicked naught!
Blind to the good there is in and to life,
Deaf to the murmurs of the hearts of peoples everywhere,
Prostrated begging, forgiving and ultimately humbled.
Pleading for vision power, nourished with hope, love
And the restoration of humanity,
These should be what man wields in life!

Jan T. Kirkman

Untitled

As I walk down the streets of the city,
what I see is truly a pity.
Aluminum cans and bags in the street,
All the trash seems to cling to my feet.
And a little bit later to make matters worse,
an old woman gets robbed of her purse.
A gunshot a mile away,
that could very well be where a dead man lay.
I continue my walk to avoid people's cries,
For I'd hate to see sadness and tears in their eyes.
When I go up my street to avoid any harm,
I see a smashed window and hear an alarm
I dive behind a truck and that's where I lie,
to try and avoid a sudden drive-by
I go to my house and in front of me,
I see bad words painted in graffiti.
I run up my stairs with some haste,
and I ask myself do I feel safe?

   Marshall Kleiber

the sound of a cry was heard

the sound of a cry was heard an innocent man was convicted
out of the greed and hatred of one man grew the pain
and suffering of another
such a thing it was said should not happen
but it did

the sound of a cry was heard a man was shot while running for freedom
that innocent man's life was taken out of hate

i looked around and saw no mourning
for this man was different he was black
and it was wrong to mourn a black man
why is it
i asked and everyone said because he was different

nobody say a man
they just saw a skin color

   Tara Zehmisch

God Created

God created me and you that's really true.
God created the air even the things made for your underwear.
God created the grass and even the instruments made of brass.
God created the flowers even the things you use for showers.
God created the sun where we always have fun.
God created the trees so that we can breath.
God created animals that are reptiles, birds, amphibians and mammals
God created the Heaven and earth
   and made our mothers go through birth.
God created love so don't push and shove.
God created hope so don't mope.
God created joy and even boys.
God created pearls and even girls.
God created gold, he will help you when your old.
God created feathery things because God created everything!

   Danielle Dickerson

As We Go

Walk, run, go, fast, or go slow,
We all laugh, we all cry, yes sometimes it hurts,
But it won't make us die.
We fall, we fall out, and live with self doubt.
Some are painted, some are tainted, and others go without,
Others have beauty, so tattered and torn,
They dread the daylight of each coming morn.
So we do what we can, we do what we must
to make our lives work and keep out the rust . . .
Yet once in a life time we do find our reason
That very special someone there for all seasons.
So take a few moments and bask in the glow . . .
You see, there are some rare treasures we find as we go.

   Ray DeLotell

Don't Pass Me By Without a Nod

Don't pass me by without a nod or a tip of the hat,
Or some sort of recognition for all of that,
Or just a look in my direction, even of pride,
While you pass me by with a quicken'd stride.

I'm on duty for all the day and sometimes all night too;
Sometimes I'm weary and worn, sometimes I'm new.
But I've been through a lot and command some respect
Whatever my condition or neglect.

I've been to all corners of the sphere since Philly;
To Europe and Africa twice, even Sicily; and after the calm,
New Guinea, Philippines, Okinawa, Iwo, Tarawa . . .
Yes, and Korea, and those unforgettable years in 'Nam.
I'm well known in the Middle East, the strife there engulfed,
And I was recently sent to the Persian Gulf.

So don't pass me by without a nod.
For our country I stand, our sod.
I said I'm known over all the world;
I am your flag, so keep me unfurled.

   Ron Graeser

Tomboy

I don't wear dresses, I don't wear skirts,
I like to run and play in the dirt.

I don't throw tea parties, I don't play with dolls,
This isn't my way, this isn't my style.

Outside is where I like to be,
I'd like to go and climb a tree.

I don't wear shoes, I don't wear socks,
I don't have any curly locks.

All the other girls just laugh and sneer,
They whisper in each other's ear.

But I don't cry, I don't care,
Even though they sit and stare.

The boys think that I'm the best,
They say I'm better than the rest.

The other girls are jealous of me,
Like I, they want to be.

With my baseball cap that's very lucky,
And my dirty shoes that are very yucky.

To know this it brings me great joy,
Because I'm not just a girl, I'm a tomboy!

   Jennifer Williams

The House Where I Was Born

As I sort through old familiär haunts
No one knows me anymore
Looking down dusty avenues of years . . .
Floating along transparent halls
Bumping into unforgotten walls
Childhood memories stick like cobwebs,
Deep within the corners of my innocent mind.
Unevenly, I have walked before, through remembered
Treasured places in my heart
My beloved house is gone . . .
And long supplied my meager needs and wants
I have struggled so hard to keep up life's pace!
I often wonder why?
Fear seems to drive me away
By the Grace of God
I am learning to accept,
So much has changed
Or
Is it I?

   Sandra E. Kimber

Unyielding Ambition

An old woman rocks in a rickety chair
Her tired eyes are transfixed in a stare.
To some her eyes look far away and blank,
But to me they speak volumes.

I see a young girl, a handsome beau at her side
And I can see emotions like the ever changing tide.
Two people devoted to the thought
That the other will always be there, no matter what.

A single tear drops from the old woman's eye
She exhales slowly, releasing a quiet sigh.
No longer is she immune to feelings from her past
It is in thoughts and feelings that memories exist.

Too many memories are alive in her mind
She can no longer hold on, can no longer fight.
Again a sigh escapes from her lips
Silently she rises and walks across the porch.

The land is dry and unyielding
As the woman's life has also been
But what can one do in life
Without a dream and ambition?

Beth Kucheruck

His Right Hand Shall Hold Me

Jesus make himself nothing for you, for me,
Sing oh heavens and be joyful on earth,
Break forth into singing you mountains and rills,
His right hand shall hold me as He wills.

He said Peace I leave with you,
My peace I give unto you
Let not your heart be afraid,
My right hand shall hold thee, He bade.

Show me now the way I may know thee
That I may find grace in thy sight.
I will love thee oh Lord my strength,
Thy right hand shall hold me at length

He offers us the riches of his grace
That I might live my life in him.
Though I dwell in the uttermost parts of the sea,
His right hand shall hold me

I fear not for he is with me,
He will help me and uphold me,
I will find grace in his sight,
His right hand shall hold me to eternal light.

Mary Rose Entriolo

Depression

Depression is a dreadful place indeed
Hate and fear fill the air
Dispirited souls flood the world
Sunlight stolen to a cloud of never
A deserted place may meet the eye
But many are here
They hide from their fears
The fears that have hurt them before
Many drowning in tears
Their cries were never heard
The dust hate air carried them away to no one
Lost souls wander here and there
Looking for an exit that doesn't exist
Some find disguises
But later discovered
Sobs and screams are the only sounds heard
Depression is nothing but the screams in the night
A nightmare in a child's dream
The pain and sadness of all depression
Is a dreadful place indeed

Felicity Pauline Ann Hernandez

I'd Like to Remind You of My Rights

I have the right to sing out loud
And do the chicken dance
Down your well-paved paths
Without your thinking I am crazy
Without your poisoned breath on my back
Without your judging me
By the length of my skirt, the bagginess of my jeans,
Or the brightness of my sun-colored tank-top

I have the right to be the president
Regardless of my sex
Even if your parents warned you that I might start a war
When I have P.M.S.

I have the right to make own my choices
Without your trying to exploit my body to win a campaign

I have the right to eat a red juicy apple
Without your comparing me to Eve
And condemning me for all the "evil" in your world

I have the right to let my heart lead my tongue
In a battle to change you

Sherry Zarabi

Black Girl

I am a black girl
Who's hair is thick and black.
I am a black girl
Who don't sit in the back.
I am a black girl
'Cause the content of my skin brings me joy.
I am a black girl
'Cause I'm a person, not a toy.
I am a black girl
Who stands for her rights.
I am a black girl
Who knows how to write
I am a black girl
Who set the matter straight.
I am the black girl
Who makes no mistakes.
I am a black girl
Who strong and wise,
'Cause it don't take me long to realize
That I'm a black girl.

Marcee Traylor

My School Teacher

Hello, and honor to you my teacher!
Today is another day at school. The classroom is still the same:
quiet, interesting, with its usual black board
and its row of desks firmly standing on the clean floor.
Teacher, you did not change either:
The multiple expressions on your face and your irritating
strictness are always the same;
They denote your concern and your strong desire
to teach me properly all your knowledge.
From your compliments and smiles,
I could see all good wishes and real gold medals.
Your job is great. From my desk, I often observe you:
You are not only a devoted teacher, but also a good parent.
You are one of the most important people in my life.
I promise you that your pain will not be in vain:
I will be good;
I will focus in learning more and more;
I will stay away from drugs, alcohol, violence and all other bad things;
I will be a potential garden for our beautiful society.
Very grateful, I thank you from the bottom of my heart.

Ibrahima Diallo

Untitled

To Jenna
Hello dear flower,
Hello strong hearted one.
Pain may wash all around you;
But remember the sponge of God
waits only for your prayer of invocation.
Sadness may cast a shadow on your soul;
Yet without this melancholy,
the summit of joy crumbles to pebbles.
Valleys and peaks prevent a life of flat sand.
Embrace the hurt, welcome the clouds,
For a beautiful day needs not a sky
of glistening sunlight, only the presence of love.
So release your fear,
Abandon the chains of your disease,
And bask in the light
that permeates a sky of grey marshmallow puff.
Never forget with each valley
there thrives the healing green of vegetation;
And with each peak there is a union with the Divine.

Jamie Mueller

Are You There God?

Are you there, God?
It's me again.
Have you seen the world, God?
You do know that something's wrong.

Guns, gangs, sex, and HIV
All of it affects my friends and me
Everyone is on the run
Something must be done

No one can leave his door unlocked
People are afraid to go out at night
In a construction site they found a sock
A shoe, a woman dead from a terrible plight

They all have lost their innocence
You can see it in their eyes
They're running, jumping the fence
There's nothing left but lies

I know you let people make choices
But can't you hear the children's voices?
The world is no longer a beautiful piece of art
For it's trying to mend its broken heart.

Jennifer Kawasaki

War

It's an ugly word as we all know
To write your friend or even your husband to tell them
that you miss them so. We wish one day, We hope and pray
That one day he'll be back home to stay.

Out there in the jungle, the stink and the smell
It's like living in a prison cell.
No one to talk with, no one to laugh with, you're all alone.
But you hope and you pray that someday, someday,
you'll be home to stay.

Your parents, your friends, and even your pals
Say a prayer to keep you alive and well.
When they listen to the radio of the men who have died
They hope that your name isn't mentioned, but it is.
The tears start to flow down from their eyes
As they all bow their heads and say their last good-byes.

To a man with bravery, intelligence, and guts
Who had to leave us with the bravest of luck.
The torture, the hate and the smell of it all
Not life, but just a preview of hell!

Marian Macek

The Changing of Seasons

The sky is snowing leaves,
across the windy autumn breeze.
The white puffy clouds are rolling along the vast open sky,
the sacred time of summer is already about to die.
Across this nippy autumn day,
my respect to God I will pay.
The times of summer are past and gone,
the memories are still here, but they are done.
New memories will be made,
but summer is gone and my debts are paid.
The coldness of this season and the times it will show,
for a new season is coming, as we all know.
A time for "Jingle Bells" being sung over a warm winter fire,
these are the times for which I aspire.
I yearn for Christmas and fall to be done,
but fall is here and Christmas will come.

Michael L. Bourgoise

Love

Like a river it flows
Deeper and deeper it goes
As strong as an old oak tree
But, it can break so easily
Tender and sweet like a newborn child
A flame of passion burning wild
Feelings so intense we cannot hide
But yet we keep them deep inside
Fearing loneliness will surely come
We keep our feelings concealed from everyone.

Nikki Poush

Thinking

As Space wraps her blanket about her baby
Earth, who is slowly drifting off to sleep,
She thinks.
"Why can't Earth have a bright future,
Like all the others?
Could my Lord have erred in creating humans
To live on my baby girl?
All my other children are going to love so much longer
What am I to do?
Do I stand by and let my child die
Or step in and do something?
Space goes to see the Lord. He says
"My dearest Daughter, your celestial children
were each given a destiny
even before you conceived them.
Earth has been chosen to bear the humans
Until I decide their fate."
So unto eternity Space sits
Her millions of children in her wide arms
thinking of her poor daughter Earth's plight.

Alledria Ebony Hurt

Abandoned

The sun goes down another day,
And still I have no place to stay.
People pass by and gaze with pity,
But none stop to do more; not in this busy city.
They have things to do,
I'm of no importance to them.
So I lie here and dream of a better place.
A place of warmth and food and rest
And a family, yes, a family would be the best.
Mine has gone long ago with everything else,
And now they are just vague memories.
Faded and gone like I will soon be.
But no one will care,
They've all abandoned me.

Travis Harwood

God's Domain

Oh God, how great is Thy domain,
The earth, the sea, the sky, the wind's refrain;
The wondrous beauty you gave us all to share,
While you embrace us in your arms of loving care.

Oh God, how beautiful are the rolling plains and hills,
The brooks, the fields, the rivers, rocks and rills;
Where green fields stretch as far as the eye can see,
And fruits and berries abound for the likes of me.

Oh God, how beautiful are the mountains high,
The peaks of which reach out as if to touch the sky;
The valleys green and floral colors bright,
The Master's touch that glorifies our sight.

Oh God, how beautiful is the deep blue sea,
The whispering waves speak so softly to me;
Until great waves by blowing winds are renewed,
And the fury of nature, the wrath of God, is in us imbued.

Oh God, how great is Thy domain,
The sky so blue, the peace and quiet remain;
Where we feel Thy presence on our Journey's way,
To Thy great kingdom where for all eternity we shall stay.

Walter L. Bost

Reflections at Three in the Morning

I am old
In years perhaps
But mind and spirit soar
To places not explored in youth
Because of time or circumstance

My world once confined
To children's cries and laughter
What a wonderful world of love and devotion
It was a happy time
Thank God for children

The years go by
The children grow
My world becomes blended with their dreams
I feel their pain and rejoice in their good fortune
It is like watching a butterfly unfold to life and beauty

The babies come
Life cycles renewed
I hold these little bundles
Created by love and say
What a wonderful life

Edna Marie Nodl

Little Things

Little things mean a lot.

A kiss on the cheek.
A touch of the hand.
A smile from your face.
A sly and sexy wink.

Little things mean a lot.

A call from you, for no reason.
A cup of coffee waiting when I arise.
A wild flower picked as a surprise.

Little things mean a lot.

A hug in the kitchen when I'm cooking.
A song played to reminisce.
Playing footsie under the dining room table.
A glance across the room, when no one is looking.

Little things mean a lot.

For no greater thing will you ever know, but to be
loved and love in return.
For little things mean a lot.

Marianne Shanks

3 Wishes

If I had 3 wishes, what would they be?
Would one be for a ton of gold? I doubt that I prefer
your warm, loving, tight hold.
Would another be for all the money in our atmosphere,
or would I prefer to have you as my peer?
Would the last one be for me to be accepted
into a really great university?
Maybe it'll be for us to share our love for all eternity.
If I had 3 wishes, what would they be?
Don't ask me, just look and see.

Kelly Kaptain

No Time to Rest

Some see me as a vein of life,
Carrying nourishment both far and wide;
To creatures living within my bowels,
And too, all that approach beside;

Rippling over my earthly bed,
While peace and tranquility steady my flow;
Nature has cause to change my rapidity,
Rising me above my familiar footing,
Thence I have no control;

At best, I offer to some amusement,
An oasis to refresh and pause, if need;
Yet, sometimes my body is carelessly polluted,
By those who don't take heed;

I run shallow and I run deep,
Through variable countryside I wind;
No time to rest in my pursuit,
To unite with one of my own kind.

Gay Phyllis Nagle

The Poor Rich and the Rich Poor

People of riches usually seek to accumulate more.
Their greed is something God will not ignore.
But we are poor in wealth and rich in faith;
Our treasures are stored in a heavenly place.
We have little money and little in salary,
But Jesus paid our debts one day at Calvary.
The accumulation of wealth is not our concern,
Our focus is on Jesus and his return.
For all his blessings and his gift of love
We owe our everything to the Lord above.
The more we love him and the more we find
That the Lord is good and he is kind.
The more we give the more we receive,
It has been that way since we first believed.
Faith, hope, and love has replaced our greed,
And our works of charity have eased our needs.
The word of God is the bread of life,
And it keeps us free from hunger and strife.
Now, it is the love that we give away
That makes us richer day after day.

Glen Larkin

A Toast

To you, for all the times we shared.
To you, for all the minutes spared
To you, for all the love you show.
I love you Steve, more than you know.

To us, for putting up with each other.
To us, for not giving up when bothered
To us, for building what we have.
We've learned it's not all take, but give.

To our friends, for all the things they do.
To our friends, for putting up with us too.
To our friends, who brought us both together
We'll always remember you, because we've got each other.

Angela Cross

Gang Peace

We live in a world where it does make a difference
Of how you do your hair, the color clothes that you wear,
And the color skin that you have.

Peace will come when no colors tie us, and no borders divide us.
Peace will come when neighbors walk hand in hand
And we have friends in every land.
Peace will come from our heart, only if we all do our part.

We live in a world where people can't see past your race.
If only they'd look deeper than your face,
They'd see the beauty in it all
And think you the most beautiful thing of all.

Peace will come when all the directions of the wind meet
And stumble down to our feet.
Peace will come when we all listen
And hear the cries of hurting children.
Peace will come when we help people
Even if they pray under a different steeple.

Peace knows no colors. Peace knows no race.
Peace knows no borders. Peace knows no face.
Peace knows love. Hopefully one day, peace will know You!

Brandi Young

A Lady Is Created

A women is born
But a lady is created
A women listens not to her man
But a lady listens to her man's every word
as if his words are the laws of her life provisions,
for his words are the sound of many waters.

A woman buys clothes to fit someone else's personality,
and when you see her, you see someone else's clothes
that she ignorantly expresses.
But a lady takes her man with her when she is buying her clothes,
for she only buys what pleases him,
and when you see her, you know she belongs to her man.

A women talks back when her man is speaking,
with tight-fisted hands, for a battle at any moment.
But a lady smiles and waits until asked when to speak,
for respect is the law of her being
and patience the character of her soul,
she is a lady.

David A. McCoy

The Lesson

Golfing principal, preacher, and parent
Discussed a principled child's apparent features
"Teach discipline, even to the baby!"
The parent demanded, all teed off.
In the rough seas, ship him to the navy
They have more drivers than the game of golf.

The principal swung through the drilled debate,
"My students need manners and straight examples
Delinquents need truth and ethics ample."

But the preacher chipped in, "Oh Lord please wait!"
"Where's religion, pride, purity and sin;
These are the clubs that showcase and win."

Then a pure young voice, asking passage, spoke strong,
"I'm playing behind my father just today
He's ahead of me now but not for long
I've wondered how long I'll follow his fair way."

The moral age learned that day in July
Was not how birdies die and score cards lie,
But how youth's iron will can drive past par
To wedge through traps to be where eagles are.

Richard Crum

Tombstone

The moon casts your shadow across the field
The willow dances slowly to the beat of the cool night breeze
Slowly the night welcomes me
As I lay on my back
As I lay awake—staring out the window
Thinking about the hours when I rose to the occasion and
Stood up for myself
I am who I am going to be until the day I die
And then I will still be me but with a dark taste of death
With out luster or shine
But dull to the core
You will never leave me
Housed in my heart
Consumed by the night
Casting your shadow across the field.

Nicki Nichols

Futile Search

That is where you find your solace
In that shiny green bottle of hopelessness.
You cry until it becomes you.
It crawls inside you and strangles your spirit;
You cannot breathe.
Your heart is wasted—cherishing it.
You wander down the narrow neck for peace.
Tip it trying to get free, you only get deeper inside.
It has power and strength that you crave.
Cloudy green glass is all that you see.

What about what you taught me to be? Is it all green glass?
I can see its truth:
Evil and lusty
Shallow and vengeful.
I have what you lost when you married it.
Is that why you look at me so?

With sorrow

Ellen Schrecongost

Half Empty

I was going to catch a rainbow for you,
but now everything I have is only blue.
I've sucked the puff right out of your clouds,
and filled the heart with all you've allowed.
I was going to sit out in the sun,
and wait until you said it was done.
There is a pool of water
that sits lonely for you,
Only wanting one more drop
Half full with memories of you.
Away is your heart,
No more colors on the floor.
Can you find me?
Probably not—
Since you don't know
What to look for.

Molly Plazak

Alone

Sometimes I lay, alone in my bed,
with thoughts of you, stuck in my head.
Alone in the darkness.
Alone in the cold.
Dreaming you're here,
your hand I could hold.
I think of the day, you told me good-bye.
As I remember the sparkle,
I saw in your eye.
I wouldn't have opened my eyes if I'd known,
that when they were open,
I'd feel so alone.

Christine A. Torelli

And Then the Rain Came

The day started and it was full of life.
Everything seemed to have a new flair.
A man walks down the street beside his wife.
The pungent smell of freshness filled the air.

And then, all of the sudden, the rain came.
Drops hit the ground like bullets from heaven.
They hit with such force that trees became lame.
I made animals run and hide even.

Then, as sudden as it came, it was gone.
Through the chaos, flowers began to bloom,
And all signs of life began to move on.
Gone were all fears of their imminent doom.

All life goes on without much of a care,
But aware that rain could again come there.

John Peterson

Distant Lovers

The package, I wondered
what's inside the mind
patiently I tried to wait
looking from a distant,
I wonder what I would find
intense from waiting to be free
the package, I opened it before time
not disappointed of what I've found
wishing I had waited until the time was right
knowing that a package like you,
beauty within and out sparkling like a crown
would have waited to be open by me
only to win your heart
and forever, to set you free

Clarence W. Jones Jr.

Wild Horses

Wild horses galloping through my mind
Wild horses racing through time
Don't know where they've been
Don't know where they are
Don't even know where they're going
Sometimes feel alone and sometimes feel ashamed
Don't know who they are and don't care
Wild horses galloping through my mind
Wild horses racing through time
Don't know where the line is
Don't know it they passed it
They push things past 'em just like
They weren't there
Living life o that's the life for
Wild Horses
Don't know, don't care, free to be
Wild horses galloping through my mind
Wild horses racing through time

Valerie Daru

Thoughts

Down winding paths of friendship
Through forests of memories,
Wanders a soul lost in thinking,
A mind full of contemplation.
Pushing aside the cobwebs of the past,
Opening closed doors to the future,
Lost in a maze of golden dreams,
Caught up by glimpses of today.
What glory lies beneath the unknown,
What hidden secrets have past by,
As he mingles with his endless reveries,
And seeks calm seclusion in his unknown mind.

Dorothy F. Ayer

Picking Cherries

"Almost full," I said, "These will be yours,"
As I looked down at her resting an empty
Bucket on the bottom rung of the Ladder.
Good therapy, I had thought, picking cherries,
But there was still sorrow and hurt in her eyes.
Loss of a daughter on the Ides of March,
An aneurysm at thirty-five.
And three young boys left motherless.
Deftly averting my eyes upward,
As if looking for more cherries,
I felt the warm tears begin to fall
And mingle with the cherry stains
On my faded, worn shirt.
Hateful, late shroud, I thought,
I will bury you again, in some dark corner
Of my closet, until the hurt does not come anymore.
Maybe next year there will only be peaches and pears to pick,
And I will adopt a new shirt until there
Are only pleasant memories
She was a favorite Niece, you see.

Harold Hoskins

Obsession

What is it called when you don't love someone,
But you more than like them?
What if I enjoy staring into his
Big, brown puppy dog eyes and hope he notices mine.
What if I crave to run my fingers
Through his black, silky, long hair?
How I want for him to grab me and hold me tight in his arms.
But I tell myself I can't be in love, because he doesn't know it.
I wonder if every female in the whole wide world feels
What I do, or am I just some freak who they'd call a "stalker?"
You talk and laugh, but does he feel the same way?
If I dream about him am I in love with him,
Or does he dream about me?
I sometimes wonder what is he doing today?
Why doesn't he climb up my window
And leave a rose on my pillow?
Why do I feel this way about him? He's not that great.
I've figured it out! I have a disease and it controls my life.
It's called obsession.
And I'm not talking about the perfume.

Leah Selinger

The Candle Box

Dust gathers and shows its age,
Sitting there for many days,
This candle box that holds nothing,
But shards of wax rubbed off against the wood grains,
Decorated by random, discrete candle stains.

Empty like the eye of a storm,
Calm, stagnate air no longer passioned warm,
Settles against the embroidered box,
Once fostered by a thriving need,
Now only time must it heed.

No longer filled from within,
Now the representation of sin,
Covered and shrouded from about,
By this dust that shows its age,
Not a having been used for many days.

The crime of passion long lost,
The box never to be filled, but never tossed,
Sitting to show those who would see,
What happens when love's flame of lust,
Has turned to a fine, waxy dust.

Jeremy Glesner

Bag Lady

Jostled through crowds, or alone,
you pace onward to fulfill your assumed purpose,
neglecting the curious stares directed at your unwashed clothing,
pity at the scale-covered skin and matted hair;
you pluck up plastic bags abandoned by people
unknowingly negligent, and thus, carrying fewer plastics.
Downward you are looked upon;
never acknowledged by anyone as simply a variant,
a different form of itinerant, traveling the same streets,
doped with the same ambition.
Never have I seen you stop on your aimless journey,
to rest the burden of your mission—
plastic bags crammed always with more plastic bags;
nor have I seen you smile.

Michael-Lyn Scott

Weekend of Love

Beautiful weekend I must say,
The sun was shining on a cloudy day.
My love still with me, Damn, it feels good.
Hope it last forever; I hope, it should.
Showing me his style of work and were he resides.
What a wonderful feeling, I cannot lie.
Making me feel like I'm important in his life.
Thinking to myself, can he love me for his wife.
Is this true; can it be, that I was
made for you and you was made for me.
Boo, I hope your love is real, that's for sure.
Cause I have much love to give and so much more.

Ramona Cash

The Unwanted One

Her skin is soft as velvet.
His touch coarse like sandpaper.
It grates between her fingers
Leaving grit that will not wash away.
She feels dirty, besmirched, put upon.
When he touches her, it is a sacrilege.
She flinches as he backs her up to the barbed wire—
Nowhere else to go.
Trapped under his muscled arms,
He pulls her into his web as she mews pitifully
Like a defenseless kitten.
Yet he seeks her consent to be his.
Even in the drunken haze of unremitting want, the unwashed
Savage with crooked, dirty fingernails
Seeks what cannot be found—the
Morning dew of his beautiful, blooming
Red rose of desire.

Marsha Newman

Because of Me

I pass you in the hall and catch a quick glimpse
I see you walk past, quiet and stunning
Your hair gently laying across your shoulders.
You stop and turn when you hear me call your name
You look at me, and I stare into your eyes
They're beautiful, they shine and sparkle more than any diamond
Your face, your lips, how perfect and special they are
We stand close, together, a warm feeling passes over me.
And to see you there, smiling, it makes me happy.
I can only hope that you're smiling because of me.
When you are there, but not close I stare
I wonder if you see me, I wonder if you know.
I look at your face and dream
I think of you and picture us alone, together
Walking, holding hands in a park at night
Nothing around, silence, only us.
I wish that someday this will be reality,
But for now I can only hope that you're smiling because of me.

Ryan P. Neary

Road Trip to Nowhere:

It's coming to the point were my memories I despise
My life is a chain of lies.
Sometimes I just want to run,
The open road, the chance of fun
Is reason enough to fill the tank and go
And disappear into the unknown.
I tip the bottle and bite the lime
And look towards the empty sky.
I pray for clouds, thunder, and rain;
Let the lightning clear my head of pain.
Passing through towns, looking for friends
And maybe the chance to start again.
But with a Marlboro in my teeth
The city limit sign I soon reach
So I continue to ride the line,
For there is nothing to leave behind.

Grant Sourk

A Warrior's Tale

There was once a maiden of golden hair.
Whose skin was soft as silk and fair.
Yet she was strong and would fight without a care.
She would cross swords with any who would dare.
The only thing left, of her adversaries was their screams,
and her battle cry left hangin' in the air.
When she entered a room all heads would turn,
as she took her chair.
She is the most beautiful woman I have ever seen,
all of the men would declare.
We wish she would leave our town, all of the women
would say, as their tempers would flair.
But the maiden would only sit and eat and drink her fill,
without stripping her soul bare.
This beautiful fighter's name is Zendare.

Jessie D. Winkel

My Perfect Man

My perfect man is like a Teddy Bear,
Who is warm and hold me close with care.
He is always there for me,
And very romantic at night by the sea.
My man is sweet and warm hearted,
And always kisses me before parting.
My perfect man is loving and strong,
And we take drives that are long.
He brings me flowers,
That smell great and over powering,
He spends Sunday with me in bed,
As he kisses me, "I love you," is what he said.
The day we met, I ran to him,
And as I ran,
I ran to my Perfect Man.

Arlene L. Grodski

The Deadly Descent

Life, is a dark, endless pit.
Every year carrying you farther down,
Plunging through the dark pit,
Unaware of the directions it will carry you.
The pathway down, a journey.
When will this journey conclude?
Reaching for life, only to be denied access.
The only thing obtained from this fatal abyss,
Is the strength to endure what life grants you.
Until, that one day,
When you are no longer necessary,
And the speed intensifies,
Only to send you crashing down, to hit the bottom,
Where all life is lost.

Jasmine Jacob

Winter

The cool crisp winter wind
Makes the bleak, brown leaves of fall
Dance gaily in glimmering light of the setting sun.

Each delicate snowflake takes its place
On the graceful white blanket
That cloaks the ground with an elegant beauty.

Every child takes advantage of this glorious day
The first falling of snow has
Kindled their spirits of adventure and fun.

Ellen Bird

Holocaust

The tears and screams are buried here.
The grass grows over the agony.
The blue skies have come back
and the sun shines down among the graves.
They finally have the sun they wanted so long ago.

This place is now peaceful.
Never, never forget what is under the grass.
What the sun covers up with its long rays of light.
Never forget the night of tears, screams . . . Never Forget!

Erin Tam

My Sun

I felt lost as if I could not see,
because of the darkness surrounding me.
I felt as if I had no soul;
I felt distant and separate
as if I were hollow.
I had no sight of what would follow.
I was lost to the sense of touch
as I wandered aimlessly for more than just lust.
Then I saw it creeping over the horizon,
for it were my own Sun.

Shedding light upon me, finally alleviating this darkness,
which caused me not to see.
Taking my soul carefully, and
placing it where it could be free.
She is brighter than the sun
for only she breathes life into me.
As the sun breaks the night into dawn,
so she broke the darkness where I once had gone.

Cary Vucinich

Untitled

With passion she carries her delicate treasure
No jewels, no pearls, no flowers of measure
Moonlight sparkle direct from her hair
Hints of silver beautifully glare
Childlike innocence pure as a dove
Gently serene demure sweet love
Guarding her virtue, besieged in her soul
Evening darkening, on a sidewalk she strolls

Nina Green

New York Windows

The fog rain roll around the large silent buildings,
surrounding them in a cloak of mist.

They are tall and straight with window eyes,
some shining with life and others dark.

They are stacked against me,
lining up to close me off from the world.

To combat them I think of your smile,
the smell of your hair and your love for me.

Martin L. Murphy

Sweet Angel Supreme

A halo of light surrounds thee
A crown of stars sits thy brow
Sweet Angel Supreme whom I see in my dreams
How I long to speak with thee now

My heart cracked and bled when thou left me
Such a wound time never can heal
Sweet Angel Supreme whom I see in my dreams
Can thy death truly be real?

I picture thee sitting beside me full of joy, laughter and love
My heart drips tears of ice, pain possesses my life
Sweet Angel Supreme whom I see in my dreams
My Cathryn, my daughter, my child

How cruelly thy life was stolen, torn away by one whom thou loved
Thy place can never be filled
Sweet Angel Supreme whom I see in my dreams
My Cathryn, my daughter, my child

When at last that dark river I cross
Towards the light of blessed Heaven I see
The Sweet Angel Supreme whom I saw in my dreams
Waiting lovingly, joyously welcoming me

Lois McLaughlin

Helen

Helen was a girl who was already married.
But along came Paris and away she was carried.

Husband found out and boy was he mad.
But Helen, the girl, that Paris had.

So Paris and Helen sailed off to Troy,
And their lives were always full of joy.

And Paris and Helen lived in a castle.
'Cause living with husband was such a hassle!

But then husband started war,
And the village people were full of horror.

Then husband captured the beauty,
The village was sad, 'cause she was such a cutie.

Then husband did away with Paris,
(In other words, he's dead!).
After the war, Helen and Husband fled.

And that's the end of the story of Helen, the beauty,
And the war with the cutie.

Megan Gravenstein

Aftermath

Past midnight now.
Thinking of earth's holocaust,
thinking of the lost ones I love,
thinking of you . . .
Smoked my last cigarette,
killed the last of the booze.
Snuggling deep into this oversized sofa,
the room is silent and deep, murmuring sleep.
The oil lamp flutters rhythmically back and forth;
laced eyeglasses crash against a wooden floor,
and the wall's seascape picture is now your face.
In the Sirens of old I hear you call,
eerie music in the harmony of waves,
whispering to me, beckoning me, oh, loving me . . .
In delight we dance and dance in shadows on the wall.
Then morning, suspecting,
probes our space with sinister sunbeam scanners—
and I rise and kiss your fading shadow on the dusty floor.
You are but a dream, a fantasy that won't come true;
And I am but a dreamer, in love primarily with dreams.

Barbara Ann Martell

Birth!

Written for the birth of my nephew Justin.
Screaming and gasping for dear life,
You announce your painful entrance into this world.
Nine months of you growing inside me,
Building your strength and drinking of my life's energy,
For the road you must travel which is humanity.

Your destination draws near
And your eagerness to be released
You have made quite clear.
My womb expands, I convulse with spasms of pain.
I feel you move and rip and tear
Wanting to taste the sterile air.

Soon it is over.
Exhausted and relieved, I lie in bed
On my bosom rests your head
And in that tender moment when I held you,
I realized that never can there be a love more true.

Melba Phillip

The Spheres

A kindred soul, a lonely heart,
Two worlds alone, two worlds apart.
Searching forever, lost from the start,
A kindred soul, a destined heart
Not to be found, but to be torn apart,
Lost forever, one of a kind,
no likeness of heart, and not in mind.
A death so fleeting, so icy cold,
A death with a story, that will never be told,
Death so silent, so strong, so old
but so weak and brittle, a shattered soul,
And so it ends, and on we go,
not quite dead, and not quite whole,
Searching forever, and lost at heart
Severed at birth, from the worlds afar . . .

Dana Martin

She's America

Come one, come all, let's celebrate in style so grand
The birth of this great nation, this beautiful land.
My heart fills with joy as I look in proud manner
At the colorful sight of the star spangled banner.
With broad stripes and bright stars see how beautiful she flies
Spreading good will and freedom o'er our crystal-clear blue skies.
As my eyes gaze admiringly at her red, white and blue
I think of all she means for me and for you.
She's America the beautiful, America the sweet
And to say I'm an American is really quite a treat.
She's America, born on the fourth of July
And for her I would gladly be willing to die.

Jesus F. Oliana

Honorable Man

And there he lied, this honorable man.
And there he died by these people's hands.
He hit their town and tried his best,
But they brought him down
And laid him to rest.

He tried so hard, I know not why,
For in the end they watched him die.
The rain came down, not leaving a trace
Of the pain and age on this young man's face.
He tried so hard for what he believed,
But in the end he'd only been deceived.
But did this man really know deception,
For I feel he's a guest at heaven's reception.

Randy L. Schneck

Rider of the Night

I love to watch my shadow grow in the yellow glow
Of the street lights
When the sun goes down I ride across the town
I'm a rider of the night
I see my shadow grow in the coming flow
Of someone's headlights
When the sky grows dark I make my mark
Riding in the night
I'm a rider of the night

I never wanted to be the early bird, you see
I prefer the night
I never cared to catch the worm
It wouldn't be right
For a rider of the night

I have my sleep while most others keep
Alert in daylight
But then I awake when others their rest take
And say, "Good night"
'Cause I'm a rider of the night

Yes, I'm a rider of the night
Michael Rue

Untitled

The seconds turn the minutes, turn the hours, turn the world
Another day, another lifetime, another thousand years.

And still we search.

Our thirsting quest for knowledge
has only multiplied our ignorance

We hear the voices crying, crying.

Pleading voices of pain, regret, agony.
They want only to be heard, remembered
But no one listens. If only we would listen.

For in some tomorrow not so far beyond today,
We will see the voices are our own,
And in our endless pursuit of progress
It is we who have silenced them.

Have we been made so blind!
Into what dangers would we be led
That we would be made to search ourselves
For that which is not in us!

Yet still we search.

Through the minutes, the hours, and soon our time is done.

In our efforts we have come so far as to murder who and what we are.
Sherri Kay Brokopp

Deer Hunter's Lament

The ice cracks and I begin to hurry
My boots start to fill, first one then two.
The cold water wreaks vengeance, I should soon start to worry.
I'll be saying it's my last, before the day is through.

Let me gather my lunch and hunting gear
And go out to the red brush edge.
Let me bag the biggest one, of all the deer
As I shoot from my ladder stand ledge.

I placed my stand in a likely spot
Where brush and runways are entwined.
There I sit and wait, some years not a shot
For I'm not the quitting kind.

The wind and cold often drives me mad
Just deer hunters luck I suppose.
But I'll be back, it's not that bad
To see how the hunting goes.
Larry C. Ott

Cansado

You look so sad
The deep frown lines on your face
tell the tale of a hard life, working in the hot sun
Discrimination, Oppression, and low wages, were your life
Now, an old aged man, you ride the bus like us
with a working man's lunch
Your hands are calloused worn and torn
Your dark hair has grayed
Time has conquered your handsome face
Your eyes are weary
Your hope has dulled dwindled and gone
I'm sorry old man
For the life you've led
I'm sorry for the injustices
and the things they've said
I apologize on behalf of this cold cruel world
To you and your ancestors
To your hopes and dreams . . .
One apology for a million things.

Olga Chavez

Losing You

Once, I had a dream where I envisioned losing you.
It seemed that it was a movie, but so much was true!
I saw the times we loved and the times we fought.
The many hardships we went through, but the love we sought.
You never told me how you felt. You knew that I knew,
Cause through your sea like eyes you gave me the clue.
I was an exception and could tell exactly what you meant.
People told me to stay away but when you called, I went.
How could they tell me what to do?
They couldn't have known about the real you!
Then suddenly my dream changed into a nightmare.
You started running from something, but you wouldn't share.
I asked what was wrong but all I'd get is your common answer,
"I don't want to talk about it right now, maybe later."
That ended up being the end of all our confrontations.
Occasionally we'd have the old, enjoyable conversations.
Then suddenly I realized everything I was seeing was true.
I am confused but now I know that I have already lost you!

Betsy Reeder

Thanks Be to God

For the breath of life, and the forgiveness of sin
For a tablet of stone, and the commandments ten
For your son on the cross of Calvary's tree
Who paid the great debt for others and me.

For ample fare, and my daily bread
For a comfortable home and a roof o'er my head
The fellowship of friends, cool water for thirst
Light for my way, when the problems seem worst.

A semi-long life, plus the joys of good health
And hopefully guidance around the worship or wealth
My freedom and church choice with friend of kin
And blessings for the America, that I live in.

For the wonderment of nature, the sunshine and rain
Fruits of vine and tree, the waving fields of grain
The grandeur of the mountains, the birds, and fish of the seas
For doctors, nurses, flowers and trees.

Our democratic laws, and the age of outer space
For songs like "The Old Rugged Cross" and "Amazing Grace."
Then when the trumpet sounds, may the clarion call be clear
"Peace and well done, my son, eternity's up here."

Thomas "Tombo" Mitchell

Untitled

In the eyes of my God
Death was so clear
I dared to reach for it
To clasp my broken hands
Around the raw uncensored death
But he, my God, closed his eyes
And I, a lowly mortal,
Fell into a nightmarish slumber
I remember the glorified essence
I reached so far to attain
But my God, oh once again I am lost
Can you find me?
Save my murderous being?
In the blackness of my soul . . .
I puke out the life from which I try so hard to escape
And I run so fast, so hard that I trip
Only to fall into the hands of my God,.
The dirty threads of my being faltered
With the rendezvous of the devil himself.

Kelli N. Roettger

Perfect People (In Society)

Men and Women,
of pale profiles with two vast optics
containing crystal pools of aquatic water,
a centered, slender slope above an opening
surrounded by roseate blossoms brightening a smile.

Men,
of immense stalking figures.

Women,
of doubled, immeasurable limbs
completing a slim stature from the scruff down.

Both,
topped off with golden strands;
Women's carpeting to the ground;
Men's clean-cut.

None,
with hearts of gold,
filled with love and sympathy,
nor with care for the human race.

Yet,
one calls them, "Perfect People"

Margaret S. Lima

Life

There's somebody looking, and about to appear;
Somebody locked up inside, very safe, very dear;
A gift sent from God, a miracle it seems;
A girl or a boy to share all our dreams;
This someone so frail, so helpless, so small;
Who needs so much care and love from us all;
The birth of this little bundle of joy;
Swells you up in the clouds from what nature's employed;
Someone so innocent, will look up to you;
Their eyes look to yours, so wide and so true;
Someone who will laugh and someone who will cry;
And this someone who will need us everyday of our lives;
Someone who looks up to you, yearning to learn;
Hungry for knowledge, you'll try to return;
Someone you can play with someone you will teach;
This someone you'll give all that you can reach;
And thank you Mother, for giving us birth;
For you are the reason we're all on this earth;
And Lord, we proudly accept what you've done;
For this gift of life, of our daughter or son.

Gregory Hunkele

This Strange World

Finally a break form the killing, the mass suicide
It is time, time to return to my home
to see my world, my past, my memories
yet I do not remember me, who I am.
I arrive home to a distant land.
All of these things, are they mine?
Who owned these things? Certainly not me.
These people all talk but do not know.
Can't they leave me alone, in peace?
Quiet is all that matters, all that should matter.
It has been very long since my last quiet time.
I look at my pictures but don't see me.
My family talks, who are these strangers?
These people aren't my family, my family is my
comrades back home on the front
I have no business here, in this strange land with these strangers.
All that I know is war, kill or be killed
My leave is over, I am happy yet sad
All of my hopes are shattered by the realization that
I Have No Home.

    Brian Danko

Pins and Needles

Under the eye of the sun,
He makes love to his nun,
Offering more than darkness.
Language ceases to exist.
Sand becomes alive.
Torn down he still grovels
With cardboard bones that crumble inside.
His flesh-light burns off her hair,
Hurt, hurts her delicate care.
Bread is enough to keep
His stomach from thinking.
Why is touching himself so sickening?
Under the eye of the sun,
He makes love to his nun.
But she's impotent today to enjoy . . .
The white alive sand.
The limb that becomes his hand
Or the darkness that can't cease to exist the language.

Who turn him down
With cardboard bones folding inside.

    Alex Cruz

Whatever Happened?

Whatever happened to poems that rhyme,
Old porch swings, and clocks that chime?
Where are the standards of a bygone day,
The parents that work, and the kids that play?
I'd like to go back to an era when
Morals and honesty meant something then.
A man's word was his bond, and if he said
He'd "treat you right," you had nothing to dread.
I'd like to go back to a saner time,
Whatever happened to poems that rhyme?

Whatever happened to poems that rhyme,
Songs and stories of a happier time,
A contract sealed with the shake of a hand,
Parades that were led by the high school band?
Right was right and wrong was wrong,
Folks had trouble, but life went along.
Dedicated people fought the good fight,
To start a new country and show others the light.
We need more commitment, and a lot less crime.
Whatever happened to poems that rhyme?

    Trula Raynes

Sometimes . . .

Precious moments of kissing and hugging last an eternity.
Tender words and whispers of affections are endless.
Soft touches and lustful looks are everlasting.
Loyalty and fondness are undying.
Happy times and pleasant feelings are infinite.
Tranquility and respect towards one another are unending.
Passion and desire fulfill one's inner yearning, always.
Soothing phrases and compassionate understanding are unceasing.
Gentle Love is Forever . . .
Sometimes . . .

    Virginia I. Rodriguez

Dear Father

Give me a sign,
Show me the way,
Help brighten up my lonely day.

Praying to you
Gives me Peace of mind.
The most lifting feeling I'll ever find.

Giving thanks to you,
My love to you too,
Makes me feel up lifted and my soul renewed.

Your light is all around
Radiating from within.
Giving me the faith and power to start over again.

The power to renew my faith,
To let your will be done.
Give all my love and faith to you the father and the Son.

    Joyce Balla

A Message for Someone Special . . .

In memory of Denise
There are special feelings I have inside
Feelings I never wanted to hide.
For now you've been gone many years
Thoughts of you fill my eyes with tears.
You were a beautiful part of my past
But I'm sorry, good things never last.
Your life was short, but a happy one
Seems it ended even before it begun.
A few minutes was all the time it took
Your life was shattered, our lives were shook.
We no longer saw your smiling face
The memories of you, we'll always trace.
You know you were mommy's little pearl
But you'll always be daddy's little girl.
On February seventh, we mourn your death
Not knowing you now is all I regret.
My thoughts of you will never cease
For I love you more than a sister
My sweet Denise.

    Rosann Verone

Untitled

I once lived life upon this earth before,
Not knowing why life gave me breathe at all.
Within myself saw blood and times of war,
The vision saw was to be my call.
Ashamed not of what I've done or become,
Though I am dead I must still deal with strife,
Left love and anger with the body one.
Within I fought, no happiness to find
My dreams of nothing which made me something.
I am my soul for life of another.
The lake caught fire so therefore I can sing.
In life that's past was anyone ever sober.
I know that in my heart the stars above,
Is only where I can find truest love.

    MaryRose Grech

Money

Money won't get you to heaven,
And when you're sick, it won't buy you health,
It won't buy you the happiness you want,
So, what are you going to do with your wealth?
Money won't get you to heaven,
Regardless as to how hard you try,
You got it here, and it's perfectly clear,
That you'll leave it here the day that you die.

Kenneth R. Richter

When I'm Gone

When I'm gone, here I'll be
Right in your heart, you'll find me

When you feel sorrow with no smile to be found
When you've lost all hope, please know I'm around

You'll feel a kiss from me to dissolve that frown
When you least expect it, I'll be around

When babies run toward danger, then suddenly stop
When things happen without reason, they're not

When you feel warm and full of love inside
Remember I'm here right by your side

When I'm gone, here I'll be
Until were together for eternity

Linda Segui Spencer

My Quest for Peace

Anger and hatred—hope and love.
All these drowning my soul.
Covering up who I am and
Changing me inside and out.
I can never go back,
I can never be the same.
A feeling of emptiness swarms over me,
But who can I blame?
No one! Everyone! Or maybe myself?
Tears of rage fill my weary eyes as I
Try to find my soul that I have lost.
Did I call the angels of Hell to put a curse on me?
No, this . . . what we call life, is the Hell.
I will never know why this happened to me.
The one who could have helped me is gone.
Until the day I leave this Hell we call life
I will go on being confused and alone.
I pray the day will come soon when I shall say,
"Good-bye"
So I can ask my loving father: Why?

Nell Ann Buzaki

Letting Go

I
have sensed you watching.
Why can I not watch you?

Will
to play hard—you instilled this in me.
When will you teach me more?

Always
In my memory.
How come it is fading?

Love
you showered me with—it still keeps me strong.
How many days must I suffer from this loss?

You
are a part of the earth.
Where does your spirit wander?

Amy Gagne

Falling in Love

The pages of my life go by like the hands of time.
Each day goes by quicker, and as I try
To make sense out of it all I start spinning.
It all turns into a blur.
I struggle to come down from this uncontrollable high.
I try to keep my balance, but I fall.
Farther and farther;
Deeper and deeper
Until I realize what I'm falling into—Love.

Monique Sampedro

The Oak

Our family home with old southern charm,
bright white wood, black shutters, lazy and warm.

In the front yard stands the water oak tree;
hundreds of years old, her massive limbs
spreading free.

Beautiful green grass, pink azaleas in bloom;
but the old oak tree takes most of the room.

A breeze blowing softly off the great
sandy beach as the oak's leaves gently
move from everyone's reach.

She seems to be smiling letting all of us know;
This place is my home—I love it;
I shall never let it go.

Jane De Angelo

Black Is Beautiful

Black is beautiful black is proud.
Are you proud to be black will
You say that out loud.

Our ancestors strived to make a
Good life for me and you.
It wasn't a choice it was something they had to do.

There weren't any schools or education
For blacks in restaurants and buses we had
To sit in the back.

So the next time you feel ashamed about
Being black remember this poem and
Take a look back.

Because white maybe bright and sky
Blue may look cool, but black is a
Color that is beautiful.

Shatonda Cephas

Life Begins

There's a story that has begun before
you, and in a perpetual cycle leads back to you
It all started when the first arrived on the shore
erupting from the ocean's deepest blue,
to where the sun shined in the mist of dust,
helping give forth growth in the very center of us

Realize that life is a play for the universe,
An eternal script strange and diverse.
It tells us life is the character of emotion,
It's times' committed devotion.

Life is the suit of explanation.
It is the very spark of a stars sensation.
Life is the breath of a comet,
It is the very light that everything's in common.

Now maybe you'll find,
That the beauty of existence is spiritually divine.
It will enlighten you with a grin.
All in all you'll learn in you life begins

Jonathan Morrison

Emotions

When you fall in love, it's like a high,
You're light as a feather and float to the sky,
Then bad times cause a strange reaction,
Stops your growth without satisfaction,

Overloaded with emotions you try to hide,
Makes you weak as you slowly subside,
Your body starts to feel nothing but pain,
From emotions held in, your suffering will remain,

Life changes in so many ways,
Soon it will end with no more delays,
You try real hard to get those good feelings back,
Without any energy it's hard to get back on track,

There seems to be no way of getting it out,
Buried emotions only cause you to pout,
If you choose to give-in and except the bad,
You'll wind up going through life alone, empty and mad,

So out with the bad and in with the good,
I only wish there was someone who understood,
Throughout your life you need to grow,
and feel the energy, as you let your emotions flow . . .

Diana Costello

My Parents

My father is aged . . . my mother is too
I know that at times they knew what to do

But time, as they say, has taken its toll
and now they look out from a deepening hole

As death 'proaches nearer they tighten their grasp
on things to let go of . . . on things of the past

Let me teach you, dear father, the things that I know
Please listen, my mother, how I've learned to let go

You've taught me most caref'ly to seek and to find
the truth of existence is in my own mind

So know that the things which you hold so dear
are things to let go of . . . the message is clear

Your earthly plane presence has been very grand
but it's time to release and reach for God's hand

Chastise yourselves not for no error was made
God's ever watched o'er us as in creation we've played

But this play time is over . . . 'tis time to move on
We know that you're carried on wings of a song

We love you . . . we bless you . . . we bid you good-bye
and know that forever in God you are nigh

Martha Thomson

I Am Poem

I am smart and shy
I wonder what I will do someday
I hear the sweat sound of dolphins in the horizon
I see the ocean glistening in the bright sunlight
I want to have fun
I am smart and shy
I pretend to be rich and glamorous
I touch the waves as the crash against the shore
I feel the smooth horn of a unicorn
I worry I won't pass with an A
I cry when I get scared
I am smart and shy
I understand my family
I say to never give up
I dream of unicorns witches and goblins
I try to play my flute
I am smart and shy

Shelly Dickey

Love

Love is like a wildflower
garden that thrives and grows in our hearts.
To be in love, the feeling must come from deep within you.

Love is more than just a feeling,
it's a gift and one that people
often take for granted.
Love cannot be bought,
shared, or joked about.

When you fall in love,
it's not because you are
popular, smart, and cool;
but because you are a trusting,
loving person with a good heart and soul.

Jen Kammler

Afternoon in Honduras

In the sweaty, sultry hours
Between one and three
When life is too hot
To endure any longer,
We women gather
On the big beds in the adobe room
To lazily fan ourselves and
Talk of men, the price of onions, mango jam
And the unbearable heat.
The absolute stillness of
The smoke-filled sky and orange-colored world
Surrounds our heads and invades our dreams
Of men and mangoes
As we slip into the siesta, hoping
That sounds of rain will saunter in
And awaken us.

Liz Peyser

Faces

Some are strong, young and bold.
Some are lined, fragile, old.
Who knows what stories would be told.
Would they sing or would they scold?
I see them on the train, on the street, in a store.
For each one I see there are hundreds more.
The fact is we don't need to keep score.
We simply need to be aware; to care.
To know inside each face a soul is there.

Marilyn Huffman

My Kaleidoscope

When I'm sad and lonely
When I'm feeling bad
I try to fight but I am still so very, very mad
I look in my kaleidoscope
I see a world of new
A world of peace
A world of magic
A world of me and you.
I feel myself relaxing
I feel my body's heat
I cover my ears
I close my eyes
I guess I go to sleep
I dream of mother nature
I dream of glory too
I dream of magic
I dream of peace
I dream of me and you.
Now if you're feeling bad or really, really mad
There is not so much hope but there is a kaleidoscope.

Li-Ann Kaye

Dance of the Serpent Girl

The ultimate cycle
transcends time in endless revolutions.
Uncommon beauty in a dead world
obsessed with image and tension.
Must be some whirling serpent
wrapped tight around her blazing soul
unleashing her when she finds rhythm
leaving her swirling in a forbidden cosmos.
Her body uses color pure.
A turbulent brilliance in some wasteland.
A Van Gogh in motion amid the flickering strobe
where a base-line vibrates still figures
and the inhabitants eye one another
without respect for the blood curdling rhythm
that breaks her free from white dragons
leaving the whirlwinds trapped inside her.
The twisting hues of bliss and torment
are the only warmth she has felt.
Alone, she waits for the meltdown.
It will never come.

Chard Herrington

Eternally Bound

Breathless have I been left forevermore
Living in a misty dream world;
A realm of endless possibilities.
Mine eyes whom grasp no truth of you;
My heart knows not a lie, having sensed your presence;
Ever so heavenly.
A glimpse of you never seen, endlessly felt.
Your sacred trace engraved in my soul
The path slowly fading now before me.
The sands again slipping through the fate of time;
For only seconds and infinite realms separate us.

Breathless have I been found evermore since our eyes met.
Our souls embraced,
Bound together by life; An eternity.
Having met my deepest desire in a dream-world, no more.
Thy self hath been captured in my heart, my life
Never again shall the desert grip the endless grains so cherished.
Forever is too brief a moment that we shall be
Having engaged eternal bliss.

Pamela Castillo

Places of Dreams

Some people say it's wrong
To want too much—
Wishing for things you see
As the world passes by.

Dreaming of doing so much
And winning and growing,
Loving.

I think it's saddest when there's
Nothing left to want.
Emptiness lives in place of dreams
And the only wishing you do is
To wish you felt that something in your life
Was worth wishing for.

The only feeling left
Isn't pain, or frustration, or defeat.
The feeling is just a confusion.

Like tears falling only on the inside.

Delores A. Hussong

Grandfather

Grandfather went home for good today
God came and took his spirit away
To where the heavenly light forever shines
His earthly body was left behind
To suffer no more pain, sorrow or tears
No more of those earthly fears
His life had been an open book
Upon which all of us could look
His Christian walk was straight and true
Leading many others to life anew
Now the family is filled with sorrow
But we know that joy will fill the morrow
As we remember this godly man
And how he led us with a guiding hand
We thank you Jesus for his life
And we know that he fought the good fight
Please bring to us a measure of comfort today
We thank you dear Jesus for providing the way
To life everlasting, loving and true
And an eternity spent worshipping you.

Jade Fisher

High on a Mountain

Hearing the cars from the highway, looking outside, see the
mountain reaching the sky, keep asking myself why? Why?

What happen to this love of ours?
True love, like no other, not found in another!

So divine, so entwine, deep as the deepest ocean!
A love potion, so unique, formulated, just for you and me!

Gazing at the mountain, seeing the birds flyin' free.
Taking a journey to the heart . . . wishing, hoping, and praying
We befriend, true love again!

Hearing the cars from the highway, hearing my beating heart.
Hear yours?
What's it saying?
Meeting high on the mountain of love!

Marlene A. Ryan

Dear One, the Road Is Long . . .

Dear one, the road is long that has no turn;
We all must come to where the turnings end,
For in the compass of what thinks, is borne
The knowledge that the best life does is lend.
These senses now that seem in me most keen
Will weaken and grow dim by time's decrease
And all the forms of beauty I have seen
Will go like breath and all my rapture cease.
Dear one, your voice that gladdens all the year
In time will change and from my hearing fade,
But did you know that voice deceived my ear
And settled in my heart where since it stayed?
If God be good, eternal be His part
To keep you singing in my buried heart.

McKenna Byrne

Silent Warrior's

We are the voice that is unheard
We are silent warrior's standing alone into the night
Waiting to be heard
But hoping that we won't
Our flag flies over our launch centers as a warning to all
That we have the will and the might to defend our country
And pay the final price
But our flag stands as our best hope for our children
That mankind will unite as one
But until then, we are the silent warriors
A voice unheard

Anargyros E. Economou

The God-Fearing Man

He is strong and bold, a man of his word;
He is a God-fearing man, or haven't you heard?
He takes care of his family and is good to his wife;
He realizes that she is most important in his life.

God is his head, and he answers God's call;
For he knows that without Him, he'd stumble and fall.
He takes pride in his work and does his best;
For he realizes that this is just another test.

He doesn't smoke or drink and he doesn't do drugs;
He's not a whore-monger, nor hangs with thugs.
He puts God first and seeks His advice;
He calls on the Lord without thinking twice.

He prays with his family and supplies their needs;
These are just a few of a good man's deeds.
He's a God-fearing man, no question about it;
He loves to praise Him, he'll stand up and shout it.

The Steps of a Good Man are Ordered by the Lord,
But the wages of sin, No man can afford.

Sheila S. Holt

Sweet Memories

It seems like only yesterday,
That I was just a tot.
With all the beauty in this world,
I just loved a lot.
Mom and Dad were full of love.
They taught me from the start.
To always share your love to all,
That is what is in your heart.
So now that life has made me grown.
I'm sure I'll always be,
As nice and as happy as my Mom and Dad were to me.

Gloria Manges

To a Friend

It's been a while since you have gone,
But we all know life goes on.
It's not the same without you here,
And sometimes we think of you and shed a tear.
We're selfish because we want you back,
Because in our lives there is something we now lack.
A friend that's gone, but always will be,
In everyone's memories.

D. A. Martin

Walking Stick

As I watch the dwindling sunlight,
Filtered through the oak leaves,
I think back on a day that I had forgotten.
It had rained recently,
And the stiff fall gusts brought a fresh shower
from the branches of the forest.
As I loped over branches and through brush,
I could hear the creak of cold trunks
and the rush of the swampy brook.
I had been there many times,
But every time is unique.
The forest is dynamic, ever changing.
On this day, a deer stood where before there had been none.
Its rack dripped from the drizzle
And a single maple leaf was impaled on a tine.
It looked through me as it chewed the brown ferns.
Occasionally, its tail would flip,
Disturbing the black flies which rested there.
Suddenly, with a shift in the wind,
My companion started, and bound away.

E. Alan Bishop

A Mother's Kiss

Labor pains, my feet to the floor,
I knew I wasn't ready, but you wouldn't wait anymore.
They said you were way too little to survive,
2 pounds, 2 ounces, but you were alive.
I saw your little fingers and toes,
It brought tears to my eyes, I knew you had my nose.
Everyday I stood by your little bed,
I watched you grow, I leaned over you and kissed your head.
Soon you were bigger and then I could see,
Soon I would rock you and hold you close to me.
I would sing you a song and hold you tight,
I vowed to loved you from morning until night.
Now you are older and everyday that I see you grow,
I remember a pain that you will never know.
The fear of not having you is now replaced by love,
My life is filled with joy, you are a kiss from above.

Michelle Kellogg

My Master

When times are tough, as they are today
It is as though I don't know what to say.
The only thing that really rings true
Is to ask God what I should do,
Because no matter what the time or season
You can talk to the Master for any reason.
I then find I have been given the key
And have untold blessings bestowed upon me,
You see, no matter how hard the fight
God will be there to make things right.
It is with Him that I set my goal
Since he is the owner of my very soul.
I pray as the ocean rolls upon the beach
God will always be there within my reach,
And tell me never to feel despair
Because He is around me everywhere.
An angel blush with a tender moment sweet insures me I'm proud to have a seat
in a dimension where love and light ride the wind through the darkest night.
My Master, My Guardian, and My Friend
with whose love there is no end.

Benny Firestone

Green

Green is a color surely everyone has seen
From the color of money to a very long string bean
Young apples, tomatoes, leaves in spring on a tree
The grass around my golf tee
A shiny car, pine trees rising high to touch a star
A tongue from a lick of a green pop-sickle on a stick
A traffic light
A blouse totally out of sight
An after dinner mint to an occasional piece of lint
Peas in a pod
Newly cut sod
Nature around us, clothes that make a fuss
Lettuce, spinach and kiwi
Gangrene of the knee
A friend's jealousy—immaturity
A jewel like an emerald
Inexperience, I am told
Unripened fruit to a funny suit
And so, a color such as this can never be mean
As having a lot of "green," is truly kinda keen

Frank J. DeNiro

I Am Still Alive

From the first day of your origin,
I've held you in my arms I'm still alive.
Throughout the times you have cried,
And I have comforted you I am still alive,
Watching you grow and hearing your thoughts
Sometime brought tears to my eyes, and joy to my heart.

I am still alive.
Although time has ripped us apart,
And we no longer have our little heart to hearts.
Fear not be strong, and rest a shore
You will always be a part of my heart.
No matter what the costs even if time loses
No earthly forces will ever tear us apart.
So allay your fears and live your life with care,
And always bear in mind that daddy will be there.

I am still alive.

Timothy R. White

Sanctuary

Yesterday's appellations are today's regrets.
Stares in consternation at our requests.
Oft the indication what we deem best
Rises in conflagration to consume the rest.

Enter the realization, impact of things said.
Lack of contemplation for whence we tread.
Fools cite incantations to raise the dead,
Destain the implications for what was read.

Headlong to starvation and cultural demise.
Dull minded in formation, we fail to realize
Our steps in cadence passion led to a dismal prize;
Complete, rapine destruction now greets our bloodshot eyes.

We scoffed at education and didn't count the cost.
Worshipped indoctrination and grieved not for the lost.
"Our lives as reparation!" heralded Heaven's hosts.
A stone's our last salvation. "Hide from the Holocaust!"

Oliver Kim Vandagriff

Forgotten Love

What would happen if we passed on the street.
Could I look into your eyes,
Would my heart skip a beat.
You've been out of my life for so many years.
Could I fight the pain,
Even hold back the tears.
The distance grows shorter
As you're headed my way.
Should I cross the street,
I won't know what to say.
Do you remember our very first kiss?
Or when you think of me . . .
The night we called it quits.
Forgotten love—can we start again?
Do we stand a chance . . .
Just say when.
Forgotten love—I still love you.

Charles Blumberg

An Evergreen Forest

I wander through the evergreen forest across a muddy trail.
The birds sing out soothing songs.
A bush full of deep intense red roses catches my eye,
Each flower has a clear drop of morning dew.
Trees stretch out toward the light sky that seems miles away,
Lizards scatter around as fast as light.
I breathe deeply, inhaling the fresh moisture air.
A river with clear, pure water twists around the forest.
A peaceful and quiet place.

Emily Silverman

Time's Journey

Time passed through my window today,
As in the shape of dust, with a damp smile.
It passed with the scent of forgotten sorrow,
As worn-out as children stories told again and again.

Is it the blink of an eye?
Is it a living too swift?
Is it a dying too slow?

He can be a cruel executioner or a loyal companion,
And the footprints he leaves behind
are the history written in the book of men.

For he takes with him the beauty and the strength of the mighty.
And we can all see him in the tiredness of the old,
For he rests in the silence of arms crossed.
The years not in vain struggle
For time brings them on to us.

Edith Farfan

I'm Going Home, If I'm Wanted

When I was a child, I had not a care
Just happiness and no one could daunt it.
I never did question the who, what, or where,
I just always knew I was wanted.

The teen years were different 'cause I knew it all.
The others, they teased and taunted,
I thought I'd be happy, that I'd have a ball
If I did those things they all flaunted.

Then came adulthood, I had to get real.
I searched for the truth, I was haunted
By the things I had done. I wanted to heal,
But I didn't think I was wanted.

The older I get, the more I believe
There's never a time I'm not wanted.
I yearn for His comfort and total relief.
I think I'll go home, I am wanted.

I know I can never go too far from home.
God's love is true and undaunted.
I'll pray for forgiveness and never more roam,
I firmly believe I'm still wanted.

Pat C. Hancock

Mother's Day, and Dave

I wait, and I wait and anticipate,
For possibility of pending stomachache

I toss and turn, and lay and fake,
For rules are clear, this mother's fate.

My son is young, his love is true,
But what kind of meal, do I see due.

The coffee, original, at least, incredible
At times I found it—positively edible.

The meal it comes, the time has too,
What kind of meal, my son's scene through?

I begin to eat, but without haste,
For certainly nothing, should be left to waste.

I remember the love, remember the favor.
Forgotten the taste, the memories, I Savor.

My son has grown, I must have too,
Did I ever give thanks, for his love, now due?

Our differences are many, some accounts for our gender,
How could we have known, he would be a bartender?

But, I hope he remembers, as I know that I do,
That my son is my son, that my love will hold true.

Therese Feser Garcia

Life

I see the man enter the emergency room
I see the look of death upon his face
I see the doctor rush to him in a maddening pace
I see the nurse enter the room
I see them desperately trying to revive him
I see the man's face is blue
I see them administer O$_2$
I see the man's skin is moist and appears so cold!
I see the nurse touch his brow
I see the look of despair which comes to those who care
I see the man open his eyes and look about
I see him open his mouth to speak
I see the doctor and nurse give a sigh of relief
I see how important it is to care
I see Life. How beautiful!

Betty Baldwin

Heavenly Home

Heavenly home, heavenly home
Our reward is that heavenly home.
Tho' on earth there is strife; God promises life
In that wonderful heavenly home.

Heavenly home, heavenly home,
There is peace in that heavenly home.
Lord Jesus is there, so radiant and fair
In that wonderful heavenly home.

Heavenly home, heavenly home,
How I long for that heavenly home.
No storm clouds appear, Angelic voices we'll hear
In that wonderful heavenly home.

Ralph O. Knapper

Gemstones

Your eyes are like diamonds,
Shiny as can be.
When the sun touches them,
They glisten like the sea.

Your heart is like rubies,
Just diamonds in the rough.
If I catch you lying,
You knows I'll call your bluff.

Your lips are like aquamarines,
Delicate to the touch.
That's one of the many reasons
I love you so much.

I wish everyone in the world could set eyes on,
The precious gem
That I cherish so much,
The precious gem is him.

Amber Topping

A Father's Love

A father is an important man,
Who plays a special role.
He gives you all his love and joy,
And only has one goal.
To keep us safe and love us,
But this is not his only gift.
When you're down he says kind words,
To give you a special lift.
This comes straight from the heart,
And is his one true part.
A father could be described
As the main character in a play.
But one thing that is different,
Is that he practices his role day after day.

Brittany Akins

No Support

An Jargon Time as ones would
Share an intellectual space
For one or more self's
Time is now, time has always been.
Thoughts of these continuance possibilities
Will only bring out the true essence.
Do you know right from maybe wrong?
Homemade knowledge is the essence of creating Peace in time.

Meaning of
Transpose
Issue
Material
Era

John Wayne Whitworth, Jr.

The Blue Ball

I saw a blue ball, in my long hall.
When my brother picked it up,
And put it in my dads coffee cup.
The ball started jumping, jumping, jumping in the air,
but I didn't care.
I thought it was bouncing,
but really was pouncing,
towards me where I couldn't see,
I fell to the floor and I was no more.
I was just turning eleven when I was in heaven
from that blue, blue ball.
He met me up there,
in the gymnastics lair,
and the ball said "look here!"
I wouldn't look there or anywhere,
but to my surprise,
just before my eyes,
was my dad trying to wake me up.

Casey Spitnale

Lunch

Filling the emptiness,
like a cool breeze on a hot and humid day,
like a reassuring light in the darkness of night,
like a satisfying drink for parched lips,
like a child's laughter for a frowning face,
like a bird's beautiful song in an empty valley,
like a twinkling star in the black of night,
like a warm smile in a cold and frightening place,
like a budding flower in a crystal vase,
your love fills my heart!
So I hunger no more.

Cecelia A. McLennan

What Is Love Supposed to Mean?

I sit and I think to myself,
what is love supposed to mean?
I suppose it can be anything
from the sounds of birds chirping
to the sight of a beautiful sunset
upon the ocean waters.
Love between two people
can feel so many different ways.
One, the way you feel when he has you
tightly wrapped up in his arms.
Yet it can be when you are sitting alone, heartbroken,
because his love for you has disappeared.
Love can mean that you have a happiness
of being secure within yourself.
This is a love everyone wishes for.
Although, I imagine,
I will never know exactly
what love is supposed to mean.

Cassandra Adams

Sand

Lying quietly in the gentle light of his love
I reach up to touch his soft hair
And melt into his warm smile
He is my true love
The one and only star lighting up my dark sky
I stand on the shores of my mind
And watch him soar above me
While I am trapped in the sand
Now he reaches down to take my hand
And pulls me from the grip of the past
He helps me fly high above reality
We race across the sky
Splashing sunshine on the world
With his loving hand in mine
I bear the strength to carry on
And together we will take flight forever
Never to return to the burden of the sands far below us.

Nicole Kanaby

Why

We are all alone, we are all sacred
We were taken away from our families' good care
They say it's our color and our race,
But in reality we are just another face.
They make us work and sweat all day,
Why does it have to be this way?

Colleen Mclaughlin

Alone in the Ghettos

I used to have many friends, but now I am alone
I used to live on a nice street, but now I live in the Ghettos

I hear gunshots and screams
I see people running and being rounded up like cattle
Then I am alone

I sit next to Papa and Jacob
While Mama tends to David

Papa pushes me into a hole
I hear gunshots and mama screaming
I hear boots
I feel alone

Then, everything is still
I hear David crying, but I do not hear mama or Jacob
I can not hear papa either
There is smoke, I can not see them
I see David in the corner but no mama or papa
I am alone

I can not hear David anymore
I can not see him anymore
I am alone

Jamie Clearfield

Yesterday Today and Tomorrow

I remember yesterday as if it were today and I know
Tomorrow will bring a brighter day.
Do you remember all the times we laughed, we joked,
And cried, that was yesterday oh what a happy time . . .
Today is quite different it's a lonely and sad time,
Waiting and wondering if you'll ever be mine . . .
Tomorrow will bring wonder I hope for you and me,
Tomorrow will bring longing down deep inside of me.
Yesterday seems far away distant as can be,
Yesterday was wonderful home and serenity.
Today we must go on to bring our dreams to light,
Today we must go on like birds in flight.
Tomorrow will bring sunshine for all of us to see,
Tomorrow will bring new hope,
I know for that I promise thee . . .

Mary Ann T. Keeley

Mama, I Sure Do Miss You

Mama, I always thought you'd be here for me,
I know if you could have, you always would be.
There are so many things I wish we could share,
The gleam in Toms' eyes, and your laughter at my attempts to
Curl Jenny's hair . . .

We were only a phone call away, sharing little things like;
Guess who I saw? Do you know what the kids did today?
Very precious moments that make a mother and grandmothers' day.
All too soon you were taken away.

The kids are grown up now, Tom has a loving wife and Jen has
Two sons of her own.
I'm happily married almost 20 years now, living in a cute little
mobile home.

I think you'd be proud of how we all turned out.
We've made the most of who we are and what life is all about.
What I wouldn't give for one of our phone calls or two . . .
Thanks for everything, Mama, I sure do miss you.

Sharon Schlereth

Another Place, Another Time

If we met in another place or another time
would things be different? Could we walk on
a sunny beach hand in hand as lovers? Maybe
in another place and another time. Is there
forever going to be distance between us
where we can share our bodies with abandon
but not out feelings? Maybe not in another
place and another time. Will there ever be a
time when I can miss You when were apart
and not have to lie about why I'm so sad?
Maybe in another place and another time. Will
there ever be a time when I'm as important
to you as you are to me? Could be in another
place or another time. Is it possible one of
us was born to early and the other to late?
Could it be that one day we might be soul
mates, friends, and lovers? Could be anything
is possible in another place and time?!!!

Mary Ann Miller

New Home

With open arms God beckons me by whispering my name,
"Come," he says, "to your new home, a home devoid of pain."

By his mighty hand I'm lifted up, eternal joy now found,
The peace I've sought since my rebirth, a love that knows no bounds.

Now knelt at God, Almighty King, Creator of my soul,
My burdens now so far away, for once again I'm whole.

G. Ross Fernandez

Good-Bye for Now My Love

When you wake up in the morning
And see the sunlight shining thru your window,
It is my smile coming to greet you.
When you look out upon the ocean
And hear the waves beating against the shore,
It is my heart beating for you.
When you look up and hear a bird singing,
It is my song of love for you.
When you touch the dew drops on the petal of a flower,
Press it to your lips my darling,
For it sends my kiss to you.
When you feel the rain drops falling upon your face,
It is my tears longing for your embrace.
When you go to bed at night and
Look up to see the moon shining,
It will be me, my darling, saying
"Good night my love. I will see you in my dreams."
For then and only then will you belong to me.

Patricia M. Koback

That Was My Child

That was my child, nor cradle nor grave
That was my child, her life I must save
That was my child, her little body so frail
That was my child, "dear God, where did I fail?"
That was my child, to wait was all we could do.
That was my child, this only happened to few.
That was my child, I wanted to hold her so tight
To breath on her own was too much of a fight.
That was my child, it was near impossible to leave her side
But then one day her eyes open wide
That was my child, not expected to completely recover
But she walked out of the hospital and into my arms, her mother
Now this is my child, there's not much she can't do
To take advantage of good health, without realizing we all do.
I feel so lucky to have two healthy children,
I love taking that extra few minutes to hug and love them.

Robin Cruickshank

The Earth

The night sky shimmers with brilliant stars,
I sit and watch the passing cars.
My thoughts wander to times long ago,
When people knew all that they needed to know.
They were wise instead of smart,
They paid attention to their heart.
They made the things that were necessary,
And material things they did not carry.
They were too wise to build things of pollution,
And so they came up with a better solution.
They realized the outcome of objects that we have today,
That is why they concluded a wiser way.
But all people have done as the years have gone by,
Is create unwise things without thinking of "why?"
I wish deep within me to have lived then and not now,
But I know that won't happen, so why ask myself "how?"
The earth was once a more lovely place,
And what I have just explained to you, I see when I look
upon its face.

Arielle Lee Becker

Oasis

I stand before this vision,
The grand representation
Of what I once was:
A dark, beautiful mare
Stands among a sea
Of white and pink apple blossoms
That seem to have
Come from nowhere.
The rain clouds above her
Pour out the blood of Life, Innocence, Joy.
I stand before this vision,
Unclear through the foggy glass of its prison.
I stand in a desert alone,
Peering into this oasis,
Seeking the rungs
With which to scale
The prison walls.
The ladder is not there.

Heather Renee Courson

Miracles

Mysterious instances of divine intervention,
Imparting hope over expectations.
Renewing strength and faith within,
Answering prayers; perhaps unspoken.
Continued assurance of God's own care,
Love expressed beyond compare.
Every life is a miracle from the start,
Savor and cherish it in your heart.

Bonnie D. Barile

Parisian Rain

A small flower quivers in the morning sun
Waiting patiently for the giver of life, the rain.
Drops fall in a seemingly haphazard fashion
Each one giving the promise of life,
Yet it's never enough to nurture its growth.
The flower collapses in on itself
Persevering through the drought
For each day brings with it
The promise of another rain,
An opportunity to bloom in full again.

Garrett Jensen

Broken Wind Chimes

If I could turn things around would I make you smile?
If I could slay your high horse, would you still be better than me?
If I could press stop, would you stop rewinding?
Replay after replay of the same scene in your life
One thing after another and I never did it right
And the same old scene plays again and again
The scene of your life in the same old town
One place after another until they all look the same
Reruns of a discontinued show
Blurred by the pain that's welling up in your eyes.

Cassie Daley

Mournful That Day—Grant Them Rest

Proceeding among weather worn,
etched, crumbling and stumbling stones;
Statues stand—gravely guarding ancient bones.

Parading incense purifies the damp air;
winter oaks stretch crippled limbs—
sorrowful, for life that's trimmed.

It's journey started the first day of breath;
Borne to shadows that linger fast,
returning among ages of the past.

Oh! Call me among the Blessed!
The eye hath failed, so has the breast—
now, forever, my soul shall be caressed.

It would be vain to try to hide;
within this bleak and somber tide
here, eternally, I shall not reside.

After a kind word and brief prayer,
the quick place me under temporal stone—
thus embarking the journey into the Unknown.
I Walk.

L. Brian Owens

Single Parent, The Father

People say that a man shouldn't raise a child
Regardless of that; I've been raising mine awhile
I love my daughter with all of my heart
Sometimes it's easy, sometimes it's hard
From crawling, to talking, to her ABC's
I've taught my child to believe in her dreams
When looking into her eyes; I can see her soul
The laughter, the pain and even her goals
Sometimes she mentions something about her mother;
Everyday she says how much she loves her father
Men can't give to a child the same as women can
But on my hands and knees; I can put it in God's hand
Still they say that a child really needs it's mother
I have no problem with that, except I'm her father
The pain spoken about in this poem above
Didn't come from a father, but the lack of mother's love
So the next time you see
A single father holding his child's hand
Thank God up above for that kind of man

Michael F. Clark

The Trinity

Why, oh Lord, can man not understand the Trinity?
Do we not understand that man can be a father,
Brother, son and husband?
Each one aspects of one individual.

Do we not understand that woman can be
A mother, daughter, sister and wife?
Each one aspects of one individual.

Therefore cannot our Lord be Father
Son and Holy Spirit?
Each one aspects of one God

He who is above us all; Leader of all
Leaders, Father of all, Maker of all things,
One who loves us all.
Cannot He who is one be also the Trinity?

Lois C. Gulbrandsen

Vampire

The passion begins to unfold
Tender kisses passed back and forth through a heated embrace
I feel his heart beat racing
The bite, I feel him quiver as he deeply moans
I taste his life, I see his blood streaming down his chest.
He is mine, I am his
I take him in my hands, pulsating, throbbing
I am in control as we share each others lust
His heart beat stops, the fire and the hunger
Fill him, it replaces his blood
As I begin to cum he lunges forward knocking me from him
I feel his fangs drive deep into my neck
I begin to cry, for now our blood, our lives are intertwined
Joined as one, one person, one passion, one life
We are vampire.

Angela P. Kogle

This Thought I See

In my minds eye I see
A pleasant thought that upsets me
Does it upset me this thought I see
For it was never meant to be
Or does it upset me this thought I see
For my own two eyes are too blind to see
When I open my eyes I reach out to thee
This thought I see, This thought I see
When I open my eyes this thought eludes me
I dream a pleasant dream
Thanks to this thought I see
But it's just a dream to me and will never be
All thanks to this thought I see

Phillip Diaz

Seed of My Seed

It's a long story to be told,
about this thing called getting old.
You begin life with the pinkest cheeks,
taking each day in the passing weeks.
No one warns you when youth dies,
then one day a tear swells up in your eyes.
Suddenly you know that youth has fled,
you cup your hands and hold your head.
Just when you're feeling empty and almost dead,
a sweet small voice startles you instead.
You raise your head to see who has spoke,
it's your precious grandchild who gave you a poke.
The youth you mourn now starts to revive,
all of a sudden you again feel alive.
This glorious child who is seed of your seed,
has now given back your youth indeed.

Ron Feasel

Grandma!

There's someone I lost in my life,
who left three years ago,
My friend and my angel I loved her so much,
I loved her touch
She made me laugh and smile,
she also loved me for awhile.
Then a day came I found out she was gone.
My heart just shattered into pieces one by one.
I cried so much I wanted to die
She was the best thing that there was in life.
Now that she's gone, I feel so lost,
I never know what to do when things go wrong.
There's never really anyone to talk to.
I now just figure it's all up to me to decide on my own,
Yea! There's my parents and my friends,
But it's not quite the same.
I wish she was here today to get me through life OK.
But either way dead or alive,
She's my number one friend,
and she's always by my side

Jennifer Shubert

The Tree

Climb the tree to see where it may lead.
See and hold.
Look through yourself.

Grab on tight it maybe your last look at light.
Chaos, it's at its peak and now everything will fall.

Held by the light of your eyes.
Will bring on the gift of cider and wine.

Let it sit let it be.
Climb the tree to the new world.
It's time to dine.

George Arritola

Heart's Prayer

For so long now,
my heart's been waiting, hoping,
expecting, praying,
for someone like you to fall into my life.

Since we met,
my heart's been racing, dashing,
shouting, rejoicing,
that you walked into my life.

Now that we've been together,
my heart's been laughing, smiling,
loving, thanking,
someone up above for guiding you into my life.

For days coming,
my heart's been hoping, pleading,
asking, praying,
that you stay in my life for a while.

Michael H. Losk

A Mockingbird Sings

I was serenaded by a mocking bird today,
And I hope it has come to stay.
Please mockingbird do not go away,
Because you have many different songs to sing,
And they have such a beautiful, lovely ring.

It is so good to hear you warble the many different tunes.
Build your nest in the month of June,
Stay at least through September,
And your songs I will always remember.

Hayden W. Higgenbottom

Untitled

I do not understand
why Romeo had to die with Juliett,
why love hurts like a bullet through the heart,
why people kiss.
Is it show they're affectionate to each other?
But most of all I do not understand
why heroes die and his or her loved ones cry
(like a flower withering away after it was just planted,
it withers away because no one cared for it.).
What I do understand is music.
How beautiful and soft it is.
It whispers through the trees,
keeps people happy and peaceful.
It tries to keep love happy and peaceful.
Sometimes it fails from its duties.

Stephanie Ruff

Green Famine

I choose not to be alive in the green of yesterday.
I only survive by the rain that has washed my hope gone clear.
I am the only female in the family,
I have to do these things to stay alive.
The sleep shadows dance in my thoughts.
I am here, that makes me strong.
To yearn for nothing that keeps me awake.
To be silenced by the wind and to laugh at my existence.
I have to escape from the destitute of the chores of the land.
The hunger that has no sympathy, the silence that has no ending.
But the journey has just begun.
It is the thunder of the white mans fire.
The night cries and everyone goes away.
To be unafraid of dying, if it is a proper death.
If I stay, will honor live on?
The silence has arrived and I am but a mirror standing.
I am consumed by birth, marriage and death.
The three miracles of heaven.
I am but one with many faces.

Marie Bowen

I'm Going to Have a Party

I'm going to have a party
A party today, oh I'm going to have a party
Hip, hip, hooray! At my party
We're going to hop, sing and dance
We're going to have so much fun
They might just lose their pants
But at the end they'll stop and say,
"Ahh Mom do I have to go"
I had so much fun today,
I'm standing here looking at my watch
They should be here by now.
Is there something I could have possibly forgot
Yes, I simply forgot to pass the invitations out!

Sara Elaine Brevard

Strong Mother

There once was a woman who was strong, bold
She was very wise and wasn't nothing
But 36 years old
She raised a child all by herself
By raising her on love, truth, and health
This lady had ways that a tiger heart could bare.
In her mind she had everything and yes she loved to share.
Her family called on her
When they thought their lives were going to fall
They called on her when they had a problem or gossip to tell
When her brothers let her down
And the only thing she could say
"That's all right, you will need me one day"
That lovely, strong, bold woman
was no other than my mother!

Elstress Key

Special Day

As a member of this community, I feel I have a say
I want each and everyone to have an excellent day

We have been through adversity: It's all behind us now
Let us rally together and envision with cheer
A better day is at hand
Oh yes it is near!

Let us rally for a superior day!
For a day of gentle effulgence,
A day of shared blessing, prosperity and plenteous too.

Begin the day with a prayer and end it there too
Go about your way
Doing specifically this and particularly that and
Whatever you select: Deem it the best!

May your day be fruitful, filled with abundant joy
Flourishing with progress of measure and prolific by far

And let us not stop here
No not with this new plan
We will try this over and over again

Ernestine Hamtion Lathan

Twice Blessed

T is for the Twins I carried, unbeknown to me,
W is for the Way they came, five weeks early,
I is for Identical, for that is what they are,
C is for Colleen, I know she is a star,
E is for Early childhood days, always putting on a show,

B is for how Blessed I am that God gave me two—to go,
L is for the Love we share, sometimes hard to say out loud,
E is for Every time they make me feel so proud,
S is for Shannon. She's now my "Little Mom,"
S is my grandson Sean, who is her firstborn son,
E is for Every day I thank God I was Twice Blessed,
D is for my Daughters, they are the very best!

Barbara Langham

Lost Prayer

On nights when its dark and beautiful,
When the stars hang like paper lanterns flickering on a fence.
I roll up my trousers,
Take off my shoes
And dip my toe in the warmth of the swirling Milky Way.
Then, jumping from moonbeam to star tip to moonbeam
I gently reach under a puffy cloud and
Collect all your prayers that didn't quite make it to heaven.
These beautiful lost prayers can be picked out right away
Because they twinkle and sparkle brighter than all the other stars
Around them.
Lost prayer are just resting or
They may be trapped under clouds or
Knocked off course by a wayward dove.
Bending down,
I spoon them up into my heart
Where your prayers become so bright
It lights up the sky.

Tony McGeorge

Fall, Star, Fall

"Read this," they say, and I am awakened once more
to the horror of every waking day.
You walk down the street and are shot from a car . . .
But we still wish upon the star.
The star, we hope, will save us all.
The star, we hope, can prevent a fall.
But we still fall all over the place,
Pushed down by greed and the human race.
Why we kill our brothers is a mystery to all,
Except to those who will fall.

Sarah Kennard

The World and the Father's Home

Outside there is storm, inside there is calm
Outside it's windy, inside it's still
Outside it's snow and slippery, inside dry and sure footing

When prodigal son was out he was eating with the swine
But when he returned home there was father and blessings divine

Worldly stocks and shares are umbrellas, you hold to protect
But blessings and salvation are from Jehovah Jireh
Where all your needs are met

How can you compare God Almighty and man
How can you compare the body and soul

One perishes and is there no more
The soul is forever
And lives with the everlasting creator

Will you still be out my friend?
Or will you choose the Father's Home
Manzoor Victor

East African Plain

The antelope graze on the grass
They are joined by the zebra
An elephant trumpets, a baboon cries
The herds run off to escape the predator
But they can not escape the cheetah
A loud crash echoes through the Savannah
As an antelope has hits the ground
The meat is devoured quickly by the cheetah and family
It is not eaten quickly enough
Scavengers have arrived
They will finish off the antelope
All the scavengers scatter
Hyenas have arrived
Others will be destroyed
For the hyena does not share
Many animals have died
On the East African Plain
Elizabeth Keller

Within the Night

As I sit here in the deep dark night,
Everything is still and out of sight.
The emptiness that you feel inside,
Comes out within with a deep dark cry.
As the moon shines from way up above.
The peaceful sensation makes you feel free as a dove,
The leaves whisper with the whistling air,
The chill you feel rushes up your spine with despair.
Now as the sun rises and a new day appears,
The night time secrets stay locked inside with all your fears.
Till next time we meet in the deep dark night,
All my secrets and fears will stay out of sight.
Michelle Calise

Untitled

If you do drugs you will have no future
You drop out of school and have no friends
You feel singled out, lonely, scared, cold, sick, and hurt
You will be homeless, with no one to turn to,
No parent guidance, no friends to help you
You will be sleeping in an alley or on a park bench
It is painful to see you begging for food
and steeling money to buy drugs
Just because you don't want help
You think everything is great
You have your drugs and that's all you need
Well it's not
Do you know why?
Because you were stupid enough to even start
Megan Lambert

Who Are You

Who are you, do I know You
You seem like a stranger to me
Did You say You knew me
I can't recall who you are
You're just like a distant star
Were we ever friends
Did we ever share secrets before
I'm very sorry
but I do not remember You
I wish I could recognize your face
It's combined with so much beauty and grace
You seem like you're a very sure, caring person
Maybe we can get to know each other better
so we can share some good times together
Since the old ones were lost in the past
I wonder how long our friendship would last
I wish I could remember who you were before
I wish I could find the key to unlock the door
To remember the special moments we spent together
My New Friend
Sara Ashbaugh

King

It has always been my dream
To someday be crowned a king.

So a vote for me and Billie Jean
Will help us become king and queen.

Now my grammar ain't so fine
Otherwise that wouldn't rhyme.

I try to live a cheerful life
Because I never took a wife.

Some say I missed a lot of joy
Because I didn't marry and raise a girl or boy.

Now you may not know it,
But I am a poet,
Because my feet show it,
They are long fellows.

So I'll go on my merry way.
This is all I have to say.
Ross Carter

When I Was 12

Dedicated to all youth who are without a parent.
I was without my father but . . .
I had a mother, 3 brothers,
1 sister, 13 cousins, 4 nephews, 2 nieces;
I had the time to be a child
and to do childless things;
I had spankings and praises.
When I was 12

When I was 12
I was without my father but . . .
I had the love and patience from my godparents;
I had aunts and uncles to help me to learn how to relax;
I had friends to fight and to make peace with;
boys to chase
and to beat at marbles.
When I was 12

When I was 12
I was without my father but . . .
I had love abundantly.
Carolyn V. Hardy

Memories of Mom

My best friend has gone, so far from here.
She has left me feeling, so many fears.
I now feel a very empty place, where my heart was full.
There's now an empty space, she left me here to make it alone.
Oh yes, I know she had to go, because God called her to his home.
Her time here was up, she could not stay, not even for another day.
To laugh, To love, To work or play.
She had to go and leave me here, to bear my sorrows for many years.
My loss was great, so was his gain, yet I know she still watches me
maintain. This life she gave to me, not so long ago.
Is filled with sweet memories of her smile all aglow.
She could no longer stay with me, you see;
To wipe away my tears or lend to me a listening ear.
She was my very best friend, and my love for her will never end.
With her help and grace, she made this a bearable place.
She still managed to leave to me her face.
She gave to me her feet, hands and legs, so I've been told.
She even left with me her spirit and soul, and yes even her grace.
But none of these things could ever take her place.
Nor can they fill that very empty space!

Jackie Robichaux

Because You Are Mine

If the birds never sing another song,
And all my dreams are gone.
If the flowers never again bloom,
And winter comes too soon.
If the moon should hide its light,
If all my days turn to night.
If all the world should end this very day,
I couldn't stop this love—there's just no way.
If I never hear another song,
If all the rainbows are forever gone.
If I never wish upon another star,
My greatest wish has come true by far.
For this love is more than you can know,
Far more than I can show.
If the sun goes down never again to shine,
I will still be happy as long as you are mine.

Michele W. Jump

Awareness

Days go by, then months, then years,
The wait is long, I shed my tears.
I once was young and now am old.
"Life is tough." I'm often told.

My hopes run high, then soon are shattered.
Despair creeps in, but what does it matter.
I long to succeed. Define success? I ask within.
To share, to give, to care, to love.
No stealing, no lies, no hate, no sins.

The night brings sleep so thoughts can rest.
Soon rays of sun shows dawn at best.
I am alive! I have success!
I have it all, it's me, I guess.

Anna M. Barry

The Sea

She lays down in the sand,
Listening to the wind and sea,
She gets up and walks for miles,
Looking at the blue sea, and the sky,
The green trees seem to be saying something.
The orange sand is whispering a secret.
The birds sing a love song.
She walks into the sea and drifts away.
Her dress is moving back and forth,
The sun doesn't know what to do except shine.
Then everything is calm and quiet.

Nicole Brown

Waiting for a Friend

I hate to be so heavy hearted,
But my life seems so intolerable

I know I have friends, but they don't understand me
Like they don't even care

It's like I'm in a world,
Of my own out on a limb with nothing to hold onto

People see me but can't do anything to help me
Friends and family comfort me
And say it's just a stage you'll grow out of it

But it seems much more than just a page
Of my life I feel I'm worthless like I want to die

I want a friend that will always be there for me
When I'm upset and when I'm unhappy

To find such a friend is really hard,
Not a friend that gossips about you,
But truly loves you for who you are

I wish I had this friend but he's just not there
and since I haven't
This friend there is a space
Waiting to be filled.

Christopher Lyon

Crossing Pulaski

I drop you off at Lawrence and Pulaski
among the Korean shops, corner cleaners
Mayfield's food and liquor
and the fantasy adult bar
And the car reeks of smoke and coffee
as parking lot dust blows through the cracked window
the sun glares into my eyes
and my hangover pulses harder
And I'm startled by the tinkle of a rolling forty
the crinkle of garbage bag
and the blast of a Toyota all at once
And everyone's trying to get somewhere
three small Asian boys running for the light
that bag lady pulling her cart into the alley
the bus driver bearing down on a slow Cadillac
But I just want to sit here a little while and smoke
watch you cross Pulaski with that heel n' toe walk
see the wind catch up your blazer and flip your hair back
and breathe in the exhaust the dust the sun the smoke the you

David McMillen

On Nostalgia

Of late, I think of a time when things cost a dime
and life was dusty and slow;
In our house by the rails we awaited the mails
as we heard that steam train blow.
Came REA, "We have lights!" we could say,
"and even a party-line phone!"
Sunday School and church were the rule;
we wanted to be counted God's own.
Our school oh so quaint with its shiny red paint
was blessed with all of two brooms.
It's hard to believe how we tots so naive
learned so well in those drafty old rooms.
Today we look back at those times and their lack
and we think how little we had,
But while we fret with our Internet
in some ways it's today that is sad;
We have drugs, we have sex, and the crimes they do vex;
our time and its wealth cause us shame.
We must learn from the past that it's our soul that will last,
but our things will burn up in the flame.

Lindsey D. Few Jr.

United Love

Love: My love for him was so pure
I knew at once it was I lay here
Now like a bird shot down,
My heart punctured with emptiness,
And the only thing I see is the face of him . . .
He is always there . . .
A lonely memory drifting in my head.
It's a love I can't forget
But the more I remember, the more it fades
Like the warm glow of a late night moon—
It fades out of my brain,
But it will forever be etched upon my heart.
Like a needle and a thread,
Put them together and they become one . . .
Put us together and we become one—
One mind . . . one love . . . one heart . . .
One soul . . . united.

Jennifer Scalzi

What Am I?

My branches reach the sky,
Without the sun I would die.
Sometimes you can find a nest of birds in my hair,
Without me you would have no clean air.
My roots sink deep into the earth,
From a little seed was my birth,
I can grow over fifty foot tall,
My leaves change color in the fall.
Without me everything would die.
So don't cut me down without a sign.
Please let me grow and have my years,
Cause if you cut me down there will be many tears,
I make oxygen for you and me,
That is because I am a tree.

Tabitha Powell

Feelings of Music

Music flows through the air, darkness all around.
Music like a swirling mist surrounding forms of noise.
Notes piercing the air both high and low.
Making a mix of good and bad better here than below.
A ghost listen to the night in the song of one's heart.
Of their dreams and hopes and theirs doubts and fears.
Of their wish to be loved and good
And of their fear of being hated and cruel.
Music is expression of all that we feel.
Anger, happiness, excitement, depression, sadness, and hope.
That is all we can feel with are unknown.
Music plays a great part in our lives.
Our lives like a play being staged out for all the world to see.
As we act out our part of this untitled play
We listen the music to feel and see.

Nicole Brooke

Journey to Darkness

The journey to darkness; we all must face,
The journey to darkness; to the unknown place.
To once know the beauty of life and love.
It's all just an illusion concealed above.

The journey is coming, for me, no more.
It is now a relief; peace will fill my core.
I have lived out my life and seen all I need.
The darkness is peace; a quieter deed.

I searched long and hard to find my ideal;
But she has found another, her love is for real.
There is nothing for me, my light has come to an end;
She no longer looks back as I travel the bend.

There are few things that make it worth living,
I had the best and took without giving.

Jennifer Updyke

Inheritance

Today is the last day of my inheritance.
The day is covered by the dark clouds of death.
The bell rings, I move.
Towards my sentence of torture, I move.
No longer know the difference between night and day.
This is going nowhere.
Stuck in my dreams.
Am I dead or alive?
What's the difference—I can think of none.
Blood, to bring life, drains through this lifeless body.
Ironic isn't it?
I write from the blood that has been taken.
From my heart, the tears pour out.
Memories haunt the life I attempt to live.
Blood stained fears.
The Devil that killed God will forever remain
burned in my mind.

Jennifer Alberg

God Help Us

America, the land of the free,
Isn't all it's cracked up to be.

We need a new anointing
given from the heavens above,
Bring down the rain from up above.

Lord, help us I pray to reach out
to you every day.

We can't start to straighten out this mess,
We need you to look down and abundantly bless.

The violence we live in every day,
Keeps us from sending our children out to play.

When little ones can't play at the park,
Paints a grim picture of the nation and that's pretty dark.

I pray that soon America will be back to where it was
when we all felt a lot more free.

LaDonna Dufur

Raining in New York 2

Livid yarns streaming from her throat
cracked, tarnished from the years of clean living,
melodious eyes
blue crescents
just past the new moon of believing.
She easily could have told the truth
and let me make the wrong decision
for the right reason
but that would have been too easy.
The pop songs swagger through the sweet room
standards for the moment,
things we swear we'll never forget
we remember,
the familiar beat
so comforting
and as deadly as a clandestine shagging in the rain.
And about as fascinating.
What were we talking about?
Oh, yes, the death of innocence.

J. René Guerrero

Grandma's Gremlin

There is a small gremlin that lives next door to me,
Whenever I open wide my door he comes inside you see.
He whirls and twirls and knocks things down and makes a big old mess,
I find his hand prints everywhere but I really must confess.

My life would surely darken if he ever left,
without my tiny gremlin I know I'd be bereft.
Of all the joy he brings each day with his cheerful grin,
so I open wide the door to my heart and invite my Grandson in!

Naia S. M. Hodge

Only a Dad

Only a dad with a tired face, coming home from the daily race.
Bringing little of gold or fame, to show how well he played the game.
But glad in his heart that his own rejoice to see him come and to
hear his voice.

Only a dad with a brood of four, one in ten million men or more.
Plodding along in daily strife bearing the whips and scorns of life,
With never a whimper of pain or hate for the sake of those who
at home wait.

Only a dad neither rich nor proud merely one of the surging crowd,
Toiling, striving from day to day, faring whatever may come his way.
Silent whenever the harsh condemn, and bearing it all for the
love of them.

Only a dad, but he gave his all, to smooth the way for his children small.
Doing with courage stern and grim the deeds that his father did for him.
This is the line for him I pen, Only a Dad, but the best of men.

Lucinda Pendleton

Trapped in a Box: Your Life on Drugs

Trapped in a box, who's in there?
Trapped in a box, does anybody care?
In a lonely place, with no life to live,
With nothing more at all to give.

Trapped in a box, alone and away,
Trapped in a box, here to stay,
In a state of depression, forever again,
How to start over, how to begin.

Trapped in a box, to live such a hatred time,
Trapped in a box, you aren't feeling fine,
With nothing more to give or get,
You do nothing at all, but sit and fret.

Trapped in a box, can you see the way?
Trapped in a box, with such an awful day,
Your life is a bore,
With an un-open door.

Please don't do drugs, they will ruin your life,
your strength, and everything.

Katie Coulter

From a Mother's Heart

Giving birth to you daughter brought such joy to my life
I was a mother now, not just a woman and wife . . .

A beautiful baby girl, with the right amount of fingers and toes
I had feelings of joy and happiness only a mother knows . . .

I wasn't prepared for the hard work ahead
The feelings of joy and sadness I'd feel after I tucked you into bed . . .

But through the laughter and sorrow, the learning and growing
We both became individuals to each other worth knowing . . .

I wouldn't trade one moment that I've shared with you
My only regret is that there were too few . . .

I was so concerned with raising you right
I lost my perspective, I held on sometimes too tight . . .

Now with age and maturity a wiser woman am I
It seems by letting go I've become the apple of your eye . . .

The Lord has truly blessed me, the insights are clear
My world is much brighter because of you dear . . .

We as Mother and Daughter share a special Love
You will always be my most precious Gift from Above . . .

Suzanne Flaherty

Laura

Laura is a friend of mine
she puts me on the bus
She locks my wheelchair to the floor
never with a fuss.

She picks me up in the morning
and drops me off at school.
Then comes to get me in the noon
because she is never fooled.

There never is a dull moment
because she laughs and sings.
We put our chairs into gear
and do wheelies and other things.

No one knows the fun we have
while riding the yellow limousine.
Eating popcorn, cokes and candy bars
and reading magazines.

So if you have the chance to ride
don't hesitate to go.
But ask for Laura if you can
cause she's the one to know.

Jenna Patterson

Amanda Dances

For my granddaughter, Amanda Lynn Scull
Amanda dances
Happy and Free
"Watch me! Watch me!"
Coaxes she.

"Life," I plead—
"Let her soar,
And fly and float
And laugh. And more."

The song is her's
that Amanda sings
Of sun, of Spring
of toys and things

And, World, say not
"Behave! Be still!"
Sing out, dear child
My heart you fill.

Frances Spackey

New Life

It's been broken many times before
And it's not that it won't heal
but the mending it must go through
Is so far from being real

The pain inside is torture
And the memories are hell
I want to fall in love again
But I bet you couldn't tell

Remembering all the pain I felt
And all the tears I shed
Replaying words in my mind
Of all the things you said

But with each day comes new life
I won't be looking back
Not on you, nor I, nor anything
That took place where we were at

Once again I'll be happy
Without you being near
I was fine before I met you
And I'll be fine without you here

Michelle Chaffin

Tomorrow

Tomorrow's yesterday begins today,
So here's a little sump'um-sump'um I'd like to say.
If I were to live until tomorrow and get rid of today's weighty sorrow,
I should spread the day with happy cheers
And cry with the wish of joyful tears.
One week is linked with day to day as we humans go on about our way.
People wonder and think, why so many men are here to slay.
God loves us, loves us he does, why can't life be like it was
(before the original sin).
Jesus Christ while here on earth, showed all what life is worth.
To continue this way is to do God's will, till death,
From the start of birth.
Holy Spirit alive in we, sustaining our lives with ease.
Don't forget our father God and Jesus Christ, OK, pray,
Pray, pray . . . please, because yesterday is gone,
And today is here, I know what I'll do tomorrow.

Anthony E. Williamson, Sr.

The Grants of Dreaming

Dreams come in many forms to many peoples.
They come as day dreams, night dreams, induced dreams and fantasies.
Premonitions, nightmares, voices from the past.

Déjà vu and rendezvous, which dream is for you?
A sweet flowing meadow, a rose garden with happy children,
  or jewels galore?
Raging memories, wishing to be stored, come to taunt you once more.

Running from your dreams? Or do you restore?
Properly collecting your dreams—placing them forevermore?

Sweet dreams of friendship, and sunshine, or a tender love longed for.
Loved ones from heaven, reaching out with forewarn,
 are some of God's blessings,
For which We are adorned.

Although, some are believers, as others do not—
dreams do encompass one's life lot.
From a child's Christmas, to the Angels in Heaven,
dreams are around us, to enjoy, if we, choose to be given.

Shirley Jones Quintiliani

I Think

Every time I hear the word Cancer
I think of you.

I think of how even though Cancer curled up in your colon
and slept for three years, but you still managed to smile.

I think of all the could's, would's, but's, and if's.

I think of how someone so beautiful and so precious as you
could be taken out by anything.

Then I think if you are watching me from the amazing place with God.

Then I stop thinking, but know that you are in a far better place,
a place that now you curl up in and sleep.

A place that also has a name, Heaven.

Joseph Carvalho

Lost Love

You only lived for a month inside the body.
But you never really lived.
You never saw the sky, hear birds sing, or feel the warmth of the sun.
For you had died before your time.
I'm really sorry for that.
For I wanted to know and love you.
Hopefully one day we'll meet, so I can tell you how I feel.
I can also hold you like I never held anyone before.
So please wait for me.
For I'm your mother and I love you.

Brandy M. Graham

Rock Scissors Paper

As dumb as a rock.
Kick me, throw me, roll me.
Step on me and crush the giving soul in me.
How naive of me!

As dull as a scissor.
Use me, tease me, please me.
All of your lies, they cut me.
And put me in a drawer of useless things
Until you need me!

As flexible as paper.
Cover me, mold me, fold me.
Bend me and break me.
Tear my beating heart right out of me.
Rape me!

Denise K. Knudson

The Dionysian Sage

In Memory Of Ezra Pound
The Dionysian sage comes forth
Revelling—as if Bacchus—to piss
On the Apollonian fall.

Whoreson dogs of science.
Techno-diviners of the false magic.
"Miracle of science" blasphemers.

O', the air stinks grease—the steel beams
The constant rumbling, Divine night hidden
Stolen by arms of electric light.

Revel! Revel! Revel! Ezra!
As the turn comes near-boorish opposing
Doubt not the madness of your ancient heart.

Lee Ryan Gregory

Our First Christmas

Silver tinsel and shiny lights
Atop a tree of green
Are just another memory
While I share with you my life.

Christmas is a special time
To share with those we love
And we have something special
That has come from up above.

Our love grows only deeper
As each pretty light twinkles
While we share our special love
That was given by our keeper.

Sharon West

Poison

You strike a match
and one starts to burn.
Its curling smoke
twists toward the ceiling.
You place it between your lips
and breathe deeply.
Then you exhale with content
and the poison floats away.

You've had your joy.
You've had your fill.
You do not care
what it may kill.
As you put it out,
you look away.
And think not of who
you've hurt today.

Travis Briggs

Looking Back

Oh, to look around to see reflections of things that used to be,
Of days that seemed so long ago,
When time stood still and wouldn't go fast enough for my
youthful soul.
Why was I in such a hurry to reach life's solemn end?
Oh, to go back and cherish each precious moment given to me,
To adore life's every trial, every challenge, every triumph.
Oh, to go back,
To glow in perfection.
Oh, to go back.

Agnes Witt

The Wind

The wind blows softly, sweet, and gently.
A moan of peace; a calming effect blows across thy face.
Lay upon the hill at night, feel the grass and flowers beneath thy feet.
Gently, cooling breeze comes brushing by; sweeping thy moods
and sky clean and dry.
Fears, sadness, happiness good bye.
Play among the leaves and wind, a carefree life is ready to begin.
Sing a song of pure joy, let thy heart sing along with thy tune,
and thy mind.
Kiss the stars that lay upon the field good night as a harsh
breeze warns you that day is not that away.
Fall asleep upon the hill and let the wind carry your dreams away.

Melissa Dolan

My Need to Live

There's a dream which follows me as a phantom, once I believed
such a dream reachable; Promises which derive from deep down,
unwrapping my soul nakedly and displaying my confused
thoughts, a conscious that bears no shame . . . The living be
damned, bless my misery and heal, oh no, damn the living; my
need to live . . . From the ringing liberty, freedom called; my need
to live . . . hell reached above ground, the screaming voices
penetrated each dripping drop, my blood stood as a cloud,
dreams and promises from afar applaud as a dying child that
recognized a miracle; my need to live . . . The pride I once
embraced died with the shame I felt, yet from afar voices spoke;
"Freedom and love" like a God scented vision from a grave bed;
zombies for our future crippled emotionally and walking heard the
voice; my need to live . . . I share a ditch from morning till noon
refusing to perish, as a herb of zombies dragged me down, the
dream shared; once a bleeding child, now a grown man indistin-
guishable, the reality of life though cruel and sweet unclouded
my vision. Small dreams appeared, my soul weeps, the mind no
longer escapes while the heart renews itself; my need to live, my
need to survive, my need to love . . . That voice, the ringing bell,
oh liberty, calls from above my grave bed, freedom is near,
freedom walks, freedom or death till night . . .

Gabriel Hernandez (1952–1997)

Through a Child's Eyes

Looking through a child's eyes
they see destruction that seems to never end

Looking through a child's eyes there is no peace and tranquility therein

But yet there is hope as they face reality that Jesus Christ our
Lord and Savior is in the midst of saving thee

Seeing through a child's eyes that he makes his presence known
by waking us up every morning and allowing us to breath his fresh air.

But the awareness of our youth is not yet at hand still our Lord
and Savior holds out his unchanging hands

Wanting to assist us with our lives you see
knowing only his assistance can make a new life for thee

Then only through a child's eyes will he or she be able to see
great hope and peace with tranquility

Lynette R. Jones

The Civil War

One month and twelve days after
Lincoln was elected, he faced a disaster
He had to go to war; but this was no first, he had done this before
The war was bloody, and gruesome too,
it lasted four years, believe me it's true
The North had more guns, and more men,
but the South won battles again and again
Lincoln had a way with words, he gave a speech at Gettysburg
Freedom was his demand,
but Southern slave owners wouldn't obey his command
He wrote his plan and called it the Emancipation Proclamation
But hardly a single slave left their Southern plantation
It's not that they didn't want to be free, owners said they couldn't leave
Then along came General Grant, who was now in first command
They took over Gettysburg and Vicksburg too,
You would not believe what the South was about to do
Lee surrendered to Grant, and the war was done
Lincoln's dream finally happened, North and South were one
Then there were lots of hoorays and cheers,
The country had been waiting for this moment for four long years

Daniel Gray

Impermanence

An unheard fallen oak echoes more loudly than the sound of
one hand clapping, cragly, snagly elbows and fingers bent in
tired arthritic knots crushing cedarlings and small hickory trees
beneath a hollow, yet still sturdy trunk.

You hollow trunk, once a seedling, how long have you felt ill?
Seeing and hearing the changes of the ages, winged creatures
of the north and south, perhaps creatures which no longer rest
in cedar sweetened air of these rocky hills.

You listened to bright trills of cardinals red, salamander
slithering sounds through leaves like light water lapping
perhaps, to the sensitive ears of an oak on a quiet evening,
like the roan spotted white dog's tongue slapping water.

Saliva drips from the dog's mouth, old oak, slippery
like the mossed rocks, rain soaked and the muddy roots which
once anchored age to space, life to earth and back again.

Under the watchful eyes of the stars this oak predicted
changes in the heavens. This oak loved the red rocky clay
soil it ate from and dropped its red yellow green leaves,
feeding green leaves, arthritic arms, fingers, and feeding
other cragly snagly trees some years off.

Bruce Charles Antrim

Just Let Me Be Me

There is no doubt my poor body's wearing out, my bones, my
eyes, my heart
At times I feel like I'm falling apart.
I can't rush tomorrow or want yesterday back I live for today
For soon I could be going away
From 50 to 70 that's our golden years
They're supposed to be special that's what I hear
When you're young and married
You feel like this will last forever, things happen and we change
Sometimes we loose . . . sometimes we gain
I know I'm single and all alone, and you worry when I'm not home
Please don't make me feel guilty or turn your back on me
I'm enjoying life and trying to be me.
I want to do whatever I want to do
But family that does not mean that I don't love you
I've worked hard and long
I just want to enjoy my life before it's gone
I know what the doctors say
But the Lord will let me know when I'm going away.
Just let me have love, joy and laughter
But isn't that what we are all after?

Mary Bratton

Untitled

Sympathy is not what it seems.
Sympathy is not what everyone thinks.
Many people believe that sympathy is when you help someone.
But in reality it is not. All it is, all you're saying is
"I feel sorry for you. I am glad that it didn't happen to me"
Sure you may believe that you are helping and who knows, you may be,
But I can see through your charade. I want nobody's sympathy.
I do not need the aggravation and the false hopes it brings.
I need not the sorrow and sympathy of those around me.
I need not the temptation of false security that it brings.
I do not need to know that other people are judging themselves
Upon me and my problems.
I do not need to know that they are laughing behind my back.
I can see what it really is.
I know exactly what sympathy really means
And why I need to stay away from it.
Sympathy is just another word for "caring."
I wish to have no part in it.

    Elisabeth Fesi

Venus of Simple Miracles

Circumstance: as there were seven restless veils
There were ten stars and ten candles before the dance
I watched as signal, outside the window, as if you rent me
I will not die but submit, others sought the cars parked
Sauntering on the pavement, with different human urges
A living lie, taut and constricted like the hand that
Holds a foreign coin.

Where she lived and why she danced is unknown,
She danced for cigarettes from the underworld
In the science of seduction, hanging on tight,
Scratching the constellatory roof with rhythms of the zodiac.
Penultimate, before crawling into the abyss, she showed all
A sirocco in the trade winds that brought a sudden streak of recovery.
Penultimate: where the stick man bounces in beggar's slang,
Where the cusp in rags is defined as something in me
That life was not denied in the dance that is the flag and ticket.

    Michael Igoe

Untitled

If I could embrace you all together, then lead you to the oceans
edge, I would whisper the meaning of a wave in your ears.
For I see each wave as a human life, molded and shaped differently,
each there for it's own purpose, to leave its markings on this
earth. Every wave has a beginning and must come to an end, as
life itself. Some come in mellowness and leave with hardly a trace.
Others are overwhelming and leave great markings in the sands.
It moves us in a way no other wave can and when we look at each other
as these grains of sand we know it has touched us.

His wave has come to an end. But looking out over the ocean,
we know he's been with us, for mist of him are everywhere to be
felt and the music coming from this great ocean is of him.

    Carol Ann Bush

The Fireside Chats of Roosevelt

The Fireside Chats of Roosevelt lent comfort to a weary people.
His talks helped soothe anxieties giving hope as tall as a steeple.
His ideas of pride in man's labor coupled with Hopkins' help, it's true,
Gave impetus to recovery after a depression never again to renew.
The hardships and struggles of our people, undeserved and sad,
Were enough to make depressed, lost men sometimes go mad.
Through losing farms, home, stock and money
Some patient people bided their time, still others cried,
Roosevelt's sympathy and understanding formed plans that he'd abide.
Giving faith to our people who were sadly spent.
He raised their focus on a new deal showing many the way as they went
To work on several projects assisting people in our great land
Fulfilling the God given destiny
To be a great nation in command.

    Elsie Mae Lukens

Rain From My Tears of Love

As the sun was just entering out of its deep slumber.
I gasped at the beauty of your lips,
as the sun gently grazed its fingers across them.
I noticed the creation of water. I saw your eyes, then the ocean.
The skin of your body exposed and defenseless,
pure and adorned by thought.
You are my world, and I evolved from you. . . .

I lay beside you only to be greeted with a kiss.
The softness of your lips, like walking on white golden sands,
sending shivers of warmth all over my body
as the waves rush through my toes.
Music came to my ears. The harmony of your voice,
whispering the words of love. I felt passion overcome me swiftly.
I took you gently into my arms, and like that of your skin
picturing the smoothness of rose petals.
I began to mold the land with my hands.
Admired and overwhelmed by your creation,
as the ground began to shake.
With the heat so intense inside me,
it sears my heart into beating flesh once again.

    William P. McQuillan II

Falling From Grace

Angels' voices are silenced, because we do not listen.
Their breath is wasted on most of us.
We all have visions of our future world,
but if we do not realize our mistakes and change,
All roads lead to our destruction.
Take a moment out of life and listen to the sound of lost
and tormented souls crying out in agony.
We think that our future is radiant,
but genuine goodness is so exotic in our everyday lives
that we are beginning to not notice
that the very fabric of what makes us all human is beginning to fade.
We all have dreams and we all have wishes that drive us from within.
Hunger is good, if it makes you strive to relinquish it,
but becomes twisted when greed enters your soul.
We fight each other and cause horrible pain with no remorse.
We are not listening!
If we listen, things can change.
If we listen, things can get better.
If we listen we can survive together.
If we listen . . . but for the time being, Angels cry.

    Shawn Hamlet

And Then It All Changed

Dreams I had many. When I spoke of them they laughed.
Somehow you can't lie to yourself, I know I've tried.
Another day goes by and the garage still echoes and re-echoes
with the sounds of my escape.
Just because the words lost their meaning in a fit of obscurity
Doesn't mean I can't yell.
Just because we're only here to fail doesn't mean we can't try.
If it keeps me going the downfall will be uplifting.
Because in a field of roses you can't run without getting cut.
Maybe it'll be okay; sure—whatever—you know.
The angels sing and schools bells ring and things don't seem so bad.
The sun sets low and clouds below know the night has come.
Locked in bed the fears you dread melt instead
   to dreams of pure white hope.
Looking back I remember
Everything was perfect
Everything was fine
Everything was there for me
And then it all changed

    Justin Sorg

My Hen

Full of life, my glorious hen, a Rhode Island Red in her prime
Strides out of her coop one sunlit spring Sunday morn—
I elect not to go to church
But to rake our yard full of winter debris
Friends walk by the house, I go to greet them, we talk
Perhaps hearing my voice, my chick wonders from her flock
To the field, toward me, pecking gently, minding her own business
While we banter amiably among ourselves, the neighbors and I, catching up
An unknown dog jumps on her—my friend hollers, "The dog!"
Instantly, I run to her, lovely red feathers everywhere cover early green grass
She comes to me, slightly wobbly but upright, dazed I pick her up
Blood streams from a gaping hole in her side
It rolls warm and harrowing over my comforting arm to the ground below
I gaze upon her knowing full well that though she looks all right
Her face perfectly normal, her comb high, eyes alert
She lives preciously now between life and death
I take her to the barn, our temple upon this earth, where, one minute later
In the simple solitude of soft hay, without fanfare,
She convulses three times and is dead.

George Delany

Allison

My dear sweet newborn Allison, you were never given a chance;
To wear ribbons in your long black hair and twirl, and prance, and dance.

You really would have loved us, good parents we would be;
How I pain at the thought, that I cannot hold you close to me.

I question if there is a God, who would allow such grief and pain;
Or if I ever really will, see you once again.

Is life really that unfair—to take you away without a care?
Is life really that indiscriminate—that our deaths are any second imminent?

I close my eyes and see your pink mouth, baby fingers, and ballerina legs;
Time will heal, so they say, but still my broken heart begs.

At the strangest times, you haunt me. It is an element of surprise.
Because I never know when it's going to hit me; what form or what disguise.

Your struggle for life was defeated;
You, me, the world, we all were cheated.

So all I have are sweet thoughts of what could have been;
And deep in my heart, I know, I will never see you again.

Mary Ann MacAfee

Braced Fastened Inextricably Linked

My sanity is a girlfriend I have cheated on with the mysterious and
Unnatural, at night I keep a loaded gun under my pillow while I sleep
Afraid of the darkness and anxious to see the night creep away from the
Advance of day, afraid that if anything confronted me it would not fear a
Weapon made by the hands of man

I wanted something different than what I have, something to make me happy
Something to make the machinations of my brain rust and cease to turn
something that tastes like forgetfulness and death mixed together without
the aftertaste of loneliness

Born to suffer bemoan be sick with life I never asked for or wanted born
live died here on this very spot where the gravestone makes a very small
shadow, till the evening when the shadow grows and encompasses the entire
World in a black blanket where I have transgressed here there everywhere.

Blessed are those who have what I have not, peace love meekness
Satisfaction humbleness happiness salvation these things I lack and have
Forsaken, mention me no more in your greetings salutations brief hellos

Turn away unburden me from the penalties tributes obligations I must
Make a social creature, unmake me responsible for anyone's jubilance or
tears, make me a rock in a forest that no one ever notices existing for a
Million, billion, trillion years and no thought to eternity, I want that.

Sherman L. Mayle III

Daughter to Father

I make a difference in this world,
If only you could see,
I don't need much, but I know I need you,
So won't you be here for me.

I made my point nice, and clear,
Now I can only hope you can hear,
As I pray for you to love me too.

I used to see you everyday, but now you drifted far away,
You weren't just my father, but my best friend in heart,
You never made me last, you always made me start.

Now season's changed,
You moved away, and my life went on from day to day.
You didn't call or even write,
You just left that gloomy night.

It hurt to see you leave and go so far away,
But even through this misery,
Your loving daughter I will stay.

Kelly Schneider

This I Understand

A total confusion lays upon your heart.
Not knowing where to go or what to decide,
This I understand.

Trapped in a large corner
Not knowing which way to go.
You feel for two and can't seem to choose,
This I understand.

The sweet person you are
Not wanting to hurt anyone
Or to be hurt yourself leaves you blind to the truth,
This I understand.

You say you love me and trust me,
But yet you're still confused.
Even though I'm in your heart
You still partly feel for her,
This I understand.

The gentle soul you bare and the heart of gold you share
Is what makes me care for you so much,
That I could never hurt you,
This you should understand!

Christy Blackburn

Memories in My Heart

On the early morn of a summer day
Grandma's soft voice awakens me
Reminding me it's another summer day
My eyes open to grandma's loving smile
Memories in my heart, memories in my heart

I hear the musical sound of birds everywhere
As I smell the sweet fragrance of grandma's flowers
Leaves rustling with the soft breeze
And the sun shining so bright in the morn
Memories in my heart, memories in my heart

Another summer day awaits me
My heart starts to sing as I burst out of bed
To greet the early morn of another summer day
And embrace my loving grandma
Memories in my heart, memories in my heart

Grandma I love you, Grandma I love you
For being there every summer morning
Your smile is like the sunshine
Your voice filled with kindness
Memories in my heart, memories in my heart

Patricia Ellabelle Mae Yomes

The Wind

Sitting here in between nowhere and destiny
I talk to the wind
As she runs her fingers through my hair
And whispers the secrets of the places she's been; sitting here,
My pain becomes another secret
For the wind to whisper to somebody
Chambers of pain flow from my eyes
Straight from my heart
These are my messengers to the world
That this heart is alone
Each day walks right by me never stopping
Each day passed never even glancing
You see, the wind is my only friend.
But even the wind can neglect me
Even now, she is still
As today walks by, a child follows him
Today's child is hope, she stops to kiss me.
A secret the wind won't have to carry from me.

Frank Hernandez

Friends

You tell me your secrets and your fears
When you're hurt inside you show me your tears
You confide in me with all of your dreams
And I help you out with most of your schemes
We share the gift of laughter and hope
And when things go wrong we learn how to cope
We're such good friends that I can read you like a book
And I've learn you have faults that I can now overlook
We talk about of futures and what we will be
I wish the best for you and you wish the best for me
One day we'll look back and remember the adventures we shared
And I'll always remember just how much you cared
The fears will be forgotten and the tears will be dried
And neither one of us will remember all the times we cried
We'll laugh about the past and our mistakes
And we'll even look back at our dreaded first dates
And if ever something should break us apart
Remember this best friend you'll always be in my heart

Veronica De Casas

To Tie a Knot

When I saw the little girl alone outside my door, I took just a minute to
stop and ask her to tie her shoe. She looked at me and gave me a sweet
little smile. "OK" she said, "but I don't know how." I showed her once,
and then she bent down and untied the shoe, preceding to tie it twice,
two different ways. I showed her then how to knot the shoelace. I made a
new friend, and she got a little bit of recognition and feeling of accom-
plishment. Or, was it that she wanted a little bit of attention that she
didn't get at home? Talecia was a beautiful little black girl. What a little
sweetheart! She said she was a friend of Danny's and that she knew he
had lots of friends. When you touch the lives of these little adults they
tend not to forget your special moment with them. They are a big part of
making America be an equal, non-prejudicial, fun place to live. Children
make life worth living.

Diana M. Billadeau

The Journey

You start at the beginning, as you do all the time
The road is never easy, it twists, and turns, and winds
You must continue on, if you hope to achieve
The goal which you are seeking, all you have to do is believe
Once you've reached the halfway point, your journey is almost complete

Your confidence should be building up,
for you have almost accomplished your feat
You should strive on, you are almost there, don't give up the fight
If you give up now, you'll never forget it,
you won't get to sleep at night
When you've made it to the end, you should feel that you have won
But it is the first of many journeys, the next has just begun

Marcus Purcell

Only You

You are the sun, which shines in my face.
You are the gold in my hair.
You are the softness, I feel on my skin.
You are taste, on my lips,
and you are the only to share.
For you are the man, I dream sweet dreams of.
And you are the man, whom will share,
The kindness, and sweetness, and ever
So deep, the love that I have is to keep.

Peggy Baker

Rain

What is rain? Is it the tears
Of the Lord when he is in pain?
Or is it the clouds telling us to be
Fair, because we are polluting their air?
Or maybe it is the answers of peoples prayers
When they are in a drought. Then when the rain
Comes they have one less doubt
What is rain?
Rain is tricky, when you are picky.
One who says there is always too much,
Or there is never enough, is a person
Who needs to be taught a life long lesson.
What is rain?
Rain is a gift. Rain is a privilege.
Be happy with what you get,
And don't abuse it.

Heather A. Beier

The Old Man's Music

The old man is playing the guitar
Tara trim trim tar, tara trim trim tar.

Spring is back again
After the cold winter rains.
Is it the sound of his guitar?
Tara trim trim tar, tara trim trim tar.

There is joy, there is sorrow, today and tomorrow,
Amidst sickness and health, poverty and wealth.
There is day, there is night,
Darkness follows the light.
We can be civil, we can be rude,
Sometimes evil, sometimes good.
Life is full of contrast
Tara trim trim tar, tara trim trim tar.
These are the notes of his guitar.

Pain and pleasure, these are the measures,
Life and death, form the essence of its breath,
Of the music the old man is playing on his guitar.
Tara trim trim tar, tara trim trim tar.

Kalyani Choudhury

The Bench

I remember the Bench
Where I sat, while waiting for the Bus
Soon someone appeared
There was a smile, and a few words were said
And life seemed so tender and warm
Now I stared alone, and the silence in deep
For I dare not smile or speak for fear what anger
It might bring.
Gone is the smile
Gone is the Bench
I sit alone, and I mourn for that piece of humanity
That was so tender and warm
The Bench is gone
Yes, gone forever more.

Helen Sharron

Lost Child

A Lost Child, is a never ending heartache,
A Lost Child, is an empty void that can not be filled or understood.
A Lost Child is a tear in your eye, and a knot in stomach that will not ease;
Why is a Child Lost the reasons are many but too insignificant to matter.

A Lost Child is joyous laughter drowned out by the hideous sounds of silence.
I know oh to well of the heartbreak and pain of a Lost Child,
for you see the Lost Child I speak of is mine.

　　Allan Michael Quirk

The Rose in You

When I Look at this rose in front of me I see the women I fell in love with.
When I smell this rose I can smell the wonderful fragrance of you.
When I caress this rose I feel like caressing your face with my hand.
When I kiss this rose I feel like I'm kissing the soft texture of your lips against mine.
When I walk with this rose I'm walking with a graceful love
When I hold this rose I'm holding the love of my life.
When I care for this rose I care for you from deep inside my heart.
When I love this rose I love the passion that flow's between you and me.
When the moon shines on this rose it shines on you like a light from an angel.
When I look back at this gorgeous rose I realize that the one gorgeous rose is you.

　　Shamika Magee

My Life Is a Poem

Here's a short, descriptive story,
About my life and its long years of glory.
Gravity controls my flaccid bod,
what once was firm is now soft and flawed
I have a cadre of docs, medicinal talks,
childhood diseases including the Pox.
My mind's sorta fuzzy, my head's full of rocks.
I take what life gives me, the good and the knocks.
"Que sera sera" explains it all. Some folks yell "Disaster!"
My life's been a ball.
I curse at the bad news that I'm growing so old
Then I realize my good news is growing old, not cold.
Like the dentist I've visited for ten years or more,
The going's the bad news, the good is having teeth to bore.
My hubby and I have passed fifty years since we wed.
Two boys joined our household, gray hairs top my head.
Three grandkids are carrying on our good name.
They're exceptionally handsome, and subject to fame.
So help me celebrate this long, happy life,
Artist, teacher, mother, athlete and wife.

　　Esther Mahannah

Upon Returning From the Graveyard

Mourning is in the air, pain is always there
Those who've borne their mortal wound force you on their graves to care
That down beneath in coffins hither
All but bones that rot and wither
And all remains of one's toil, trauma, and despair

Ethereal lives with no hope, leaving those who have to cope
Minds whose memories fade like a burning rope
Eternal comfort their souls sought
A preexistent joyful thought
But 'tis nothing but a river lying in the desert taupe

A realm of Nothing is where they are bound, an idea chillingly profound
For the greatest thinker ever born cannot be in blackness drowned
The mind needs a resting place
It cannot comprehend its eternal waste
Its destiny of empty room where never will it hear a sound

Nor ever will it dream a dream, smell a rose, nor feel a stream
Feel the heavens solar warmth nor see its ultraviolet gleam
Nor ever experience again
For all life ends in vain
The Eternal Lie is not; what be is nothing's empty theme

　　Dan Tierney

Mom

You work two jobs everyday;
One at home, the other at work,
Both thankless with little pay,
But somehow, you make it work.

To you I am always thankful:
You make sure my underwear is clean.
You find "the missing sock"—I'm so forgetful.
I never left the table without eating something green.

So thank you for all that you have done,
And all that you will do.
Raising me is surely tons of fun,
I know I will always love you.

　　Julie Smith

The Handshake

She is reaching out to me—
should I take this gnarled,
twisted, oversized hand?
My hand may be crushed in its grip.
A sense of panic makes me want to pull back
as her hand slips into mine.
At the moment of contact,
I am surprised at the smooth softness of her touch.
A thought flashes through my mind,
"Yes—that's it her hand feels
so like that of my Mother."
I am reluctant to let go,
for fear that this moment will pass.
Although she withdraws her hand,
I know the tenderness of her touch
will stay with me.

　　Jean A. B. Robertson

The Park Bench Crazies

We sat on the park bench
arms crossed
hands gripped above our elbows
staring stupefied
as though mesmerized by flame.

A man was positioning catatonics
for a game of human croquet.

"Pwaying fwoo," laughed one of the impatient
mongoloids
whacking a soccer ball with a large stick
against the legs of a disheveled
frozen woman in her twenties.

"That's what happens sometimes,"
remarked the young man seated beside me.

I grimaced
blinked
and swallowed,
then took
rapid shallow breaths
until I fainted.

　　Tierre Avery

For All We Have

Parallel are our lives as we long for their bonding.
Unknowing whether they could ever be.
But cherished is the borrowed time, reminding.
Dismiss it not for what we cannot see.
For all we have—
Brief moments of pleasure,
Suspended in time,
Remembered forever,
Treasured in passing.

　　Jenny O. Crupper

Mother's Hyacinths

Brightly colored eggs, baskets filled with chocolate bunnies and jelly beans.
Adorned our Easter table year after year, as long as we were able.
And oh, the centerpiece, must always be a hyacinth by every means.
'Cause it just wouldn't be Easter, Mom said, without its sweet scents encircling the table.

It didn't matter what the shade—pink, purple or white.
Dad or I presented Mom each year with this aromatic delight.

But Dad went to be with God two years ago and Mom joined him there last year.
For Mom lost her forty-four year long partner and it was too much for her to bear.

Easter came and went this year, and I moved far, far away.
And out of the clear blue, a marvelous sight graced my new driveway.
A fresh, purple hyacinth in full bloom did I see.
'Twas a sign from dear Mom, that she would always be with me.

Barbara Balogh

ODE   TO   THE   WASTELAND

Empty.   Silent.   Still.
    EMPTY: as a dish licked clean.
      SILENT: with quietness so complete it does not even hear
            Speech, nor Sound, nor Word, WORD, Word, word, word—
      STILL: so motionless that the very wind, not being a part thereof,
                  but, driving dust and tumbleweed before,
                  hurries on, lest it too stiffen and grow still.

THE DESERT: So empty!   So silent!   So motionless and still!

O barren waste: What stories can you tell?   Of cataclysms vast and fierce;
Of cataracts and lava flows, Flaming mountain and the deluge roar;

Of forests green, and grassy plains; Of pounding hooves and migrant herds.

Of homes, where play and work and happiness lived on,
And child, and love, and pleasure: each was there.

    Now all have passed,   And you alone remain;
            Yet tell us naught;   Nor even our dreams.
    O Desert Bleak: I like you much!   But it seems you do not care;
So now I too must go, and leave you there alone—there alone—alone—

Empty.

Silent.

Still.

Norman L. MacLeod Jr.

Sweet Kisses of Summer

The slow, majestic rising of the morning sun spills its glorious rays over
Millions of tiny dewdrops, left behind by the cool summer night now ended.
The glory of the sun covers the bright green grass,
Each minute dewdrop sending their bright sparkle throughout the prairie.

Carefree days of ponytails and shorts
And wisps of hair lining the laughing faces of small children.
Cool, crisp glasses of real, ice cold lemonade held tightly
In their delicate hands turned golden brown by the sun's bright rays.

The clear, blue sparkle of the old backyard pond
Comes alive with anticipation and seemingly becomes a magical place
As it turns into a world filled with handfuls of smiling faces
And countless memories by the old twine rope forever swinging
Over the water, sending over a million laughing children
Splashing to the sparkling water below.

Running barefoot through a rainbow of brilliant colors,
The soft moss of the ground squishes through my toes.
Millions of wildflowers dot the earth and rolling plains
As the soft breeze of the afternoon sends them rolling in the sun
And blows a cascade of golden hair around my sun-kissed shoulders
And gently licks the sweat off my brow.

Konni Haverman

Lifescape

She floated in on air spun wings
and offered me a feast of kings.
I opened my heart with my arms
and said, "Come in and stay awhile."
She took me instead to float on promises
of gossamer airships at dizzying heights.
With hypnotic ease
my life was telescoped in gauzy clouds
and I, encased in the womb of comfort,
faded into oblivion.
Until, with jagged jolts of stormy wakefulness,
I found myself at the door of death,
arms empty and heart wanting.
Gossamer was gone.

Marlene Peoples

Precious Life

There are times in our life,
When darkness surrounds us.
We feel like we are falling down a deep well,
And no one will be able to pull us out.
But the next thing you know,
You feel a strong hand pushing from behind.
As if to lift us towards a brighter day
And when it does we need to embrace it,
As though we embrace a lover.
Holding on tight and praying it won't slip away.
For each precious moment of life is a gift,
And should be treated as such.
Therefore I will open my arms,
And wrap them around it,
And hold on to this precious life.

Jamie L. Brower

In God's Hands

The skies have turned sullen gray
Ever since the Lord has taken you away,
For the angels have started calling,
And our tears of pain are falling,
But deep in our aching hearts
We will never be very far apart,
For your memory will always beam bright
Within each and every one of us all through the night,
For you will be missed and you are dearly loved
For now you are in the heavens way up above.
I know the Lord has taken you for His very own
So you will never be standing there all alone
For He will be there to guide you through His open land
Now He is waiting for you to take His extended hand.

Sharon Sullivan

Cloe

I have a dog who is as black as night.
When she begs she looks at me
With adorable
But sad brown eyes.

When I'm sad or feeling sick
She cheers me up with a tender lick.
She's always there to comfort me.
Cloe Patricia Patre Marie.

Sometimes she gets me so frustrated that I yell.
Other times I grab her otter-shaped tail
(Playing, of course.
Except when she's barking at a horse.)

I would never sell her:
No!
She's my precious puppy,
Cloe.

Matthan S. Staerkel

GulfWar

I scan the faces of these young men going off to war
Just as I've looked for you on playgrounds, school yards and playing fields
For thirty years. I've searched for that three-day-old face, matured.
Years of yearning for some sign of you.
It is different now. I feel my heart gripped by an icy hand.
Will I feel a psychic bond break if you die there in the sand?
Will I search for you no more?
Joyce W. Miller

Broken Promises

As long as the grass grows of the waters runs was
Promised to my Indian people concerning our native land;
But as history shows and you know our land was taken away from us;
We were herded like cattle to the slaughter and placed on God-forsaken
Reservation to scratch out an existence;
The land we now live on is harsh and bitter not green
And fertile as it was promised to us; our souls and loins cry out to be
Free to roam our native lands like our fathers before us;
To ride the green valleys, plains and wooded land upon our painted ponies;
To hunt the great elk, deer, and buffalo;
To chase the wind that blows across the great river waters in our canoes;
To gaze into a starlit night around the great campfire;
To sleep in peace in our teepees or adobe dwellings;
To walk proud upon the earth among all men
Without fear of death or imprisonment;
To be free again to dwell upon our fathers land
In peace with God and nature;
But no more as long as the grass grows or the waters run shall we see that
day when we can live as a people, seen as a people, and be treated
As a people upon our native land.
Al Harven

Addiction in Youth

Abandoned by childhood, possessing no wisdom of age, he's assaulted!
Waves of self doubt lap ceaselessly, eroding his, as yet unset,
pylons of confidence.
Threatening to expose his weakness.

Ah! One true friend soothes the pain.
Together, allies, they proclaim his foundations firm.
Trusted companion taken to the very heart in dark corners.
Sacred ritual.
Dancing merrily, leading him down paths of comfort.

An honored guest, invited, welcome, time makes a permanent lodger.
Controlling his mind, consuming his heart.
Before fades, all but forgotten.
Choice now beyond his grasp,
he continues the hypnotic dance to near exhaustion.

Trapped, terrified, dying!
Laurie G. Barnhart

Voice in the Wind

He is like a wild stallion, standing proud and running free.
Only the voice in the wind knows he.
In time of quiet, a loving heart he gives, in his own time and at his own pace.
And then I see the voice in the wind call upon his face.

It's like "desperado" who can't stay with one true love.
He pushes hard away, he's afraid of love, and to only once be true.

The voice in the wind calls again and his thoughts turn only to running free.

It takes time for me to get my balance once again, to this Desperado's freedom.
Then he wonders back, I knowing it's only for a short time be.

The voice in the wind calls again and that look in his eyes to roam and be free.

My heart stops, only to start again and remember the voice in the wind calls again.
No place to be still for him in this life, where my love can reach out to him.

The voice in the wind is stronger than any love could be.
That lonely, lonely voice in the wind calls again.
Danelle Whitson

Life

First the seed,
Then the tiny stem—
A little flower bud emerges.
It opens up.

It reaches for the sunlight,
But the tall trees stubbornly grab it all away.
The little flower is sad.
It wilts and dies.

First the seeds,
Soon the vines are quickly creeping,
Creeping up the trunks of the trees
And grasping firmly on the way.

The trees reach for the sunlight,
But the vines steal it all from their veins.
The trees fight fiercely, but are afraid.
Slowly, painfully, they die.

A new flower forms and reaches for the sunlight.
It slowly drinks the kind warmth.
The flower is strong.
The flower is life.
Jennifer Smith

Lonely

Not a day goes by
Without me asking why
I don't have a girlfriend

What can it be
That they don't see in me?

Is it my silence
Due to shyness?

Or can it be the fact
It is in a weird way that I act?

The answers to these questions
May never be found.
Like a hidden treasure buried deep in the ground.

Was I predestined to be lonely
And never meet her, my one and only?

Or has she passed me by
Like a roaming stranger, without saying, hi!

I say to you once again . . .

Not a day goes by
Without me asking why
I don't have a girlfriend
Veda Ruiz Jr.

Disillusioned

Silently moving inward
A place often forgotten
Doubt, confusion, fear
Erratic thoughts washing throughout
The hour, the moment,
Standing still unfulfilled
A distant heart yearning for discovery
Slowly embracing the need for change
Realization of the rainbow beyond
Cautiously pursuing the light within
Transcending over the shadows of time
Learning to listen to the depths of the heart
Approaching the answer within
Grasping for eternal peace
Shannon Vogel

No Longer

My soul has died I am no longer here,
everyone around me are fading memories.
I feel no pain no hate and no anger,
I can no longer feel my empty tears as they fall down from these eyes
that have seen too much to mention.
Just as this heart that has felt to much to explain,
I no longer feel the need for happiness because it always seems to fade into sadness.
No longer do I feel the need to fall in love because that too goes away,
just as the sunlight fades into the darkness of the moon.
No longer will my face form a smile because for every smile there follows a frown,
no longer do I feel the need to see loved ones because they all will leave one day.
But I have already left so I have become "no longer."

Michelle Ead

The Tree You See

Don't ask me to explain why,
all the trees are condemned to die.
Don't rub your eyes or gasp your breath,
this air pollution will bring on death.
Don't frown at the water you taste,
because burning it can't remove the waste.
It's up to us, yes you and me, to be responsible for all we see.
Our journey began upon that first step,
along life's path we are hurriedly swept.
At different times we find a fork in the road,
until it's traveled we won't know the load.
Finding the path which is true, depends on what's important to you.
The trees, the air, the water you see, is what brings on life's diversity.
The trees do more than we think, without them the level of air would sink.
Without air there could be no evaporation,
no rain would mean and end to vegetation.
One by one the weak would die,
starvation would be the reason why.
In the end we would blame God for the theft,
because how could we blame the only man left.

Larry A. Genson

The Sound of Her Voice

It getting worse, a little worse just about everyday,
The strangest malady I've ever known—it's not a disease,
not contagious in the least—
And yet, it gets worse for me with each passing day.

I suppose there's a cure, but if I am cured,
I'm really afraid I'd be worse off than before.
The sound of her voice fills me with joy and exhilaration,
Hearing her voice once each day is no longer enough,
And twice a day just makes it much worse,
Leaving me wanting to hear her ever more.
I doubt if hearing her every night and day,
would I eventually find myself happily satiated.

It's getting to where I'm hearing her voice when there's none to be heard,
Then the awakening, the disappointment from loss of the joy, the exhilaration.

I must try for a cure, I really must,
I must wean myself away from dependency upon her voice,

I'll start tomorrow . . . well, perhaps not tomorrow, but the tomorrow after.
I must wean myself away, I really must, or face the reality . . . of insanity.

Tomorrow, I'll start.
Well, at least soon after, maybe the day after I'll start?

Frank D. Dunkel

Seize My Sanity

Dear darkness of midnight,
Your passionate power owns my envy
as a friend, not as your enemy.
Those taunting streaks of moonlight,
Which haunt with such spellbinding spite
victimize virgin visions
in the dead silence of fright.
Their appealing adaptations
have polluted my subversive sight
awake I . . . incoherently scrawl,
from soul to paper as my emotions fall,
the edge of my eye spies
your sly streaks crawl . . .
Reaching out to seize my sanity
stretching across
my bare bedroom wall . . .

Keith Anthony Francese

I Will Try Again Dear God

I pray dear God my soul you'll keep
while in your loving arms I sleep

Forgive the things I did today
when from your glorious path
I'd stray

And as I slumber through the night
please take my hand and hold it tight

And when I wake to a bright new morn
I will try again dear God
to be the person you would hope of me

Amen

Janet Jacobson

Colors

Each one of us has colors
That we harbor deep down within.
So why are you obsessing
About the colors of our skin?
Red is the color of rage,
In which we all have seen.
And envy is the lovely color
By which we all call green.
Not one of us is free from fear,
This one is known as yellow.
And even on the coldest day
I've seen you turn blue, dear fellow.
So all of you filled so full of hate
And titled as a racist,
All you really do is show
How much that you disgrace us.

Shelley Brockish

grey-green skies

grey-green skies and honey dives
bungalo spreads and spider webs
neon sights, fascist bites
traffic fights and warm warm nights.

Peruvian devils, sunfish speckles,
iridescent poppies and lollipop mommies,
Sad leap tides, silken sun shines,
crocagators wallow in wild marshmallow.

Yellow-painted monks and spiritual healers
dancing to the Sugarfoot Reelers
Saving grace with plasticoid lace
diesel trains without no pain.

Sad leap tides and Friday's sky
Ham sandwiches with mustard and rye
Yellow bluebonnets and a-rhythmic sonnets
Sing are a favorite of my fewest things.

S. George Miller

Trapped Here

When you think you're there,
You are actually trapped here
to stay,
away,
from there.
My life isn't very clear,
my family isn't anywhere near,
they're there not here.
Now you see how clear,
it is here?

Heather Erickson

Kicking the Stone

Walking along the road was I
Ambling along was I
At twelve years old
I was beginning an adventure
measured by one lifetime

Look at that nice stone
let me kick it
Let this little stone be my companion
through this life long adventure

I kick the stone
It goes askew
I must break my stride to retrieve it
Let me break my stride

What does this life long adventure
have in store for me
what coat shall clothe me along the way
what sense of excitement stirs in me
as I kick the friendly stone along

Stick with me little stone
we shall experience it together

Raymond Messina

Nature

You shall ask
Why do birds fly
And I will tell you
So they can be free
You shall ask
Why do beavers build dams
And I will tell you
So they have protection
You shall ask
Why do bees dance
And I will tell you
Because they are happy
You shall ask
Why do buffalo roam
And I will tell you
Because they have no home
You shall ask
Why are animals free
And I will tell you
Because that was the way it was meant to be

Melissa Gajda

Mask

A man
Steady foot and strong
Broad shoulders and weathered hands
Solid arms and thick necked
A virile look in his eyes
Lips like steel, in a firm straight line
Masculinity, he wears it like a mask
A mask which falls away
At the mention of his lover's name
And tenderness shows through

Jennifer Atkinson

Two Hundred Thousand Steps

A hundred thousand times I stood
A hundred thousand times I fell
A hundred thousand steps I gained
A hundred thousand steps I remained

A single step I make
A spiral when I fall

Two hundred thousand steps in all
Wishing I would fall
Poor, lifeless, there they lay
Watching in dismay

Jesus BenHur R. Torres

World of Hate

There's no hope left
Nothing worth believing in
We have finally realized
That this is a reality
All our dreams are now gone
Only the pain remains
The hate, the fear
That's all that's here

A world of hate
Has left us here
The love we once knew
Has long disappeared
All the feeling has faded away
Replaced by this emptiness
This emptiness so unreal

This world full of confusion
Answers deep within
Too late, for everything's gone
It disappeared in a world of hate

Ashley Wagner

The More I Listen to Men

When the revolution of evolution
Pushes a mans' instinct past
The continual degradation,
And pollution,
Of a woman's soul,

When a man can care about children
Before he has his own.
(Not caving to peer-pressure
Amongst brothers to disown,)

When a man can say it,
And mean it,
And make it happen,
Then will we be whole.

Time waits for no man.
Distances damage
Relationships beyond repair.
The 'Y' chromosome needs
A revolution,
Till then,
We're not going anywhere.

J. Gates

Untitled

By day she is a queen
By night she is every mans dream
So much of a beauty
So delicate of hand
Yet she is more
Than just a mere drop of water
Upon the lips of every thirsty man!

Ronald L. Ghiotto

Cloudy Days

The rain has come
the end is near
Your voice is quiet
never more to hear
We walked and loved
for so many years
Now I walk alone
In a field of tears
By your stone I stand
My head full of pain
Wondering how much
more of this
I can withstand
my head I must clear
Before my poor heart can mend
I hope this happens
before I end it my friend

Gary Lewis

Tomorrow

My mind is clear
My mind is bright
Just before the morning light

I look around and all I see
Is nothing but humanity

I know not why I understand
Why God loves every man.

Tammy L. Sorrell

War

It happened once, so long ago,
An ancient battle, a vicious foe.
It happened once without consent,
For the lives it must have spent.

And now it happens once again,
Same old battle, same old den.
And now it comes, again repeating,
For the lives it is depleting.

And it will happen yet again,
That very battle, that very sin.
And repeated, yet once more,
Like the words of forgotten lore.

Robert A. Buchanan

Jimmy

Hello, you're born,
with blue-grey eyes
so cloudy,
just like threatening skies.

If only you knew
those eyes foretold
your future,
the wonder the world would behold.

You're a singer in a band,
charisma with curly locks,
but your shocking display in Miami
a successful future has blocked.

If only you knew
those eyes foretold
your future,
the hate the world would then hold.

You calm down now,
like an unknown soldier.
Rest easy, Jimmy.
Your war is over.

Patricia Marie Colacicco

Love Thy Enemy

It was a hot August afternoon,
when a stranger came to our town.
He didn't like what we believed
and he came to burn our church down.

We watched the black smoke roll!
We saw the windows shatter!
The firemen fought valiantly
but all their efforts didn't matter.

The tears really stung my eyes
when I saw the cross melt down.
Long it had stood atop the dome,
Which was so high and round.

Before the night was over,
the whole town came to grieve.
The art work was irreplaceable.
The loss was so hard to believe.

The arsonist is in jail now;
A man we must forgive,
It isn't easy for us to do
but it is the Christian way to live.

Patricia Hohn

My Friend

How are you feeling my
Kind dear Old friend
You look at me and say
"Pretty soon you will understand."

Your fingers are in pain
As you hold on to your cane
Your walk is so slow
Your spine is like a bow

Remember when we laughed,
You slowly held my hand
Now I watch you groaning
And struggle day by day

I must keep on going
While your life is at an end
Speak to me my friend
Come and hold my hand

God will carry you on golden
Wings of love
You deserve to be happy
And that I understand

Carmina Lalama

Spring in Fairview Cemetery

I glimpse forsythia bushes first.
Their desert thirst assuaged
by last week's splattering rain,
they leap alive
and, just as plain as fire,
fling yellow sparks up every twig.

The park lies still.
Three lesser finches dip
and chase
and flash their feathered flame
across green graves.

No loss so big this Spring
that living color cannot quell.
I kneel
and smell the yellow sweetness everywhere,
until, with Sun inside, I cross all time
to grasp the Void
where Lightning dwells.

Elizabeth Richardson

Summer's Wealth

Rising sun, a ring of gold, casts
Amethyst and amber beams.

Clouds of pearl grace the horizon,
A turquoise and lapis sky.

Emerald shoots of winter wheat,
Diamonds of morning dew.

Promises of summer's wealth
From the onyx and obsidian soil.

Lauren Hyde

Untitled

Goodbye lovely Lady
We know you must leave.
Your time here is over,
and now we must grieve.
It was so easy to love you,
And so hard to say goodbye.
God must need another Angel.
To Heaven your Spirit will fly.
And when you are there,
surrounded by Gods light,
Have kind thoughts of us
when we cry in the night
You will know that we miss you
by the splash of our tears.
Your memory lives with us
through all of our years.
So Goodbye lovely Lady
Till we see you once more.
For I know you will be waiting,
when I come to Heaven's door.

Glen L. Sauerbry

Dreaming of a New Century

On dreaming of a new century,
I didn't know that I would see.
I'm gazing at the beginning
Of a new world soon to be . . .
The coming twenty-first century.

Will it be too high-tech for us?
Everywhere people staring at web sites,
Hardly a call until they're done
To friends or family.
Is that all?
No indeed!

All the while in the forests and parks,
The lakes and the rivers
Are at home with the larks,
Safe and secure because everyone cared
What happens to our world.
Thanks to all who dared.

Gloria Wilson Kaplan

Ballad in a Near Empty Tomb

It is strange
To see under the steel grey pipes
A black woman
Singing melodies from within
One is shadowed by the other
One will survive
The pipes sit above the wood floor and wait
While upon that lighted floor a
Single pipe
Has gone 1,000,000 miles farther than they
Can ever go
Can ever know
I do not know which one

Mark Spence

Meant to View

Sleep? Explain . . .
How many hours,
Now, remain?
A clock 4 U,
That ticks too fast,
Relationships,
That never last.
Happiness . . .
Meant to view.
I could've lived my life with you . . .

Movie? . . . My life?
So dramatic,
In my strife,
So unfinished,
So unseen,
No audience,
Would only mean . . .
Happiness . . .
Meant to view.
I could've lived my life with you . . .

Michael Anthony Lopez

Shive

A little boy reaching for affection
A grown man seeking a direction
Needs cannot be shown
Truths must be kept unknown
Fear startles the weary heart
New love provides a jump start
But unknown the truth remains
So fear can make no claims
Only when you my eyes behold
Will my truth readily unfold
This truth you'll never see
For fear won't let it be
Yet it stands firm and strong
Desperately wanting to belong
Unfold my weary heart I say
Even if turn away they may
In the heart all things prevail
With the wind the truth will sail.

Ira Godinez

Gray Walls

Evil lurks in every room
Gray walls surround each tomb
Watch your step
As black night turns to gloom
For tomorrow
You may be the evil bride's groom

Ida Huntsberry

Enjoying Our Senses

A sculptor pent in a windswept city,
Calder sketched the tossing trees,
inventing mobiles with such ease
he drove a rhymester to this ditty.

A poet embracing all of outdoors,
Keats adored orchestral crickets
building on voices from the moors,
saving costs of concert tickets.

Whenever bouquets are lovingly tossed,
scents remain on giving hands.
Nothing in nature ever is lost;
This truth survives from ancient lands.

Vain is my quest for a decent line
When I am blind to the grand design.

Howard Derrickson

Hello

Why? I don't know,
I'm sure you don't care,
Oh, your question was how,
How much should I share?
Would you listen at all?
Would you deafen your mind?
I will mute my beliefs,
my reasons, my rhymes.
You really don't see,
I really don't care.
Did you hear anything?
Hello! Are you there?

Teresa Marie Small

Flipper

She has a blue and green eye,
That she uses to keep herself safe.
She has a nice white coat,
That keeps her warm at night.
She has short hair,
That she keeps very clean.
She has a little pink nose,
That twitches if she is scared.
She has two pink ears,
That look like radar dishes.
She has nice long white whiskers,
That tickle my face.
She loves to be hugged and cuddled.
She is one of a kind.
There is no other that is like her.
I don't want another cat.
I want Flipper.

Becky Fisler

Shattered Dreams

Whatever happens to dreams
That are not accomplished?
Do they demolish into thin air?
Or do they flutter
And fly away to heaven?
Where God sends them back
Out for some other
Soul to accomplish them.

Or does it sit in your mind
And expands to its highest
And in the end
What do you get?
Not even a taste or a feel
Of what your dream
Could have been.

Gena Shellman

Dream Land

A few hours before dawn.
I found myself far beyond,
the limitations of my mind
eager as to what I should find.
I found more that I expected.
I had no map to be directed,
through this vast land of green,
it appeared to be a dream.
Although I cannot be very certain
I couldn't see another person.
Apparently I was all alone,
I quickly drew up a plan of action,
to search the world without distraction,
looking for a way out
and I would find it without a doubt.

Nicholas Adams

The Stream

Water flows through the stream
granting visions of a dream
lost forever in the clouds
lost today and never found

Fish swim in the stream
not as bad as they may seem
swimming to bring us home
a friend when we are alone

Bubbles bounce around the stream
giving air for us to breath
hope to lead us on our way
try to get us home some day

Trees hide away the stream
make it hidden, thus unseen
keep us searching for a path
try to find a way to last

Randall Shelley, Jr.

It's a Shame

Welcome into this world
So innocent and pure,

But as life goes on
We get kicked in the rear,

Our heads get filled
Full of negative thoughts,

Then our brain becomes twisted
And tied up in knots,

We begin to get confused
About the right things to do,

And the world raises us to become people
Like me and you.

Joseph A. Beard

Saying Goodbye

Standing alone at the gate
A tear in his eye
He waves goodbye.
His duty now is
To comfort and care
For those small ones
Left behind
Without their Mom at their side.
Is now grandpa and them
To fend for themselves
Can they do it?
She thinks as she leaves
Of course they can,
It's the way it's been planned.
She waves, says "I love you"
His expression is the same
She knows
He wants to come too.

Judith Holen

Seekers

If time came to an end
What will we do, what will we see,
Is it that we see something
We like or don't
Is it that our confusion
Takes over and our minds
See only what it wants to see,
For all the things that you see
Take all of your abilities
To know all of the unknown
Parts of life's mysteries

Aliece Marie Endress

To My Twins

You are my twin daughters so fair,
To whom I gave all of my care:
As babies you were so cute and cuddly,
Always cheerful, smiling and bubbly.

I nurtured and loved you each new day,
While watching you at your games of play:
But you began to grow so fast,
I could not make your baby days last.

You danced, cheered and went to school,
Trying to live by the "Golden Rule";
then emerged two lovely young ladies,
Getting married and having your babies.

You must go on now with your lives,
Becoming more sage and somewhat wise;
Try to forever help each other,
You will not always have a mother.

So my dear girls I have this to say,
As I finish writing this poem today;
That God will bless you with a happy life,
And keep you free from harm and strife.

Bonnie Ryan Nickleson

Roses

Roses are red,
Roses are white,
Roses are pink too!
Some roses have thorns,
So be very careful!
I love roses, don't you?
Roses are sweet,
Roses are lovely
Roses are nice to look at too!
Some roses don't have any smell
So don't be disappointed!
I love roses, don't you?

Felicity Keeley

This Guy

I liked this guy so very much.
He had a warm and gentle touch.
I liked this guy couldn't he see.
I hoped this guy really liked me.
I wish I could've won his heart.
Then only death took us apart.

Melinda Ingoglio

Dancer in My Mind

Body crescendos, innuendos,
Delicacy in form.
Weaving limbs sing unsung hymns
Escaping all the norms.
Stepping, whirling, ever twirling;
Matrix of expression.
Healing motion, artful potion
Cures sore depression.
Muscle stories; aesthetic glories
Are traced within your grace.
Fingers mime, add to the rhyme;
The theme is on your face.
I relate as I simply wait;
Your dancing arcs will fade.
Dreams are filled, your heart has spilled
The loving that you made.
Rhythmic steps from the depths
Soothe the soul, it's timeless in time.
You're so real, you make me feel,
Dancer in my mind.

Dave Cummings

Imagination

Come away with me.

I'm going away to a wondrous place,
It is filled with magic,
There is no such things as hate.

Come away with me.

There, time has no meaning,
It's a place to laugh and play,
It's a place to trust,
There is no deceiving.

Come away with me.

Enter mine and then to yours,
Each one is different,
Something new to see.

Come away with me.

        Andrew Bergeron

Death

I often sit and wonder
"What it would be like if was not here?"

Would people be happier and more
joyful?
Would there be less yelling and scream-
ing
At my house or where I go?

I can see my funeral in my head,
Not many come but the ones that do
Really care, I see my boyfriend and
parents
Crying what seem like rivers,
Wishing I was back in their arms.

As they lower me into the ground
All these thoughts floating around
Wondering who am I, and where I am
going.

I can feel the dirt thrown onto my casket
Now I know I will never return
To the life I once had.

I lay in this coffin wondering
"Is that good or bad?"

        Nikki Fowler

With You

Enclosed in your arms
The world disappears
No hates, No harms,
No hurts, No fears

All melts as snow
On the first day of spring
You're all I know
You're everything

The storm rages outside this port
But I feel only serenity
Joy and glee fill this resort
As well as tranquility

I long for this embrace
Each day as night falls
To gaze upon your lovely face
And surround you with loving walls

To you I give my life
And my everlasting love
Thank you for being my wife
My angel, My turtledove

        Murray Fugate Jr

Summer's End

To sit and watch the days grow short
Lies heavy on my heart
To know that summers at its end
And winters about to start
With winter comes the wind and snow
Loneliness, death and pain
And everything seems so dark
When the winds begin to sing
So in these days I'll watch and pray
And sing, be still my heart
It won't be long, the sun will shine
When springs about to start

        Lela Gayles White

Storm

As the lightning flashes
A lost dog runs,
Trees f
    a
      l
       l
Children play
On the driveway,
While others are in school,
As the roads flood and others close,
The cats play under a leaky roof,
As I watch from my front porch.

        Shilo Caley

To Whom It May Concern

I've been on special diet
to chase some pounds away
I don't care where they go to
Just so they go to stay!

I want to feel quite young again;
Full of Vim and Vigor.
Then too, it sure won't hurt me
To have a slimmer figure!

There were time when pangs of hunger
Made my stomach writhe in pain.
And tempting thoughts of luscious food
Would drive me most insane.

But then the taunts of friends, who said
"You'll never stick it out."
Determined my persistence
(Though even I am still in doubt.)

But diets they are wonderful
I feel so light and gay.
I'm sure I've lost a lot of weight;
I've been on it One Full Day!

        Lillian Gip Pritty

For You

I promise you
I will cross the ocean for you.
I promise you
I will give you wisdom.
I promise you a winner.
I promise you
I will move a mountain
If you want me to.
I promise you
I will bring you the moon.
I promise you
That I will give you my loving heart.
I promise you a very caring soul.

        Christal Lemasters

For Tony

An arrow flies and hits its mark
A fire starts from just a spark
The greedy keep the flame supplied
The archer finds a place to hide.

Vulture gather 'round and feed
Fulfilling a perverted need
If they can live on others' woe
Their own may fade, and sometimes go.

Although the pain that's felt today
Seems unsurpassed in every way
Much greater tragedies could be:
Loss of health—friends—family.

A silver lining's always there
Our greatest wealth is those who care
Your worth and value are still whole
Don't let the devil steal your soul.

A shirt that's stained can still be worn
A coat give comfort when it's torn
Machines can run with surface marred
A man can live, though he's been scarred.

        Susan Ruggieri

Beseech

Beseech to us,
It would be wise.
We postpone,
Or impel your demise.

Look in the mirror,
Run of the mill.
And as for us,
King of the hill.

We smile at you,
And tip our hat.
Knowing who would win,
In combat.

If you're in our way,
Best accede.
Do not interfere
With our greed.

For we are the ones
Who supervise.
Beseech to us,
It would be wise.

        Roland T. Bowler IV

And You Are Here

When day is just beginning
I call upon your name
To thank you for my blessed rest
To lead me through the day
And you were there

Midday I seek your guidance
For strength to see me through
And thank you for your wisdom
For all the times I needed you
And you were there

Serenity flowing through me
When in spirit now I pray
My gratitude is deepened
As I reminisce about the day
And you were there

My prayers have all been answered
My heart has found blessed peace
For in your love my life is anchored
In your hands, I've found release
And you are here

        Freda DeBonis

Love Storm

As I listen to the wind,
And pitter patter of rain
All I think about is,
It's driving me insane.

I listen to the wind,
Whistle out his name
But then here's the rain,
To drown out his fame.

I start thinking of him,
And repeating his name
But then comes a thunder,
Not saying the same

Another name is what I hear,
Someone whom I know
I've had this feeling all along,
But hoped it wouldn't show.

Here's the roaring thunder,
To bring this secret out
I hope the rain comes back,
To hide and drown it out.

Erika Saviano

Forest Cathedral

The carpet's a pattern of ferns.
The organ's played by the brook.
The sermon's preached by the trees.
And scripture's wherever you look.

There are no stained glass windows,
Nor hand-carved altar rail.
Yet here in this quiet reverence
Is the feel of the Holy Grail.

Men build cathedrals of granite and glass,
With tools and clamor and toil.
But for His sanctuaries, God needs
Only seeds, the sun and the soil.

Roberta Garrett

The Photo Album: A Visitation

(To James And Chase)
Today
I kissed your little baby brother
Blissful in slumber
And I watched you jumping on the bed
Over and over and over
The laughter
The screams that I used to mind
Now merely precious fading echoes
Suspended in buoyant carefree play
You sweep me into dreams of flight
A glimpse of angelic light
This visitation
My transparent childhood relived
somehow
My precious sons
Yours I'll keep for endless replays

Jayme M. Uy

Heart of Fire

Heart of fire,
Burns so bright,
Filled with anger,
And fierce fight,
Do come so near,
So the Heart of Fire,
Will lose its rage

Keeley Pascucci

The Lover

In the silence of the night
My mind is numb with pain
The pain of frustration,
The pain of shame,
The pain of defeat.
The stillness of the night
Broken by heartbeats
And the air conditioner that grumbles
I lie crumpled in my bed
Weary bones, flabby flesh
Only one could love me
God
Would he come I wonder?
With his old walking stick
Aged and gaunt,
The ancient master of time eternal
Then I hear the Tap tapping so clearly
Coming nearer, nearer, nearer . . .

Vinodini Jayaraman

My Arms

He tugged off his pajamas
He pulled on his shirt.
He helped brush his hair and his teeth.

He picked up his teddy
He went down the stairs.
He helped put on his jacket and his hat.

He giggled and laughed
He stood tall and proud.
I a big boy Mommy.
Yes, you are a big boy.

And he stared—
I not hold you any more?
And I stopped.

With my heart pounding
With my gaze fixed with his,
No matter how big you are
My arms are always there for you.

And we hug
Together—
With my arms wrapped around my big
boy.

Lynn C. Kraus

The Color of Love

I met a little child today
Her eyes were as dark as coal.
Her mom brought her to school
And she did what she was told.

When we talked about our families,
She became so very still.
But I knew in time I'd learn about
The space she needed to fill.

Her brown skin told a story
Which set her apart from the rest,
And as I grew to know her,
Her story became my quest.

It seems she was the product
Of her mother's agony.
A rape took place four years ago.
Shall we call it destiny?

I met a little child today,
Whom I shall never forget.
She spoke about her mom with love,
And a father she'd never met.

Karen Verderber

Waves of Muriwai Beach

No longer so young the man
Out of the window looked
Wistful at the rolling waves
Slowly moving in

So many years in motion
His weary eye surveyed
And down a restless past perceived
The sightless action gone

Then the distant roaring heard
Below on crashing rocks
Gave out those seried breakers
Tones expiring

Now in the vast sea bounded
Pitch and roll without cease
Here the senseless goes observed
A remnant in time

Stephen C. Callaway

Untitled

I saw a sign by the street
it said to go and greet
so I went in the meadow
and saw a big shadow
and it scared me off my feet!

The shadow was of a girl
she looked as white as a pearl
her hair was black
and she carried a sack
and I greeted the black-haired girl.

Bonnie Alarie

The Inevitable

And his face fell
Like autumn leaves
That float sadly
To rest on the ground.

She saw what was to come,
And with a scream,
To her knees
Was she forced to rely.

Bye and bye,
The wails,
The cries,
The tears did fade
Into the silent night.

Mary Ann Skipper

All Hail the Belly Button!

When women take over all science
Acknowledged—at last—mental giants
They will proudly proclaim
Without blushing or shame
Canonical truths for their clients:

They'll offer substantial reward
To anyone who can record
From a female womb purged
Any male who emerged
Without an umbilical cord . . .

Yes—the belly's small button's the case
That confirms for the whole human race
One small fact (though uncouth)
Fully proving one truth:
Namely, womankind's primary place.

H. W. Edwards

Lost

Lost in isolation
seeking refuge from desperation
Between the darkness and light
cradled by the night
I ran to an obscure place to hide
with no one by my side
Smiling through a thousand tears
she pretends to hide her fears
She hides herself inside me
grasping at all she can not see
The true verse of life
pierces me like a knife
I stood beside my self and words were none
love lies bleeding when all is done
We live to love another day
as we pass along the way
My heart silently cries
as the dream dies
The ghost of another day
is here to lead the way
            Tammy Lota

Untitled

He
She
She
He
Be
Me

        John P. Gusdon Jr.

The Dying Rose Bud

I feel like a dying rosebud.
I wither in the fall.
I feel my petals leaving my soul.

As each day goes by,
My petals fall slowly to the ground.

When spring comes once again,
I bloom into a beautiful Rose
That feels my love
And my heart of a rosebud.

I will die one day again,
Return to the soil of the earth,
And may never return again.

I'm the dying rosebud.
        Sandra K. Willard

A Votive's Song

Teach to me the vows of your love.
Hold me naked.
Hold me and never let go.
Whisper to me the words of desire.
Caress me.
Feel me.
Touch me.
Graze me with hands so soft.
So smooth.
So immaculate.
It is my heart you feel with each kiss.
Yes!
Salute my soul.
Wrap these words I speak
And let not your warmth take cold.
Sleep now
And know that when you wake.
Here by your side I will be,
And loving you more with each smile.

        Jeffrey S. Smith

God Gave Us His Son

God gave the Sun to warm the day,
He gave the moon to shine at night.
He gave the stars to light the way,
God gave the birds to be in flight.

How precious was His Son that night,
In Bethlehem they came to worship Him,
On that cold and winter flight,
Angels sang a merry song that night.

He grew up as a carpenter's son,
Learned how to live and preach,
He gave His life to save and teach,
His sermons were sent from God's thrown.

It was Joseph and Mary away from home.
His enemies sought to kill Him from Rome.
Soldiers sought Him to take His life away,
But God gave Him a throne of strife to pay.

They killed Jesus, God's only Son.
He arose from the grave to save mankind.
He is gone to Heaven that beautiful place,
Someday I'll see Him face to face.

        Glenn M. Baker

On the Wings of Change

One day, I looked up at the sky
And wondered, why can't I fly?
Like the birds soaring up above
The lark, the eagle, the dove

Against the dewy blue horizon
There is a show they put on
For poor souls like me
Who desperately want to be free

They are circling and flying in formation
Wings spread out in a wonderful fashion
While I struggle with my innermost fear
Trying to hold on to life so dear

I stare up at the fresh blue sky
Still I wonder, why can't I fly?
Then a lightning flashes from above
A stroke of wisdom not from the dove

It did me a lot of good
When I realized I could
Soar over a mountain range
If I fly on the wings of change
        Coleen Robbie M. Magno

Love's Skylight

Midnight comes by lonely feet,
Hear the pace, pick up the beat.
Water runs a darkened path,
Just like love's aftermath,
Light soon reaches our lonely eyes,
Lifts our spirits up to the sky.

And as we sit here bound as one,
Together, forever,
Our new life has begun.

Oath bound,
Love bound,
Never to part.
You were sent here,
To heal my bleeding heart.

Love forever,
Ceasing never,
Time heals all wounds.
        Tamisan Latherow

Untitled

As I watched the sun go down,
The sky is blue and golden brown.
I think of all the things gone wrong.
I think of all the sad, sad songs.

I sit, and stare into the sea,
And think of what is wrong to me.
I think so hard it makes me cry.
And all I say is, "Why? Why? Why?"

I can imagine what could have been.
A world at peace and not a sin.
A world where love is all you hear,
And walk the streets without a fear.

I wish to say it's just a dream.
It's not as bad as it may seem.
It will get better, you wait and see.
But the truth is there for all to see.

A world where war is all you hear,
But war is not the only fear.
But as the sun comes up once more.
A new day begins with no more war.

        David Falzone

Praise God!

Lord Jesus, I love you.
And this you know, is true.
Because You, gave Your life for me
You died on the cross at Calvary.

You've blessed me in so many ways.
You let me wake to see another day
So happy I'm, I do
serve You, Lord
For in serving, there's
a great reward.

When I think of my
heavenly home.
I picture You, Lord,
sitting on the throne.
And all that are Yours
are praising thy name.
You are my light, my eternal flame
        Frederick Leon James

To My Husband

No more walking down the road
To look for tracks of deer,
No viewing gorgeous sunsets
Every season of the year.
The growth of tall and stately trees,
The beauty of field and flowers
The awesome works of nature
You enjoyed hour by hour.

These things for you are past and gone,
But a far more beautiful place,
No more sorrow, no more pain,
Ever beholding the Master's face
So we will look beyond the clouds
To the bright and glorious sun
And trust the future to the Father
'Til His noble work is done.
        Anna Lee Lackman

Caterpillar

Caterpillar, caterpillar, climb a tree
Caterpillar, caterpillar, meet a bee
Fly all night, fly all right
Caterpillar say yippee!
        Veronica Prosser

Our Child

The Robin chirps merrily at thee,
My love,
my eternity . . .
So warm in thine womb,
As dark as a tomb.
But soon to arise,
lift your soul to the skies,
    and become our compromise.
A part of me, a part of him:
Growing, maturing deep within.

Our love gave you life . . .
But you will live it:
With a passion all your own . . .
That will shape your existence
Into a new unique being
that we may call Son
    or Daughter . . .
But will always call with Love.
    Our Child . . .

Lynn Goodwin

This Day

To my dismay, as I awoke today,
The sun was slow to rise;
So, for a brief time,
I sat in this near-total darkness
Allowing its softness to settle
around my shoulders,
Like the warmth of a treasured
Quilt, a friend.
This dark—perhaps not always as
Appreciated as the light.
The rare gift of This Day has been
Fashioned by my sweet Jesus,
And granted to me, so that I might
Continue the journey of my life.
I will endeavor to fill This Day with
Busy and with happy and be worthy
This Day is precious
Thank you, sweet Jesus.
But a little sunshine would be nice, also.

Dorothy O'Brien Williams

Love

I used to think love wasn't real,
It happens in movies and novels.
It doesn't come to people like me,
People who don't fit in,
Drifters
But as I look at you
I realize,
Even drifters who don't fit in,
Deserve to find a piece of heaven,
Deserve to make someone happy,
Carving destiny in stone
As they look into the future
And there is a light.

Rachel Cecilio

Nottingham's Ghost

In the midst of Nottingham
among the trees and starry skies
lurks the ghost of Nottingham
watching with his spyful eyes,
remembering his life that's past,
recalling his death,
enjoying new life at last
while haunting those at rest.

Geraldine Lesso

The Flower

The flower standing,
Watching over the world,
Like a proud and strong soldier.
Standing with grace and beauty,
Living in groups of beauty,
Hoping and dreaming of being free.
Free from the prison,
The prison of the ground and vases.
Dreaming of being free,
Of the painfully killing pollution
Made by humans.
Humans that take the flower away—
Away from their prison and to their death.
The flower—so delicate
And beautiful in every way.

Nicolle Tsertos

The Letter

The soldier at the front
A letter from home did receive

Of its contents most proud was he
Of four lines that said

You and I we got ourselves a daughter
Her smile is sweet
She has perfect feet
And her hair is a brownish color

He shared those lines with all about
And you could hear him shout
Good news from home
I am a Dad

The bullet that ended his life
Tore through the folded letter
Tucked lovingly next to his chest

His last words were
I got a letter today
I am a Dad
Tell my daughter
I was so glad

Robert F. Zahradnick

One Fine Day

So many times I feel like the
world is closing in on me.
So many times I feel like an innocent
prisoner longing to be free.
Every moment in time for me
seems like forever
If only I had something to hold on
to, something to endeavor!
Days go by and nights seem longer.
With everyday that passes, I
grow a little stronger.
With a little hope and a little
luck, things may go my way.
I only hope I'll be around to experience
this one fine day!

Tresa Tuinstra

Nanny

There is a twinkle in her eyes,
That makes her strong and wise.
Her smile is big and bright,
That makes me glow all night.
And when you see her there,
Sitting in her chair.
She hugs me warm and tight,
And makes the world all right.

Amanda Kessler

The Beginning

Being cause
Total cause,
Static.
Static, or ubiquitous
But, certainly,
Certain.
All-powerful,
Everlasting.

No impossibility:
Total cause.
No difficulty,
No problem,
Can do, can see,
Can create
Anything, or,
Everything.

No barriers,
What goals?
No game.

No fun.

Manuel F. Vianna

The Moons Play On

I've travelled far to believe
beyond the stars I've never seen
To touch the beauty of your life
and the alien coolness of your smile.

And the night closes in seductively
as the moons play on with the sea.

The silence shatters as you call
to hold me breathless as I fall
The red and gold in your eyes
drive the wild softness of my cries.

And the blue daylight covers the dawn
as the moons play on with song.

Memories that whisper in the flight
take away the emptiness from time
And the tangled shadows that we weave
bring us safely closer to our dream.

And the fires color the dark
as the moons play on with our hearts.

Gary Lahner

Nocrya

Shock,   bewilderment set in
as the small scarlet specks
yank at me from the dimly lit corner.

Anxiety,   terror creep
into my pounding heart
as I descend upon the
pale motionless heap.

Ruination,   devastation.
Scooping up the small warm lump,
I can feel the heat escaping
from this inner pristine mass.

Revelation, comprehension.
Minute pieces of the destruction
crumple in my trembling palm.
Reading aloud to make sense of the word.

Realization, relief.
Uttering the letters N-O-C-R-Y-A,
the chain of events make sense
Red crayon melted in the white laundry.

Linda Osborn

They Dropped the Bomb

They dropped the bomb,
Now even they are gone.
They promised peace,
Delivered death,
A quiet, new beginning.
Sit and wait for evolution,
Hastened through the old pollution.
Space embraced and lacking face,
A new solution coming.
Weapons gone, along with song,
A huge, surrounding silence.
Slow dispersal,
Now we're universal,
Grow with molecular violence.
More new arrivals crowd around
Bent on survival in a filling void.
Busily making unheard sounds,
A new solution coming.

    Carey King

One Day

When I was young my mom would say,
A special someone will come one day.
I don't know when or who it will be,
But my daughter just wait and see.
As the years passed in endless awry,
Be patient my daughter please don't cry,
I know someone will come is all she'd say,
No more tears could I cry,
Feeling for sure love had passed me by.
Then one day with great surprise,
There he stood before my eyes,
He smiled and, he winked I knew it was him
Not a word could I say,
But my heart stopped looking that day.
I knew this had to be,
My true love had found me.
So Mom was right in what she had to say
True love did come one day.

    Karen R. Cox

Oh, Surf Dude

Oh, surf dude, oh, surf dude, catch a wave.
Make it the best around.
Don't ever use the string,
And never get down!
Oh, surf dude.

    Chris R. Thompson

Bumble Bee

Bumble bee,
Bumble bee,
Now fly away,
And don't sting me,
Bumble bee,
Bumble bee,
Ouch!
You stung me,
Bumble bee,
Bumble bee,
You were a bad bee,
Now you belong to me,
Dead!
Bumble bee,
Bumble bee,
You didn't die,
Now fly away,
You big old bumble bee,
Ouch!
You did it again.

    Heather Taylor

My Granddad

I love him gentle.
I love him sweet.
But when Jesus took him
I wept and wept.
But now I know
I will see him again.
When Jesus takes me
Just like he took him.
He will be waiting
To lead me down the golden path.
Laughing, singing, and playing too.
Just like we did
Before Jesus took him
By the hand
And led him
To the promise land.

    Kristina Worline

Look at Me Grow, Mom

I've found my smile, Mom
Look at me coo!
All my smiles and my coo, Mom,
I've learned just for you.

I've found my feet, Mom
Look at me run!
I know you're chasing me,
Aren't we having fun?

I've found my wings, Mom,
Look at me fly.
I know you're watching out for me
trying so hard not to cry.

I've lost my heart, Mom,
Look at me in love.
She'll keep it safe, Mom . . .

You showed me the world, Mom,
You taught me to reach for the sky.
You'll always have my heart, Mom,
You had the courage to let me fly.

    Donna M. Bowser

Thirteen

It seemed she graced a magic place
Of exotic, mystical array.
But no—she was near to me;
Near—and yet far away.

A vision to me,
So beautiful and graceful at play,
A delight for me to see,
And I saw her most every day.

Alas! age thirteen does not discern.
I did not understand. Alack!
She was over there,
And I was across the track.

    Bernard C. Halstead

Halloween

Haunted Houses
And
Loud noises and
Loch Ness monsters.
'Ooting owls and
Whispering ghosts and
Elizabeth the witch.
Electrical spells in the
Night of horrifying monsters.

    Matthew J. Ducote

Nirvana

There is a Magic Kingdom,
Far beyond the glistening sea.
A land of merriment and magic,
An Enchanting Odyssey.

Knights in shining armor,
But with no battles to fight.
Children, safe from any dangers,
In the meadows fly their kites.

Wizards in the turrets,
Reading stacks and stacks of books,
To find the right formula
For wisdom's why he looks.

Bunnies hop, dragons fly,
And fairies spread 'round peace.
Princesses dance, eagles soar,
As sways the lush, green trees.

Pearl flowers, diamond castles,
Like a wondrous dream.
I've been there many times before.
An Enchanting Fantasy.

    Briana Dell Villafuerte

Love's Bitter Pain

Love for some is special
But few have much to gain.
For most of its poor victims,
Have felt loves bitter pain.

Your life was filled with joy.
But now it's all in vain.
The joy has turned to hurt.
From loves cold bitter pain.

It began with something special.
Couldn't stand to be apart.
But then loves bitter pain.
Has taken another heart.

You walked into it blindly.
Couldn't see what lies ahead.
The love that you once felt;
Is broken dreams instead.

It's shattered all your hopes;
You feel your passion drain.
You're a victim once again.
Brought down by loves bitter pain.

    Dorris Burks Gaston

Who Am I?

Odds are against me, so they say
I am woman, that's the way
Cook, sew, clean, and more
Going about the daily chores
I am strong, I can go on
I stand tall, I'm not alone
I am not a bore
And that's for sure
I have a choice
I can use my voice
I can do anything I want to do
I am no different from you
Think of me as proud, but not headstrong
You won't go wrong
Think of me as gentle, but firm
Striving to learn all that I can learn
A better person I would be
If you talk to me, instead of at me
Look in the mirror can't you see
I am that woman you know you could be

    Lisa Jordan

My World

Simplicity—disturbs me.
Complacency—provokes me.

Tenacious oblivion
In silent execution
Chokes the light from life.

Duplicity—surrounds me.
Adversity—assaults me.

The feisty apparitions
Of vengeance and suspicion
Mangle virtue into vice.

So turns my world
Desperate for redemption
Destined to extinction.

Still, beyond this chaos
There is purpose.
And amidst this terror
There is peace.

So long as one,
If only one, believes.

Kimberly McCreery

Untitled

Father is to mother,
Like sister is to brother.
What I want to know is,
Why can't we love one another?

Many people hate each other,
Arguing 'bout appearance and color.
What I want to know is,
Why can't we love one another?

Nobody can decide,
Who will be their lover.
What I want to know is,
Why can't we love one another?

You can't erase the hurt.
You can't erase the hate.
The only thing I know is,
The subject isn't open for debate.

We have to stop the violence,
And bring it to an end.
What I want to know is,
Won't somebody be my friend?

Amanda Pape

Dedicated to Leaves

See the Trees, the Trunks,
The vines, the branches,
The flowers, but see the Leaves.
Leaves in clusters, in bunches,
Angling downwards, upwards,
Touching Mother's earth,
Swaying in cloud and Sky.
What color leaves,
Only the artist brush can define,
In green, all shades of green,
And brown, yellow, vermilion,
Red, purple, some of all such colors.
Leaves shaped like spears,
Others domed Little Tea spoons,
Round, Long, needle like, curly, twirly;
And look, flat green plates floating
In the pond.
And diamond dotted leaves
Of dew and raindrops, twinkling
In the sunlight, all reaching out for us.

Peter T. BaccHus

Fact Or Fantasy?

Spotted was a Leprechaun
upon my lawn one day;
Awed by this sighting,
Not a word could I say:
But when he smiled at me,
I offered him a drink;
upon request for "grog,"
My composure began to sink.
Being an Irish gent,
he sensed my dilemma;
"A cup of tea," quipped he,
Which I did quickly simmer.
This visit was to me
a fantasy of my heart;
How could one appear
Then suddenly depart?
This tiny mythical dear
Will never, ever conceive
that in his existence
I do truly believe!

Lucy McMaster

Why Me?

As I sit here in my bed,
Dying of a disease.
Going all over my body,
Each and every second, minute, and hour.
I think of all the fun times
I've had with my friends and family.
We did so much together.
And now it's all over
Cause I didn't think before I did.
Everything's gone down the drain,
And no one can help me now,
Not even myself.
My strength is gone, I'm gone myself,
So one thing must be I'm dead!

Lisa Polley

I'll Always Remember You

I think of you and I can't speak.
I think of you and I grow weak.
I see your shining face each day,
Whenever you need me,
I'm not far away.
I love you so much
If only you knew.
Soon we'll be apart, and
I'll no longer be with you.
I'll never forget you
Though, while we're apart.
Because you'll be in a special place,
Right inside my heart.

Noelle Feliciano

A Tear

A tear is running
Running down my face
It gets to my chin
But I don't wipe it away
I let it fall
Fall to the ground
I don't care
'Cause I feel so down
The tear left a spot
A spot on the ground
This is where I sit
When I'm feeling down

Kimberly Williams

What's Up Above?

Love
Yes nothing but pure
Love
There are stars in the sky
That sparks in the night.

There is a moon that shines
Like a spot light,
Round and bright.
There is love up Above
And it feels so right.
When you look up in the sky
You wish someone was there
Holding you tight.
Feeling the wind blowing through your hair
Saying to yourself, this is not fair,
Hoping that someday love will come
Flowing in the air.

Trina Partee

Dream Come True

Meeting you
    was a dream come true

You stole my heart that day
    with just one look my way

With your beautiful eyes
    rivaling the bluest of skies

With your tender loving heart
    more precious than Picasso art

I dreamt and prayed for someone like you
    someone special to talk too

Someone with which to dream
    or just to split an ice cream

Someone to share the joys in life
    and to help in times of strife

I want you to know
    my love continues to grow

Today, Tomorrow
    and will for the rest of my life

I Love You!

James B. Nicholson

When I First Met You

When I first met you
my heart took dip.
Now that I love you,
I turn monkey flips.

When you said that you loved me,
I took to your arms,
Now that we're sweethearts
you've lost no charm.

The best I recall and the happiest
night of all,
Is when you kissed me
one night in the hall

You held me close to your
trembling heart,
You looked into my eyes and said
"Darling, I hope we'll never part."

But When I first met you
My Darling Dear,
I would never have thought
we would now be so near.

Maggie Estelle Bowden

Spiritually I Feel

When I am down and feeling low
I get on my knees
And on the floor I go
I tell the Lord what's on my mind
And I wait for his answer
Before I mourn
Oh but once I get up
And stand up on my feet
I feel like dancing
To my own spiritual beat
And when it's all over
I'd go on with my day
With a smile on my face
And nothing mean to say.

Melinda E. Young

The Goal (Flight of the Arrow)

Search, struggle, strive
for that goal so aimed.
Elusive target even when still.

Infinite attempts straying
from its ultimate path
as the cycle continues.

An abrupt interruption,
numerous distractions
frays concentration,

Until at once regained,
linking with destiny—
The goal to be attained.

A cessation of time and space.
As limitlessness takes its place,
action simultaneously is launched . . .

Time and space again manifest.
Limitedness returns—
But too late—the goal is gained.

Rory Grady

Untitled

Our daughter is golden
Her hair—in the sun—
Shines and sparkles
Like diamonds under light

Her smile comes in a flash
Making one believe in
Fairy princesses and little elves

The beauty and rhythm
Of her small body in motion
Reminds one anew
Of the miracle of creation

God was good
to bless us with—
A daughter who is golden

Ann Lauson

Achooo!

Once there was,
A fuzz.
He was one and only,
And he was very lonely.

So I looked at him and said,
"Come live under my bed."
Where there were many like him.
So he married one named Kim.

Lillian Faye

Salvation

There came a doubt, distrust and fear,
Then came sadness, a blinding tear:
A hope forlorn, a prayer unheard,
Unceasing prayer—but just the word.
Awake! Awake! To see
The Truth, an Angel said to me:
Then came the light and Spirit true
Dispelled the night, then came the view.

John Frum Keeling

Pilgrimage Around the Holy Cathedral

To See the Body of Cardinal Bernardin–1996
Today I went walking
Many people were walking
Many people were talking
Walking, talking, walking, talking
Trying to find a pathway to the Lord.

Many people were praying
Many people were saying
Bernardin has gone straight to the Lord.
Walking, talking, praying, saying.
Following a pathway to the Lord.

Many legs walking, walking
Many lips talking, talking
Many hearts praying, praying
Many tongues saying, saying
Follow our Cardinal to the Lord.

Catherine Granberg

Child

Thin ice cracks beneath my feet.
Crisp air bites my nose.
A new adventure lends,
I turn 'round another bend.
Each dusty trail an avenue.
One lonely tree a friend.
Great wealth held by tiny hands,
All coming back to me.

A forest vast within my sight.
Where shall I venture next?
Will it be to old "Clay Mountain"?
Or the waters of its creek?
I love you, oh, you bounding oak.
Wild daisies sweet perfume.
In the memory of that security,
How I long to be with you.

Sharon E. Bradley

Angel of Mine

As I sat here thinking, and wish
That you were here.
To hold close to you so, so near
Angel of mine,

Thank you for being near to me,
And directs me thru the days,
I know who you are, there's no
Mistake, you guide me
To your voice.
I love you so, so please don't let go.
Angel of mine

Without you, life is nothing
Nights, and day's stands so still.
With you Angel of Mine beside
Me, gives meaning to life at will.
It's you that spark my thoughts
For living in every way.
Please, please, stay with me this day.
Sweet Angel of Mine

Mary N. Horn

The Boy Next Door

I saw the child pick up the toy—
He seemed like such a lovely boy.
Alone he stood, his clothes all torn,
A sight of hope all too forlorn.

The years have passed, the boy has grown.
His worried look, his face is worn.
He plays no more with the old toy,
For now he is a "Big, Big Boy."

Days go by Oh! so fast—for—
The boy with the battered past.
One last look, I did take
One lasting look of heartbreak

I saw the light of flashing red—
A boy so limp upon a bed.
The boy is gone—his life has past,
A forlorn look upon his face.
The sad thing is—another boy
will always be there, to take his place.

Elenora Tijerina

My Martena

Old and crippled, overshadowed gloom.
Twisted, stroke-inflicted wounds.
Arising now at half-stance height
We get a glimpse of inner light.

Lucille Land Arnell

Mirror

Bedroom of blindness
staring back at me
Blankets of color
only darkness can see
Wardrobe of props
lay between folded sheets
Scripts of this life
tucked in corners discreet—
Proudly standing with
its power of reflection
I timidly look into
that pool of inspection
Solitude unmasks
this deceitful disguise
Nakedness reveals
the truth in these eyes.

Tammy Winters

Aug. 11, 1996

What can be learned in a day
That makes living it worth while?
Establish a reason for being among
The throbbing of the earth:
To feel the pain of living,
To feel the depth of despair,
To see the despair in eyes
Old in the ways of the world.

'Tis hopelessness that puts it there.
The sight of nothing ahead,
Chaos in future happenings
Despair without hope.

What we need is a seed of hope
To save us from utter despair.
To be lost for all eternity
To stay connected with heaven and earth.
So in transcending the planes of this life
To ascend into the Love of God.

Doris Tobias Coy

After My Demise

When I have left this earthly life,
Free from the struggle and the strife,
I wonder if they'll say of me
"She had an ear for poetry;"
Or if my heart they will lay bare,
Showing the things that are hidden there,
Things, that are written in poetry,
Revealing the very soul of me.

Clarissa R. Myers

Seaside Soul Soak

Endless rhymes beautiful rhythms
washing ashore crashing waves of wonder.
Soothing sirens' songs freeing the
mind's tides of tension,
loosening the grip of pain.
The sounds of freedom's magic love
calling from the Kingdom of Neptune.
The urging caws of the birds
giving you that last push onward.
Cold, wonderful, refreshing waters,
exciting the heart, seducing the soul,
cleansing away all the impurities
of the body, purifying the depths of skin,
scars forgotten,
fading phantoms of forgotten wars.
Timeless tides of treasures tell
tales of titans and tomorrows.
Mythical, mysterious mermaids
motioning us to the alluring and
ancient Atlantis.

Christina L. Stone

Party Babies

Party babies in the sun,
Party babies have some fun,
Party babies look alike,
Party babies never fight!

Shannon Cummings

Things

You have seen
That my hands are clean
You took a look
After you've read my book
I see the flame in the wind
I always knew I could win
I want to touch your flesh
I know it would be fresh
A flower so very bright
Just like the stars in the night
A long breath of air feels so good
War is something to protest
Just like a baby falling from her nest
A boy knows a girl likes him
But he doesn't have to tell her

Suzanne M. Cirincione

L.O.V.E.

L is for the love of life
    Forget the battles of strife.

O is for the love of others.
    Especially our Dads and Mothers.

V is for the life of virtues.
    Always try to improve your nurtures.

E is for the goal of eternity.
    Remember the love for our Trinity.

Tommye Reese

Symbol of ✓a22 Love

✓a22 Love means (Jazz Love)
(alpha) Thee beginning of
2   Solid Gold heart
            To Create
1   Solid Gold heart
            To feel
        The Sound of ✓a22 Love
        flowing through Your Veins
            And flows through
        The Vine as Wine,
        Through thee Entwine
            of
        Thy roots to Fine. X
(omega)

Shelly Shelton Ankhesenamen

Along the Water

As I sit here by the water.
I gaze into the sky.
I look all around me,
I seem to wonder why?

Can't people see the colors,
that God gave the trees?
Can't people see each other,
and help a brother who's in need?

The air is cool and healthy.
The water moves so fast.
Yet people pass along the water.
Just about as fast.

Duane E. Weilnau

Drugs

Drugs make us unhappy and sad,
And sometimes make us really mad;
We get really weird and wary.
And sometimes get really scary;
We make our friends and family sad,
And drugs make our brain work bad;
Always know that you can say no,
Anywhere even in the snow;
Way up high like in a tree,
Or maybe down on earth like me;
In a house three stories high,
Or in a car waving bye;
At school and home and on the phone,
At the park a walking;
Or when you are a talking;
I'm telling you this cause you
Ought to know all you say is,
No! No! No!

Samantha Wilson

Reflections

I look into the pool of water
    And I see my reflection
I look into the pool of water
    And I see a child looking back
I look into the pool of water
    And I see the child smiling

I have grown
I have made my decisions
I have made my mistakes

I look into the looking glass
    And I see my reflection
I look into the looking glass
    And I see a man looking back
I look into the looking glass
    And I see the man smiling

Kevin T. Hathaway

Being a Man

I saw you in a dream
As clear as the light
With glimpses of the dark
You bolted like a lightning
And there,
I stood just watching.

Scared and unrelenting
I knew you'd keep fighting

Tired and discouraged
You always had courage

Trying every night
You waited for the light

Quiet and uncomplaining
I knew the pain was unending

I woke up crying and perspiring
Then smiled,
That even in my dream
You never gave up praying.

Imelda Loreto Stivala

Understanding

From birth you try to do your best
To teach your child to pass the test
With love and hope you help them grow
And pray someday that they will know

You did your best to show the way
How to become a man someday
Your love has been there from the start
No matter how much you broke my heart

Whatever path your life may run
You will always be my son
I've made mistakes as parents do
Mistakes were also made by you

One thing I know will always be true
Dad and I will always love you
When you become a parent too
Understanding will come to you

Pauline Wilson

Cinquain

Tears
Empty, lonely
Sorrowing, wrenching, mourning
Oh, bring back yesterday!
Regret

Heidi Bennion

Time

If time could be stopped
Every one would have a watch
If intelligence was operated with a dial
Everyone needs to turn theirs up a notch.

Forget the world, let me be happy
'Cause when I'm looking for it
Ain't none of y'all gone give it to me
Be to yourself and stay out of mine,
Look at yourself I'm sure some
Fault you'll find.

Whisper in my ear the trash you say
Instead you talk and smile in my
Face the very next day.

That's okay the stuff you do to
Me, cause when that bright light

Shines down, let's see where you'll be!

Barbara Fuller

The Great War

Two great armies gather and cover the sky
they cover the sun and its light
Creating a gloom over all of the land
which knows they are going to fight

The deafening battle cry
is heard throughout the land
The creatures run for cover
for they know a battle is at hand

They fight and they fight
for hours and days
Shooting bolts of fire
the onlooker amazed

They cover the ground
with their transparent blood
Feeding the plants and creating the flood

A strong wind begins blowing
pushing the great armies away

As the sun regains its position
an arc of triumph soars through the air
The light of peace is true

Dan Walker

The Window of My Soul

Look in my eyes
And behold my soul.
Look in my eyes
See secrets never told.
Look in my eyes
And see deep pain
Look in my eyes
And see love never gained.
Look in my eyes
And see my wants and desires.
Look in my eyes
And see my hearts passionate fires.
Look in my eyes
And see dried tears.
Look in my eyes
And understand my fears.
Look in my eyes
And see your reflection.
Look in my eyes
And see our perfection.

Deborah E. Doherty

The Purple Shadow

The blanket of darkness
That billows down deep
The agonizing thump
Of the heart that still beats

The rush of the tears
That leave a mark on the face
The number of fears
Contentment cannot erase

Splintering on the rocks below
With up the only way to go
Impossible is to fight the weight
That holds but caresses and lulls the hate

I shall never escape what binds me now
It will follow wherever I go
If I should happen to outrun it somehow
I will yield to it anyway I know

Below is a darkness to never be known
Unbelieving it surpasses the black
By which I am now held
And it is mine for keeps

Jessica Reid

A WINTER SNOW

WINTER SNOW
DRIFT AND SPIN
WAY
NORTH FROM
DOWNWARD
SPURRING ANOTHER'S
BELOW

Michael J. Barone

A Journey

No stranger dwells
In this place called hell.
The door is always open,
The admission free.

The only cost
Is a soul that's lost.
Though the door is open,
You cannot leave.

The pounding begins
It gets louder and louder.
The door flings open,
Peace of mind.

Roseann Modak

In Love

Once I fell in love with a boy;
A boy who looked at me and smiled.
Then the day came and I had to leave;
I had to leave that boy of mine.
When the day came and I said goodbye;
That boy just looked at me and smiled.

Once I fell in love with a guy;
A guy who loved to talk and laugh.
One day he talked till he broke my heart;
I wished I mistook what he said.
But it was clear, he was not "the one."
The guy who loved to talk and laugh.

Once I fall in love again;
I want to fall for a man.
A man who will look at me and smile.
A man who is full of love and truth.
Then I can end my search here
and just be. Just be in love.

Awilda Aponte

Untitled

No one should say you're 80 years old
Much rather 80 years young
Considering all that you've been through
You're a mother second to none

You raised us eight most by yourself
Of that you can be proud
And prouder still the original eight
Produced for you a crowd
And you remember all their names
Their age and place of birth
Surely the brightest Octogenarian
To ever grace this earth
And I do love you mother dear
Though not oft said aloud
A thought I'm sure reverberates
Throughout the Hanna crowd
So enjoy your day dear mother
And after all is said and done
You're not 80 years old today
You're exactly 80 years young

Richard R. Hanna

First F

I fell asleep at school today,
When I will not say,
I dreamt that I had bought a cake,
I dreamt that I was awake.
I dreamt I flew in a spaceship.
I dreamt I went on a trip.

I dreamt I was a millionaire,
I dreamt my sister pulled out her hair.
I dreamt that I had won a race,
I dreamt I made it to third base.
I dreamt I didn't have a care,
I dreamt that I went to the fair.

So that is why I flunked that test,
I really think that you're the best,
So I give you this suggestion;
I should be grounded that's no question,
I think an hour would do fine,
What, ten days? How 'bout nine.

Joseph Suarez

What Mother Means to Me

Mother means the world to me
She combed my hair and kept me clean,
Made me say thank you and please.
And made me get down on my knees.

My prayer was said every night.
She tucked me in and held me tight.
I don't know why she had to go,
Because you see, I miss her so.

She was gentle and kind and loved me so.
God had a purpose for her to go.
His love was greater than mine,
So he took her to heaven to shine.

We have to love Jesus. So we can see
Our mother some day at Jesus's feet.
We know we will join her some day,
For our debt we will have to pay.

Wilma Gaines

Snow Flakes

Snow flakes are falling
My heart is calling
Snow flakes bring memories of you
I still remember
That lonely December
When the Snow flakes
Were falling for you.
We loved together
It didn't last long
And the snow flakes
Bring memories of you.

Margaret Egan

Untitled

Vessels of bodiless whispers,
how is your wealth yet so vivid?
Are not dreams fleeting memories
and hopes of your creation?
Then how does a heart touch a heart?
A spirit brush a spirit?
Over the trestle of space,
the tower of isolation in barren land,
the lonely dove in nighttime air,
You link two souls.
Keep holy their silent tryst.

Ellen Wingo

My Mommy

When I see your face.
It brings warmth into my heart.
When I get a hug.
It brings your heart into mine.
When you smile.
It bring joy into my eyes.
When you cry.
I feel the pain.
When your there for me.
I am glad you're my mommy.

Jonathan Pertile

Racist Grudge

There is a racist grudge,
That just won't budge.
You're black or white, day or night.
If people could see,
I think they'd agree
We don't need violence,
And we don't need silence.
We can live together,
It's not our skin color,
Or if we wear a feather.
We can work it out
There's no reason to shout.
If we start today, later we can say,
We did right, without a fight.
That's my dream
That wants to scream.
Let our heart be the door,
Open it and we will soar.
It's not to late,
To change our fate.

Tom Stadler

My One Love

My love, my heart,
my soul, my every thought
He watches from above

How I long to hold and
nestle close
But cannot I am told

His face I see with
shining eyes
My love for him never dies.

When time and meaning
are all gone
Our love and dreams will
linger on.

We'll meet again
When time is spent
To love forever, in heaven
When we are sent.

And even tho' my love I see
From near or far he'll always be
So close and watching over me.

Marian Frasco

And the Dark

Shadows, from the other side of the light,
Comes peeping through his window.
Conscience sleeps here.

Bewildered, I ask,
Can I come to you?
Silence reverberates.

The dark night begins.

Amitava Ganguly

I Was Walking

I was walking in the street
When a little girl came by,
Said she couldn't stand the heat
I asked, "wish you could fly?"

The little girl jumped in surprise.
And she walked up to me
She was so very wise
That girl, "oh yes!" cried she.

So I took her for a ride
In my special car.
"This will fly you," I replied,
And it did—so very far.

So the little girl and I
We had this lovely car
The girl dared not ask why,
If flying is the way we are.

So I am walking down the street
Being just what I am.
Just me and my own two feet
And no girl called Tam.

Allison Higgins

Memories

I look out my window,
A hole in my wall.
What do I see?
Time stands still, still for me.

I see—birth of a world,
The birth of all life . . .
I see with blind eyes.

I lose my father,
A thousand times over.
Not once, said goodbye.

The demons; lust, cocaine,
Made my father go away.
He'll be gone; yesterday, today.

I looked out my window,
A hole in my wall.
What do I see?
Time stands still, still for me.

A black nothing . . .
A ghost yesterday,
Memories that won't go away.

Tara Piowaty

The Cold of Death

In loving memory of Charles McCarthy.
The cold of death has left you dying
For why so stilly would you be lying
The cold of death has left me crying
For your last breath am I espying

The cold of death has cast her wings
Past the threshold of far off beings.
And come in close, next to me
For I am watching but I cannot see.

The cold of death has taken you
Past what we know is true
We can believe and speculate
When our time comes we'll know our fate
Our fate that is the cold of death

Brian Hollenbeck

The Weeping Willow

The weeping willow is a depressing tree
With its branches drooping to the ground.
All around it no happiness can be found.

I tell my problems to it
Though I know it doesn't really care.
It helps comfort me
Even with the hint of sadness in the air.

Maybe it weeps out of loneliness
For it is always seen alone.
Will it ever stop sobbing
Or will it forever cry and moan?

Why it weeps is a mystery
No one will ever come to know.
Now I truly must confess
I am that weeping willow.

David Schneller

Suddenly Lost

I wondered blindly through the darkness
And the silence surrounded my soul
I called out to you
My cry a strange and eerie sound
But I could not find you Oh Lord
Lost and forgotten
Which way to go
Which way to turn
The tears stung my eyes
Oh how they burned
And then I felt your presence
My heart was overjoyed
You gently took my hand in yours
And wiped away my tears
Then you whispered softly in my ear
My child
You only closed your eyes
And thought I wasn't here.

Annette Joseph

Mr. Mem's Time at the Pond

With a furry paw he pats the water
Staring at rippling light

Time dances on and on and on
From mystery to delight

Mr. Mem becomes a spirit
And contemplates the fates

Lying in a lion-like pose
Each day he meditates

And has his feline world revolves
Into both day and night

Time dances a round again, again
In mystery and delight

Ellouise Collins

Trees

Rainforests are getting cut down.
Trees are falling all around.
Right now an animal is losing its home,
While you are reading this poem.
Garbage piles are forming everywhere
They are also forming bad air.
We have to stop this madness
Can't you feel an animal's sadness?
If you have a heart then do your part,
Recycle!

Sarah Biermann

A Bride's Wish

Dressed in my white gown sitting on a pink cloud
Thinking of you because you mean so much to me.
Remember on the beach, where we first kissed?
That was when I knew that we were meant to be!

When I hold you in my arms,
I feel like a rose because you handle me with such care
And I can fall asleep feeling so loved and safe
Because I know that in the morning you will be there!

I knew that my prince would come for me
One day when the time was right.
That day became a reality when I met you
Because my dreams came true and I loved you with all my might!

You listened to every dream that I had
And you began to make my wishes come true
By standing beside me and encouraging me
With so much love that grew and grew!

We will say our heartfelt vows,
As we look deep into each other's eyes
And we will be happy in our paradise
Because everyday will be like dancing in the skies!

Kamylle Santiago

Sweet Slumber

During the twilight of the evening,
I feel the cool, gentle breeze sifting
Through my opened window.
I hear the soft hum of the night
Inducing me to sleep.
And then I think of you,
A constant thought that frequently
Invades my mind.

I fantasize myself being curled snug
And cozy in your arms.
Your warm touch gently caressing my body.
Our hearts simultaneously beating as one,
Strong and loud,
As to pierce the stillness of the night.

A whisper suddenly escapes my lips—
I love you—
And I immediately drift off to sleep,
Graciously at peace in the web of your arms.

Pat L. Daniels

Golden Days With Granny

Down on the farm with Granny in times of long ago;
Watching her work with fervor to make her gardens grow,
And delighting in her busy and her energetic ways,
Were a most exciting part of my tender childhood days.

Granny rose up early 'fore the rooster's morning crowing,
And soon the wood stove embers were red and hot and glowing.
Warm French toast of homemade bread, she'd fix for me to eat,
And sitting down to breakfast was a truly tasty treat.

In my play-suit (made by Granny), I'd follow her out the door,
With an eager heart right ready to go wander and explore.
I could amble to the dairy barn 'fore milking time was over.
Or maybe wade instead through an inviting patch of clover.

The chicken yard awaited with some eggs for me to gather,
But climbing to the hay loft might just be the thing I'd rather.
The stream way down the hillside, could be the place to go;
Where lots of little tadpoles were starting then to grow.

By chance, our horse, old Charlie, who was fun and big 'n' strong,
Might would beckon me to ride him and sing him a happy song.
The day would end so quickly and Granny then would call.
Those days on Granny's farm were some favorite times of all.

Mary Bass

I Heard an Angel Cry

I heard a sound above me, it sounded like it came from the sky.
I turned my face toward Heaven, for I heard an Angel cry.

I saw the Angel coming toward me, and He came with a shining light
I asked him, "Why are you sad?"
He said, "My friend, Fred died last night."

"Why so sudden?" I asked him,
He answered with a tear in his eyes,
"The Master had need for Fred, way up in yonder sky."

What a friend we have in Jesus,
Way over in Glory Land.
We will all have to leave this place,
Just like this humble, friendly man.

The bittersweet is just for a while,
'Til our time to go be with God above.
Our empty hearts that beat so fast,
Will be filled with everlasting love

So cry if you like, and let it out,
But don't stop looking into the sky.
For one day I may hear you say,
I heard an Angel cry.

Ben Clements

Untitled

In loving memory of my grandma, Katherine McGee Shorb
A great woman just left me today
A wonderful woman who knew no bounds
Her love and affection were strong enough to cure all tears
She gave all of herself and expected no return
There's so much more I could have done
We all have our cross to bear
I just wish I could have carried hers for her
But I remember all of the little things
Time will never erase those memories
The ones of the holidays and of the family
The vacation to Colorado seems like yesterday
She was such a caring woman
Soft-spoken yet stronger than everyone
She had seen success and failure from two generations
But her love was unconditional
She tried to please all and succeeded
She is my grandma and she always will be
I love her with all my heart and I will always carry her with me
For all the days of my life and I just pray that I could, one day,
Be as beautiful, strong and as great as she will always be.

Michelle Shorb

Why Does It Have to Hurt?

I love him with all my heart,
But he can't see the way it hurts.
He says he'll spend some time with me,
But he spends his time with everyone but me.

Why does it have to hurt so bad,
Why does it have to hurt . . .
Why can't it be someone else instead of me.

I'm so stubborn, I can't give him up,
Not even for someone else.
He says he'll spend his nights with me,
So I won't have to be alone.
But he rather spend his nights with anyone but me.

Why does it have to hurt so bad,
Why does it have to hurt . . .
Why can't it be someone else instead of me.

Rose A. Knickerbocker

Torn Soul

You must forgive this mournful sigh,
The trace of tears upon my face
Old thoughts came windblown by
And whisked me to that other place.

A place where home meant joy of living
With warmth and laughter en surround,
And time was love coined for the giving
Through spindrift days, blithe spirits bound.

Now you are gone, and all my world is muted.
Church bells toll through softly falling rain.
I lay a rose upon the marble legend,
Then close my eyes and softly call your name.

I've been told, "time would bring a healing,"
But the sages never seem to know
A panacea to calm a vortex—reeling—
In voiceless anguish of a torn soul.

Doris J. Stevens

Dream Keeper

Sleep tight my baby,
All curled up in your bed.
And may the most pleasant of dreams,
travel through your head.
In your dreams I'll sprinkle star dust,
With the lightest touch.
To let you know,
I love you so much.
Hold the thought of me close and near,
So while you sleep you will have nothing to fear.
So have pleasant dreams while you sleep,
My heart is forever yours to keep.

Rob Bruner

Sensations

Tonight I dare to dream of my pen saturating the paper
with thoughts of love for my lady. Oh, I can feel it as my
emotions explode onto the paper; like a river plunging over
a waterfall. Yes, my feelings are as pure, but a thousand
times stronger. Nothing can contain this flow. The longer
you wait the stronger it will grow. This is the same body
of water that filled your very walls and seeps through your
soul. Soaking you with long forgotten desires and emotions
that you've been craving. Come ride my waves of passion and
you'll never grow thirsty. The moisture from my body will
keep you wet. Sip me, feel me as I intertwine with your
innermost desires. Let me cool your body and quench your
thirst with a whole new kind of liquid desire and wet sensations.

Paul Mitchell

I'm Alive!

For a friend that died!
Because I'm dead inside.
Hey! What's going on?
Why am I laying in this casket?
I'm not dead! I'm alive!
What are all of these people doing here?
There's my Mom and Dad, my aunts
And uncle, my boyfriend, my best friend!
Hey, you guys! I'm alive!
Don't cry. I was just one of your ordinary kids.
I want to stay alive and enjoy all the fun there was in life.
I can't even bear this,
Let alone my family and friends.
God, if this really is
Happening, I know I'll be with you,
But it can't be happening
Because
I'm Alive!!!

Donna Jarrell

Where the Clouds Reach Out and Kiss the Trees

You'll never know how I wish I could be,
Where the clouds reach out and kiss the trees.
Where morning skies layered dark and lite,
And sun spots on the mountain, shine so bright.

The joy in my heart, from this harmonious view,
Could only be because of you.
You lift my spirit and you fill my soul.
You bring to my heart peace untold.

Please take me back to the place I found,
Where beauty and life so abound.
Where the clouds reach out and kiss the trees,
And you with your love, bring me to my knees.

Glenna Garcia

Today Tomorrow

Today is today
And tomorrow is tomorrow
Live today today not tomorrow
Because life is too short to live today tomorrow.

Just look around the world today
Look to see what you want,
What's stopping you from getting it
Life is too short to live today tomorrow.

We may not understand what's going on in this world
Because it's not meant for us to understand,
Even though we want to know what the future holds for us
We've got to live today today not tomorrow.

We cannot worry what tomorrow is going to bring
We cannot worry about next week or next month,
We've got to live today today
And let God worry about tomorrow tomorrow.
Make the most of today today
And spend today the way you want to spend today
Because today is today
And tomorrow is tomorrow.

Angie Lea Anderson

Sunshine When It's Raining

9131 Days since 1969, when we all went different ways
Everybody just scattered
All that really mattered was going out to find a new trail to blaze.
9131 Nights, I stumbled along the way but now everything is all right
My philosophy takes good care of me;
It led me out of the dark and into the light.
No one can say how much time there is remaining
I could explain, but it would take too much explaining
Just drink the wine and try to have a fine time
Remember your friends, they are the sunshine when it's raining.

Janie Holder

I'm Lonely

I'm lonely on Monday the first day of the week
Because I can't see, dear, your sweet blushing cheeks
I'm lonely on Tuesday but not quite as blue,
As on Monday, my darling, after Sunday seeing you.
I'm lonely on Wednesday until five thirty nears
Then I look up the road and know you'll soon be here.
I'm lonely on Thursday as if it were "Blue Monday" again,
For I have just seen you and I still think you're grand
I'm lonely on Friday for your smile I can't see
But tomorrow night, dear, you will again be with me
I'm lonely on Saturday until you're by my side
Then I worship and love you until you whisper "Good night"
I'm lonely on Sunday, but why should I be?
For I know, my love you are still true to me.
I'm Lonely, my Darling, I'm lonely for you all the time
I won't be lonely long, dear, soon you can say "Darling you're mine"

Estelle Bowden

My Forever Friend

A friendship so rare. A friendship so true.
This all comes from the friend, I found in you.
The sharing of a smile, or maybe some tears,
Part of all we shared over the years.
A touch of laughter, over a joke or two.
All from the friendship, I shared with you.
A bond we shared, like no other.
Giving birth to Krystal, you too became a mother.
You shared in the nurturing, loving and care,
Of the beautiful baby, we began to share.
From infant to toddler, now a little girl.
To you she was as precious as a pearl.
As you pass on to the heavenly land.
Krystal sends a gift, you now hold in your hand.
Though she will miss you with all of her heart.
I told her your souls will never part.
For the forever friend I found in you
And the mothering touch you have given Krystal, too.
No other person could replace the forever friend I found in you.

Jeanne Wetherby

A Great Hope

Another day, another week, another month
Meditating, hoping a dream would become, a reality
Within reach with minor obstacles, yet assured
An excitement mixed with emotions and unending
Balanced with a touch of support, and circular network

Climbing a ladder, step by step, looking
The top in view, within reach, with precision
The mission, possible, but not yet accomplished
A mother, a father—a springboard
A cushion, landing without damage, its presence recognized

The sky, a changing format, yet certain
A reminder, searching, hoping and extending
Family, friends—an opening—heart to heart
A reservoir of strength, filled and overflowing
Today, tears and sadness, joy removed, a cure in view

Memories of reflection, possibilities or options
A Source, looking and hoping, focused
Nevertheless, a chain, yet unbroken, intact
Circular and strong—link to link, hoping
To the One and Only; our ultimate hope, final arrival.

Henderson T. Headley

In Memory of Grandpa

I took a rose from your grave today
Eventually it will die and go away.
Although it can be pressed and saved for a while
Its beauty is gone just as quick as a smile.

So many frowns and so many tears
Because of the wonderful memories accumulated throughout the years.
We're all sad that we had to say our last goodbye
But happy cause we know we'll see you again up in the sky.

So I'll hold on to that thought and every night I'll pray
I'll thank the Lord, for in my mind, letting your memory stay.
I'll never forget all the things we did
or how you used to call me your personality kid!

One more thing before your journey toward above
Tell Grandma Mers I send my love.
I know we'll all be together again someday
When it's my turn to die and go away.

Until that day comes I'll hold on to what I've got
I'll hold onto the memories of you that I love a lot.
Grandpa, one last thing I want to say, I'm sure you know it's true.
Even though God had to take you away, I will Always Love You!

Melinda Wingenbach

October 18, 1951

It was early one morning before dawn
An auto car diesel was on the run
He run over saplings and he knock down pines
He run through Wilson's house and demolish mine

He must have been driving in a reckless way
To end up into my house that time of day
My wife and I, we were thrown to the floor
What in the world had happen we didn't know

We thought the world was at an end
And that they had drop the atomic bomb again
Just imagine how close we were to dead
With a huge diesel three feet from my head

I'm running short of words, and don't have much to say
But that truck is too big to be on the highway
This like to been a sad story; I like to been unable to write
You'd know what I mean if you were me on that night

When you kneel beside your bed, don't forget to pray
Because you don't know the hour and you don't know the day

Sam H. Mattix Sr.

Angel on Your Shoulder

As I ride into the light, not darkness,
Don't grieve for me.

I now travel on a higher plain,
Under no stress, under no strain.

As I ride into a new dimension,
Think of me as a vision.

My road is vast, uncomplicated,
I am at peace, my quest is sated.

Although I miss the days we shared,
I do not ride alone.

Each time you ride,
I am by your side.

Time may pass, memories keep.
I'm an angel on your shoulder, 'til again we meet.

Patti Paz Wickham

O So Tall

If I were not so tall I could not touch the sky.
I often have to wash my ears to get meteors out of them.
I am so tall that if an airplane is falling I can catch it
before it is even falling.
I am so tall that they put one million king-size beds for me to sleep on.
Sometimes for fun I climb up on the moon.
Don't tell anyone but I've been in another galaxy.
I hopped from planet to planet.
If I polish my nails people would ice skate on them.
If then I fell apart by some unknown force
pieces of my body would cover the whole earth.

Dina Yavich

It Isn't Fair

It isn't fair the earth is getting destroyed.
It isn't fair animals are losing their homes.
It isn't fair birds are getting oiled.
It isn't fair we're losing rain forest.
It isn't fair people are destroying their own habitat.
It isn't fair we're ruining our lives.
It isn't fair people don't love the earth.
It isn't fair most people won't help clean the earth.
It isn't fair we prefer paper instead of trees.
It isn't fair our world won't turn.
It isn't fair one day our earth will crumble.
It just isn't fair.

Abbey C. Sanders

I Did Not Know About Death

I did not know about death,
Until it came knocking on my door.
It took away my beloved's breath,
Yet it took nothing more.

As I set fire to his body,
I thought of our lives together.
I knew that I could never forget
This man who had changed my life forever.

We had seen each other across a room.
We both felt love at first sight.
He was my first love, I loved him with all my might.

But neither of us knew, the doom that was to come.
That my beloved would be taken, and leave me feeling numb.

I yearned to see him once more,
For I missed him so very much.
But yet I could never again feel his beloved touch.

Yet I knew I had to go on, for I had a life ahead of me.
And when that life comes to an end,
In heaven, we both shall be.

Rachana Satija

Sulla and the demon-god spring

Each day, the same question:
who is this child?
This bare-chested boy of ten,
dark-skinned and silent,
fire-brown eyes and a tuft of hair.
Who is this child that plays in the vineyard
among the houses of the older spirits?
Each day he comes a little closer to the pile
of aged equipment behind the shed.
I offer him cinnamon sticks, confectioner's sugar.
He will not touch me, though.
Occasionally, my children find him, throw rocks
and pebbles . . . and it snows.

I hear you Metrobius. I hear your constant exclamations,
know well your pale skin and ripe body. Once a year,
I force myself to see you, out in the open,
under God and the heavens. I am too easily teased.

It is the one night I do not sleep
in that bed of pomegranates and rust.

David Sobel

Generations

My message herein is to keep going strong,
In rearing your children it doesn't take long,
For them to grow up and all too soon leave,
To seek their own way and what they believe.

Grandchildren will come before you know,
The next generation is here for the show.
We all do our best to bring up our young,
And look to the past before we've begun.

Our parents old fashioned, misguided and wrong,
With all the tradition they just went along.
We know how to do it all properly now.
Old ways shall not be repeated, we vow!

Our own set of problems fate soon does devise,
Alas, we grow older, alas, we grow wise.
It has been written and indeed it is truth,
Time makes ancient good seem uncouth.

Soon our children to their children will say,
We shan't make mistakes our mom and dad's way!
Their ways so old fashioned, we know better now.
Old ways shall not be repeated, we vow!

Marilyn S. Adkins

Weather

Drizzle on the sidewalk sizzles,
mean old Mister Twister, gets a windy blister.
Just when Mister Rain started to become a pain,
what was there to gain, from pouring, pouring rain?
In the fog I lost my dog, he was found by the bog.
When the weather turns bad the wind gets mad.
That's winter norm,
she's in rare form,
students run for the dorm.
Then the snow will start to blow,
sometimes fast, and sometimes slow.
Then I wake up to find it a dream,
I look outside the snow looks like cream,
the stream is frozen,
all the fish are dozin',
It's the weather, it's explodin'!

Robyn LeBlanc

To Dawn

If, just for a moment, the word of a friend
Could actually give you a spine,
Or turn on a light in the muddle and haze
Of what's otherwise known as your mind.

If, just for a moment, the smile of a friend
Could beat out the flames in your heart,
Or pour the cement, (when you've given up hope),
That keeps you from falling apart.

If, just for a moment, the hand of a friend
Could scatter the rocks from our feet,
Or humor the madness, churning inside
Of a heart that's pursuing retreat.

If, just for a moment, dear Jesus Himself
Would acknowledge that such a friend be,
I'd have to proclaim that I know her by name,
Cause she's sitting here, right next to me.

Libby Sterba

Untitled

An intimate smile to my own true love
Like Romeo and Juliet, too young in love
In my heart a lonely cry of loneliness did utter from inside
And my heart slowly cried and something great inside of me died
From within my deepest soul
Something, a familiar Sorrow did arise
And corrupted me and took over
I lost control and my heart
Slowly muttered to itself within my
Essence and my very being
A cry of loneliness and of help
But only God could do what I have done to myself
I reply with no words but the regret that my life has met
I rejected the loss I face
God gave me a chance at love that I did waste
And now I am all alone in the world and in my own life

Denise Gail

Glorious Morning

Golden sun rays filter in the clearing,
God has painted the forest with a snow dusting.
The pond glitters with snow diamonds,
A solitary bird sings to the rising sun.
A tender veil of love floats in the air,
Their fingers and lips dance with butterfly flair.
Between heaven and earth,
On the magical bridge,
Leaping across the wintery pond,
The lovers become one in a kiss of passion.

Marinette Hutchinson

A Parade

The flag passes by and men remove their hats,
ladies touch their hearts, it's as simple as that.

I'm standing tall, serene and still and suddenly against my will,
my heart skips a beat and down my cheek a tear slides.
It always happens when the flag passes by.

The feelings are deep for sacrifice has been made.
This is why we fly "Old Glory" at every parade.

Marilyn Fields-Kretzer

Eloquence

You've got it together. Your sociability runs high. The
language you speak is elegance in itself. Yes you are in a
class of your own. There's not one thing that's imperfect
about you lady. When it comes to style, you're a teacher.
Every woman learns from you. You have direction. You
are the height of fashion, and you being the
grandiloquence that you are, you don't live in seclusion.
You live in honor. Ethics show, even the birds sit in the
dog wood tree speaking softly in whispers of love, come
live with me you beautiful girl whose speech is like
Ever flowing music; How can I touch your beautiful soul . . .

Phenia M. Hudson-Moore

The Face in the Mirror

I look into the mirror and there I see
A reflection that looks happy, sad,
Angry, stressed, and uptight.

So much to deal with, to say, to think.
And I stare and wonder,
"Is that really me?"

The face so like mine, the smile fake.
The eyes reflecting pain that no one else knows of
For she will not tell.

The heartbreak and harshness of her features
Making her seem indifferent.
And I wonder, "Does she really even care?"

And I know that she does, she tries to show it.
But something holds her back from expressing herself
So she is quiet. Saying nothing, just looking.

Maybe she is afraid, her fear is there on her face.
She doesn't want rejection from friends and loved ones.
And I stare and wonder, "Who is this girl?"
But my heart knows the face in the mirror.

Britonya D. Banks

Untitled

Have you ever wondered why the sky is blue?
Or why each morning the grass is covered in dew?
Why is it that flowers bloom in the month of May
And the sun, instead of the moon, shines in the day?
What causes trees to change colors in the fall?
And why is the earth in the shape of a ball?
How do we see the stars if they're so far away?
And where does lightning come from on a stormy day?
Why do chickens lay eggs but not cats and dogs?
Who decided that there would be white sheep and green frogs?
In spite of all these questions, I must ask a few more
For I have several deeper questions in store
Why do people only call on God in their time of despair,
And when things are better, for God, they no longer care?
How do people believe that evolution is really true?
There is no way I used to be a monkey; were you?
If there is no God then there is no water in the sea
For without God there is no you and there is no me
God made the earth and everything that it holds
And if you say it isn't true, a lie has just been told

Christie Freeman

An Eagle's Prey

Shhh . . .
Listen to the beating of the air against my face
While you lift me higher and higher from the warm water.

I see you above me
Rhythmically, gently, pulling me up to you,
Your penetrating eyes submerging into mine.

I cannot look away
Yet I know my world is disappearing,
And if I dare look back you will lose me,
But I don't, for I am not one to fall.

Was that the sun
That just flew past us
Causing your wings to beat as fast as my heart
And sending electric jolts through our souls?

I quiver.
You gently lay me down.
You eat me as your prey
Singing me your blessed eagle's song
As I die in ecstasy.

Shannon Burnett Kim

Reflections of Grandpa

His eyes have seen what most men fear.
His hands have accomplished what most men dream.
Experiencing war, never losing his mind,
Grandma knew then she had found a good find.
His heart of purple and heart of gold will grow never old,
For one resides on a ribbon and the other in his soul.
With eleven kin not counting his wife,
He worked his hardest to give all a full life.
His hand was always there, soft and gentle to the feel,
But when wrong was done, his hand soon turned to steel.

My grandfather was so many things to the world,
But the one thing he wasn't was a quitter.
He believed in the good Lord through thick and thin,
And when diagnosed with cancer he knew it was time for him.
With twenty-seven grandchildren and two of them great,
He looks down from above, protecting our fate.
I want to thank him for the good times we had,
And the fact he's not with us is really too bad.
We all hold an empty spot in our mind,
Because he was nothing, but all too kind.

Matt Bingham

Signs in the Skies

On a bright and blustery day
As clouds move in from the east
And sun sets in the west
A double rainbow brilliantly appears

Splashed across dark and heavy skies
Winds bend palm sentinels
Standing proudly on Jefferson Way

As I walk with steady steps
I rejoice to take another breath
And rise to live now as I will again

I've read there will be signs in the skies
To be a harbinger of Christ's coming
As comets fill the heavens and glorious sunsets
Rejoice at prophetic promises

I wonder why 39 misguided souls
Would leave this glorious earth
To chase a phantom UFO

A higher source they say—
I find heaven's gate in my gaze
As I embrace God's glorious world

Kathryne Whitford

Resuscito

battered, bruised, broken
like a crushed flower surprised by an unexpected frost
melancholy, like a blanket of snow, settles upon her and
life recedes into the darkness within.

shrouded in silence
entombed by the sepulcher of depression
a fragile seed, her life balanced precariously
on the fulcrum of faith.

within the shell of her wearied soul
darkness quells hope, the tenebrous milieu
threatens to choke anticipation of viability
only surrender can quicken her jaded spirit.

the divine, gently, ever so gently
reaches down beneath the crust of her wounded heart and
infused with love and courage
the seed submits to a power greater than herself.

her husk shattered by the brightness of love
the seed bursts forth, pushing upward
straining, stretching toward light and life
renewed, redeemed, resurrected.

Ginmarie Rodondi-Huhn

The Colors of Life

When I look at the bright yellow sun,
I just know I can run.

When I look at the blue, blue sky,
I just know I can fly.

When I look at the tall green trees,
I just know I can feel the warm summers breeze.

When I look at the red beautiful rose,
I just know my eyes will close.

When I look at the purple violets,
I just know I will grow silent.

When I look at the dark black dirt,
I just know I wasn't hurt.

When I look at the clear gentle waters,
I just know I have no need to fear.

When I look at the full white moon,
I just know I'll grow older soon,

When I look at that pretty golden road,
I just know in his hands I'm in hold.

When I see all these precious colors,
I shall know that these are truly the colors of life.

Joseph F. Snyder Jr.

The Realm of Dreams

Here is where so many battles I have fought.
The place of a beautiful girl I have sought.
Where there is a castle on top of a mountain,
And statues of heroes past highlight its fountains.
Here is where I walk with my love by a crystal stream.
Surely you know this is the realm of dreams.

Rainbows flow down from the skies,
The sun casts its shadows like watchful eyes.
I've walked with my love hand-in-hand in a field of green,
It feels like she's mine forever, so it seems.
Surely you know this is the realm of dreams.

You've all been there with stars in your eyes,
Where each day starts with a beautiful sunrise.
Where time and space become as one.
As will you and I, It shall be done.
All this can happen, I have the means.
Let me take you now my love to the realm of dreams

Robert Brando

Set It Off

Sound the alarm
for the children
whose screams are not heard over the ignorance.
Sound the alarm
for the women
whose hearts crystallize they've sold their souls.
Sound and alarm
for the men
whose souls are encased in the metal bars of jail.
Sound and alarm
for the communities
that are crumbling with the weight of need and neglect.
Sound the alarm
for the sun
as it rises on another day, another chance to
Set It Off.

Debra Clarke Rafih

The Path

As I find myself reflecting on the path my life has taken
The truth that emerges is clear;
The door to discovery of my very soul
Was through my own fear.

To allow all events in life their full range of emotion
Was the key to the door, I believed.
My worst fear became my strongest ally,
In letting go, I received.

Fear of loneliness led to solitude
And in silence . . . the miracle birth!
There I came to know a sense of myself
That transcends the limits of earth.

There are many who have traveled before me
And my guides have come and gone.
There is a method in the madness of life,
And my path has brought me Home.

C. Alan Heald

A Woman's Love From Within

It always amazes me how very mysterious love can be.
Hiding its every secret with passionate intervals,
And then, by chance, taking allowances
For our own secrets of lovers had and lovers to be.
Though much love is yet to come,
The love within, we hold so dear.
For every heart there is but one cache for love to live,
Which is in a lover's eyes.
The Lord provides such graceful emotion
That the dirt from which He hath made man,
And the bone with which He hath created woman
Is my root and my foundation.
Our love is because His love lives.
Shall our lover's hearts remain thine for all of eternity
And our love be a gift of Yours!
For the love he possesses me does not have mark
To the love I bare him and shall all of my days.

Brandie L. Smith

Mothers Are Special

To a mother there is so much to say.
A mother is a special person that deserves this special day.
To all of the mothers throughout the land,
When God made woman it was a great master plan.
I salute mothers all over the world.
God bless them, they are like a precious pearl.
So God Bless the mothers young and old.
God Bless your contributions and God Bless your soul.
But don't forget to let the Lord have His Way,
Because it was Him that gave this day.

Curtis Williams

Mulch

Dig into the crumble of oak leaves,
Work your heels down into the loose, soft rot
And roll it back like a comforter.
Roll it up and carry away a blanket of rot for the garden;
A wormy crumbling sponge.

Lay it out across the hungry beds
before the hard freeze comes.

First stay; crouch in the shelter of the forest,
facing the sun.

Come out at dusk, arms empty, quiet-footed
as the doe.

Follow the doe and drink deeply in the sweet dusk.

Spread the wild earth across the gentle gardens—
Cover with fir boughs.
Kneel and pray.

Sharon J. Griffin

The Flower

A dog would see this flower as an object
To chase as it sails in the wind

A baby would see this as a small toy to play
To smell the sweet scent of spring

It would be a gardener's dream
To have this grow in his garden

A seventh grader might pick off
The petals for hope of love
"He loves me, he loves me not"

Amy Herber

Heartless

Unnoticed have I gone since the beginning of your existence.
Pumping you with fresh oxygen,
keeping the blood coursing smoothly through your veins.
Stranded on a never ending mission to keep you alive.
Have you no gratitude?
No sense of appreciation?
For many moons have I longed to be free of this wretched body.
Free of this duty to serve a master
who has never given me a second thought!
So now you hand helplessly at the end of your rope.
Hoping someone will give you an extension of life.
Hoping your heart will beat again!
But—I think not!!!

Rosemary Garrison

So Maybe

Maybe I wanted it to work,
So maybe you did too,
But there was so much pain beyond the hurt,
Pain that was each our own, pain which neither of us knew.

Maybe I wanted you to go back to how you always were,
So maybe you wanted to go back too,
But time changed all that had occurred,
And we moved on holding memories that were few.

Maybe I wanted to be a good kid,
So maybe you wanted me to be good too,
But that all disappeared with the invalid promises
we both used for the bid,
And we fell, too hurt and scarred to be made over with the "New."

Maybe I wanted an unrealistic reality,
So maybe you wanted one too,
But dreams don't understand causality,
And so we're still playing the wrong parts right on cue.

Rachel Conger

I Weep for You, Dear Francis

I weep for you, dear Francis,
When our flag is mocked and shunned.
When vilified in the name of peace,
It leaves me shocked and stunned.

I think of a night long ago,
A night of gloom and sorrow,
When the only thought in your heart was
Will Old Glory wave tomorrow.

And yet there are those who take shelter
Beneath our Banner's shade,
Who are first to claim their American rights,
But are last to extol its fame.

I weep for you, dear Francis,
May your good soul rest in peace.
But I'm sure you know, with the help of God,
Our Star Spangled Banner will never cease.

Moshe Sobel

My Daily Prayer

Today Dear Lord I thank You, I know that's not enough,
for all the things You've given me and never asked for much.
I don't deserve Your kindness or even sympathy,
but when I asked for happiness You sent her down to me.
You told me I should love her and treat her with respect,
You've never asked much of me but this You did expect.
My friendship I should offer her, my kindness she will need,
show thoughtfulness in helping her in some small but loving deed.
Dear Lord, I pray for Your forgiveness if I've failed in any way,
if sadness I have caused You by not loving her each day.
Down on my knees I beg You, please grant me one more time,
so when You look my way again, You'll smile when You find
the one that You have given me, You know I'll always love,
I thank You Lord for sending her to me from above.

Louis P. Ramirez

Bitburg

This cemetery is for the living, not the dead.
The living come here to commune with the past.
I come to ease the pain of a future never attained.
Searching through headstones
Surrounded by flowers in a sea of green.
A gentle breeze tousles my hair.
The scent of new mown grass fills my lungs.
We should treat the living with such care.
My heart pounds, my temples ache.
Somewhere out there in this rigid grid is my . . .

Oh! God! What's my boy doing here next to Fritz?

E. Warren Bruce

Walking in My Shoes

Walk a mile in some of my shoes
to see how I feel.
Some of them are tight on my feet,
and sometimes I'm in pain.
So when I'm short-tempered with you
blame it on my shoes.
Some of them are old and comfortable
and feel great on my feet.
So when I'm smiling and helpful,
blame it on my shoes.
Sometimes they are too big and slow me down.
So when I can't keep up with you,
blame it on my shoes.
Sometimes they may have holes in the bottom,
and my feet are cold and wet.
So when I put them next to you to keep them warm,
don't push them away, just buy me a new pair of shoes.

Diane Emery

Grandma's Quilt of Life

Grandma had an album she called "The Quilt of Life."
She said, "It keeps me warm on cold and stormy nights."

When I was younger, I would sit at her side looking
at photos she would call "Grand Ole Times."

Once while we were talking, I asked her to explain
what was it she was thinking to give it such a name.

She said, "One little piece of cloth can't save your pain,
but sew another piece to it and it's a whole new game.
Yet add another to it you've got something to hold on to.
The story of your life you should pass on for you're through."

Gram's been gone which seems so long
and now I have what she had to keep her warm at night.
That old torn up book she called "The Quilt of Life."

Lawrence F. Jones

Life's Examples (Letter from the grave)

Though I have only lived a few years
I have learned many things from this world.
From the time of my birth,
to when I exited this earth.
I learned to love, to hate, to be strong, to give up.
I learned to always have hope
even when it may seem
that even hope has lost its focus.
The things I achieved were small,
the things I lost were the greatest of all.
Few could have contradicted my thoughts
but many knew my faults.
I learned happiness is a shortcoming of life.
It only disappears,
when you artificially try to make it appear.
As I remember my last days on Earth,
I think of all of life's examples.
The pain. The heartache.
All the things that bring you down
but somehow make you strong.

Holly Arjune

Another Burnt Bridge

I lit the match and screamed my silent cry
The bridge was tendered well
The fall of it was greater than the emptiness inside

I choke on smoke and lost high hopes
My back is black with ash
Red embers flare and hit the night
The river numbs my soul

With distress I bore my inner roar

A surety of life is gone
Why can't I cry out loud?
When I'm right the pain is more
A banshee from my core

Ben Harmer

Answer to a Wish

Once I was told by a very old soul
That no matter how great the gain
Never live life in vain
Dry and scorched the desert floors remain.
A thirsty miserable life you will surely obtain.
In hope this message reaches one of you
And puts an end to your masquerade of arrogance and blame.
You may find, you were left behind
Lost yourself for a spell
Lessons taught by an old brick wishing well
Play a different role reach out and wish your life well.
A tale set to sail.

William Davitian

The Comical Clown

There I stand, a comical clown
For everyone to point and laugh.
They don't know who I am
Beneath this smile and the paint.
They stop and watch
And I help hide their problems.
While I, the comical clown,
Have problems, too.
How could they know
That my act is just an act?
Or, in truth, I'd rather wear
Dull colors than these bright,
Flashy colors I don?
And when I put on my smile,
I'm just hiding my frown?
No, they can't know this.
I use these people to hide from
My problems, just as they use me.
But why should I hide?
I'm through being everybody's comical clown.

Kate Green

Change

Nothing in nothingness;
calm within calmlessness.
A still life painted, as mindfulness vented succumbs
to the trance of elongated glance,
as transform completes

A song without beat.
Likeness of cellar!
Dampness in color! Lightless and vague!
Love inside hate . . .

Grey behind shadows,
only to have those execute wrath,
as none other hath such menacing power yet,
nurturing hours of recovering days
'midst lingering haze.

Then settling profoundly
with brightness abound thee,
blacks and whites fade,
though soon to replace are delicious reds
and sweet smelling yellows,
Unchangeable changes yet bound to create those.

James D. Brewer Jr.

For I Am a Girl

For I am a girl who dances
In a twirl and is happy with
The world around me.

Now I am older and getting much bolder
And the world seems real to me.

Now I tear and have much fear
Of all the things that will arrive me.

I have hard school work which
Makes me berserk and I have no one to guide me.

My mom is mad and I have no dad
So no one is beside me.

Now I'm grown and I have two
Of my own and they make me groan

Now I'm a widow and my
Children have grown up
And left me in my co-op
With no love around me.

I once was a girl who danced
In a twirl and now I have pain that I dread
And now my soul is dead.

Marisa Bischof

A Child Is Born

Two hearts that became one
Brought to this world a wonderful son
A gift of love, the miracle of life
The best gift there could ever be
The most beautiful baby, is he

A newborn so alive and new
Wondering how I could ever be blue
A lot of happiness is certainly due

Such an innocent look
One glance is all it took
That first breath of fresh air
With skin so soft and fair
Knowing that I'll always care

Those tiny little toes, that cute button nose
And with hair so fine
I'm so happy that he's his and mine

Seeing life through brand new eyes
The love you feel you can't disguise
The love I feel will always be
A special feeling between you and me

Kimberly Ann Donovan

Ode to the Cow

This noble beast has no choice in a mate,
We force a bull to her side.
This is an act she possibly hates,
But she still puts up with the ride.

The newborn is frolicking through the meadow,
In the late days of Spring.
While the mother looks on with adoring eyes,
It is quite a beautiful thing.

During cold, winter months, there is hay in the barn,
Where she sleeps, and the grain keeps her full.
And though she's content with her calf by her side,
She dreams of her ride with the bull.

Oh, the simpleness of the life she leads,
Yet, her ability we push upon her.
The terrible things that people will do,
When it comes to the love of butter.

The cow needs to be milked, day after day,
If not, she could explode!
For the life she endures, to keep us all plump,
To The Cow, this poem is ode.

Monique Brusse

Motions in Momentary

The first encounter, the glance
The thoughts, the words, the eyes,
The aura, the expression, the anxiety,
The response, the rush, the inner peace.
The touch, the feelings, the walk, the talk,
The promise, the plans, the commitment,
The sharing, the exchange, the vows,
The sharing, the new world, the dream.
The connection, the tenacity, the life,
The endurance, the expectation, the joy,
The embrace, the kiss, the love, the living,
The pride, the presence, the movies,
The candlelight dinners, the sunrise brunch,
The sunset desserts, the morning dew, the evening rains,
The midnight pleasures, the songs, the friends,
The enemies, the pretenders, the jealous, the empty
The pain, the trauma, the littlest Angel,
The spirit, the struggle, the fight, the wailing siren,
The faces, the places, the bed, the room, the doctors,
The nurses, the IV line, the stainless table, the light.

(Paul F. DeVané)/MAXMAN

Hard to Say Goodbye

In the loving memory of my Grandpa, Kenneth J. Sweeney.
I thought you'd never leave,
I thought you would always be there.
Now that you're gone, boy am I scared,
scared for what the future holds.
The only thing I can do is be bold
and stand tall,
or I know I will just fall.
I'm afraid to fall,
because you won't be there to catch me at all.
You're here in my heart and that's where you will always be,
but I still wish that you were here with me.
The time to say goodbye has come so fast,
I wish it would always last.
Since it can't, the time has come to depart,
just remember, you'll always be in my heart!

Kristin Pepitone

From Slavery to Freedom

The weight of sin is hard to lift, the rope is hard to break,
And all the pain that holds us down, we physically can't take.
We often try to find a way to free ourselves and run,
To find a path to travel on, we think we're having fun.
But we forget to follow God so we get taken in,
By lusts and pleasures of the world, we are a slave to sin.
The one who has control of us is not a man at all,
Instead he is a careless beast that's broken every law.
He cares not if or when we die, that's not his big concern.
He knows his time is limited and wants to see us burn.
There is one person strong enough to wring the devils throat.
That persons name is Jesus Christ, he wants us in his boat.
The only thing we have to do is grab his outstretched hand,
Then he will gladly pick us up and put us on dry land.
We have to take His loving hand to live eternally,
With God in Heaven, our new home, where we can then be free.

Jon Mauldin

Anniversary

. . . And here we all are,
some very near, some from afar . . .
To celebrate, to commemorate all the years spent
And join in the happiness

Through this journey you have seen
. . . Hard times
. . . Good times
. . . Bad times
. . . Sad times
With smiles, with laughter, with happiness ever-after,
with tears, with fears, with or without hesitation,
with determination and consideration, with apprehension
and condemnation, with hope and gratitude, and an
enlightened attitude, with prayer, with promises, and
sometimes solemn demises, with a little help from God,
may you have many more years to come . . . So embrace them . . .
cherish them, for they will never be again . . . Love and
comfort each other, above all the rest . . .
For the years ahead are most likely to be your best . . .

Bonnie Luinski

My Child, My Love

Who was to think one could love so completely
Give of oneself ever so deeply
It's a feeling I feel that's so deep within
It's all so consuming, It's way under the skin
Who could have known
This love I've been shown
It's forever so real
This love that I feel
It's the love for a child that let's you know
This love that your feeling will continue to grow

Julie Spataro

Untitled

Pictures in my mind
of senseless pain,
Tears of blood shed in vain.

A hero, a change is needed.

Actions and consequences hand in hand
like darkness and light, like good and bad.
This world we live in—who knows why, what,
where, when, and how . . .
But . . .
Struggling for dreams, so few seconds,
Piercing screams in agony beckon.
Inside us all, I truly believe, is something wonderful,
but lack of heart and courage
condemn us all to a lazy lull.

Rony Armas

Hourglass

"How far shall we walk?"
"Until the shore runs out, the beach no more."

Sun, a single shabby Christmas ornament hovers low
Paler at season's last mile
Misty mauve cloud-wisps linger awhile
Satin-soft breezes wearied by travel from afar and
Scented with salt pungent secrets
Kiss our white-capped lips.
We walk together.

Gulls cartwheel above
Black cormorant twisters swirl seaward
A harvest of sand dollars scatters the sand
Tepee limpets dot the shore
Foamy sea tickled toes in a land we can't see and
Wets our soles, whets our souls.
Hourglass journey ebbs as twilight drips dry.

"How far shall we walk?"
"Till the sand disappears."

Maggie McMillen

The Mirror of an Endless Blue

The mirror of an endless blue
I visited when I was two
And again and again as I grew
And I cried when I walked away;
I maybe feared the sky would fall
Or the ocean wouldn't hear my call
And the fish and seamen and waves so tall
Would cease when I walked away;
Two years ago, my thirty-fifth
My wife and daughter whom I took with
They accepted the sea with joy and blithe
But my son and I cried when we walked away . . .

Joshua Seth White

I

I am the love born in wrong times,
I am the time of the left hearts.
I am a dead heart that very suddenly loved,
I am the death of a sick heart.
I am the way for slow steps and for someone to step on,
I am the slowness of a way that remains to this very someone
   to come back.
I am the space seeking for a wider infinite,
I am the infinite that makes me smaller.
I am the poem that is missing one verse to get to an end.
I am the lack of verse and life because it is missing me in myself.
I am a mistake made at right moment,
I am a wrong moment——but I am a fact!

Carmen Pereisan

Just Imagine

Just imagine if your life were perfect,
And you never had to hate it,
If you could spend your life with the one you love,
And he was your match dove,
If you could have two girls,
That had hair of golden curls,
If you could have two boys,
That didn't make much noise,
If your house were a big palace,
And if your maids name were Alice,
Do just imagine if your life were that perfect.
Would it be worth it?

Jill Staniszewski

Pepere

My Pepere is very special to me.
I visit him often and my happiness grows.
I leave for home and my happiness dies.
I am sad now that he is sick.
I pray for him to get better.
I fear for him.
He has suffered enough.

He died.
I am sad and happy.
The suffering he went through is over.
The wondering if he will live or die is over.
He is still in my heart no matter what.
I am sad that I have no more
Grandfathers to visit and love.

Monica McLean

Flight

Now where shall I go today, where will it be?
The ocean wide, the great divide?
Snow filled slopes, or the land of popes?
London, Egypt, Asia, Spain or
The middle of the great rain forest?

Friends surround me, awaiting my choice,
Slumped in wheelchairs, bedridden! Cheeks moist
Minds trapped in bodies with no way out,
The end of great lives, existence, no hope, but

Oh, what joy to possess the use of hands,
To hold a book, peruse, and plan
To see the wonders of this great earth
Created by God, enjoyed by man.

My daily travels are wide and far
Allowing me to roam without use of plane or car.
Releasing my legs to move once again
On the wings of a book, the balm of all men,
I take flight!

Willena T. Nunn

In the Past

In the past, I thought I couldn't
and I wouldn't

In the past, I seen defeat
and it was there

In the past, all seemed lost
and it was

In the past, everything seemed to always go wrong
and it did

In the past, I could not see my way
so I was lost

In the past is where I left my past and the past is now just that,
The Past!!

Cynthia Bell

A Passing Moment

The fancy of a look in my eyes,
  of such deep innocence.
As I passed by, I looked back,
  I found you looking at me too.
In a passing moment you smiled so sweetly,
  your eyes sparkled so.
In time our two hearts grew together,
  an act of love to remember forever.
Your touch is so soft and gentle,
  passion rages inside of my soul.
Your words linger in my mind,
  your heart is imprinted inside me forever.
A passing moment was all it took,
  to melt our two souls as one.

Andrea Jane Currier

A Summer Evening Date

As I stroll down a small country road
As the sun sets in the west
As the moon rises in the star-lit sky
As the night cast its shadows in silence
As the cool breeze gently brushes against my cheeks
My thoughts encircle my mind
As I gaze up at the star-lit sky
I watch shooting stars go by
I can hear the sounds of the warm summer night
The life around a glimmering pond
The call of the night birds settling
down for a nights rest
And I say to myself, "Oh! What a beautiful,
wonderful, peaceful world to live in,
And how lucky I am to be alive."

Janice C. Wiesinger

Untitled

The trinket show boat curves its painted wood
To storm cluttered river's smacking lips
The black-capped captain scurs water
With his vigil o'clock lamp
As red paddles battered gills
High in the backward air
He whistles through a cobbed pipe
The tunes that three loves taught.
(Unmarried, that pitch with water)
Until this storm-centered ride
Clings the song as its own
And stamps it to the sea-breasted hull

Dale Michael Erwin

Anything But Me

They say for every rose, there is a thorn
They say for every cloud, there's a silver lining
I want to be the moon, and come out at night
I want to be the sun shining
I want to be the crystals glistening
I want to be an ocean or sea
I want to be just anything.
Anything. Anything but me.
If I'm a cloud, where's my silver lining?
If I'm a thorn, where is my rose?
Where's my leaves if I'm a tree?
I want to be anything.
Anything. Anything but me.
They say every night has its dawn,
And they say if you fall, to get back on
Who says that two is better than three?
Oh, I just want to be anything.
Anything. Anything but me.

Devan Jennings

The Lover

They met and as everyone said fell in love at first sight
But on those nights,
It was such a scary sight.
They seemed to be perfect to everyone around.
But the beatings ended at the ground.
The bruises, the bumps, the blood, the gore,
Every time she woke, there appeared yet another sore.
The pains she had to keep inside.
It hurt so much.
She winced from every forceful touch.
No one who knew would tell,
Waking the lover from his spell.
Ending this so-called love the lover choked.
And ending his other with a bare bodkin.
They went down in smoke.
Now the love that once was there, still remains.
But the souls of the lover and his other rest.
They rest in bed, a bed of silk, or a bed of guilt.

Jennifer L. Norris

Untitled

Somehow you make it all come together
Bring out the sunshine and make me feel better
Without you I don't know what I'd do
There's no telling where I'd be without you

You to console me, counsel and guide
Put things into perspective when I just want to hide
You to lift me up when my heart breaks
And I don't know which road to take

Always assuring me you're my biggest fan
Your words of encouragement I've heard over again
You'll never know what it means to me
To know beyond a doubt who you'll always be

The someone who believes in me
And the someone I believe in too
Where love is there steadfast and true
I'm so lucky and blessed

Because no matter how old I get
I'll always be your little girl
And you'll always be the best Dad in the world!

Cathy Whitten

The Ballad of Air Chetcos

The whistle announced the start of the game
his presence assuring his opponent's loss
he prepared himself for the pride and the pain
that were sure to ensue in this game of lacrosse

They fought each other and dove for the ball
Air Chetcos coming out with possession at last
the defense stood like an impenetrable wall
but Air Chetcos up and ran right past

He ran the gauntlet with unrelenting will
the goalie becoming overcome with fright
as he dove in the air, time seemed to stand still
he shot at his target with all his might

The ball flew through the air with incredible speed
the crowd jumped up, the goalie got set
Air Chetcos soon pulled his team to the lead
as the speeding bullet sailed into the net

He brushed himself off as he rose from the ground
and looked to the stands toward many a fan
the stadium roared with a deafening sound
"Air Chetcos," they shouted, "we love you, Man!"

Mark A. Taurence

The Real Loser in the Race

I ran the race with life and at the end
I expected to get a blue ribbon,
for saying I beat Him and I beat Him.
Look at me and my, life the treasures I collected
from others as I stole their dreams
and tripped them up in my journey to be first at everything I did.

I laughed at him also as he tried to be my competition
and when I surpassed him in all the meets.
He stood on the side lines still smiling
and I could not understand.
The fool even hugged my neck,
congratulated me and shook my hand.
What happened didn't he feel bad
as they called out my name over and over?
Didn't he feel bad when I drove off in my fancy chariot?
Didn't he feel bad when my parade of friends came to see me?

How can he stand so tall but be so small?
I really don't get this but I'm sure I can fix it.
Next meet we race I'll put my defeat even deeper in his face.

Pamela Saxton

Odyssey of Existence (Mental Intelligence)

Rolling hills of laughter permeate,
But where are the smiles?
Madness all about, without
Thrill of kill, as crocodiles!
Candles move in the night
Yet nothing is right!
Help from four corners of Earth
All said to be contrite.
Where is the credit, where
Credit is surely due?
See I am true, all through the day and night.
Secrets abound, without service thoughts.
Independence is Moffit or so I
looked and saw nought!
Family looks away so close,
"Carpe Diem," this we know!
The love hastens to leave, the darkness covers the light,
The life slowly descends, until nothing is left.
I fight to honor truth, honesty, and the freedom to live life!

Michael Wilson

My Mother—My Friend

From the time I was little always knew,
You were more than a mother, you were my friend too.

When I'm sad and when I cry,
You don't push me to tell you why.

You love me just as I am, I'm free to grow,
What a mother, what a friend.

You always find time in your busy day
To make me feel special, in your own caring way.

Mother allows me to make my mistakes,
Do you know how much courage that takes?

She allows me the freedom to be,
The person I am, inside of me.

Sometimes we get angry and sometimes we fight,
But we work together to make things all right.

Being a mother isn't anything new,
But a friend and a mother is what I have in you.

A mother is a mother, and friend is a friend
To me you are both, What a gift for God to send.

Our bond is forever, and always will be,
A special love for my mother, my friend and me.

Natasha N. Wick

My Spirit in the Wilderness

Here the air is crisp and cool
As the wind whips through the trees
Here mountains are like majestic images
And the largest mountain is tipped
with lacy, white snow
Here a house is a warm refuge
With a stew boiling over a red hot fire
Here rivers are blue and glisten in the sun
With a sound like roaring thunder
Here when rain falls it looks like
clear teardrops
Which has a fresh scent coming down
off the mountain
Here the clouds are like cotton candy
And the pastures go on forever
through the hills
Here I write this poem sitting in a tree
As I listen to the sounds of nature
And here I feel satisfaction in knowing
I'm in the calm, quiet, peaceful, primeval forest

Alan Roeder

One Word

One little word, that nobody ever wants to hear;
One little word, that sooner or later everyone will start to fear;
One little word, that is not all too few;
This little word, could leave anyone blue.

If you say that you're in love,
You may think that you can fly.
If you say that you are happy,
You may smile without ever knowing why.
If you say that you are sad,
You may sit down and begin to cry.
But if you hear this single word,
You may just simply want to die.

Prepare yourself for this day.
Otherwise, you may have to pay.
Some people do not truly see,
That it's part of life—it has to be.
One little word, I cannot lie,
And I'll never be able to explain why,
Will simply make you want to cry,
If someone ever says, "Goodbye."

Stephanie Lynn Martell

A Little Inspiration

Over the horizon the bright morning sun greeted me
Quietly I sat watching the spectacular sunrise
Promising yet another beautiful day to come
Certain that a creative story I would soon surmise.

However, my imagination appeared to be dormant
My anxious mind then became frenzied with anger
Because its desperate search was to no avail
Appearing that my writing endeavor was in danger.

My eyes then wandered beyond the ocean shore
At the breathtaking colorful array before me
I listened to the gentle waves breaking on the sands
And the distant cries of hungry gulls out at sea.

Slowly I strolled to the remote edge of the shore
Noticing the incoming tide swirl about my feet
Cool, misty droplets lightly splashed on my face
I felt immense happiness inside beginning to heat.

Numerous compelling emotions started to flow
The outlook of my quest became suddenly clear
Instantly inspiration surged all through my body
Eagerly I reached for my pen without any fear.

Linda Crowel

The Arrival of the Alien

Perspiring very heavily, I extend my hand in greeting,
Every muscle trembling at the enormity of this meeting.
My life-along has been granted, I now stand face-to-face
With a living alien being from some far-off distant place.

I know not the world from which the stranger came.
No known distant galaxy occupies that domain.
I see not his face, his form so bathed in light
That even shadows cannot take shelter in the night.

He claims that he was here before, and now had come again
To deliver a special message to each and every man.
"Your world is doomed to a cataclysmic disaster,
Unless it swears allegiance to the kingdom of my master.

No resistance will be permitted, those who oppose him will perish
In a devastation so total, it can only be called nightmarish.
To spare your world, I myself will be sacrificed.
Yes, I am he, the one you call the Christ."

Randy C. Meyer

A Lifetime Friend

Lifetime friends, don't come along everyday
That's why I thank God, for sending you my way
We've built a friendship, through smiles and tears
We overcame our differences, and conquered our fears
In you I found a friend, who's special and very rare
You guided me through life, and showed me how to care
You were there for me, in times of joy and stress
I thank you with all my heart, and wish you happiness
So during this brief hiatus, don't let it be forgotten
As good as friends we are, friendships never rotten
One thing is for certain, of my friends you are the best
And nothing will ever change, until the day we rest
I thank you for the years and I pray for more to come
We'll always stick together, like paper does to gum
So from this day forward, remember you have a friend
A lifetime friend in me, one that just won't end.

John Ewing

It Takes Two

Today is the beginning, your hearts and souls meet.
Bonded together forever, love just can't be beat.

Toward each other you're so kind and dear;
Loving and caring and so sincere . . .

Tomorrow is another day, together still,
to pave the way; to get started on your brand new life,
Together as man and wife.

Remember love is a big part of your marriage
and can help you through and through . . .
But love is not everything,
For it takes two.

Misty Jane Clark

Solitude

There's a moment of solitude
Found in the heart of the mind's eye
Crystal clarity of peace sublime
The light of infinite kindness
Reflected back through the mind's eye

It is all of the world, pure essence of truth
For all to gain
Open ended light of goodness
So simple, so kind
There to grasp
In the oneness of the mind's eye
Love unaltered

Judy Tyson

The Belly Button Tree

Once, I saw a belly button tree.
It was as silly as could be, that belly button tree.
When I saw it, I said, "Gee! what a funny looking tree!"
Me and my dog Lee, sat down by this tree.
And then we were visited by a big honey bee.
"Hello, I am Z," said the bee, to me and Lee,
"What are you doing by this belly button tree?"
"Well," said me, "we were just walking you see,
And then we saw this belly button tree."
Then honey bee Z, looked very mad at me and Lee.
He buzzed up very close and said, "Look, you see,
You and me, stay away from My belly button tree!
For you are a flea, smaller than a pea, and you
Have no use for a belly button tree."
Then, the tree moved, and scared Z, me and Lee.
It moved until we could no longer see.
Honey bee Z, followed the tree. And from that
Day on we never saw Z, or another belly button tree.
But me and Lee, will always keep looking you see.

N. Rose Jackson

The Graduate

Who is a graduate
A graduate is one of the best
Anyone who isn't is just one of the rest
He endures all the bad times
And cherishes the good times

He takes advantage of every breath
Because he knows there's no more after death
Will the world take him in a warm embrace
Or given him a harsh slap to the face

Even with the risk of a great fall
The graduate goes for it all
Don't wonder if he will succeed
Because inevitably he will indeed

For a graduate it is inevitable
That by trying his life will be incredible
People think that he's lost his way
But he's already there to stay

When they tell his story
It will be one filled with glory
That is a graduate

Juan Orozco

To You, My Love

Love be gets sacrifices, leaving behind piercing seeds,
A force to announce, definite boundaries in need.
A workshop to inspect, causes in careless way,
Evidence of entertainment, love and honor at bay,
To express protest, at best in primitive hearts,
Completion to pursue, captive ending distorting starts.
"Guilty to Guilty," our assign either self brags,
"Covered with Blood," circumspect clothed in rags,
Acting our roles, heart matters to natural laws,
"Doing my Best," characters in the garden calls.
A sweet vine, pierced with vinegar and sin,
A wooden upright, shouldering nations to win.
One worker declares, "There's ash on my head,"
But Simon shouts, "Dust Should Be There Instead!"
Question to request, "Let Me Go Free,"
Soldier from wall, "I Hear A Rustle, A Breeze."
A seed dies, the temple curtain is rent,
A test memorial, upper-room-joy is sent.
Sacrifices in love, reminiscence in attending,
Worship in silence, broken bridge are amending.

Jerry Ragsdale

My Brother

My brother's name is Joe. He died three years ago
He was my special friend. To him my love I send.

He left this earth without a warning
The weather outside was storming.
He held his chest and fell to the floor
And now his pain he feels no more.

I know he's in heaven where else could he be
But why did God take him away from me
I know he finally found everlasting peace
But my love for Joe will never cease.

There was five of us children we were like one
And when Joe died it hit us like a ton
Me, my sister and brothers miss him like no other
Joe's always been our baby brother.

I wish I was by your side, that rainy night when you died
There's so many things I wanted to say
But now all I can do is pray

My brother, Joe you're always in my heart
Not even death can keep us apart
Oh, Joe can't you see, you will always be special to me.

Josephine Vieira

A 50th Reunion Salute

I salute you, my classmates, where'er you may be
On this our 50th reunion, the class of '43
And especially to all gathered for this gala affair
I bid you all welcome on this day to share.

A half century has passed since we left Wakefield High
Together we have seen some bad times go by
Wars, recessions, losses of classmates and others so dear
But with spirits high, let us face the future without fear.

We stand on the threshold of a new millennium age
With new promises and problems for us to gauge
Let us fervently hope and earnestly pray
That peace and prosperity will rule the day.

And so my dear classmates of Wakefield Cardinal fame
Let us spend this day in reverie, our alma mater to acclaim
May "As Time Goes By" forever be our refrain
And may God bless and keep you 'til we meet again.

Glenn M. Wood

A Rose

A rose
Its soft scent can bring a smile to the hardest face
Its delicate beauty can brighten the darkest room

The sculpted petals so unique
Each one glitters with such grace such elegance

The magnificence of that single rose
Tender as a swaddled infant
Pretty as a summer morning
Soft as a baby's skin
Red as the blazing sun

It radiated happiness
Eyes soften at its sight
Lips curve at its smell
Hands ache to touch its fragile splendor

How I wish to possess that single rose
My thoughts never leave it
Its image is engraved in my mind
Forever

Shauna McRoberts

Forever?

Did we have our forever?
The forever that we pledged to each other.

Did we endure all the triumphs and troubles that
Naturally come with forever?
Or did the trials shorten our forever?

Did the promise of forever have conditions?
Why did forever mean maybe?

Weren't the words spoken, "In good times and bad,
For better or worse," meant to mean forever?

It's not important who the words were spoken in
Front of but why can't we remember forever,
They were spoken to each other.

Why did we forget our promise?
Why did we let go of the promise?
The promise of forever.

Norman C. Perkins

The Topic of Disease

Her mercury-belly protrudes itself against my aluminum chest,
however we both are seated . . .
amidst these middle-back contusions
A prolonged breath—performance of sadness
to encounter our next victim?
No longer is the orange-softness of your neck as innocent,
the merciless nape, so abrasive
space becomes the sum-total of her sex-appeal
aplomb, aplomb
Forsooth, the pardoned interference
and so much train of thought
What can she profess? What can you display?
Other than the three-fifths of your [public flesh]
Late-afternoon seduction and indeed
She is the sole-proponent of phallic injustice.
She holds a mock-marriage in her beak.

Hesse McGraw

Daddy's Love

Isn't it strange?
How your thoughts God can rearrange.
It was Daddy's smile down on the range.
He was there for a while, and
I liked his style, and even when I was a child
He was always mild, and
Hardly ever acted wild.
Our phone number he dialed, and our nails he filed.
He often told us when we were loud.
He sometimes told us when our clothes were piled,
And he told us when he was aroused.
He made sure our plates were mild and piled.

Barbara Newberry

Be Calmed and Restored

There's no need to hurt or be afraid,
For loved ones with us or who have gone away.
The Lord is with them as He is with us.
We just need to believe and give Him our trust.
You may wish there was something you could have changed;
Problems resolved or rearranged.
Or feel there should have been more you had done,
To make their lives easier or at least more fun.
But their soul or spirit is happy and free.
They don't hold you to blame for what was to be.
Just remember the bond of love we all share.
Until the end of time, it will always be there.

Melonie O'Meara

Freed From Pain

Lying in bed, shaking in fear
Crying, crying for the nightmare is here.

Living a nightmare, praying for sleep.
The fear in my heart goes ever so deep.

Your presence is evil, evil as sin.
I see your face and cry again.

The scars you left will never heal
For the hatred and pain is oh so real.

You've stole my childhood, took it away.
You will pay for that on the reckoning day.

I'm older know and much more strong.
With you gone form my life I can once again sing my song.

I'm freed from pain, Freed From Pain.

Charlene Adams

Just Friends

Why did you leave me in such great sorrow?
I always think it'll all be better tomorrow.

But there is no tomorrow it's always today.
Why do you always seem six worlds away?

It was just you and me, but now I'm alone.
Since you left me, my heart has been full of stone.

Do I choose to love? Or choose to hate?
I know I can't predict my own fate.

I want to be with you forever, until the end of time
I want to be yours, and you to be mine.

To be with you again, I've only dared to wish.
Could it be that our love is truly finished.

I guess I'll never know until you tell me how you feel.
You're the only one that will make my bleeding heart heal.

You're the only one that can mend my broken heart.
I knew that right from the start.

I never thought you'd be the one to break it.
I'm starting to think that I can't take it.

I guess I'll never be in your arms again.
So I'll have to settle for being Just Friends.

Evelyn Boss

Thinking Back on Yesterday

Thinking back on yesterday, when we were young and free,
The jungle was our kingdom, the river was our sea.
We played that we were mermaids and we did only good,
And we even knew some golden elves who lived out in the woods.
Our laughter rang from tree to tree, we climbed their every limb,
Yes, we were young and happy, when we lived way back then.

Now we are no longer mermaids, the elves were only in our minds,
We find that things are different, our dreams change with the times.
But, now, even though we're older, when there's a chance to be . . .
The jungle's still our kingdom,
The river's still our sea!

Sandra Dawson Jank

Untitled

I ran through a hall of flames
I thought I heard you call my name
It was faint but still the same
I screamed and cried, let it be true
that at the end of the hall, I'll be with you
And I run until the end,
never to find, my Lover, my Friend
once again I awake, once again my heart breaks

Betty Metzger

The Time to Poetize

Inspiration is surely needed to "poetize,"
From deep within the mind, time and time again,
Spring forth thoughts we all realize,
Stir the best and the worst in men.

Certain events and seasons arouse the mind,
A defeat or a victory, a loss, or a gain,
A fortune lost or a treasure find,
Better stature or health or strength that wanes.

Romance that leads to the joining of two,
Separation of lovers and loss of friends,
Clouded days of sorrow or skies of blue,
Happy days or hours the heart with grief bends.

Writing must be done from the heart,
Wisdom, experience, and emotion dictate how,
Yet it's most difficult to find a time to start,
But if one is to "poetize," he must begin right now.

Franklin Roop

Home Sweet Home

After school, I go to my Home Sweet Home,
When I get sick in school, my Mommy comes and takes
me to my Home Sweet Home,
When I'm out of school on break, I get to take sometime
to be with my family in my Home Sweet Home.

Whether you go to a baby-sitter's house or not, eventually,
you will be in your Home Sweet Home,
And whether or not your family is divorced and
you have two homes, they are both Home Sweet Homes,
and so eventually, you will come to a Home Sweet Home.

Lauren Michele Baugh

Hungry for Life

He told me sweet lies of sweet love
Heavy with the burden of the truth
and he spoke of his dreams
broken by the burden of his youth.
Thirteen years he said, "I couldn't look into the sun."

Then she came and saw him lying dead at the end of her gun
"I remember his hands."
And the way the mountains looked.
Light shot demons in his eyes.

Confused why his life I took,
Like the fear of age written all over my face.

When I wake up I will be in a better place.
The war is still rapping inside of me
I still feel the chill hunger for life.

My shaman, to you I reveal.

Sabra Baker

Untitled

Of the same blood we are not,
Yet somehow we do favor.
She gave me not birth,
Yet she gives me life.
Changing my diapers,
She was never given the privilege,
Yet she is my mother.
Holding my hand for my first step,
That taken from her also,
Yet she holds my hand through every step,
Feed me my bottle, she never got to do,
Yet she feeds me the knowledge of the world.
My first word "Momma" she never heard.
Nor did she know, that I would consider her
"Momma" until the day I die!

Teresa Pilkinton

Why Didn't You Say Goodbye
In Memory of Lucy Maselli
I remember coming home from school one day
And there was no one home,
Not a sound in the house but the ringing of the phone.

Thinking who could it be, why aren't my parents here.
I had the most terrible fear.

My cousin answered, said she's not doing well.
The doctors have been saying it's really hard to tell.

As I was walking to her home
All I could remember was all the fun times we had together.

Thinking I was so young and naive,
Thinking one of my parents would never die or leave.

I arrived at my cousin's home
And she said they don't think she's going to pull through.
I said no, I want to go to the hospital, this can't be true.

I was in a room with my best friend crying
And so many thoughts came in my head.
They said I'm so sorry she didn't make it, your mother is dead.

Oh God Mom! I wish you were here, I just want to cry or just die.
My mother, my friend, the one who gave me life.
Oh, why didn't you say goodbye!
Kim Maselli

Gawky God

One day many years ago, God created animals
To roam the earth, to and fro.

She noticed that they were all very dull,
Even the very elegant sea gull.

God decided to give them all color,
So that they would not be any more dull.

Even though God was a Saint,
She managed to spill all of her paint.

She caused a colorful arch to fall in the sky,
That any animal could see as they were passing by.

God decided that this problem had to be fixed,
But she did not know how to wash out acrylics.

She painted over the colors with invisible ink,
So that no animal would notice, even the bright pink.

This solved her problem, for a short while,
Which made God happy, and made her smile.

But when the rain came down,
It washed the ink to the ground.

Revealing what we now know,
As the very colorful rainbow!
Amanda H. Crawley

Forget Me Not

Forget me not, when I'm gone
I'm leaving you this, to carry on
I'll be back, before you know
I'm giving you this time, so that you can grow
I hope you miss me, as much as I'm going to miss you
I hope after this, I will know what to do
What you did, I drew the line
Now that I'm gone, I'm going to be fine
I want some space so we can see how we feel
To make sure our love is real
We need sometime, so we can mend
Just know whatever happens
I will always be your friend
The time apart, will help a lot

So please dear, forget me not!
Nicole Fox

A Daydream

I once stared out the window, without hearing what was said.
I dreamed of trumpets blowing, as I heard God in my head say,
"This, my child, is the Book of Life, in which your name I've read,"
And overcome with happiness, I cried and bowed my head.

And with a heavy heart, I looked at Him and said,
"But Lord I'm not deserving of all the blood you've shed."

With tearful eyes He held me, and said He cried for me,
For all the pain I'd suffered in my life was needlessly.

"As a child how you loved me, and we spoke every day.
And as your life went on, I watched you slip away.

And not once did you call on me, except in time of need."
And as He spoke those words, I felt reality.

As I stared back out that window, I knew God spoke to me.
If my name was to be in the Book of Life,
That's where my heart should be.
Deborah Wilson

A Very Special Girl

It is written somewhere in a book on a shelf
that young girls think of only themselves.
I know that is not the whole truth
for I live with a young lady that is my living proof.

She makes friends who will never forget
that this young lady is one they are glad they have met.
To her coworkers she is a rare kind of breed
and they can't help but follow her lead.

She gives a kind of love you have to feel
and to me that love is so very real.
Others who know her can attest to my claim
that the way she shows her love to each is not the same.

I guess I'm kind of slanted about the way I feel
and all this fuss that you might think is a big deal.
But you may have guessed by this time
that the little girl I'm talking about in all mine.
Edward E. Wethey

Toe Freedom

When I take off my shoes and socks
I wiggle my toes
I imagine they say to me
"Come run in the dark green grass,
Come bury me under the warm pale Florida sand
And let me wiggle my way out,
And let the waves of the oceans
Lakes and seas run over me."
"When it is winter outside
Don't let me out of the warmth of the fuzzy
Socks you put me in when you get bored.
Try to write your name with me
For I love to be as free as I can be.
Jenny Jann Sayles

If Only You Knew . . .

If you only knew how it feels to get divorced
If you only knew why God actually put us here
If you only knew why there is so much war
If you only knew how it feels to be an adult
If you only knew how it is to walk in space
If you only knew how it feels to be a parent
If you only knew how it feels to be an infant
When no one knows what they want
If you only knew how our parents felt when we were born
If you only knew if animals can really understand us
If you only knew that my baby cousin
Was born on November 5, 1996
If you only knew how cute he is
Jamie Hills

Only You

When our eyes first met there was
something special there;

I knew then it was with you, my life I
wanted to share.

As time goes by we grow closer together;
And I hope we both want this to last forever.

So let's open our hearts to one another;
New and wonderful things we will discover.

'Cause I love you more and more everyday;
And it's our love I will never betray;

So on this one of a kind day;
Always remember, it's only to you,
The words I do, I will say.

Jeffrey Scott Clark

"Now That I'm Old"

A Parody Of Yeats' "When You Are Old"
So I'm sitting here, tired and half-freezing,
Trying to warm myself by this small fire;
And suddenly, I remember the words
Of this really old guy I once used to know.

My God, he would go on about my face,
And how everybody used to love me;
I don't know, it was kind of flattering,
But, God, I wish he could have lightened up.

He gave me a book a long, long time ago—
Told me to read it when I got real old.
Damn, I wish I remembered where it was;
If I could burn it, I might not be so cold.

Stephanie J. Stiles

Doin' Time

As I lie here at night my loneliness is clear.
Thinking of your beauty and my eyes start to tear.
I hear your voice in my head and it puts me at ease,
I love everything about you, even your cute little sneeze.
I would walk a thousand miles just to touch you again.
You are not only my lover, but also my best friend.
Your very essence keeps me alive.
Knowing I'll still love you when we're ninety five.
So don't cry for me, instead wear a smile.
Because I'm almost done walking that first mile.

Howard Beam

A Voice for Endangered Animals

I am a small part of the mystery of
creation because I was never produced through
human imagination.

It has been my misfortune to rank beneath
the human species, though some kind humans
have been known to show me tender mercies.

In some human habitations, my presence
is a threat. Sometimes I'm considered a
pest; though, sometimes I'm loved as a pet.

Someday I may cease to exist; I'm already
a part of an endangered species list, while
the land I once called home is shrinking
day by day. If I survive another century,
What price will I have to pay?

Will I be tortured in the name of science
or mass-produced for human consumption?
Would I be wrong to make such an assumption?

Jeanne K. Mears

How Do You Weep

How do you weep when you have no tears,
When the ache wells up inside and struggles to overflow,
When the war between peace of mind and great anxiety rises
To the surface but has no outlet?

How do you release yourself from the box of frustration
When your hands are tied,
When all you can do is sit, watch, wait,
And hope someone else is free to lend a hand?

How do you help carry another's burdens
When more than miles separate your lives,
When the weight knows no boundaries or limits,
And threatens to tear hearts apart?

How do you pray when you have no words,
When all the heart feels cannot be expressed,
When no human words seem adequate enough
To voice all the emotion welling up inside?

How do you weep when you have no tears?

Beth Hollopeter

Mom

You've been there for me since I was born,
From what you tell me it was early morn.
You've been my best friend from day one.
To love with no question is what you've done.
You've been the best mother the world's ever known,
No brighter than you has the sun ever shone.
To hear your voice, to see your face,
Makes this world a better place.
You must be an angel from up above,
To be so full of kindness and love.
So when the time comes for you to go and leave this worldly place,
I know that God will be there waiting with a smile upon his face.

Lisa Ritter

Life's Lessons Learned

I have learned of men and things—a little
Known fear found courage and spread my wings—a little
Of politics or law and such not much
Yet enough I feel to grasp the wheel
Of life a little stronger
For life's a journey calm and rough
On which we all are travelling
But the love of family, friends and God
Have kept me form unravelling

Robert L. Meyers

A Prayer for My Little Boy

Oh, God in heaven above, I pray
You'll watch o'er my son his everyday.
He's so very helpless and so very small
There isn't much of him at all.

Give him Thy care while he's awake,
And when he's asleep, for Jesus sake,
I ask Thee to guard him from every care.
Teach him with us Thy love to share.

His hands are so tiny, oh, Father above.
Please guide every movement with Thy love.
His feet are so small, oh, please dear God,
Watch them wherever they may trod.

His lips are so rosy, no words yet they speak
Oh, teach him the words that are kind and meek.
With his tiny blue eyes may you teach him to see
All things that are lovely and wondrous—like Thee.

Oh, Father in heaven, watch over my child
And make him like Thee, Mary's son, meek and mild.

Louise N. Johnson

My Gift to Your Unborn Child

Can I be strong enough
to do what I must?
Mind and morality
over body and desire?
Eyes must be opened to reveal
that a night of lust cannot compare
to a lifetime of Love.

Youth is made up of
unthinking, recklessness and rationalizations.
"I am only human . . ."
can only cause
undeserved pain and destruction
to the trusting.

Let us grow older at this moment,
find wisdom together
and preserve our sanctity.
If the longing must continue,
be it from a distance;
sparing the ones we love
by denying our indiscretions.

Mary Ann Grace Maciel Turman

The Fire of the Light

Make me a fire, Lord, always burning bright,
Warming hearts, warming lives,
In the coldest of all nights.
Never let me stop burning,
Though some may smother the flame.
Make me Your light in this dark world,
Proclaiming Your holy name.

Make me a fire, Lord, always burning bright,
Warming hearts, warming lives,
In the coldest of all nights.
May people gather 'round me,
Longing for the love,
That comes flowing through me
From the heavens up above.

Make me a fire, Lord, an everlasting flame,
Changing hearts changing lives,
Through Your most-powerful name.
And when the blaze is finally through,
the final ember's spent,
Take me home to be with You, eternally content.

Jill Christine Kissinger

Little Wings, Our Angel From God

Your mother held you oh, so tight
The moment you were born
Suffering throughout the night
God took you that next morn

Yes, we grieved, our hearts hung low
And God's purpose wasn't clear
He made our sorrow overflow
But from you, an angel did appear

In our soul and in our hearts
We've replaced sorrow with godly things
The knowledge that we're never apart
That's why I've named you, "Little Wings"

Your little sister, Katie star
Always kissed you while you were growing
Feeling Mommy's belly everyday
Talking to the brother she thought she'd be knowing

I know you're with us here right now
I know this above all things
I can't explain exactly just how
So God bless you, our "Little Wings"

Judy Pariseau

Heaven

Heaven is a place that I cannot see.
But, heaven is a place where I long to be.
You see, my Father and his heavenly hosts are there
But, the fullness of his Spirit can be felt everywhere.

Do you see the greatest miracle that he has wrought?
How that your soul and my soul, he magnificently bought.
Yes, the price tag on us was very high.
But, "Oh" my God worked it out without a sigh.

My sisters and brothers, we are very precious in his sight.
So, hold on and keep the faith and most of all, continue to fight.
So, heaven is a place; we can't naturally see.
But, heaven is a place . . . you and I long to be.

Deborah Johnson

Lonesome

Tears do not come as I wish them to,
to free my crying soul
My heart is breaking as each second ticks by
Daydreaming my only friend
Eyes closes tightly against reality,
colors alien to my grey world
Love withers away like a blackened rose
My fate lies within the stars
I sing to at night
The present unwanted,
past forgotten
Words unspoken, have meanings misunderstood

Kathleen Pedro

Wanting to Die/Live

Someday's I feel lonely and sad inside
Although I really don't know why,
I am confused as you can see
This creature of the night has been searching for me.
I can feel him watching from far away
And then at once he is standing beside me.
I can feel his breathe on my neck
Chills start creeping up my back
All at once I feel the pain
The creature is taking my life away.
Why have you waited so long I asked
I'm going to be on his throne at last
Take my life as you see
Then remember this phrase I am saying to thee
You can take a life everyday
But is it the same when they don't flee away
Is the satisfaction there when the blood is cold
Thank you for picking me I didn't want to grow old
Now I live forever in your black soul.

Lonna D. Darrah

Untitled

My family is a rainbow
We all shine in different colors
When one is a happy color
Maybe another is sad
Sometimes one shines
While the others seem dull
During the rough times
Mist might sprinkle on the rainbow
But when the mist is gone
Everyone shines through brightly
Mostly the rainbow is metallic
Polished to a bright gloss
All the colors flow together
As each color is a part of the others
You could think about it one way
The rainbow would never be the same without one color

Andrea Krause

The Storm

It starts out a sunny day,
But then it goes away.
The clouds come in and overtake the sky.
The blue turns into gray.
Then the gray is filled with flashes of the yellow.
The rain comes down,
With the yellow and the gray in the sky.
Out of the blue comes a rainbow.

Love is like a storm sometimes;
It can end as fast as it started.
The blue sky is the clear beginning,
The gray is the arguments to come,
The flash of yellow is the ending coming near.
Then hope comes from a rainbow radiant and clear,
Suddenly the hope is clear
The blue sky,
The love, reappears.

David Bauza

Daddyhood

With a love that is deeper, than darkest of nights,
For patience and wisdom, we always will fight.
The days troubles we've had, when we put them to bed
Leave only the love, with that kiss on their head.
It's so hard to discover, that we've misunderstood,
When having them here, is always so good.
All the pride and the wonder, is seeing them grow,
And a constant reminder, that we're feeling old.
We commit to a life of hard work to provide,
Seems so simple for them, just along for the ride.
We hurt and we fear, but we know all will heal,
But what's under the bed, is to them just as real.
It's so hard to convince them, that father knows best,
When they've heard what they know, from some of the rest.
We feel that at times, all our efforts are shot,
Then "I love you Daddy," say's probably not.
What was it we did, the first twenty odd years?
None of that matters, we know why we're here.

Mark Rynd

Spring Shine Day

*(written after near-death auto accident,
April, 1997, as I felt God's presence)*
"I'm grateful for each leaf I see
As I lie beneath dear verdant tree
Looking up to heaven's sea
    of white foam clouds passing by
    against an azure ocean sky

Thank God I'm alive this spring shine day

As trees clap hands as if to say
    seek Me He says in every way
    I am here with you this spring shine day."

Jeanne-Helene Wattel

Believe

All that you wish for that is honest and true
The Lord will certainly give it to you

Not always the way you most desire
But, He always gives what you most require

So accept what he sends, be bitter or sweet
For God knows best what makes your life complete

Great is your gladness and rich is your reward
When you learn to accept the will of the Lord

The future is yours; it belongs to you
And with faith in God and in yourself too

No hell too high; no mountain too tall
For with faith in God, you can conquer them all

Sheila Netherton

Fear

Fear laid upon me that day—
His devilish mask glared through,
As his flamed body hovered
Above my tense and trembled soul.

Fear moved in my body,
Stopped to examine my mind;
For the intellect of himself,
And walked into me knowing,
I couldn't compete with him.

Fear healed back my goals,
Intimidated his other family fears,
And laughed with Ryan
On my chickened ideas.

Fear is a mental image
Figmented into my open mind.
It lingers as I allow,
Fear, I must conquer thou.

Fear disrupts my inner self
In order to overcome.
I must hold a mental edge, to pursue my goal, No Fear!

Aaron Moe

The Tunnel of Life

The shadow of darkness
The picture of death
I must walk through the tunnel
to get to the light.

I must open doors that are normally closed
Challenge people on new ideas proposed.

Look beyond what I can already see
touch things new to me.

Cross the ocean
run across the sand
jump out of a plane
travel across foreign land.

Change the only part of the world I can
my own life, my own future.

Make my dreams reality
cherish what God has given me
love the person I know I can be
love myself just for being me.

Christina Binder

Canoe Ride in Mobile Bay at Sunrise

The canoe rides uneasily in the bay waters past the calm sloughs.
Sloughs have no interest, the bay has life.
Waves cluck against the canoe.
The beach, the destination not straight ahead. Turning over
Would result from a direct approach.

Terns sound alarm crying out of our approach
Beside the reserved pelican.
Pelicans are here in spite of us
They survived all that man could
Do to them, And. Here they are.
The quiet reserve comes from knowing they will survive.

Piles of wood rest on the island.
Smoothness out roughness
The bay, the wind, the sand beat upon the grains.
To produce the art of the wood.
The poet sees life; the worker sees a table.

Islands exist for what is brought and left.
Mud flats from the tide.
Wildflowers among the driftwood from another place.
Clapper rail announces his territory is the island.

Robert C. Zeanah

Isolation

Barrenness; at peace with its desolation, soaks feverishly
against the wash boards of a child's tub: a vessel without
a sailor lying in despondency, and at sea a wake crashes;
lacking a captain to conduct its assembly of elements, and
in turn it rolls away discharged.
Taking in the old sea with a youthful wheeze, the boy
dresses himself in navy blue, and like his father before
him; the boy shall fear only the point of return.
Port side to the sun, the young captain spills what's left
of his father's garden through the hands of his mother;
reminding her of his once wearisome way of love upon dry land.
Into the boat the boy settled; sipping from pools of sea water
he wondered how long he could last at sea, from which
tapered end of the arrow would point north and which one
of his father's watches could keep time in a monotonous sort.
At sea, the tiny craft sails into a righteous voyage, rendering
its confidence carefully passed the wreaked waters of those
who drowned along the way: Dying fathers not sailors, men
with rafts not boats at sea for the salvation of their hearts;
to elude their isolation for death.

    Victor S. Salvador

Union, Never Again

In memory of Kam Shan Fung, March 18, 1997
It's misty, foggy; umbrellas tag along.
Drizzling on windshield, the wiper pendulum stops.
A bus of friends and families, a gathering of unforeseen agonies.
Peers only; seniors lonely.
Traditional ritual forbids the aged.
Twenty-six, ready to roll; twenty-six, too soon to go.

Hospitals house the sick; Doctors save lives at stake, if
they show up in time.
Nothing's too late; yet it is too late.

Mom, I don't want to die.
Mom, I don't want to die.
Mama let go of his hands;
Doctors grabbed hold of his arms.
Thro' double door, mama
Mama was left behind. Mom, I don't want to die.

Fire cleansed his body; fire set him free.

A kid he was, I left home.
A married man he became, we met again.
At wedding banquet, a bouquet of giggles and laughters;
As he lies dormant, another family reunion.

    Cora K. S. Fung

A True Friend

I am weak, but you replace my inability with triumph.
I am tired, but you give me the strength to do your will.
I am ill, but you heal all my wounds with your mercy.
I am depressed, but your love fills me with joy.
I am rejected, but you embrace me with never-ending love.
I am lonely, but you send your people to fill the emptiness.
I am lost, but you find me, take my hand and guide me
    on the path of your light.
I am afraid, but you surround me with comfort.
I am unhappy, but your love overflows me with a stream of joy.
I cry from the hurt that binds me, but you take me in your
    loving arms and wipe my tears away.
I am saddened by the ways of the world, but you have shown me,
    only through you can there ever exist harmony.
I see evil, but through your eyes, I see goodness.
I am selfish, but you show me the needs of others.
My heart is filled with mistrust for people, but you show me
    that trust in you conquers the deceit in others.
My mind is closed, but you unlock it with the key of understanding.
I want to die, but you give me precious air with which to live.

    Debbie Schwartzman

She Is

She walks, tall and proud,
Among the scurrying beings on the Avenue.
Slowly, deliberately, she moves,
Aware of her surroundings,
But detached in her purpose.

Head held high, she pursues her path,
Determined to achieve her goals.
Unaware of the stares of many passersby,
Her regal demeanor precedes her.

Unbowed by the past, hopeful of the future,
She has her sights set on the pinnacle.
Praying to her God, faithful to her beliefs,
She knows, all too well,
The joys and pitfalls of Life.

She is A Woman,
She is African-American,
She is strong,
She Is.

    Margaret R. Harris

His Time Had Run Out

There once was a man who was happy and gay,
Not a care bothered him all through his day.
Toil nor sweat interfered in his play,
And he never bothered to help anyone along their way.

He cared for nobody, only himself,
He liked nobody, only himself.
He taught no one, for he had nothing to teach.
He guided no one, for he had nothing to preach.

And "oh" said he, I've got plenty of time,
There'll be a day when I'll let my light shine,
I'll help others with my whole self
But now, I'm only concerned about myself.

May I leave with you this parting thought;
He had plenty of time. But without giving thought
To the future and that time was passing by,
He wasn't really very ready to die.

    Virginia Hart

God Gave You to Me

Will I ever know why you came into my life,
What I did to deserve your love, kindness and respect?
Your love for me is there in so many ways
When I laugh, you laugh,
When I cry, you cry,
My happiness is your happiness.
Even at my worst you stayed
Never leave, oh Lord I pray
Trials and problems even still
Staying with me saying, "I'm doing God's will."
I love the respect you give me
But also the same for others I see
I wonder sometimes how this could be
It's all because gave you to me.

    Margaret Boadu

Time

My heart bleeds since that night he left me.
He's so cold with the way he dumped me.
Hatred runs wild in me . . .
Since that cold night he left me.
I stand in the cold dark world all alone.
To find myself in a world unknown.
Emptiness is all around me.
My head and heart are messy.
What to do is still unknown.
The only thing I know is time . . .
Might help me.

    Sharee Adkinson

Flower Garden of Life

In the morning as the sun slowly appears up over the horizon,
I can see the shades of color in all forms and sizes.

As I sit and sip my morning coffee,
I realize a flower garden is so much like life at its best.

The tiny plants come through the warm soil, just like
children that are born and nurtured with love and care
they grow into a beautiful sight to behold.

As Spring turns into Summer and slowly into Fall,
others take on their brilliance and start to show their beauty.

By late Fall, we know by the coolness of the soil,
as the colors slowly fade, we need to get them ready
for the coming of Winter.

Some will find it a perfect resting place,
while others will grow and multiply
and then I can look forward to them
being more beautiful than ever the following year.

     Pauline Thomas

School Girl

I am a crazy depressed school girl
I wonder what the world will be like for my kids
I hear people crying all around
I see many angels flying
I want to fix the world
I am a crazy depressed school girl

I pretend that life is a dream
I want to feel no pain and hatred
I touch the fiery depths of life
I worry that I will be stuck in this H - - L we call life
I cry at the drugs, gangs, and violence
I am a crazy depressed school girl

I understand that our world is corrupt
I say "Lord save us"
I dream that one day he will
I try to do my part to make this world a better one
I hope this world will be around to raise my kids in
I am a crazy depressed school girl

     Amanda Huigen

For Georgia

Time falls rapidly.
The future is already the past.
These paths ahead are vast.
It is almost to difficult to choose which one to take.
The umbilical cord that attaches us to the ones we love;
Stretches and springs back every once in a while.
Memories linger in the mind.
Tears taste bitter after a while.
It is unconditional love that is true,
And I love you.

Our time together is short, but meaningful.
It is me that ventures in and out, unknowingly.
These thoughts are creases in the paper meant for you,
And I love you.

Sometimes I think I am not thoughtful enough,
But thoughts are too much and are embedded within.
I am aware of my faults,
Longing to be the best for my family,
But I am me and you except me for me
And I love you.

     Christine Myers

Untitled

The night of the party had come—
Fun and laughter for everyone.
Everyone looked really great
Ready and eager to stay out late.

What? You didn't see me anywhere?
Oh, believe me, I was there.
I saw you laugh, and dance, and drink.
Seeing you with her caused my heart to sink.

You looked handsome—so very fine.
You were certainly having a very good time.
She was having a grand time too.
You were looking at her the way I look at you.

What? You still cannot recall—
Seeing me last night at all.
You might not have noticed me above the din.
I was outside looking in.

     Jamie M. Cordrey

Dreams

Sometimes as unreal
As a childhood fairy tale

Able to be crushed and destroyed into nothing
Though unable to touch or feel

Pillow soft clouds of intangible thoughts
Beaming as colorful as a rainbow

Dreams are special thoughts
Meant to be shared with someone you love

Moonlit walks along the beach
Romantic candlelight dinners for two

Moonbeams shining on the incoming tide
As we watch the white caps subside gracefully

Sunshine sparkles through the trees under which we walk
A fireplace glowing, warming two winter hearts

Taking years to build
Though only moments to destroy
Dreams are something we live for

     Patricia Bieszki

The Face of a Stranger

This is a story of a baby born with no sadness
She wasn't aware yet of her coming madness
She never saw the problems around her
Until one day she lost her father
Sometimes she dreamed of some magic force
Then she learned the meaning of the word divorce
The sound of daddy grew fainter and fainter
When finally daddy became a stranger
She felt all alone so she picked up the phone
And invited the man to come to her home
So they set a time and a day
If the man was excited he didn't say
Finally the day came
But the girl didn't know it was just a game
Hours came and hours passed
That's when the girl learned on his mind she was last
And then one day the girl moved away
And the man had nothing to say
Now the girl's left with confusion and heartache
And a daddy who turned out to be a fake

     Alexis M. Taylor

I of the Tornado

In the I of the tornado, is a peaceful center, safe from the
violence and destruction of the outside world all around.
Safe from the whirling of conflicting winds,
there is a place to objectively watch,
untouched by the witnessing.
There is a place to dream,
unshaken by the
sleeplessness.
In the I of the
tornado is a
peaceful
center.

Kathryn Yarborough

Beauty

Beauty is the heaven that lights up at night.
Beauty is the dawn with its Sun so bright.

Beauty is the rainbow that crosses the sky.
Beauty is the colorful flowers that greet the eye.

Beauty is the sight of a mother's smile
as she holds her tiny newborn child.

Beauty is the mountains covered with snow.
Beauty is the rolling valleys spread out below.

Beauty is the ripple of a gentle stream
wrapped in a field of glorious green.

Beauty is true love shared by two.
Beauty is a lifetime of dreams come true.

Paul Baker

To Our Four Children

Not much help can we give you dear
When you have problems we don't seem near
Not much sympathy when the tears show clear
A cruel hard parent we must seem to appear
The young and the old are so far apart
When one life nears end the other will start
But our darlings you are all in our hearts
We give you so little and wish we could give more
You have a father that you should treasure
Just knowing he is yours is a priceless treasure
He is working his body and fingers to the bone
So his children can be proud of the place they call home
Someday when God has called us both away
We hope you take the time to pray
Remember the things we tried to do for you
And may God grant your wishes
When it comes to you

Sophia Wolfinger

The Other Side of Man

Some say that they are devious and don't mean what they say.
But mine is warm and charming and more loving every day.
When he is late I get irate and jealousy sets in.
Only to find that he was searching for my favorite chocolate tin.
I can be sad or all upset and ready to throw in the towel.
And he shows up with flowers for my garden and a trowel.
I find some money missing then get so angry I could scream
Then he shows up with something I've been wanting, what a dream.
Some say that they are selfish, condescending, chauvinistic.
But mine is always complimenting, fair and realistic.
It's said they don't have feelings, they're too busy being cool.
But I believe for many men this is untrue and cruel.
Lots of women will tell you romance ended with the marriage.
But ours continued on and on even past the baby carriage.
It isn't fair to judge them all by those who cut and ran.
Because I have the first hand scoop of the other side of man.

Delia

Fractured February

February's here and so
Goodbye to January
January with her biting winds, elongated nights
Extending
Into time's deep mornings.

And then
Before expected and much too soon
The light of day leaves us,
Leaves us to draw into our cocoon-like existence
Pull down the shades—pull up the comforts!

This February especially
With fractured foot, crutches, shuffling.
Ordinary tasks taking everlastingly long
A painful time—a trying time.

Ah! But then the pets, they play.
They bring the chuckles, laughs and love
Seemingly
From the past when children played
And danced and sang
And into mischief too!

Mildred Ardys Harrington

Rock-n-Roll Poet

Silver cat crawled in the alley way, just before the dawn.
Sandy's wearing dead flowers, from last evening's prom.
Lawrence of Arabia, was free fear of fame,
Me, I'm sitting at an old card table, trying to guess the game.

Look at all those people, running in the race.
The lovely ladies with their low bows, putting them to waste.
Tried to get Ray Davies, I couldn't reach him on the line.
Sometimes, some stars are too bright to see,
when you look into their shine.

Some bloodshot eyes are stalking sweet, there's nowhere to run.
Your sister, she keeps calling me, wants to borrow my gun.
I'll have your party sometime, but this can't be the day.
Because anything I ever wanted to keep, I had to give away.

So I'll play your guitar, you can lay in my bed.
You never listen to the words I sing, the lyrics in my head.
Tomorrow you'll go to Pittsburgh, I'll drop out of school.
You always try to make me look second best, well now
    let's look at you.

Ryan B. Bleck

The Parson

While on my way to Canterbury, one hot spring day,
I was dying of thirst along the way,
When I noticed a poor, frail man,
Of the Lord's Gospel lying in the sand.
When he heard my horse's hooves clattering,
He woke with fright, eyes battering.
Noticing I a poor, thirsty, hungry man,
He offered bread and wine with his hand.
"Friend" said I, "what brings you this way?"
He ignored my question and did not say.
Instead he spoke of Christ's gospel, fluently preaching it,
And to I, he was teaching it. After night began to hover,
He offered a spread so that I could cover.
When I woke with the sun, I noticed he had already begun,
His journey onto the unknown land, for he no longer lay in the sand.
In place of where he was lying, was bread, wine and a note implying.
I gathered myself and mounted, and found I no longer doubted.
That there are some good men on earth,
and that gold is not greater than their worth.

Nancy L. Ferguson

The Fisherman

It's raining
Out the door he ran with his worm can
Bare feet . . . up and down the street
Night crawlers everywhere . . . WHAT JOY
THIS BRINGS THE LITTLE FISHERMAN.

A little older . . . a little bolder
Rod and reel . . . carrying a creel
WHAT HAPPINESS
THIS BRINGS THE YOUTHFUL FISHERMAN.

Years later . . . load the car
Load the kids . . . to the lake
My children and my wife . . . THIS IS THE LIFE
THINKS THE MIDDLE-AGED FISHERMAN.

Time moves on . . . he's a little slower
Not as strong. Friends stop by
Oxygen in tow . . . IT'LL BE A GREAT DAY
THINKS THE GENTLE OLD FISHERMAN.

New home . . . old friends
He's moved on . . . rod, reel and creel
WALKING HAND AND HAND WITH THE *FIRST FISHERMAN.*

Karen S. Harrison

Love Defined

It's a warm feeling of sunshine
Sunbeams playing on my face
I am yours and you are mine
This spot in my heart is your place

It's a strange pain inside
Whenever I have you near
Don't be shy; you have no reason to hide
You have no reason to shed a tear

It's a stabbing pain
As my love walks out
My life begins to rain
Was there ever any doubt?
I can't keep up with time—
Instead of slow, it moves fast
One minute, us together is fine
Though right now suddenly turns into the past

It's a feeling of absolute faith
Utterly trusting that one
One and the other is kept safe
The hope that binds is never undone

Denise Magditch

The Hour Glass

To my loving husband
There's an hour glass of time.
It sets upon the table.
It resembles the time we have to share together.
How fast the sands flow, and so does our time.
If I could stop the sands that flow in the bottle.
My time with you for 1 hour would be 1 year,
and 1 year would be an eternity.
You are my friend,
My father, and my mother.
You are my lover,
My enemy, and my mate forever.
Sometimes they say absence
makes the heart grow fonder,
It doesn't make it fonder.
It makes it find the things that everyday life
causes you to set aside for something less important.
My heart is as much in love as the first time we kissed.
So even though my hour glass of time still flows as before.
Just occasionally turn it over, and remind me what it's for.
I love you forever.

Barbara Jezior

Mother's Day

Mother's day.
Mother's day is coming near
And I think her hair is
Pretty and weird . . .

My mother is nice
She is like mice
The reason is she is a sight

Mothers are just for you
And I love you too

In the sun she is fun
And she does not like to cook buns.

Last but not least she is so sweet
She is sweeter than a flock of sleeping sheep.

Robyn Harris

Someone New

Meeting someone new is so exciting.
It puts so much fun back into your life.

Sometimes life seems so plain.
How can someone new bring it back to life,
You know the one you hate so much?

They do so much with just a smile, special touch,
Open arms and loving, caring open heart.

They can help you to learn to breath and relax again.
Learn to sit back and talk what even comes your way.

So always go with whatever makes you happy
At that time and always learn from the good or bad times
And points of life.

Myra Istne Cruchet

Oh Divine Source, I Thank Thee

Oh Divine Source,
I thank thee for creating me in the image of yourself
Thank you for the life you have given me
I thank thee for free will and the
Power to create and recreate
I thank thee for loving me unconditionally and
Paving the way for me always
I am so grateful to have thee as my ˮ
Support and my Father/Mother
I am thankful for the abundance of
Unlimited supplies you have provided for me
My will is to use this good to bless all of
Life, as you have blessed me
I Thank thee, O Divine Source

Zandra Samuels

The Desolate Mother

No one can describe the pain of the sad desolate mother.
Tell me how she remains sane trying to raise our brothers.
The man leaves her home alone to play the role of Poppa.
Even when the money was low that could never stop her.

Because she really does love you!

She can teach the child good manners and self-respect.
But there is that mile that the man must show the steps.
And without the man around to be the fatherly mentor.
I'll be you'll see the kid downtown at the justice center.

Don't even try to deny the truth!

At night I can hear her sad tears expressing her stress.
Failure is the feeling she fears deriving herself some rest.
But she still stands tall through it all every single day.
That's why we must crawl on our knees for her I pray.

Because I have a desolate mother too!

Jason E. Tucker

Remember When . . .

Remember when you said, "smile," and I did?
Remember when you listened while I cried?
Remember when you said, "don't give up," and I didn't ?
Remember when you said, "try," and I tried?
Remember when I said, "I can't," but I could?
Remember when I needed someone, and you were there?
Remember when I said, "it's hopeless," but it wasn't?
Remember when you said, "I care?"

I remember when your smile helped me to smile.
I remember when your listening helped me not to cry.
I remember when your not giving up on me helped me to continue on.
I remember when your trying helped me to try.
I remember when your faith in me helped me to gain faith.
I remember when you were the one I needed.
I remember when your hope helped me to renew my hope.
I remember when your simple, "I care," was all that I needed.

Remember when . . .
I do . . .
Now, and forever.
          Patty M. Schulz

"Gently day dons her cloak . . ."

Gently day dons her cloak
And shadows hide her face
Her streaming blonde ringlets are hidden from view
Until the time comes for their next debut
Braided with golden lace

Night sweeps in with a chilly air
Her icy fingers grasp the breeze
It shudders with cold, utters a moan
Then scrambles away chilled to the bone
Tripping over streaking leaves

Though night's terror seems unending
Her reign is quickly past
For day's soft fingers unwinds the mist
And her warmth embraces rolling hills sun-kissed
And night's darkest hour is her last

Night's harsh shadows swiftly flee
And beauty is found in the light of day
Her golden banner is quickly unfurled
And her love shines warm upon the world
As night's terror fades away
          Stephanie Willing

Rest . . . Rest . . . My Dear

Rest, rest, my dear,
Now all things are coming clear.
As I take my one last glance,
I think about having just one more chance.
I take my last breath,
And I think of death.
How bad can it be?
I just lay there with a smile on my face,
And slowly die at a medium pace.
I feel a holy force upon me,
Then I see the peaceful glowing light coming down,
And my loved one laying by me, crying silently without a sound.
I see my life flash before my eyes,
And I feel a heavenly rise.
As I descent into the clouds above,
I feel a powerful burst of love.
I lay there pale and blue under the midnight moon,
Knowing my loved ones will be joining me soon.
My last words to all: Don't look into the eyes of death with fear,
And her last words to me: Rest, rest, my dear . . .
          Wyatt Townsend

Release

Wanting a certain thing in your life yet kept arms length away
for many years and days.
Upon change brought about through death giving what could not
be obtained time and time again.

Effort set free not just for you, also me.
Best happening of the mind this I claim being mine.
Perhaps making a sign big letters saying, "Free"!
Just for you and me.
A vast ocean carrying away troubles with each wave.

Worries sifted away through sand carried far from land.
A special soul given release of pain seemly with ease.
Chain wrapped around a mind and heart from the very start.

All ashes washed away before dark letting go being given a
wonderful calm with open arms.
Release for you, also me.
          Maureen M. Potts

Fish Fry

Gnats, Quitos and Lovebugs,
Frolicking and cutting-a-rug . . . ha, ha, ha.
At the Saturday night fish fry.
Where sister Fannie Mae was seen,
Stealing a kiss from brother Sprye.

RC, Strawberry and Grape,
The best soda water on the make!
Were chosen to wash the fish sandwiches down.
Banana, Orange and Honeydew, having a quarrel because so few,
Were brought by patrons all around town.

Roasted and boiled peanuts, homemade ice cream too,
Were also sold to help pay for the church pews.
Sawdust floors, oil burning stoves, accomplishing
Hush puppies doing the slide,
Record player thumping, kept things jumping,
While sister Rosetta sang on the side!
          Laura P. Gray

The Bridge Between

I've come to a bridge
Where I must make a choice:
Stay in the land I'm familiar with,
Or visit a new one, and hear a new voice.
I stand in the middle
Not knowing what to do;
Stay safe with the old
Or live dangerously with the new.
The time has come for me to choose;
Will I go forward or will I go back?
The fish all share their opinions
Understanding in my position, is what they lack.
I will soon choose
But no one will ever know
Because my bridge will soon fall
And no where will I go.
          Ashley Stevens

Untitled

Staring down into the glassy lake, the water winking in the moonlight,
showing what's wanted, not what is.
Thinking it deceitful, night after moonlight night, sitting there staring,
wondering, dreaming. Feeling the cool water,
the slight breeze. Reality slowly blowing in the wind, kissing the
wake, becoming daylight. The dream broken, reality
becoming vibrant. The cool breeze giving way to the warmth of day.
Returning home, sleeping, slowly slipping away
from reality, as though giving into the darkness of make-believe.
          Jessica Post

Steel Stealth

Steel stealth, spritely spring sweetly surprises, single-handedly
supplanting, warrior white winter's barren blanket. Why wheel
and deal in worthless, worldly wealth? Treasured trinket,
trickling teardrops—buoyant, bubbling brook borne of blatant
joy. Overtly overflowing. Silently, secretly smile, steel stealth,
transforming, towering tree of knowledge nebulously nearing,
holding out. Healing hands, heeding helpful history, hearing
scathing stories sadly strewn
Leaves lie lifelessly limp, in strangely supine silence.
Sudden seclusion, svelte snow; Such soft strength spirited
spring showers show. Steel stealth, ignominious ignorance in
gentle gestures of genuine genius. Refreshing, rejuvenating
rivers run rapidly rampant; Reach remote repose in reason. Halt!
Harvest hearkens! Will willing wayside workers wax wondrous
wonders by the water's well spring? Innovative, imaginative
images, intrinsically interconnected;
Rising reasoning resonating, rippling.
Reality repeatedly rejected, steel stealth. Instill real riches,
wealth of wisely wielded words, swiftest swords scaring, sharply
swiping, savagely slicing atoms agelessly, automatically aligning.
Airy, artful allusions assessing, caressing complete, chaotic calm.
Paradoxical, profoundly puzzling perplexity, steel stealth.

Alexis Renee Steel

Untitled

A woman trudges through the rope ladder with a broom full
of webs—full of experience. She paves no trails—shares no
short cuts—she is a believer in a discovery made
alone—anonymous—in a terror known only when dealt with.

A fly shoots by with a verve we expect will cut through
the string. It is stopped dead in the web—many eyes darting
in anticipation of doom—it does not struggle—but remains
still as it seems to slink into the elaborate design of the trap.

John and Mary walk hand in hand during their ritual called courting.
John—being vicious—rips his hand across a web in the way.
He tosses the spider and smashes it—a laugh is heard.
Hands are wiped on faded jeans and then rejoined.
They are walking home. Tumbling to the ground—free—a lone
fly trots on a burning sidewalk—future is in clear view.

With a sky so blue and clouds so defined—the suburb comes to life.
The grass seems so green when the children tumble upon it.
The next door neighbor boy—Teddy—comes to a
gallop down main street—and on his way he kills a fly.

Cheryl Louden Kubin

You Know

Have you ever looked into your soul and seen pure despair?
Have you ever felt pain, that consumed every bit of your strength?
If you have, then you know.
You know that there is no place as lonely as yourself.

You maybe surrounded by love; you maybe in the midst of a crowd—
but still there is nothing—no sound, no emotion, no light.
If you have, then you know.
You know that there is no place as empty as yourself.

Time stands still.
You function and move, as if pulled by a string with no idea of
who's in control.
If you have, then you know.
You know that there is no place as cold as yourself.

Emotion cannot survive.
There is no hate—there is no love.
And yet you know that despair is only as strong as you allow.
So how strong are you?

Can you face the devil?
Can you dispel the darkness?
Can you feel the hug of a child? Only you can know.

Clare M. Bello

The Lost Generation

My brother and sister confused from addiction
Walking with satin and lured by temptation
Running day and night for a hit; dripping in perspiration
Living lawlessly but dodging the law and avoiding litigation
Yet, smoking that pipe day in and day out without hesitation
Won't work—can't work full of aggravation
Living and working the streets, shameless and insane
With lust for the sensation
Brother living for days in insanitation
Sister unkempt, unclean and unconcerned of the degradation
From morning to night an endless rotation
Mind stirring and plotting on how to maintain participation
But wait! Brother and sister there's hope even in all the frustration
He's called Jesus, the Son of God—Maker of all Creation
And He will set your soul free by the Grace of Salvation!!

Karol L. Jackson

To Cookie

I thought of my "Cookie" for a long time today. Her laughter, her
Smile, and things she would way. I thought of our friendship from
Years gone by, and remembered I loved that gleam in her eye.

She's gone from me now, forever to rest. Gone from the man that
You said she loved best. I hope she took with her a memory of
me, Because I loved her in ways that no one could see.

I pray that God keeps her close by his side, and hope she can dry
The tears I have cried. When thoughts of her seem to fall from the
Sky, I'll regret that we never said our good-bye.

I will visit her grave site, I will bring her a rose, and think of life's
Pathways that each of us chose. Her pathway was sometimes painful
And sad. My memories of her are of good times we had . . .

You gave me her picture and a lock of her hair, small tokens of love,
That we used to share. I will cherish these things till the day that I
Die, her smile, her hair, and that gleam in her eye . . .

Michael Miles

I'd Share This Body With Your Spirit (Mother)

If it were possible for me to share this body I have with thee
To house your spirit that slipped away I'd move you in this very day!

It's not a mansion this earthly temple of mine.
But you and I would manage just fine.

For nine whole months you shared yours with me.
I'd gladly share this one with thee.

I'd move over and let you in, give you the penthouse apartment
And with a grin I'd be your chauffeur from now until the end.

For you were truly my best friend! We would travel both near
And far with you as my guiding star!

If this my dream could but come true.
I'd gladly share this body with you!

Charita L. Germany

A Cry for Help

There's a battle raging deep inside, it encourages me to run and
hide. I need someone to guide me down life's winding road. I'm
young, but still my heart carries a heavy load. Becoming a
teenager is a big step for me to take, confusion and frustration
cloud my mind and I sometimes have difficult decisions to make.
I have a problem, liking myself you see. I need help bringing out
the good in me. I'm not a child and I haven't yet reached
adulthood. I'm trapped in the middle at a time where all parents
once stood. Hold my hand and listen with your heart. You can
mold and shape me, for life could be a form of art. You can teach
me how to use my mind, but please do it with a loving heart and
a face that's kind. If you fail to understand some of the things I
do, please remember that's one of the reasons I need you. I'm
really not a bad kid.

Lillie Mae Chandler

Love

Love is a four letter word that's been scattered around since the beginning of time; it has blind and confused many of great minds.

I was young and spry and free as a bird;
so I set out to find the answer to that four letter word.

What is love? Where does it start? Is it in the mind or does it form within one's heart? Is it sex, money or having a good time? It can and has brought pleasure and sorrow to all mankind.

Love can be beautiful, it can be sweet,
but most of all it has to be a two way street.

I found love is a word few people understand,
it could cause the birth of a child or make one kill a man.
I also found if love was something only money would buy;
The rich would have all of it and the poor would die.

Love can make one act like a fool, because love is a very powerful tool.

During my many walks trying to find the true meaning of that word love,
I looked up at the moon, the stars in the heaven above:
I looked at the trees, the grass, the lovely swans,
the buzzards and the beautiful doves;
and there's but one answer that I could find, God is love.

John P. Reed

Heard the Chatter

Rain on me with hate and love
Touch me with gossip, take me with rumors, break me with lies,
But know I am here.
Regret I wasn't a day ago
When the world stopped a thousand times and glamor was ours.
Now is here.
Never afraid to live this way the second that eyes shift to my actions
with God and you and the audience that always waits
for me to turn them on to their lives.
Be impulsive with me.
Make them sweat for no other reason but now.
Let the world watch you be a man inside me
Above me
Blasphemy for the masses to feed on
Turn on hard on
Move on, is what they say.
But this second is ours and today talks loud
So you better inhale the moment and hold your breath
'cause the people are too many
And I can feel their eyes.

Tarah Talasek

A Night Poem

Night was here, the day was over.
The birds were singing to the cold shivering clover.
The bees were saying their good night prayers.
Hoping they would not see any bears.
The flowers were tucking their babies to bed.
While little frogs were being fed.
The squirrels were chattering.
And the chipmunks were snoring.
But their babies thought the night was boring.
The wind swept down, and said goodbye.
While the sun sank deep into the sky.
The stars were shiny and very bright.
And the wind sang, "Don't get in a fight tonight."
A petal blew into the breeze.
And made a tiny gray mouse sneeze.
All the little snoring and sleeping sounds.
Woke up the very tired hounds.
Everything was calm and still.
As the bright yellow moon peeked over the hill.
Good night!

Kariann Bubb

People

People on the rise with bundles of endless hope,
And a basket of plenty lies.
Some are a success, and enjoy publicity, fame, and fortune.
Many can endure certain levels of stress,
But others need lots of rest.
People are curious with devious eyes,
And show smiles to sunny skies.
Everyone loves to spend and shop,
But childish games will never stop.
Hearts are broken, there is no trust.
Attitudes are composed; while feelings are often exposed.
People are lost in a pool of rage,
Because their life is the next topic on the last page.
Creativity at the highest cost, but respect and dignity seemingly lost.
Poor people; filled with madness and strife,
But value the precious gift of life.

Vanessa M. Chattman

James At . . .

Jimmy died and some people laughed,
but they were only fooling themselves.
They led him to believe it would be okay,
as they all turned and walked away.

When you are no longer welcomed
it can become very hard and so lonely,
If help finally comes to you,
you'll never be able to see, for you are blind.

No peace is there, if you are wild, but some joy
you brought and didn't know
You helped so many and they never said thanks,
Now it's too late, but you are at God's side.

Be glad, dear one, that the pain is through,
and if we could have done more, we would have,
We'll all remember your grief and sorrow,
and pray that you will survive in that beautiful world.

Lynne Donahue

Borrowed Angel

For only a brief time, to us she was sent
This angel from God, to us he lent.
Sweet little angel without words to speak.
Yet her Father's voice could be heard so sweet.
She taught us how to love, to give, and to care;
Even when life seemed just too much to bear.
Once we learned, it came her time to go
To join her Father; to heaven, her home.
And like a gust of wind, she blew into our lives;
And with this wind, to heaven she'll ride,
With outstretched wings, upward she'll soar,
Where pain and suffering are no more.
Though her body is gone, the spirit will stay
Of our borrowed angel, who's not so far away.
So for now, little one, we won't say good-bye,
But, "See you soon," for our time, too, is nigh.

Sheila Canada

Memories of My Blankie

When I crawled into my comfy bed, you closed in all around me.
You tucked me in so tight and snug, so I could sleep so soundly.
You protected me from the monsters in my closet and under my bed.
You shielded me from those nightmares that I feared and that I dread.
When I got cold, you were there to keep me warm all night.
When I got scared, you were there to there to scare away my fright.
When I started to cry, you soaked up all my tears.
And you were always there, right underneath my ear.
I still have you to this very day, except you're all folded and put away.
When I have children I'll give you to them,
So you can be their hero now and again.

Jennifer Kreutzer

Saw the World Today

I saw the world today
On New York's lightened and frightened city plain.
Then I saw Africa's lean starving people.
I saw the world today
Then I saw Bosnia's thundering bombs,
And ended on Australia's silk-sanded beaches.
I saw the world today
On Russia's sorry begging stage.
I looked around and then I found I was in the USA
Just lying there sleeping in a dream land far away.
The world I've seen drifting away
Like leaves on a cold fall day.
All the bad stages of life.
I wake up and Oklahoma City's bombing will fall upon my soul
I look and walk.
I walk and look.
Then I begin to see how much this world
Must really mean to me.

Christine E. Johnson

Thunderstorm at the Close of Day

At the close of day
I hear the clouds clap together.
A bellow, a shout, a resound . . .
A peal, a roar, a roll, and a crash!

The silvery blue shaded sky captures my glimpse,
while the weather and climate surrounds my aura.
The rise and fall of the barometer stirs the air
And I explore for a funnel.

I hear another clap, bellow, resound, peal, roar, roll, and crash!
Again and again!

The silence—

Now, I see a rainbow in the distance
and hear the sound of tiny raindrops on a tin roof—
and the music of mating crickets.
I smell a fresh aroma scent.

Across the way, I see frogs plunging in and out of the flowing gutters.
There's glistening leaves and breezy windows.

It's an unjaded cleansing of the Earth, and more . . .
It's an introduction of spring.
It's thunderstorm at the close of day.

Stacey D. Winters

When Through Silence I Speak

When through silence I speak and words can no longer
express passionate sentiments, my thoughts like music flow
with you as the master of their composition.

When through silence I speak, I see doves perched so peace-
fully upon my window sill. Accompanied by a nightingale whose
sweet melody enraptures me with a love of soothing sound.

My silence speaks through my heart and soul and touches in a
way that words could never say. So many times I have wished to
confess my soul hoping for a kind exchange. Need I be too
forward? Or let time play its tune.

How many have fallen prey to the same slow demise
I feel every time you pass by. My silence can be heard so very
clear, if only you have the heart to listen.

When through silence I speak, I listen to hear what all has been said.
The birds sing sweetly in the morning air. They are joyful,
chirping harmoniously, for they see me holding you silently in my arms.

Melody T. Cochran

Can a Furling Turn to a Pea By Drinking Tea

A Furling sitting on a tuffin,
Eating a big brown muffin.
With glossy eyes like silver.
Sitting next to a white pillar,
with a dog named Miller.
Miller with black sapphire eyes speckled
with fairy's dust.
Fussed at the Furling for a piece of his
big brown muffin.
The Furling sitting on his tuffin said what
will you give to me?
I will trade you a cup of French tea.
Oh my! If I drink tea I will turn to a pea.
Come my friend, we will see if a furling can
turn to a pea.
They went to a shore by the sea and drank
French tea.
Surely enough the Furling with glossy eyes
turned to a delicious round green pea!

Rekha Kumbla

The Preacher

God sent you to his children,
To help them find their way.
Some appear to be lost;
You can teach them how to pray.
Some may be rebellious,
And don't know what to do!
You can sit them down and tell them
Some of the things that you went through.
Some may be discouraged and have nothing to say,
Encourage them to wait on Jesus,
And he will lead the way.
Some maybe a help to you,
Willing to stand up and fight,
By helping you to spread the word
That Jesus is the light.
I just want to encourage you,
With the words I say,
"Stand up for Jesus,
He is the way."

Mary E. Weems

Is There a Spot for Me God?

Lost and confused, used and abused. If I die, what do I have to lose?

Dear God, I don't know what's holding me down.
I'm a lost soul never have been found.

My life has been torn apart. I'm cursed until death do me part.

Never did do anybody wrong.
Will there be a spot for me, when I'm dead and gone?

Can I enter into your gates
While they are busy burying my estate?

Wiping away the sins I've committed,
I tried to avoid the B.S., instead I got sucked up in it.

I had some trouble; I tried to get some help.
Because at some point I can't help myself.

Looking up at the skies asking God to give me a spotlight.
Because sometimes my life isn't acting right.

I see everybody life's turning out perfect.
Wondering now, why my life got short circuited.

Everybody is dead in your kingdom.
Getting a taste of absolute freedom.

Is there a spot for me God?
'Cause my life is turning out to be quite odd!

Marcus D. Green

Sitting on the sand,
The waves come crashing in.
The dark clouds rolling overhead bring the breath of their cries.
A collision of the clouds leads the rain to me,
As a fierce bolt of lightning strikes the water sending it to its fury.
I, fish below the surface, struggle to get free,
As the water is tossed about,
Spinning,
Twirling,
Like a washing machine.

Soaked from their anger,
I feel a quiver from below.
The earth begins to open up,
And dissipates the anger from the sky.

Their loathing voices launch the rush of
The vile sloshing of the
WAVE.
As it drenches me with their bitter wrothy bicker,
I bob amidst their infinite tears.
Cascading over me the timeless ripples of the abhorrence.

Lisa Wiley

The Skies Moving the Rainbow

I ask the skies to move the rainbow to protect you.
I believe with all my heart there's no one out there to get you.

And if we believe together the rainbows will never miss from
protecting you, this is why I give the skies a kiss.

Understanding things may appear to be scares, but look up in
the sky and you will see, a rainbow protecting you for me.

The sky will move the rainbow where ever you go, even at night
although, you can't see the rainbow.

The colors you have been feeling inside,
has been coming from the rainbow in the sky,
giving you comfort and tender care,
this is why the rainbow follow you everywhere.

When you lay down to close your eyes,
you know you need a peace of mind.

This is why I send the rainbow to you,
so you may feel comfy and warm too.

Always keep your eyes for the colors of the rainbows in the skies.
Now you know who I am sending you the rainbows to protect
you again and again.

Althea Trantham

A Taste of Victory

As the ball flows toward the hoop,
it bounces and makes one giant loop.

Up for the rebound we all fly,
for there are no limits, just the sky.

Soaring down the court in a mad primal rage,
like we've all been released bound up in a cage.

Towards the hoop we all fly,
trying with all our might to get the tie.
Up, up, higher and higher
it seems as though we'll never tire.

Through the defense we all go,
which team will win, we soon shall know.

The game is tied with 20 seconds to go,
seems like we've got it all wrapped up with a nice big bow.

So much pressure, like a ton,
three, two, one, the shot . . . Yes, we've won!

Ryan Ippolito

Choices

I was born of white folk,
Didn't have a choice,
Neither did you.

I was born on the South side of Chicago,
Didn't have a choice,
Neither did you.

I was born in forty-three,
Didn't have a choice,
Neither did you.

But I do have choices,
Choices—where I go
Choices—what I do
Choices—who I become,
And so do you!

Marianne Newton

Something Has to Give

No one understands this pain I feel inside.
I continuously hide my feelings because I don't want to lose my pride.
I don't have enough tears to keep crying my frustrations away,
And it seems like my problems grow more and more each and every day.
I need someone to talk to, but I can't figure out who.
I feel like no one can relate to me
because they do not know what I go through.
From the outside looking in, everything seems to be all right.
But what no one knows is how I cry
when I lay my head in bed each night.
One question I need answered is how long will this pain last?
Is it going to be here all through my life or will it just pass?
I need a way to escape this pain, something has to give.
Because if this pain goes on much longer, I will not be able to live.

Fatimah King

Puppy Walkers

Puppy walkers are people who take puppies bred at the
Guide Dog Foundation and raise them. We also teach them
basic commands such as sit, stay, down and come. I'm a puppy
walker. We keep them for twelve for twelve to fourteen months.
Then we give them back. This is our third puppy. Our first
one's name was Robin. She made it to become a guide dog.
She went to Arkansas with a young man named Danny.
Our second puppy, Luffy, is still in training. Now we have a new
puppy, Flo. It's hard to give them back, but, as long as we know
we're helping someone, it's alright.

Kristen Wade

Sea Dreams

In reality you cut me—you loved me in a dream
You saved me from the afterlife and heard my dying screams
You're fire in an icy world
And I don't mind your sting
You know as well as I
They punish me for everything
My view of you is changing daily, though in one place we all are sailing
Through the ocean of our tears passing up the land of fears
Forgetting our insanity in the rocking motion of the sea
Suffering is miles away
Left us with the moonlight
I see you sleeping in our bed
I'm losing an internal fight
We're together again within our dreams—you're not angry anymore
You look peaceful, and I must leave—turn off the lights, I shut the door
I'll take care of you from within
Now I must get off the boat
My voyage is over now
You still have some time to float

David Graham

I Am the Reason

Old Glory, Stars and Stripes, I stand for an American dream.
Do people even realize the blood behind my beams?

I awaken every morning risen briskly to my place.
And end every evening with a slow ceremonious pace.

As I lead the town parade veterans shudder to their feet,
while local school-age children remain quaintly in their seat.

Widows clinch me to their bosoms as their husbands lay to rest,
while anti-war activists burn mine cloth in protest.

Will Americans ever realize I'm the reason that they're free?
Understand their right to speak and right to vote are due to me?

I cannot bare the thought of their actions made in vain,
I've touched the ground, flown at night, and been left out in the rain.

I see not your flesh color so do not claim that you see mine!
I symbolize America, United and Divine!!!

So next time that you see me, do not shrug and pass me by.
For millions have given their lives for your "right" to see me fly.

Kerri M. Lucken

Luke and Duke Stuck in a Hoop

Sleepless nights and wishful days, to eat the dish of plenty,
Oh if we may! One twin, one sis, plotted against Viola's locked niche,
Filled with confectionery sweetness and candy cane twist!
Their craving tooth sent Luke and Duke flying under the coop!

A lonely backyard, a loose plank jarred,
Beneath the storehouse floor, beyond a narrow porch door!
Out of sparkling eyes, with wagging tongues, A child's paradise
Sprung! Gushing odors of coconut taffy charmed like a bomb,
The feast of a marathon wrecking crew lunch rung!
Jaws too full too stuffed to chew,
Still Luke and Duke raced to consume the conquered loot!

Twelve bars and several boxes later,
Pot-bellies stood high like a rising elevator!
Chocolate, sweet and messy teeth, shortly disgust each sour face,
While the shaft-hole in the shed house floor, firmly held aching
Stomachs in place! The room grew cold, scary and dark,
Sobbing for Mama were two repented hearts!
When the tiny key unlocked the tiny chute,
There sat Luke And Duke stuck in a hoop!

Captain Sir Charles

Life

Few are the days that exceed our expectations,
Many are the days when our dreams are only imaginations.
Weren't we supposed to walk before we run,
And weren't games invented just for fun?
The changing times evolve so fast,
That suddenly our future becomes our past.
Time forbids us to stop and smell the roses,
If we stopped could we imagine what a panic this imposes.
Our schedule does not allow us to waste an hour,
Just to stop and smell a flower.
But because I stepped out of the fast pace for a minute,
I caught a glimpse of the world and realized what's in it.
I saw a blue sky, family, friends and did I mention the flowers?
I realized time doesn't have to be measured in hours.
There were children playing, and birds were singing,
In the distance I could hear the bells of a church that were ringing.
Perhaps they were simply my wake up call.
I was bound to a schedule and nothing else at all.
Accomplishing this and getting ahead in that caused me such strife,
I suddenly realized what I was missing was Life.

Shirley RushingUntitled

I look deep into those blue eyes
And I see a stranger
Someone whom I can't recognize
She lays up all night, head in hands
And just cries and cries.

She wonders why she's all alone
With no one who will help her
No one hears her screams.

She then meets a Greek stallion.
Who makes her feel like one in a million

She's finally happy she has someone
He listens and cares about her
She can't see herself with a man no other.

He has brought so much happiness
But she feels alone again
When she's not with him.

She finds herself in a weird state
Of nothing which she can relate.
She now realizes what it is
She's fallen in love with Angelo Asprogiannis.

Christine Seremet

The Great Oak Tree

From a tiny sapling, it grew
Into a big oak tree
On top of a little grassy hill.

The tree watched over the children
As they played hide 'n' seek
During their summer vacation.

As the summer days became hotter,
The tree provided shade
For the children to cool off.

When lunch time came,
The tree let the children recline against its trunk
So they can relax and eat.

The tree watched the children grow up
Every year, getting a little taller
Being able to reach a new branch

Until one day, the oak tree was gone
And all that was left was a stump
Upon which the children would sit and cry.

Rebecca Miko

A Black on a Golden Diamond

Fifty years to the day when Jackie Robinson
Broke Major League Baseball's racial barrier
His widow, Rachel, joined President Bill Clinton
In N.Y.C. in a stadium, called Shea
Where he was retired for all time from the Majors
Uniform #42 worn by this great Dodger star
Honoring Brooklyn's first black Hall-of-Famer
On April 15, 1997—a golden day.

Play was suspended after the fifth inning
Of the night game between the Dodgers and the Mets
For ceremonies memorializing this courageous man
Of color who defied our national attitude
Of immoral racial segregation
And second-class status for blacks; No one now forgets
This pioneering athlete who dodged ugly death threats
And racial epithets: The nation showed its gratitude.

I'm convinced that this fierce diamond competitor
Who in the face of injustice never did flinch or yield
This same week smiled as a great, young golfer, Tiger Woods,
Won the Masters, the first black ever to lead that field.

Norman R. Nelsen

A Viking's Raid

As we go along the whales road
Traveling to pillage the gold
Our Fjord Elk is tossed in the whales bath
Nothing will stop
the blood branches wrath

As we drop the one with the cold nose
Our warriors draw their fire of battle
And ready to sun of sea-kings
They will stop at nothing to live up to the Viking reputation
By pillaging farms and killing those who fight back

We load our Fjord Elk and return back to Denmark
Awaiting a feast for our victory
As we dock on the bones of the sea
Leif welcomes Ottar with his falcons seat
While Ak gives Ragnar a snake of wounds for his victory

Later in the evening after the feast
We thanked Odin and Thor for our victory
And prayed they would gives us the same amount of luck on the next raid

Mike Roe

The Wondering Why's

Questions! Questions! Why do you ask so many questions?
My folks ask me all the time.
I never knew I ask so many questions
they say I do every time that I'm around.
As I sit thinking on the floor, things come to my mind,
things that I just cannot ignore.
So I get up and run and ask someone.
Mommy, Daddy where does my voice go when I begin to blow?
Why do the sun shine that it makes my eyes blind?
Why are oranges orange and squares are square?
Why do people talk when no one's there?
Questions! Questions! why do you ask so many questions—my folks say.
I don't think I ask so many, but they say I ask a plenty.
Brother, Sister why are you older than me?
Why couldn't I be the first to run you crazy?
Why can't I play with you, when you or I have nothing to do?
Are you being stingy and mean? Or are you like that because it's me?
Quiet! Quiet! they say little child,
you ask so many question it's driving me wild.
Somebody, somebody I must know—do I ask a lot?
Please help me to figure it out.

Alberta Tylia Dorethea Battle

Special Thanksgiving

Thanksgiving is a special day, it's when people pray
for the things they love. And the blessings came from God above.

Thanksgiving is a special date, when pilgrims and Indians ceased all hate.
They put a turkey on a plate, then they kindly sat down and ate.

This is how Thanksgiving came to be, when people then began to see
how to keep peace and happiness, without nastiness.

Most of the world today is at war and fighting
while everyone should be giving thanks,
but instead the world is frightening.

As time goes on, people agree less and less.
Most of the world has to live without the sweet, loving caress.

But my family doesn't live this way. We live with blessings every day.
We might disagree with each other, and sometimes I fight with my brother.

Seriously over-all, I'm thankful for a lot of things,
but I'm especially thankful for all the gifts that life brings.

I wrote this poem to remind others of
all the loving and caring blessings from God above.

So everyone should pray on this very special day,
for love and happiness, without nastiness.

Dalia Erney

Growing Old

When I look into a full mirror
It occurs to me
That my body is like a mushroom
Big on top and short stem
It has a bland color
So do I
It is fragile
Just like me
I like the taste of mushrooms
Makes it easy for me to accept
Looking like one

Ceceil Siegel

Untitled

He straddles my waist.
His soft hair brushes at my skin.
I reach for his hips and pull him closer.
He responds and rocks forward
hiding the hair that still touches.
My fingers feel the smooth warm skin
that will soon be wet with sweat.
I watch him watch me. We move.
This man, with me.

Clair G. Campbell

The Coals of Old Nostalgia

Late in the night
when thoughts take flight
toward home where the heart is yearning
I lay my gaze
to the former days
where the passions of youth were burning
to the days behind
where the fires I find
lie smothered in the ashes of age
and I stir for awhile
in the warmth of a smile
the coals of old nostalgia

David L. Camp

Wild, Wonderful, West Virginia

West Virginia is wild.
West Virginia is wonderful.
West Virginia is beautiful.

The air is fresh and clean.
The sky is clear and bright.
The trees are tall and wonderful.
The animals are just as nice.

The old Appalachians go on forever.
They are more beautiful than anything else.
The rivers and lakes are large.
And more clean than you have ever seen.

The coal miners are hard at work.
Never stopping to rest.
The people here are peaceful and kind.
This place is one of a kind.

Amanda Lynne Davis

Five Little Snails

I have five little snails
who live in a cup
they wiggle their tails
and try to stand up.
I've taught them to climb
out of an old rusty pail
now please help me to find
my five little snails.

Jacqueline Ouellette

Reciprocity: An Ode

To him I trust, my thoughts, I must, when I speak my mind
Aesthetic, poetic, and prophetic he reciprocates in kind
A friend to mend or lament, to dissuade or to inspire
Audacity, sagacity, and his capacity to entreat me in my mire
A friend to lend or to send his support, although in strife
Limited, inhibited, and revisited by his reverent vows of life
With wings he sings and flies the skies with little effort borne
But smiling, willing, and beguiling are the friends who secretly scorn
Deceived and bereaved he's left to bleed, he wears a masque of pain
But he fends, and mends, and then ascends to a higher plane
Often pining, ever whining I wallow in mediocrity
Blind, supine, I've left behind my friend in agony
With haste I waste and have effaced a friendship dear to me
I sought, and caught, and duly brought to myself this tragedy
But I will fight to make it right, I've found a remedy
To assist, persist, and coexist in reciprocity

Chris Williamson

Shine Brightly My Sweet Friend

I had a dream about you last night.
You were so real, and your spirit shone bright.
Lately the bad memories have been coming back to me.
I really miss you a lot, if only you could see.
That time keeps coming back to my mind each day.
If I had only been there, I probably would have been near your way.
Because you always encouraged me to step out,
You have shown me what life is all about.
Why it had to happen to you, I don't have a clue.
You were always so innocent, so true.
My dream seemed so real that when I woke up
I thought maybe your departing was a dream—enough,
Enough of me wondering if you're really gone,
Enough of me trying to figure out what went wrong.
Because I can't bring you back, as much as I want to,
I have no clue on what to do.
There is no explanation as to why, so why do I even try?
To figure out life's mysteries which often lead to tragedies.
Maybe you were too good to be on earth, maybe you're heaven, for what it's worth.
I do however know that you're an angel—so shine brightly my sweet friend.

Virginia Hooks

Blue . . .

Blue is the tenacious sea trapped in the iris of his eye;
It's the free and endless air among the white clouds in the sky.

Blue is the ripple-rippling feathers of the Chirp-chirp-chirping Jay,
      perched contently in his nest;
It's the petals of a newly blossomed tulip,
      placed over her cold body when laid to rest.

Blue is the color that represents their forever echo—echoing school pride;
It's the face of bitterness, and depression, and grief, that you can no longer hide.

Blue is the miracle that never-ever takes shape;
It's the realm from in your dreams, which you cannot escape.

Jeanette M. Basirico

About Dying

If I were to go out there, and rest on that patch of grass
If I could remain completely motionless, detached from the world
Do you suppose the birds would peck at my flesh, a feast of human essence
Splashing about in my blood, like small children playing in a mud puddle
The veins of my throat, threaded through their stained beaks
Producing an eerie steam from the chill of the night
A mist to raise my soul to the heavens, to rest in the presence of God
To be with Him in the beautiful serenity of eternal love
            and with those who are residing in His grace.

Diane Beck

Flight

Door firmly locked
On the crouched Lares and Penates
Well entrenched within.
Back turned on the weight
Of relationships.
Things left undone.

Through the pall of gray
Over the city,
Shedding the sullen pull of earth,
Into the blinding blue,
Where all seems possible,
The Titan lifts.
Spirits lighten.

Barbara Roth

Puppy Love

Don't let his incessant
Outer appearance
Deceive you for what's
Really in store
If you're not careful
You might get a broken heart
Just when you're about to fall apart
Remember the way
You once were
Even if it's a slight blur
Hold your head high
Get over it
He's just a guy.

April Harrington

Wonder

Finding myself wandering the beach,
I sit, the sand climbs up between my toes.
Looking upward, there it is.
Color ablaze,
Each evening an original.
Supreme beauty no one has yet captured.

Christine Lehnardt

Untitled

Growing inside
Beautiful life
9 months to bloom
Meet your mom and dad
We love you now
As you are so so tiny
We love you always
Beautiful life

Nikki Bettenhauser

Untitled

The sea
Like a mirror
Reflects the sky
Not even a breath of air
To give warning
And off in the distance one can see
A few wispy clouds
Like a scouting party
And fear holds me
In its freezing grip
As I watch the glass plummeting
And I feel on my face
The icy breath
Of the "angel of death"
As he whispers "hurricane"

Harold Atlas

Untitled

In memory of Lawrence E. Payton
You were enjoyed, respected and loved by family, friends, and staff.
They always knew that you were good for a laugh. When spirits were low,
Fun you would poke, and like many of us you enjoyed a good joke.

When the eye of Mickey you caught with a glance,
talking of marriage during your very first dance.
From then on, it was love, devotion and romance.

You always found time for a wayward soul with an open heart to deploy.
Poetry, song and music on the piano you did enjoy,
even a duet in your home with Miss Illinois.

God knew you were getting tired and a cure was not to be,
so he put his arms around you and whispered, "Lawrence come with me."
A caring heart stopped beating.
A joyous spirit with hard-working hands came to rest.
God proved to us he only takes the best.

Like the American Indian, you loved to hunt and fish,
with your trusted dog thru nature's wild you would swish,
in hopes of getting a special meal's dish.
No longer this land your soul will travel,
for now in the heavens your journey of life will unravel.

Lee Newtson

Ghost of Halloween Past

Remember stealthing through the streets and fearing other moving sheets?
And hoping other sheets would hide a pal, a childhood friend inside?
Did rustling leaves seem louder then? And did we think of goblins when
No ghosts or spirits could be found? Did shadows move without a sound?

The fearsome fun of Halloween, a child's world of scares unseen;
Of whispered words and laughing fright; a haunted house with ne'er a light
But iron picket fences round its spooky, ghost infested ground.
Want any Halloweeners, Sir, Or, "trick or treat," if you prefer.
And tricks were gentle, window soap; or 'tricks' were cutting, clothesline rope.
A doorbell rung, then run and hide and laugh as people looked outside
And found no callers at the door! Was this your Halloween of yore?

It's not all gone—you'll see and hear the ghost of Halloween each year;
In children giggling as they run, all costumed, sheeted, seeking fun
And laughing, sharing prizes won with friends who had collected none.
And wishing that the night would last; and wondering why it went so fast.

Robert J. Connolly

You Must Acquit

The charge they made just wasn't true,
They tried to say I murdered two!

They searched and found a bloody glove,
And said the motive "must be love."
They made me take the witness stand, then asked me how I cut my hand.

I said that when I heard the news, I started then to be confused.

I broke a glass within my hand, "You've got to know, I'm not your man."

Then where were you that fatal night?
"Just ask my friend, I took a flight."

The cap and glove belongs to you.
"A lie! I say it's just not true."

The (DNA) is traced to you, from blood within your Bronco, too.

Now tell me where did this come from
When you boldly say you're not the one?

The cops, you see, were after me,
They planted blood, it's plain to see!

You ask me why, when, how and where,
When I plainly state, "I was not there!"

So base the facts on what you know,
You must acquit and let me go!

Glory D. Slayton

Bataan

A bayonet away from death
fear is his only friend
but he believes in God and country
and that soon the war will end.

But he walks a thousand miles
and the days turn into years
and he starts to doubt his country
and he wonders if God can hear.

"I am a battling bastard!" he yells
"I fight for freedom, for you"
but his voice is lost in the silence
as his country abandons their youth.

After the shackles are broken
after the wounds have healed
freedom doesn't seem so free
and reality seems so unreal.

Now the war is fought inside his mind
and the little girl's face is bleak
as she cries to God and country,
"How could you take my daddy from me!"

Virginia J. Krolikoski

To My Parents on Their Golden Wedding Anniversay

We may not often tell you
How much you mean to us
But in our hearts we're very glad
We want to shout and fuss
And tell the world we think you're swell
And tops in every way.
Our wish is nothing but the best
For you this special day.

Then too, we're truly grateful
Believe us when we say
We hope the years ahead for you
Are great in every way.
Our thanks again for all you've done
This wish is most sincere;
May all good things head down your way
For years and years and years.

Marilyn E. Yergey

Wild Things

The clash of the rain,
Beats hard against my window.
The firm trees sway
Freely in the air.
The bee fights with
The flower for pollen.
The sun warms up the outside,
Yet chills the inside.
The grass grows, gets cut,
Yet grows again.
The moon closes over us,
The warmth is gone.
They are all wild.
They are all free.

Camilla Yamada

Beach

Big waves crashing in.
Endless days of beauty begin.
A mist so sweet and a wonderful smell.
Countless hours of sweetness.
Ohh! So swell.
Have you ever been to the beach?
If not what have you missed?

Courtney Kemmerlin

Friend

For you I am willing to lay down my life and die
No task you ask will be too great, nor too small
I'll support and protect you when you tell the truth, or lie
I will always be there to catch you if you should fall
My hand I will always lend for you are my dearest friend
I will shed a tear for you in times of joy and sorrow
I will go through life your hand in mine
Whatever you need I will gladly give or borrow
Whenever you need me just give me the sign
No matter how far backwards I must bend, you are truly my dearest friend
Our bond for each other will never break, for it is too strong
My trust and love for you will never erode
I'll stand beside you regardless if the outcome is right or wrong
My strength will carry your burdens, no matter how heavy the load
For I need not pretend, you are my dearest friend
I will always stand by your side
If you need a shoulder to cry on, a kiss, or an embrace
All your secrets I will never confide
I will be there for you anytime, anyplace
Until the very end you will always be my dearest friend

R. L. Saylor

Naked Thoughts

Crimson tears extend across my porcelain face
As broken images of your genuine smile play in the crevices of my mind
Our arid meadows of tranquillity and completeness are gone
Separating me from the soft interpretations of your thought perfection
Memories of our togetherness bask in the emptiness of my sorrow
As emotions ooze past the numbness and cradle me in their arms
Nostalgia for the withering days are molded into my ever blackening heart
Unknown—is the future and the empty dreams I hold in my hands
Valiant though are the impressions left and engraved my soul
Shadows touch upon the clamminess of my broken heart
Vigorously trying to attach to the naked void protruding
Yet, in the midst of my nakedness I long for you and your soothing voice
To nestle beside sensitive waters in your tender yet masculine arms
To gaze at the ironies of life in the dancing stars that held our dreams
As we would lie under our private mystical world of phantom clouds
Interpreting the paths taken and the meaning of the moment at hand
Absence—though is strangling and it smothers my every lost thought
I am naked without you and our togetherness.

Cassandra Borton

To a Friend With Love

How do you choose the proper words to convey the things you want to say,
To tell the friend this note I give to her how very much she means to me
and how much I love her and care.

Let's just forget the fancy things, and come down to earth, and say, I thank
God for a friend like you.

You are always ready and willing to do the best you can seeking to help
someone knowing need has no respective man.

You never seem to grumble no matter what the task.
Would that we had more like you is that too much to ask?

God put us all on earth, He expected us to be a friend. Without doubt you have
proven your worth, your reward to receive in the end.

Long ago you made the promise to the one who means the most, that when it
comes to doing His work you'll be glad to be His host.

That promise you have kept maybe sometimes it was hard to do, but God
helped of the goodness, and kindness there is in you.

I am sure you will reap your reward when at last your work is done and when the
Master offers praises you will say I enjoyed it, Lord, really it was fun.

Why should I wait any longer to speak it loud and true,
"When it comes to choosing friends I am glad God gave me you."

Geneva Buckland

Dreams of Yesterday

There was stardust in the night
When my love and I first met,
There were love songs on the wind
When you said "I'll not forget"
We saw diamonds in the leaves
When the sunshine followed rain,
Yet my love—you did forget
I'm alone in memory lane.

Now the stardust is all gone
And the songs have died away,
Where once diamonds shone so bright
Leaves have fallen in decay,
Yet my memories linger on
Though the years have gone their way,
Life and love cannot return
To the dreams of yesterday.

Anna L. Cook

Animals (a new baby)

I see it opening its eyes.
I see it nuzzling for its mother.
I hear it try to make a sound.
I hear it when it's frightened.
The smell of a cool, crisp air is upon it.
The smell of a new life learning.
I taste the touch of its mother.
I sense the touch of trust.
I feel the loving kindness of a new life.
I feel her mother wonder where she's at.
This is like a miracle working its magic,
It is new generation going on forever.

Kizzy Benson

My Love Is Free

I am loved, this is known
But sometimes I wish it shown
With kind words and thoughtful deeds
Rest assured, that's all I need.
No gifts, money, or guarantees,
Please believe, my love is free!

So remember for the ones you love
There's nothing better under the sky above
Than a smile, your time, and simple joys
No need for flowers or expensive toys
Try saying "I love you."
There's nothing better that you could do.
Just give your time and trust me
Let them know, "My love is free!"

Lynn Riedel

Ode to Women

Women have been through
many things
Both great and small
Both good and bad
They come from being owned
to be the owners
They come from being quiet
to speaking up
From the bottom they rose
straight to the top
From the kitchen they cooked in
To the desk they organized
From being led
to being the leaders
From following
to being followed
They come from being over powered
To giving orders.

Helen Kaplan

Friday Night Is Oyster Night

Friday night is oyster night, ye bring 'em home an shuck 'em.
Ye rinse 'em good an' bread 'em light,
'er otherwise ye'll muck 'em.

Ye take large quantities of ale,
'ter git the juices flowin',
And when ye've sliced yer lemons right, ye know ye've got 'er goin'.

Ye drop sir oystees in the fat, an watch 'em boil and bubble,
An when ye drain 'em, dip, an chomp,
Ye know 'es worth the trouble.

Ye finish up an wipe yer trap, ye guzzle more some strong brew,
A be'er meal ye couldna' have,
An this aye tell ye true blue.

So Fridays are fer oysters friend,
Forga' the steak an lobster,
An why ye wanna dress that way? Ye look jus' like a mobster.

So let 'em primp an shave an snoot, an sit in li'l cloisters . . .
Me Friday nights is thus reserved . . .
'fer heavy drink an oysters.

Charles M. Cody

Of Me

And I, the individual, walk unknown to the world.
They who recognize, respect, and acknowledge my being, don't know me.
Amid the crowd I still remain untouched;
Even the friend so close cannot be near
Unless I, the individual, choose to share.

Then coming to know one another:
The opening of that inner door which keeps us hidden
And sacrosanct from the world;
The sharing of that secret self;
The knowledge of you, and me, our universe,
And beauty, and God, and God is Love.

No they don't know, and they can't know
Until they are you . . . and you, maybe me.

O. Avaris B. Williams

Compound Composure

The desert is a tranquil place.
The bird flies high in the open space.
The succulent lies with moisture stored for the sultry day ahead.
The wind wakes the sand from its sleepy bed.
Little movement from the sky above for the cloud feels at home and love.
The sun is strong and radiates the heat.
The ground is flat until it makes a mound that goes so steep and then
Straight back down.
As the sun slowly departs and the stars bursts out to caress the moon.
Activity continues, a flowers blooms, and the heat breaks.
The desert's night is the past leaving little trace.
A recycled canvas recurring that can be painted upon
By the moments of the next day.
The desert is a tranquil place.

Sherry Polnicki

The Two Purest Loves

In this day and time love comes and love goes,
but there's two loves that you can always depend on to be there for you.
One is the love of God the purest love of love all.
For there is no purer love than this love of God's.
The second purest love is the love of a Mother,
for a mother's love comes from the love of God and her heart.
For God's love is always with you, just as a mother's love is always there for you.
God's love will never betray you,
a mother's love will never desert you when all other love fails
God's love will heal you from sickness and pain.
A mother's love will help and comfort you through sickness and pain.
God's love will save your soul, a mother's love will soothe your soul.
Now you have the love of God, and the love of a mother,
so now you will find you have the two purest loves of all.

Keith Anderson

Burnt Sympathy

Worthless creeps
Depreciating emotions
Into the soft glow
Of the moonlight;
Sinking further
Down into
The forbidden pit,
Sympathy goes;
Countless, heart wrenching
Soul diggers
Volunteer as
The ashes hurl;
Watching the fire,
Gut feelings
Of intolerable trauma
Grow;
Hardened hearts
Share the pain,
As sympathy left.

Cara Lundt

A Flower a Guinea Pig

So beautiful things are, if we
can take care of what is there,

Breathe the air.

Feel the drops fall upon
us from heaven above.

Earth, you know, we walk on is not
there.

What is? Hell!

If you can't touch the air, you must
breathe.

If you can't be in
Heaven
You must feel the drops.

Fernando Valtierra

Flowers

Women are like flowers
They are beautiful in their own way
Roses may bloom all season
Orchids, Irises only in May
Even the weed that flowers
Is beautiful for Her Day

Albert S. Chmielak

Unfound Love

I find myself wondering
If love is real.
Always escapes me
The way that love feels.

When I think I'm in
Love, it slips away
And I have to face
Loneliness another day

I can find myself
When I am alone
Asking if love, to
Me, will ever be known

Where can I go to
Find my greatest need?
Will I ever find love?
Or, will it find me?

Crystal R. VanHyfte

Love

I am in this dark cave alone. Each time I try to go near the sunlight, I fail.
I want to be out there where everyone else is.
I want to be touched by the sun's heat.
Everything is so beautiful under this light that it seems too good to be true.
I was acquainted by it several times though.
It opened its doors to me long ago.
I went closer and closer, but dare not go into it.
For I knew when the moon came out I would end up in darkness again, and I
would be alone.
Even when I'm in daylight I still see darkness through my eyes.
I am still alone, still untouched, and still unloved.
The love I see in people's eyes is just a stranger to me.
The emotions and feelings they share was never given to me.
I observe and envy their love, but yet, I still choose to keep it unknown.
I know there will be a day when I finally do succeed.
I will join this world of light with the others indeed.
I will be given this thing called love. And only then will my inner hurt
and anger be gone, will these tears of sadness turn into joy,
Will my pain and suffering be forgotten.
I will wait for this day patiently, but for now, love is just a stranger to me.

Berna Seman

The Person You've Judged Is an Image of You

Darkened by mystical shadows, engraved by footprints left behind,
you defined me not divine,
But as an outcast by my past, stereotyped me as one without class.
Maybe ya brother, sister, father and ya mutha;
never judge me by my cover; I'm like no other.
Perhaps ya foe, friend, or even ya lover.

Deeply rooted by my heritage.
Morally, spritually and uplifting harmonies,
playing defense against the vague pictures drawn of me.
God, my soul, heart and mind, not hard to find,
but something within my breast, inside my chest; Now I'm able to rest.

As you can see, you are no better than me.
For I have no one specific color; I'm all that you see.
Sparkling like white crystals of sugar;
Mysterious like the splendid darkened shade of mahogany.
I'm sugar coat, mahogany wax, chocolate dip,
or amongst the satin caramel cover drink you sip;
What you've defined is the person you see;
no other than your inner self that's what it appears to be.

Note, all that you must uncover;
ye must seek and then shall find.
You are the mystery everyone awaits to discover.
Your change is the cause of frightened minds, left behind and undermined.
Generating mistakes left untouched.
For you are the one whose changes make us wonder,
about things that leave us in ponder.

Nikki Lacy

Mysterious Eyes

Mysterious, mystifying, yet sometimes misleading, puzzling eyes
Are meandering about. Stroking the day with a deep, glistening dazzle
Like the sun at daybreak shines with a warm salutation.
Suspicious, indecisive, completely perplexed, these vivid and blazing eyes,
Encounter a radiant
image, perceiving the knowledge into the mind.

Friendly, dark, deep, yet never causing derision; they
Sense and perceive like a satellite in space.
My eyes are a gateway to the field of knowledge,
And always are ready for radiant excitement.
They search, stare, and glance. Waiting.
Sometimes I wonder, will my eyes ever witness a happening
Of great importance in the world?

Rachel Rife

Divine Love

"Alas!"
"My love for you so great,
forsaking all others; till eternity's
end I will wait."
"If not in this lifetime of flesh
should we meet,
At the gates of heaven;
there shall I seek."
"As in life, so too death;
our souls do entwine.
My hand in yours; Your hand in mine."
"Together forever Divine"

Bradley O. Gruwell

Sunshine

The sun is gone, it leaves no lust.
What am I to be but dust?
Alone I walk, on my own.
To a place I call my home.
There the sun reappears.
There the sun warms my fears.

Stephanie Potter

A Baby's First Prayer

Please don't make me go to bed
Don't want to rest my sleepy head
Mommy and daddy don't make me do this
Think about all that I'll miss
Please don't make me shut my eyes
You'll have to listen to my cries
I'll take a glass of water please
I'm begin on my hands and knees
Let me stay awake some more
And please don't shut my bedroom door!

Mary Yanni

Heavenly Eyes

When I look into his heavenly eyes
I see much surprise to realize
It feels good to be free
I see all the love surrounding me
When I want to be free from sin
it's always in,
his heavenly eyes

With his power
blooming like a flower
He will take your worries away
just get down on your knees and pray
All the way up there
he hears your little prayer
To feel the heaven's above
You have to learn to love

His love will never die
You'll see it in his heavenly eyes

Becky Hartman

Free My Heart

With hair golden brown,
And eyes as blue as the ocean,
My heart yearns for your forever embrace.
With skin as smooth as silk,
And desire as hot as fire,
My heart craves for your burning passion.
With laughter as pure as the wind,
And a heart as big as the heavens,
My heart longs for your undying love.

Jennifer Bell

Waiting

Sitting here waiting, trying to stop my hands a-shaking,
can't get it off my mind
I wanna be with you all the time.
Seeing your face just makes me wanna cry,
I wish I could be back where I belong,
there with you, together all along,
I wonder if you're thinking 'bout me too!
All I can say is please O' Lord, lead me to your face,
I need the light
I need not this horrible fight,
please let me rest, my heart is beating through my chest,
my mind is going crazy without you here beside me,
my soul seems like it's kind of miserable,
how much longer Lord?
I don't know if I'm able.
Please Lord take me back to the good ol' days,
please listen to what I say,
save my soul out of all this waiting!

Justus John Caleb Mothorn

Plumeria Kingdom

In Pearl City, when I was young,
I would walk barefoot everywhere, down
the dirt road to my Auntie's, where ceiling nook
geckoes chirped, sunlight peeked through walls
which Uncle never mended. It never got cold,
insulation wasn't needed.

I would suck on dried squid and pickled plums,
walk the tracks to eighteen bridge
where Grandpa wrestled hammerheads
when he was young. Past the graveyard
where Baban saw fireballs, phosphorous ghosts
that would follow her home.

I would weigh fallen mangoes in my palms,
scoop green coconut meat with my fingers,
and string plumeria into crowns, so by night
I would be nectar sticky, pollen dusted,
and my Aunties would be queens
who would carry me to bed.

Amanda Price

Thank You Dear Mom

Thank you dear Mom for wanting me and for giving me life.
Thank you dear Mom for holding my hand in my times of strife.
Thank you dear Mom for being patient during my "Awesome" teen age years.
Thank you dear Mom for being near when I went through all my phases.
Thank you dear Mom for always singing my praises.

God knew that I would need someone to listen to my cares
Someone who would always remember me in their prayers.
So in His boundless wisdom from above
God gave me the best and most precious gift
That of a mothers unending love.

P.S. I love you dear Mom

Joyce Malaske

The Rainbow Comes Behind the Rain

There are too many wishes.
And far too many tears;
Not nearly enough kisses,
To ease the doubts and fears.

We often need someone to care,
But find, only hurt and pain;
Perhaps because we're not aware
That Rainbows Come Behind The Rain.

We want too much, we feel mistreated,
When all our wishes we can't gain;
But really we should not feel cheated,
'Cause Rainbows Only Come Behind The Rain.

John Arthur Goetz

I Miss You So Much

I miss you so much,
That everything I do . . .
Is haunted with your laughter,
And the love that I once knew.

I miss you so much,
That every time I sleep . . .
My mind is filled with dreams,
Of the memories that I keep.

I miss you so much,
That when I sit to rest . . .
I can hear the mournful crying,
Of my heart within my chest.

I miss you so much,
That the only thoughts inside my head . . .
Are of the times we spent together,
And the "I love you" that you said.

Andrea Marie Eaton

Addiction

I'm helpless, in every way
It controls me each and everyday.
I try so hard, so hard to stay away,
But it makes me feel so very gay.
All I can do is pray and pray.
But I still feel helpless every day.

Forever and ever it will only be me,
How could this ever be.
For it is my everlasting desire,
In mind, body and whenever I perspire.

Jamie L. Hogue

My Mama Said

My mama said there'd be no use
for me to go ahead
and hang up my stocking this year
because Santa Claus is dead.

She said some folks had been up north
looking for the pole.
They searched all around where Santa lived
and never saw a soul.

I asked my Daddy what he thought
and he just laughed and said.
"I haven't heard a single word
about Santa being dead."

Maybe he is ill,
or perhaps he is sick.
But if Santa doesn't come this year
he will send his good friend St. Nick!

Jackie Skinner

Teach Me, Touch Me

Take my life
Take my all
Teach me to be
Wholly thine
Touch my heart
Touch my mind
Enlighten me to thy will.
Touch my mouth
Touch my ears
To be open to thy word
Take my hands
Take my feet
Teach me Lord
To do thy will.

Phyllis Zarzyczny

Abandoned

Once I believed in Santa Claus
And that wishes on stars came true
Once I believed in fairy dust
And I even believed in you

I thought you'd always be there
Like a pot of a gold at rainbow's end
I thought that you'd forsake me never
Through all that is thick or thin

I needed you and you weren't there
Surprising me without a doubt
I wished for you and you were gone
Like birthday candles just blown out

I once thought we were special friends
As true as the truest dark blue
But colors fade when put to a test
And so it appears do you

Rochelle Burdine

Untitled

Lovers are holy saints,
who can be a little quaint.
They roam the world,
with a heart full of gold.
Making mubblefubbles turn to sand,
with the wave of their hand.
Changing nithe to kindness,
instead of hatefulness.
If you need someone
to make you snirtle,
That someone will be there in a hurdle.
They are the holy saints of the world,
whose love is dateless, and far above.

Denise Joseph

Chrysalis

Butterfly, butterfly
Where have you been?
I've been in oneness
Out on a limb.

Butterfly, butterfly
What did you there?
I found what things
I have to share.

Butterfly, butterfly
What did you then?
I took a leap of Faith,
Now I am free again!

Melissa Sorensen Upham

A Father's Love

To My Daddy Christopher Lee Honse
A Father's love cannot be spoken,
Only thought through the heart.
A Father's love cannot be broken,
No matter what may happen.
A Father's love is always fending,
Especially for his daughter's sake.
A Father's love is never ending,
Lasting for always and ever.
A Father's love will lift you up,
When lying down upon the ground.
A Father's love is like a cup,
Holding all his love inside.
A Father's love will always be there,
Even when you're gone.
A Father's love will never tear,
Even in the worst of times.

Corina Honse

My Teddy Bear

I have a special teddy bear,
Sunshine is her name.
She used to go with me everywhere,
And play in every game.

But now this bear is tired and old,
She needs some special care.
Sunshine sits on my bed all day,
Way to worn to share.

Wherever we went, wherever we go,
Car trips, vacations, and much, much more,
Cuddling, crying, laughing, and mad,
This old bear is never a bore.

Sunshine's smile is now gone,
Her fur is not all white.
But she will never be replaced,
Because she is to me a caring light.

Amanda Bonnes

Angels Dance Around Us

Angels dance around us,
All throughout the day,
They see and pray for us,
In a very special way.

Angels dance around us,
In moments of everlasting love,
Even though sometimes,
It comes from way above.

Angels dance around us,
In times of great fear,
They watch us and occasionally,
Will shed a little tear.

Angels dance around us,
Seeing us with friends,
They know we are loved,
For that's what they intend.

Sarah McDowell

Forgiveness

Forgiveness is the true test of love
It will carry you through the darkness
And to the light above
And without forgiveness in the heart
The soul will grow cold
And stand far apart
from those who have learned
To give enough love
And help spread the peace
We're all so deserving of.

Diana Balogh

Grandmother

On her final day on this earth,
came a typical midwestern
thunder, lightning, wind and rain storm.
Grandmother chose that time to go out
to the well, draw some water.
A lightning bolt struck the well,
tore her arm off, and caused her to fall.
She was dead when they brought her up.

I never had a boy's chance
to develop memories of her.
To draw water from a well
in a lightning storm took
a certain challenge
and disdain of nature.

Aaron

The Progressive Promise

A young earth,
seeds planted.
Prophecy is born!
Adam first name.

A mature earth,
sound unheard.
Justice is conceived.
Light is received.

A dying earth? Quest
for a thief.
Institutions flagged.
Life brand new—bureaucracy ends.

A dawn breaker rises,
twins appear.
Promise kept while kings wept.
Unity unfurled.

James Robinson

Untitled

Far away my heart seems to drift
so far that I can't get a grip
sometimes I think I have it
but then it just slips

Growing darker and darker
like the setting sun out of sight dips
darkening my world
and sealing my lips
through the corridors of my soul
my heart wonders and rips

From the sea of sadness it sips
then to the sea of forgotten dreams
it goes by to cry and sit
waiting patiently for someone to visit

Ciarran Deahl

Behind the Door

I wonder who's behind the door.
Is there someone there
I knew before?

Do I have to run and hide?
Or will I be
Allowed inside?

I wonder what's behind the door.
And will I see the light
Of the shadowy figure
That comes in the night?

With a halo that shines
So bright, so bright.
With a halo that shines
So bright!

Harriet Browne

Crow

The crow is a gentle bird
It flies over mountain tops
Of green flesh
The crow is a beast flying
In the wind high in the clouds.
It sometimes hunts itself
But other times eats
What others devour
This bird, this beast
Has common enemies
The crow is like you and me

Matt Kline

A Mother's Unhealing Wound

Motherhood began in the womb . . .
Nurturing began when conceived.
As years went by, day by day
Unselfish love was given
to the one she bared.
With anguish and fear she lived,
that something would happen
to the one she loved so dear.
Suddenly an awful awakening occurred,
The day, that the life she gave
Was abruptly taken away.
No less, by the hands of the child . . .
"She conceived, carried in her womb,
Nurtured and loved."
Just to be left with such a vague feeling—
With a wound that will never know,
The meaning of "Healing."

Jennie Vázquez

My Heart Has a Key

For my mother on Mothers' Day.

My heart has a key
You're the only one who can open me
When you do, I feel so strong
Our love will last real long.

My heart has a key
You're the only one who can see
We have lots of fun
Even with no sun

My heart has a key
You're the only one I'd like to be
I might be a pain
But I can push away rain

My heart has a key
You're the only one that likes my tea
I have stars in my eyes
That used to twinkle in the sky

My heart has a key . . .

Hayley Lynn Miller

I Believe

I do believe that God above
Created you for me to love.
He picked you out from all the rest
Because He knew I'd love you best.
When I saw you I must confess
I didn't even have to guess,
You were the only man for me.
You were all mine for eternity.
You've been with me through every way
You've been with me through everyday.

Christy White

Black Mother

There once was a poor
Black mother who lived
Alone with struggles in
Hand trying to make it
Alone she had five
Children to feed and
Clothe, people said she
Would never make it
Alone well she taught
Them a lesson with
All struggles in hand
That Jesus had her
In the palm of his
Hands!

Valencia O. Fuller

Reflection

Seeking God with right intent
Takes us down paths bent
Far from any human plan.
Yet, looking back when at a gate,
His ways seem straight somehow,
And only those false starts of
Ours spread nowhere, like a fan.

Marta S. Weeks

Respect

To me respect means:
sharing, playing,
helping, caring.

Be kind,
Don't hit,
Be nice,
Don't throw a fit.

Play games,
Play tag, or just run,
But remember to do this with everyone.

So all of you listening,
Spread the word,
Plant the seed,
listen to what everyone needs.

Gabrielle Bruno

Suicidal Dreams

My suicidal dreams
What do they mean
Are they about future tendencies
I hope they don't influence me
My suicidal tendencies
They really got a hold of me
I have no reason to live
My grip on reality is starting to give
They got me
And now my life has ended
It was probably for the best.
I had no friends or family
My suicidal dream.

Joshua Johnsen

So Let the Nature Be

So let the Nature be
So it always is for others to see
Clear blue skies keep me mesmerized
Beautiful like a young girls eyes
We try to fly like bird of wing
Fly so high you start to sing
Waiting in patience by the dozens
Trees and rocks who are our cousins
To take a walk and not come back
Find yourself, pick up the slack
So you'll always be free
So let the Nature be

Scott Bullard

Bottled Up

Anger deep inside my soul,
an anger that I can't control.
A rage that's kept deep inside,
a rage that I try to hide.
Fears and lies buried side by side,
secrets that I can't confide.
My mind is set on just one thing,
sadness is all that it can bring.

Jessica Balmer

Waiting

I'm always waiting, it seems
For something better to come along,
For the anger to pass,
For doubt to disappear,
For someone to love,
For compassion to return,
For the chance to feel good again.
I'm still waiting.

Robin A. Hartsell

There and Back

To the outer regions
Of the world of Hate
To the inner regions
Of the land of Hope
I have been there and back.

To a life of death
And a dead life
To a life without hope
And a hope without life
I have been there and back.

To the darkest dark
And the brightest light
To the open gates of imagination
And the closed doors of reality
I have been there and back

David Rothchild

Rain

I watch the rain pour down and down
I watch the clouds turn round and round
I watch the rain pour down the side
I watch the rain dry up and hide

Roger C. Ferreira

Cryin' Eyes

Life is unfair,
change is frightening.
Feel the air,
the tension tightening.
We all ask why,
we all ask how.
And when we cry,
all our heads bow.
Down fall the tears,
closer together,
all through the years,
forever and ever.
Cryin' eyes,
untrue lies,
It hurts so bad,
to feel this sad.
I want to stop,
and not go on,
but what's life worth,
If we're not strong

Stephanie R. Ernest

Untitled

All my life I search
I wander and I find
Many empty people
And all their stupid lies
Hating them I realize
I'm looking for some truth
God only knows what makes me think
I'm finding it with you

Crystal Hazelton

Simple Innocence

On a swing
Of a tree
Of a cloud
I will sing
To the bee
Crooning loud
Of the spring
Feeling free
Sun my shroud
Shawl I fling
Look at me
Soaring proud
On a swing

Janice A. Suwyn

My Little Friend

To Leanna
How time goes by
Seems like yesterday
I watched you out of the corner of my eye

Now your life begins at eighteen
You can go and face your dreams

My little friend

You're not that little girl anymore
Through my yard you would go
Coming over for a meal or two
Sharing my corn bread
Just me and you
Remember the long talks we had
Most of the time you never left sad

No matter where you go
No matter what you do
I'll often think of you
Cause you are my
Little friend

Ella M. Cales

I Was Meant for You

As I sit and cry I ask myself
Why don't you get the clue
that I was meant for you

Don't you see
we were meant to be
There isn't nobody but me

You look at me, I look at you
And I know I will always
have feelings for you

Alicia Simones

City of Angels

You take the long way down
to the underground City of Angels,
you realize you won't survive there.
You won't even be able to go home
with one head light.
As you die in the City of Angels
a man comes toward you
and extends his arm to lead you
to the right path.
He leads you to a fountain
and tells you to drink.
You drink back your dignity
and wipe your mouth,
and hold your head high,
and take his hand
so he will lead you back home.

Leandra Lea

Jazz Morning

Murky shades of azure
Slip in and out
Of my consciousness
Twisting and turning my mind
Until it is stretched beyond
Its elasticity.

Hearing the echo
Of sugar-sweet sax
And silky-soft trombone
I rise to greet the day.

Craving an adventure
My journey beings
When I sit
In the sunshine
Close my eyes
Feel the warmth
Holding me
Intoxicated by the
Wonder of imagination
Flying.

Michelle Ingram

A Ten Year Old's Favorite Place

Quiet, still, calm
Water reflecting the trees
That rustle with the gentle breeze
Sitting on the biggest rock
With the sun shining on my back
And the wind blowing in my face
I feel the smoothness of the rock
Hear the birds chirping softly
Smelling the warm, country air
Sitting here thinking
Of all the good times
This place and I shared

Heather Newswanger

Go Placidly Into the Night

Go placidly into the night.
The morn has long since passed.
The brilliance of the noonday sun,
Which forever seemed to last,
So quickly changed is hue
And gloriously filled the sky
Then silently faded from view,
Another day gone by.
When day is done and life is o'er
We'll find eternal peace,
As we embrace the velvet night
In deep and quiet sleep.
Go placidly into the night.

Mildred H. Tims

A Star in the Sky

One night I looked up in the sky,
What I saw made me say, "Oh my!"
I saw a star,
Yes a star I say!
The star I saw was up so high,
And that's no lie!
I watched that star all through the night.
While I watched, it gave off light.
Soon morning came,
And it just wasn't the same.
My star left me as I could see!
But, I wasn't sad, or even mad.
Because I knew at night,
My star would again give off its light.

Erica Dykstra

Green Gold

She smiles,
creases of pain lingering
in the corner of her eye.
Black and white faces
circled in green gold
smile back.
They laugh at her
alone,
knitting memories
with yellow, white ,
orange flowers
for warmth.

Miranda Tompkins

Finding a Way

Into a cave,
Through the sea,
Around and around an apple tree.

Over a hill
Onto a plane,
In and out of a chugging train.

Around the world,
Avoiding a dart,
I found a way to your very own heart.

Alyson Dusseault

Loving Hands

Please Lord let me know the way
Through each and every day
When I'm feeling down
Help me not to frown
Put Your loving hand upon me
And let me be the best that I can be
Life can sometimes get tough
I don't feel like I do enough
But then I hear a voice inside
And You pull me to the side
You give me the strength I need
To continue on each and every day

Kaley Wells

The Heart of Defeat

As long as we remember
Being defeated is not our goal,
It just keeps us humble
Our humanness to show.

Just so we keep on trying
Defeat's not what it seems,
It's more of a strengthening power
To help us reach our dreams.

Phyllis Gail Allison

Bold Emotion

O' sadness
O' boldest of all emotions
Do not pursue me
I cannot face the emptiness
Rise above me
Pillow my face
Shower me in short response
Creep not over me
For I am lost to you forever
O' sadness
O' boldest of emotion
Leave me to my sorrow
This too shall pass

Pam Loveday

Untitled

Here I sit,
I came to write a poem
but couldn't get Started.

Here I sit,
my mind blank,
can't think
of anything to write.

Here I sit,
all broken hearted
my mind still a blank
I don't like having
a blank mind.

Here I sit,
on My own trying
to think of a poem
to Write.

Tasha Perry

Life

Life is so brief, like a wave
    tossed upon the shore.
Do we, like the wave, return
    o'er and o'er?
Or is this our one chance to prove
    our worth,
Before ascending to Heaven, or
    entering Earth?

Mary Morris Kalbaugh

Why Me?

My heart throbs for him
Perhaps he will listen to me
Trust for an eternity
Remembering yesterdays
Asking questions
My brother, his sister
deep secrets
with him is like heaven
I would sacrifice my life for him
Our lives are never easy
Longing to be with and to embrace him
He can be cold at times
Sadness and joys
I speak all of this from my heart

Corey Villines

At 15

An empty beach,
A lone dove,
An empty sky,
A girl without a beau,
An old man
With a story in his eye.
No one can be as lonely
As when you left I.

Maybe I'll fill that beach,
Or find that dove a mate,
Or fill that sky
With dreams and thoughts
And find that girl a beau.

Maybe I'll listen
To that old man's stories
Or maybe I'll just
Forget about you
And the love we shared
And act as if
I never cared.

Courtney Hodges

Ode to the Inner Light

Shining, shimmering, glistening,
The inner light gleams,
Just a flash and it's gone.
Was it there?
It seems so ephemeral, so ethereal
Like fairies in the glades
Dancing lightly from flower to flower
Woven hues of rainbow shades
Their multicolored gowns surreal,
Flashing, sparkling, enchanting,
Enticing all to the inner realms,
To the pool of blue,
Deep to infinity like a cloudless sky
To rest within the subtle hue,
To find solace, rightfully due,
To leave all cares and start anew
In each moment fresh as dew,
To start each day in a new way,
Nothing exists but the infinite now,
Deep as the ocean, tall as the sky!

Catherine M. Stack

Time

As summers die,
We learn to go on.
Getting stronger,
But always aging.

We ponder time,
Always asking why.
There are no answers,
Only more questions.

Time can fly,
Like birds on the wing.
Time can also drag,
Like the slowest of snails.

Years go by,
And we still feel despair.
But summers still die,
And we learn to go on.

Brian Skillman

Loneliness

As the river of love flows
through my heart,
Seeking for a passage way
to the depths of my soul,
Trying to get over the walls of loneliness;
With each assault upon its existence,
It struggles to find its way,
but with the memories of you,
the river of love flows
over the walls of loneliness
like a waterfall!

R. J. Fairbanks

Untitled

May the wings of life always rest on
Your shoulders,
And the dreams of tomorrow carry
You on.
May happiness always nip at
Your heels,
And love reside in your hearts.
May your eyes see what others
Are blind to,
And always capture the beauty that
Surrounds you.

Sarah McGee

A Single Tear

As the single tear,
Runs down my solemn face,
I feel the wetness,
The painful hatred,
Fill my needless fate.

But when the lovely girl,
Comes to the heat of my soul,
I feel the never-ending coolness,
Hold all of my control.

For where there had been a tear,
A glamorous smile had risen,
Yet in the hopeless face of a shadow,
One realizes I have been forgiven.

Eileen Soltes

End

Her stories were tragic
Her demise was long
She pulled the trigger
As she sang his song

Ever punished by grief
Almost killed by strife
This man was hurting
As he took his own life

The gang was his family
His life line at best
He gave them his soul
And was then put to rest

She lived on the street
Her body for sale
She slept for a living
But hung in jail

None of these people
Had to descend
They used different means
But reached the same end

Corrie Thomas

Butterflies

Up and down, round and round
They gracefully dip and twirl,
Away in the sky, way up high
They dance the dance of the butterfly.

With graceful wings they swoop and glide
In summer fields big and wide.
With bright colors, a beautiful sight,
They seem to glow with their own light.

They pass the farmhouse by and by.
I feel to touch one; I'd touch the sky.
All across the land they fly.
I'd love to touch one way up high.

With spots or glitter I don't care,
I love butterflies everywhere.

Amee Looney

My Valentine

I'm really not into Valentine's Day,
but I am this year.
Because you are my Valentine.
I have a reason to be your Valentine,
Not because I did not have a Valentine
Before you asked me. It's because
You are nice, and a sweet person,
You are loving and caring. That is why
I am now your Valentine!!!

Selina Droz

My Son: A Boy, a Man, a College Grad

To Erik

As you grew from within
I knew that God would hold your hand
On your birth
A day of glory
Moms' heart would hold
Your life's story
I chose your name with greatest care
A baby boy with golden hair
A gift to me from God above
A son to give all my love
You took your lumps
You sometimes faltered
My faith in you
Was never altered
School days came
The years flew by
You graduated Senior High
College came
And now that's through
I am so proud of my son—you!

Terri Perrigan

The Unborn

I never got to feel you move,
Or to feel your little kicks.
Never got to bring you home,
And give you tenderness.

I'll never get to cradle you,
Or sing you lullabies.
Never get to tuck you in,
Or teach you to wave Bye.

I'll never get to read to you,
Or teach you to say your prayers.
Never get to give you presents,
Or buy you things to wear.

I'll never get to comfort you,
And wipe away your tears.
I'll never get to protect you,
And take away your fears.

I'll never get to name you,
Or to touch your little face.
I'll never get to show you love,
Because of my mistakes.

Lillian Lack

Divine Stream

Mortals look ye skyward
for blazing faith
Be wary lest ye die
Fulfillment of the mind
the soul the body
Enriched with chocolate
gorged with Dante
Brimming with Christ
Only to know that one survives
One eternal
Look toward Nazareth
and let the rivers flow
over my dead and bloated body
Read the Word and soar
then wonder fall
deeper ever deeper into demons
One survives
Don't dwell on life but give me up
Take me home
So I may survive

Matthew Trujillo

Pal of My Cradle Days

Pal of my cradle days,
I've needed you always.
Since I was a baby upon your knees,
You sacrificed everything for me.
I stole the gold from your hair;
I put the silver threads there.
I don't know of any way I could ever repay,
Pal of my cradle days.
Dearest friend, dearest pal,
It was I that caused you
All the lonesome heartaches you knew.
I never knew what a mother goes through.
There's nothing that she wouldn't do,
My pal of my cradle days.

Thomas Perritano

Trees

You see them everyday.
Whether at work or at play.
They are important to us,
So saving them is a must!
They take in what they need,
And give off oxygen for us to breathe.
We have to share our Mother Earth,
And give them the respect they deserve.
When we cut down one, we should plant two.
It's the right thing to do.
Because trees have feelings too.

Julie Hinrichs

Thoughts of an Infertile Woman

I have always known my body
(though not intimately)

Only as a barren desert
(full of wind and sand and empty spaces)

Where no seed could grow
(disconnected)

But look in the sky
(my heart is beating)

And I see myself breathing there
(in the rustling of the leaves)

My body becomes one
(I am the lush green riverbed)

And I will come
(into this knowledge of myself)

Susan League

Not-So-Smooth Sailing

My ship set sail
A long time ago.
Where it went,
I don't quite know.

So all day long
I sit by the shore,
Watching the horizon,
To see what's in store.

As for my ship—
Not one sign today.
Lost at sea
It's there to stay.

It hasn't returned.
Wasn't meant to be.
I guess I'll keep hoping
For all eternity.

Karlie Thate

Polka

I see how happy the children
Dance to the music
My hot, sweaty hands
Clapping together
I hear how they laugh
And sing along
I think about how I used to do
That
But now I'm too old
Too weak
But I enjoy watching
My grandkids and kids
Dance to the ancient music—
Polka

Amy Shollenberger

Love

Love is great
If you have a mate
Love is sad if you get mad

Love can be exciting
But can also be frightening
Love is blind
Love is kind

Love can make you go out of your mind
If your love is true
It will be returned to you

Sharing someone's love
Can be a blessing from above
Love is new
Love is true

Love can be old
And also can be bold
Time to care
Time to share

If your honest with your love
Then you know it comes from above

Shannon Hunt

What Am I Doing?

What am I doing?
Handing in my words
For the audience to take
For what they are worth
What am I doing?
Opening my mind for now
Forever expressing what I'm about
Letting the people know
How my pen flows
A representative of my thoughts
Though my mind had fought
What am I doing?
Leaving my mark on this earth
Value my work
What am I doing?
It is time that I tell them
What am I doing?
Writing you all a poem.

Brian Horton

The Loss

It is a cold day,
The people are silent,
Women cry into their handkerchiefs,
The men fight back their tears.
It is over. The people leave silently,
With only the broken hearted family
Left to mourn over their loss.

Angela C. Kelton

Two Little Children

John and Linda
So much in love
They couldn't wait to grow up
But when they did, life got rough
A little baby was on the way
They had to work,
But still didn't have the money to pay
The mother died while giving birth
To a beautiful baby girl
The doctor came out and said
"Congratulations, but you'll have to leave"
Cause the mother's fading fast
Johnny hit his knees and said
"Oh God it can't be!

Tammy Wheeler

The Cage

I am watching life
From within my cage.

A cage wrought of flesh,
Housing my soul
In a wretched exterior.

I cry out with my eyes,
But no one hears me.

I decorate my cage
With the foppery of joy
And the finery of laughter.

I hope you will be fooled.

For this cage protects.
As it imprisons.

Brian Jerome Dunkel

No Joke

Prom night was so cool
Was a get together for a few
Some could act like drunken fools
Smokin' pot, sniffin' coke
What was this, no joke

Just about two
The party was through
Tim and Sue only had a few
Got in a car
They thought, what could we do.

Guess what happened, just a mile or two
Two drunken lives had been taken
Drinking and driving was only one clue
But two, Tim and Sue
Just a casket or two
Whose headstones read:

Tim—1977–1996, Sue—1978–1996

Don't be mistaken, this is no joke
Prom night is cool, but don't drink,
Smoke or sniff coke

Shannon Denise Barger

The Friends

The friends watch
The moon go over
The hill and slowly
Meet the stars
And go to its
Place in the sky
And all the stars
Around it.

Amanda Torres

Shadowed

The crumbling walls
And the fading dream
Of Babylon
In an uncalculated scheme
Pressing on through the cold dark air
I can feel the inevitable stare
Of Death looking in on me
Waiting to steal the key
Unlocking the door
To my reality

Joseph Carroll

Untitled

It is such a slow love
You make me wait, so long.
And I shall wait as long for you
As bridges take to build.

For now I gain the sleep I'll lose
While you are here with me
Constructing just how high to go
How far that one could reach.

It is such an urgent love
Because I wait, so long.
And I shall wait as long for you
As bridges take to fall.

By then I'll gain the ground I'd lose
In choosing someone else
To lay each brick and span the lengths
Of river beds and fells.

Laurel Ann Hardy

To Wonder . . . To Know

Am I the only one looking up
Always thinking . . .
Will I ever know . . .
Will I ever realize . . .
Will I ever feel . . .
Will I ever see . . .
How dark the light really is
My solitude swallows my
hopeful interlude of colorful thoughts
That are deep without shallow meanings
And feeling this I realize in a world of
Ten million, still I stand alone . . .
In love.

Renée Jackson

The Love We Share

I will send you red roses
To match the blush upon your face
These roses I send you
My heart I'll use as a vase

You will find them entwined
With threads of gold so fine
To show the world of our love
And that you are mine

Each year I'll add a rose of red
Each five a golden thread
At twenty five a silver bow
All trimmed in gold and red

At fifty a golden crown
For my queen so fair
To show the world of the love
That we had to share

Ralph J. Veach

No Interruption

Here's a very different poem,
from dinosaurs to soda foam.
It might change subjects from line to line,
but, don't worry, I'm sure you'll be fine.

I met a man who had a joke,
but, once in a while, he'd give me a poke.
Daisies lived on the hill of life,
but animal's words were all full of fife.

I'll say it backwards to confuse you more.
Back then, life was all galore.

But animal's words were all full of fife,
daisies lived on the hill of life.
But, once in a while, he'd give me a poke,
I met a man who had a joke.

But, don't worry, I'm sure you'll be fine,
it might change subjects from line to line.
From dinosaurs to soda foam,
here's a very different poem.

Sarah Davie Silvey

When?

When the last leaf of summer falls
And the trees become bare;
When the foggy mist of autumn calls
And the sun refuses to care.

When little birds no longer sing
And church bells no longer chime;
When the world itself stops turning
And the stars no longer shine.

What then is the reason for living?
What is the reason to be?
How else can I go on believing;
If truth I couldn't see?

When sweet wines don't mellow
And flowers no longer bloom;
When butterflies no longer follow
The scented trail of doom.

When all good things have ended
And all the rules are bent,
How can the hurt be mended
If souls do not repent?

Nida Ines R. Natividad

Life; Me! Yes; You!

Life is my help in every need
Life does my every hunger feed
Life dwells within me, guides my way
Through every moment of my day.

I now am wise, I now am true,
Patient kind and loving too,
All thing's I am, can do and be
Through life the Christ that is in me.

Life is my health, I'm well and strong,
Life is my joy the whole day long,
Life is my all, I know no fear
Since life, as love is here!

Life, I thank you for the night
And for the pleasant morning light;
For rest and food and loving care
And all that makes the day so fair.

Help me to do the things I should,
To be to others kind and Good,
In all I do in work and play,
To grow more loving everyday!

Maria Sostenita Giron

The Tree of Life

Years of spring with branches budding
Time of wonder and delight
Suckling roots seeking mother's nourishment
Gaining strength for summer's plight.

Summer years with branches searching
Reaching for the God above
Flourishing leaves, simmering passion
Restless in a thunderous love.

Autumn years with branches rooted
Colorful leaves of red and gold
Attaining peaks of untold beauty
In their beauty growing old
Silently growing old.

Winter years with branches brittle
Colorless days and endless nights
Lingering dreams of past summer's madness
Fading in the dimming light
Coldness comes
Darkness calls
The time has come to rest Good night!

Frank A. Arrigo

An End to Darkness

The Darkness came
afraid to move,
one wrong step,
alone,
I waited in silence for you
to bring the light.
Not knowing the enemy,
no clear path,
no way to turn,
Restrained—I begin to fight.
Restless, floating in limbo,
fumbling through this starless night.
Gave into myself and realized
you were, it was,
I was there all along
Just had to open my eyes.

Jennifer Shelton

To My Mom

Roses are red.
Violets are blue.
Your are pretty,
And I love you!
But,
Best of all;
I know you
Love me too!

Ashley Nicole

For Mom

You were my childhood
You made me dance
You gave me my music
Every turn—every chance—
Every time—
I think back,
And I can see you smile,
I can feel your hug,
If for only a while.

But I see you slipping—
Your life—slipping away;
Mommy, I'd give it all back
If it would make you stay.

Kristina B. Nelson

Beloved Grandma

Grandma, sweet Grandma
Your smile is a treasure
Your laughter, sweet music
And your joy shows no measure

Grandma, beautiful Grandma
So fair of face
Your eyes, how they sparkle
With the light of God's grace

Grandma, delicate Grandma
So tall in love
Your devotion is steadfast
In our Holy Father above

Grandma, gentle Grandma
You comfort me
With words of wisdom;
Laced with Love, from thee

Grandma, beloved Grandma
You inspire all others
With integrity and compassion
I will love you forever

Carol Padilla

The Edge of Heaven

My spirit soars high over the earth
as I stand peering over the mountains' edge.

The beauty of the land before me
is nothing in comparison to God's
Handiwork in the clouds which sit
hovering
upon the peaks of the mountain tops.

Here is where I feel free,
where I feel peace.

All aspects of life are but a
distant memory . . .
quite possibly I have reached
the edge of heaven.

Kristi Neace

The Sunset's Love

In the still of the night,
When no longer bright,
The sun went down,
Without a sound,
As I relax I see the rays,
I am often in a deep daze
And then just then he came over here,
I knew it was true love,
Sent from the sunset's love.

LeeAnn Shelton

To the White Dogwood
and the White Azalea

Distilled essence of shooting stars
Crowning the outburst of spring
Your dazzling whiteness
Whittles us down
To our essential oneness,
Hinting a
Unity!

But do we dare be,
That pure, that dazzling, that white.
That committed
That free?

Dr. Ouide Bilon

Spirit Happy

Thank the beggar
Dressed in daisies
Offer roses
To a thorn
Carry castles
For the queenless
Bless the bishop
For his scorn

Plant sunflowers
In the morning
Leave wild horses
By the sea
Gather children
Lost to darkness
Scorn the lizard
Long last free

Michael Revere

The Old Man

The old man says
We are doomed.
He says
You have killed the land,
Murdered the animals,
Poisoned the streams.
You have upset the great balance.
Now the Gods are angry.
Not at me, but at you.
You must change your ways.
Yet we laugh. Why?
What are we afraid of?
Maybe he is right.
He is not, they always say.
He is just an old man.
What does he know?
Still, I believe him.

Stenna Michelle Hinson

Pennies for St. Peter

Two pennies in my pockets
For St. Peters at the gate
Open the doors to heaven
St. Peter take my pennies
before you close the gate.

I see before me all
The angels and the saints
Mom, Dad, sisters, and brothers
Just beyond the gate
St. Peter take my pennies
Before you close the gate.

Thank you for waiting
Let me rest inside
Close your arms around me
Close the door St. Peter
I am safe at last inside.

June M. Sperske

Untitled

At the first quarter of the moon,
I saw your golden eyebrow;
At the second quarter,
Your heart illuminated my night;
At the third,
Your hand on my shoulder was a feather;
At the fourth,
I started to see.
Then the dark night,
No more, you and me;
Goodbye!

Annette Lorant

He Cared

A clown laughs at me. Who Am I?
Standing alone being afraid.
Don't laugh at me clown, for I'm sad too.
He reaches out his white gloved hand.
Takes my hand and places it on his heart.
I look up and into his eyes, they were sad.
It was the painted smile around his mouth
That made it appear as if laughing.
He draws me to him and strokes my face.
This clown knew I was sad and in his way
Without saying a word, he gave me the
Feeling that the cared.

Gillian Leach

Twilight

The flaming sun sinks low in the west
To meet the far horizon
Like a child cuddling in its mother's arms
For a moment before retiring
The heat and work are done for the day
Our troubles and worries seem smaller
As we pause for a while and enjoy
The merging of day and night
The cricket in the field starts chirping
The frog in the pond begins croaking
As if to show their delight
In the calm that comes at twilight
And this is the peace we feel at twilight
The time between day and night

Charles M. Langen

Sturm Und Drang

Sometimes it's tiring to say no
When yes would seem more fitting.
But yesteryear I let the yeses go
So freely that they choked the way.
And now my steps, so carefree then,
Must needs be slow and more in tune
With cosmic thought.
Or else results will once again
Come thumping on my head and heart,
Reminding me that only I can take
The blame, and follow through . . .
Or not.

Donald Clyde

Lava Moon

Killer bees swarm the streets;
Night lights no more.
Millions buzzing—people shoving.

Execute.
Execute!
The green flash of ash;
Soaked and soaking in dry miniature
leaves,
Now in a jail.
Hallowed red horizon over an exhaustion.
I've spoken of
Crossing that seasonal line.
Many amazing laws—a million flaws.

Prevent.
Prevent!
Gunfire and thunder;
Needle thread nerve in a blackened box.
The middle of this morning exhibits
A cold sweat; a short-fused breath.
Remembering the spidery sunset death,
In the life of this lava moon.

Clint Gray

Evenfall Spews Venom
Or So It Seems

Evenfall spews venom
Nightmares are mute and
without hue
Dusk inks fear into the soul
of twilight
Nocturne charms the horizon
with black and rue

The dawn erases the phantoms'
tour of terror
Sunflower is a beauty bush
enhanced by happy sunbeams
The dark horse loses to the
celestial favorite
A sunny disposition is a wonderful
thing or so it seems

John Duran

Mother's Day Is Everyday

Do all mother care?
They can't all be as mine,
Such a heavy load to bare.
And who would take that time?
No, that's not even fair.

But mine has never wavered,
Never, not been there.
Through years of pain and suffering,
And oh, so many failures,
I doubt that many would hold true.
I've often wondered,
"Maybe it's just me"
But no, she's that way with all,
That take the time to see.
Yes, I just happened to be blessed,
With a one in a million,
Mother you're just the best!
And we love you . . .
Me and all the rest . . .

Forest Martini

The Plant

In a tiny garden
There is a corner.
A small flower waits.

Christopher M. Martin

Only If . . .

The look of his eyes
The gentleness of his touch
The warmth of his caress
and the sweetness of his kiss

The calmness
the comfort
the security
and the love they bring.

These could be mine
If only I could
If only I would
Enable myself
To open up and release
My heart
To feel love
and to be loved

If only I could
If only I would
These could be mine.

Michelle Wilson

The Death of an Angel

A cool summer night
A cloudy sky, no stars to be seen
Another one of the angels gone
Taken to heaven forever
Close your eyes and listen carefully
The sound of beating wings
Softly fluttering back and forth
Whispers of love and of loss
Cries of agony and of pain
Raise your face to heaven
Offer your tears as a sacrifice
Your pain will slowly be erased
Memories will take its place
Thoughts of joy and of laughter
Numbing the aching pain of loss
The loss of love and the taking of an
angel.

Sarah Smith

Life's Friendship Flowers

So perfect is a flower,
While in a field it bares,
Its colors ever vividly,
Showing happiness as it shares
Itself with another.
When the wind blows a flower cares
To entwine 'round its neighbor,
And whisper healing prayers.
Then tilt its head so gently,
Celebrating, it tosses front to back.
It's a splendid blessing
To hear a flower laugh.

Traci L. Hollingsworth

Difference

We're each different;
Oh how true!
As different as a new,
Or a well worn shoe.
Well let's not hide,
That new is shiny;
But not comfy inside.
Each has a purpose;
Each in its time.
Only God knows
The rhythm and rhyme.
Left to one's self,
The going's so hard;
Only God's spirit
Gives peace by the yard.
And joy is God's spirit,
No time for boo-hooing
There's much to be giving,
Life's really worth living.

J R Gerhard

Hand in Hand

I can smell the rain
Coming in the southern sky,
And I can see the tears
Streaming from your troubled eyes.

If you'll believe in me,
Then I'll be there for you.
And if you need a shoulder,
Then you can have that too.

Whatever the problem you have to face,
I'll help you all I can.
We can make it through together,
Walking hand in hand.

B. J. Murrey

Best Friends

Beginning to
End,
Sharing
Together
Fond
Remembrances of
Innumerable
Experiences,
Never losing
Devotion or
Sincerity

Lisa A. Kafka

Alone

Some things are large
Some things are small
But I know
The largest things of all

It's always with you
So beware
For it's something that
Shouldn't be allowed too near

It comes out mostly
When you're sad
And sometimes even
when you're mad

It's strong and tough
You must break free
But don't expect help,
For it's hard for others to see.

Holly Hadden

Alone

My heart has gone black.
My soul has disappeared.
My life is in chaos
with no hope to reappear.
I gaze the world with eyes
that do not see.
Forever searching
for others like me.
I know that life is over
because it never really began.
Soon we will all be swallowed
by the sand.

David Pasternak

A Lament of Spring

I stood in the midst of spring
Behind walls flavored with dolor.
Stupidly, with my arms outstretched,
I sway in the airy freshness
Of its fragranced breath
As the spirit of my eyes
Streaked down my face like a
River of melted mountain snow.
And it embraces me.
Then it soars high, floats, dances,
With the newness of life.
Showing my imagination
What my soul yearns.
I smelled, I tasted, I felt.
I, for the briefest of moments,
Was one with it all.
But like my spirit water that
Carried my eyes, words, and pain,
I too now fall, dissipate,
And die along with the old.

Neil J. Miller

Survivor

He's a blind old bear
Alone in the winter woods
With only the smell
Of his breath for comfort
Too mean to die,
Too lost to care
But show some caution,
He's still the bear.

Reid Lewis Nelson

Mama

Mama, I know the timing wasn't right
And you think of me each night
All the things I could have done
The missing joy, and the fun
We could have had
Please don't be sad
When you think of me
And what will never be
The cure for Aids I'll never find
These things I know, they cross your mind
But, I still love you anyway
Just wish I had the chance to say
But the timing wasn't right
And we'll never know what might
(Have been)
Can't really say that it's a sin
But then again
Would've liked the chance to say
Mama, I love you, everyday.

Eric J. Pirtle

Untitled

Star-crossed lovers
That by chance crossed paths
Once longing for togetherness
Now wonder of the past
What could I have done
To make us grow apart
I watch her slip away
She's the girl who stole my heart
I once had thanked fate
For bringing her my way
Today I curse that evil being
For taking her away
I wish that I could change the past
I'd return to the day we met
And take you again into my arms
My forever Juliet.

Joshua McNellen

Who'll Be a Volunteerocrat?

*Dedicated to Norman Katz Shearer
and his family*

A volunteeronomist, volunteerologist
A volunteerosophist, I'd like to find.
So, who'll be a volunteerocrat
And a volunteer at that,
Who'll be a volunteer linguistically?
Who'll play volunteeropoly
With volunteericity?
Who'll eye volunteerometry
Quite volunteeronically?
Who'll entreat the volunteerees
To learn volunteer, expertise,
Only to find surprisingly,
A volunteer may suddenly be
A volunteer-put-to-sea
Yet, transmitting messages rejoicingly
Oscillographically!

Esther Shearer

A Child's Time

We don't have time
we're sorry dear
We don't have time
to draw you near
We don't have time
to teach you love
These things you'll learn . . .
when the time comes

Cathy Rae Martin

Biannual Thought

As I sit here by the hour
As I'm gazing at this little flower.

I see a little teardrop of dew
I see a little tint of blue.

And now I often ask why
This little flower has to die.

If by chance it should appear
I'll see the little flower again next year.

Amanda Mueller

For You

For you I gave my best
For me you stood out from the rest.
For you I went through such
For me you meant so much.

For you I have betrayed myself
For me you were reason to persevere.
For you my mind is torn
For me you never shed a tear.
For you I fear I'm wrong
For me you were always strong.

For you I long . . .

Matthew R. Boggs

I See

I see the world
Spinning, rotating, reeling,
Through the universe.

I see the men
Crying, fighting, dying,
In a world
Of their own creation.

I see myself
Falling, calling, slipping,
Deeper into my inner mind.

I see the world
Spinning, rotating, reeling,
Through the universe.

Tracie Springer

Untitled

Now I'm feeling sorrow
Now I'm feeling pain
Shall I look to tomorrow
To step out of the rain
Or dwell in sullen melancholy
But, would that be too great a folly?
Sense the sickness is in my head
My only possible cure is to be dead
For death is life's own remedy
To be gone and forgotten,
As a poorly written comedy

Stark Raving

Untitled

Love is like a
Candle . . .
It can sometimes burn
Strong
It can sometimes burn
Subtle
It can sometimes burn
at both Ends
When that happens
It usually Dies out
Fast
Leaving Nothing but
Flames of
Smoke . . .

Narice West

Friendship

Friends are there
When you need them
They can't wait for
your arrival
When you are down and
very disappointed
They will try to get you
more joyful
And sometimes when
You are disappointed
They get disappointed too!

Ashley Light

Untitled

Come then quietly, without a sound
Sit thee softly on the ground
In the evening's dimming light
Nature's lanterns take to flight

A circle forming 'round about
Vines entwining in and out
Hear the laugh of faerie things
Heed the song the Phaedre sings

Lost thyself, and time is still
Join their dance against thy will
Music like a heady wine
Blurs the mind like pale moonshine

Dawn comes slowly, without warning
All is lost in early morning
Curse thy life until its end
Searching for that time again

Kathleen E. West

Keep on Talking

Keep on sweeping
And talking
My Lord with do the speaking
Just keep on talking

On his time to
Cause he see that one
Whose heart is aching
Keep on seeking for that one

Because one care
God does the changing
Keep on sweeping around my door:
One who is changing!

Keep on sweeping around my door
And talking
Who being molded?
One who do the talking (me)

Letha I. Graham

Life at Eight

Eight years old and full of fire
her daddy's youngest child
soft brown eyes like the sand
waiting to learn life's mysteries

One fateful day her life was ravaged
when a freak storm stole her daddy's life
his little girl's dreams there vanished
as her daddy's boat went out of sight

More than twenty years have past
and still day turns to night
his little girl is now a woman
with a daughter of her own

Eight years old and full of fire
her mother's oldest child
vast blue eyes like the sea
she fulfills life's mystery

Nancy Ann Bell

I Can't Stop Thinking of You

My love for you cannot be measured,
In inches or feet or yards.
You've captured my heart,
And one by one, overcome my guards.

Hour by hour, day by day,
My love for you still grows.
How big it will get, how large it will be,
I don't think anyone knows.

Whenever I hear your wonderful voice,
Or see your beautiful face,
I think of how you are so much
The jewel of the whole human race.

When I look up at the twinkling stars,
Just hanging in the sky,
I think that if I were with anyone else,
I'd probably rather die.

I end this poem from me to you,
With one last closing line.
You're the nicest girl I've ever met,
And I think you're really fine.

Dan Dutcher

Forgiving

I walked down to the peaceful pond
At the closing of my day,
And found a leaf where thereupon
My troubles I could lay.

Once upon the leaf I blew
My sorrows from the shore,
To find a home in the water's depth.
And torment me no more.

Sean Kelly

Wings of an Angel

At the moment you die
On the wings of an Angel
You get to fly
She takes you to heaven
To our maker in the sky
On the wings of an Angel
You get to fly
Your soul, she takes to Heaven
So high-up into the sky
Therefore you shouldn't cry
On the wings of an Angel
Your son will forever fly

Vanessa Gilkerson

Long Ago Dreams

When she was young and full of dreams,
she planted these—and now it seems
in memory of her love and care,
here they bloom with golden flair.

Amid the silence and unkempt lawn,
they bow in reverence, and still bloom on.
Then all together in full array,
hundreds of blooms greet break of day.

With inspiration, their heads held high,
they bloom for her—not passersby.
The old house stands in rain or snow,
Knowing secret dreams of long ago.

Eunice Skelton

The Stranger

There was a portrait on the wall
That frightened me when I was small.
Tales of this icon Mom would tell
About this man she loved so well.
My mom, the widow, was his wife.
His only gift to me was life.
His seed was planted—so I grew
The daughter that he never knew.

Mikki Zadrowski

Black Cat

You look at me,
black cat,
with bright, golden,
glistening eyes.
Seeming to
read me,
sad and alone
you stand there,
wanting and wishing
to be let
inside.
But you can't
come in,
no matter how
much I want
you to.
Oh, beautiful
black cat,
can you ever forgive me?

Allegra Long

Music

Sense the silence, hear the sound;
Combinations quite profound!
Integrated melodies,
With the rhythm . . . thank you, trees.
Short durations, long ones too,
Set a mood . . . depends on you.
High and low the sounds are pitched,
Up and down, durations switched.
Intelligence within is found,
Pleasing to the ears, the sound.
Anything that resonates,
No one now does hesitate.
All together, beat prepared,
Start at once, the ear is spared.
Juxtaposed the sounds occur,
Forming a delightful blur.
Stopping, starting, fast and slow,
Instruments his pleasure know.
The composer does create,
Audiences celebrate!

Leonard A. Martin

The Duffer

He stood upon the second tee,
the marker showed that par was three.

He thought this hole would not be tough,
then hit his shot into deep rough.

He gave the ball another rap,
it sailed into the nearest trap.

A wedge was placed into his hand,
but all he did was move some sand.

Three times more he tried his luck,
and finally the green was struck.

He found the putting just as hard,
and entered ten upon his card.

He's very happy with that score,
his playing partner had two more.

John J. Celesnik

Untitled

A dry, blustery day
The wind sweeping through the grass
The soft sound it made in the trees
Is it calling?
No, it is scurrying by
Leaving its mark
A quiet farewell

Laurie Petty

Over Me

Oh if I could only tell
The feeling that fell
Over Me
When I dreamed of you
And how you'd Be
When I stand there next to Thee.
The slightest image that I See
Depicts your love of Me Sweetly.

I know I dream such hopeless dreams
Of you and Me and how we'd Be,
If only I'd confess to Thee
Those feelings that fell over Me.

Sandra J. Flynn

Seem to Be . . . But Really
(Use of Pronouns Only)

I seem to be smart
But really I am confused

You seem to be kind
But really you are very mean

He/she seems to be true
But really he/she is a liar

We seem to be close
But really we are so far

They seem to be serious
But really they do not care

You seem to be decent
But really you are disgusted

Venus Lee

Boys

My boys are joys,
With toys
And ploys.

Lisa Christell-Sandri

Father

He is a guardian
Of all he surveys
He loves all the people
In the home he maintains
His children look to him
For his leadership and guidance
He is upright and honest
And a good father
Is loved by all

Rose Zizka

Grandpa

I speak in silence,
When it comes to you.
I can't bare the thoughts,
Of you being gone!
Gone far away . . .
From the ones;
Who care the most.
I believe in angels,
Just like I believe in you!
Someday, I'm hoping that
I can reach out my hands,
To touch yours,
And I'll feel the warmth.
The warmth is near . . .
Somewhere!
I can feel it, near!

Melissa Shreckengost

The Empty Bottle

The bottle is empty,
It's memory lingers on,
It's a crying shame,
Since I found it's all gone.

It was given to me by my brother,
Who at the age of 64,
Said "Take it easy Don,
Because there won't be any more."

So I nursed it along
The best that I could,
But I found it got empty
Just like I thought it would.

The only thing I have to say
To the makers of this fine brew,
It just don't last long enough
I'm sure you know that's true.

So keep up the good work
Since your product is so very fine,
I'm sure other people would like some
Jack Daniel's #7 I sure enjoyed mine.

Donald T. Miller

On Intimacy and Fidelity

My neck is stiff . . .
The guilt of having my head turned.

How the mind punishes
And the body receives its instructions.

Why not rejoice
The spirit kindled
From another source
Or is just the light within
All the more glowing
From the contact
Soul to soul?

Dr. Wendy Satin Rapaport

Coral Reef Hall

Fishes dancing, octopi prancing
Let's all go to Coral Reef Hall.

Clown fish amusing, gambling sharks losing
Let's all go to Coral Reef Hall.

Piano fish playing, groovy crabs swaying
Let's all go to Coral Reef Hall.

The fishes say, "Come and play and
while you're at it, why don't you stay."
So here's your invitation to
Coral Reef Hall.

Emma Marie Wnuk

Dream

Dare to dream of love so strong,
That it fills your heart feelings so warm.
It could twist your mind—
Till what you see is blind,
Yet dreams that I have are pure and kind.
But to wish on a dream could never be sure,
Yet to love in my self could be my cure.
So that's what will be,
Just you and me, in a dream of love,
For none to see.

Laura El Sayed

Afterglow

My head rests upon your shoulder.
Your hand gently strokes my hair.
A blanket of peace covers us.
Understanding is everywhere.

A gentle kiss between us,
Love has left us weak.
Oh, the sweet and blissful feeling
Of almost being asleep.

Tamra Dickenson Keeth

Untitled

To death, surrendering my
soul, easier would be,

Than, to a lover, entrust my
hearts key.

Intimacy, sweet maze, unrivaled
by natures honey comb,

In whose catacombs I
blindly wander,

Every dying step impaled
with pleasure.

How much kinder deaths
embrace,

In one last kiss, my breath
he takes . . .

Martha L. Arredondo

Me and My Guitar

I have a friend that sits so still
It waits for me and does my will
The sounds that we together make
Are so intense, not one is fake
The music can be fast or slow
Whatever I feel, it lets me go
Maybe some day we'll be in the show
Until that day you'll never know.

Mario Vigil

Me

In my mind many problems
are there to find,
I'm hoping to find a way to
make them somehow go away.
Away! They don't they just get
worse with each passing day.
My heart is in pain I've tried
to explain, but it's only in vain.
Why do I feel lost and not needed?
Maybe because of how I've been treated.
Please help me find the way to be happy,
all I want to be is me—Kathy.

Kathy Van Norde

Love, Everything

When I die,
I want to be happy
With a smiling face
'Cause life is nothing even die!

When I live,
I want to be happy
With my living life
'Cause life is nothing
If only live!

When I love,
I want to be happy
With a loving life
'Cause life is nothing
Without love!

Alfonse T. Nguyen

Barbara Ann

I've never seen the Grand Canyon
Or looked upon the Mile High Falls
But they never could compare,
With my Love for you.
I cannot explain it
Or why it lasted so long.
I can only accept it
And grow with it
And continue to nurture it;
Bask in its glow
And say once again:
I love you—now and forever.

Alvin Jan Bakun

A Tribute to Walt Whitman's
Leaves of Grass

Walt was seeing, seeing;
Seeing; then, word painting;
And was singing, singing;
Writing poems so haunting.

He was hearing, hearing;
Hearing; then, relating;
And was singing, singing;
Using words so sating.

He was ranging, ranging;
Ranging; then, recalling;
And was singing, singing;
Ringing words so telling.

He was aiming, aiming;
Aiming; self-imaging;
And was singing, singing;
Writing poems of living.

Walt was loving, loving;
Loving; self-revealing;
And was singing, singing;
Loving words of feeling.

William Thordarson

Untitled

In loving memory of Austen Alexander Sanov
A young boy,
So innocent at heart.
It seemed as if
We'd never part.
He loved all sports,
Skateboarding, and roller-blading too.
He loved little puppies
And me and you.
Now that he's gone,
All these memories have entered my mind.
We miss him terribly right now,
But we'll heal—with time.
The accident was tragic.
I can't believe it was someone we love.
If only he'd taken a different road
Is all I can think of.
It shouldn't have happened,
He was only five.
If only it had happened differently,
He might still be alive.

Jolynn Powell

Yours and Mine

I have a story I want to tell
You may not want to hear it
But if you listen to me well,
The story is not a secret.

My story is old, a little bit
It was born on "Golgotha's hill,"
Beneath a crown of thorns, it lay awaiting
The master to pay our bill.

It lay there silently, afraid
The sun went down in shame
The lightning flashed, the thunder roared
And we, were the ones to blame.

My story is, I hope you see
That Jesus was hanging there for me,
The crown of thorns upon his head
Should have been on mine instead

But we could not hang upon the cross
Our souls were already lost,
But Jesus, Precious Saviour, Friend,
Hung there for us, my story ends.

Lucille Orr Freeman

Black Like Me

They say—
You don't belong here
You ain't like one of us
Your skin ain't black enough
Your hair ain't kinky enough
You don't talk black
You don't walk black
What you tryin' to prove?
You've lost your way Girl
Get back to your roots!

I say—
I know where I've come from
I know who I am
My skin is Black And Beautiful
It's what I'm comfortable in
But there is more to me
Than this here skin
I am, who I am
I do, what I do
I ain't got nothin' to prove.

Danielle Hubbard

Gymnastics

Gymnastics is fun
I like to practice in the sun
Bars are the best of all
Watch out because you just might fall
Beam is the trickiest one
If you fall you might be done
Floor has lots of passes
You can't miss any classes
Vault you have to run very fast
If you do you won't take last
If you do good you might get a medal
They are not cheap or look like a pedal
If you don't get one
That is okay
Just be happy that the meet is done
Then you can say, Hooray!

Phylicia Hixson

Honesty

There's a special kind of person
When words need not be said
To know your every inner thought
Through your eyes it can be read.
It's that simple look or gesture
Not just anyone can see
It takes an understanding
It's called total honesty
Sometimes it isn't easy
It takes a lot of work
To make a person see your point
Without their feelings hurt.
Once you give up trying
To please your special friend
A relationship starts dying
And next will be the end.

Audrey Chiodo

The Sea

Do you see what I see?
I see the sea
Full of fish and splashing, waving water
Curly shells that last forever
Relaxing on the sandy beaches
picking fruits like plums and peaches
Shells that curl round and round
Waiting, waiting to be found
Palm trees that wave in the wind
Ocean currents oh, how they spin
Wishing I will never have to go home
This is where I shall forever roam.

Anna Youells

Thoughts of a Caregiver
(A Farewell)

There lies her scintillating rainbow
Standing in a row they shimmer so
Bright pills, dull pills
To cure her ills
Gulp each one and down the hatch they go.

Expectant is the hope in her eyes
Faithfully each prescription she tries
Will this one fail
Will it prevail
And succeed where often failure lies?

Medi-cal had put me at her side—
One of the strangers she met with pride:
How dear to me
She came to be
And I've grieved greatly since she died.

Alma B. Laurens

I Got My Wish

I got my wish.
I wished to be single and it came true.
I wished to live alone and now it is so.
I wished for a peace of mind
And received that blessing
Also, along with unpaid bills,
No help with the kids
And a broken down old dog!

Kim G. Joyner

Drug Euphoria and Prevention

A drug a day,
Keep the healthy away.
Fools drug and perish slowly. But
Wise refrain and relish evenly.
Slow death is sure to fall, on
Whom drug has taken ill toll.
Hallucinogenic drug for sure,
Spoil your health and wealth assure.
Euphoria of drugs is short, and
The effect of ill-health is long.

Cocaine is joyful, but
Its effects are painful.
Heroin, Brown-sugar are their names, and
Calamity is their game.
To drug is human, and
To recover is divine.
Drug addict is a reject, and
Treat him kindly to revert.
Finally, to know is to aware,
To aware is to beware (of drugs).

R. Krishnaswamy

That's What Friends are For

When you need a shoulder, I'm there,
When you need someone who cares,
If you need a laugh, or a cry,
And you don't really have a reason why,
Just come to me, cause that's
What Friends are for!

The door stays open to my heart,
When you're ready, you can start,
I'll always be there for you,
'Cause that's what Friends are for!

You've been so good to me
And I'll do my best to be a Friend,
You'll see.
And Best Friends forever we will be,
'Cause that's what Friends are for!

Jennifer Doran

Rain

He takes his hat and coat off
And spreads his arms,
Looking to the sky
For some answers.
Instead he gets rain.
He opens his mouth,
And feels stronger every time
A drop trickles down his throat.

The darkness and clouds
Only make his shining heart
Look brighter.
The flowers drink and
The dirt is washed from his hands
As he spins around,
Trying to catch as many plump beads
As will fit in his overturned umbrella.

Casey Kirchhoffer

~The Snakes That Take~

~~~~

*Tell me . . . Tell me . . .
What to do?
I work for snakes
that take—
~LAWYERS THAT'S WHO!~*

*They Slither and Slide
Get ahead on their pride,
and
The use of people like me and you.*

*Whatever your talent they
swallow you whole,
To make for themselves
their ultimate goal—
MONEY-MONEY!!*

Elaine M. Cioffi

Words Are Funny Things

I'm sitting here with pen in hand
To write a song for the local band!
The more I try to make it rhyme,
Those words refuse to make a line!

Well, maybe if I have some tea
By chance, a verse might come to me
Writing songs is not much fun,
But then, of course, I've just begun!

Words come tumbling through my brain,
And then they float right out again.
They just don't seem to stick around
Long enough to write them down!

Well since I don't know how, indeed,
To think of all the words I need,
To keep me always from complaining
I think I'll just go back to painting!

I don't need words to paint a tree,
Or barns or ships upon the sea.
But when that picture is completed,
Words of praise flow unimpeded!

Margaret Barbour McClain

Lyrics From an Indian Summer Idyll

"Beloved," whispered my love to me,
"See there behind the tall pine tree,
On the lake the ripples call,
There, beneath the water fall . . ."

"Come now, my own, and follow me,
Feel the waves that o'er you be,
Deep within our midnight pool,
So soft and clear, so kind and cool."

Splashes by my lover's swimming,
Shadows over lake waves skimming
Faintly hid our nudity . . .
So young, so old in love were we!

Upon the banks we quickly lay
As though we might be caught by day.
Precious hour, precious minute!
Precious is each second in it!

The night was still, the moon was high.
The pines were black against the sky.
In this, I loved and slept so nigh
My lover when the moon was high.

Louise R. von Paffen

The Little Girl

The little girl I see before
My very eyes I do adore.

Her puffy cheeks a shade of rose
A pinch of silk her tiny nose.

Her crescent smile which mystifies
The chocolate color of her eyes.

That meet my own upon a stare
Beneath her darkened satin hair.

Upon which lies a pinkish lace
That tops the beauty of her face.

The little girl I see before
My very eyes I do adore.

Michael McDonald

Untitled

It's about all of us
Though often we fail to see
Our focus refined to
Our own space and time
Asking, "What's in it for me?"

We all seek peace and freedom
And love and safety on our way
But pleasant words spoken
Won't repair what is broken
Until we really mean what we say

It's about all of us
Some day we'll be forced to know
We plant different gardens
And secretly plead for our pardons
While praying our crops will grow

Steve Spencer

Who Is She?

Who is she?
She is love.
Can you describe her?
She is you, she is me, she is us.
Had you known her for long?
An eternity.
Where did you meet?
She came through my heart,
We met inside a smile.
Do you see her often?
Every time I breathe.
Do you have a photograph?
She cannot be captured,
She must be free.
Will you see her again soon?
Yes, when she is willing.
When she is free.

Beverly D. Baecher-Lowery

Sarah's Smiles

Stars fall through in softly felt sighs
Every time you shine your light
Captured by your alluring eyes
Roses blush with just one sight
Enveloped by smiles you magically wear
The angels' jealousy grows

Ambivalently the heaven they share
Dims as your's tepidly glows
Mirror images never before seen
In the sun's proud ascent
Refulgently shown of a beautiful queen
Ebulliently I'm no longer confident
Remembering my undelivered kiss

David Boothe

Peas in a Pod

We were like peas in a pod, my imagination and I,
We soared to new worlds in a blink of the eye.
We wrestled with dragons, put up with jesters' malarkey,
Then headed to South Africa for a daring Safari.

We'd take long walks from 9:00 till noon,
But because of the horrible heat we'd swoon.
Our days were full of questions and befuddle,
Like a sudden downpour and a titan of a puddle.

We found ourselves floating in the center of the ocean,
We had to abandon ship from the queasy motion.
The sea was full of spectacular fish,
Which sailors would find a most appetizing dish.

We zoomed through space above and beyond,
Until I realized I was on the front lawn.
We were like peas in a pod, but that was before,
Those joyous days are no more.

Kinsey Labberton

Black Spiritual

Be given a friend on the long path.
Jesus the shepherd along with his staff.
Emmanuel, being interpreted, God with us
Ashes to ashes, dust to dust
Resurrected to life, an spiritual being.
With joy in our hearts we will be singin'
Praises to God, three in one
The Father and the Son
And Holy Ghost;
But for life will our gratitude be most.
Singin' to God for our expression
Livin' our lives with God in the blessin'
Giving thanks to Jesus our advocate
To the "One" living God "the Spirit"
Living Father who created all.
Past present future for our sins He has paid
Crucified, in the tomb He was laid.
But victory in Jesus His resurrection we share
And all is well on this here fair.

Justin Eriel Herring Wright

Untitled

Deprivation
Laborious and acquisition.
Something gained by one's own efforts.
Deprivation in a moment.
Very flency in explaining.
Not only it was methodical.
But required authoritarian.
Requiring unquestioning obedience to authority,
The streets very graphic.
Leaving all behind consolidate strength to go on.

Edna Harris

Easter Symbols

New Life begins in a garden as:
Small seeds send up beautiful flowers
And the trees' dead looking branches
sprout tiny leaves.
In a chicken coop on a nearby farm,
eggs crack to release tiny chicks,
While in a rabbit hutch newborn bunnies
tumble over each other;
And in many places in this rural area
seemingly lifeless insects emerge
from their metamorphoses—lovely butterflies!
All these wonders of nature are symbols
of Christ's glorious resurrection.

Sister Theophane Guilfoyle

Struggling With Poetry Assignments

I think so hard, I try my best,
This poem puts my mind to the test,
The words I think they don't come out
I don't understand what my poem's about,
My words won't rhyme, my thoughts won't flow,
There's something about poems, I just don't know.

My thoughts are like soldiers marching on,
They're there for a second and then they're gone.
My mind is stubborn, it just won't try.
I think and think, and then I sigh.
This poem to me was not a friend,
So I'm happy to say that this is the end!

Amanda Luther

Three Little Pigs

We are three little pigs.
We weren't always little pigs.
We were born as beautiful babes,
The pride and joy of our parents,
Delicate little girls, innocent and untouched . . .

Until the wolf came.
He taught us to roll in the mud.
He fed us slop.
He made us dirty.
He made us grunt and squeal.

Maybe he wanted to make purses of us,
To carry his pride in.
He was so proud . . .
He could turn babes into pigs.

Kelly D. Liverett

Avalon Memories

Tomorrow I reach the beach—
I reach the lands I must find to save me . . .
(the resurrection)

In these lands lie
The sea of broken men—
The composer who cannot hear
The artist who cannot see
The writer who holds crippled hands;

And to this sacred shore they are an island,
An island of pain and freedom
They walk hand in hand through
The sands of time
All in constant effort
To place their mark upon history
With the deepest footstep . . .

It all begins here.

Cassidy James

Jule

A precious stone used for personal adornment
The consistent search much time is spent
The rare excellence is persuade every single day
Years, months, minutes are all carelessly thrown away
But, I have no need to continue the search anymore
Since I have found this virtue in the one I adore
At times she cares about others over herself
This single quality is worth more than any wealth
Her intellect consumes her every thought
With her immense serenity is also brought
A smile that glistens like the sun across the horizon
She is one definitely blessed and breathtaking creation
I'll never forget the solitary moment I saw her
But when I spoke to her soul's the moment I treasure
There is no other like her, now or even ever
This sparkling Jule's radiance will shine on forever

Eric Walters

Easter Sunrise Meditation

It does seem a bit strange to gather this way,
Amidst the darkness and chill at this time of day.

Yet gathered are we by a wonder foretold,
Whose joy and beauty we have only begun to behold.

The followers of Jesus had seen the horror of it all,
The grisly culmination of evil that began with humanity's fall.

Their hopes and dreams were destroyed that day,
As wickedness, evil and death had their say.

How they had longed for Jesus to reveal God's power and might,
Yet the crucifixion of Jesus was such a disappointing sight.

"Why do you seek the living among the dead?
Jesus has been raised just as he said."

Jesus who had died on the hideous cross,
Has rescued all creation from death's dreaded loss.

Sin, evil and death will no longer enslave creation,
God's love in Christ has fashioned the gift of salvation.

Life is now more than a futile march to the grave,
Our destiny to sin is no longer enslaved.

A redeemed creation bursts forth in music and song,
Embraced by the Savior, creation to God now belongs.

Rev. Gary Weant

There Is a Hero

He's a hero that I love so much who gave me all.
His my whole entire life
He knew me even before I was born

He promised me that he will always be there for me.
I love Him more than anything
He is my strength when I am weak.

He comfort me with his words
When I am sad. When troubles come around
He told me not to be afraid because he loves me.

He took my arms and taught me how to walk.
He taught me the rights from wrongs
He prepared me for the bads
He smiled at me and told me that he loves me.

I want to give my whole life to Him
Work as hard as I can.
Share His love with others till I die.
This hero is the new born King
Jesus Christ the savior of all
Nations, why not try Him.

Jocelaine Julmis

Come Tea With Me

God in His mercy, gathers all of us to share
The grace that is ours, through His tender loving care.
With this time together, we truly have been blessed,
For in the eyes among us, God surely is our guest.

He has passed His ways, He's passed them through the ages.
"How do we really know?" We look through life's torn pages!
For some of us the journey, it has just begun;
But for some it nears the end, for VICTORY we have won!

But in God, as He has promised, He will not let us falter.
He shows His loving care, as He passes it, mother to daughter.
But "Fear not!" For God is in control,
Sharing, caring, loving kindness, comes from within our soul.

It is our FAITH that guides us, So come and share His tea;
For it's truly a loving Grandmother which "God would have us be!"
God's wishes are set before us, they're simply there to take.
Daughter, Mother, Grandmother, are words we all will make.

Anita Kay Miller

Parents

You loved me as a baby,
You cared so much for me.
You taught me everything I know,
That starts with "A to Z."

You also loved me through those years
When I thought "I must be free."
I know it was so hard on you
And you had to punish me.

But now that I am older,
I have come to realize,
For all the hurt I caused you,
You had to "cut me down to size."

One thing I'd like to say to you,
Mom and Dad, to make you see;
Without your love and patience . . .
I don't know where I'd be.

Thank you
Jacki Lynn Levinson

Time

There was a time
When youth was mine.
Convinced I'd never grow old,
Show a wrinkle or a line.

There was a time
I stood straight and tall;
Grace, poise, and beauty
I had it all.

There was a time
I was vibrant and free;
All things were mine
To be.

Now the time
Is slipping past.
Youth and beauty,
Fading fast.

But I have made
The most of time.
My memories I keep
Until the end of time.

Maria Schlager

A Battle

Oh, it's me again . . . why?
Why me?
I try my best but my best
Is not good enough.
Though I keep trying,
I never give up.
Just a beautiful thing; life.
That's why I've got to try.
I wake up in the morning,
Fighting the evil.
Though I fight and fight . . .
He always gets me.
Why me?
Oh God, give me a spear
And a shield . . .
So I can kill this evil thing.
That's all I ask.
It's me . . . It's me again.

Oscar R. Gonzalez II

Anger

Anger drifted across the sea.
His cloak hung limp with ecstasy,
Black scythe held tight by bony hands,
And a ghostly face under hood.

He spread like a dark mist throughout white lands,
Handling to victims utter fear.
One by one, friend fought with his friend
As Anger passed over his day's work.

Anger stopped by an untouched child
Who uttered prayers to deaf wild.
From an unknown place, Anger wept
As he grasped the child's holy soul.

His soul shouted out, "I am free,"
And Anger's black heart stopped beating
As it lost hate, and filled with glee
As Anger left and love entered.

Anger is a powerful force.
It spreads quickly throughout harsh lands,
And can even be touched by heart.
There is good in all hard anger.

Jeff Hall

Today's Prayer

Begin each day with an idea,
So the world is never faced with fears.
Take that first step and you will find,
By opening up your eyes, heart, and mind.

The world has many twists and turns,
Cherish each obstacle; even the ones that burn.
You must learn from every failure and achievement,
Because it brings a new meaning of acknowledgment.

To some a wish maybe,
A simple phrase or action to see.
Others it is a jester at best,
But are put through some tests.

Now, I wish for me to find,
A gift within myself and mind.
The heart has a mind of its own,
So follow the path all alone.

Time to fly or sail away,
So you can begin to pray.
May the wish you want to say,
Bring peace to you on this day.

Patricia Dempsey

Bright

Bright is the sunshine that shines above.
Bright is the smile that says I love.
Bright is the color yellow.
Bright is helping the other fellow.
Bright is studying your lesson every day.
Bright is making things right when they're done the wrong way.
Bright is understanding why we're here.
Bright is coming together with good cheer.
Bright is saying your prayers every night.
Bright is thanking God with all your might.
Bright is a family filled with love.
Bright represents a white dove.
Bright is happy and always glad.
Bright is polite and never sad.
Bright is a color everyone can see.
Bright is bright, as bright as can be.
Bright is the child that can read and write.
Bright is the teacher that breaks up the fight.
Bright is the look of caring.
Bright is the look of sharing.

April M. Leonard

Flower

Love is like a flower.
The seed is that first awkward moment . . .
When Romeo meets Juliet,
And fate has not yet been determined.
Then the seedling develops,
As do feelings . . .
Leaving a couple breathless,
As if a constant breeze blew around them.
Soon the flower blooms,
Shining its beautiful colors
As passionately
As lovers on a starry night.
But a flower be a tender object,
To be handled very delicately,
For if the flower withers,
The love will slowly fade and die as well.

Adriana Kosovych

The Broken Hearted Man

He's out in the wilderness, so desolate and sparse.
The lonely little man with his broken heart.
He cries oh God won't you help, as he picks up a drink,
Now meek and bitter as he grows so weak,
I tell of God's miracles to Him can come this day,
But you must abide by his laws or you cannot pass this way.
I try he responds but God just doesn't hear.
You're wrong little man for he is always there.

Just try not to drink and pay heed to what you say,
Your mouth is the door way to your soul to be saved.
Now months have gone by and years slip away
I pray of his deliverance to the Lord someday.
Dear God please intrust him is how it should start.
For the lonely little man with his broken heart.

Dawn Miller

Happiness in a Bottle

Seven people laughing
A little boy starts to cry
All the pain and agony of a broken heart
Beating down at his tiny body
When the seven people laughing
Look to see where the little boy has gone
All they can see is an island inside a crystal ball
They have no feelings and no sense at all
But when they find out why they're laughing
They forget it all
And on that little island
Where the boy has gone
You can find him laughing
Because they forgot it all

Paul McCollin

Daddy Must Go

This was written for my little boy during my divorce
Although I sit here with my wife and son
I wonder if he knows, he's my number one
For I feel a sense of remorse
As I ponder the outcome of my course
Will he or can he ever understand
Oh God, if so that would be grand
For my love for him is greater to me
Than anyone can possibly see
I am not trying to cause anyone pain
Even though I seem to be the target of their aim
It's just something that had to be
So son, one day I hope you'll see
That this is the hardest thing I ever had to do
So please remember son, that I'll never stop loving you

Russell Edward Karrick

Signs

Total darkness
Just following the signs, the dots, the dashes
That's all I see, all I think of
What if I blocked the signs out?
Just follow the dots and dashes.
Where would I end up?
Far away?
Would I be missed?
Would I be remembered?
We all want to be missed.
I could do it
Just follow the dots, the dashes
Just disappear
But I will miss
I will remember
I'll just follow the signs first
The dots and dashes second.
I want to be home
Where I am missed
Where I am remembered

      Nathan Smith

Similarities of the Heart

Both so alone, and so confused
Both hearts have been beaten, battered, and bruised.
So much different, yet so much the same
Both have been hurt by life's little game.
Both still young . . . yet wise beyond years
Learning through suffering and tasting bitter tears.
Both searching for reasons, trying to understand
Why life has dealt them such a bad hand.
Was it something they deserved—what did they do
Wishing they had answers—wishing they knew.
Tired of everyday life—needing to get away
Responsibilities holding them back—making them stay.
Being brought together—was it destiny or fate?
They found a friend in each other and begun to date,
But what now, where do they go from here?
So many roads to choose from yet, none of them seem clear.
She doesn't even know if he likes her
What they want—neither are sure.
Right now, friends is how they will remain
To help each other through life's bitter rain.

      Tera Speer

Evil Is in Government Everywhere

Evil is in government everywhere.
In other countries evil is there.
It is not just in the good old U.S.A.
Evil is all around.

It is on and under the water.
On the land or underground.
It is in a father, mother, son and daughter.
It is in the sky—with animals that fly.
Evil lurks in the shadows of the night.

In homes and business it can be found.
Making people of countries want to fight.
Having us humans do wrong instead of right.
It darkens the soul and the mind.
Sometimes it puts us in a bind.

All evil will end on "Judgement Day."
Because God the Almighty is here to stay.
Evil breeds off of the poor.
It comes knocking at our door.

Enslaving us to work here or there.
Evil is in government everywhere.

      John S. Griffiths

What Is an Educator to Do?

The bell rings, the noise starts
Yelling, screaming, crying "West Side"!
The running begins.
It's a morning full of noise with no discipline!

Sit down, be quiet please!
But, they think we are just a tease.
Our voices go unheard . . .
We are insulted and disrespected.
Yet the board does not even answer our pleas.

What is an educator to do?

Hammers, Guns and Knives that's what they have for us,
But all we have is the ABC's and a school bus.
There is a madness within
When and where does it end?
The real question is where does it begin?

Character begins in the home so I thought.
They are our future.
I hope I get rich!
Because teaching is a B—!
So . . . what is an educator to do?

      Gaynell Scott

The Courtship 1938

Let me take you by the hand and walk along
the ocean shore and feel the awesome power
of a turbulent sea.

Let me take you by the hand and walk along
a mountain path and feel the might and majesty
of a towering peak reaching to eternity.

Let me take you by the hand and walk along
a country road and see the bounty of the planted fields
and feel the piece and serenity.

Let me take you by the hand and walk along
a crowded city street and feel the throbbing
of a teeming humanity.

Let me take you by the hand to that quiet running
stream to mind recall—our first kiss, fond embrace,
clasp of hands and treasured memories.

Let me take you by the hand and to the altar walk
with me to pledge our love forever to endure and
I too give thanks to God for his gift of you . . . to me.

      Michael Guy Sectish

Comfort in Salvation

I know I am getting older, my hair is turning gray.
My eyes are getting weaker, but I am okay.
The Lord came down from heaven and took me by the hand.
Gave me peace and joy and now I understand.

That although I am getting older I do not have to fear,
For Jesus walks beside me.
He is always very near.

I lean upon my savior, as I go along life's way,
And He guides and keeps me each and every day.

I go to church on Sunday and honor Him in prayer.
For He's my God of mercy and he does always care,

When my journey's ended and I leave this world of sin.
I'll be somewhere in heaven with many, many friends

I know my Jesus said it, and what He said is true.
So I'll be with Him in Glory.
Somewhere beyond the blue.

      Jimmy J. Draves

Velma, Velma

Velma, Velma, where has it gone? The zest
Of laughter in your voice and in your eyes.
Two of your qualities which exemplify first Prize.

Velma, Velma, where has it gone? That shine in
Your eyes that could light up Broadway. That
Girlish grin, and resilient attitude, your carefree
Spirit meandering in the wind in such a seductive Way.

Velma, Velma, where has it gone? Who tampered
With that zeal, that noble will? Is it hidden
Behind the disappointments, lies, misunderstandings,
Or has life for you become too demanding?

Velma, Velma, retrieve that gala in your smile,
That gleam in your eyes, that pep in your step,
That hardy laughter that sends the room
Into an uproar. Don't lose those qualities
Given you, which makes you that special
Gem in a rough cut diamond and never a Bore.

Jeannette Cunningham

Untouched Thoughts

We see it as a mark on the wall
Only a shadow in the back of our mind
Small and almost out of reach
We tend to dismiss it,
Paying no attention to the strength of its birth.
The knowledge we know not of can change
The direction of which we are leading.
Thoughts will run through your brain
Like a storm in the night.
It will make you look back and see that
It just wasn't right.
This thing that can you, everyone has
It's called your conscience,
This you will learn, after you've done
Something wrong.
Your conscience you will surely earn.

Connie Bristow

Cherished You Are By Me

Hypnotic as water from a faucet tickling a marble tub
Aromatic as your silky raspberry lotion
Crisp as a mandolin string

I lay in bed at night
    thoughts tangled in your auburn hair
My love for you is as blue as the skies
    on a cool spring morning
If you were one in a sea of a thousand—
I would know you with a glance,
your aurora borealises shine much brighter.
To lovingly caress the soft texture of your hand
    cradled in my palm.

Cherished you are by me.

Robbie Clark

The Touch of Life

I became from love,
I cried, was held and nurtured.
I crawled, walked and talked.
Learned and earned my life.
Family influenced but never controlled.
The path was fate.
Not born with a silver spoon, which is best.
I can walk straight, talk high and love with passion.
I have seen, been seen and have done a lot that most will not.
In all of this he has been with me, I know what he can do.
I know of his sacrifices and miracles,
Through him I became alive and from him a touch of life.

Keith E. Alger

Street Light

Dusk falls on a summer day.
It draws a child's innocent eyes towards the street light.
To some it may only symbolize a source of energy
That luminates the dark night.
To a child it means something different.
As a child I too had my eyes on the street light.
A summer morning breaks, I'm up with the sun.
I gather with friends for a fun filled day.
As the sun glides across the sky and evening
Falls, my joyful thoughts are interrupted by
Thoughts of the ominous street light.
A game of hide-and-seek is over quickly.
The street light pops on, signifying the end
Of that fun filled day.
That's what a street light means to a child.

Pamella Jean Engravalle

To Breathe in a Morning

In the morning sun is where I step,
I slowly breathe in the early morning virgin air.
The sweet peppermint breeze feels as though millions
of candy kisses sweep innocently across my skin.
The morning's subtle brightness with her colors of
warmth invite me into her realm with her outstretched
arms of multicolored rays.
She beckons me with such a sweet spring song of chirping
birds and crickets and all unnoticed things during the busy,
loud day.
It is about then that I realized that I was saddened because
in such a busy world, those who live their lives by the clock
above their heads will never understand what it is to
breathe in a morning.

Jessica Levine

Sequoia

As I look out the window of my laundry room
I am feeling tired.
I lift up mine eyes to look, as if you bade me to
do so, and gave me strength to carry on.
There I see in the far corner of the yard,
the grand and stalwart sequoia.

Oh, sequoia, you grow so straight and tall,
travelling to reach the sky, in the
straight and narrow path.
Go on! Reach up and touch the hand
that planted you.

Sequoia, reach the outstretched hand of the one
that nurtured and watched over you,
as I too will reach and touch the blessed
hand one day.

Oh sequoia, you have inspired and comforted me
this day.

Myrtle B. Phillips

Dream

An endless tunnel of desperation

Panic
Longing for the taste of love

Happiness,
Or just the taste of bitter chocolate on a bad day

Sailing with life's sail
Through the tunnel of the lost

Armoring from the pain of failure,
I hear the trumpets of victory:
I have rediscovered the taste of youth

Aris Michalopoulos

Raven Night

The wind howls,
As the trees wave their ghostly figures
In the blackness.
The spirits come alive, for it is midnight.
There's a sudden silence
Over the ebony plain.
Whispy, white figures rise from the ground.
Aaahh! comes the scream,
From a haunting victim's throat.

A flock of ravens
Cast their spells over the forbidden land.
They cackle in their diabolical way.
The clouds come rolling in,
Disguising the serene light of the moon.
The thunder rumbles,
Shaking even the strongest structures.
The wise owl screeches his spells to all of the possessed animals.
The fire in the sky rises,
After the cursing of the evening.
There will be another night!

Christina Yi

Wronger?

I know it is good, when I write to a friend,
To use proper words that will never offend
But lately I used one that may have been wrong,
In the statement I made, it was very strong.

So I'm puzzled a bit and I don't know why
That now, the word I wrote should raise Hew and Cry
For it's very much like other words that we use.
It means what it says so we've nothing to lose.

We say stouter and slimmer and thinner, too
And taller and shorter and blacker than blue
And that days in June are oh so much longer,
To say otherwise would be a bit "wronger."

There is bigger and littler—larger and smaller,
And fatter and leaner—shorter and taller,
There's darker and lighter—dimmer and brighter.
You must decide if it's "Wronger" or "Righter."

So let's add "Wronger" to broader and wider,
Upper and lower—and good apple cider,
To weaker and stronger—and all words like that.
So for upgrading "Wronger," I'll go to bat.

Horace M. Johnson

Love in the City

We have a ball . . .
Stress and all . . .

Not because we can cope, or believe in hope;

Others in the city,
should look beyond pity

To the beauty around us, and the
desire within us . . .

We have a chance to sing and dance.

Come, just imagine, feel the heat,

Peace in our dreams,

Fire in our groins,

Love in our hearts.

We can inspire, some other's desires to have

Love in the city . . . like we do
Baby!

Shirley Young-Hodges

Tomorrow's Song

Today I tore the bird nest down.
Its gray emptiness had for so long
echoed the last robin's song.
Almost taunting in the barren tree,
reminding me of family
loved, nurtured, fed and taught,
Giving strength to one another;
anticipated freedom each tiny creature sought.
I had hoped they would return in spring;
any spring, filling silent boughs
with lovely notes only birds can sing;
bringing with them color
to the soft paleness of winter's end.
But God in His wisdom decides
who will be denied and who,
perhaps someone lonelier than I,
will awaken at break of dawn
to trees amply supplied
with tomorrow's song.

Lynn Williams

The Time of Wishes

I was hearing always: "You must not"
Here "you must not" and there are prohibitions
And suddenly this morning disappeared "you must not"
And now I am free as wind, for all I have permission.
I will immediately go there, take all of that
And doing thus and so always,
I will be standing on my head, throwing away all wrong,
Forever I will burn the doors and castles.
But why I am not running from my bed?
Why I am not doing those and that one
Maybe I can't? Not! Worse—I did not want
Locks are inside of me, and doors do not matter.

Larisa Matros

Family Tree

Oh mighty family tree, you give me cause to wonder;
With all your grace and splendor,
Can I truly be—
The fruit of your long and mystic story.

History has nurtured your mighty branches
To grow under any circumstances.
Whether by fate or happenstance,
I too have grown from your branch.

Looking now in retrospect, at me—a little speck;
Like acorn growth to mighty oak tree,
Is this the cause for my family?
To grow from twig to sculpted limb,
To help lend shade and symmetry,
To you—my family tree.

Gary W. Hanson

No One

The world is a strange, strange place to me . . .
As I stand all alone . . .
No one's next to me . . .
As I look up in the sky . . .
I see a butterfly . . .
Then I wonder why . . .
The flowers have to die . . .
I think the world's alone . . .
As so I think am I . . .
This world's a strange, strange place
It make's me want to cry
No one seems to care . . .
About the world at all . . .
No one seems to care
This world's about to fall.

Robert Tymony

My Twilight Years

When I look back at all the years,
That I have just come through.
The years behind me are many,
But the years ahead may be few.

Then I ask myself if I have been
An example for one or two,
Some one to look up to, and hear them say,
"I'd like to be just like you."

Have I been kind and considerate
To those who've had less than me?
Or have I just taken for granted,
That these things should always be?

As I look back at the road I've been through,
Have I done the best I could?
Have I wasted my time on useless things,
Instead of doing things that were good?

I think of the things that I should have done,
A helping hand or two, to do unto others
As the "Good Book" says,
As you'd have them do unto you.

Per Weggum

Sweet Sorrow

Life is hard at school and home,
Please don't leave me here alone.
My heart is breaking everyday,
And every night to God I pray.
My friends are always there for me,
My family argues constantly.
Sometimes I wish I might just die,
Then God would raise me to the sky.
My grandma says "think positive"
My grandpa says "you'll never live."
My family tells me that I'm lazy,
But then when I cry they call me crazy.
There are people out there with hearts made of coal,
Such as people who come and rip out your soul.
Well God's on my side so there's nothing to fear,
But now in my heart I have a huge tear
Well like I said life is hard,
So if you're looking for your life be on your guard.

Love, Melissa M. Creek

Two Weeks Ago Today

It was two weeks ago today,
Two weeks ago that he passed away.
The last time I saw him we had nothing to say,
Now, as a mortal, I sit and slowly decay.
I often wonder if we could have kept in touch,
But writing letters seems to be a burden of such.
These thoughts I seem to use as somewhat of a crutch,
A crutch to ease the pain I feel from missing him so much.
So as I walk out the door to visit his plot,
I know that even though he's the one who died,
I'll be the one to rot.

Chris Markus

Alone

I run through this life scared and alone.
I walk through this life lost and unknown.
I sit in this life with hopes and with dreams,
Then proceed with this life and they break at the seams.

I look to this life with love in my eyes.
I talk to this life with fear in my cries.
I question this life and wait for replies,
Then proceed with this life and the truth turns to lies.

James Edward Powell, III

A Wounded Little Lamb

A wounded little lamb has wandered astray
Disillusioned with others, trying to find her way
Through the mountainous terrain she trod, fearful and in despair
I'm all alone, she sobbed, no one really cares

Then the great shepherd looked down from above
And poured out open her, his compassion and love
Little lamb, little lamb, do you not know
My name is upon you, wherever you go

Little lamb, little lamb, do you not know
We walk hand in hand, there's no need to fear man
Come little one, come unto me and you will surely see
My love pouring unto thee, security is found only in me

There in the shelter of the O Most High
Close to his breast will I abide
Until I am strengthened and nurtured again
By the spirit of Jesus, in the arms of my friend.

Linda Donohue

Winter Is Past

Winter is past,
Spring is here at last!

Jesus is risen,
New life He has given!

All doubts and fears are gone,
To him who has faith all good things belong!

Winter is past,
Spring at last!

Hail to the King,
Abundant life he does bring!

My life is made anew,
And you can have it too!

Winter is past,
Your cares you can cast!

God's love is so great,
It can wipe out all hate!

I'm renewed in Him,
We are all made kin!

Winter is past,
Face to face I see Jesus at last!

Gary E. Davis

The Deserted Mansion

Shadows from the depths of night,
In curving lines around the old house form.
The walls, now gray and peeled with age
Are vacant . . . It stands alone . . . forlorn.
Vast is the mighty crystal shattered hall,
Where once there echoed laughter of a Ball.
And rooms, resplendent in an older day,
In dusty, broken ruins lay today.
No more this Lovely Mansion shines with light.
No more do people wonder at its sight.
This house whose beauty once was rare,
In golden memories stands forever drear.

Margaret Christopher

The Meaning of Life

Living in the land of life.
It is full of strife with grief and despair.
People think and act without care.
Of all the pain,
There is something that is always the same.
That when death comes
You will never be whole again.

Robert Gall

Suicide

There was a time I had a life,
Now I look at a silver knife.
My life is spinning uncontrollably,
I count the times I tried before, I count three.
Once to escape the constant pain,
Of fists I tried to block, but in vain.
Twice when all left was fear,
Fear so twisted and so sheer.
Thrice will be the charm,
I turn the knife, I slice my arm.
I watch the blood flow crimson,
I watch the slowly fading sun,
Dark, darker, my life is done,
My head sinks slowly with the sun.

Eric Panter

The Wonder of Autumn

As summer fades out and autumn slips in
You can see the magic of nature begin
Green leaves change to a beautiful
Rustic shade of brown
And then start falling to the ground
Musical snapping of twigs under feet
With a cool breeze as you walk
Down the street
Soon the trees are completely bare
Stronger winds sweeping and scrubbing the air
Nature is cleaning and preparing the earth
For the future's beautiful and
amazing rebirth

June E. Young

Hand Held Silence

There's a silence that kills, eats a child alive,
A plummet to death through a never ending dive.
Your silence is loud on its journey through me,
I need a revolution and to find someone to be.
Come sit down beside me I have lots to tell,
Here! A bag full of pennies for my wishing well.
The stars and the moon hold my secrets steadfast,
But such uncertain things can't promise to last.
They know when they'll come to never be,
And then my secrets are history.
Lost forever, forever untold,
In your Hands, the silence,
The silence you hold.

Brittany Salmons

Looking Down From the Cross

You know God was not color blind.
He did not choose black or white.
God chose the colors of his rainbow
then added a few more.

God never picked which ones he loved the best.
He never chose one color special from the rest.
For you see, this was one time
God chose to be color blind.
For you see, he wished to leave all hatred behind.

This day is one of his special days
when his son gave his only life.
Not for a white man, nor a black man,
this wasn't in his plans.

But you see, somehow this all got lost
hen people no longer thought of his cross.
But maybe one day we all will see
what his only son saw
looking down from his cross.

Lillian M. O'Neal

Feelings of

Madness, in a world where nothing matters
Victory, never found but always fought
Love, is something we all search for
Even though sometimes we were not taught.

Loyalty, tell me is there such indulgence
Honesty, what's the truth in someone's eyes?
Forgiveness, do you know the words I'm sorry?
I'll give you one more chance as long as you will try.

Happiness, it brings it all together
Sorrow, right before you're torn apart
Laughter, makes it all look simple
But sometimes something easy, isn't what you want

So, maybe if you have a little hope
You'll happen upon all that you deserve
For we were not put here to be lonely
Never to be stingy, keep a little on reserve.

Rebecca Parsons Johnson

Blackened Heart

Look inside this blackened heart and tell me what you see.
Is it the mirror of your soul telling you to hold on to reality?
Can you see the thorns that weep the blood
of a thousand wasted years?
Or the pain you hide deep inside, held onto by all your fears?
Look a little further, past the waters of life and death.
Don't be afraid, we have nothing to hide
except your pain not spent.
Witness the birth of corruption on the weakening mind.
The souls of others just like yours,
searching for a soul just a blind.
Search on in vain for what you'll never find.
Search for all eternity, decimation of the mind
Look inside this blackened heart and tell me what you see.
That black soul you are looking at, it was yours. Never me.

Mark Rossiter

The Road

The time has come to cross the bridge on the road that
We call life.

Sometimes that road is long and hard being filled with
Bumps and strife.

Though if you would but let me I'll walk this road with
You.

At times it won't be easy no matter what you do.

But never fear for God is near to guide every step of
The way.

He'll keep you safe step by step when to him we always
Pray.

Virginia Toney

Practicality and the Butterfly

My father and I are talking about my life again:

"You know how a butterfly
just floats through a meadow in no
particular direction, just kind of
wanders along?" he says.

Yes.

"You are that butterfly."

He chases me, waving his butterfly net in the sun.
I fly away.

I can,
I am a butterfly with enormous orange and black wings.

Mike Michaud

The Forest

I saw things in there that night
That the owl could not explain
Nor did he want to prowl

Before his very eyes laid the answers
But to my disclosure
That wise old owl was blind

The power of his mind was so great
He could kill you with a glance
And take your soul to the heavenly gates

But he stood on his redwood and preached
He preached to all the animals his knowledge
And they silently stood on his path

As the owl said
I can quench your thirst with my tears
And let you feed off my body
But I cannot fill your mind with the knowledge
The knowledge you'll need to surpass the demons
And live in peace with your maker
The animals cried
As I stood in awe

Shaun Trosky

Untitled

Dancing girl
Pirouetting across the faces
Knowing only when to leap
But not where she'll land
Must land softly
Never be heavy. Delicate, gossamer
Keep her eyes open
Harrison her dream King
a survivor she's told
Curtis was not so, happiness his own
The eyes all focused on the motions she makes
Stage fright perhaps? Caused that last trip?
Not in the routine which she had practiced for years
Drilled into her head
Repetition repetition repetition
Daily redundance caused this fall
She gracefully glides in the space provided
And as she closes her eyes
She takes her leap into the darkness
The last one she'll have.

Kerrie Clifford

Black Elk's Vision

If not for you

As I lay here in my Unconscious, I wonder where I am
As I lay here in my Sleep, you wait for me
If not for you, I would have no Beginning
If not for you, I would have no Direction
If not for you, I would have no Future
For you are me and I am you
We are Connected
We are One

Dedicated to my son, Jason.

Julie A. Baker

Baseball

The smell of turf.
Dirt on their cleats,
The players silently stride to their positions.
The sound of wood meeting with leather.
A few seconds.
Wop.
The ball meeting glove.
The silent triumph of the infield.

John Mark McIntosh (age 11)

Wind

Stared fascinated at the drapes
Being pushed repeatedly, back and forth
   with a steady regular rhythm
Timing itself to my heart beat.

Outside trees are swaying gently
Each branch at its own rate, different than and
   unaffected by each other
Yet responding to the same wind.

Muriel Cohn

Henry's New Face

Henry's new face is similar to his old one.

Midst his ninth decade he saw his family's health fail,
Yet still he moved slate tabletops and tilled his back yard.
Scientist ever, he prepared his career award speech.
But still he grieved for his family,
Acutely recalling the last days of his first wife.

Suddenly Henry found himself in the hospital.
He ordered a basin of water and a straight razor.
With clinical care he shaved off his beard of 25 years
(His son didn't recognize him),
Maybe to survey the stroke's damage,
Maybe just to see his own face again before he died.

Henry left the hospital after five days,
Cooked me dinner at his house to celebrate,
And argued a scientific detail I'd forgotten . . .
His family begins to rally: there is hope in the darkest corner.
Henry has a new face, but it is similar to his old one.

Michael H. Brill

Spring

A blossom slowly opens,
Touching the wings of the wind,
Its fragrance releasing to the radiance of day.
The morning stars sing together.
A humming bird, tiny, suddenly appears,
Vanishing as quickly as it came,
While treasuring in the blossom's sweet nectar.
Mysteries play with the light and the shadows,
As the wind gently flows through the leaves.
Love birds join the symphony in song.
Each entrance of life substitutes joy from our strife
After winters unsympathetic weather.
Now, arise from your dream,
and follow it.

Patricia N. Richards

Demise of My Friend

We met when you were but a few weeks old,
On a day that was oh so cold.
Some remarked it is a canine,
Oh no! It is a feline;
I reminded them of my borderline.
He was so lively and frisky,
That I called him Frisky,
Immediately I was asked did you say Whiskey?
Then one fine day in May
Or so I thought it was hey!
I had a premonition
But paid no attention to my intuition.
The door was ajar
So he leapt out afar—
Then came a land rover
Which ran him over!
You are suppose to have nine—
Oh maybe that's just another line.
To be no more, for you were ran over
My poor, poor friend from Dover.

Joan Thompson

New Birth

Violence produces a brokenness which,
Like a seed, must be . . .
Submerged in the soil's darkness . . .
Immersed in redemptive waters . . .
Warmed in Christian love . . .
Ruptured by the agony of change . . .
Born a new being. Then be . . .
Nourished by the communion of the saints . . .
Drawn by the light to manifest fruits of
wholeness.

Linda Weant

Untitled

This round and dimpled ball,
Placed on a tee.
Hit with a mighty power,
Soar, soar, soar.

Down it falls,
With frightful force.
Not knowing where it will land.

As the dimpled ball hits the ground,
A few feet from a hole.
The mighty club lightly taps the sphere,
In hopes that it does not miss.

The tiny ball rolls,
Its path following the contours of the land,
Hits its mark.
The shot is done.

Robby Permenter

Rain

If I were rain I would come gently upon you.
Each droplet would be a caress falling softly by your feet.

If I were rain, I would be heaven sent.
I would bathe your being in glory;
you would know ecstasy from above.

If I were rain, I would wash from you all sadness
And replace it with rainbows of happiness.

If I were rain, I would hold your heart forever midst
the warm waters of my love.

If . . . I were rain.

Harry B. Briggs

My Little Angel Girl

You bring such sunshine into our lives.
How can I deny you anything when you look at me
With those big blue eyes?

God has granted me such a wonderful treasure.
Because of you my life is filled with pleasure.

The joy I felt when you came into the world was beyond belief.
A healthy, happy, beautiful baby, what a relief.

As time goes on, and the years unfurl,
You will always be my "little angel girl."

Cheryl A. Globig

Thinking

When you think of wild, wild you see.
When you think of flowers, flowers you see.
But when you think of thoughts,
you don't see.
You don't see.
Your mind is like a river flowing on and on.
Never fixed.

Catalina Iannone

The Purpose of Life

Love can only be measured by how love is perceived.
If you love with your whole heart, no love can possibly be greater.
But to be in love, you need to be in it with full strength
You need to love mentally within the mind
physically within the sight
emotionally within the heart and soul.
Greed, selfishness, hate are not part of love.
Infatuation, helplessness, jealousy
cannot overpower you, if you are truly in love.
To be truly in love is
to fit into that missing part,
to fill in where love is lacking.
True love is the security to be in love and to be loved.
To be in love is to live it.
Life is love if you perceive it.
If your love is perceived to the highest extent,
you have truly gained the purpose of life:
Love!

Megan C. McLean

Island

Surrounded, yet all alone
Admired by far for her strength,
To stand alone.

The few who know her well,
Know all the faults and all the fears,
That dwell beneath the surface.

She puts distance between her and the rest,
For she is a quiet one underneath all the glitter
Many try to come aboard and understand her better,

Yet soon they find they are not strong enough.
For the Island needs a strong anchor,
To keep her afloat.

Kim Donahue

"Exist"

In my quiet solitude, I ponder upon
my existence,
my purpose?
Holding on to the "love of life."
The beauty of the day,
The bloom, of the day's extensions
Fading into the pinkin' horizon.
The music of the outside calamity
Fill my thoughts of what is taken for granted.
I focus on the melody of a sun warmed
bird calling for nature's way.
I see the billowy puffs in the sky as a
Stairway to a more peaceful journey.
I know whatever my purpose maybe;
I will carry my faith in my heart and know
"All is Well"!

Cynthia A. Kreider

The Soul

To love someone as they are,
For love is bonding of the soul.

There is more beauty to behold,
One may not have the power to behold the soul.

For everyone will learn in time,
It's a secret of the mind,
To have them all unwind.

You will go blind,
Until time finds the beauty of the soul.

Shaneon Adkins

Big Brother

You stood before me, looked up at me.
Brother, I knew, you knew.
I screamed, but no sound was heard.
I shouted, but no voice came out.
Your sensitive soul shined like the sun in my eyes.
Only you, my beloved brother,
could touch my sensitive soul with yours.

Patricia Ann Faison

Edwin Arlington Robinson

Because, for him, language was stern and bare
You down-played his artistry. You still found
Truth in a vagabond's jacket walking down
Amidst a diverting carnival fare,
Hand in hand (interlocked with human care)
Enraptured with multitudinous sound,
The echoing citizenry of Tilbury Town:
Its alluring importunate air.
His art, with a throbbing shaft recreates
His characters' hovering hopelessness:
Its attendant paralyzing chasm,
Tunnel-deep! Insidious sleeplessness
Robinson's verse with wary vigor relates
Transcending its blurred, flickering spasm.

John Schmiel

Mother

She is now old with a few wrinkles,
but how come to me as a star she twinkles.
She has not curls or nails you'd envy,
but she has the hands that mould success.
She is not music, she is not on stage,
but as she speaks, courage and honesty I see.
She is not a friend, she is not The Lord,
but like a shadow, she is always there.
When Thou pay heed to my every prayer,
she is there as a solution to every trouble,
    for she is my Mother.

Dr. Natahsa Buckshee

Storm

Thunder and lightning roar outside my window,
Rain pelts hard against it too,
Wind whistles unfamiliar tune,
Oh how I wish it would be over soon.

Lindsey Spitnale

Look Over Me Lord

Look over me Lord when I am fast asleep
Look over me Lord when I am walking down the street
Look over me Lord where ever I may be

Look over me Lord when the world don't care
Look over me Lord when trouble times are near
Look over me Lord from this day on and forever more

Clarita Mitchell

The Winds of Change

A golden blanket of wheat in mid summer,
Mounted on the blue background of the imagination.
But in this blissful, state a disobedient cloud,
carries an ominous force, disturbs your perfection
This black wave of destruction suddenly hits,
ripping the imperfect scene apart;
harboring death, disease, and famine.
And what was once fruitful is now desolated.
All that is left to hope.

Sean Wilson

Lost Love

When I see your smiling face
Or hear your voice,
The feelings I have for you
Become forever stronger.
With each passing moment,
My heart feels the void
Of not having you in my life.
Time and time again,
I think of all the special times we shared.
Special moments that I could never give anyone else.
Like two ships that pass in the night,
We pass on the road of life.
As we pass, I can feel the love and passion
We could share, beyond compare.
But, when I look into your eyes,
I see eternity.
I see my dreams
And just the way my world should be.
I'd give anything just to be with you
And have you in my world.

Derek L. Johnson

Sadness in the Night

The sky is silent tonight,
The moon is shining, the stars stand bright
Across the sky; on the lake the moonlight
Brightly gleaming out in the night air.
Join me outside with the beautiful moonlit night.
Only from the long line of shimmering stars,
Where the lake meets the horizon;
Can you listen, and hear the cry
Of the wind blowing through the trees,
At their return, up the high peaks,
And down again.
But you must listen closely to its voice
With your heart and soul,
To the silent sadness breathing through the sky.

Janna A. Loken

Good Morning Sweetheart

Good morning sweetheart
Look to the east,
See the sun breaking across the land
Feel its rays beaming my love into your heart
Tho' the stars may fade from the skies
My love for you will never demise
As you look at the sun let the color remind you
Of that band of gold I placed on the ring finger of your left hand
When we pledged our love to each other.

Kenneth L. Robinson

I Am Alone

I am alone in the dark fields of loneliness
No one laughs or has a smile on their face
I am alone in this fearful world
Where people cry
Where pain fills you with anger and rage
Where the sun never shines and stars never flow through the sky
I sit alone in a field of withered flowers that died of neglect
and no love
I think of all the happy times before the death of loved ones
and all the anger and rage the world became
Life if lonely and filled with no love
There is no care in the world that will bring back the past
I am alone in the dark fields of hate and ruthlessness
Where love becomes pain
Where hatred becomes rage
I am alone.

Olivia Stewart

Untitled

You opened up to me and let me share your life.
You've showed me so many things.
Things I never knew

You offered me yourself;
your inner being.
You reached your hand out to me.

Now come share my life, let me offer
myself to you; my whole self.

Take me totally, as I will take you.
Let us share our lives as one,
and receive all that life has to offer.

Laurie Palffy

Shadow of a Day to Come

Quietly, in the dark, I await again,
Waiting, anticipating, what is to come.
I stand in adornment in dark array,
You see, I am the opposite of the day.
I wait in silence, but I'm not shy,
I'm with my friends, the moon and the sky.
I am bold and faithful, I will always be there,
I clothe the skies with much tender care.
But now it is time to say our good-byes,
as you see the light come up in the sky,
that is the day with his friend the sun,
I am only a shadow of a day to come.

Olivia Wallis

Just Because of You

My heart's felt true love . . . My life was complete
My days were filled with love, by my angel from God above . . .
You gave my life meaning and purpose too . . .If it weren't for you
My life would have been over long ago . . .
Now I'm alone with my thoughts on you
Have you found another love to take my place
Have I lost you without being able to see you face to face . . .
Or are you alone with your thoughts on me
As mine are on you continually . . .
Do you count the hours for the day to end
So you can start tomorrow, all over again . . .
For that is how my days go by
Waiting for one to end, so I can start all over again . . .
My love is lost with nowhere to go
I put it in prayers and letters for you . . .
Just because my love belongs to you
It's all I can do to give it to you . . .
So my "C" accept it from me
It's all I can do
Since I can't be there with you . . .

Robert H. McMurray Jr.

Untitled

My darling, I begin to think that you
Are one on whom I never can set blame,
Although I find it clearly plain to view.
As old alumni fix the mark of shame
On coaches for the looses of their teams,
So have I sought a scapegoat for your crimes.
Blaming your deceits, in foolish dreams,
On all those football players who ruled the times.
The game you favored was too rough for me,
Requiring one of stronger stuff than I.
But while I wasn't what I had to be,
It never was for lack of old school try.
And I was on your side, more than you dream,
Although I only made the second team.

Douglas R. Smith

Perfect Harmony

Oh, my dear, how I long to see,
You and me in perfect harmony.
I live for the day, when you'll be mine,
When that day come, the sun will shine.
For now until then, It will be me,
No one to help me, no one to see.
I'll be all alone, without you to see,
Soon, you and me in perfect harmony.
I don't know what to do, for I'm in love,
The sweetness you are, is just like a dove.
You fly up above, so sweet to see,
Soon, you and me in perfect harmony.
You are so sweet, a beauty from above,
So sweet to see, for someone in love.
I love you my Dear, with all my Heart,
I want to be with you, I don't want to part.
I wish you could see me, see how I feel,
Come touch my heart, so it will heal.
You are the one, the one I want to see,
Soon, you and me, In perfect harmony.

Daniel C. Riggio

Love

Respect and trust
Which one has for another.
It is the little things that count!
Just ask your mother.

So you ask what is Love?
It is a change.
A wanting to be with someone
Close and a lifetime of togetherness.

Then you ask what is a friend?
Well it is liking someone
Keeping in touch!
And caring and listening.

But sometimes not agreeing.
It is liking a person a lot
And keeping in touch
Caring and listening!

So true love is different
As you both have common goals.
A meeting of the minds, togetherness!
Cultures are different but goals are the same!

Jean K. Mathis

Then I Realized

I was all alone on this cold winter morn,
I sat silently listening to the frightening storm.
I was shaking in fear and cold with no fire,
I decided to lay down in my bed to retire.
A shadow of thought, entered my mind,
I lay half asleep, was this a sign?

Was I all alone? Or was I not?
I woke suddenly as I heard a gun shot!

Someone was outside or somewhere within,
I could tell by the sound, he wasn't a friend.
I suddenly rose from my bed to my feet,
and silently ran to find what I seek.

I was terrified and startled as I heard the whispering wind,
the door was partially open and this man came bursting in.

What was I to do with a gun to my head?
I knew now that soon, I would be dead!

Then I realized . . .

It was my time to go.
He pulled the trigger,
and with a loud blow, I was gone!

Becky Garrett

Young Abe

Young Abe was here so long ago
He lived here as a boy.
He roamed these fields, and walked this land.
He didn't own a toy.

He longed to learn all about the world,
A world he thought he'd never know.
He borrowed books from all around,
No matter how far he had to go.

Knowledge that he got from books
Certainly did serve him well,
And a lawyer is what he became.
Knowledge mixed with his natural wit
Got him into the political game.

Since with his opponents he did debate,
The brilliance of this country boy
Soon was to seal his fate.
He won debates, he won elections,
And off to Washington he went,
The boy who grew up in Indiana
Became our 16th president.

Miriam Rembold Schnapf

Year 20/20

Lush forests disappearing fast
Healthy plants a thing of the past.
(Save our forests now)

The atmosphere once lean and fair
Now thickly polluted beyond repair.
(Save our air now)

Fish, in millions, once swam contentedly
In lakes and rivers contamination-free.
(Save our rivers now)

Oil tankers that carelessly spilled
And endangered species needlessly killed.
(Save our oceans now)

Land for living and what farmers need
Sacrificed for concrete cities at alarming speed.
(Save our land now)

The deterioration of our environment
From unnecessary exploited development.
(Save our wildlife now)

Our planet becomes smaller day by day
We all must be responsible to lessen the decay. (Save our world now)

Nona Green

My Mask

Alone in this world, that is how I feel
Trapped, a blinded victim of my own mind
I am lost, In my journey to stay real
A missing link, that link is hard to find
Who has the answer to the mystery
I constantly look back and reminisce
Why is life full of pain and misery
My death, my body only few will miss
Life is complicated, I am confused
Everything is wrong, but still I maintain
Society has mentally abused
Me being insane, is what keeps me sane
I stand alone, eyes seen too many lies
Scales, Fangs; Lord take my hand and guide me through
Bless me with the strength to where I can rise
It is me and you, me and you are true
I feel hopeless, time is my enemy
Who will win, I ask, who will win, I ask
My short years, blood and tears, I shed many
To survive and last, I must wear this mask

Andre C. Best

Emptiness

The emptiness within was a place once filled with happiness and joy.
But now it is like a black hole
Down from the deepest darkest corners of my heart
The pain and the darkness still taunt me.

Thoughts of death and ultimate depression,
A few of the things which lurked.

Out of nowhere they took control
Slowly destroying parts of me with every passing hour.
Along with the emptiness emerged a cold and heartless creature,
With no love and compassion left for the world outside.

Like a plague, the emptiness spread
Causing pain and sorrow to all it touched.

The battle soon begun.
Forces of hope charged to defeat this mental state
The only terror that remained is the emptiness,
The emptiness that dares return.

It hides within and dares return
The emptiness returns.

Patrizia Duca

Change

As the sun rises
and touches flower's seed,
a lark pistons through the morning
quandaring for feed

The buck bounds gracefully,
its doe cautious and sure
consuming enough grasses
for winter's long endure

Trees negotiating
to drop or to hold
leaves of fire, crimson
and shimmering gold

The last emerald blades
of earth's downy, untouched bed
standing erect—soldierly
in winter wind's icy thread

Fall's glory passes
in what seems a single day
yet, if we have the courage
we will see more beauty in tomorrow's crisp wintery day.

Shawn Banks

Mirrors

I have no more yearning; I feel that I'm complete
It's because I'm learning I'm Part of the Elite
Part of the Master Plan, part of all there is
And finding me that perfect man just isn't where it is

I used to need to have a man to validate my worth
As if his touch, his words of love, could trigger my rebirth
I never thought to look inside, but when I did, you know, I cried
All we are, we can create; there's little one should blame on fate

It's not that I don't like the thought,
for years "true love" is all I bought
But now I have a higher cause, to live by Universal Laws
To thrive and grow on my own esteem,
instead of living up to some man's dream
To be all that I was meant to be, to love myself and feel so free

But this journey is for sharing; sweet souls they come and go.
The trick is knowing who to touch and when to let them go
And not to hold them quite so tight for fear that we might lose them
Remember, they are all "just right;" they're our mirrors,
and we choose them

Bonnie Blazak

Seventy Six Lambert Avenue

The Old Homestead where dreams were planned . . .
A spot on earth when only land
Adorned by trees and grassy knolls,
Was spirited to structured goals.

The house was built as to enhance
The barren slope into a glance
That stirred in its foundation
Seeds of love and admiration.

Oh! Tears are shed and joys abound,
The cycle going round and round,
Where children come and children go
And memories there forever grow.

The homestead wears a brand new look!
So thus begins another book
Of memories and family love . . .
God's special gift sent from above.

Estelle Caron

Tomorrow

Some think it's fun to run from the life they once knew,
You may think otherwise, but you've done it too,
Sometimes life brings hardship and sorrow,
If that is so than just look for tomorrow,
There's bound to be days of fun in the sun,
And that is where you must run,
So no matter how hard you think life is for you,
Just look towards tomorrow and you'll make it through.

Robert Dearing

Dangerous Games

It's dangerous, yes the games we play
My hearts at stake, I fear
Despite my flirting ways you find
I long to hold you near

I see more than a handsome face,
Mystery in those eyes,
A smile on a mouth,
Who would never tell me lies

You lay so gentle on my mind
A simple thought of you makes me smile
I long to make this game be real
But, I wonder all the while

How would you take all of this?
Can you even guess, or would it be a surprise?
I wonder how it would feel to look,
And find the love in your eyes

Alecia R. Pickett

I'm Glad I'm the One

I'm glad that I can be the one
To hold you close at night.
The one to kiss away the tears
And make everything all right.

I'm glad that I can be the one
To walk beside you every day.
The one you'll take with you everywhere,
The one to love you in every way.

I'm glad that I can be the one
To make your dreams come true;
To help you build your future plans,
For I love no one but you.

I'm glad that I can be here
Through every step of the rest of your life.
To one to make you happy,
For you're the one I'll love for life.

Marilyn Lyons

Please Stop

When will it stop?
Why do they do it?
Grown people
Claiming to be adults.

Small child, boy or girl,
He isn't a punching bag,
She isn't a football to kick.
He isn't trash to be thrown out,
She isn't a disease to destroy.

Why don't you love her?
Why don't you treasure him?
How can you, an adult, hurt them?
How can you turn away from the screams?

So small they are,
So trusting of you to care for them.
When will you stop hurting them?
When will you, as an adult, start loving them?

Judith M. Marr

I Don't Know

The sun sets, the nights falls,
The city breathes the fumes of her automobiles,
Rushing, passing, trying to get home
The day is over, night has begun
As I sit in my watchman's booth
I wonder, who am I?
Feelings of frustration overtake my thoughts,
Yet sadness fills my heart.
The laughter, I used to have is gone.
Who am I? Where do I go from here?
I wonder, who am I? What am I?
I don't know! Do you!
I wonder! Does anyone really know.
Who they are,
I don't know.

Rodney T. Walker

I Have Never Known Love

I have never known love.
Love that comes from heaven above.
Love that floats high above the world and everything within.
I am waiting for that love to begin.
Love that makes you not see straight.
Love that controls your fate.
Love that will never break my heart.
Love that will not let my world fall apart.
Love that stays with me day by day.
Love that will never go away.
I have never known love.
Love that is true.
Love that comes from you!

Kristy Martin

Beyond the Lilies

Oh! The beautiful signs of spring
Once again drapes our gardens green.
With colors so vibrant and pale,
And lilies that blossom pure white in the dell.
Dear lilies your scent is a breath of fresh air
Flowing calm and peaceful without a care.
"God is the lily of the valley, our Rose of Sharon,"
At times we drift away, feel desolate and barren
Yet, he woes us unto himself in tenderness and love
Always forgiving with kindness, and compassion,
Preparing our home above.
My hope lies beyond the lilies
Where time and space are no more
When eternity begins, across that Jordan shore.

Kathy L. Felknor

The Man for Me (That I've Yet to Meet)

The man for me (that I've yet to meet)
Will able to stand on his own two feet
Because of the work of God above.
This man will have a deep, and lasting love
For Jesus his Savior Who's plan for his life
Will include me—being his wife.
Christian is a name that comes to mind.
It could be his 'cause in its meaning we find
The words "follower of Christ"—this means a lot—
A life of service and more than not—
Sometimes of hardship in the midst of the joy
That is like that of a little girl or boy.
So, right now I'll call him by that name
Since someone called Christian should bring true acclaim
To God's purpose and will for the people of earth
(The purpose and will that brings second birth).
You see, faith in God is very important to me.
With faith in God one can make anything be
Much more special and meaningful, too.
It can save someone's life—maybe even you.

Irene Carol Chattaway

Wondering, Pondering

Wondering, no place to go
Pondering, I do not know

Wondering, no place in particular to stay
Pondering, trying to bring my life back from astray

Wondering, can't seem to excel
Pondering, were is the line between heaven and hell

Wondering, no one really to blame
Pondering, knowing that tomorrow will only bring more pain

My hands are dirty
My face is clean
From the tears you've never seen

So try living the life I've lived
We'll see were you set
Your outcome will not be any better
I have already lived the hell you will soon get

Wondering.
Pondering.
Were has my life gone

It all seems so meaningless

Shannon Frisby

Bed of Roses

I once had two beds of roses
I gave one to Pharaoh and one to Moses.
Moses said thank you but Pharaoh said, "go away!"
He banished me for 40 years that very day.
So here I wait in the desert for Moses,
The only one who really appreciated my bed of roses.
Moses never came, so here I lay,
In the scorching desert, waiting day by day.

Kelly Effinger

Just a Prayer Away

Every living moment, every hour of the day.
I think about life's situations that seems to come my way

I look up toward heaven and say a soft prayer,
Believing God hears and knowing that He cares.

My prayer may not be answered that particular day.
By faith I feel much better knowing . . .
God is just a prayer away.

Joseph Patrick Davis

How Are You

Leaping whales from the deep blue arctic shore.
Eagles, eagles, eagles I did see soar.
The elk, the moose, the caribou and the bison too!
Oh no, not me did they ignore.
The wise old fox asked, how are you?
The mountain big horn sheep—my, my,
did you see how they could leap?
The sky never darkens in the land
of the midnight sun, from spring 'til fall.
Oh, what wonder Mother Nature brings to us all.
Alaska, the Yukon, the rivers wild, old Mother Nature
And her blessings shall always keep us as her child.

Jerry L. Peel

Valentine's Day

On Valentine's Day, I share some of love,
It soars up in the sky's high above.
I wish your heart would open up wide,
You could hug me tight and be at my side.
For this time now, we are apart.
But I wish you happiness and send you my heart.

Jennifer Izzo

In Softness

Soft as a mothers first kiss upon the brow of her first born.
The sweet scent of new cut hay in the early morn.
Soft as the lace surrounding the face of a bride newly wed.
Soft as the fuzz upon an infants head when placed upon a velvet bed.
Soft as a puppy's eyes while loving hands caress his head.
The soft flutter of angel wings while leading
us with caring grace to an unknown softer place.
Soft as Gods tender hands wiping away our tears.
These are a few of the things I feel as I live my own soft years.

Louise Mossholder

among the bottom

i'd give myself to the ocean,
and sell my soul to the sand.
flesh alone becomes water.
i am one mortal man.

toss my body upon the surface.
lead-drop to the flooded ocean floor;
inhale death among the dank animated seaweeds.
fade to black as the liquid around me.

my last breath exhausted sole at the bottom.
gagged and drowned among the raging calm:
the bloody, sadist ocean of the Atlantic.
the sand—my grave—a dust cloud, blinding.

i am no more or less of a man
for wishing my tomb into this massive abyss.
upon the earth's continents, a man may die with many.
upon this cavernous trench, i am eternally alone.

Michael Richard

A Delightful Untruth

I wish I were not so cool.
My popularity makes it so difficult, I make girls drool.
At McDonald's I can't order, don't you see
Because they give me everything free.
Tom Cruise is sad and about to pout,
Cause Alicia Silverstone just asked me out.
It's sad to be trapped on earth envied by all,
perhaps on another planet I could escape being mauled.
If I were to be taken away by a UFO,
the alien girls would be after me also.

Chris Baldwin

Lovers

He ran in the morning
and his world was blue
colors washed clear
sky separated from earth, and he
strong in the center
his body very strong.
She ran in her head
roads unwinding like magical balls of string
more than one, more than one way to go.
He ran brave as a bird
she ran quiet
he
could hear his footsteps beating like a heart
and she could feel, could hear
her heart beating.
He ran in the morning, sometimes thinking of her
and she
in her soft blue morning bed
ran too.

Rose Leiman Goldemberg

Granddad

If I had a life time to tell you all he's done for me,
I could write a book or even make a movie.
He loved me in spite of the trouble and stress,
But I have found no words to start to express.
He raised me with love, patients, and pride as I grew.
We build a bond so strong that no one knew.
Every time I cried, every time I'd shed a tear,
He was always by my side and told me not to fear.
He gave me courage and strength to walk.
He opened my mouth and taught me how to talk.
He picked me up every time I'd fall,
Made me walk every time I wanted to crawl.
He raised me from baby with the love in his heart,
Then sent me into the world to make my own start.
I know he isn't God, nor did he ever claim to be,
But in my eyes, he is as close to perfect as can be.

Rodney Price

Inside/Outside

My inside self and my outside self are
as different as can be.

My outside self is friendly,
And very popular indeed.
Kind, easy, and gentle am I,
With words of peaceful love.
Everyone around knows me,
Because I am as peaceful as a dove,

My inside self is different as you can see.

A hatred beast,
Always snapping at others around me.
Tough, angered, enraged,
And never giving up.
People stay out of my way,
Because at any moment I'm sure to erupt.

Huey Boyle

Sweet Dreams

Sweet dreams little one, sweet dreams
Lying in the warmth of your bed
Your beautiful eyes so gently closed
Your silky hair soft with a gentle flow, sweet dreams
So innocent, so much love in your tiny little heart.
So much joy and beauty lie ahead, sweet dreams
No worries in your precious little head
No sorrow or pain lying in the warmth of your bed.
Sweet dreams my little one, sweet dreams

John Hinojosa

Through the Debris of Time

In the debris of time, we hear voices.
Sounds of the day and nights.
Uncle Dick with a playful grin,
Showing us the Northern Lights,

Noise of laughter along the Waddle pike,
That winds through Paradise.
Watermelon feasts, enjoyed by those
Who picnicked there.

Adventures with girls like Simone,
Along Paris Streets, the Riviera, Rome,
Climbing Mount Fujiama,
With Kip, a son, seeing sunrise, on heights unknown.

Boisterous reunions with
"Gray-haired soldiers," stories of Comrades
Who died too young.
Prayers to keep the faith for heart and mind.

Through the debris of time, stumbling
Now and then, to a banquet hall
With ancestors seated at the table,
Smiling, laughing, waiting.

John Hunter

Angel in Disguise

You do not realize the love you have
Imparted to others—family and friends.
It is a love that endures all,
The memory of which never ends.
A gentle smile, a twinkle in the eye,
An admonishing voice, all to keep us straight.
Because of your caring, in our lives there is no
Room for hate.
To yourself, you are nothing, but to us,
You are everything; you have so enriched our lives.
We can see the true self inside of you;
But you are blind to the angel in disguise.

Harry E. Swinney

Oasis

Life is an oasis,
Filled with pleasures and sorrow.
It contains the river
For which our conscience grows.
When it rains,
Our life soaks up the dampness in our minds.
We become filled with knowledge.
Knowledge to achieve our goals,
Knowledge to conquer all obstacles
Set before us.
Our life is what molds our personality.
The joys are our smiles,
And the sorrow our tears.
Life is an oasis.

Stephanie Rogers

I Would Have Called But . . .

I would have called but,
If you were not there to answer it would have
Caused my heart to break.

I would have called but,
To have the sound of your voice and not the
warmth of your arms would be too difficult to bear.

I would have called but,
To have the memory of your smile and not the joy of
your being would leave me somewhere beyond
sorrow and past despair.

I would have called but . . .

Anita Gill Anderson

I Cry!

My lonely eyes weep the tears
Of effervescent sorrow,
And my pillow once again becomes
blindly saturated with
Once-loved emotions of my glassily
Hazed eyes.

How could have been so blind?
Why could I not see the
Trap of love, set to catch the dreaming heart?

Did I not try to bring hope to the
Wondering soul?

The rays of desperation shine on me,
Like a glimmering lake
When the sun peaks itself above the tall,
Yawning trees.

Now a dead love weighs itself in my chest,
And emotions become hard to achieve.

Happiness and love escape me now
Like a hot burning fire's smoke,
Suffocating me to the point of sheer death.

Brian K. Seay

Nature Cries

Devils with guns, animals being slain
Mothers and fathers crying for their young
Without these creatures, the world will feel pain
This has to stop, the animals have sung

Does the world know, we're not the only ones
So many animals have already paid
So many mothers without any sons
Many extinct animals have been made

So many fathers begging for just one
Humans who like to show off their fur coats
So much damage has already been done
Dolphins being slaughtered in tuna boats

Why can't everyone learn to just stop
People don't always have to be on top

Richie Lee Davit

Alone at Last

Alone at last, away from it all.
Away from the city with its buildings tall.

No hustling or bustling to worry about,
No more problems, to work out.

Out in the country, where the bluebirds fly.
At the top of a mountain,
I could almost touch the sky.

And here I am, away from it all,
Alone at last!

Cindy Balcom

Day By Day

How can I change it and what must I say,
then my mind answers; you can't change yesterday.
Yesterday is like tomorrow the same as of today;
With joy, grief and sorrow for life can be that way.
The pain for tomorrow is borrowed from today—
The hurt takes forever, forever to go away.
The oppressions cut deep a hurt from within—
No one can see them, not even a friend.
But there's hope for tomorrow for a new and brighter day
Because God is our hope—and he will make a way.
Now, how can I change it and what must I say—
Then my mind answers. Today is a great day!

Richard Clyde Lewis

I Am Proud to Be a Senior

Look how fast time has past.
I tried to enjoy everyday, but
Many difficulties got in my way.

Childhood hard without a dad;
Mom was there to untangle the snags!
Had few clothes and run down shoes,
Never missed a day in school.

All this helped me to understand
That life ahead would be filled with pain.
Sometimes young and a lot when you're old,
It takes all this to reach your goal.

Now a senior and filled with pain,
I'm so busy I can't complain.
The Senior Center have a lot for me to gain,
A balanced hot meal for my body to sustain,
Games and exercise to keep me maintained.

Trips we wouldn't be able to take.
Thank you Lord, for this wonderful break.
Keep the Center open to give us a break.
It sure makes life easy for us to take.

Pearl Ballard

The Mariner and His Ship

Sun-stained and wind-worn skin;
Eyes full of stories from the places he's been;
Rough hands, tough as leather;
Strong sea legs that stand firm in stormy weather;
Scars the reminders of yesteryear,
The trophies of courage that conquered his fears.

Barnacled beauty slicing the sea;
Long since surrendered to tall tales from history;
Sails full from the breath of the sky;
With the belief that, like the birds, she will one day fly;
Chipped, and nicked, and blown away;
The evidence therein from centuries of salty decay.

The mariner and his ship, then,
Do make an awesome two—
One, the captain of weaker men;
The other, a follower true

Deborah L. Carter

I Once Had a Friend

I once had a friend that helped me carry my books down the hall.
I once had a friend that pushed me and made me fall.
I once had a friend that stood up for me.
I once had a friend that laughed as he teased.
I just remember that friend that made me fall,
that friend is no friend at all.

Krystal L. Cleary

A Tragedy

A hundred years ago, on a frigate out of Italy,
Two hundred Stradivarius violins and cellos
Sank beneath the ocean with a big doomed thrum.
In seas of silent symphonies the angel fish were plying
Varnished crypts of melodies unsung.

Where is the music of us all?
Fathoms down in tears? We poets make no wills.
We leave to a peopling world
Old pearls from a mossy chest. So I leave mine.
But I would gladly lie
Fathoms from the sun's green eye
Among the weaving weeds
If I could leave one singing line.

Norma Laut

A Special Thank You

We came to you with open hearts and minds
Not knowing the mysteries that first grade would unwind

Specials, music, gym and art were
Such a wonderful way to start

Singing songs and playing games
Made we children praise your name

You have taught us all to read and
Write so well

Because of your patience we shall never fail

Geography, social studies and math
Are sure to help us in life's path

And though we may not always understand
You gently guide us with a smile and helping hands

Because of you we try our best . . .
Nothing more and nothing less

Your teaching and sharing have given
Us a great head start

Thank you teacher for caring with
Such a big heart!

Deonna Heintze

A Cry for Love

There is a cry not soft and tired.
Yet it's left to be desired.
Some can not hear, some do not care,
But yet we know that it is there.
'Tis a cry of pain, a cry of sorrow.
A cry that wants to see tomorrow.
Do we help, or do we ignore
That cry from a not-too-distant shore?

They say to us "Carpe Diem,"
But days are short where we come from.
The nights are long, and full of sadness
Because our future is being dismissed.
We carry guns, and drugs, and knives.
What will we leave for our babies lives?
This teen is pregnant, that one is dead.
This one used drugs, that messed up his head.
We all need to cry, so open your ear.
You might be amazed at what you will hear.
Do not get mad when you get a shove.
It was probably just, a cry for love.

Melinda Mueller

Nature

I love to see how nature blooms
In all her beauty splendor and hue
She sends the rain, the sun, the dew
We see the little fish that swim
And all the pretty birds that sing
Let us then be willing to share
Our bit of love and care

We must remember everyday
She is the one that directs our way
The sun, the moon, the stars that shine
The air we breathe are all sublime
We thank thee for the life you give
All the wonderful things each day brings

As we walk through fields of grass so green
It's fun to stare at insects small
The animals so big and tall
As they romp and play among the trees
Then when the evening shades come down
The flowers bow as if in prayer
And silently they disappear

Phyllis Greenidge

Classic Jazz: A Poem in 3/4 Time

Come with me and you will hear;
The music America has.
It sings and blows and swings
And waltzes, and some call it classic jazz.

The orchestration plays in the background.
The saxophone's sound is mellow.
Although, it's not a common thing;
There's a musician playing cello.

The bass and drums keep the time,
And the beat and the rhythm steady.
The trumpeter will play a solo;
So he is making sure, the instrument is ready.
He is now quickly riffing . . . Classic Jazz! Classic Jazz!

Now that I have waltzed you through;
A musical celebration.
I hope that you can feel it too; a great exhilaration!
Oh, listen to the piano pound; saxes blow; trumpets blast.
All the instruments are now playing in concert . . .
Classic Jazz! Classic Jazz.

Frances M. Johnson

Success

I've tried all types of methods,
Materials and ways.
We've worked and worked since September first;
It seems like a million days!

We've used tracing paper and finger paint
And even wet spaghetti noodles;
But all it's looked like afterwards
Are someone's daydream doodles.

Chocolate pudding, sandpaper,
And gray school modeling clay;
And finally something registered
'Cause today you made my day.

You came in the room and sat straight in your chair
And with a gleam in your eye like a flame,
You picked up your pencil and paper
And legibly printed your first and last name!

Arlene Rosenblatt

Happy Go Lucky Sunshine

Oh happy go lucky sunshine,
you're a wonderful thing
You put me in a good mood each morning,
Which makes me sing.
Oh happy go lucky sunshine I love to feel your rays;
They keep me warm and tan each and every day.
Oh happy go lucky sunshine you are lucky to me;
For each day of sunshine brings help in track to me.

Jennifer Patchen

Always Together, You and Me

When I need you the most, you're there like the sun.
Hovering over me, through darkness or light.
You guide me to safety, when I'm lost and can't run.
You give me my will, you give me my might.
I want you to know, I'm your sunshine too.
I'll be here for you, like you've been here for me.
I'll be your light, when you need something new.
Friends forever, that's what we'll be!
Together we'll always fly higher and higher.
No matter the weather, we'll keep on trying.
We'll take the path, that is the most winding.
We'll fly side by side, till at last we retire.
Friends forever, that's what we'll be!
Always together, you and me!

Amber Wold

There for Me

He was always there for me
Through the endless medical tests and medications
Through the gut-wrenching psychotherapy and evaluations
He stood by me

He was always there for me
Through my countless rantings and ravings
Through my excessive overreactions to small things
He calmed me

He was always there for me
When I doubted his love and sincerity
When friends were a rarity
He reassured me

He was always there for me
When I gave up on my career
When my future was so unclear
He guided me

Because he was there for me
I am beginning to reclaim my life
I am proud to be his wife
He loves me

Catherine Richardson

A Mother's Love

These perfect flowers are from Heavens love,
And the summers soft breezes that blow from above.
They were nurtured in raindrops and warmed by the sun,
And their scent fills the air each and every new dawn.
Each bee and butterfly drew life from its stem.
And returns it to us with pleasure again.
They were preserved with love and each petal you see,
Was placed with thoughts of you from me.
So remember each time you see a flower from above,
Even they can't compare to a Mother's love.

Melinda St. Jean

Nature's Fireworks

Breathless
Countless
Darkness upon empty
Momentary perceptions so bright
See the offering, the heart is felt after death
When the skyline falls motionless
Perspective unattainable
Security without demand
Miles seem nothing, coordinates no help
My aura disappears
And before hopelessness; destruction widespread; vast
unknowns
Fueled by interactions of opposites
Demise—never it seems—is a choice
Too far from human capabilities
Too concentrated the energy
Pretend the nonexistent; be fooled nonetheless
Heavenly flares
Heat lightning

Heath Moody

Fear in My Soul

I stand and look around
As I am surrounded by an unforgiving world.
But I fear to disclose my helplessness to any soul
For that the soul I speak
Should think of me as a coward of the world
And my respected self would no longer be.
I keep my fear to my soul
And show no mercy to the world.
I live, but fear is a stillness in my dreams.

Craig Maley

Death Before Birth

The world with its color and sound so loud and clear,
Beckons me, before my time, from my mother so dear,
But a fear to leave my bed and the warmth of the womb
Grips my being and turns me upside down as in a tomb.

'Farewell, time to part;' and my feet goes before.
And I sense in my limbs the feelings I longed for,
The coolness of the air and the brightness of the sun.
'O let me out, awake to this wonder world, full of fun'.

Not fully born, I am still in their hands like a pawn
Groping around in the deep darkness before dawn.
Soon the hard hand of an intruder brings fear and chill
And a doc's tools meet my skull with butcherous skill.

A piercing pain and a sparkling fire end the agony.
All is done, and then they leave in well-writ glee.
'Mother dear, wounded and hurt, victim of a lie,
Tell me now, if you can, for whom did I die?'

Xavier Thelakkatt

To My Lovely Arlynne

How many ways do I love thee?
Let me tell you adverbially.
I love you ardently, passionately, affectionately,
Devotedly, excitingly, emotionally, thrillingly,
Infatuatedly, impatiently, fanatically, happily,
Sincerely, fondly, tenderly rapturously, zealously,
—Even jealously assiduously, perseveringly,
Constantly, indelibly, and utterly with ineffability.

Frederick

Untitled

Why is it that life must change so fast,
and things flip around when no time has passed?

One minute's happy,
the next one's sad,
because your mind is racing
with memories you have.

And then in an instant, for no reason why,
Your thoughts switch to new and those memories die.

You try to become happy and cheerful again,
You realize someday, somehow you'll win.

Just deal with today and try to cope,
because life will never change if you give up hope.

Sonya Zebarth

Footsteps to Departure

He tried to block me from leaving,
placing his wagon, pushcart and
bicycle over my Verdi suitcase.

He filled a suitcase of his
own with shredded paper.
He hid it under the table near my empty seat.

He put a handful of wildflowers
beside the night-stand that morning.
Sleeping in, I woke to find them.

That evening, I found them again
in a glass of water on the sink.
I decided to leave them in the glass.

As we drove near the airport,
no one mentioned the flight.
After the trip to the mall, he looked for me

in the bed where I overslept
and the room where the flowers had been.
Our lives leave footprints in the sky.

William Melaney

The Unanswered Question

We sit here together, yet apart,
trying to think of that one special thought,
that will make the other fall madly in love.
Yet, I know that if we do not act upon this love,
It will up and fly away, like a dove.
For if we shall spend our lives apart,
it will feel like an eternity, with a broken heart.
I know I love you, yet the words I can not form,
even though the fear of rejection, isn't worth the pain
deep within which burns.
What I shall do, I do not know,
even though the love for you inside of me, continues to grow.
I just wish that there could be a sign, there for me to see,
so I don't spend eternity alone, and forgotten in a sad
loveless sea.

Wade Nathan Rake

The Fruit of the Spirit

The fruit of the Spirit is . . .
Love—Love is like a strawberry, it's sweet and gentle and
knows what you want and need.
Joy—Joy is like a grapevine, easily grown easily withered.
Peace—Peace is like a wild berry, growing in a field of dreams.
Long suffering—Long suffering is like an apple, sometimes
sweet sometimes sour but always good in the end.
Goodness—Goodness is like a peach, good from skin to seed.
Faith—Faith is like a cherry, you can never have enough.
Meekness—Meekness is like an avocado, unrushed and mild.
Kindness—Kindness is like a bunch of bananas,
always room for one more.
Self-control—Self control is like a pineapple, move too
quickly and you'll get a prickly!

Adrienne Lorraine Dauk

Fire and Ice

Some say the world will end in fire.
Some say ice. I desire fire, but I drink slice with ice.

It wouldn't nice if the world ended in ice or fire.
It would be nice if we died without a price.

Why do people think the world is going to
end in fire or ice?

Chris Hathaway

Black Pearls

Hidden beneath impenetrable pride,
Wrenches an inflamed, sweltering, aggression inside.

You, my friend rediscovered that uniqueness in me,
Experiencing the attainable fantasy you knew I would be.

As we merged minds, hearts, thoughts, body and soul,
And peaked to elevations of ecstasy, our ultimate goal.

Never, in all my wildest dreams did I . . .
Think you would retrieve misplaced essence, and constrain me to cry!

Your words spoke the comfort I so needed to hear,
And distinct finger lent to catch the flow of my tears.

I am that Black Pearl, once scorned and down trodden,
Only too many times that I've essentially forgotten.

Now . . . authentically cultured, my love is as vintage,
Providing completeness in you, depicting the image,

Of two once-lost people finding consolation together,
Sharing the truest-of-true in a friendship forever,

Unadulterated by the world's pollution of facade and mistrust,
Devoid of all sensitivity, as dreams turn to dust.

One day we'll move on and bring something sacred to one,
But, never will it duplicate what we to each other have become!

D'An Kelly

The Freedom of a Swallow

Here on the ground I am stuck.
My heart is as heavy as lead,
Depressed and pitted like an empty crater.
Here on the ground I am
On the edge of existence,
Dehumanized and different from the rest
Of the human race.
I know there is nothing wrong with being different,
But I wish that difference was not
In the form of an impairment.
However, if I were a swallow, I wouldn't mind being different.

If I had the freedom of a swallow,
I would rise above the tallest buildings
And shake the dust of the oppressive
Ground off my feathers.
With a new perspective of the world,
I would fly around the Earth to discover new truths.
My wings would have the strength of the eagle,
The wind would whistle in my ears
While I would climb high in the sky.

Patricia E. Plumer

Children

Children of the world
bring peace and joy to one and all.
To handle and hold, to feed and hug,
allows us to display our unfailing love.
To teach and guide through walking and talking,
creates a bond that's everlasting.

Oh no, what's that I hear?
The mourning and crying of a mother near.
For she has just lost a child so dear.
Why dear God must she suffer so,
did you really feel he must go,
To romp and play in heavenly delight,
with toys and boys of the same height.

Oh no, what's that I hear?
The crying and sympathy from a community near.
The sorrow and pain,
the anguish and suffering,
For two little boys that died while their mother did nothing.

Oh God, explain to me so I can understand.
The meaning of your plan.
Why must children of the land
Be sacrificed like little lambs.

Lester L. Ruark

Wood Fence

The snow wet smell of wood;
in a fence, taller than my head.
The moldy straw smell of last summer's grass,
that has lain all winter dead.

The seat of my pants, all soggy
from sitting on the ground;
But my senses all delighted
with Spring's arrival sound.

There's a nip in the air,
but the pale yellow sun
Warms my face with the promise
of summer fun.

Alone, I sat against that fence,
that surely is no more;
For that Spring day was years ago,
and yet my mind did store

The sight, the sound, the smell, and the feel,
like an inner burning light
That even today, can fill my heart,
with mem'ries of childish delight.

Harold Bishop

African Queen

Behold, she is the pride of all God's
Glorious creation;
The seed of her fertile womb has
Multiplied in every single nation . . .

America was built upon her strong back
And from her royal blood, sweat, and tears;
Warriors, Princes, and Kings she has produced
Looking backwards over her many proud years . . .

She's African Queen, the epitome of womanhood,
The line uniting divinity, and matter;
Through her loving care our future posterity
Is gathered up altogether . . .

O' How I do love thee beautiful,
Sister, woman, majestic African Queen;
And pray that sweet images of your
Sensual and enticing allurements continuously
Manifest and multiply in my dreams . . .

Gary Gee-Gee Casterlow-Bey

Then I Am Me

I am a student working hard to get good grades
I am a daughter helping with the chores
Then I am me

I am a sister watching my brother and sister
I am a friend hanging out at the mall
Then I am me

I am a lonely girl wondering why I can't fit in
I am trying to talk to 20 people at once
Then I am me

I am a brave quester saving a fantasy kingdom
I am an author signing her best-selling novel
Then I am me

I am a nervous clarinetist about to play a solo
I am a nervous dancer about to perform
Then I am me

I am the girl who wants to be with her friends
I am the girl who wants to be alone
Then I am me

I am all of these things
Then I am me

Allyson Schettino

Creatures of Our World

Creatures of our world, live far and near
They live in many different places
They live with many different races
Creatures of our world, their meaning is not clear.

Creatures of our world, live in the sea
They swim where it shines
But they get put on lines
Creatures of our world, why can't we let them be?

Creatures of our world, live on land
A lot of them run really fast
But we don't know if they will last
Creatures of our world, need a helping hand.

Creatures of our world, have beautiful wings
They soar through the deep blue sky
We ask ourselves what makes them fly
Creatures of our world, do many wonderful things.

Creatures of our world, love is what we must
One day they are here
The next day they'll disappear
Creatures of our world, need all of our trust.

Michelle Perrucci

I Am

Still racing my horses over the sands,
Hot, cold, devoid of water.
Seeking to sack, to kill and to rape.
I was not born, I knew no mother,
Empty of soul. I am Marauder.

Still holding my vessel before the winds,
Plowing headlong into the seas.
Many's the mate who has stiffened with fear
From my shouts upon the breeze.
Struck dead as they were with my blooded sword,
They vainly raised to defy it.
I was not born, I knew no sire,
Empty of soul. I am Pirate Marauder .

Stalking still through the bush, quiet as death,
Which I mean very soon to visit.
Upon the halt and the meek, the old and the weak,
This survival for the fittest.
I was not born, I knew no lover,
Empty of soul. I am Predator, Pirate Marauder.

Samuel S. Smith

The Love of a Lifetime

There are two people in my life,
who are an important part of me.
Sometimes we may not get along,
but they love me, I can see.
They've provided the things I've needed,
and have given me lots of love.
When I'm alone and thinking,
I knew they were sent from above.
They have stood by me no matter what I do,
and have believed in me throughout the years.
If I am scared and upset,
they've helped me overcome my fears.
Sometimes I do take them for granted,
and that I do regret.
But I do know they'd do anything for me,
and that's something I'll never forget.
When I'm having problems,
they're there with open arms.
These two people are my best friends in the whole world,
they're my Parents.

Chastity Brown

Sharon B

Sharon as a secretary is simply great,
On her performance score, give her the highest rate.

She sits at her tube punching away at the keys
Everything she prints out she does it with ease.

Sometimes she smiles and sometimes she frowns
Sometimes she laughs and sometimes she clowns.

But whatever mood that she might be in,
She always comes back with that friendly grin.

So, I don't know what to call her, maybe a live wire
Or more to the point—she's a ball of fire.

So working with her, how can you measure?
I guess you got to say it has been a pleasure!

So, when I retire and I'm long gone,
Whoever does my work please don't go wrong.

But how can you not help it to do it just great,
When you have Sharon to keep you going straight.

So, unless you don't know who really runs this place,
Keep your eye on Sharon for she sets the pace.

Well good luck to you Sharon as I leave this mess
You surely deserve the very best!

Eugene F. Franz

Sonnet #2

Midnight fades slowly as it roams to dawn;
Then dawning melts away and day is born.
Sunrise keeps splashing light 'til night is gone.
Daylight does brighten the arising morn.

Then morning stretches and unfolds to noon
And afternoons wears on to evening time.
Day dwindles down, and loses light too soon.
Sunset may paint a final scene so fine.

Dusk changes to the darkness of night.
A black, enveloping and muting shroud
Does cover up the day and deepen night;
A changing panorama well-endowed.

These phases have an everyday rebirth
From interaction of the sun and earth.

Forrest Claffy

The Fire

There I sat in total silence,
Watching the flames lightly crackle beneath the burnt wood.
The flames seemed to danced to the gentle sound of piano music
Playing endlessly in the background.
The soothing sensation eased me away from all my sorrows,
But soon the flames burned low and there was nothing left but
dull, gray ashes.
I was forced back to reality,
But I had a new hope
A new dream
A new life.

Kristen Kesser

Enlightenment

A mass of past lives marks the horrors of yesterday's battle,
the blood, no longer rushing through the endless tunnels, frozen
Limp statues whose memories were infinite.
Not a sight for longing, but one more blow into the dignity of
fellow countrymen, and a hand to help them achieve a higher
understanding. Bigoted toward no one.

In ways not explainable, the best has stepped forward.
Divine's will was done, and forgiveness the victor over hate.
Life is easier, but takes strength to go on.

Words and actions are spoken and remembered,
as if they had been etched in stone by God's outstretched finger.
Memories sadden, yet strengthen the weakest of hearts.
New life dawns once more, a better life, and chance to forgive
and let live. "Gone, but not forgotten" they're remembered by,
regrets not alone in thought.

Jeremy Cowan

Magical Memories

Oh, my favorite place to be!
The Magic Kingdom looks down at me,
I feel so carefree and happy.
The smooth touch of the railings,
as I wait in line.
The fresh aroma of popcorn and candy.
Best of all are the rides,
twisting and turning in a cartoon wonderland.
I hear the soft twang of old familiar music.
In the distance, what is that?
It is no other than my dear friends,
dressed in their jubilant costumes.
I experience happiness, and exhilaration,
as I walk through the endless maze of magic.
Trying to stay until midnight,
but afraid I might turn into a pumpkin,
I look back at "The Happiest Place on Earth!"

Michelle Cannella

Spotted Windshield

What passengers we are:
Babies of tar—
From birth carried,
Bundled, and ferried.
By mother borne—
Eventually torn.
Even dead we are taken by caring hands . . .
Like those which hold the eternal Sands.

And upon a broad girth,
We are also perpetually carried by Mother Earth.

To this lonely passenger: it fell
Ringing, ringing—the bell—
oh the bell.
The constant ignoble Hell;
It covers,
Carries, hovers.

We are all carried . . .
By the Mother, the Earth, the Sun, the Hole, the Soul,
the Now . . .

We are carried.

George Mason Tudor

Untitled

Critter, Pitter . . . underneath a log . . .
(Oh what a heavy burden!)
The rain and dew and hazy fog . . .
(Of all the guilt and sin),
Are making it hard for you to see,
Making you blind to where you should be, but
Critter, Pitter, . . . God sees. Critter, Pitter . . . God knows.
That you are slowly running away
Blindly in desperation, looking or the answers
(That are right in front of your nose),
Looking to a distant land, listening to the lies of a strange
People with strange Gods . . .

Critter, Pitter . . . the great I am is good.
He won't force himself on you—who is now being bullied,
Pulled by the strings of choices you've made.
God won't lie to you—who is now being deceived.
He's already given his truth,
His son Jesus, the word of God.
It's your choice to believe.

Denise S. Boynton

Nana's Prayer

While I held my Grandson as he slept today,
I looked down at him and I started to pray.
Wiping my tears and gently kissing his face.
"Please God, I pray You will keep him safe."

He soon will be three and he is growing so fast.
Each day it seems he learns a new task.
Stacking blocks so high on top of each other,
Sometimes just making a mess for his Mother.

Cars and trucks are his favorite toys of all.
He is very good now at throwing a ball.
He loves to swing and go down the slide.
In his wagon he laughs as Papa gives him a ride.

I look at his face so innocent and sweet.
When he hugs me it is Nana's most special treat.
My love for him is more than money could buy.
Such a treasure, his smile and his big brown eyes.

I gently touch his delicate cheek and hand.
A tear falls down on "Nana's Little Man."
Again I whisper a soft quiet prayer.
"Please God always keep him in Your warm loving care."

Sandra L. Wilson

Little Blessings

When I was young and in my prime
I wasted years and wasted time
On silly things that did not matter
Like fashion wear and non stop chatter.

Now I'm older and a little wiser
Set in my ways, some call me an "old geezer"
Little blessings everyday are things now I treasure
The love of my family, blessing that can't be measured.

A smile and a hug or just a touch
And the best of words "we love you so much."
The older I'll get, the more senile I'll be
My sight maybe dim but with my heart I will see.

My ears may be deaf, but a touch I can feel
Of yesterday's years when life was so real
The love of my children, when we were so young
The joy of my grandchildren, we had so much fun.

So enjoy little blessings and try to be kind
Just try to remember, take one day at a time
Yesterday is gone and tomorrow hasn't come
Don't waste it foolishly, not a minute not one!

Renda Hurst

Christ Is My Valentine

I knocked at the door of my Saviour's Heart
His Holy Spirit Welcomed me in;
Now, I live in His heart and He lives in mine
That is why I say, "Christ Is My Valentine."

Secret love we have shared, all down through the years
Laughter, cries and even my secret fears;
When the hurt became unbearable,
He started a flame down in my heart
That will burn forever, and we will never depart.

This "Light of Love" give warmth and cheer,
Soothing and comforting me, I know He is near;
My life becomes more beautiful each day
"Oh yes! He is mine"
My faithful, loving, Valentine.

Christ redeemed me with His own precious blood
He proved that He really loved me.
And then went on Home to prepare a Mansion
That is where He and I are going to be.

His home in Heaven is also mine
Thank you Christ, for being my Valentine.

Helen K. Felton

The Path of Disability

Life becomes a walk;
a walk down a dark and narrow path.
I know not the rise nor the fall.
Its twists and turns are as unknown as the days ahead.
People question.
Friends sigh.
Family comforts, in loving compassion.
Yet they know not the path.
Its haunting trail
Which spirals down.
Perhaps it levels, providing a small light to lead.
I fear I will stumble and fall once more,
But I rise, and continue the walk,
With stubborn determination.
Where will the path lead me?
Will I trip, taking a final fall from which I may never recover?
In the stillness of my mind, God only knows how I long to cry out.
He sees the Path.
He knows the Path.
He will not leave me.

Daniel Hedlund

The Wounded Womb

"Muthuh!" He yelled
(I hadn't started while the light was still red)
His words echoed like canyon screams in my head
reverberating through mind's eye pictures
of my happiest times
Bouncing off walls of pain
where thoughtless minds had cut the cord of dignity . . .
aborted love's labor with a clenched fist
pierced the wounded womb's placental heart
with the birth of profanity
Against that name.

Nothing seems the same

What highway can he travel worth the hit and run
of taking years of work . . . and tears . . . and dreams
and rendering them
none

Edythe Ledee Finnerty

What My Grandma Is to Me!

My grandma is another word for love!
My grandma is something so strong I can't explain!
My grandma has 4 children and 8 grandchildren living and one son dead.
My grandma is not in the best shape now!
My grandma is fading, fading, gone.
My grandma is gone and I didn't even get to say good-bye!!!

Stephanie Dowd

Roberto

Your eyes can stare no longer than seconds . . .
then they dance

I want to sing them
"Twinkle, twinkle, deep brown stars
How I wonder what you are!

Light and sweet like butterflies
You warm the dark like fireflies"

But someone else pulls away your light
clouds your sparkle
swallows you to night

Can you be a spring branch
reach to the light
be lifted out
and be again so bright?

Oh please, please
twinkle, twinkle, twinkle
big brown stars
Show the wonders you truly are!

Anne Cortese

A Friend

A friend is someone who listens with her heart
Who lend a shoulder to cry on.
A friend is a firm hand who reaches out
To give strength.

Sometimes a friend is laughter
A sharing of a thought, a sunset, a flower, or mountain
There are sad times too, but mostly,
There are good times with a friend.

A phone call to brighten the day, is a friend.
Quiet talk, just listening, a sharing of dreams
A friend is all these, and more.

If you have one true friend
You are blessed, gladness fills your heart
Faith is restored, and life has meaning.

Winnell Wade Bandy

Sophistry . . . Speciously

Now I observe not through tinted glass or cellophane.
My eyes see and believe what we now both know is true.

How excellent the timing and truths proclaimed.
The darkness of night and khaki camouflage can no longer
hide the secrets or campaigns you carefully pre-planned.

Now here, now gone I welcome that which you explain.
No bold declarations are required.
We too can celebrate the triumph of stolen time if for
only minutes, and our love that is neither apparent to
senses nor obvious to the intelligent.

Once anonymity, we can now declare. I celebrate your
life, our lives everlasting satiated with respect,
trust, truth, loyalty, Love and all we dare to share.

Behold, I fear I too am so fond and delight
in those feelings you relate.
Sorting facts from fiction knowing a planted seed,
though belated and unpretentious,
your proposal shall fulfill my every need.

     Doris R. S. Miller

Death's Tragedy

It has long been a misconception that Death,
Is the enemy of man, always hiding.
In shadows, in a dark robe, a skeleton,
Waiting to steal your life, something to feared.

But Death is a kindly soul, though remorseful,
Sad to see your body leave this mortal plain.
And Death does not kill, he only guides the soul,
To the place where all souls go, eventually.

It is not Death that makes men afraid, but Fear,
That yellow demon, wearing sour green robes.
Smelling of stale sweat, with hollow eyes, frightful,
Telling lies, dirty traitor, stabbing his friend.

In the beginning the people understood
That Death was a guide and Fear his companion.
But fear stayed behind when Death had gone, unseen,
Tricking men into believing he was Death.

So when Death came again men thought he was Fear,
In their minds Fear was Death and they became one.
Since then men have been afraid of Death, unfair,
Accused unfairly, misunderstood, Death lives.

     Brian Coleman

A Messy Room

As the sun rose to its place in the sky,
I woke up and stretched my arms way up high.
I looked around and I could see,
All the clutter that was around me,
I gave a sigh and my face lost its gleam.
Cause that messy room I had to clean.
Why did I go to sleep with such a mess?
I didn't even bother to hang up my dress.
I must think of this as an adventure!
Hey, isn't that my grandma's dentures?
If my mom sees this I'll be in over my head.
Boy, right now I really wish I was dead. Come on you lazy fool.
Pretend you're in a dual. Pretend you're with the three musketeers.
I wonder if any one ever boxed their ears. Knock knock knock
Oh no, it's Mom. What will I do?
Hopefully I'll turn into a shoe,
Click, era "Amber it's time to eat."
"Look at this room, is that a beet?"
"After we eat your going to clean it."
"Now come on beat. . . it."

     Amber Stutzman

In Pursuit of Me

In the dreary backyard, beyond my home's decaying trees
Through the drifting tall grass in pursuit of me
As night descends upon the whispering woods, dimly lit
The glow of distant stars illumine all I see

Upon the old stone, I've now outgrown, a while I sit
And ponder the moment, where upon the earth, my fallen angel hit
Following a receding luminescence, years gone by
I struggle in the twilight to know, now, where I fit

The weeping clouds drown the embered sky
As I'm speaking softly with some memories, so afraid to die
Dreaming of a world where no longer my eyes suffer a fading day
And heaven's tears mend my angel, trying again to fly

So if my mortal mind allows me, here, to stay
With my angel that fell from grace one silent spring day
I'll encounter the place time has tossed away
In the memories of the moments when my youth was made

     Jared O'Connell

On This Day

It was a beautiful spring afternoon,
he had cried all night.
She was leaving him on this day.
Yet something just was not right.

He gazed into her cold black eyes
as his memories grew dim . . .
For him it was a sad fact
that she no longer needed him.

He took his love away from her
so she could now be free.
She did not say a word,
but he knew this had to be.

He gently reached over and kissed her lips,
without any kind of goodbye.
It's true she left him on this day.
Yet she gave no reason why.

He turned his head away
and with God he prayed amen.
A tear rolled down his fragile cheek
as her funeral came to an end.

     Heidi Easter

Los Angelinos

Staring at the ebbing sea,
and disrobed by the winter sun,
like a worn-out book, fully revealed.

As the ruins of the past, of a distant tribe,
where the palm trees strip me naked,
in the arms of wave and fishes and seamen's chaos.

An aging memory, unable to flow as the rain does.
The night is approaching.
And I stand with bitter memories that kindle no lamp.

Alas at twenty!
I stepped upon the horizon,
put fire to the house, with no fear of tomorrow.

A crescent, with open arms in solitude, remote
ignores me, for hours.

I am wavering in the downstream
and the world, follows me nightly
to count the delays of my return!

Among the waves the blustering wind paddles,
my vision is blurred, and is clouded by the air
I sail recklessly, abandoned.

     Mansoor Khaksar

Silence

Silence is as precious as a baby to its mother,
It gives you a peace that no one else can give,
It can come when you want it;
Even if you're in a room full of people,
Blocking out every sound,
Entering a world all your own,
Where people are what you want them to be.
A crazy mixed up world;
Green sky, blue grass, purple sun.
Everything is unique.
Wandering all alone,
Walking on the ocean if you feel the time is right.
Floating through the air . . . then suddenly,
Slowly drifting down into reality,
Back into the imperfect place,
Back into the noise.
But always there waiting is your world
and your eternal silence.

Alicia Korosec

Imagine If You Can

Imagine if you can the pain
My Jesus bore when He was slain.
The blood He shed for you and me
His beaten carcass upon that tree.

Imagine if you can the shame
I only have myself to blame.
The nails are not what held Him there
But His love for you and me, I swear.

Imagine if you can the crown
The thorns that pierced His precious brow.
The cat-of-nine-tails that ripped His back
As He defended not His brutal attack.

Imagine if you can the cross
He carried to Golgotha for the lost.
He was beaten and mocked and raped and killed
As he struggled to do what his father had willed.

Imagine if you can Jesus dying for you
Doing what no other man could do.
I've never seen a greater love as such
Imagine my friend, Jesus loved you this much.

Barbara Monroe

Moon Times

In January, Man Moon listened
  to twin soul whispers
In March, Ash Moon glistened
  on hope's glowing embers
In April, Planting Moon perfected
  destiny's swelling seeds
In August, Lake Moon reflected
  hawk circles in Mother sky
In October, Leaves Falling Moon mocked
  hands slicing gray and skull
In December, Night Fire Moon walked
  over Fijian tin roofs.

In March, Ash Moon stilled.
  Your body lay dying;
  I chased rainbows in California.

In April, Planting Moon wept
  gentle tears amid ashes in a cardboard box.
In May, Corn Planting Moon gazed
  on barren soil
Rainbows and moon time forever lost.

Nancy L. Cavanaugh

Lie and Lay

The words lie and lay are so easy to confuse;
By most of the students they are often misused.

In comparing their difference we need us a chart;
To avoid the confusion of telling them apart.

'Cause if you say lie when you really mean lay;
You may say night when you really mean day.

And if you say lay when you really mean laid;
You may say charged when you really mean paid.

Or if you've said laid when you should've said lain;
You may have said drought when you should've said rain.

It's hard to use these verbs and make them come out right;
'Cause when mixed with other words they sound so much alike.

But when your chickens cackle you know there's no denying;
Then, the word to use is laying unless your hens are lying!

M. D. Tennessee Ralph

Of a Boy That's Made of Wood

My friend the little soldier boy,
with his brigade hat so high,

So as the nose of Pinocchio would grow,
as he would softly tell a lie,

Wishing that I'd drift away but only if I could,
If I had this feelin' of a boy that's made of wood.

With a grain of salt and no pain to gain,
I'd simply wither away,

For in due time the dust of my mind,
would slowly turn to clay,

Wishing that I'd drift away but only if I could,
If I had this feelin' of a boy that's made of wood.

Lewis R. Shelton

Little Teapot

I'm a dingy little teapot
Sitting on a corner shelf.
The others are thought to be more important
So, of course, the dirty one sits by itself.

I'm a dingy little teapot
Unnoticed by passersby.
I want to scream in frustration
But am really empty inside.

I'm a dingy little teapot
Still hoping my dreams come true;
Someone appears who cares enough
To look past my dirty hue.

I'm a dingy little teapot
Living one day at a time.
So if you think your life is bad
Look through the window into mine.

Angela Bitson

Dreams

Dreams of being with him
That is how I think.
Late at night I pray beneath the moonlight rim.
His thoughts surround me with joy . . .
But in my heart I know I would never know him . . .
Even if I was a boy.
So, as I lay
I dream of the day . . .
Of my father's thoughts.
With me, he will always stay.

Randi LeClear

The World

The world we face today is terrible
The gun situation is just unbearable.

It's bad enough we have those gangs
With kids killing kids with big loud bangs.

We all had enough
Guns and gangs and all that stuff.

It's bad enough that we are losing our loved ones
Because these people in the gang want to carry a gun.

We can't go on hating blacks or whites
We need to put this racial thing out of sight.

The world is tough
and getting rough.

LaKiesha N. Laws

Drunkard's Dream No. 44

Beyond the hissing lamppost, on the ground floor of a haze,
I watched while Paddy Nunzio polished up his blade,
At the corner of Tenth and Torment,
in the early seeds of morning,
he smiled while he stroked the edge and
reached down for more bourbon.

In an alley way of brick and mortar,
where our shadows scraped the wall,
and the rats crawl with impunity while
a cat lurks down the hall,
Paddy plunged his spruced-up shiv through
a murky swath of darkness,
carving a sliver of night from there, clean,
and passing me the carcass.

I snatched it up with sheer aplomb,
gazed down into the hole
Paddy made with his well groomed blade,
and saw a raging rum river of gold.

Charlie Burnett

I Think, I Think, I'll Think

I think, I think, I'll think,
If I think I think I'm gonna think,
Then I'll think and think and think,
When I think and think and think,
I'll be a thinking Thinker.
To become a Thinker, I must think and think.

I'll be a Thinker and think things out,
To understand what things are about,
We all should think before we act,
To avoid mistakes and over react,
As a Thinker I won't stop there,
For a Thinker can go anywhere.

Ryan Wood

Reflections

Black and white pictures scattered on the table
Shattered memories lay clearly unfolded
Stone cold portraits of what use to be
Inscribed messages left to read

Heart warming thoughts fade to ashes,
the urn she loves so much.
The sentimental song that makes her cry
Tattered home, living alone
Her family's gone, all on her own

She let time come to a crashing halt
Just to relive the moments.

Michele Minute

Behind the Waterfall

Light diffuses sharply through the wall of roaring water.
The thundering roar stings my ears.
As I grope, my searching fingers touch cold, wet slime.
Musty dirt particles seep through cracks and scratch my nose.

Through the wavy shroud I can dimly
Make-out the shapes of the moving world beyond:
Two people hand-in-hand;
They smile at the sky.

Music filters through, thrilling my ears,
Vibrating inside my body and mind.
Strange echoes bounce off every corner of my cage.
My soul hungers for the world

Beyond the Waterfall.

But the dull, monotonous roar has raped
Me of my energy and vigor and passion.
I strain to see the distorted world beyond,

And just as I separate one vision from another,
The Foggy Mist violently smears them again . . .

I am trapped
Behind the Waterfall.

Lois E. Phillips

Untitled

Countless sweet kisses and soft tender glances
murmurs of love, we plighted our troth
undying faithfulness, forever true
we wandered sun-setting beaches,
drew our names in wet sands
never quite dreaming or fearing the chill
of Autumn that o'ertook us, so sudden, so soon,
as we lay below heavens, gazing up at stars
in velvety darkness we ne'er sensed the gloom
and so Winter crept in, careful and clever,
sharpened claws tearing, leaving hearts torn asunder yet
battered and bruised, we clung to each other
steady and sure, but Winter was cunning,
she sent Spring and past the next Summer,
Autumn awaited, while Winter stood patient, gnashing
her teeth and thrice we battled, successfully
forcing her strength to the side and yet into the
fourth fray, Winter conquered, destroyed us
a love ever eternal, for all seasons, all reasons,
not separated by death but by discovery of life . . .

Ann Lamb

Grace

To my Mother
My mother is warm and kind
to help me out when I'm in a bind.

She loves and gives me all her best
but never takes out the time to rest.

She could not predict what my future would hold,
but took a chance that my choice would be gold.

My mother will hope that I inherit
all the treasures that will give me merit.

As she gives her love and support each day,
I just admire and respect her in every way.

Good times or bad, she is always there
even when I'm not aware.

All the dreams, hopes, and prayers
to the Lord for your family
is your one and only true reward.

Ann Scotto

If

If the sun shines brightly in the morning,
There should not be any mourning.
If it rains in the morning there is a lot to gain,
But then again, a lot of pain.

Most people like their days sunny and bright
With lots of light.
Some lovers like the night,
But still others would rather have the light.

If there is snow, think of all the glow.
If there is a lot of ice, it is not very nice.
If you have a nice lady to hold
Then you will love the cold.

If you wished there were more lakes around,
Then you would never be in town.
If means there is hope
And not just a lot of dope.

Stephen Berbes

Unicus Veritatis Amor Reliquiae

To wish a violent death upon someone
is far more courteous than betrayal.
It is not easy to trust anyone
when humanity gives such grim portrayal.

Love unfaithful and infidelity,
by-products of misguided affection;
so that a guiltless soul seeks clarity
amidst scars and wounds that ooze infection.

The fault of not knowing truth from cheap lust
can be a danger, but over and above,
it injects seeds of anger and mistrust
into a heart that wants only to love.

One need not administer these senseless pains.
For it is true, only honest love remains.

Allen L. Hall

Desert War

War means destruction and death,
the world turned upside down in a mess,
Operation Desert Shield has become Desert Storm,
Air defense, taking form;
ground forces checking their guns,
to all who know, War is no fun.

President Bush gives Saddam his "High Noon" ultimatum,
scud missiles, patriots, fire works, fighter bombers,
P.O.W. interrogated, paraded, threatened as human shields,
sorrow, sadness, their families must feel,
Some say Saddam Hussein, is really Saddam insane,
The treatment of P.O.W. is a crime;
Saddam feeds United States a line.

Patriotism, togetherness, long live the Red, White and Blue,
freedom for all is well over due;
Desert Shield, Desert Storm, America at War.

Kathleen Johnson Breakfield

Anniversary

Many years ago today a man and a woman joined together
and they prayed.

Our mighty Lord in heaven above, I come to you not
in purity by in love.

I have no shame our mighty one nor guilt I love this
man and how he felt, and what I have done I will do
again where there is love there is no sin.

It's with a man and woman that life begins, and only
in death will it end.

Candace Arebelo

My Only Place of Contentment

To An Angel
Close your eyes and dream with me;
to a place where no one can go but you and me.
In darkness, the wishing stars go by with a sigh;
and their dust gives us hopes and we can fly.
Beyond forever, where there is no never;
you'll forget all ever and we'll smile together.
I can help you through, but only if you want me to;
I can keep these dreams alive for you.
Just ask me and together we'll be;
just you and me in eternity's space between.
It'll take away life's hurt and pain;
and then you'll return for just one more day.
If the hurt never goes, around me your arms can close;
and I'll take you to dream once again.

Susan Noe

Me

To be or not to be me
Comes pretty naturally
As one can see
Through these eyes of glimmering light
Makes me wonder, what's going on with me, tonight
For my mind is that of a thousand parts
And it is up to me to know me from my heart
For no one else has the insight to see
All that comes to them from me
Me, me, me, me, me
That's all I can think about can't you see
For without me thinking of only me
What a wasted life mine would be
So you see how selfish I am about me
Because my world would not exist,
If it wasn't for me.

William Patton

Lost Love

It was mid-November
But the year I can't recall.
When I lost the one I love so much,
My mother the princess of all.
I was too young to remember what actually
Went on, but all I know is I never
Thought this dreadful day would come.
Maybe I should turn the tables
And ask this question to you; have
You ever lost someone you loved
And your love for them was true?
One day you're together and then
The next moment death appears.
But the only advice I can give is never forget,
Try to move on and wipe away the tears.

Felicia Thompson

To the Lost

All is lost many dead
Bodies scattered among the debris
They were once the ones we held for comfort in our tears
But are now crumpled bodies charred and soaked in blood
We cry for them
All is lost, buildings destroyed
The pride of our land desecrated to nothingness
Life smothered in black ash and smoke
Hell burns upon our spirits
We cry for them
All is lost, she is drowning
Our Lady Liberty broken to dust
Her truth once guided us beyond defeat
Never more have we felt her flame of hope burn within us
She cries to us
All is lost yet we listen and begin again

Megan Street

Lithium Blues

Running feet kiss the dew-ridden grass,
As the ground vibrates below them.
Pitter, patter in time to that beat
Pounds the heart that wants to free them.

Awh! Stop to gaze upon the root system
Of that big ol' maple tree.
Breathing heavily, taking in those deep hues
of more nature, and for free!

Onward toward the spiral of the mountain
That seems so impossible to reach.
Adrenaline rising to help you lift your feet
In anticipation of learning what it has to teach.

The drive of knowing that there is more to learn
Will turn your head; you'll see it point blank!
That long spiral up the mountain you must take
One step at a time; so as not to reach a blank!

Once you reach your destiny so high,
You'll see more than what surrounds you looking down.
It will make you gasp with each new breath
And lead you on with more space than going down.

Cecilia Eckerson

I want

I want to hold you with my life.
I want you to want me with all your might.

To not know where I end and you begin.
To be so very close to you that I can drink you in.

I want your hands around my breast
And to roam my body on a desired quest.

I want to feel your hands real slow,
As you move across my threshold.
Then slip your finger deep inside,
To discover what is yours and mine.

I want our heated energies to rise
And perform the dance of our passion fire.
And as our bodies ebb and flow,
I want us to feel God's presence grow
Until we enter that heavenly space,
Filled with ecstasy and grace.

Then while our spirits float gently down,
Our souls will feel warmth wrapped around.

Melting our hearts together as one,
Deepening a bond that cannot be undone.

Sarah O. Usher

It's a Miracle

In traveling through our lifetime
We accept the things we see
And things that we can't change, we let it be
Our day to day routines
We take for granted it seems
And the miracles that transpire, they're our desires
Concentrate on actions that you see taking place
And store your thoughts in order as you retrace

If your heart is clear and your actions are sincere
Results of what you do will come directly at you
The blessings you receive are the rewards of your deeds
And the requests that are asked
It's a miracle when it comes to pass

You'll experience for yourself
The wonders of what is felt
And all your doubts and fear will disappear

Sheron Regular

Adrift on the Sleeping Sea

*Dedicated with thanks and appreciation
to the words and music of Kate Bush*
Adrift . . . Receding.
Buoyant in the darkness . . . A sleeping witch.
Floating beneath the surface of a frozen river.
Dreaming of sheep while a blackbird is condemned to death,
its flight impaired by the stone tied to its leg.
Watching from a distance, the person I am yet to implores
"Please don't kill me for I am not yet born."
Reach beyond the surface of the cracked mirror.
Break through . . . Sink . . . or swim for shore.
Get out of the water.
The little Earth floats in the universal sea.
Through the haze of the early morning fog . . . I awake.
The dream fades.
I am lifted from the tempest to the brilliant light above the horizon.
I love you better now.

Paul Clough

Young Life

Delightful, young personalities often misunderstood.
Such a beautiful tapestry you are weaving out of life.
An inspiration when I work and rest.

It is your smiling face, vibrant spirit that speaks refreshment to me.
A song you sing, your distinctive voice echoes in my memory.
Your delicate fingers touch the piano keys,
commanding to unveil the sweetness of your soul.
Beautiful artworks created by your hands hang proudly
in the gallery of my heart.
Words expressed on a page reveal a heart to be treasured.

Young life, inspiration, sing your songs.
Play with expression your piano and flute.
Let your words touch paper when your heart longs to speak.
You are a great treasure.

Luann Jones

Beautiful Sunsets

Two months long I have lived here
I came to work to aid the needy
The days are hot, the air dry
And those I came to help, often violent
Yet with all the aggravation,
There is a part of the day that holds true peace
The sun settles with an explosion of voices
Each is different
They speak, sing and dance themselves into exhaustion
My private audience is short, for soon
Lovely Luna and Venus join to watch the final act
And with the sun's last words, Venus and Luna are joined
By their sisters and brothers
Together they watch over a silent earth
Soon I will leave this barren and violent land for the comfort of home
But the sound of my beautiful sunsets will follow only me

Robert L. Harden Jr

Out in the Night

Out in the night where only moonlight,
is shining through the clouds.
A mouse will scurry in a hurry to reach
his house in the trees.
The trees will sway in a way
to make them look like their dancing.
The dancing stars, over the cars,
skip through the dark night.
As a Mom is finishing a book,
a child takes one quick look
before he is sent to bed.
Out in the night where only moonlight
is shining through the clouds.

Abbey Smith

The Best People on Earth

Your family are the people who care for you
They shelter you, comfort you, and love you too

When you feel sad
They make you feel glad

On trips and vacations you have fun with your family
And even if you fight with your siblings, you'll see

When you get older you'll appreciate them
When they're around you you'll feel like a gem

Because if you don't see them regularly
And if they live over many oceans and seas

It will be nice to have them with you
And they will be thinking the same thing too

Two people who have unending love for you, are your mother, and father
To them you'll never be a bother

The most important thing in the world to me
Is my loving and caring family
    Timothy Berardo

Children of the Sun

Do you know what love is?

It is pain and joy all wrapped in one;
Like rain and rainbows

Sad and mournful drops pelter down like knives;
But when the sky is ever clear again, a rainbow appears

Happy and bright rays of colorful light make you smile
As does love, which also makes you cry like a storm cloud on a dark, depressing day.

There are times when the one you truly love is the best things in your life,
But then there are times when the pressure of commitment brings you this boredom and insanity
because you want to be young and free,
But you don't want to lose your love

Follow your mind with all it's anger and oppression;
Of follow it down the winding path of joy and security,
But never let it out of your reach,
Never let love possess you like it did me
    a child of the storms

God's Little Angel

Sister, little sweet sister, we'll miss you oh so much!
The world just won't be the same without your smiling touch.
You are a Little Angel sent from God above,
Filled with so much caring, and a special kind of love.
God tenderly placed you here on earth, and I'm so sure He knew,
Just how much we would benefit from knowing and loving you.
But you endured so much more than anyone could ask,
Your life down here, Little Angel, was no simple task.
The lives you touched while you were here just cannot be counted.
The hearts you warmed with your smile, continually increased and mounted.
Then God looked down and said, "Enough, it's time to bring you home.
Through the flowering meadows of heaven, without pain you now can roam."
So now, with tears, but acceptance, we know that we must part.
Though you will have left us in body, you will always live in our hearts.
Happy eternal life, Little Angel.
    Merry Miller Hinrichsen

Wind in the Night

O wind in the night,
With your weird woo,
What do you tell me?
Are you lonely and blue?

O wind in the night,
With your sounds and moans,
Have you come far?
Are you wondering alone?

O wind in the night,
With the deep mystic air,
Do you yearn for someone
To share your solitaire?

O wind in the night,
With your ghostly whistling,
Are you alone?
No, I'm here listening.

Listening, but not lonely,
Just loving your song,
O wind in the night
Our God is on His throne.
    Eunice Graham

Reminders of a Dance Long Done

Gray cold days with chilling breath,
Bare stark trees as sentries stand,
O'er a world grown still, feigning death,
On an empty haunted land.

A cold pearly blanket wraps the earth,
Snow laden limbs that bow so low,
A ramshackle house with a long cold hearth,
Fading memories of a fireplace glow.

Varied greys of unwanted scrub,
Rolling gold of uncut grass,
Skeletal remains of an old wash-tub,
A crackle under foot of long broken glass.

A weathered swing hanging by one chain,
Rusted . . . clinging . . . soon to fall,
From a withered limb seeming to blame
Its circumstance on all.

The empty promise of the sun
Sweeps across a silent crystal sea.
Reminders of a dance long done,
Orphaned memories yearning to be free.
    James F. Camp

God

God.
Is He real or just a myth?
Only your faith can decide that.
Do you believe in Him?
Is He what we expect Him to be?
Omnipresent?
Is He there when we need Him?
I think He is everywhere.
We talk to Him when we pray.
He comforts us when we are:
Alone, sad, or we just need a friend.
Is He a father as well as a king?
We are His children,
Yet we worship Him.
He loves us like a father,
Yet He is as powerful as a king.
God.
Is He real or just a myth?
Only your faith can decide that.
Do you believe in Him?
    Elisabeth Wood

The Mirror

Wow!
Now there's a guy who know's about class . . .
Look at him lying there all macked out.
Not a single strand of hair is out of place.
It's as if he never moved and will remain like that always.
Complexion tight without a smile, hands folded, and body peaceful,
It is as if his heart took a break only to begin again somewhere else.

"Don't worry. Your soul is about to depart on a trip.
It's not gone yet. I'm still here."

It's growing cold now.
You're fading to white.
Please don't leave just yet?
Everyone I know has traveled from afar to see you.
Let me stay a few minutes more.
I realize I must carry on, but this can't be the end.
It's just not fair!
The next time I see myself, it will be in another mirror.

Mark Evan Feldman

Hair Rage

Over-curled, over-colored, over-permed, oppressed
Cut, crimped, curled, and braided
Not to be a bob or a style that's belated
Weaves, tracks, and invisible braids
Remove all that's fake, keep it on the real
Dreadlocks, spiral curls, silky dreads, French rolls
Uncover the individual, hide the original
Wraps, flips, sets, and plaits
Duplicate life, sort out the nappy
Coarse, thick, frizzy, and beady
Separate us from the outside world
Curly, wavy, straight, and pressed
Cause us to wish and wonder and envy
Damaged, split, uneven, broken off
Give us a reality check, tell us what's wrong
Repaired, redone, touched up, and retrimmed
Give us hope, and prepare us for the end.

Damien Carter

A Love Lost

Love is a wonderful thing,
yet love can bring so much pain.
My heart is full of longing for you;
my heart aches to be with you.
I glance into your bright blue eyes, searching for warmth and love;
I glance into your heart and soul, hoping you can find love in me.
Everyday is full of agony, pain and love,
while I wait to hold you in my arms.
My eyes look longingly to you, full of endless love and admiration,
yet my heart remains empty because you're not by my side.
Age does not stop Cupid's arrow from piercing my heart,
for love knows no boundaries, such as a mere age difference.
Love is all around us, yet we still remain apart,
together in our quest for love; alone when it comes to love.
A face full of youth, a heart full of maturity,
your lips, alive with passion, always speak the truth.
My heart belongs to you—and your heart belongs to me—
but for now, we still remain apart—a love lost.

Michelle Mostovy Elsenberg

Unnoticed

She steps out of her shy world and looks around.
The trials have caused the wrinkles that wind around her face.
She looks so old from the emotions she never shared.
I watch as she desperately tries to reveal who is there in the mirror.
Identifying herself as someone,
A victim of judgement from the outer world.
Peaceful in every movement,
she settles herself down in a corner.
Unnoticed, she starts to think of the memories that are
"So there" from years passed.
I know she cries herself to sleep at night,
But nothing is said.
She remembers the songs she used to sing
and the way her daddy used to say,
"I love you." She turns away and crawls back into her shell,
Unnoticed, and with every bit of gentleness in her step.
She gets up out of the corner and moves on
as if she were never even there.

Elizabeth Metcalfe

Runaways

Is it problems at home? Are they confused?
Some run away 'cause they've been abused.
They run from the fire and into the pan.
Where the real world doesn't give a damn.

It uses them like trash, then throws them away.
A lot are still missing, even today.
And the families don't know if they're alive or dead.
They go to the kids' room and see an empty bed.

Please help before it's too late.
There's so many runaways that the world wants to rape.
And many kids are murdered, some suicide.
Think about the ones that have already died.

They went through Hell and didn't return.
It's time to stop, listen and learn.
Talk to your children about the problems in their head.
'Cause if you don't, then they might be the next runaway
That the cops find dead.

Stephen D. Watts

The Sailor at Sea

A sailor is gone out to sea,
surrounded by people as lonely as can be.
The secret thoughts that are on his mind,
are his wife and children left behind.
He endures every hour along the way,
keeping in mind he will be home one day.
To pull along pier side and see their faces,
can not hardly wait for their warm embraces.
It is hard to be gone for a month or longer,
but distance makes the heart grow fonder.
Today the sailor is going home,
he will no longer have to be alone.
He is packed and ready then his heart pounds,
as he watches the brow being lowered down.
Listening closely to the one M C,
waiting for what seems an eternity.
Waiting for that magical sound to fall,
then it happens; "Liberty Call!"

Christopher G. Bowser

Visualize

You have allowed me to fool you into believing
that the reflection of light in your eyes is my wholeness
You look right at me but cannot see the hurt behind the facade
the pain underneath the carefree
Don't you realize that sometimes the visual lies
that it can be manipulated into what the heart wishes to hide?
But here I am, right in front of you like so many pieces
of shattered glass, I lay exposed confronting my demons,
trying to make sense of my past.
It's been so long that I don't know my fact from my fictions.
Wide eyed innocence, replaced by deliberate contradictions,
The balance has been distorted to the point that even I can't tell.
Should I let you in, do I dare unlock the door to my personal hell?
To let you see that which has been concealed for what seems a lifetime,
My truths that you never knew,
My fears that have kept me out of your view,
My love that just ates and grows for you—it's all right—
They're vulnerable and undressed
If you will just look with your heart
And see with your mind my realness.

Anthony L. Davis

The Tornado

I was without hope, void of feeling or thought when out of nowhere,
reaching into the very core of my being, the tornado claimed me.
Without warning, it drew me up from my stillborn existence and
ripped me into a million pieces, absorbing me into its winds.
I was the tornado! It was me! Swirling, twirling, ever faster and
faster, drawing thru me again and again the essence of my being.
I was ecstatic, soaring beyond all limits for a glimpse of life's meaning.
The winds increased to an incredible speed sweeping thru me
the profound and trivial bits and pieces of existence from time immortal.
Spun from these winds of chaos and confusion emerged
understanding that defies expression—a "knowing" beyond
words. As unexpectedly as it claimed me, the tornado gently
released me, formed into a new being and returned to the earth's care.

April L. Powers

There Is a Time to Cry

For all of us there is a time to cry;
For all of us there is also a time to die.
My willingness to be the best that I can totally be,
Will give my soul the okay to soar like an eagle and forever be free.
Once we accept the challenge of an exhausted sigh,
We will find, that there is always a time to cry.
My father from up above, please teach me about true love.
Father, help me to get from the burning fire;
help me achieve the life I so desperately desire.
There is a time to cry, but for some a time to deny;
Love, life, death.
I bequeath myself to grow and to fight
And I'm forever, patiently waiting to take flight.
I wait and I so hardly try,
And I'll never forget there is always a time to cry.

Jason Scott Rand

Sunshine

I have a secret friend, I see again and again.
At night my friend comes out and smiles at me from the moon.
When I get scared she sings to me:
I see you there dear, do you feel me near?
I swear it will be soon,
But until I will continue to sing to you from the cover of the moon.
I dream of sunshine all through the night
And until I hear the Rooster's crow.
The day goes by fast Sunset at last.
I sit on my swing in the garden and watch the setting sun.
"Um, hello. " I turned around to see a girl whose face I didn't know.
Her hair was brown, her eyes blue and skin as white as snow.
Oh, how she looks familiar, but who could she be?
Wait a minute, now I know, Sunshine you found me!

Cassandra Ray

Use Me Lord

Use me Lord, day and night;
Fill me with your love, power, and might.
Use me to the fullest; I won't be ashamed
To worship and magnify your holy name.
Let my actions express how much you mean to me,
And allow your light to reveal what I see in thee.
Lord, I will give up all to be by your side;
'Cause the love I have for you, I just can not hide.
Lord, use me as your servant,
Your riches and glory to gain;
For the steps that you order in my life
Shall not be in vain.
Lord, I'm willing to be your sacrifice
To reach every woman and man;
Obedience and honor I will vow
To fulfill your holy plan.
Use me Lord to exalt you up high,
For you are worthy to be glorified.
Lord, here I am on humble knees
With one request, "Would you use me please?"

Twyla C. Miller

I Wish

I wish I could feel you,
with my hands and feet.
I wish I could see you,
as your presence,
would make my life complete.

I sometimes imagine
us being together,
and nothing seems
more real,
than us lasting forever.

I wish you could be here,
with me in my room,
as everyday without you,
is filled with gray and gloom.

My thoughts are not clear,
though my feelings seem so true,
and my heart aches,
as I am without you.

Crystal Rodriguez

Arbol

sunny sidewalks with magnetic gait
over corduroy shoulder
a monster companion awaits
stretching one motionless,
horrible thumb
over hot-to-the-touch concrete aisles
blue green gray wizard cripple handshake
stretching perpendiculars
over railroad ties:
subsonic perfect motorized.

On behalf of the workday,
let me apologize to you,
the gnarled fruit of a tangled earth:
I could stop and extract your
beauty for instant analysis
I really should
Blame it on the heat
and blame it on the short distance
between here and home.

Thomas Staley-Trull

The Wind Blows

The wind blows with her lips
Pressed like rose petals

The bloom has begun
And whispers of infinite love
Are in times mystery . . .
Invisible to the silence
Yes, the echo is loud.

My heart is filled with a knowing
A tone that is eternal.
Once again I find myself in
Black velvety richness
The space of all is-ness.

She's the voice that has answered my call
"Hey intimacy," I ask,
"Will you still be my friend?"

And the wind blows with her lips
Pressed like a rose
For I now surrender to the light, a glow.

Sharyl Noday

The Beauty of Love

Unseen visions of beauty
Unspoken words of tenderness,
Heartwarming goodness,
Your ears cannot hear.

Joy unspeakable Joy,
Unimaginable Happiness,
Indescribable kindness,
Your eyes cannot see.

Incredibly beautiful feelings
Pure and honest kindness
With wholesome goodness,
Your hand cannot touch.

An authentic and real emotion,
Full of tender-loving care,
A beautiful and wonderful feeling,
With an everlasting impression.

Unbelievable compassion,
With a never ending forgiveness.
And unthinkable touch of kindness,
Which can only be felt with the heart.

Les Grandberry

The Old Man

He was old. No doubt about it.
He agreed, and that helped out.
He'd held his youth past sixty years,
with mountains, ocean, fields, and streams,
birds, beasts, and flowers his friends.

He skied the Silver Belt and climbed
the Matterhorn and Western peaks,
He kayaked rapids, roaring rivers,
surfed the wind and played the surf,
enjoyed a life that most would shun.

In time, his strength and vigor ebbed,
pileups, heart blocks, gut knots, cancer.
He mourned his inactivity,
bemoaned his unrelenting fate.

His rescue came (to his surprise)
as love from friends and family
brought joys his macho life had missed.
No more he bowed to boats and skis;
old age became his loving friend,
despite its stalking unawares.

Earl D. Oliver

On a Midsummers Night Dream

It was on that night,
Unusual as it may seem,
How it fell upon me,
On a midsummer's night dream.

I crept into the valley,
And jogged along the stream,
As I watched my reflection,
On a midsummer's night dream.

As water fell on me,
A non-scented cream,
That seemed to touch me,
On a midsummer's night dream.

And then it hit me,
That glowing beam,
Rising me to the Heavens,
On a midsummer's night dream.

Brian Riegel

Imminent

(You are)
A pause before speaking,
one breath taken
in anticipation of thrill;
coming into your own
like a sweet flower blooming:
a wave cresting shortly,
dark clouds growing thunder . . .
as the earth before dawn
is mountain under shadow
and mighty seas at rest,
so are you too, dreaming
one moment before glory,
like the sun about to break darkness
into morning, streaked with light.

Amy L. Matiska

My Pretty, Blue-Eyed Girl

She used to be so sweet and fair;
Her eyes were blue and gold her hair.
She laughed and sang and bounced her curls;
My pretty, blue-eyed girl.

Now she has grown and changed her ways;
No longer so innocent; wastes the days.
She dyed her hair black,
And turns her back,
My pretty, blue-eyed girl.

She loves to talk about boys,
And never plays with her toys.
She's gotten contacts: colored brown,
And is the hit of the town.

But to me she is not so good anymore;
I want back my beautiful blue-eyed girl.
She's always insulting, and is no longer
My pretty, blue-eyed girl.

Eliza Dreier

My Bed

My bed is an ugly monster,
It eats up all my toys,
It can even eat up me.
Or some other girls and boys.

Sometimes it eats up my sheets.
And then it spits them out,
I am sure that it's my bed,
Surely with no doubt.

Cody

My Pet

A grey and beige
Ball of fur
Uncurled and stretched
Upon the floor.

She blinked, yawned,
And licked her paw,
When bam! She leapt,
At what she saw.

She followed the way
A ribbon moved, invading her space,
She crouched, pounced,
And caught the ribbon lace.

Purring triumphantly,
The queen tore at her prey,
Stopping suddenly,
As it was whisked away!

Furious that her prize
Was snatched from under her nose,
She mewed, made as if to rise,
But instead went back to her doze!

Amber Pearce

Indifference

"Are you dying?"
I asked calmly, flatly, coolly.
Cool as the ocean
Waving and lapping at the dock
Covered with moss and fungus.
Two eyes staring longingly, desperately.
Pleading, with no words.
The eyes close.
Bubbles erupt from the depths.
Are you dying.
Maybe I should have done something.
Maybe I should have cared.

Laura Pliskin

Despair

Dark clouds are moving across the sky,
The fog drifts softly in.
My heart feels heavy with the gloom
Depression settles in.
The wind is blowing from the North.
It chills my soul to core.
Where is the sun?
Where is the bliss?
I have been here before.
Then tiny ray of timid sun
Appears and pales again
Maybe there's hope?
Maybe there's joy?
But first it has to rain.

Irene L. Ocwieja

The Days of Wine and Roses

The days of wine and roses
have long since gone away,
today the only thing some people know
is hate and disobey.
If only we could bring back
a little tranquility;
This world would be a better place
to raise a family.
God please speed that chance to us,
as fast as you can do.
Before there is no world left,
to hand down to our new.

Deborah A. McGinnis

Sleep

"Life is like a good slumber
It may be full of letters
It may be full of numbers
Or even something better"
"Sometimes they are good
Sometimes they are bad
But you'd want good if you could
Or maybe even sad."
"Sometimes it goes your way
Sometimes it goes the other
You can never really say
Or it can even smother"
"So dream your life away
And keep the nightmares at bay."

Brian Reis

Stolen Moments

Our affair was one of beauty
When we met on darkened streets,
Each anticipating moments
We would share in private suites,

Who remembers how it started?
It just seemed to fall in place,
With a glance and playful twinkle
And a passionate embrace,

Naked bodies gently swaying
To a song no one could hear,
Moonbeams dancing to the rhythm
Two hearts beating without fear,

Lips that touched with gentle sweetness
Fingertips that thrilled,
Eyes that locked in loving gazes
Promises we had fulfilled,

Embracing arms that yearned and hungered
For stolen moments we now shared,
As fiery passion consumed our bodies
We were lost without despair.

Shirley Nesom Guerrero

Winter

Winter comes when trees are bare
and the wind blows cold air.
Firewood chopped,
all animals have hopped
into hibernation.
Oh, the exasperation!
Snow drifts in and out.
Children shout.
Oh, winter has come!

Sarah Ograbisz

How Does Love Speak?

Love speaks in quiet sweet tones,
And in words unexpressed,
Love speaks in movements
Without the symphony being played.

Love speaks in the quietness
Of a still small voice
That causes two hearts
To beat as One!

"And after the earth-
Quake a fire; but the Lord
Was not in the fire, and after
The fire a still small voice"
(I Kings 19:12)

Eva M. Thomas

Positive Thinking

My dad once told me
Who I could be
If you put your mind to it, said he.

I may not be the best
But I try harder than the rest
Can I make it?
Yes!

August Weideman

Appreciation of Two

It was a hot mid's eve,
the precious type of night
that you soak up as
much as you can, the
eve that releases your
spirits makes you free.
Moonlit gentle breaks
in a distant body of
water, water you
long to bathe in, the
smell that's so familiar,
wanted, cherished and
praised the rare times.
We've touched and swam in
it, I love these times forever.

Kevin F. Seymour

How Can I

How can I see.
The stars in the sky.
When you're not by my side.

How can I sleep.
A peaceful night.
When you always on my mind.

How can I hear.
Any one talk.
When you're always in my thoughts.

How can I eat.
Breakfast, lunch or dinner.
When my stomach is in knots.

How can I do anything.
When you walk by me.
And smile that beautiful smile.

How can I be you're one and only.
Always and forever.
If you push me away.

Oliver Hugh Martin Jr.

Untitled

You say you'd like to be a trout
With nothing at all to worry about
Consider seriously this notion,
Before you take the magic potion.
From fingerling to adult size.
The trout is always someone's prize
His finny brain he must keep sharp.
Or he'll be eaten by a carp.
He dare not dart from 'neath the moss,
Or he'll be doused with tartar sauce.
If for a fly he has a yen,
He's soon a trophy in the den,
With gaping mouth and rigid pose.
This puts an end to all his woes.
Just think of this I'm sure you'll doubt.
You'd really like to be a trout.

Doris M. Humpal

Mopar Man

October 16, 1996.
That's the day
I locked my
soul in a box,
refusing to care,
refusing love.
And what happens?
It didn't work.
I left that damn
box at home
in Pittsburgh.
I flew to
Philadelphia to see
a friend from New York.
I looked into his
eyes and I knew—
he broke into my
tiny apartment and
stole that box for
17.2 hours.

Angela Velnich

Final Destination

I look beyond the outer man;
deep within he hurts.
His soul cries with anguish;
he tries to escape
Only to be suppressed again.

I look beyond the outer man;
someone answers him now.
Is it friend or foe?
He tries to escape,
only to be suppressed again.

I look beyond the outer man;
he is sorry he was born.
He thinks he should have stayed silent;
he is betrayed,
only to be suppressed again.

I look beyond the outer man,
he is taking his last breath.
God has him by the hand;
he has escaped,
never to be suppressed again.

Dondrew C. Gibbons

The Giver of Peace

When tumults overshadow me,
And I cannot find my way;
When troubles bend my spirit low,
And all the world seems gray.

The only path that I can find
To chase the gloom away, is
Go to Christ, and bare my heart,
As I humbly kneel and pray.

I take to Him my troubles;
I ask Him for His help.
He takes my hand and lifts me
When I cannot help my self.

He is my strength, my comfort,
When I'm burdened with despair.
If I take the time to go to Him
I always find Him there.

He calms my fears, He gives me peace,
And shows me how to cope.
He dries my eyes, and cheers my heart.
He is my Greatest Hope.

Ina W. King

Free

When we leave our bodies
Our soul will be free
To fly up to the heavens
Where you'll be waiting for me.

I will still feel sadness
For those I've left behind
But remember I love you
Just keep this in mind.

For one day you'll be with me
And your soul will be set free
To fly up to the heavens
And there you'll be with me.

As for now go on and smile
Don't be sad and do not cry
For I am watching over you
My love will help you try.

Misty Stinson

Without Love

Without Love I am merely existing,
Marking time without purpose or goal.
I mourn and I suffer forever
Out of touch with my heart, with my soul.

Then Love reaches out to enfold me
And the longing I can't comprehend
Is replaced with a joy without measure,
My searching has come to an end.

Love asks that I trust without question,
That I follow wherever it leads.
It takes me to life everlasting
And provides me whatever my needs.

This Love is the Master, Christ Jesus.
He's the One that answers my prayers.
By His Blood He has bought my salvation;
My sin he so willingly bears.

Bowed down, I ask His forgiveness
And accept His divine gift of grace.
I enter the house of the Master
To gaze upon God's Holy Face.

Mary Sue Kafel

Fly, Fly, Fly Away

Fly, fly, just spread your wings
Far beyond the sky of blue.
Your mind is strong, your heart is true.

The love you feel inside is pure.
Forever more your life awaits.

Fly, fly, fly away. Spread your wings,
Let your life be free.

Soar above the mountains high
Glide upon the oceans deep.

The love you looked for all your life
Is waiting on the other side.

The wind that pushes you so hard
Will turn and carry you beyond.

So fly, fly, fly away
She waits for you with open arms.

You will stand alone no more,
The two of you will stand as One.

Face the wind
Withstand the storm
Paradise is yet to come.

Michelle Haack

I Am

I am an oasis in the desert,
the city by the bay

I am the heat that warms your skin,
the cold that chills the day

I am the ear ready to listen,
the shoulder that dries your tears

I am the heart that soothes your pain,
the grasp that releases your fears

I am the guide that aides your travels,
the sun that lights your trail

I am the path never taken,
the highway to your dreams

Daniel Casey

Yesterday

Our lives touched once,
so soft and sweet.
The memory is forever new.

One sweet moment in my life,
forever mine,
was shared with you.

Elizabeth Samuelson

Spring

Spring is hot.
Spring is nice.
Spring is warm
And hot as spice.

I like spring
because you see
Spring is everything
to me.

I like flowers.
They smell nice.
The different flowers of every color
seem nice and bright to me.

I like birds,
especially in the spring,
when humming birds flap their wings.

I like spring
because you see
Spring is everything to me.

Maggie L. McRea

Brown Eyes

Brown eyes, brown eyes, brown eyes.
1, 2, 3.
I have three dogs that are
Always looking at me.

Not quite sure what they want.
But those brown eyes tend to haunt.

But I guess there's no doubt.
If they could they would shout.
Will you please let us out.

Well free at last out
Having a blast.

But they know it's not going
To last.

Brown eyes, brown eyes, brown eyes.
Can't you see. They think they know
How to take advantage of me.

Monica Marie Raley

Choices

What is a choice?
It is a voice,
A child's song,
As they grow on.
Choices to care,
Choices to be,
Choices made by you and me.
Choices, choices,
More and more voices.
Using our mind,
To be kind.
When to love,
When to care,
When to be here or there.
Choices like a growing maze,
People choosing the latest craze.
Not caring to see
The world around us, and last of all me.

Jaime Hinrichsen

Sail On

Sail on my friend
To a place where all have tried to climb
Let your soul soar for the heavenly sky
There's a place for your spirit
Among the galaxy of stars
Let there be a wish
For the children cries
Because you departed from earth
Not with tears, but a smile
Let dominion of cherubs
Help fulfill every child's dreams
Erasing what is know to man as fear
That voices will echo throughout the clouds
With a rejoicing sound
Sail on my friend, sail on

Renee Jones

Our Cats

Small and furry they are
When they come to us as kittens,
Full of spunk, some with stripes,
Looking like they're wearing mittens.

Now full grown adults,
Surely well set in their ways,
Seem to be acting rather lazy,
Since sleeping fills their days.

Kathy Anne Tanton

Untitled

Pale, serene and shrieking silence,
waits the tomb for judgement day.
God alone know all the secrets,
held within the slabs of grey.

Carolyn M. Johnson

Happiness

The sound of water
takes me
To the woods
Its sound is so quiet
Like a bird
whistling a song
Or like rain droplets
falling down
Onto the pavement floor

Neil Hatfield

What's on My Mind

What's on my mind,
I cannot tell.
I think I'll grind,
So it will dwell.
It should be sharp,
So clear, and bright.
To tune my harp,
With much delight.

When I do play,
The angels sing.
All I can say,
Its time to bring,
Tom, Dick, Harry.
To sing the song
Here comes Carey
With bells, ding, dong.

Eugene Knaiz

Substitute Grandma

All children need a Grandma,
This was one of God's last rules,
Because yours is now an angel,
He's asked me to substitute.

My heart has overflowed with joy,
About my new position,
Because you see, God's gift to me
Was "Love without condition."

Not a day will pass now that you're here,
That my one and only goal,
Will be to see that your life is filled,
With guidance from the soul.

So know little one, that very nearby,
There's always a smile, hug and kiss,
For all the 'boo boo's' and broken hearts,
Grandmas are made for this.

Carole Malone

Kids

To watch them run to watch them play to
watch them sing along today.

To see them walk upon the road to see
them wander through a grove.

To be a part of the wonder, to share in
their joy and plunder.

To feel the power of their words in every
single thought and phrase.

To see them jump about with glee to see
them run so free.

Christopher Free

I Wonder About Her

While walking in her garden,
on a brisk spring day
I pick perfumed smelling flowers
I think about my mother
She has been gone for fourteen years
Sadness still lives in my heart
I wonder . . . did she bring me here
and sing to me?
As I grasp an undersized purple flower,
I feel her presence
My white parasol shades me from the sun
This sweet scent of flowers fills my head
Did she smell like these flowers?

Melissa Brightbill

That Lady

The lady coming toward me
From the far end of the hall
Had a dress exactly like mine.
It didn't fit on her at all.

Her hat was kind of cockeyed
And her purse looked kind of worn.
Her petticoat was showing
And its lace was kind of torn.

What can she think, I wondered
Dressed in that sad array?
I'll step aside and let her pass,
I'll keep out of her way.

But she got closer to me
And I could clearly see
That lady was a mirror.
Oh, no! That lady's me!

Kathryn M. Fisher

The Shadows of Love and Death

The Rose
Beautiful and magical
Enticing and regal
A diamond in the rough

The Thorn
And dark spot
On the beauty
Of the Rose

The Rose,
No matter how enchanting,
Still has the Thorn,
Lurking in the shadows

The Rose and the Thorn
Love and Death
Intertwined forever

Sarah Gore

Sadness

Here I am crying over you. Three
days have come and gone and now you
say we are not meant to be together. My
heart, now has broken and can never be
fixed. I am not angered I am just sad.

So much sadness is upon my
shoulders holding me down. It's like
striving for air and never finding it. The
once bright girl is now dark again. You
were my light now that you've gone it
has gone out. It's like a candle being
blown out by the wind.

Tiffany Lyn Kasper

Snow White

Once upon a time,
she slept under glass and gold
Perfect Lips
waiting for you.
Frozen until . . .

And now that you've
got her—
happily ever after—
what to do you do with her
to make her
shut up again?

Carrie Wyland

Jaime's Face

When first I glanced at Jaime's face,
He winked a dark and sparkling eye.
It touched me like a warm embrace
and made me think of days gone by.
A character from Dickens
in all his elegance and grace,
Could not show the warmth and beauty
that I found on Jaime's face.

Evelyn F. Carlo

Malady

Love is an insipid ailment
for which there is no cure.
But if there were a cure of sorts,
would I take it?

Anne Marie Warfield

The Shepherds

First came the shepherds.
The childlike always come to Him
More quickly, regardless of their age.
Wise men calculate, make plans,
Buy costly gifts, and wait,
'Til stars and signs are right.
While shepherds, trusting, travel light!
Only themselves they bring.

Anita Wheatcroft

The Kiss

I'd hoped that he would love me
and he has kissed my mouth.
But I am like a stricken bird,
that cannot reach the south.

For though I know he loves me,
Tonight my heart is sad.
For his kiss was not as wonderful,
As all the dreams I'd had.

Robin Ann Strunk Smith

Untitled

Somewhere not so far away
A little voice is crying

Somewhere on a distant shore
A child's soul is dying

In our state of self concern
Is where the fault is lying

For I know I could help this child
But I'm not even trying

Terri Sue Brown

Forget Me Not

To Daddy
He echoes through my every thought,
the memories they flow;
It's almost as though I see him there,
Standing at my door;
Those precious times, the tough ones too,
Keep running through my mind;
From the beginning, throughout my life,
Until the end of time;
Forever in my heart he stays,
and precious to my thoughts;
I hope he will always love me too,
and please, "Forget Me Not."

Rosey O'Dalaigh

Untitled

To my precious angels
I fell lost without you there
You brighten my darkness,
and wash away despair.
You are the joy in my life,
the thing that I did right.
You are the sunshine in my days,
and the stars in my night.
I'm so very glad God opened his
heart and shared you with me.
I feel I've been truly blessed,
and oh ever so sweetly.
Your smiling little faces, your
bear hugs, and kiss after kiss.
These are indeed the times,
when it doesn't get any better than this.
I just wanted you to know,
how very special you are to me.
So sleep my little angels,
And God and I will watch over you quietly.

Melanie Maples

Desert Love

Wake me, desert
With your blooming jasmine
Sweet as desire
Hold me with your twilight gaze
Night times sacred embrace
Starlit skies burn bright
Your mystic sands, wild winds carry
Aspire upon wistful ears
Sage and spice, scented ardor
Aphrodisiac of my desert love
Warm my heart
With your honey colored land
Fill this empty space
With the fruits I'm longing for
Gentle is my desert's touch
Sweetly its descent on me

Jessica Larkin

Sailing the Spice Islands

Magnificent sailing ships of the line
Their ballast laden with gold and wine

Glide across the frothing seas
Bound for spice in the island keys

Molasses, rum, tobacco and peas
A pungent odor, salt-pork and cheese

Copper skinned muscle on iron willed men
With hopes of making port again

Creaking ropes o'er turbulent seas
Topsails snap as they catch the breeze

Off sailing into gray skies destiny
beyond the horizon disappearing
Into forgotten pages of history

Paul M. Bocchetti

Untitled

The thorns,
The thorns that prick mine eyes.
Oh lover lost, am crucified.
Hammered in terrorem to wattle and daub.
Oh bearer of woes,
From felicity was robbed.
To opportune betrayal,
Insensitive lust lay ye despise.
Ye pang wear no disguise.

Shirley Pehrson

Feat

It was a hurdle,
Four feet off the ground.
It might as well have been
Twenty feet high.

It was a hurdle!
No way to go around;
Not under, nor over.
Too high! Too high!

It was only a hurdle.
One upward motion,
A step at a time.
Not, after all, so high.

Now, vault over the hurdle!
It's gone . . . it's behind!
See the standing ovation.,
Conquest is mine!

Loretta Guyan

Perfection

Perfection is the clearest call
To intelligence and learning.
It cannot be bought,
But should be sought
By all,
Especially the most discerning.

Barney L. Byrum

The Ocean

The ocean is so pretty and light
If you listen, it will talk
When you look in to it, it will look back
If you watch the ocean
It moves like a snake,
It will move, walk, and sing to you
All you have to do is Believe.

Angelica Lillie

Untitled

The first time I saw him
he looked like an angel.
Our eyes met like magnets,
Our souls wanting to become one.
I knew we were meant for each other
for he's the only one for me.
I walk around drifting back
to the time we first met.
Holding my breath and stopping my heart,
Unless I see him again!

Maria Gargiulo

Trapped

In a world of hatred,
In a world of fear,
A poor man cries out.

Thirsty for love.
Hungry for care.
He stands naked
In the eyes of his loved ones.

A lifelong maze.
With nowhere to go;
No one to run to.

Sorrow overpowers.
Drowning in his tears,
He dies.

Celeste Mott

If Evil in Between

Three goats, each thrice
Older than age two.
Each one younger than the other
Scamper around starving—destroyed—dark
Remains of rotting
Hopes. Shattered with no future
After their pasts.

Three goats feed upon
The weakest of
Hopes—prayer—until one eats well.
It grows disgustingly
Obese; eats the younger and the elder.
Alpha and omega.
Left without a beginning and end.
Starving now—out of hopes to consume,
It slowly grows weaker.
Frightened, starving:
Evil in between birth and death
Life eats itself away.

Donald J. Lee

Why Me

Why me? Why me?
Can't you see,
Everyone blames it on me.
Oooh no!
Oooh no!
Why me? Why me?
Can't you see
Everyone blames it on me.

Ashley Lauren Bland

Come Along With Me

Come alone with me, let's jump on a cloud,
A cloud waiting on the painted horizon,
This cloud, it has been reserved for us,
To take us far, far away.
From all the troubles we will ever face,
To a golden land,
With rainbows galore,
And fairies dancing by a crystal stream,
The unicorns will frolic around,
Just as happy as can be,
Go with them,
Laugh, dance, make merry, smile!
This land is carefree!
Here, you don't have to worry,
No work to do, no pains or troubles,
Just fun, laughter, and friends,
It's not your imagination,
Not even a special dream,
All you have to do is jump on a cloud,
Come along with me.

Rachel Hamilton

Still Life

Still life
Lying on a mantelpiece,

What do you know about love?
What do you feel about me?

Are you planning to stay there
Pretending to know how to live?

I made this drawing
In front of my window

And now you are
Part of me.

Arnaldo Salas

Harmony

To walk together hand in hand
Creates a glimpse of life that's grand;
It breaks down walls, it shapes the land—
Like rocks becoming grains of sand.

Removing strife can only lead
To helping mankind to succeed;
Togetherness is like a seed
That bears fruit—meeting every need.

The coward chooses not to fight,
He uses fear instead of might;
It takes real courage to do right—
To open up, and be the light.

Jane Harlow Handel

Untitled

My mind is empty
My soul is blank
Inspiration; that which guides me,
Like the wil-o'-wisp,
Has once again left me.
Death, its face so clear,
Hovers near.
But life, sweet being,
Still holds me fast.
My soul, a dried up spring,
An empty well,
Hungers to be refilled.
Where is the oasis?
In the desert of my soul.

Michael Dean Dearman

Caged Queen

The caged lioness growls
But no one hears.
They have become immune
To her snarls.
The cold iron bars are her
Fears
Tears
Stressors
And
Oppressors.
One by one they have slowly
Enclosed her into a space of
Madness.
She once was Queen of the Jungle.
Now she only whimpers for
What she has missed.

Desiree M. Berg

Untitled

A small silhouette in the universe
A child shrouded in shame
Hearing laughter from another place
In tormented and tortured silence
Can never reveal her face

Mary Pat Downing

Today

I do not often stop to remind,
Myself or others of a tragic time,
Today, I say, it makes me want to cry.
Oh the deaths that happen but we do not try
To help to save their lives'
Oh the torture but we do not strive,
And make a life that is stable. Hey!
It's going on today, today . . .

Alexandra Demshock

Sundials

Hours of glass
threaten to shatter
beneath the illusion
we call time

A fragile planet
ebbs and flows with energy
driven by One who creates

The Architect created seasons
and cessation of darkness
that we might toil
cessation of light
that we might rest

The archenemy sought to divine
to control, to seek compliance
destroying the freedom
granted by the Creator

How very sad
we allowed
another to spoil our joy
and gift us with a sundial

Anna Boatwright

Reminiscence

Strange . . .
When, in quiet solitude,
Thoughts drift back into the years
Like a rose petal
Borne by a soft summer breeze
Along a garden path.

Barbara J. Brown Barnes

Time's Awaited Relief

The hard times seemed to linger,
They never cared to cease,
Then told by you to break the stinger,
Try to find the peace.

The painful thoughts soon made me aware,
While leaving no sympathy,
My heart was left with just one tear,
And flooded with misery.

With time the wound itself will heal,
And darkness no longer be,
Soon nothing left but the scar to feel,
And the relief inside of me.

Michelle Passey

A Special Friend

A special friend is someone
Who will always mean so much,
Someone who will always care
And always keep in touch,
A special friend is almost like,
A sister or a brother,
for there are things
that you can only
tell one another.
A special friend
can help you through
on your very hardest days,
Or brighten up the good times
With their caring thoughtful ways,
That is why of all the many joys
That life could ever send,
There is no greater treasure
Than a very special friend.

Marie Boschert

Content Sorrow

I must have been mistaken
    more than ever before
I mistook your warm embrace
    for attraction, and so much more.

Shannon M. Sardelli

The Spirit Sounding

I have abandoned sight,
Though people come and go.
They live with me, I know,
But why unknown my fright?
I live for who I am,

An everlasting maze
Of nature's compromise.
The sun is in my veins.
A year of cloudy days
Is hidden in my gaze.

Brian McDonald

My Birthday!

Thank you Mother and Father
for giving me this day, not tomorrow,
not yesterday, but today!

Today you gave me the world
to explore, to experience, to enjoy.

Today, I have a family, a husband,
a child of my own,
a lifetime of precious moments
I am happy to have known.

Today, many years later,
as a daughter, as a mother, as a wife
I'd like to take a moment
to thank you for my life.

Melinda L. Hansen

Untitled

Did you ever stop to wonder
How things would go asunder
If it were not for the guiding hand above
Who upon his least desire
Could destroy the earth by fire
Or show how far extending His love

Is there such a thing as peace
Peace of heart and mind
Peace with every nation
Peace with all mankind
Yes peace is here
Peace we can find
If only we remember
Peace comes from God
And not mankind

Helen C. Reichardt

True Love

In his tiny hand,
He holds her golden hair.

Tickling his face,
As he suckles to dream.

This beautiful child,
She holds in her arms
A part of the love the share
He is everything of them,
Yet his own being.

A new soul unto this world.

Julia L. Love

The Sorrow of a Friend

My best friend was a beautiful person.
Her name was Ann.
She loved a man
Who always said he loved her.
But when they were alone,
He always seemed to hurt her.
Then one day it was too much,
And Ann could take no more.
They were alone when she wrote the note
To tell me she was sorry.
Then she took her gun,
And pulled the trigger twice,
And ended their lives of sorrow.

Crystal Cline

Echo

Blank uncurtained windows stare
From that apartment over there.
Its people left and have moved on,
Cold empty rooms now echo air.

While peeking in at emptiness
A frightening chill confronts me there,
To speak that soon my windows bare
Will softly echo nothingness
And I'll be gone . . . somewhere.

Sheila Crumpton Cobbs Barron

I Wish . . .

I wish I was a millionaire,
I wish I had a fish.
I wish I had that long blonde hair
I wish I had another wish.

I wish that I could really fly
Really, really, really high
I wish that I was really small
So no person could see me at all.

I really wish that it would snow
I wish I was in a race
Ready, set, go!

I wish I could write another poem
But I really don't have time
I wish that I could be in Rome
I hope you liked my rhyme

Emily Abrams

Ancient Eyes

Metal flecks on navy,
Pinpricks in a sea,
Pegasus and Bellerphon,
Dance and jump with glee.
Ancient eyes look down upon us,
Moving with their tide,
Seeing everything we do,
Bright eyes open wide.
In the wake of a brilliant orb,
Casting other worldly glow,
Beams and waves fall from above,
Banishing shadows far below.
Cancer, Aries, and Virgo,
Turn with their fam'lies in the sky.
Watch their arches lifting hopes,
As dreams are let to fly.
Alas, the sparkling show of splendor,
Fades with dawn's first light,
Fear not dear friend, just wait a day,
They'll soar again tomorrow night!

Christina Sears

Today

Today is near
Today is here
A new day is dawning
Every morning
The same way as before
See the sun glisten
Hear the bird's song, listen!
Today is a glorious day!

Caitlin Devlin

Questions

How many fish are in the sea,
and is broccoli really good for me?
What makes the trees so tall,
and why can't I draw on the wall?
Why is the sky so blue,
and can you help me tie my shoe?
Where does the sun go at night,
and can you help me ride my bike?
How did that cloud get way up there
and can you help me fix my hair?
What happened to the dinosaurs
and do I have to do my chores?
Why is water wet,
and are those cookies finished yet?
How did this mud get between my toes,
I'll ask Mommy. I bet she knows

Lisa L. Adams

First Snow

I've not known this place;
Fires burning everywhere,
The cold—bitter as stout,
A thousand bees sting my face,
Quickly—my hands don't work.
Which is the way?

There is no sky.
A wind built from nothing;
building,
wresting the white from my coat
like moult from a bird, yet quietly.

Quietly they lay before me;
Beneath me, like diamonds—Gods riches!
They lite upon me still.
I know He is here.
I am warm again.

The light I see ahead is my own;
I am home.
He is with me as before,
and I will sleep well tonight.

Scott Weise

Time

Time shows
When love grows
Who knows
When he will go
I'll be truthful
You will see
Then he'll tell me I am free
Oh dear love
Don't put me down
Show me that you'll come around.
If you have a dream that's new
Let me make your dream come true
Trust in me
Like I trust in you
Show me that you love me too!

Theresa Lundy

Why Should I Fear?

Why should I fear to face him,
when he knocks at my door?
Why should I hate him,
knowing he comes to do his chore?

Why should I fear and flee,
or hide and seek play?
When he comes with summons,
should I cause delay?

I do not love nor hate him,
see him not as a friend or foe,
when my savior sends for me,
I have to happily go.

As a hero on this grand stage,
I'll exit when my role is over,
leaving behind my co-actors.
I will be afraid of him never.

B. N. Shaw

Help Through the Storms

To look up into the Heavens
on a dark and dreary day
reminds us of the storms in life
and the pain some hearts will pay

Though if we look beyond the clouds
to Gods' bright shining love
new life will come into our hearts
new hope from up above

Then as we look to God with faith
and promise in our hearts
to try our best to heed His word
and from it never part

His love sustains us through it all
and brings new hope to heart
those dark and dreary days of past
from us will now depart

Evelyn M. Sorter

The Place

As I look across this field
The grass is green and the trees are still
I wonder why he made this place
I'd like to see him face to face.

For now I know the reason why
He made this place for those who die
As I read the names and dates
I know their souls are his to take.

David O. Richardson

Electricity

Zzzzap!
I'm back
100 years
TV is gone
And I am on a farm.
Get me out of here!

Gas lights have an awful smell
I think I died and gone to hell.
Get me out of here!

Computers used to rule my life
Now I have to learn to write.
Get me out of here!

America is the land of the free
Also the land of electricity
I don't think I will last
Get me out of here fast!

Nirav Doshi

Happy Day

An ominous shadow
Danced around me,
Dragging me down,
I smiled and shrugged it off.
Crushin' down the sidewalk
I was devastated by the past.
Places, faces; spaces.
I saw them here;
And over there.
A tear came to eye when I thought
I thought too hard.
The grayness transformed into sunshine,
As I shrugged
And I smiled it off.
I caught a beat,
Then a rhythm;
And I danced the shadows around.

Grasshopper Jones

A Lover's Lament

If I could be with thee my love,
For just one night alone.
'Tis all that I've been dreaming of,
To have thee for my own.

My hand doth long to touch thy face,
And press my lips to thine.
To feel the warmth of your embrace,
And know that you are mine.

My life I'd forfeit for this sake,
No sorrow or regret I'd know.
For 'tis for thee my heart doth ache,
And for thee alone I must go.

But dreams of you are all I own,
You are so far beyond my reach.
Too many pitfalls I've been shown,
That I can never hope to breach.

Laura Nunes

Dilemma

Be I myself a friend or foe
Someone to listen and still not know
Someone to hear and still not see
Be I myself thine own enemy.

Maxine Askew

The Letter

I wrote you a letter
The other day.
Full of the feelings
I never shared with you.

I reminisced, oh so sweetly,
On days of love and happiness
Between you and I.
Won't you come back to me?

I shared so sweetly
Long and forgotten memories,
For you
To remember me by.

Have you forgotten us?
All the cold nights we spent
Snuggled up in front of the fire.
Together in peace and harmony.

I wrote you a letter
The other day.
To remind you of me
And a promise you made . . .

Pamela Dickerson

Grandfather Saying Good-bye

It was in the early morning
Grandfather came to say good-bye
He sat at the edge of my bed
and there were tears that filled his eyes
We talked of all the years gone by
memories in our hearts and minds
Child don't be saddened by the news
For now I must leave you behind
He then embraced me in his arms
with his Bible held tight in hand
He sang his favorite old Hymn
saying he must leave this good land
There remains but one journey more
and in a whisper he was gone
I sat there yet thinking of him
and humming his favorite song
Take good care of this special man
I ask you—Great Spirit above
As I shall never forget him
My Grandfather whom I have loved

Lucinda Brant Zuccaro

The Warm Summer Day

The sunshine shining in my eyes
Reminds me of that warm summer day,
As I lay upon the bed of straw
With my face to the sun,
Thinking, thinking, how bright the light
Did shine on my delicate face.
A face so young and tender,
Unfamiliar with this world
Innocent, innocent, my face did cry
On that sun shining summer day.

Lillian M. Meade

The Old Man

The most in the least amount of words.
Sad things come into our lives:
Like the time I awoke without a wife.

Like the time I broke my back
And it took me ten years to get back.

Like the time my daughter was shot
And I was not.
And from this we grow.

Edward R. Barmes

The Power of Sleep

Sleep that knits up the
Raveled sleeve of care
The death of each day's life
Love labors bath
Balm of hurt minds
Greet natures second course
Chief nourishes in life's feast

Joe Kilgore

The Fury of Being Scared

I hate being scared;
It annoys me so,
not knowing what isn't in the darkness.
Oh, I hate it all—
Being scared is like a punishment
that's only for me.
Being scared is like being buried
and I feel like I'm dead.

I really have to stop being scared!

Victoria J. Winfrey

The Darkness of the Night

I'm in the darkness freezing cold
I'm in the darkness growing old
I'm in the darkness scared about
I'm in the darkness about to shout

I'm in the darkness lost astray
Will someone shine their light my way
Will someone take me by the hand
And guide me through this distant land

Creeping through the tunnel of life
Your emotions stabbing you like a knife
Will someone wipe away my tears
Will someone shoo away my fears

Now thanks to you I have the power
To grow and bloom just like a flower
And I will try with all my might
To fight the darkness of the night

Tiffany Ciesicki

A Smile to Live By

Live not in the shadows of sorrows,
try to live for the sunrise of tomorrow.
Live not in the cries of yesterday,
smile, come what may.
Live, live for the day.
Pleasure is all you have to pay.
Kiss not empty for you.
Love is all that is due.
Hugs not full of hidden spikes.
Embracing the ones just for spite.
Live not in the weeping of lost causes,
try to live by your own just cause.
Live not in what you leave behind,
try it, and what you're looking for,
you just might find.
Just try, and you might find,
a smile to live by.

Michael Daniel Muñoz

Untitled

Bosnia—War—
Skirting the facts
Old men plot and plan
To defend their illusions
Setting the course for war,
Where young men die.

T. Johanna Duenkel

A Christmas Poem

Black and white checkered tiles,
Down empty halls for what seems like miles.
High ceilings, decorative trim,
Intricate designs, lights are dim.
Glass chandeliers, hanging swing,
Lighting up everything.
Clicking heels hit the floor
Echoes ring in every door.
People fill the hallways now,
The sound of voices, clear and loud.
Spiral stairways with gilded rails,
Spicy perfumes fills the air.
Tiny lights flicker and shine,
Along the spindles in a line.
Garlands draped 'round columns tall,
People humming "Deck the Halls."
Christmas lingers in the air,
Everyone cheerful, spirits sail.
Elegant dresses, fancy food,
Christmas creates a festive mood.

Christine DeMichele

Valentines Day

Everything you say
Everything you do
Keeps me loving you
It is now Valentines
And now it is time
For you to be mine

Won't you be my . . . Valentine?

Timothy Scott Bradford

Intercession

You think you're in command of your destiny
Don't be silly be a fool
Ever live through a natural disaster
Ever with a flood had to duel?

Ever witnessed a typhoon, a tornado
Ever lived through an earthquake severe
Ever had a split second to decide
How to save those to you most dear.

Let us not brag or boast
That we are in command
Better be on a first name basis
With the one with the divine hand.

Don't expect to ignore him in your life
Then frantically appeal when in a jam
Present your resume, your introduction
Plead to become to him a lamb

Better make prayer a daily habit
Same as washing, dressing and all
Then when the need arises
He may not say, "I know you not at all!"

Florence E. Freilino

War

Constant
Never ceasing
For weapons, we use words
More powerful than the sword
Timeless, this age old battle of youth
against age
Only the strongest survive
But no one wins
Death is far superior to both

Elizabeth Eisenberg

What Is Purple?

Purple is my color
I wear it everyday
Purple are the leaves in Autumn,
When it's cold outside.

Purple is the sky,
When the sun rises so high,
Purple is my binder,
I write in it everyday.

Purple is my backpack,
I carry to school each day,
purple is like powder,
It smells like a flower.

Purple is a can of Cherry Coke
It matches Amanda's shoes,
Purple is on the Rockies' jersey,
It matches someone's hair.

Purple is the color of Love,
it makes me think of a dove
Purple makes me think of a guy
that is the apple of my eye.

Melissa Weber

Christmas Time

A blanket of snow covers the city,
And lights are shining bright,
Red, green, yellow and gold,
Are glistening in the night.

A tree is billowing in the wind,
A rustling is in the air,
A powerful gust is whirling round,
As nature says beware.

This season is a time to reflect,
On love, on souls, on purpose,
As to the future we look to unfold,
To make sense of this crazy circus.

Rosemary Saurer

Incriminating Underthoughts

My hypocrisy of worlds
is held against me now
in the courtroom I stand
to take the solemn vow.

A parliamental judge
presides over my fear
as a condescending prosecutor
screams into my ear.

Taunting me with lies
My confusions are results
He glares at me, smirks,
and I believe in my own faults.

My defense is sent to save me
to disprove all the lies
and now I come to see myself
through another person's eyes.

Julie Boom

Between Us

Look out, through the glass,
through the wall between us.
It is there to cut in two,
the love we both shared.
What can break it?
Nothing can take it
away from our minds,
away from our souls,
away from our hearts.
It is there between us,
to rip, to tear us apart,
and leave us scattered,
like sands on a shore,
like clouds in the sky,
like leaves in the wind,
forever.

Matt Money

Wonder Why

I wonder why I need you
I wonder why I believe in you
I wonder why we spend the time we can
walking hand in hand

I wonder why we were brought together
I wonder if our love will last forever
I wonder why we care so much
even about a single touch

I wonder why you're there for me
I wonder if it's possible to make you see
all the love I have for you
and all the dreams you've made come true

I Love You!

Pamela C. Carroll

Beauty of the Beast

He kills the fear
That lives inside his heart
Only to kill a foe
I will cry by his anger
But understand his pain
I reach into his soul
And find his heart
Filled with tears of joy
And inner peace
But only the beast is seen
My eyes see beauty
Through black skies
There is a light
Through horror and death
Through clouds and rain
The beauty of the beast

Jenni Enzman

Thank You Lord

I cannot thank you Lord enough
For all you've done for me,
For food, for shelter, and for love
For friends and family,
In time of sorrow you stood by
And held my trembling hand,
You wiped the tear drops from my eyes.
And helped me to understand.
Although I cannot ever know
What the future has in store for me
Your love will always see me through.
Till we meet on Paradise Shore.

Edward T. Baldwin

Love's Awakening Call

I woke up one morning and much to
My delight
The sun was shining brightly and radiant
Was its light

Why were things so different as if
I never saw
The beauty all around me just struck
Me with awe

The birds were busy eating, the pond was
Very still
I thought I'd take a better look and walked
Upon the hill

I seemed to be transported to somewhere
Far away
I felt so very peaceful like I rested
One whole day

What is it that make us notice
Things we never saw before
Why I believe it's love
Knocking on our door

Josephine Kaitbenski

Why Not Fast

It's guaranteed
The centipede
Has many legs—'tis so

What I just can't understand
With all those legs
To carry him—carry to and fro

You'd think the little fellow
Would be fast
Not slow!

Benny L. Cole

To You My Darling

To you my darling, my love, my song,
My heart sends a message saying "I long."

I long for you and your strong embrace.
Waiting to fill this lonesome space.

Throughout the day I wish you to sight,
Forgetting, you're not beside me at night.

To you Sweetheart, my life, my dream,
No greater love than this it may seem.

Except that which Christ did give,
So that you and I together may live.

He sent it to us from up above,
Knowing that it would grow into great love.

Melissa Reader

The Pipe Organ

Pipes, pipes, large and small,
Standing like a brazen wall;
Mighty monarch, staunch and strong,
Ready to sway a mighty throng.

Booming, bellowing, thundering chords;
Running, crying, screeching notes;
Tinkling, singing, ringing bells,
Dancing and playing like fairies and elves.

Drums and cymbals clashing loud—
Like conquering armies lost in a cloud,
If I had the voice of an organ too,
I'd shout to the world my love for you.

Allan Dietz Cornelius

The Daze of the Dreamer

To one day be famous
To have friends or for the ages
Like I'm living a perfect story
Life turning all the right pages
Seas of crystal waters
Mountains as far as eyes can see
Flying to the horizon
Being anything you wish to be
Perched up in the tree tops
Or swimming the river wild
Even seeing a flock of Bluebirds
While walking a country mile
Whether it's nature's wisdom
Or money that you seek
In the daze of the dreamer
All is possible life is complete

Tim Maurizzio

Daddy's Girl

I wanted to be just like you
I tried hard to fill your shoes
But when it came down to push and shove
You know I had to choose
I know I chose the wrong path
I want to get back on track
But I want to leave the past in the past
I never want to look back
You always stand right by me
You're really like a shield
You always want me to do my best
To go on and never yield
I'm Daddy's little girl
Even though I make you mad
And I just wanted to tell you
I really love you, Dad

Michelle Harshman

Rules of Love

Correct me when I am wrong
Stand by me when I am right
Think of me in the morning
Dream of me at night

Comfort me when I am lonely
Have faith in what I do
Follow me to the ends of the Earth
As I would follow you

Kiss me softly and gently
Hold me tenderly but tight
If I should lose my temper
Please do not let us fight

When you say that you love me
Say it with all of your heart
And if you truly love me
Death will not let us part

Forgive me when I am not myself
But try to understand
Just put your arms around me
And lightly hold my hand

Moses C. Lanham Jr.

The Feeling

It whispered in silently,
Floating over my head.
And into my mind.

Then silently
Into my heart whispering
And floating.

Occasionally darting out,
And back into my soul.
Yet I knew it not.
I will forever whisper outwardly,
Into the deep-blue night,
Here I am, love me, for I love thee.
At last the feeling is back.

Edwin M. Cintron

Giraffes

Giraffes are graceful
Giraffes are peaceful
Giraffes are elegant
Not like an elephant

Autumn Eve Bak

Untitled

The gateway of light,
Is only seen through darkness.
Its light shadows you.
The path is dark and twisted,
Is it confusion or fear?
Where is it leading you?
Its only pain and suffering I hear.
A feeling of imprisonment?
Where is the light? Its gone
Only darkness folds its misery around you,
Never showing face.
Its your choice of words.
You have the control, or do you?
Who shuts you up inside?
You have no voice.
You live only inside your mind,
Showing no true emotion, if you exist.
Where do you go?
Isolating yourself from others around you.
Are you in deep thought?

Heatherlynn Joyner

A Lonely Guy Like Me

I love those sad songs
They almost make me cry
Guess I'm just a lonely guy
And I'll tell you why

The jukebox played a sad song
Of the girl who set him free
And I'll bet the one who wrote it
is a lonely guy like me
The girl left him that morning
And broke his loving heart
Because he made her nervous
She told him they must part

The tune was really lovely
And the singer gave his all
It really touched my lonely heart
And almost made me bawl
Now every time I go to town
On a honky-tonkin' spree
The jukebox box plays a sad song
About a lonely guy like me

John Hank Cluff

Watching and Waiting

Restless,
Friend or foe
Look beside me
Where shall I go?

Calm,
Friend or lover
How can you choose?
Is there one, without,
The other?

Reckless,
Heart is breaking
Lost without fire
Soul is drowning
With pains of desire

Courageous,
Time is passing
We must surge on
Threatened by truth
Blinded by fear.

Colleen A. Twomey

Wings Soft As Dreams

Soft flowing clouds,
  how long it seems
Since I flew among them
  on wings soft as dreams.

Feathers of love
  and a downy of fears;
A frame of emotion
  held together by tears.

I soared in the haze
  with lovers and dreamers,
Looking down on a world
  of loners and schemers.

Then as love slowly faded,
  my wings fell apart.
Me feet touched the soil
  as I emptied my heart.

Now I walk on the ground
  'til with love my heart teems,
And I fly high again
  on wings soft as dreams.

Trudy Payne

Losing Someone Loved

I used to think us all immortal
that we would never die.
Somehow we'd miss the heaven's call
and pass our coffins by.

But I have learned the awful truth
of losing someone loved.
Now this anguish I've felt has spoke,
I too will go above.

Oh, what is there from death to gain
myself will question him,
when one so young of age is gone
how can I understand?

God has reasons I will never know
so I mustn't think him wrong.
There is a time for all to die;
it just hurts when they are gone.

Kimberly Griffiths

Terror

A long and lonely street.
No one else but you.
No idea of who you just might meet.
Footsteps behind you.
Who could it be?
Faster, faster, faster.
Are they coming for me?
What happens next is a big disaster.
He forces you on him,
He pushes you down, falling you see the limb.
A burst of pain and all the lights go dim.
Unconscious, barely breathing he
throws you in a pit.
Police find you days later.
Scrambled, horrid memories you will
never forget.

Danielle Fulmer

Journey of Life

The far side is now, near.
The mountains to climb soon.
Decisions to make, many.
The strength in love, certain.

Debra Brown

Final Choice

Be strong, strength;
No room for weakness.
Love is still here,
With images of you.

Visions, love;
From deep within the heart.
Hold me tenderly,
For there is little time.

Be brave, fear;
For which there is no place.
My heart is willing
To share your love forever.

In love, tears;
As they fall silently.
I long to have you
Show me love.

Be sure, honest;
I am the one,
The only one
Sharing your life in a special way.

Dana Y. Fiester

Over Yonder

*In loving memory of my dad, Daniel
"Dan" Lee Martin.*

A man once known years before
often known as the partier.
He was here but not no more
he lies now over yonder.

A pine tree by his grave site
put there by my grandma
fading flowers in the light
a present from a stranger.

Daddy's little girl was I
until that tragic day
they didn't force me to say good-bye.
I was real little anyway.

Now I sit and look for you
but a stone is all I see.
The sky above is all so blue
and you're still with me everyday.

I don't know why they took you
all I can do is wonder.
The memories I look through lay now.
Over yonder.

Julie Martin

A Quaint Cafe

Beside a lamp-lit cobblestone road,
A small cafe invites the eye.
Close to the window a table's set,
Enticing people passing by.

A crystal vase reflects the light,
And glasses sparkle at each place.
The warmth and cheer within the room,
The memory never will erase.

Baskets of flowers are hung outside,
Secured against the building's wall;
While sunlight streams on leaf and bud,
And dewdrops glisten over all.

Whoever enters through the door,
A magic world is sure to find;
For friendliness will bid the heart
To leave all worldly care behind.

If ever you should come this way,
To linger for an hour or two;
This quaint cafe will always be
A dreamer's wishful rendezvous.

Concetta M. Guido

The Cost

I've spent so long
forgetting your face.
Your eyes gone.

Then the snake bit.
Your eyes I saw again.
Your pain, your confusion,
I saw as real.

Then the venom struck.
Two steps, I did not get.
Up my spine, stopping my
heart, and my lungs it did clutch.

A gasp as though the last;
my innocence dead.
What betrayal has been done?
What justification has this price?

What is the cost?

Michael Owen Davis

Melancholia

With Adam and Eve came the curse,
This wretched life, this bondaged Earth,
And since that time we've come and gone,
Some here so brief, some here so long.

That God should look upon us and smile,
We walk among thorns, many a mile
And raise our eyes in desperation
To look for a sign of consolation.

The seasons change, the years go by,
Our bodies grow weak, we prepare to die.
With our Lord, looking back,
We finally realize what we lack.

Anne Roy

Darkness

As darkness falls
Across the sky
And moonlight comes
We know not why

The sun has left us
All alone
Where heat had made us
Dry to the bone

But now it's dark
Across this land
As I dig my feet
In the precious sand.

I sit and dream
Wanting to know
Why it is the darkness has to go.

In the morning
The sun will be here again
But after the day,
Comes darkness my friend

Michelle Peterson

The Love of God

If not for the love of God
Then where would I be?
Wishing I had tried my best
To spend eternity
In Heaven with the ones I love
Who have gone on to wait
For my arrival and happy homecoming
At the Pearly Gates.
For if it wasn't by the love of God
Then what is life worth living?
For me the Love of God means:
Love, peace, happiness, joy and forgiving.

Christian Wright

White Knight

I walk in silent shadow,
the dark patterned shades of grey,
knowing that black reflects no light.
And yes, chivalry is dead
upon the forever streets I roam,
but still, I offer my dead hand,
to the crying world that continues
to refuse its touch.
And now, I must know why,
even though I live in this dark world
that does not respond,
you can see that which makes sense
about this white knight in black.

Matthew Woltjer

Emperor Penguins

Six emperor penguins flowing side by side,
Each flowing smoothly with the waters tide.
The kids are wishing,
Dad would be done fishing.
They want to eat.
Shrimp would be a nice treat.
When dad gets back
They all attack.
They each have a full belly,
That wobbles like jelly.
They sit in a heap,
And then fall asleep.

Amber Dubs

Above the Clouds

Above the clouds I love to fly
No earth below I see.
But with the clouds I find
I build a fantasy.
I see castles tall
And knights if I so wish,
Or mountains very high
With yawning precipice.
Sometimes a burst of sun
Will turn the clouds to red;
A brilliant hue, and artist's dream,
To easel one is led.
When I'm homeward bound
Above the clouds for me
To dream the time away
Till loved ones I will see.

Fritz E. Johanson

The Winter Months

The sun shines so bright
But no heat comes from it
On the cold winter day
So I shelter myself
In the warmth of my lovely home
Where I lay in the dreams of others
That are not so as fortunate as I am
To be love
To be care for by others
And love and care for to others
So every morning before breakfast
And every evening before dinner
I thank the Lord for what I have
And wish for people
Who don't have what I have
To someday get
What I sometimes take for granted

LaTonya JanNell Powell

Untitled

I can't believe you are gone
And my love and life goes on and on
It hurts to think that you're not here.
You always seemed to be so near
Even though you lived far away
We went on living day by day
Then one day it came to an end
I lost my cousin and best friend
I really can't believe you are gone
And my life goes on and on
So many times I think of you
And of the things we have been through.
Good and bad we did it together
I always thought it would be forever
Then one fatal day you were gone
And my life goes on and on

Donald Branham

Darling Song

Yellow moonchild,
Groomed by the Gods;
Son of love,
Created and Recreated;
Ghost of a thousand silences,
Have you come down so long,
Have you come so far,
Have you trod these soft waters alone?

The self beyond the selves—
We are not the dead we thought we were—
Bemused by dreams,
Crushed by music,
Washed away by oceans of radiant song—
Rainbow magic
Visions, Mind dance;
Love of a thousand ages, smile of smiles—
Our now the forest, the feast, the kingship
And the ancient music of the soul.

Blake Abramovitz

My Prayer

Surround me with your arms
Dear Lord,
For I want to come home.

Shower me with your love
Dear Lord,
As i do believe in you.

Cleanse me with the blood of Jesus Christ
Dear Lord,
As I am a sinner who wants to be saved.
Amen!

Mary M. Allsup

Little Footsteps

Little footsteps
I think
I know
But you slip away . . .

Masked smiles
Empty laughter
Constant reminders
False understandings
And quiet pain
As the glimmer fades . . .

Little footsteps
I think
I know
But you slip away.
*Dedicated to all those
who desperately want a child.*

Janet Limbert Glazebrook

My Love

Once you ask God for a true heart
One that stands the test of time
To love only you and you alone
Well he sent you one mine
The love not over and the love not gone
God does listen to what you say
How can two souls now be free
When he joined them together
Before we ever meet "you and me"
He put in the stars and the heaven
Gave a pure true love that won't die
Even the angels know what God has done
No light can outshine the love in these eyes

Janice Swallows

Sorrow

The cloud turns grayer
With every heart beating step
What once is there is gone
Sorrow fills fuller hour after hour
Silence is my only friend
The walk grows longer colder and darker
Life has but one destination
The other side of reality
Getting there is the only adventure
Looking up I see the shadow of
What was once
And what is now
So I clear my head
I walk into the dark day
A loudness fills the chilly air
On lookers scream in senseless terror
And the blackness brings me home

Abigail Kelsch

The Cat and the Bat

Once there was a cat,
Who ate a bat,
No one could understand that,
For the bat was the cats best friend,
Now the cat ate the bat,
What a glorious meal,
For the bat was quite fat,
Always frightened of that,
And now all bats know,
That a cat will always eat a
gullible bat!

Aubrey Rose Norling

Clouds

Scientists say clouds are made of vapor,
but I say that they are made of dreams
or summer days flying kites
or fluffy puppies or kittens
or possibly love.
Clouds are always moving
and always changing shape.
They are peaceful
They are near God.
They are angels singing
and happy memories from the past.
When you're down,
just look up
and remember that I'm your friend.

Lindy Grone

Myself About to Faint

You left me there,
just, standing there,
myself about to faint.
Have you been this harsh all your life?

The question lingers deep inside.
It hurts me just to think,
how close we were as friends,
and me to never understand.

You used me.
We never did want to meet,
we were so far apart.
How we broke in I can't remember.

The outside world is harsh,
so it will just take a second,
for you to think how you left me there,
just standing there,
myself about to faint.

Susan Irwin

The Angel

An angel came from heaven,
And whispered in my ear
"Be very, very quiet—
Listen, and you'll hear."

So I knelt down to listen.
An soon I heard a voice
"What took you so long, my child,"
He said with rejoice.

Father and I talked and talked
"Child," He said, "I love you."
Without a hesitation,'
I said "I love you, too."

So . . .

. . . When an angel comes from heaven,
And whispers in your ear
Be very, very quiet—
Listen, and you'll hear.

Holly Taylor

Mere Words

Mere words cannot describe
the emotions suppressed inside.
Struggling to find expression
and voice my soul's confession.

Might you see through my disguise
if I gazed into your eyes?
Might you see the child within?
Would you comfort and take her in?

Might you reveal what's hidden below
exposing the love we haven't shown?
Might you whisper what I long to hear?
Would its truth ring loud and clear?

Might we dare to love again
or should we stay forever friends?
Might we yearn for what could have been
if we kept these feelings in?

Mere words will never capture
the passion nor the rapture.
So this poem I put to rest
allowing time to serve the test.

Roze Castillo

Untitled

In loving memory of Colletta Hibbett
She was walking home without a care—
there was a smile on her face
she was happy and unaware—
of what was about to take place
with her friends at her side
she was as happy as can be
with nothing to hide—
she always had such a sweet personality
but here came the mistake she made—
she hesitated as she crossed the street
with her precious life she paid—
her heart will no longer beat
she was hit by a car—
as her friends stood helpless by
she was not dragged far—
and at first she did not die
bitter tears were cried—
as an ambulance took her that day
thirty-five minutes later she died
and now the pain won't go away.

Anna Gouley

I Stay

Where is he?
Who has he chosen instead?
Will he be back tonight?
My stomach in knots,
does he feel one pang?
Oh, I want him to realize my pain.
To hurt him the way he hurts me.
But he always runs.
Left again with this malignant ache,
Only his touch, like morphine, can soothe.
But his drug wears off and I'm truly alone.
Like a defeated warrior
I wonder where my strength has gone.
But no one else can touch me like him.
And no one else will want me like him.
So you see I have no choice,
I stay.

Patricia Boyle

Starlifant

Of all the creatures in the sea,
There's not another one like me.
A starlifant I am by name,
And you may call me by the same.

Made of shell, my ears and tail,
And with my snout I never fail
To frighten off my enemy
And go on living in the sea.

I cling to rocks and climb sea trees
To find a friend and shoot the breeze,
For there are few of us around,
'Cause where man is, we can't be found.

For if found by man, I'd surely be
Plucked from far beneath the sea,
Pickled, pruned and then ker-plopped
Upon some fancy table top.

For of all the creatures in the sea,
There's not another one like me.
A starlifant I am by name,
And you may call me by the same.

Merrie Christmas Phelan

The Brother I Loved

I know you've gone to heaven
And will never hear me say
The things inside my heart and mind
That just won't go away.

I think about the fun times,
All the memories of past
And then the thought occurs to me,
"So, who will make me laugh?"

Who will tell the funny jokes
Time and time again,
Pull pranks so later I can say,
"Do you remember when . . .?"

Who will call me just to say,
"Forgot to tell you something . . ."
The silence of the telephone
Reminds me every morning.

The laughter and the closeness
That I will surely miss
Bring to mind a lonely thought,
"Now . . . who will call me Sis?"

Pamela Bollnow

I Am Jealous of the Night

I am jealous of the night

The night comes upon you
surrounding, enveloping, caressing.

It comes as a mother, tenderly holding
and comforting
Tucking you in.

The night comes as a friend
sharing your dreams and thoughts.

It comes as a lover, nuzzling close,
knowing the curves of your body,
the texture of your skin, the warmth
of your touch.

The night shares all these things with you
I wish I were the night.

Lorri Dotson

Artist

Chip away.
Sand rough edges, varied patterns,
Circular, angular, jagged, straight,
Peel, cut, reveal
New layers waiting to be born.

Trees shine, forming
Wet green networks,
Forests of leaves,
Entanglement of branches and lives,
Creeping, nesting.

Smooth their splintered curves,
Those rugged sides,
Chisel, stain, polish, seal,
Finish.

Oh struggling spirit,
Your effort and complexity
Have vanished within the process,
Refined to simplicity and truth.

Sweep away the dust.
They cannot know.

Lois Hudson

Entreaty

Please, please
Don't sneeze!
Take care,
Don't share
Your bugs.
No hugs,
No flu,
Thank you.

Barbara Liter

Strangers

You don't know me.
You have been part of my life
since the day I was born,
but you don't know me.
You watched me grow
and come of age,
but you don't know me.
I've tried to keep you
a part of my world,
but you don't know me.
And try as I might,
my father, my dear—
I don't know you either.

Christe Marie McGann

Broken Flower

The night before
the broken flower
was found
laughter and tears were heard
and talk of where
she was bound.

The night before
the broken flower
was found
music played
and the dance
went round and round.

Dawns shadows
blanketed the flower
creating dark corners
then light, then dark again
as the neon sign
blinked, then slept.

David G. Hauser

Red Tide

Waves just show up
On the shore: RED.

"RED TIDE," says the lifeguard.

Trillions of alive and dead organisms
"PLANKTON," says the lifeguard.

Don't eat the shellfish these days.
"TOXIC," says the lifeguard.

Gretchen Yates Lum

The End

How were we to know
That our youth would ever end
That we would one day be left
Without our childhood friend

When we heard the words of wisdom
If I knew then what I know now.

Would we have been so eager
To waste the time we were given to spend

And when our steps get shorter
With our vision growing dim

Will we be where we started
To begin the story again

George Brackeen

Feathers and Glass

It was a cannonball, that sneaker,
Thrown with angry velocity,
The chiming of the toy piano shatter
Awakening me
Like in one of those films
One watches
Late at night.
I ran to the living room,
Its belly laid bare
By a gaping hole
With its mess of glass and
Plant entrails.
Back arched, I picked up the shards
With pincer fingers.
And the vacuum cleaned the remains
Of dirt and splinters
While feathers danced in the air
Like they did last evening
In the warm light.

Andrew J. Rash

Volcano

As the blazing lava shot up,
I looked into the sky.
When the big explosion happened,
I got really frightened and cried.
I tried to defy it,
but it was too strong
So I ran for my life,
And I think I was wrong.

Ness Zolan

October Roses

Breathless, I open the door
Just before dawn

The newspapers, thrown not far enough
are wrapped in plastic,
Wet from the sprinkler
Still watering summer roses.

But it is October
and your beauty is fullest now:
profusion of pink.

Roses, three bushes in a row,
Braving the fall, striking in the dawn.

I see you.
You have captured summer
in each of your blossoms.

Susan G. Stein

Grief's Final Separation

I miss those days of you and me
Where I'm not so alone;
Let's go back to yesterday
Honey, take me home.
Did my hand slip from yours?
Are you lonely too?
What is this shadow of grief
Forcing us apart?
Can you tell
I'm no longer at your side?
When you look at me
You no longer see . . .
Right before your very eyes
I've become a memory.
Oh honey, take me home
Let's go back to yesterday,
The way we used to be.
Good-bye my love . . .

Patti Holter

I Am, In Them

I was born a child and a child I'll be,
till it comes time to bury me.

Wrinkles may dwell on this, my face,
and hair of brown, with gray replaced.

My outer shell is quite deceiving,
my fallow fields in need of weeding.

But let no one doubt this heart of mine;
'tis of a child's, not worn with time.

Here today and gone tomorrow.
Parting is not such sweet sorrow;

for when I'm gone, still here I'll be,
my flesh not felt, but memories seen.

Reminders of what once I was,
tucked in my children's undying love.

Kim Timbrook Miller

Sail On

Some ships leave the harbor,
To the fishing-ground,
Some do good,
Some not so!
Never quit!
If always it were a full catch,
We would stop trying.
It is not the decision of the catch.
But the desire for it!

Gary J. Moscato, Sr.

The Birth of Spring

See the pretty red rose,
Out in the garden.
The green grass coming out new.
By the small house,
Out in the garden.
Is a pretty little violet so blue.

The azaleas seem to shout,
Out in the garden.
The camellias are blooming too.
All the wild flowers have little flowers.
They seem to say,
It is time for spring too.

The trees are a shade of pale new green.
A more beautiful sight you have never seen.
The dogwood is blooming,
Out in the garden.
It is truly,
The birth of spring.

Julia Hasell

Spring

I see the earth so sweet beneath my feet.
It shows me signs of spring are near,
Nearer than before.
As March winds make their rounds,
Announcing a knock on every door.

Blossoms bright we soon shall see,
With warmth and beauty in our midst.
Then following, in all their best,
Comes Crocus first and then the rest.
Daffodils, hyacinths, tulips and all
Nod their heads in sweet respect
To forsythia so tall.

With ice storms past and winter gone,
The season renewed lingers on.
It's here for all, it's here to see
Lovely, sure, true and free.

Elaine V. DelGrosso

Theasthal

On a windswept morning . . .
The pansies in the garden were
Nodding to each other as I passed by.
They seemed to be in joyous thrall,
To weave and bow one to the other.
Though the yellow to the blue
Bowed most deeply.
Colder than usual . . . yet
Stepped I more slowly theasthal
The morning will spend their life span
In a gorgeous setting
Outside a world famous hotel.
The sweet faces curtsied to me
As I bid farewell.

Mary T. Price

My Dearest Friend

Through all the laughter
Through all the tears
You've been my friend
Through all these years

I've made mistakes
Along the way
But you stood beside me
Each and every day

Even though we're not together
As much as we used to be
I carry you inside my heart
You are always with me

When I am feeling weak
You make me feel strong again
I just have to tell you
You are my dearest friend

I truly have to say
That I could never love another
As much as I love you
My dear sweet Mother!

Patricia D. Dedeaux

This Day Is Mine

Were I to ask for bounty,
I would ask for time.
After years of endless "no time" . . .
years of nothing left for me.
Early or late,
no time was my fate.
A ten shone godly on others,
rain poured on me.
Eons of a "bad time to travel,"
a bad time to stay.
The blessedness of loving,
in time went its way.
The messenger came . . .
I heard it on a wind-drift,
saw it in the stars.
The no-times and time-outs
are gone forever, exist no more.
Hear it . . . sun, moon and stars.
I am the messenger,
this day is mine.

Mary T. Price

I Can Feel the Reign

I cannot foretell the future,
But with this I can say.
I can hear the reign coming;
For it will be here someday.

That day is nigh.
Just a sin or two away.
But doubt is filling the minds
Of the "children" today.

Will your ears be open?
Will your heart let you hear?
I can hear the reign coming;
For the day is near.

Not one of us is perfect.
All of us make mistakes.
When our names are called,
Will you flood the gates?

Can you hear the reign coming?
Can you feel it drawing near?
When the Father calls the names,
Will yours be one we hear?

David Clemans

Ambitions

With incomplete lives,
We labor for greatness;
With incomplete thoughts,
We form words.
With incomplete hearts,
We search for love;
With incomplete bodies,
We seek perfection.
With incomplete surroundings,
We toil for beauty;
With incomplete minds,
We acquire knowledge.

Michelle Hickman

Mixed Rivers

Colors of mixed
rivers weaving
in and out
fat
skinny, short
and small
all different shapes
and sizes somehow
got mixed together

Ashley Johnson

Nights Treasure

Crimson, gold and pink delight
a sunset watchers feasting sight.
Each shade in measured beauty stands.
As if, to me, outreaching hands.
A welcome to the night ahead,
reminder of life's fragile thread.
When once in darkness men did fear,
that which unseen crept so near.
Terror, once was night believed,
to bring to men and so he grieved.
But now sun's set brings thoughts afar,
for those who wait to glimpse a star.
And now from velvet case release,
nights treasure of a wish for peace.

Brenda Endicott

Untitled

I want to ride the blue waves,
Swim through the red days,
Walk with a flower,
Dance for the next hour,
I want to ride with an eagle,
Swim with a seal,
Walk with a shark,
Dance alone in the park.

Melissa Gardner

Received in Full

Dear Cupid,
I noticed the splintered bow
And
The tattered arrows
Scattered on the floor,
Writhing in anguish and wounded
Pride,
Dining on the blood
Etched in fading
Footfalls.
I thought you'd
Like to know—

I got your message.

Babette Padron

At My Bedroom Window

Outside my bedroom
Through the window
Upon the tree
With a chirp
On the windowsill
At my bedroom window
With a song
Underneath the tree
In the day
Upon my shoulder
With a trill.

Megan Michael Foran

Liquid of the Orange

Orange in hand
With fist closed
Arms wide
Comes together
River from orange
Fails to flow
My eyes are covered

Orange is uncovered
Orange in palm
Fist closed over glass
River of orange flows
My eyes are uncovered
I can see

Joe Haney

A Stranger

A stranger I walked in,
A lover I became.
Who knew that our lonely hearts
Would beat the same.
I looked at you, you looked at me.
That's when we knew, our love would
Brave the roughest of seas.
If we keep the love that God has
Put together,
Then our names shall be chanted
In the heavens,
Forever!!!

Hector Perez

Untitled

Come with me along the sea
seeking treasures of the sea.
Search with me the truths of time.
I slow the hastening of my footsteps—
listening from afar the haunting echoes
of the sea—the journey is worthwhile,
alone with whales, sails and seashells
the untold treasure of the sea.

Constance Gibbs

Regard

So much talk about self-esteem.
So much confusion on what it means.

How do you get, how do you teach,
that which seams so out of reach?

Set value on unexplored potential?
Assign rank to ever-changing growth?

Appreciate limitless self.
Care for limited self.

Accept and use limit as tool.
Reject what limitless self judges—fool.

Patricia Bernard

A Waterballoon for My Brother the Goon

When he walks past.
I'll throw one hard.
Then it will burst.
And I'll laugh hard.

Then he'll get me.
But I'll tell mother.
Then she won't let him free.
And he won't want to be my brother.
Connie Jones

The Plummet

The eyes held an empty staircase,
And watched it wind down,
Farther and farther.
Twisting around the tears,
The hurt and deceit.

People once within her grasp,
Slipped through the parted fingers,
Of her empty hand.
That was once full,
Tightly clenched around them.

The eyes held an empty staircase,
And burned with tears,
Not able to fall.
Into the darkness surrounding her,
That she had created.

The prism of mistakes,
Cast rainbows of regret,
On her shadow.
And illuminated the pebble-like tears,
That rippled through her.
Gina Burd

I Thought I'd Let You Know

I thought I'd let you know
A friend that's very near
A friend that's not too far
A friend that's very dear

Doesn't like to see you hurt
Hates to see you go through pain
Doesn't want to see you ride that
Emotional Runaway train

So I thought I'd let you know
If you need to shed a tear
A shoulder you can cry on
Will always be right here
Frank Cavaciuti

Lily

The pretty children of the night,
Painted prettily in white.
Pale skin, alabaster in the moon.
Lips of rose colored satin, kiss the
nighted sky.
Sad almost lost eyes drifting o'er the
land, ready to die.
Leather and lace twisted grimly 'round
long lanky bird-bodies.
Norse gods look down from Valhalla,
Proud and vengeful parents.
Spines to be broken,
Spines to be rent.
Pretty Children Dressed in Black.
My how the times have been bent.
Gabrielle Hawkins

"Ol-Boone"

His name was Ol-Boone
and he was so much fun,

He brought much love
and he brought much joy to everyone.

His name was Ol-Boone
and he was so unique,

He was so original
he never had to compete.

His name was Ol-Boone
and he started growing old,

But he never gave up
he was still very bold.

His name was Ol-Boone
and he started growing weary,

Some days were dark
and some days were dreary,

His name was Ol-Boone
and the day was drawing close,

Good-bye Ol-Boone
we'll miss you the most.
Maggie Wilkinson

Lonely Emptiness

I want to reach for your hand
But I don't

I want to wrap my arms around you
But I can't

I want to lie down beside you
But I don't

I want to kiss your lips
But I can't

I want to make love you
But I don't

I want to whisper I love you
But I can't

I want to sleep in your arms
But I don't

I want to stop these tears from falling
But I can't

I want to end this lonely emptiness
But I don't

I want to protect my fragile heart
And I do.
Lisa Marie Reist

Flowers

Flowers are a wonderful thing
They make you want to laugh and sing
Yes flowers are beautiful things
Make with them some little rings
Some are big
Some are small
You can draw them on your wall
Some are purple
Some are blue
Some are painted on your shoe
Some you can pick
Some you can't
'Cause if you do your hand you'll prick
So love all flowers
Great and small.
Jessy Hodges

God Is

God is the air we breathe,
The trees upon the earth.
He is every good thing given us at birth.
God is in the birds and rivers,
And all the beautiful trees.
He's down in the oceans
Where we cannot see.
God is the snows of winter,
The blossoms in the spring,
Soft music in the summertime,
And every brook and spring.
God is in all the children;
He loves them very much.
He is Our Father
Who heals with every good thing.
He is found everywhere.
He is truly the one who loves us,
And always cares.
God is the wind.
Leonard Orr

The Unknown

Their unit
was last seen dressed in dull tasteless
green, with matching turtle shell hats
and dusty boots once black.

In the field
during battle, their guns at an angle,
the men crouched low moving slowly,
while silhouetted against the brilliance
of enemy fire.

The silhouettes
were nameless and faceless.
Their uniforms stripped them of the past,
the present and the future.

They became soulless
justifying their deaths.
Donna L. Smart

The Lost Buck

I think that I shall never see,
The dollar that I loaned to thee,
A dollar that I could have spent
On many forms of merriment
The one I loaned you gladly,
Is now the one I need so badly.
For whose return I had great hope
Just like an optimistic dope.
For dollars loaned to folks like thee,
Are not returned to fools like me.
J. Megge

Mother

Oh gentle, loving mother,
Oh sweet beautiful rose.
Your petals stretched to protect us,
With soft, velvet clothes.

Oh gentle, loving mother,
Spring, summer, and fall.
Blossoming forth in glory,
Making gardens for all.

Oh gentle, loving mother,
Your petals are touched with dew.
Winter is approaching,
But spring will make you anew!
Jacqueline Narragon

Leaving

Married young in love,
Always my best friend,
Raised a precious family,
Joy that had no end . . .

Losing one another,
Growing up too fast,
Maze of emotions,
Can't seem to make it last . . .

Souls feeling captured,
In another time and space,
Living without love,
Anger out of place . . .

Pretending getting harder,
With each and every day,
Questions without answers,
Stay or walk away???

Bronwen Mary Elizabeth Crue

Believing in Dreams

I've dreamed of this moment
For what seemed a lifetime.
I was almost afraid it would
Never happen to me.
All the planning and dreams—
My patience was tried.
Then it happened—
The wait was over.
As my tears of joy drifted down my cheeks,
I saw for the first time—
What I had waited and prayed for so long.
A single yawn, the slightest of movement,
And my child was fast asleep in my arms.
My new born baby was here
And that day all my dreams came true.

Debbie Fortier

Untitled

My life is like a blur,
as skin before the eyes.
The happiness I've lost,
has came as no surprise.
I awoke one morning in misery,
it was jumping at my face.
I thought I was the problem,
I was everyone's disgrace.
I have no place I can call home,
no castle in the sand.
I have no true friends to talk to,
or no one to hold my hand.
Has all life become this evil?
Has everything gone wrong?
Now is everyone similar,
miserable all day long?

Kelli Scott

Untitled

Take my hand child
do not fear its firm embrace
for many times you've heard my name
but never seen my face.

The road that I have traveled
leads to a greater height
My name I know you'll recognize
they call me Jesus Christ.

My father is the universe
his love for all to see
Compassion in his promise
of life eternity.

Harry Johns II

Learn to Follow

Have you learned to follow,
Or must you have to lead;
Have you learned to serve,
The ones who are in need?

Must you be first in line,
At the top of ever stairs;
Or can you sit in second place,
Or must you be in first chair?

Have you learned to call on God
If happy or sad today?
Have you learned to look to Him
And to guide you all the way?

To serve, to work, to learn,
Makes us grow day by day,
Living, teaching, doing our best,
Then turn all to God and pray.

Yes, life is full of sorrow,
But we must learn to stand in line.
And learn to serve God and others,
Then we'll see things are all just fine.

Carl Banks—Guymon, Oklahoma

Heaven

Have you ever wondered
What heaven looks like?
Me? I can't even come close,
To the beauty of that wonderful place
Full of angels. Made by grace.

If you look in the bible
It will tell you of that great place.
I wonder, I wonder what it will be.
You can read the B-I-B-L-E.

With pearly gates of gold
People enter when they're deceased
They enter to that place
To receive a home from grace.

We can never decipher
What God has in store for us
But I know I will go
To that place called heaven
Made by grace.

Tommy May

True Life

You my love.
Born this day.
Here in the world
A place to stay.

Yesterday morning.
To me you came.
To tell of your troubles and life and pain.
Two of us now.
Some day must be.
A perfect example for all to see.

Though hopes and dreams.
Be yours and mine.
Let's tell the world of this love divine.

I speak my mind of the truth I know
Now goodness come.
It will never go.

Let's go to sleep
See a new world to come.
Build our precious lives.
Smile when all is done.

Gordon Isaacs

The Journey

As I contemplate my journey
Toward what you've planned for me
I cannot help but notice
How Your love has set me free.

At times it's been a struggle
To focus where I should
Fear and misdirection
Often clouded what was good.

You never let me linger
In valleys, oh so low
Your presence would announce itself
In ways that made me grow.

Throughout this life You've given
To creatures great and small
A healing reassurance
To those who heard your call.

Keep my motives pure, Lord
Be ever at my side
I know how much You love me
My faith won't be denied.

Marie B. Haynie

Wolf

With an alarming tune you sang my name.
Your merciless notes reached the people
And they came. The song made you laugh
So you sang it again, and again, and again.
Don't you know I'm always near?
Quietly, waiting
To bring you fear.
How dare you employ my name
For this infantile game.
The people no longer believe your cries,
The time has come
For my surprise. Calmly
I'll creep down the hill.
When you see me
You'll feel a chill.
Cry out my name as loud as you can,
Those people
They won't help you again.
Hum—lunch
For a week or two

Amanda Leonard

Untitled

God doesn't judge us by our skin
He judges us by what's within
Our hearts must pure and simple be
If heaven we expect to see

After all, he made each man,
White or yellow, black or tan.
We each must fit into his plan
And each must love his fellow man.

Vivian McInroe

Angels in My Life

Angels, Angels are oh so good,
they keep us doing what we should.

God sends all his angels here,
so we don't have to live in fear.

Angels help the sick and dying,
they encourage us to keep on trying.

I want to be an angel in heaven,
but is hard when you're only eleven.

Maryann Walston

Memories

Memories are like stars shooting
from the sky creating a memorable
sensation for the mind.

Lasting like the delectable taste
of one's favorite food.

Giving permanence, a mere
facade, like roses in June.

The feeling of eternity, yet lasting
a minuscule of time.

Changing like blossoms and
aging like fine wine.

Memories, delicate, beautiful, memories,
are etched in our souls.

Folded laid in passion, garnished
in sheer gold.

Forever in our hearts, capsulated
in time, staying young until
eternity, ageless, memories, body and mind.

Brigitte Moore Ward

My Thoughts

I am living in a world of
Enchanting things, where all things
Are beautiful, even the last leaves
On the trees that fall and become
A part of this enchanted world.

To be drunk is not a sinful thing,
When you are drunk with the understanding
That life can be beautiful,
Come what may.
If you take a lonely heart and
A non-lonely heart, blend together
With true love and understanding,
You will know this is not an
imaginary thing, but reality.

J. Bernice Wormley

I Love You

I love thee
For you are more beautiful
Than a sweet dew-kissed morn,
Caressed by fiery rays.

I love thee
For you are greater
Than a mighty flashing blade,
Swift and sure in each stroke.

I love thee
For you are gentler
Than a flutter of butterfly's wings
On the lips of a lover.

I love thee
For you are all of these
And yet, you are so much more
You are everything to me.

Angela Gramkow

Direct Experience

Among the smaller things
I make my questing way.
The towering trees are not for me today.
The lesser things of earth
Will make their message clear—
If I but pause to sense them
As I go near.

Pink fairy flowers
On graceful wands,
Hold my eyes with
Beauty's bonds.
Other flowers hanging there
Waft priceless perfume on summer air.

Madcap hopper, robin, bee
Join in Nature's symphony
With all of these to hear, smell and see
Who would choose learning vicariously?

Frances Dempsey

Can You Use Me Lord

Can you use someone
Who once had gone astray?
Can you use someone
Who learned how to pray?

Can you use someone
Who has surrendered all?
Can you use me Lord
I'm waiting for your call!

Does it matter Lord
How people look at me?
Does it matter Lord
How my enemies treat me?

Tell me Lord Jesus
Can you use me?
Is there somewhere
I can work for thee?

Alonzo D. Easley, Sr.

Roses

Roses
Small Red
Growing Blooming Dying
Flowers Buds Stems Thorns
Shedding Falling Sprouting
Pretty Beautiful
Roses

Brittany Clisso

Blue

Blue is the color of my bike.
Blue is the sea.
Blue is the sky.
Blue is shirts.
Blue is rain.
Blue is the color of my folder
Blue is books.
Blue is the color of playground balls.
Blue is paint.
Blue is paper,
Blue is crayons,
Blue is jeans.
Blue is flowers.
Blue is eyes.
Blue are dishes.
Blue is stain glass.
Blue is blankets.
Blue is hats.

Tyler Mareel Pullens

Wonder If . . .

As the lips that once
told me they loved me
claimed to
love me no more,
I wondered how to stop
the tears that flowed
so freely to the floor
As the eyes that once
held a look so warm
could no longer hold my stare
I wondered it there was
a time when those eyes
really did care
As the arms that once
held and comforted me
Now just push me away
I wondered why my time
was through and why I
could not stay.

Vicki Ann Clark

When

I think of you the whole week long;
And suddenly, you're there—
three nights is all I have with you;
I long to keep you, dear.

This what remains of yesternight,
must carry for tomorrow;
And still four days in misery,
with only thoughts to borrow . . .

No, weekends won't remain enough;
You're mine for every day—
Your face, your touch, your all of you—
must take me to Friday . . .

Then when I see you on that
night, it will be oh so good;
we'll marry, yes, oh, won't we love?
Remember? You said we should.

Brenda Ray

Mental Menopause

The human mind is a powerful tool
It can make you a king or make you a fool.
It can mesmerize and concentrate
Or wander off in a mindless state!

And when this jellied mass of gray
Decides to fool around and play,
Creating visions that aren't really there;
Instilling within me a bona fide scare

For lack of sleep or such distress
As simple physical duress—
Can propagate its fertile soil
To kink this jellied mass of coil.

And so I'll take it far away
And let it be and hour a day
To ponder thoughts and fantasies,
And other mental congeries!

Judith M. Gemeinhardt

To Hear the Angels Sing

When you hear the Angels singing
You know that's where I'll be
In that sweet Cherub chorus
Of Heaven's jubilee

I've had my share of troubles
And I've fought the fight of faith
I've done the will of my Savior
Though I know I've make mistakes

My time on earth is over
But don't you cry for me
For when you hear the Angels singing
You know that's where I'll be

To hear the angels singing
You know that's where I'll be
Listening to the Angel Chorus
Of Heaven's Jubilee

Can you hear the Angel voices
Singing in perfect harmony
Oh, what a Heavenly chorus
That's come to comfort me

Tammy Carter

The Long Road Back

From graven sight
To manic moods,
Confusion and plight
As madness broods

Simple steps of wholeness
To strive for,
And no mistakes
Coming through the door:

Making friends and learning
To trust
For sanity, this is a must

Coming from the darkness,
And into the light
Can be very fulfilling,
And bright

Jeff Elliott

The Queen of Heaven

If there is a King of Heaven,
Why not also a Queen of Heaven?
Evidence abounds history.
Yahweh had his Asherah.
Biblical archaeology confirms this.
The great Church of Rome sings
The praises of the Mother of God,
Celebrates her assumption and coronation.
India and China build temples by the
Thousands to honor the Heavenly Mother.
Mother in Heaven was not lost by
Egypt, Greece, and Rome.
She is still with us in so many ways.
Watching, blessing, and loving.
Mother Earth, Mother Nature, Hear, Athena,
Medusa, Hathor, Astarte, Mary,
Names and forms unlimited forever.

Dr. Alan Albert Snow

Untitled

Love is money
Love is life
Love is what is thoughtful and right
So if you want a life of lust, then people
Should be your biggest must.

Michael J. Giannini

The End

I thought about you day and night,
I whispered happy thoughts,
My love for you was so real,
You tied me up in knots.

Yet as you walked on day to day,
You stared right through my heart,
And if you would have noticed me,
My soul would then jump start.

In my dreams were fantasies,
That we should soon be wed,
The next day when I went to school,
I found out you were dead.

So on that day my soul did die,
As I began to cry,
And when I thought about your love,
I hoped death was a lie.

Linann McDonald

Sleepless Soul

I'm spun:
It's Sunday
Winter chill is on the wind
Cold and gray

And I'm restless

I could keep the pace
Of breathing if I
Only had enough air

The smoke caught in the light
Moves to the beat of the music

Who am I? Is this defeat?
This dog's not dead

Yet I'm so hollow—vague

I won't give up—I'm near
This end—coffee's finished—
Stash cashed

The sun is poking through
The clouds—candle flickers—

Finally—I cry

Kathleen Koltz

Santa's Express Delayed

Black track around
Our Christmas tree
Atop a skirt of white,
Reflecting back our
Love of life
With every blinking light.

Santa's express
A train of red
Lying on its side,
Wrecked among the needles
That our pretty tree has shed.

Our little village
Beneath the tree
Has met its end,
Because of our puppy
Who is our two week
Old new friend.

Sharon West

Our Love

No joy can compare
to what we share.
No one can understand
until they've been there.

A gentle touch
a caring smile,
an understanding
that "goes for miles."

There are no words
that can describe
the lasting love
we hold deep inside.

My only hope is
that God above
let's everyone
find their real, true love.

Sharon West

Mama's So Fine

You are so fine
A gentle touch, soft
like a baby's behind.
Your voice is quiet and strong
Just like a quiet storm
When you speak of love
You bring the heart so clear
Who made me so special
To be blessed with thee
Mama So Fine
There are times when I feel
So far away
You step in to help
Steer the waf
Mama are you the only
Mama So Fine

Because if you are
I know I'll be just fine.

Brenda Williams

Twenty Plus

I try to imagine
What's on a youngin's mind
For it's far too many
Out in the streets dying

It's not a funny sight
Seeing so many mothers cry
Being told their sons (so young)
Died victims of a drive-by

Drugs—money
It just their way of life
If not selling drugs—in reverse
They're smokin' the pipe

Kids should be studying
Somewhere in school
But instead of education
Guns are their golden rules

If only they read the Bible
And see that in "God we trust"
I'll promise a lot more youngin's
Will reach that twenty plus

Robert Robinson

Words

American women can never be free,
Our language blinds what society sees.
We're classified by the way we live,
Demonstrated by the names they give.
Friendly with men, you're called slut, whore, harlot.
A glamorous beauty is a model, actress, starlet.
Tough, demanding women are ball-busters and b****s.
Mean, nasty uglies are banshees, hags, and witches.
The Marilyn type are ditzes, twits, bimbos.
Chick, bird, fox, use of animal symbols.
A farm full of women, hens, heifers or cows,
Let's not forget nags, vixens, shrews, sows.
The Bible, too, have women to hate.
Beware of Jezebel and Delilah on dates.
One was a tyrant, the other a traitor,
The moral of the story is "death awaits her."
How hateful are words, demeaning and wrong,
But these are everlasting when the person is gone.
We have dreams and ambitions, of visions afar,
Of which these words say nothing of who we are.

   Gain G. Lu

The Washing of the Dead

In the morgue at Sarajevo
The new corpses seem beautiful, innocent:
poised like dancers frozen in time,
Their eyes stare.
They smile the strange smile of the newly dead.

Let it begin.
Lay them out.
Close the eyes.
Stuff cotton in mouth and anus.
Strip them, wash with soap and water.
Disregard the smells.
Dress them again or fit winding cloth around them.
Prepare them for their journey to a silent grave.

All those dead and wounded, they are the rum raisins of war.
Refugees, orphans, widows, they are its honey, its oh-so-sweet honey.
Burnt-out towns, wreckage among ashes are its creamy, chewy slaw.

Come to the washing of the dead.
A war is on.

   James L. Gardner

Untitled

It came down hot and wet
like summer rain
soaking through me covered
shining drops of love I see
glistening like diamonds enter sigh
oh soft arch
say my name, faster pounding
the waves wash over
and I am weak
and this is heaven
and it feels good
and the tile is getting closer
and that summer rain is coming, faster
and this steam is blurring my eyes
and I'm seeing more clearly than ever
so I'm letting go
and can't get a tighter grip
cause I've lost all control
of this shower with you
towel please.

   Jeffery N. Green

Father

As tribute to our father Herman H. Chapman, Sr.
Father ours is one of the greatest
Always there for us is He
Thoughtful, considerate, loving, kind
Also is He
Happy is what he will always want us to be
Enjoying life to its fullest
Is what he will forever want for my brother and me
Respect, love, appreciation for our father
Shall always and forever be
Among our highest priorities

   Virginia L. Chapman

Love at First Sight

I met her when I was 17 years old. It was love at first
sight. She was everything I wanted; all the curves on
her body in the right places.
My brothers told me that she was too much for me;
she was too wild and other guys wanted her. They
stared at her with lust; some tried to take her from me.
No matter what, she is always with me wherever I go.
I can't stay away from her. Sometimes we go for a
ride and she goes too fast; the police catch us and
give us a ticket for speeding.
I don't care, I love being with her. I have to work hard
to make enough money for her. I like to buy her things
so she will always look good for me. I still take good
care of her; I love to bathe her often so I can put my
hands on her smooth body and watch the lather from
the soap slide down every curve of her body; then I
gently wipe her off with a soft white cotton towel.

   Willie C. Ng Sr.

The Bride

Know little while, liked his style, "let's get together!"
Time flew by, biological clock loud, "it's about time!"
He popped question she said, "yes!" They set date.
She picked ring, he bought ring, she wore ring.
They told parents, she picked bridesmaids, he picked groomsmen.
Down the aisle, dressed in white, the groom awaits.
Everyone in place, gifts are piling, what a day!
Eyes are misting, hands are trembling, is she rethinking?
Is he it? Is the real? Am I ready?
Is he ready? Love or lust? Should we continue?
Call it off! Are you nuts? Got my pride!
Did God ordain?

   Lorna L. Morris

Untitled

The light grows dim, my mind's retreat;
My heart beat cloud, it's time to meet.

Off in a cloud, my soul flies free;
My love takes form, and it's you I see.

The sparkle of your eyes holds me in place;
A tear tracks my cheek, reflecting your grace.

So tender, so sweet, your smile brings peace;
My struggles, my grief, all seem to cease.

Time stands still, our beings intertwine;
A marriage of love, caring, hope, forever combined.

Then light slowly comes, our dream about to close;
Your tears splash my hand, forming a single rose.

My eyes slip open, once again in this cell;
A new day dawning in my lonely, four-walled hell.

Resigned to the routine, I rise, to block out the pact;
When I realize with a smile, the most beautiful rose,
Is still held in my grasp!

   Jason A. Saldana

Endless Nights

If I knew what to sing in the morning light,
If I knew what to sing under the stars so bright,
I would sing them to you, with all my heart,
Spending endless nights in Love, with you . . .

Beautiful and so romantic,
You and me and nothing frantic,
In the quiet candlelight alone . . .

Wine and Rose with our dinner,
Oh! Darling you're a winner,
And your charm sweeps me off my feet . . .

Grapes and oils and other treasures,
Indulging in our deepest pleasures,
In each other's arms all night embraced . . .

Would you walk on the beach, hand in hand,
Would you play in the water, by the sand,
Darling come and spend some time with me . . .

If I knew what to sing in the morning light,
If I knew what to sing under the stars so bright,
I would sing them to you, with all my heart,
Spending endless nights in love with you!

Coni Thompson

My Forbidden Love

It was a gratifying stealthy love
while it was to bear.
Vigilant he was beneath and above
guarding the truth from his only scare.

How we wanted
things to proceed,
But his superior haunted
the way he perceives.

He couldn't take the aggravation anymore,
and he didn't want to break my heart,
So in denial he changed to the way it was before.
Now I am all alone trying to part from the start.

My only questions are . . .
Will his superior ever see
It is not wrong for us to be?
Or that it is not that far
our age differences really are?

Erin Kerting

Mary Gould Descartes

In the search for sweetest truth, younger Mary had turned
To the treatises and treasures that the Queen ordered burned
To the Gibbons and the Humes, and the Jean Jacques Rosseaus,
To the studies of St. Aquinas and the persecuted Huguenots.
In well-lighted libraries she became well-learned.

She saw atheists beheaded by the conquering Quakers
And rationalist gravestones paving miles for God's acres.
And there within the gloom cast by the queen's evil 'democracy'
Shone the withered light of hope beyond empiricist philosophy.
Her innocence of heart amidst the bedlam of hate,
Whilst voices of her ancestors struggled to fill the vacant room,
She heard her own sing softly, 'Cogito Ergo Sum . . .'

And as she scaled the summit of enlightenment,
She found that the soul of one so pure cannot be so easily bound.
Now her missives are the bibles of the righteously-inclined,
They're potent as narcotic and they're not as hard to find.
Just as Attis is revered by Cybele, I take heart
Having recorded the facts concerning Mary Gould Descartes.

Aaron Black

Darling

Darling when you leave,
Please turn off the light
That shone so bright.
And darling when you go,
Don't think I won't hear.
Just turn off the night,
While I pray for a better day.
But darling if you think I'll forget
What you put in my head,
I'll only remember what was said,
And that was,
"Darling I'll be with you tell you're dead."
Please erase that from your head.
And darling if you say you understand,
Just leave right now, let go of this hand.
'Cause it's much more then what's been said,
It's just something between us we can't comprehend.

Willie Reisinger

Lessons of Life

Life is a gift not to be taken lightly.
To make it through without mistake is very unlikely.
'Tis important that in mind you keep,
other people are affected by misfortunes you reap.
They will cast you out among the stones,
leaving you lost, and wandering alone.
However, in learning from those mistakes,
and by giving repentance,
enemies will be turned into friends,
and relationships will go the distance.
In life, through mistakes, you either fail or succeed,
so make use of the lessons taught,
and good advice you should heed.

Dale Charles Armbrust

Open My Ears Someday . . .

There are times . . . I want to hear . . .
Choirs singing beautiful songs . . .
Of Jesus . . . and hear people singing . . .
All together . . .

There are times . . . I want to hear . . .
Birds singing on tree-tops . . .

There are times . . . I want to hear . . .
My beautiful little girl's voice . . . calling . . .
Me . . . "Mommy . . ."
But . . . I told thee . . .
I don't mind . . . not hearing anything at all . . .
'Cause . . . I'd rather . . . wait . . .
'Til thee . . . take me home . . .
And hear . . . the sweetest sound . . .
Sung . . . by his heralds . . .
All around me . . .
Oh . . .
I can't wait . . . someday . . .

Shannon Regis

Pan's Paradise

He danced through lush fields of variegated hues,
dappled with sprinkles of scarlet dew,
to his own perverted tune.

He played his reed at bacchanal feasts
and slaked his thirst on exotic treats
which solicitously collapsed at his cloven feet.

He slept on pillows of supple breasts,
then, in the morning with a final kiss,
danced away to newer flesh.

Anne Bradley

Small Hours

Sheets, dirt, pillows, foam, ashes,
protruding springs
One sliver of night light, sharp.
Eyes stretched unnaturally open.
Books, papers, pen, open unfinished
whispering voices almost inaudible
waiting, clinging sweat . . . fear
knife left—right—light on
light off—knowing . . .
Knowing the figment is here
eyes behind that can't be there
shadows move . . . knife
night life, knife light.
Kill the fear with sleep,
sleep with the sweating fear,
the chemical smell dream, point, smoke, nose
knowing the present will soon be gone.
I'll be blowing my nose and wiping my a**
Normal

Christopher B. Sharkey

Gunpoint

Beeped the garage door to let us in,
Home from our dinner at about ten.
Clean-cut, white athlete slipped in behind,
Both hands on his gun, aimed at my mind.
"Give me your **** billfold" he said,
Raised my hand, said, "You don't need me dead."
And, "You got it," gave it with left hand.
He lowered the gun, turned and he ran,
Helped me feel better, not so alone,
With Carol, and 9-1-1 on the phone.
Quickly, deputies with two dogs came
To collect clues for this deadly game.
Hot on the scent this skilled team began,
But lost track at getaway sedan,
Traceable evidence, prob'ly trash.
His loot was a small amount of cash,
And not worth his incarceration,
Nor trashing of civilization.

George W. Guthrie

Modern Times Stagnant Winds

There is no moral ending to this tale;
As callous men pollute the land and air:
Soon, there will be no ears to hear a wail;
No teary eyes of children or despair.

In changing times, from renowned days of old;
Lingering forces still overtax the poor.
True Americans, lie on the winters cold;
Our Veterans, cry in alleys pained from war.

Buying stock in Reno, foiled the good sleuth;
No longer is there honor in Words worth.
When honest lies are spoken as Sam's truth;
And the spoils of Pols lie beneath their berth.

Long past are the days of Security;
One law for the poor, and one for the rich;
Be damned! Don't try to beg for charity;
Or it's off to the dungeon if you b****.

While the voters eye an old empty fridge
Some laughed at the tube, Oh! their aching side.
Wild Bill, looking over his Cooler ridge;
Missed a step to fall on his Demo pride.

Edward L. Thomas

Untitled

Insanity is pain. Insanity is pleasure. I feel it smothering me. I welcome it, teasing my mind. I feel the coils of madness slip through my fingers. Rage. Undying rage burning deep inside my screaming soul. Voices of pain, voices of pleasure. All I hear in my mind. They're all that comfort my tears of insanity. How do I overcome these antagonizing cries? How will I overcome the deathening grip it has hold of me? I will never know. I will never be freed from these chains that bind my tired, my weary body. I find myself trapped in my own insanity.

Holli Mowatt

The Real Dream Catchers

The birds fly across the tinted sky.
Whisking, swooping; darting over the treetops as warriors.
Peaceful, peaceful, graceful warriors.
I question myself "Why do they even have wings?"
So I watch these angelic creatures dance in each others unseen,
untold shadows and stories.
Enveloped in their tiny, mighty wings my dreams are made and stored,
   sealed and hidden from you behind their nestful doors.
Soul saving, love working, goal making, religion finding, heart healing,
sorrow eliminating, life restoring;
spirit shaping birds perch on the branches beyond the mountaintops
where the rain clouds catch my sins, hold my strife and meet the
Heavens.

Melody Nicolle Haller

We Are All God's Children

We are all God's children
All the people, living and dead in all this Universe
Our God is the Creator of all creations
Our God always cares for all of us, always understand us,
never likes to punish any one of us
We are given and we accept unconditional freedom
to think and do good to help one another
We are aware of the blessings of God, the Creator of all creations
To be able to accept and appreciate them
Individually and/or collectively we tell so
to our God the Creator of all creations.
Our God the Creator of all creations is and will always be
the Creator of all solutions to all our problems
Because we always think and feel secured
We have no problem, we have peace and joy
We always let go and leave everything to God
   the Creator of all creations
And so we feel that we are back again in Paradise
Because we have regained our former selves

Lolita Pornasdoro Habito

Life's Last Wishes

When someday we leave this earth behind;
and, we all know we will, unless we are blind;
to the realities of life that face us each day;
it's not what you do and it's not what you say;
that will matter in the last moments of life;
but rather what we have done in our entire lifetime
walking through cemeteries is interesting to do.
The older the graves, the more they should mean to you.
How long ago did these same people walk the same path as we?
How did they lead their lives until they took their leave?
To be buried in the ground, leaves those behind a place to go and talk;
to wonder about and let your mind's thoughts,
take over and wish you away from this place;
for it's the one that we all dread
and it's the one we'll all one day face.
In my mind I've always wanted to be buried high above,
in a tree's flowing branches, with the wind and the sky, which I love.
The winds would gently rock me, as my Mother did as a child,
and, I'd rest in that bosom of a tree peacefully in the wild!

Catherine Ruedy

Undertow

Holding only breath
Where to go
Deeper, but the past
Kicking and screaming
For each his own future
Twisted by the current
Further out to sea than ever before
Fish swim by, kiss on the face
Showing love, he pets them
Again in a flash they are gone
Swallows salt
Eyes close, consciousness gone
Existence erasing
Floating up not much time
Only thought
Sweet cool air above

    David Masters

Untitled

When I close my eyes
I call you again, in the shadowy realm
where you dwell.
Softly, like our first ethereal kiss,
opening like rosebuds against
my dream lips,
more real than sunlight,
you speak without words.
In defiance of the coming dawn,
I savor you like droplets of wine or sweat
still feeling you,
Your imprint on me like
the rumpled spot in my sheets
where I felt you
in my sleep.

    Amy L. Gruss

BIOGRAPHIES
OF POETS

ABBOT, CAROLYN T.
[b.] January 12, 1913; Brazil, SA; [p.] Katharine Eastmand, Joseph Tyler; [m.] Sydney G. Abbot; may 2, 1942; [ch.] Carolyn G., David K.; [ed.] Gr. Billerica H.S. 1930, Gr. Wellesley College, 1934, Summer Schools of Music in Middlebury, Concord, Cambridge, Boston Art School, Harvard Summer School; [occ.] Writing; [memb.] Billerica Historical Soc., Massachusetts Poetry Society; [hon.] Editor H.S. Magazine, Class Poet ('30), and prize for essay, "Congratulations, Churches, and the Church" (1962), Poetry reading— Billerica Library; [oth.writ.] Poetry Books: Tapestry of Time, Poems of Progress, Live and See, The Reality of Christ, These Things and Those Things; Prose Books: Our Christian Beginnings, One Church, A New President; [pers.] Pre-school poems from swinging and making thoughts fit the rhythm pattern. Youthful poems write on ribbon paper creating the long form and the hope to write a yard a day. Now, probe inner thoughts.; [a.] Billerica, MA

ABRAMS, EMILY
[b.] March 31, 1987; New York, NY; [p.] Gay and Harry Abrams; [ed.] El Rodeo Elementary School entering 5th grade; [occ.] Student; [a.] Beverly Hills, CA

ADAMS, LISA
[b.] January 10, 1965; [p.] James Lawson, Sara Lawson; [m.] John Adams; August 13, 1983; [ch.] John Nelson, Jennifer Lynne; [ed.] Coal City High School; [occ.] Housewife; [a.] Helenwood, TN

ADAMSON-MCMULLEN, TAMMY
[b.] April 15, 1959; Springfield, IL; [ed.] B.S. Journalism, University of Illinois at Urbana-Champaign, 1981; [occ.] Freelance Journalist; [oth. writ.] Articles published in Various Magazines throughout North America.

ADKINS, SHANEON
[pen.] Sean Wallace; [b.] October 28, 1983; [p.] Kendall and Tammy Adkins; [ed.] 9th Grade HS; [occ.] Student; [hon.] 4.0 Honor Student; [oth.writ.] The Game, Life: Death; [pers.] My poems are based on my personal feelings mixed in with my friends' feelings.; [a.] Midkiff, WV

ALGER, KEITH E.
[b.] August 19, 1955; Binghamton, NY; [ch.] Keith/John; [occ.] Technical Services/for a packaging company; [pers.] Life is wonderful in hard times and good times when you have the Lord, Jesus Christ in your heart, nothing is impossible.

ANDERSON, ANITA GILL
[b.] September 2, 1956; Nashville, TN; [p.] Mrs. F.J. Gill (Frances); [m.] Monroe A. Anderson Jr; September 8, 1984; [ch.] Monroe (Albert) Anderson III; [ed.] Graduated from College with a B.S. in Speech and Hearing disorders and political science, and a minor in Psychology; [occ.] Subrogation (insurance) Adjuster; [memb.] Member of Heritage Fellowship, United Church of Christ, member of Potomac Associate Women's Coordinating Committee-UCC; [hon.] Awarded the "Living Legacies" from Reoston, VA. Links Inc., Founder and Director of the theatre troupe, "A New Voice"; [pers.] My poetry is an honest and open reflection of my heart.; [a.] Herndon, VA

ANKHESENAMEN, SHELLEY SHELTON
[b.] September 25, 1954; Louisiana; [p.] Mary and Maurice; [ed.] University of Houston, a lot of workshops, including poetry; [occ.] Special Talent Director, artist; [memb.] Film writer for special talented Kids, Karate Angels Sister (9 lives, Moments of Intimacy); [hon.] Wynton Marsalis, Cab Calloway, Maya Angelou, President Clinton, thee, Special Talent "teens," Director, director for Miss USA 1997, Ali Landry and 35 other students during age 74-18; [oth.writ.] "Jazz Love," title to a movie, is being looked into by greatest Jazz man, Kenny G., Wynton Marsalis, Herbie Hancock and other interested; [pers.] "Chasing the Bird" was born when I was raised with thee Wynton Marsalis as a kid since age 4—14 years. We chased birds, together with bread crumbs. My African Grey is named "Sir Wynton" in honor of Marsalis. "Kaytee Productions" complimentary to "Jazz Love" and "Birds."; [a.] Breaux Bridge, LA

APONTE, AWILDA
[b.] February 18, 1971; Bronx, NY; [pers.] And Away we go; [a.] Queens Village, NY

ARCHIVILLA, MERLIN
[pen.] Merlin Archivilla; [b.] January 31, 1931; Philippines; [pers.] Philosopher, psychic, writer-poet and connoisseur, advocate of the doctrines of the self, of individualism, of humanism, and of personalism. A self-taught philosopher, he taught himself philosophy, he learned from himself philosophy, philosophy is his way of life, he lived philosophically, "A man of the 21st Century."; [a.] Los Angeles, CA

AREBELO, CANDACE
[pen.] Candy; [b.] June 7, 1962; Gardena, CA; [p.] Fred Nash, Vivian Nash; [m.] Richard Arebelo; March 27, 1984; [ch.] Selina, Shelly, Richard Jr; [ed.] Long Beach City College, Pacific Coast Highway Campus, L.B California Somerset High, Bell Flower California Class of 1980; [occ.] Cashier; [hon.] Long Beach City College Certificate of Achievement on IBM Computers, High School Diploma; [oth.writ.] I have several other poems written, but have never entered any of them in a contest before. I would be happy to send in copies of my work either for future publication, or just for viewing.; [pers.] I want to thank my husband and children for believing in me.; [a.] Long Beach, CA

ARMAS, RONY
[b.] May 30, 1977; Los Angeles, CA; [p.] Elizabeth Romero; [ed.] Graduated with scholarship from Amelia Earhart High School/Currently Attending Los Angeles Valley College; [occ.] Amateur Photographer and Student; [oth.writ.] I have written several other poems but this is the first one ever published. Hopefully the others will soon follow.; [pers.] My personal note is more of a question: What keeps us all from living up to our fullest potential? Ask yourself this!; [a.] North Hollywood, CA

ARREDONDO, MARTHA
[b.] January 27, 1950; Selma, CA; [ch.] Dax, Renan; [occ.] Home Care Provider; [pers.] Remembering Victor Hugo, Tianna, Camille. With first breath, looks and stares from strangers we encounter, approaching death all become our intimates. I've been given that "gift" of intimacy, through my occupation.; [a.] Santa Cruz, CA

ARRINGTON, TASYA MICELLENA
[pen.] Tasya; [b.] August 8, 1966; Spring Hope, North Carolina; [p.] Brenda Joyce Ellis; [ed.] Associate in Applied Science—Business Management University of Maryland (College Park) honor student, Damascus High School, Damascus, MD; [occ.] Big Sister of Washington D.C., Metropolitian Area, Febrauary '94 to present; volunteer with organization So Others Might Eat, to feed the homeless. Member New Southern Rock Baptist Church; [hon.] Employee of the Year 1989—Mastercraft Interiors; [oth.writ.] Poetry for weddings, birthdays, graduations, funerals, retirements, etc.; [pers.] "Who I am is God's gift to me, and who I become is my gift to God." — Pamela Turscott.

ARRITOLA, GEORGE
[b.] September 29, 1979; Miami, FL; [p.] Noemi Intenzo, Vincent Intenzo; [ed.] Coral Park H.S. Junior; [occ.] Student, Museum of Science; [oth.writ.] Numerous Poems, unpublished; [pers.] I have been influenced by music specifically Jim Morrison. My favorite writer is J.D. Salinger. I strive to be a student athlete.; [a.] Miami, FL

ATKINSON, JENNIFER
[b.] November 2, 1982, Florida; [p.] Lynn and Suzanne Atkinson; [ed.] Freshman at Niceville Senior High School; [occ.] Student; [hon.] 1st place winner of the Okaloosa County Poetry Contest for School Year 1996-7.

AUKERMAN, ROBERT B.
[b.] April 16, 1939; Cincinnati, OH; [p.] Charles R. and Louise H. Aukerman; [m..] Cecelia; [ch.] Judy, Arlene, Robert; [pers.] "Humble Majesty" is dedicated to the memory of my brother, Charles H. Aukerman, who lived with his hand extended in concern and help to many others.; [a.] Littlebon, CO

AUSTIN, MARIKA HEIDE
[b.] April 21, 1958; West Germany; [m.] Christopher Austin; November 29, 1986; [ed.] German High School, 3 Years Trade School, 2 Years College, took 2 1/2 Counselor, USA Schools: Trade and 1 year College; [occ.] Self-Employed, Control Technology for 10 years; [memb.] I am a distinguished Member of ISP and the Delmarva Pilot Association; [hon.] Editor's Choice Award from ISP, 3 years class President, 2nd Place in German County, "I Was Born Reading," 9th grade, U.S.M. Award and Certificate as Pinch Hitter Pilot, Certificate in Medical Terminology, Award for High Achievement in Medical Terminology in Spain, Certificate—Scuba diver, Award for Nursing, since English is not my primary Language; [oth. writ.] I always wrote, however I never published, with the exception of one very popular magazines for "men," I gave my piece of mind, which got published. I was very exited to see you published my poem in Essence of a Dream and the following new ones.; [pers.] I usually unite from me, as published in Essences of a Dream "One Word I Will Never Hear"! Which I won Editor's Choice Award, Also past lives and I am inspired just by everyday life goings-on!; [a.] Dover, DE

BACCHUS, PETER TERENCE
[pen.] Ter Bacchus; [b.] August 9, 1942; Georgetown, Guyana, SA; [p.] Father (deceased), mother—Veronica; [m.] Claudette Avis Bacchus; June 18, 1966; [ch.] Pauline, Maria, Susan, Naudia; [ed.] Queenstown, R.C. Primary, Indians Trust High, Wandworth College—London; [occ.] Statements Processor—Bank Atlantic—Lauderhill; [memb.] National Geographical Society, Roman Catholic Church; [oth.writ.] Many poems and essays, mostly as a hobby; [pers.] I see beauty in simple things of nature, especially in animals and plants. To share such thoughts could generate deeper love and understanding of own surroundings. 'Ode on a Grecian Urn' was inspiring.; [a.] Lauder Hill, FL

BAILLARGEON, JESSICA S.
[b.] May 2, 1982; Milo, ME; [p.] Cherie, and Donald Bryant; [m.] Boyfriend—W. Everett Sanborn; [ed.] I want to be a lawyer and part-time writer; [occ.] High School, work Day Summer Camp; [hon.] 2nd Place for poetry at the Unified Arts Fair; [oth.writ.] Eighty other poems that I have written; [pers.] Writing is a great way to deal with conflict through life. All writings should be saved because someday someone may like your style. Smile.; [a.] Ellsworth, ME

BALDWIN, BETTY LOU
[b.] September 25, 1930; Mobile, AL; [p.] Mr. and Mrs. Jesse Baldwin; [ed.] Registered Nurse 3 yr. Diploma plus AA degree; [occ.] Retired R.N; [memb.] NARFE; [hon.] Superior performance Award, Heart and Hands Award while employed as an R.N. with Veterans Administration; [pers.] God has Blessed me with the ability to serve others as

a registered nurse. The poem I wrote was the result of some of my experiences.; [a.] Los Angeles, CA

BALDWIN, EDWARD
[b.] September 16, 1902; Ottawa, IL; [p.] Mr. Baldwin is deceased, I, Mrs. Baldwin submitted the poem that he had written; [m.] Edwards Baldwin; July 28, 1934; [pers.] Mr. Baldwin was with A L an L. Inc. For 39 years. He was manager of Patent License until his retirement.

BALMER, JESSICA LYNN
[b.] October 25, 1981; Scranton PA; [p.] Harold and Geraldine Balmer; [ed.] Mid Valley Secondary Center (still attend); [hon.] 1991-92 reflections winner (music), softball trophies 1993-96; [oth. writ.] Several other poems unpublished and unread and books I wrote when I attended Dunmore Elementary School.; [a.] Dickson City, PA

BALOGH, BARBARA
[b.] June 8, 1958; Miami, FL; [p.] Deceased—Emery and Ethel Balogh; [ed.] B.A. in Communications from the University of Miami, with a major in journalism and minor in music; [occ.] Freelancing and seeking other employment too; [memb.] Currently none; [hon.] None recently-in college, was in Golden Key National Honor Society and the German Club; [oth.writ.] "Christmas Without Candy" published in December 1994 issue of "I Love Cats" magazine; [pers.] I write about personal experiences, and am currently working on inspirational and spiritual accounts that have touched my life.; [a.] Olmsted Falls, OH

BALOGH, DIANA
[b.] January 15, 1959; Copenhagen, Denmark; [p.] Evy Mortensen; [occ.] Retail Sales; [oth.writ.] "Gone Forever" published in National High School Book of Poetry in 1975-1977; [pers.] What a better world this would be if we could only put ourselves in other people's places . . . So much more understanding so much more harmony.; [a.] Goiden, CO

BANDY, WINNELL
[pen.] Winnell Wade Bandy; [b.] July 27, 1919; Olney, TX; [p.] George Hollive and Pearl Maude Wadep; [m.] James R. Bandy (deceased); November 12, 1946; [ch.] Jerry J., Gregory S., Dana W., David W.; [ed.] High School, 3 years College, Grad. Trade School, grad. of a Secretarial/ Acctg. School; [occ.] Retired; [memb.] (past) President Zonta International Bd. of Dir. Boys Club, Bd. of Dir. of Food Service Executive Club; [hon.] High School Athelatic—Public Speaking—Organizing, Planning and Establishing a Girls Club—11 Senior Community Service Awards—15 years as a volunteer for disabled, certificate 8 ribbons and medals from Army Air Corps. I served from September 1, 1945 to November 22, 1945; [oth.writ.] Short Stories (unpublished), Published articles for Air Corps News—Published poem for local volunteer groups; [pers.] I try to help people to "stop and smell the roses" each day.; [a.] Margaret, FL

BARMES, EDWARD R.
[b.] November 30, 1938; Chicago; [p.] Irene Novacke and Marion Barmes; [m.] Divorced; June 8, 1963; [ch.] One daughter; [occ.] Driver-Messenger; [pers.] With the help of P.M.A. a fourteen week course given by Clement Stone at the University of Illionis. Helps me to use a positive mental attitude in my life.; [a.] Chicago, IL

BARNES, BARBARA J.
[pen.] Barbara Brown-Barnes; [b.] April 20, 1939; Redding, CA; [p.] Alta Hannemann-Brown, Wayne Brown; [m.] Merrill Wayne Barnes; November 7, 1965 widowed in 1987; [ch.] Marshall Ward Barnes; [ed.] PhD in Counseling Psychology in 1986, PS. PS., San Diego, CA; [occ.] Psychospiritual Counselor Hypnotherapist/Regressionist; [memb.] A.R.E., A.P.R.T.; [oth.writ.] This is my first

published poem. Currently completing a first novel, titled "Darias, Łegend of a Wolf"; [pers.] It is my prayer that my writing will be "As A Light Unto The Darkness." I hope that the reader will find some measure of personal peace, joy and truth in my words.; [a.] Banning, CA

BARNHART, LAURIE
[pen.] Laurie Barnhart; [b.] December 2, 1941; New York City; [p.] McDonald and Peggy Gillespie; [m.] Harry Barnhart; May 25, 1984; [ch.] Amy Ledbetter, Amanda Arnone, Edward Wyslick Jr; [ed.] 2 yrs University of Conn., poetry writing classes at Greater Hartford College; [occ.] Writer and homemaker; [memb.] Trinity Epicopal Church, Collinsville. Education For Ministry—Practically Christian; [hon.] Second place in the greater Hartford College poetry and short story contest; [oth.writ.] Poems have been published in local publications.; [pers.] I try to address the emotional experiences of my own life which I believe may have universal connections.; [a.] Collinsville, CT

BARREIRO, JOSEPH
[pen.] Joe Brado; [b.] June 7, 1933; Pittsburgh, PA; [p.] Florencio and Mary Barreiro; [m.] Alice, Jean Barreiro; January 11, 1953; [ch.] Joseph, Florencio, Michael Anthony, Cheryl Marie; [ed.] High School, Penn State 1 yr., Robert Morris 1 yr.; [occ.] Retired Insurance General Agent; [memb.] Universal Athletic Assoc., WM Penn. Assoc., I.S.D.A; [oth.writ.] Short story: Can I Make One More Call, Hey Angelo!; [pers.] We can only give what we have—to keep it to ourselves makes it worthless.; [a.] Pittsburgh, PA

BARRON, SHEILA CRUMPTON
[pen.] Sheila Crumpton; [b.] October 10, 1935; Little Rock, AR; [p.] Rebecca Shepard Crumpton, Oliver Wendell Crumpton; [m.] Divorced; [ch.] Elizabeth Cobbs Graves and Joseph (Bill) Barron; [ed.] Little Rock High, Little Rock, AK and Draughon Business College Little Rock, AK; [occ.] Retired Management, Asst. Secretary from U.S. Army Finance Center of Indianapolis, IN; [memb.] Quill and Scroll, International Honor Society for High School Journalists of Little Rock High School, Little Rock, AK, Member of "Tiger" staff, school newspaper and co-author of Tiger Tales with Dean Faulkner Meadow (niece of the famous William Faulkner of Mississippi); [oth. writ.] Numerous other poems since age 17 (My mother who is deceased wrote verses for greeting cards in 1920's); [pers.] Was diagnosed with disease of Multiple Sclerosis 20 years ago but with determination and will-power I am blessed with conquering it and am able to remain active instead of bed-ridden as many afflicted with "MS." Through my mother Rebecca Shepard Crumpton I am 12th generation American.; [a.] Indianapolis, IN

BARRY, ANNA M.
[b.] October 22, 1934; Worcester, Massachusetts; [p.] Matteo and Isabel/D'Errico; [m.] Richard J. Barry; August 14, 1953; [ch.] Richard, Joseph, Dawn (Grandchildren) Andrew, Keith, Connor, Briana, Reed ; [ed.] High School Grad Shrewsbury High School in Massachusetts; [occ.] Semi-retired; [oth.writ.] Write children's stories, and I keep a daily journal; [pers.] Words can inspire, they can comfort, they can encourage. That is what I want the reader to feel.; [a.] Standish, ME

BARTRON, HARRY
[b.] December 26, 1917; Van Etten, NY; [p.] Margaret Cranmer and Fernando iBartron; [m.] Inez Fortner; June 1942; [ch.] Stephen Bartron, Liz iPittenger, [ed.] B.A. In English, M.A. in speech, B.A. (Eqonalancy) in iTheology; [occ.] Actor, singer, and writer; [memb.] Screen actor's guild, iSeculab Franciscan Order (Catholic), Equity, American Federation of Radio iand television artists, dignity, the I Am Foundation; [hon.] Who's

who iamong students in American University and colleges, Dignity Archangel iaward; [oth.writ.] Poems: book of poets entitled "Poems of Protest, " A inovel entitled "Drummer Boy," book of poems entitled "Quite Another Place," iA treatise on the teaching of the Catholic church of homosexuality: "you ican be a bird, but you can't fly; [a.] Los Angeles, CA

BATTLE, ALBERTA TYLIA DORETHEA
[b.] July 31, 1978; Nashville, TN; [ed.] McGavock High, TN State University; [occ.] Full-Time Student; [memb.] Pre-Fellowship Program; [hon.] Dean's List, received scholarships from the following: Townsend Press Inc, Corey L. Harris Foundation, and the PFP Foundation. I am also a Residence Assistant at Tennessee State University; [pers.] I strive to write through expression and feelings that come from the heart.; [a.] Old Hickory, TN

BEAM, HOWARD
[pen.] H Thomas Beam; [b.] July 4, 1974; Condell (Mundelen) IL; [p.] John and Suzann E. Beam; [ed.] Graduated from Johnsburg High; [occ.] Life; [memb.] Hippocritical Society; [oth.writ.] I have several other writings. Some written down on paper, some still in head. This is my first publication; [pers.] Everyone wants the answer to the meaning of life but no one is willing to live a life to get the answer. Because by the time you do get the answer you're too old to remember the question but that's life.; [a.] McHenry, IL

BELL, CYNTHIA
[b.] Chicago, IL; [m.] Divorced/Single; [ch.] Adult children/Grandchildren; [ed.] Four year degree in Liberal Arts, considering seeking a Masters in Social work in the Near Future; [occ.] Community worker w/ Chicago Housing Authority; [memb.] Member of the Apostlic Church of God in Chicago IL; [hon.] Several plaques for community services donated in kind to non-profit organizations focused on inner city youth; [oth.writ.] "I've God My Mind Made Up," "Do They Really Know," "A Letter To My Heavenly Father"; [pers.] "My philosophical out-look on life is avoid becoming a problem, by joining those with the solution." God Bless The World; [a.] Chicago, IL

BELL, JENNIFER
[b.] May 26, 1977; Lansing, MI; [p.] Mary Geirland and John Bell; [m.] Erin Wagner; [memb.] Reconciliation Metropolitan Community Church; [pers.] May God be with everyone.; [a.] Walker, MI

BENNET, RACHEL
[b.] May 2, 1982; Reno, NV; [p.] Rick and Rosanne Bennet; [ed.] Currently enrolled at Silverado High School in Las Vegas, NV; [occ.] Student, jane-of-all trades, comic, aspiring writer; [memb.] Silverado Tennis Team, National Honor Society; [hon.] Editor of school paper, nominated for American Legion Award, Honor Roll; [oth. writ.] Four novels in progress, one fiction, one collection of poetry, one collection of short stories, one collection of insane babblings from my head and the minds of my compatriots; [pers.] I would like to thank the following people: Nancy Thompson, for her encouragement, Susan Thornton for her guidance, Aubrey, Heather, Ted and Melissa for their support, Jane for her inspiration.; [a.] Las Vegas, NV

BERBES, STEPHEN
[pen.] Steve; [b.] January 25, 1943; Baltimore; [p.] Angela Berbes; [ed.] College Graduate-1976 University of Maryland Other Colleges - Penn State, Tennessee, Brigham Young, Cornell; [occ.] Government Security; [memb.] American Legion, Church, Book Clubs; [hon.] Basketball Trophy Security Honor Awards, Certificates of Achievement From Colleges in the Arts, Literature, History, Business; [oth.writ.] Health Versus Wealth, Wrong Idea of Success, Nice Thoughts, Simple Things, Spring, America, Greener Pastures, The

Boxer, The Ocean, The Town, Missing His Lady, Night Time; [pers.] I started getting interested by reading great poems, from great poets. I would lean toward Romantic Poetry. I lean also toward mankind poetry.; [a.] Baltimore, MD

BERG, DESIREE MAUREEN
[b.] December 18, 1979; Fairmont, MN; [p.] Tim and Marsha Berg; [ed.] Mankato West Senior High; [pers.] My poetry is a window into my opaque inner world. I want to thank Maya Angelou for inspiring me to write.; [a.] North Mankato, MN

BERKSHIRE, PATRICIA A.
[b.] May 7, 1943; Los Angeles, CA; [p.] Frank R. Berkshire, Dorothy M. Muth; [ed.] Our Lady, Queen of Angles High School, Los Angeles, CA, San Diego Community College, San Diego, CA, University of Portland, Portland, OR, The Professional School of Psych. Studies, San Diego, CA; [occ.] Masseuse, musician, teacher; [memb.] Sociedad National Hispanica, Delta Epsilon Sigma Honor Society (U. of Portland), Alpha Gamma Sigma Honor Society (S.D. Community Coll.); [hon.] Philomathean Honor Society (U. of P.), College Scholar, 1969-1970 (U.Of P.), Who's Who Among Students in American Colleges and Universities, 1969-1970 ed., Dean's lists; [oth. writ.] Poems in College Poetry Journal; [pers.] I am complex, but not complicated.; [a.] Oxnard, CA

BERNARD, PATRICIA
[b.] August 7, 1944; [p.] Grace and Dan Collins; [ed.] Bachelors Degree Anna Maria College—Math; [occ.] Project Manager—Systems; [oth.writ.] Working on Science Fiction Novel; [a.] East Windsor, NJ

BERRIOS, MARIO EFRAIN
[b.] March 28, 1973; New Haven, Conn; [p.] Mario Berrios Jr. and Patricia Stewart; [m.] Kathleen Berrios; December 17, 1993; [ch.] Breylan John Berrios (son); [ed.] Corona High School, Embry-Riddle Aeronautical University; [occ.] Loadmaster, USAF; [pers.] Our lives are controlled by that which is around us; if we learn to love our surroundings, we can begin to learn to love ourselves.; [a.] Spanaway, WA

BEST, ANDRE C.
[pen.] Dre; [b.] May 4, 1977; Rio De Janeiro, Brazil; [p.] Marilda S. Best; [ed.] Chandler High School, Chandler-Gilbert Community College; [occ.] Student; Song writer/Composer and Performer; [hon.] Who's who among American High Scholl Students '94-'95; [oth.writ.] The Search, Eyes on the Horizon, A Man's Plea, Complicated and Confused; [pers.] Everything that I write is a reflection of society and life interpreted through my eyes. They are my feelings and deep thoughts.; [a.] Chandler, AZ

BIESZKI, PATRICIA
[pen.] Patricia Marie Kelly; [b.] March 21, 1960; Chicago, IL; [hon.] 2000 Notable American Women, The World Who's Who of Women; [oth. writ.] An Incomplete Childhoods, Whispers of the Heart, Do Teddy Bears Sing; [pers.] Words are whisper of the heart—created by one, yet felt by many.; [a.] Huntley, IL

BILLADEAU, DIANA M.
[pen.] Little Indiana; [b.] October 26, 1949; Evansville, IN; [p.] Gilbert and Pauline Kuhen; [m.] Roland F. Billadeau; August 14, 1994; [ch.] Danny (12 years old); [ed.] University of Miami and PCDI. (Professional Career Development Institute), Atlanta, GA, Career Choice: Medical Transcription; [occ.] Medical Transcription in Colorado. A Small Company, New in the Area; [memb.] ABWA, Alumnae of University of Miami, Methodist Church, and KK (A Philanthropical International Organization, U.S.A., Republican Party); [hon.] Dean's List, '71 (Bachelor of Ed), Sweet-

heart of Sigma Chi, College Board (University of Miami, '69-70), FCC Counsil Hostess; [oth.writ.] "Teacher of Leisure"; [pers.] I Teach and Believe. Everyone has a complete knowledge. Everyone will be the benefactor of their own will and testament. Smiles only show our outward "Peace Of Mind." May we all age gracefully, hopefully, and love of the living prevail.; [a.] Colorado Springs, CO

BILON, DR. OUIDE
[b.] November 23, 1915; New York, NY; [p.] John F. Russell Jr./Elizabeth Taylor Russell; [m.] George Bilon; June 25, 1953; [ch.] Jane Ann Bilon; [ed.] AB Bryan Mawr College '38, Union Theological Seminary, M Div '42 George Washington University, Elin MA '53, George Washington University Elin Ph.D. '67; [occ.] Pr. Practice of Elin Psychology in Washington DC 25 years of experience; [oth.writ.] Article on or direction to the Priesthood for Wovel the witness 1942, Louisa R. Bilon have written many other poems not yet published; [pers.] I am creating my own intervition of Philosophy and dept. psychological or a psychological compose with a spiritual enter hataged "Ouide" Wheel and currently writing and soul suit it.; [a.] Washington, DC

BINGHAM, MATT
[pen.] Bingham; [b.] July 22, 1979; Stevens Point, WI; [p.] Jim and Kathy Bingham; [ed.] High School Diploma Graduated from Central Gwinnett High School; [occ.] Sales Clerk at Seans; [memb.] St. Margurite D'Youville Softball Team; [hon.] GPA Awards for School, trophy for Baseball (1st place team); [oth.writ.] Essays and poems writen for school assignments; [pers.] If people would take the time to acknowledge the beauty and wonders of the world instead of the downfalls, it would be a much better place to live.; [a.] Lawrenceville, GA

BISCHOF, MARISA
[b.] April, 1985; New York; [p.] Stella and Richard Bischof; [occ.] 6th Grade Student; [hon.] St. John's University Program for gifted and talented children, Talent finalist in Pageant for singing; [oth.writ.] Many poems and songs; [a.] Fresh Meadow Queens, NY

BISHOP, HAROLD
[pen.] Hal Bishop; [b.] June 18, 1916; Black Duck, MN; [p.] Deceased; [m.] Patricia (Patti) Bishop; December 28, 1953; [ch.] Lynda Joyce, Jana Petruzon; [ed.] Central High School, Superior, WI; [occ.] Carpet Business, ex-Professional Ballroom Dancer; [memb.] Writers of Kern; [oth. writ.] Selected poems from the library of Harold A Bishop. Novel (in writing) Black Wolf Moon; [pers.] Dishonor lies behind the door, paneled with greed, whose latch is opportunity.; [a.] Bakersfield, CA

BITSON, ANGELA
[pen.] Angela Bitson; [b.] November 10, 1975; Shelby; [p.] Robert and Carol Bitson; [ed.] Shelby High School Baker Colleg of Muskegon; [occ.] Office Administrator; [hon.] Dean's List; [oth.writ.] Other poems published in class publication project.; [a.] Shelby, MI

BITSON, GARY A.
[pen.] Lance Pentagrasp/Lance Freeman; [b.] September 04, 1953; Shelby, MI; [p.] Arthur Bitson & Cista (Rought) Bitson; [m.] Cindy L. (Boes) Bitson; January 05, 1974; [ch.] Wyatt Arthur, Benjamin Franklin, Rebecca Lynn, Joshua Clay, Betsy Lou, Mary Bell, and Samuel Mead; [ed.] Shelby High School/Shelby, MI; [occ.] Freelance Writer, Poet, Lyricist, Philospher, & Christian Preacher w/Friar lifestyle; [memb.] The International Society of Poets, The International Poetry Hall of Fame, God's Church in Christ, Universal; [hon.] Nominated & accepted into The International Society of Poets, Elected into International Poetry Hall of Fame; 2 National Library of Poetry Editor's Choice Awards; [oth.writ.] Poems in several NLP's An-

thologies, past articles in local newspaper; [pers.] I promote the reality of God; Divine Providence; God's grace and salvation to mankind upon repentance to requirements of truth as delivered via Jesus Christ and the Prophets.; [a.] Baldwin, MI

BLAZAK, BONNIE
[m.] Chris Auer; [ch.] Erin Rowan; [pers.] Having spent the first half of my life in service to others, my wings are now spread for the flight of a life time.

BOADU, MARGARET G.
[b.] February 17, 1952; Ahoskie, NC; [p.] Ellen Givens; [m.] Yaw Boadu; July 12, 1977; [occ.] Nursing Asst. UNC Student Health Service; [memb.] Eagle's Summit Christian Fellowship Church; [pers.] This poem was written for my husband for our 20th anniversary. (Wedding); [a.] Durham, NC

BOGGS, MATTHEW RYAN
[b.] January 27, 1979; ForthWorth, TX; [p.] Paul Boggs, Glenda Boggs; [ed.] G.E.D.; [occ.] Student Pilot Sun Point Aviation Longview, TX; [oth.writ.] Ghost Of The Past to be published by Sparrowgrass Poetry Forum in anthology Poetic Voices of America, in February 1998; [pers.] I hope "For You" touches you as much as it did me when I wrote it. It is truly from the heart.; [a.] Gilmer, TX

BOLLNOW, PAMELA
[b.] September 7, 1956; Chicago, IL; [p.] George Diandrea, Shirley Reamer, William Reamer; [m.] Karl Bollnow Jr.; February 14, 1989; [ch.] Matthew Raymond, Brian Joseph; [ed.] Morton East High School Cicero, IL; [occ.] Data Processing MGR, THK America, Schaumburg, IL; [oth. writ.] This writing was my first Artistic Endeavor; [pers.] This poem was inspired by the recent death of my brother. In my heart, I know that we wrote this poem together.; [a.] Addison, IL

BOSHEARS, KIM
[b.] September 10, 1966; Joliet, IL; [p.] Loyd and Kathleeen Martin; [ch.] Jeremy and Jessica; [ed.] Joliet Central High School—School of practical Nursing—Joliet Junior College; [occ.] LPN; [memb.] ISP; [hon.] President's Roll of excellence—Joliet Junior College; [oth.writ.] The weathered souls, Elemental consciousness—published by NLP; [pers.] Poetry is a way to view the world through your soul. It always speaks honestly.; [a.] Joliet, IL

BOSS, EVELYN
[pen.] Robin; [b.] January 29, 1984; Good Samaritan West Islip, NY; [p.] Michael and Ann Marie Boss; [ed.] Junior High Robert Frost Middle School-Deer Park, NY; [occ.] Student; [hon.] Presidential Award; [oth.writ.] Other poems not published; [pers.] Forget the past, don't think about the future, live the present; this is life.; [a.] Deer Park, NY

BOST, WALTER L.
[b.] February 19, 1927; Kannapolis, NC; [p.] Theodore L. Bost and Myrtie Bost; [m.] Ruby Bost; August 11, 1951; [ch.] Judy Frances, Walter Lee, Jr; [ed.] J.W. Cannon High, Davidson College, North Georgia College, Georgia Institute of Technology, Southern Technical Institute; [occ.] Retired Architect, Real Estate Broker; [memb.] American Institute of Architects, Lions' Club, First Baptist Church, Prior Member Toast Masters, Charlotte Chamber of Commerce, Cancer Society; [hon.] North Carolina Board of Architects—10 years, 3 years Pres., Vice Pres., Sec., and Treas. one year EA; CHM of Southern Conf. of Nat. Council of Architectural Registration, BDS—2 years, State Director to Region—5 years. (1985-1995) Participant in International Construction Symposium, Seoul, South Korea, 1996, Continued Travel Around the World; [oth.writ.] I have written a number of professional papers for presentation, as well as poetry, but have not submitted for publication previously.; [pers.] Poetry to me is

simply an outward expression of an inner emotion. I have written a number of poems, all of which evolved from high emotion, some happy, some sad.; [a.] Kannapolis, NC

BOWDEN, MAGGIE ESTELLE
[pen.] Joyce Morton; [b.] July 5, 1925; Martin, TN; [p.] Bertha Leora (Jackson) House, Earnest L. House; [m.] William Bowder; May 24, 1947; [ch.] Steven Lynuel, Mark William, Pamela Jean, Joyce Renee; [ed.] High School; 1947 Martin TN; [occ.] Housewife, retired; [oth. writ.] "I'm Lonely " Estelle Bowder, "Sea Shells," Pen name Pamela Jean Russell. I purchased one book already of the Ever-Flowing Stream under my other writer's name.; [a.] Garden City, MI

BOWSER, CHRISTOPHER G.
[b.] July 14, 1968; Salida, CO; [p.] Marvin Bowser, Sandra Bowser; [m.] Vickie Bowser; May 1, 1987; [ch.] Jessica Bowser; [ed.] Moffat County High School Colorado Aero Tech; [occ.] Aviation Maintenance Technician; [hon.] Received several letters of Commendations and Appreciation from the U.S. Navy; [pers.] I have found that for me it is sometimes easier to write about feelings from the heart than to speak about them.; [a.] Clifton, CO

BOWSER, DONNA M.
[b.] February 23, 1946; Baltimore, MD; [p.] Eugene A. and Josephine F. Peach; [m.] George C. Bowser Jr; May 8, 1965; [ch.] George III, Eugene, Jerry II, Jason; [ed.] Woodlawn SR High; [occ.] Tournament Director for editor of several Bridge Books American Contract Bridge League and monthly newsletter; [memb.] Reisterstown Chapter—Women of the Moose, Maryland Bridge Association, Nunt Maron Woman's Club, American Quilters' Society; [oth.writ.] Several short stories, 2 children's books, poems, etc; [pers.] I try to go through life enjoying the good in the world and its inhabitants.; [a.] Reisterstown, MD

BOYLE, PATRICIA
[b.] May 19, 1965; Pompton Lakes, NJ; [p.] John and Joan Boyle; [ch.] Jazmin Alise Boyle; [ed.] Mommouth College; [memb.] Alpha Sigma TAU Sorority (AET); [oth.writ.] Poem published in Great Poems of the Western World, called "Why Do I Cry"; [pers.] I'd like to thank God for my greatest teachers, experience and my daughter, Jazmin.; [a.] Newark, DE

BRADFORD, TIMOTHY SCOTT
[b.] January 17, 1982; Ukiah, California; [p.] James H. and Nancy L. Taylor; [ed.] Intermountain Adventist Academy, Currently 10th Grade; [occ.] Student; [memb.] Seventh-day Adventist Church of Grand Junction; [hon.] A honor roll. 3.80 G.P.A. Presidential Academics Awards Presidential Fitness Award; [oth. writ.] "It Is Love" (not published). "Are You the One?" (not published); [pers.] I do the best I can with everyday life and if that isn't good enough, I do better.; [a.] Grand Junction, CO

BRADLEY, SHARON E.
[b.] July 5, 1951; Philadelphia, PA; [p.] Albert and Charlotte Bradley; [ed.] High School (Bishop Conwell) Some College (Bucks County Community College Christian Counseling Education Foundation); [occ.] Disabled; [oth.writ.] Working on children's stories, a book of poetry and an autobiography; [pers.] All things are possible through Jesus Christ.; [a.] Langhurne, PA

BRADY, DEE
[p.] Anne and William Smith Atl. Hglds. NJ; [occ.] Early Childhood Ed. Teacher Mt. Hill School, Atl. Hglds. NJ; [hon.] Editor's choice award for 1996, and editor's choice award for 1997; [pers.] Learning to deal with the many emotions of life will need all the strength of how well you've developed your inner soul and heart, for when your heart is hurting,

the back-up of a soothing soul is desired for healing of oneself.; [a.] Atlantic Highlands, NJ

BRANDO, ROBERT
[b.] March 22, 1964; Bethpage, NY; [p.] Thomas and Dorothy; [occ.] Police Officer, New York City Police Department; [a.] Long Beach, NY

BRANHAM, DONALD
[b.] June 15, 1972; Torrance, CA; [p.] Irma Marie White; [ch.] Albert Anthoney Branham; [ed.] Hamilton High School Anza, CA; [occ.] US Army, Stationed Ft. Irwin; [oth.writ.] "Time after Time" and other poems not yet released; [pers.] I wrote this poem in loving memory of my cousin, Albert H. Rameriz Jr. (November 19, 1971 - July 21, 1990). Thank you to the people who believed in me and helped me to believe in myself.; [a.] Ft. Irwin, CA

BRAUN, RUTH JOLENE
[b.] September 15, 1937; Apple Creek, OH; [p.] Ralph and Lorna Roberts; [m.] Richard; April 30, 1955; [ch.] Michael, Steven, Jolene, Karen, Henry; [ed.] Finished 9th grade; [memb.] National Library of Poetry; [oth.writ.] "Old Lady All Alone" was in National Library of Poetry's Anthology "In Dappled Sunlight" in 1997; [pers.] I have always written poems for family and friends, for many years. For birthdays, anniversaries, holidays and just for fun. I have done them for about 25 years or more. I think it is a relaxing thing to do. And all of my family enjoy them; [a.] Wooster, OH

BRILL, MICHAEL H.
[b.] January 26, 1949; Bay Shore, NY; [p.] Henry and Wenonah Brill; [ed.] BA, English, Case Western Reserve University; MS, Physics, Syracuse University, Ph.D, Physics, Syracuse University; [occ.] Vision Scientist, Sarnoff Corp, Princeton, NJ; [memb.] Inter Society Color Council (ISCC) Optical Society of America, American Society for Photogrammetry and remote sensing; [hon.] Phi Beta Kappa, Omicron Delta Kappa, 1996 ISCC Macbeth Award; [oth.writ.] Technical articles in physics, psychology, geology, and recreational mathematics; [pers.] I strive to look at truth unflinchingly through science, and to communicate it memorably through my writing.; [a.] Morrisville, PA

BROCKISH, SHELLEY
[pen.] Shelley Brokish; [b.] November 14, 1965; MO; [p.] Homer and Hilda Steffens; [m.] Rick Brockish; February 3 1990; [ed.] Fort Osage High; [occ.] Country Club Emp; [oth.writ.] Others (not published) however enjoyed by family and friends; [pers.] I enjoy reading and writing. I try to write feelings understandble to most.; [a.] Independence, MO

BROLSMA, SHEILA
[b.] November 24, 1903; Jamaica under British Rule; [p.] Charles Condell-Elmo Bryce; [m.] Deceased, married into Lawrence of Arabia Family during the War. London in America to Clarence Brolsma June 17, 1964; [ed.] Tutored by my Father, Professor of Languages and Mathematics. At 12 could read and write in Latin; [occ.] Retired and give a helping hand wherever necessary. Very interested in the state of the country and send articles to the local newspaper; [memb.] Member of The English Speaking Union; [hon.] My greatest Award is to belong to The National Library of Poetry; [pers.] I try to keep my mind on a high level of thinking. I have traveled in Europe and seek my inspiration from the great Cathedrals and Art Galleries.; [a.] Glendale, AZ

BROWNE, HARRIET
[b.] August 7, 1932; Chicago, IL; [ch.] April Browne, Renell Gonsalves; [ed.] Engle Wood High School, A.O. Sexton Elementary, Sadie Bruce Dance School; [occ.] Professional Top Dancer,

and Choreographer Chairman of the Board of Directors of Black and Latino AIDS Coalition—Bx. Council of the Arts, and others such as the Silver Belles, Ladies Who Danced, International Women in Jazz; [hon.] Citation of Merit Pres. Fernando Ferrer Bronx Borough, Certificate of Recognition, Columbus, Ohio Mayor Gregory Lashuika, National Tap Dance Day in Honor of Bill "Bojangles" Robinson, Gen. Assembly, Ohio Senate Senator Ben Espy, Pres. of Ohio Senate Stanly J. Arnoff; [oth.writ.] From Della Reese to Mama Reese, Sugar Hill Gang, Pearlie Whites; [pers.] I am interested in all art forms, writing, and tap dancing being my favorites, but I also love jazz singing.; [a.] Bronx, NY

BRUCE, E. WARREN
[b.] July 1, 1921; Salt Lake City; [p.] Calvin Leroy, Ruth Mildred; [m.] DEV; April 10, 1943; [ch.] Tamara Jo, Jillana Susanne; [ed.] Self Taught Architect U.S. Air Force Pilot Training- Rated pilot; [occ.] Retired Architect; [memb.] American Institute of Architects; 2nd Air Division Association; 8th A.F. Historical Society; 446 Bomb Group Assoc.; [hon.] D.F.C.W/O.L.C. Air Medal W/4 O.L.C. AIA Inland Calif Chapter Honor Award for Downtown Plan-Riverside CA; [oth.writ.] 4800 Horses (WW II Air Combat Story), Goombah (a fantasy), The Golden Chord (creation-evolution fantasy), Christmas Story: How the Moon Saved Christmas, Many Haiku, Tranquil Eve—addendum to first Christmas Eve; [pers.] Write what you feel, tempered with honesty and simplicity.; [a.] Moraga, CA

BRUNER, ROB
[b.] June 19, 1980; Kansas City, MO; [p.] William Bruner, Christine Bruner; [ed.] Liberty Senior High School, planning to go to college; [oth.writ.] Many other poems, essays, and short stories; [pers.] I watch what goes on in daily life, and record what I see. I write what I feel needs to be written down.; [a.] Kearney, MO

BRUSSE, MONIQUE
[pen.] Monique Brusse; [b.] June 8, 1956; [p.] Wilfred Brusse, Marguerite Brusse; [ed.] Merritt Davis Business College; [occ.] Unemployed; [pers.] This poem is dedicated to my mother, who inspires me and encourages me to use my humor in my writings.; [a.] Kent, WA

BUCKSHEE, DR. NATASHA
[b.] December 11, 1972; New Delhi, IN; [p.] Mr. M.M. Buckshee and Dr. Kamal Buckshee; [m.] Dr. Amit Kumar; March 13, 1996; [ch.] Nil; [ed.] M.B.B.S. (Bachelor of Medicine and Bachelor of Surgeon) - Maulana Azad Medical College Schooling - Modern School Vasant Vihar, New Delhi; [occ.] Clinical Research Coordinator - Columbia Presbyterian Hospital - N.Y.; [memb.] Indian Medical Association; [hon.] Letter of Recognition by Secretary General of Russian Communist Party for poem and called "Upon," by Prime Minister of India for same. Swaran Deep Singh Medal For Excellence in Science, Certificate of Merit for Shankar's On-the-Spot Painting Competition.; [oth.writ.] Several poems published in Local newspapers.; [pers.] I strive to reflect human emotions, their depth and value in my writings. Greatly influenced by my own personal experiences in life and, my mother.; [a.] Irvington, NJ

BULOW, LORI LEE
[b.] April 26, 1978; Hermiston, OR; [p.] Jerry Bulow and Claudia Bulow; [ed.] Riverside High School in Boardman, OR. Blue Mountain Community College in Pendleton, OR; [occ.] Student; [memb.] Desert Spring Foursquare Church; [hon.] Dean's List; [oth.writ.] I have written numerous poems and short stories, but this is my first published work.; [pers.] I love nature and through writing I try to express how beautiful and pre-

cious it is. I truly believe that people need to stop and enjoy life's simple pleasures. There are so many of them, and so much that life has to offer.; [a.] Irrigon, OR

BUSH, CAROL ANN
[b.] November 7, 1949; Bronx, NY; [p.] Edward and Dorothy Majka; [ch.] Matthew, Shannon, Brian; [ed.] North Rockland High School; [occ.] Assistant Athletic Director, Ticket Management, West Point, NY; [pers.] Inspired by music, written with love; [a.] Highland Falls, NY

CAMP, DAVID LEWIS
[b.] September 9, 1993; Waunetta, KS; [p.] Fred W. and Ruthie B. Camp; [m.] Laritta Janiece Camp; July 22, 1960; [ch.] Cheryl R., Michelle L., David N., Lisa J., Justin W.; [ed.] ThG. (Graduate in Theology), Baptist Bible College, Springfield, MO; [occ.] Facility Management, Supervisor, Painting Services Dept.; [memb.] Grace Baptist Church Wichita, KS; [oth.writ.] Compiling a book of Poetry Stories and Philosopy for my children; [pers.] Ordained Baptist Preacher, My work is Christian in Philosophy. My purpose is to awaken, initiate, and excite the reader to the truth of Biblical teaching, and introduce him to or strengthen his faith in God of the Bible.; [a.] Wichita, KS

CAMPBELL MCGANN, CHRISTE MARIE
[b.] March 31, 1968; Baltimore, MD; [p.] Richard and Kathie Campbell; [m.] Robert A. McGann; March 6, 1993; [ch.] Carolanne Katherine, Ian Richard, Sarah Jennifer, Moira Leigh; [ed.] High School graduate currently college freshman at Lake City Community College; [occ.] Full-time student; [pers.] I wish to thank my parents and my husband, who have always encouraged me in any endeavor. Special thanks to Dr. Yvonne Sapia, Professor of English, my teacher and inspiration.; [a.] Lake City, FL

CANADA, SHEILA
[b.] November 1, 1968; Memphis, TN; [p.] James Patterson and Sophie Branton; [m.] Taylor Dale Canada; October 10, 1992; [occ.] Registered Nurse—Pediatrics; [hon.] Phi Theta Kappa, Dean's List; [oth.writ.] Wrote a 5 min. speech that won a national competition in 1990; [pers.] When we see with our souls and listen with our hearts to those who are different from ourselves, we truly become wise.; [a.] Elk Grove, CA

CARDWELL, VIVIAN ANN JOHNSON
[b.] July 22, 1953; Texas; [p.] Nola Mae Johnson Brown; [m.] Richard R. Cardwell Jr.; March 17, 1972; [ch.] Maurice and Richard Cardwell III; [ed.] Redando Unified School District and Redlands Senior High School, 25 year GTE CA Veteran; [occ.] GTE Administrator; [memb.] ABWA Pomona, CA Avante Chapter; [hon.] 1971 GTE CA President's Life Saving Award. 1990 GTE/ CA WMBE Award, 1995 GTE CA ERS Customer Service Award; [oth.writ.] The Day, Whales, My Wings, The Extraordinary Life Of Vivian Cardwell; [pers.] Live each day as though it were your last and give thanks for each blessing you have.; [a.] Rialto, CA

CASE, COLLEEN
[b.] July 14, 1957, Geneva, OH; [p.] Broughton M. Williams, Georgene K. Williams; [m.] Daniel Arms Case; May 10, 1983; [ch.] Matthew Daniel, Thomas Monroe; [ed.] Sue Cleveland Elem. Woodmart High, Greenville Tech; [occ.] Forklift Operator Warehouse; [memb.] Westminster Presbyterian Church, International Society of Poets and Tommy's Save the Turtles Club; [oth.writ.] Several poems written, first published - Beverly (Silence of Yesterday); [pers.] Life itself has been a poem to me. When I couldn't speak my feelings, I could write them. It's OK to be different.; [a.] Piedmont, SC

CASE, MICHAEL D.
[pen.] Michael D. Case; [b.] January 2, 1952; St Louis, MO; [p.] Veryl D. and Mary L. Case; [m.] Divorced; August 23, 1972; [ch.] 2 Branden Lynn and Kevin Shawn; [ed.] 2 yrs. at Belleville Area College; [occ.] Disabled R.R. Conductor; [pers.] The world is a big round poem that sparks the interest of a single mind, just enough to share it with a friend.; [a.] Snellville, GA

CASH, RAMONA
[b.] July 27, 1968; Brooklyn, NY; [p.] Frank Cash, Joyce Cash; [m.] Byron Pierce; July 28, 1989; [ch.] Anthony Wilson, Byron Pierce; [ed.] Grover Cleveland High, College of new Rochelle; [occ.] Student full-time, and housewife; [memb.] Good Samaritan Church; [a.] Brooklyn, NY

CASTERLOW-BEY JR., GARY ELLIS
[pen.] Gee-Gee; [b.] November 25, 1956; Indianapolis, IN; [p.] Gary Ellis, Audrey; [m.] Tonya Casterlow-Bey, October 13, 1996; [ch.] Gary Ellis III, Rafael David Louise; [ed.] Associates Degree/ Cosmotologist; [occ.] Greeting Card Producer; [memb.] Moorish Science Temple of America/ Antioch Baptist Church; [oth.writ.] All inscriptions done for the Casterlow-Bey greeting card line.; [pers.] If you can conceive a thought and believe in your ability to realize your dreams, then there is nothing too impossible to achieve. The human being is the marvel of the universe, born with unlimited capacity for growth and development.; [a.] Tacoma, WA

CAVANAUGH, NANCY L.
[pen.] Caitun K. Chaomhanach; [b.] January 8, 1942; Gallipolis, OH; [p.] Richard M. Cavanaugh, Helen L. Eads; [ch.] Karl Scott, Keisten L., Elizabeth H.; [ed.] Compton Sr. High, Coastline Community, University of Redlands, University of San Francisco, CA., LaSalle University, LA; [occ.] Writer/Consultant CA, OR, CO; [memb.] Women's Health Leadership Faculty, American Hospital Assoc., National Wilderness Soc., Nat. Geographic Society, American Assoc. University Women; [hon.] Alfred North Whitehead Honor Society; Outstanding Female Executive, Academic Excellence and Dean's List Honor Roll, Outstanding Civic and Community Leader in Health and Leadership; [oth.writ] Technical Projects for Public Health, Non-Profit Agencies, Native American Indian Clinics, Ed./Publisher of several state and national newsletters, essays, poetry, prose in local anthologies, short stories in National Spiritual Newsletter; [pers.] I write from the heart, sharing experience and stories from the female perspective based on Ancient teachings. I have been influenced by writings on strong women.; [a.] Cassel, CA

CHAPMAN, VIRGINIA L.
[b.] Januanry 11, 1917; Detroit; [p.] Seth M. and Rosie L. Williams; [m.] Herman H. Chapman, Sr.; August 8, 1937; [ch.] Herman H. Jr. and Seth M.; [ed.] Graduate of Northwestern High School Equivalent Experience was given Credit of 2 yrs. College by having and living with our two mentally impaired children wife and mother; [occ.] Retired from Wayne County Intermediate District—as an Instrudional Aide, Member of St. Stephen A.M.E. Church Since 10 years of Age; [memb.] Sunday School Teacher Since age 14, Founders of Loyal Hearts Club of A.M.E. Church Oak Grove, Organized First Mother Club, Customer Elementary School, one of several Area Chairpersons of United Foundation of Retarded Children; [hon.] Honored Times by Loyal Hearts Club of Oak Grove, A.M.E. Church, Chaired Many Fund Raisers for my Church and The Detroit Association for Retarded Children; [oth.writ.] Several Birthday Name Poems: Poems of Sympathy, Poems of Friendship to Personal Friends; [pers.] All of my knowledge for writing and life's experiences comes from The Spirit of the Lord in my Heart.; [a.] Detroit, MI

CHATTAWAY, IRENE CAROL
[pen.] Joy Chattaway; [b.] July 20, 1959; [p.] Harold R. and Grace E. Chattaway; [ed.] B.S. Computer Science/Social Science, 1985, William Paterson College of New Jersey; [memb.] Church of Christ; [pers.] I believe in the power of God's Love which can help us "rise above" into the power of "the living water" and, truly, "the ever-flowing stream."; [a.] Woodbury, CT

CHOUDHURY, KALYANI
[b.] August 11, 1933; Calcutta, India; [p.] Dakshina R. Bakshi, Kanak P. Bakshi; [m.] Pushyendo S. Choudhury; February 22, 1951; [ch.] Shikna, Abhi and Mita; [ed.] Mahila Kalyan Girls High School, Asansol College, West Bengal, India; [occ.] Homemaker, mother and grandmother; [memb.] United Nations Women's Association of Ethiopia, African Women's Association of Ethiopia; [hon.] 2nd Place Winner of the District Essay Competition (1949); [oth. writ.] Poetry published in Sparrowgrass Poetry Forum, U.S.A., several articles published in school magazine; [pers.] I write poetry as an enjoyable pastime. It helps me to divert my mind from the worries and anxieties of daily life.; [a.] Fremont, CA

CHRISTOPHER, MARGARET
[b.] August 23, 1926; Kearny, N.J. [p.] Fred and Margaret Christopher; [ed.] First Street School and So. Orange Jr High, So. Orange, NJ, Columbia High, Maple wood, NJ-Newark School of Fine Art, Newark, NJ, and Art Students League New York City; [occ.] Free Lance Artist; [hon.] Honorable Mention So. Orange Library Poetry Contest at age 16, Second Prize—Graphic Art, So. Orange, NJ Outdoor Art Show; [oth.writ.] Poems printed in newspapers, earliest one at age 13. Cartoon mouse drawings published in writing tablet by "Vagabond Creations," Dayton, OH; [pers.] A love for the beauty of nature and the fascinating world around us inspires me.; [a.] Long Pond, CA

CLARK, MICHAEL
[oth.writ.] This poem is only on expression of my feelings, and is in no way meant to harm her mother (Judy E. Goodoll); [pers.] This poem is dedicated to my lovely daughter Klasy K. Clark whom I love with all of my heart. Forever and forever; [a.] East Chicago, IN

CLIFFORD, KERRIE A.
[b.] June 22, 1978; Carmel, NY; [p.] Arlene Turner, Gary Clifford; [ed.] Roselle Park High School, and School of Visual Arts; [oth.writ.] "Kate," a short story to be published in Words by SVA, many other shorts and poems, My Final Hour and Breathe for My Life, both films; [pers.] Carry with you always the strength to support what you feel is right and your life will not become so common that it disappears.; [a.] Roselle Park, NJ

CLINE, CRYSTAL
[b.] April 21, 1983; Pennsylvania; [p.] Sherry Cline and Dale Cline; [occ.] Student; [a.] Shippensburg, PA

CLYDE, DONALD E.
[pen.] Don Clyde; February 27, 1942; Augusta, GA; [p.] William E. (deceased) and Mary P. Clyde; [m.] Divorced; Spring 1965; [ch.] Candace, Sara, Sam, Tim, Tom, Jacob, Joseph; [ed.] BA—1966, Baylor University, last two quarters Dean William Boswell's tenure, Baylor Law School; [occ.] Owner/ Operator (long-haul truck driver), Carpenter and substitute teacher; [a.] Kankakee, IL

COLE, BENNY L.
[b.] January 24, 1947; Laurens, SC; [p.] Ryan and Mary Cole; [m.] Beverly Behling; May 31, 1969; [ch.] Daughter—Nedra Paton, son—Mark Cole; [ed.] Spartanburg High School, Spartanburg, S.C.; [occ.] Public Safety Officer—Trident Tech College, N. Charleston, SC; [hon.] South Carolina

Criminal Justice Academy, Retired US Navy; [pers.] Live, love, and celebrate each day. Inspired by the writings of Ogden Nash; [a.] Goose Creek, SC

COLLINS, KELLY S.
[pen.] Sean Kelly; [b.] January 12, 1960; Dekalb, IL; [p.] Kenneth and Mary Collins; [m.] Patti; November 17, 1979; [ch.] Ryan, Cristin and Vance; [ed.] Plano High School, Plano, IL; [oth.writ] None published; [a.] Somonauk, IL

CORDARO, JOSEHPINE
[pen.] Josie; [b.] September 30, 1923; Syracuse, NY; [p.] The Late Mary and Angelo Cordaro; [ed.] I attended the Overbrook School for the Blind in Philadelphia from which I graduated with an Academic Diploma at the age of 18.; [occ.] Switchboard Operator at Allies Services for over 30 years.; [memb.] The Blind Association of Scranton, and Sears Department Stores.; [oth.writ.] I have been writing poetry and attending national poetry conventions for many years.; [pers.] One of my lifelong dreams has been to have my book of poetry published. I hope each of you gains as much enjoyment from reading this collection of poetry as I have in writing it over the years.; [a.] Scranton, PA

CORNELIUS, ALLAN DIETZ
[b.] August 14, 1911; Chesterfield, IL; [p.] Orson B. and Cora E. Cornelius; [m.] Deceased; August 28, 1941; [ch.] Allan Jr, David L, Donald W. Phillip J; [ed.] Elementary, (Springfield) High School; [occ.] Retired Letter Carrier; [memb.] NALC (National Ass'n. of Letter Carriers), NARFE (National Ass'n of Retired Fed. Empl.), IBM (International Brotherhood of Magicians), FCM (Fellowship of Christian Magicians), SVC (Southern View Chapel, Springfield, IL); [hon.] Presidential Service Award from Springfield Municipal Opera Association (Oct. 17, 1985); [oth.writ.] Editor of several monthly church publications (in states and overseas). Produced dozens of writings, editorials, short stories, poems; [pers.] I love to pass on any good thoughts or ideas before they're lost to posterity.; [a.] Springfield, IL

CORTESE, ANNE B.
[b.] June 17, 1961; Chicago, IL; [ed.] 1984— B.A., French (University of IL at Chicago); 1997—M.A., Adult Continuing Education (National Louis University); [occ.] Italian Instructor; [pers.] From the heart, Poetry is to "hit" hearts to identify with them, to hopefully bring strength and healing.; [a.] Chicago, IL

COWAN, JEREMY
[pen.] Jeremy Cowan; [b.] August 16, 1981; Tulsa, OK; [p.] Riley and Auleen Cowan; [ed.] Entering 10th Grade at Mauldin High School; [occ.] Soccer Referee; [memb.] South Carolina Upstate Soccer Referee Society, Volunteers for the Special Olympics (VSO) at Mauldin High; [pers.] I write from the heart, that is what the Lord lays on my heart. I just do my best to glorify him and put it down on the paper right.; [a.] Mauldin, SC

COY, DORIS T.
[b.] January 5, 1918; Kokomo Ind.; [p.] Nora Bellwilson and James Oliver Tobias; [m.] Carl E. Coy Sr; March 12, 1944; [ch.] Four; [ed.] Graduated Kokomo High, Attend Kokomo Bas. College, Attended Purdue, W. Lafayette, IN.; [occ.] Retired from City of N.O.—EMS Supervisor; [memb.] Christian Children Fund 5 Sponsor, Cornerstone United Methodist Women and Church; [hon.] Reporter for 'Hall Talk,' Dept. of Sanitation, New Orleans, LA; [oth.writ.] My Golden Days and An Interlude; [pers.] Thank God for His grace and discovering hope is the faith in God.; [a.] New Orleans, LA

CROSS, ANGELA
[b.] July 11, 1968; Monticello, IA; [p.] Richard and Ruth Pasker; [m.] Steve Cross; September 25,1993; [ch.] Alexander Sean, Christopher James Colton Lukas; [ed.] Central City Community School; [occ.] Secretary, Banks Heating Springville, IA; [memb.] Broken Bit Saddle Club; [oth.writ.] Several Poems written about or for family and friends; [pers.] I want to thank my mom for "making" me write all those poems;. [a.] Marion, IA

CROSS, PAUL L.
[pen.] Paul Cross; [b.] July 8, 1970; Desmoines, IA; [p.] William P. and Joyce J. Cross; [ch.] Cameron P. Cross; [ed.] Indianola Senior High; [occ.] United States Postal Service; [oth.writ.] Unpublished; [pers.] Give God the glory and you will prosper. My love to you, Mother and Father.; [a.] Indianola, IA

CROWEL, LINDA
[b.] September 6, 1957; Dania, FL; [m.] Robert Crowel; April 7, 1986; [ed.] North Miami High, Miami Dade Community College, Miami, FL; [occ.] Administrative Assistant; [memb.] World Wildlife Federation; [oth.writ.] Currently working on a children's book entitled "Patsy's Garden." This story is about a pig who wants to fly but realizes she has many other special qualities.; [a.] Miami, FL

CRUICKSHANK, ROBIN
[b.] May 13, 1968; Decatur, GA; [p.] Wayne and Brenda Adams; [m.] Glenn Cruickshank; April 25, 1992; [ch.] Tiler and Amber; [ed.] Norcross High School, Currently enrolled in photography school ICS, School at home program; [occ.] Full-time mom and wife; [memb.] National Parent to Parent Support and Information System, Inc. "NPPSIS"; [pers.] "That Was My Child," was inspired by an almost tragic end with our daughters rare brain infection known as Encephylitis.; [a.] Colbert, GA

CRUZ, ALEX
[pen.] Joel; [b.] November 20, 1975; Mexico; [p.] Estela Cruz; [ed.] High School and College (Long Beach City College); [oth.writ.] All worthy of publication, but yet undiscovered; [pers.] Reflect on your past, for it's a glimpse of your future. God bless you all.; [a.] South Gate, CA

CUNNINGHAM, JEANNETTE
[pen.] J'nette Cunningham; [b.] July 14, 1957; Greenwood, MS; [p.] Beatrice Cunningham, Daniel (d); [ch.] Antoinette Cunningham; [ed.] Jackson State Univ., University Southern CA. (USC); [occ.] Aspiring Writer, Playwright; [memb.] Outstanding Young Women of America 1986, Alpha Phi Omega, Tau Beta Sigma, NAACP; [hon.] 3rd Runner for Ms. New York (1988), Dean's List; [oth. writ.] Several plays written; [pers.] I strive to make a difference in youth's life through my plays and writing, and inspire others to just do it. And instill in my daughter the importance of humanity and self-respect.; [a.] Wilmington, DE

DADDONA, CHARLOTTE R.
[pen.] Charlotte N. Michael's; [b.] Aprial 16, 1972; Miami, FL; [p.] Paul and Sharyn Daddona; [ed.] General Education Degree, Concord Career Institute; [occ.] Administrative Assistant, Engineering Order Processing; [memb.] Florida State Young American Bowling Alliance; [hon.] Young American Bowling Alliance: "National Youth Leader of the Year—1993," F.S.Y.A.B.A. Youth Hall Of Fame—1995, Greater Miami Jr. Bowling Association: "Outstanding Youth Leader of the Year—1991"; [pers.] I write about love won and love lost, about how love makes us do strange things. Wherever love is, pain is sure to follow, even after a lifetime of loving someone.; [a.] Miami, FL

DARRAH, LONNA D.
[b.] August 24, 1967; Whichita, KS; [p.] Sarah June Hood and Earl Kay Hood; [m.] Pat A. Darrah;

March 17, 1997; [ch.] Thomas R. Ertz, 10 and Amanda D. Ludlow, 5; [ed.] Taft Union High School, want to continue college courses in a few months; [occ.] Housewife; [oth.writ.] Several poems for personal reasons, nothing published; [pers.] I write what comes to mind by what type of mood I am in. I get a lot of ideas from my husband and friends.; [a.] Wichita, KS

DARU, VALERIE
[b.] February 19, 1987; Carmichael, CA; [p.] Judy and Peter Daru; [ed.] Shalom School; [occ.] Student; [memb.] Mosaic Law Synagoge; [hon.] School Treasurer; [pers.] I love horses and that's why I wrote about them in my poem.; [a.] Carmichael, CA

DAVIS, ANTHONY L.
[b.] Chicago, IL; [pers.] The evolution of mind brings forth revolution in time. Against archaic ways of thought, and the types of solutions that are sought.; [a.] Chicago, IL

DAVIS, GARY E.
[b.] February 12, 1954; Taylorsville, NC; [p.] Everette and Ruth Davis; [ch.] April D. Davis; [ed.] Alexander Central High; [occ.] Pastor and Mechanic; [memb.] Wildman Ministries, To Know God's Love; [oth.writ.] Maybe Not A Shed A Tear Today, My Treasure, Canaries Are Yellow, Memories Of You, Thinking Of You; [pers.] Everyone should come face to face with Jesus.; [a.] Taylorsville, NC

DAVIS, SANDY
[b.] February 18, 1958; Richmond, TX; [p.] Maurice Tucker, Claudia Tabola [m.] Steve Davis; August 4, 1988; [ch.] Colby and Kalum Davis; [ed.] Bellville High School; [occ.] Administrator Kings Avenue Baptist Church, Kings Avenue Christian School; [memb.] Kings Avenue Baptist Church, Riverhills Country Club, Society of Poets, Christian Business Women; [hon.] Fine Arts Awards in watercolor, pottery, oils, black-and-white pen drawing, poems, speeches and narative stories; [oth.writ.] Various poems and speeches; [pes.] All worthless in vain is any life without Christ. Find him now. My purpose is to help anyone who seeks his beautiful face.

DAVIS, WILLIAM R.
[b.] April 13, 1926; San Bernardino, CA; [m.] Maria T. Davis; July 24, 1965; [ch.] Robert, Peter, John, Christina, Elizabeth; [ed.] Ashland Oregon, High School University of Oregon; [occ.] Sales Manager; [memb.] Knighs of Columbus; [hon.] Acknowledgement from Pope John Paul II for the poem "Glory" to whom it was dedicated. Acknowledgement from President John F. Kennedy for the poem. "The Death Sentence on Communism"; [oth.writ.] A Voice, Trust, The Plunge, A Rose, Iwo Jima, Redwood Empire, Tall Pines, Strangers, Flying Revelation; [pers.] My poems reflect my thoughts and inspiration.; [a.] Petaluma, CA

DAVITIAN, WILLIAM VICENT
[b.] October 30, 1970; Glendale, CA; [p.] Joseph and Eileen Davitian; [occ.] Housecleaner/Writer; [oth.writ.] A Poem for North, Everyone's First Time, Tears Roll Down My Face, Thoughts of You, Nightmare, Foreseen, Answer Me, (currently unpublished); [pers.] Every person, every place, everything has influenced me; I write about those things. Love and thanks to Eleonor Turner, G.M.; [a.] Verdugo City, CA

DEANGELO, JANE
[b.] September 23, 1947; Gulport, MS; [p.] C. Roland and Frances Martin; [m.] James DeAngelo, September 4, 1976; [ch.] Jaimee N. DeAngelo; [ed.] Elementary and High School—Pass Christian, MS, Phillips Business School Gulfport, MS; [hon.] Poem Published 1964, "Young America Sings," National High School Poetry Anthology;

[pers.] Instead of writing letters, my father and his cousin used to write poetry to one another. This is how I inherited my gift.; [a.] Moss Point, MS

DELGROSSO, ELAINE V.
[b.] December 31, 1933; Pittsburgh, PA; [p.] Amelia Albanese-Michael Albanese; [m.] Richard M. Delgrosso; August 27, 1955; [ch.] Rita Marie, Doreen Ann, Linda Richelle; [ed.] Westinghouse High, Community College of Allegheny County (CCAC)—Boyce Campus (2 years) Fashion Academy (3 Semesters), Art Workshop—University of Pittsburgh; [occ.] Freelance artist, taught art in several local schools, in my homes—2 years; [memb.] Art Club—CCAC, Penn Art Association, Local Club, Boyce Campus Choir—3—Fall, 1996 voice class, several semesters; [hon.] Association in Science Degree, 2 years (art), Deans List Honors, Received several various awards in painting, and other medias incl. ceramics, 3 design patents for butterfly pkg. bows; [oth.writ.] I have never submitted any of my writings before, but I do have a private journal of other poetry and private thoughts and feelings about life.; [pers.] Both my parents love poetry and came from families with an abundance of talent, both in art, writing, and music, back to vaudville days. It makes me very proud to have been left such a wonderful legacy. It has enriched my life.; [a.] Pittsburgh, PA

DELOTELL, RAY L.
[b.] June 5, 1954; Dayton, OH; [p.] Phyllis and Charles Delotell; [m.] Ellen Vance Delotell; June 5, 1997; [ch.] Victoria(7) Laura (6) Ryan (12); [ed.] University South Florida Ringling School of Art; [occ.] Auto Sales Consultant Arnold Dalmer Cadillac; [pers.] My poetry reflects my personal observations, and life experiences. Hopefully, they cause the reader to reflect, and relate to their own experiences.; [a.] Gastonia, NC

DEMPSEY, FRANCES
[b.] November 15, 1911; Dixon, IL; [p.] Frank and Bertha Scholl; [m.] Fern (Jack) Dempsey; March 1, 1996; [ch.] Mary, Robert, Richard, Carol; [ed.] I was within 8 hours of receiving my Bachelor's Degree. I had one year of teacher's training. Then taught 4 years. I went back to teaching and college at age 49, after my children were in high school or college.; [occ.] Homemaker; [hon.] I spent it. I was lucky to be challenged to go back to teaching. Many parents and pupils appreciated my teaching. Those were my honors and awards. Later, I did Arts and Crafts and sold them at about 25 different shows. Again, the appreciation and income from them made me feel honored. It was hard work but worth the effort!; [oth.writ.] I took several nature courses at Loredo Taft near Oregon, IL. I wrote poems, and painted many pictures inspired by nature.; [pers.] I taught for 10 years and went to college during the summer to pay for installing a bathroom in my farm house and other things I needed. My husband said I didn't know how to handle money.; [a.] Polo, IL

DENIRO D.C., FRANK J.
[b.] December 28, 1957; Youngstown, OH; [p.] Frank and Catherine DeNiro; [m.] Lori DeNiro; June 20, 1992; [ed.] Cardinal Mooney High School, University of Cincinnati, Youngstown State University, Palmer Chiropractic College; [occ.] Chiropractic Physician; [memb.] Ohio State Chiropractic Association Eastern Ohio Chiropractic Association; [hon.] Who's Who, Dean's List; [pers.] "I strive in my poetry to reflect everyday life and nature around me."; [a.] Youngstown, OH

DERRICKSON, HOWARD SICKEL
[pen.] Derrick Van Bummell; [b.] September 9, 1913; Philadelphia, PA; [p.] John Henry, Carolyn Sickel; [m.] Whinifred Cox, July 5, 1945; [ch.] Fred Cox, Ann Lenore; [ed.] Church Farm School; Harvard College, Washington U. in St. Louis, U. of

MO in Normandy; U. of MO in Columbia, Harris-Stowe State in St. Louis, MO; [occ.] English and Latin Teacher, Whitfield School, St. Louis, MO. etc.; [memb.] St. Paul's (Overland, MO) Episcopal Church Scholarship (Harvard) Committee; [oth. writ.] 100-plus paid-for and volunteer bits of rhyming verse in a score of daily, weekly, fortnightly newspapers, NYER (unsigned "Talk of the Town" in '32), Time stringer material '44-46; regular art reviews in New Art Examiner, ART News, 4 other art mags; poems and verse translations from D'Annunzio in Cadence: A Magazine of Verse Appreciation (Associate Editor); 1,000-plus book reviews, art reviews, when ('42-'52) full-time St. Louis Post-Dispatch staffer on rewrite, copy desk, ed'l page and acting bk ed.; Frank Jewett Mather art crit. citation of College Art Assoc.; book prizes for addled adages in Harvard Alumni Magazine; very nice rejec ltr from SEP.; [pers.] My spiritual ancestors are Shakespeare scholar G.L. Kittredge, Keats, Byron, Browning. I believe in naming chief expressive metrical and in teaching the diagraming of sentences, but now only acting sub throughout Marin County on rare occasions.; [a.] San Rafael, CA

DEVANE, PAUL F.
[b.] January 7, 1947; [m.] Elsie M. King (deceased 1988); May, 1977; [ch.] Tonka DeVane (deceased 1985); [occ.] Engineer; [memb.] National Association of Power Engineers; [oth. writ.] Personal reflections about events that I have witnessed and participated in (continuing); [pers.] As a hearing impaired person that just emerged from a disgusting civil litigation against a corrupt municipal government, I wanted to express my thoughts, paintings and words about real life without pretense.; [a.] Washington, DC

DINKINS, TERESA
[b.] August 10, 1982; Lynchburg, VA; [p.] Dreama Semmont and Gary Dinkins; [ed.] Brookville High School; [occ.] Student; [hon.] Cum Laude, National Latin Exam; [oth.writ.] "The Journey" published in The National Library of Poetry's An Evolving Secret; [pers.] "Don't compromise yourself. You're all you've got."; [a.] Lynchburg, VA

DONAHUE, LYNNE
[b.] December 14, 1950; Providence, RI; [p.] Rita and Cosmo D. Mirando; [ed.] Grad. Seekonk High School 1970; [occ.] Self employed; [memb.] Humane Society, Assoc. of Handicapped Artists, Doris Day Pet Society; [hon.] Gold key (RISA), abstract wall painting; [oth.writ.] This is the first poem I have ever sent in like this.; [pers.] I write from mostly personal experiences, be they my own or those around me.; [a.] Narragansett, RI

DONNER, ISAAC C.
[b.] November 28, 1899; New York City, NY; [p.] Moses Aaron and Tilli Esther; [m] Deceased; September 21, 1931; [ch.] Rose-Anne D. Colt, Judith D. Hancock; [ed.] BCS, NYU; LLB, NY Law School; CPA, N.Y; Member NY State Bar; [occ.] Retired; [memb.] NY County Lawyers' Assn.; National Lawyers' Guild, NY Law School Alumni Assn., World Jewish Congress, American Jewish Historical Society.; [hon.] BCS and LLb (above) both "With Honor"; [oth. writ.] Many poems short stories, lectures, many briefs in NY State and Federal Courts; [pers.] That of me, as is plan to say, is simply flesh and will not be when I am tucked in 'neath the God stretched stiff and lifeless as a nod. But that of me that's part of you or is contained in all I do, or is inbred—a daughter, son—will live 'til all of these are gone; [a.] Bronx, New York City, NY

DONNER, JOHN PAUL
[pen.] Christopher Free; [b.] February 5, 1976; Tulsa; [p.] Jim Donner, Jean Donner; [ed.] Condry Christian Academy; [occ.] Youth Pastor; [memb.]

Vineyard Christian Fellowship; [oth.writ.] "Do You Understand," "A Painting"; [pers.] Do not be afraid to be who or what you are, because you can always ask for help.; [a.] Vinita, OK

DONOHUE, LINDA
[b.] May 23, 1956; Vermont; [m.] Daniel T.; September 15, 1979; [ch.] Patricio Lyn (4) and Ryan Daniel (3); [ed.] Associates Degree—FLCC "The Arts" Canandaigua, NY; [occ.] Homemaker and "My Kids' Mom"; [oth.writ.] Our Love Affair (encs.), Calvary (encs.), Life (encs.), Peace (encs.), The Bridgegroom (encs.), The Architect (encs.); [pers.] My main goal in life is to encourage and closer walk with our Lord and Senior Jesus Christ to all who will listen. Without him, there is no hope. With him, all things are possible.; [a.] Canandague, NY

DOOLEY, ALEX
[b.] November 3, 1974; St. Louis; [occ.] Youth Leader, Fire of Life Youth Group; [pers.] Psalm 91:1&2: "He who dwells in the shelter of the Most High will rest in the shadow of the Almighty. I will say of the Lord, `He is my refuge and my fortress, my God in whom I trust.'"; [a.] High Ridge, MO

DORAN, JENNIFER
[pen.] Jennifer Doran; [b.] June 8, 1983; Tampa, FL; [p.] Diane and Jim Doran; [ed.] I've gone to Brandon Heights Christian School, (K-5-3rd), and Grace Christian School, (4th-8th). I'm going to attend Coweta High; [occ.] Student; [memb.] Drama, Arts and Craft, Arts, Bell Schools Baptist Church, and New Creations Choir; [hon.] Honor Roll, Pres. Award (For Grades), Missions Awards, Spiritual Award; [oth.writ.] I have lots of other poems, some are named most aren't. Named ones include "Mommy," "What Is a Prayer," and many about friendship.; [pers.] I am a Christian and I love the Lord. He died for me and you. I love children and to act and to sing. I am a part of the choir, drama and nursery.; [a.] Smurna, GA

DOWNING, MARY PAT
[pen.] Mary Pat Downing; [b.] March 18, 1936; California; [p.] Helen Ruth and Lyke A. Downing; [ch.] Chuck, Carol and Laurie; [ed.] High School with some college; [occ.] Retired from the city and county of S.F. Airports Commission; [memb.] ACLU, The Southern Poverty Law Center, Sierra Club, N.O.W., National Parks and Conservation Association, Gorilla Foundation; [hon.] While Working for San Francisco City and County: "Employee of the Quarter Award" and "Certificate of Recognition" from the CAO's office; [oth. writ.] I just finished writing a novel. My poem is included at beginning. The novel is entitled "Feathers." I have not found a publisher as of yet, but I will try.; [pers.] Joy and suffering are both a fact of life. Never give in to the hardships of life and enjoy whatever there is to enjoy.; [a.] Denver, CO

DRAVES, JIMMY J.
[pen.] Joe; [b.] December 4, 1941; Pacific, MO; [p.] Herbert and Elizabeth Draves; [m.] Julie J. Draves; September 25, 1971; [ch.] Linda Sue, Danny Earl, Lisa Suzanne; [ed.] 12 years graduated in 1959 from Pacific High School; [occ.] Automobile Worker, Chrysler Corp., Fenton MO; [memb.] Pacific Pentecostal Church, United Automobile Workers Union (UAW) Local # 110; [hon.] 30 years membership plan with UAW, also plan for 30 years employment with Chrysler Corp.; [oth. writ.] Some other poetry about family, friends and Christian subjects; [pers.] I love the Lord Jesus and writing poetry. I like reading and I collect knives.; [a.] Pacific, MO

DUFUR, LADONNA MARIE
[b.] August 19, 1940; Moline, IL; [p.] Brooks and Ruby Allcock; [m.] Lloyd D. Dufur; October 31, 1990; [ch.] 4; [ed.] 3 years Scott Comm. College, Bettendorf IA; [occ.] Secretary at L and L Gutter,

Davenport, IA; [oth. writ.] I've written numerous poems since February 23, 1997; [pers.] I love to write and share with others what God inspires me to write.; [a.] Davenport, IA

DUSSEAULT, ALYSON
[pen.] Sam Peterson; [b.] July 6, 1984; White Plains, NY; [p.] Barbara and Peter Dusseault; [ed.] I am going into the 8th grade next fall. (Stanley School and Swampscott Middle School); [memb.] JCC, Kernwood Country Club, YMCA; [hon.] Published in Kids Review Kid's Books by Scholastic; [a.] Swapscott, MA

DYKSTRA, ERICA MARIE
[b.] November 12, 1986; Grand Rapids, MI; [p.] Randy and Denise Dykstra; [ed.] 6th grade—Northern Trails Forest Hills School District; [occ.] Student; [hon.] Continental Math League Finalist, President's Education Award Program, National Physical Fitness Award; [pers.] I enjoy reading, tennis, playing with my friends and writing poetry.; [a.] Grand Rapids, MI

ECONOMOU, ANARGYROS E.
[b.] July 31, 1964; Lakonias, Greece; [p.] Evanelos and Sofia Economou; [m.] Melodie L. Economou; June 22, 1985; [ch.] Evangelos; Dimitrios; Sofia; [ed.] B.S. in Vocational Education—Southern Illinois U., Master in Aeronautical Science—Embry Riddle Univ.; [occ.] Officer in the U.S. Air Force (rank of Captain), GPS Navigation Officer; [pers.] The future of mankind depends upon our integrity, excellence in our endeavors, and service towards peace.; [a.] Colorado Springs; CO

EGAN, MARGARET C.
[b.] December 25, 1915; Paris, IL; [p.] Robert and Vanna Downs; [m.] Widow; February 1933; [ch.] Five; [ed.] 8 grade; [a.] Waukegan, IL

EISENFELD, ELIZABETH
[b.] August 14, 1944; Bombay, India; [p.] Simon and Mary Jacob; [m.] Melvin S. Eisenfelf; July 7, 1968; [ch.] Joseph and Simon; [ed.] High School—Haifa Israel, BA—NYC, Nursing Medical Asst. Teaching Professional in Long Beach City College; [occ.] Teacher—Early Educator Center; [memb.] Temple Kahal Joseph, AARP; [hon.] Outstanding Teacher of the Year, gymnastic performance, classical dancing; [oth.writ.] Working on children's book and some more poems; [pers.] Life is full of spiritual skills. If one can make a true expert of their field with the values and morals, that they will able to inspire challenge and bring out their best to achieve their goals.; [a.] Long Beach, CA

ENTRIOLO, MARY ROSE
[pen.] Mary Rose Entriolo; [b.] December 13, 1922; Cleveland, OH; [p.] Joseph and Mary Consiolio; [m.] James Entriolo; June 7, 1973; [ch.] Two; [ed.] High School-Business School; [occ.] Home Maker; [memb.] St. Francis of Assisi Church Knights of Columbus; [oth. writ.] 10 Prayer poems; [pers.] You have filled me full of joy. The Lord has inspired me to write these prayer poems. My son puts them to music and uses them in his concerts.; [a.] Mayfield Heights, OH

ERWIN, DALE MICHAEL
[b.] February 15, 1951; Louisville, KY; [p.] Donald DC. Werwin and Marlys V. Wearren; [pers.] This poem was written by Dale and survived a fire at his residence on January 17, 1977 along with hundreds of others poems. Dale died during this fire and this poem is submitted posthumously by his family with love and honor of his talent.; [a.] Louisville, KY

FEASEL, RON
[b.] November 19, 1943; Topeka, KS; [p.] Leon and Ruth Feasel; [m.] Jackie; May 28, 1965; [ch.] Cassandra and Jack; [ed.] B.A. in Economics, Washburn University; [occ.] Salesperson; [oth.

writ.] Several unpublished poems; [pers.] To live is Christ, to die is gain.; [a.] Meriden, KS

FELTON, HELEN KENNEY
[b.] April 29, 1929; Paris, KY; [p.] Helena Rice-Harvey K. Rice; [m.] George W. Felton; October 20, 1951; [ch.] Brenda, Jukube and Fred J.; [ed.] Graduate-Western High School Paris, KY, Graduate-Cortez Peters Business College Chicago, IL, graduate Baptist Institute; [occ.] Retiree from the University of Chicago; [memb.] Bethsaida M.B. Church; [hon.] The University of Chicago Certificates of Achievements, Service Award—Fifteen years, Service Award—Twenty Years, 5 Recognitions for Perfect Attendance, 2 Pins (Emblems of U of C), Department of Christian Education, Progressive National Baptist Convention Inc., First Diploma of Achievement, First, Second, Third Certificates of Progress; [oth.writ.] Friendship Is Precious, Do It God's Way, Thank God For My Husband; [pers.] The beauty of life is loving and sharing "Life's Experiences" with the people in the world.; [a.] Chicago, IL

FERGUSON, NANCY L.
[pen.] Nanner; [b.] May 1, 1957; Great Falls, MT; [p.] Juanita and Ivan Davison; [ch.] Jamie Lee Ferguson; [ed.] High School; [occ.] Manager Retail; [oth.writ.] Private Journal; [pers.] I wrote "The Parson" 22 years ago and frequently used it to uplift spirits in this ever-changing world.; [a.] Bozeman, MT

FERNANDEZ, GARY R.
[b.] September 5, 1947; San Francisco, CA; [p.] Maxine and Ross; [m.] Divorced; [ch.] Matthew R., Josh A.; [ed.] Some college; [oth. writ.] None that were ever published. But when I was younger, I really enjoyed writing short stories and writing poetry to girlfriends.; [pers.] I try to be kind to everyone I meet because there is no one who isn't struggling with something in their life.; [a.] Charlotte, NC

FERREIRA, ROGER
[b.] February 12, 1949; Oakland, CA; [p.] Raymond Ferreira, Anne Ferreira; [m.] Sharon MacLachlan-Ferreira; February 1, 1982; [ed.] Skyline High, Chabot College, Contract/Procurement Administration Department of Defense (DOD); [occ.] Contract Administrator Department of Defense (DOD); [hon.] Air Force; Defense Intelligence; Navy (hon.) Special Award from Lieutenant General, USAF Commander dtd 9 June '97; [memb.] Guide Dogs for the Blind, Screen Actors' Guild (SAG); [pers.] I rise to the defense of the powerless and to the protection of the weak. I dedicate this poem to my wife and our three guide dogs "Pukka," "Jacques" and "Duke."; [a.] Arcadia, CA

FESI, ELIZABETH
[pen.] Helen Kiyonis; [b.] May 4, 1981; Delware County, PA; [p.] Michael Fesi, Lynne Fesi; [ed.] Dr. Charles Brimm Medical Arts High School, just entering junior year; [occ.] Student; [memb.] Yearbook, newspaper at school, all-city program, secondary bond for about 4 or 5 years; [hon.] Creative Writing Awards, Computer Science Awards, Band Awards; [oth.writ.] Been published once before with the Creative Communications Inc. in Smith Field, UT. The book was called A Celebration Of New Jersey's Young Poets and the poem was entitled 'Falling' and for school newspaper.; [pers.] Be who you are. God made you the way you wanted to. Don't try to change for any one person but yourself. Be true to yourself. God made you the way you are for a purpose, live for that purpose.; [a.] Camden, NY

FEW, JR., LINDSEY DURHAM
[b.] February 3, 1938; Dekalb Co., GA; [m.] Johnnie Sanders Few; December 24, 1961; [ch.] Christopher Wesley Few, Cynthia Few Phillips; [ed.] Apalachee Elementary, Morgan County High

School, Madison, GA, West Georgia College, Carrollton, University of Georgia, Athens, Georgia State University, Atlanta; [occ.] Retired from Georgia Public Schools (Foreign Language and School Counselor), Front Office employee with Ramada Limited Motel, Newnan, GA; [memb.] GA Assoc. of Educators, National Education Association, Retired, First Baptist Church, Newnan, GA, Gideons International; [oth.writ.] Poems in school yearbooks and to honor fellow teachers on special occasions, poems in local newspaper in memory of family members; [pers.] Virtually all of life's experiences are to me an inspiration for poetry. So many find my poems with their rhythm and rhyme very enjoyable and this is a great reward.; [a.] Newnan, GA

FIELDS-KRETZER, MARILYN
[b.] April 18, 1930; Seward Nebraska; [p.] Corteonigkh, V.D. (Jim) and Edith; [m.] Neil Kretzer; [ch.] James H. Fields; [ed.] High School, Hasting Jr. College, San Jose State (CA); [occ.] Retired to a Texas Ranch; [memb.] Beta Sigma Phi, Green Thumb Garden Club, Texas A and M Extension Club, Word Runners Writers' Group, American Legion Aux. Post 240 and Lutheran Church; [hon.] Many various awards for presentation and offices held and flower ribbons; [oth. writ.] Never tried to publish before but I have boxes of poetry, written over the years since age 7, and I have written (while Amer. Legion Aux. Chaplain) a small book of prayers I may try to have published.; [pers.] Live by the Golden Rule so you can enjoy a clear conscious in your Golden Years.; [a.] Stephenville, TX

FINNERTY, EDYTHE LEDEE
[pen.] Edythe C. Ledee; [b.] January 21, 1945; Jamaica, NY; [p.] Christian and Alice Curschmann; [m.] Eugene J. Finnerty; July 30, 1995; [ch.] Qui Qui and Louis Ledee; [ed.] 1.) Catskill High School 2.) SUNY Frodonia 3.) Columbia-Greene College 4.) SUNY Purchase Conservatory; [occ.] Musician, Music Director: White Plains Coalition for Cultural and Racial Harmony; [memb.] White Plains Coalition for Cultural and Racial Harmony, West Fair Chamber Singers, New Wine (singer); [hon.] 1.) President's Award For Excellence—SUNY Purchase 2.) Award For Leadership and Musical Composition Excellence—White Plains Coalition for Cultural and Racial Harmony; [oth. writ.] Published poet and published music books of own compositions, published by the United Methodist Church, The Purchase Review, The Catskill Daily Mail; [pers.] I would hope that my writings would make people think about how we should treat each other, and cherish each member of our race.; [a.] White Plains, NY

FIRESTONE, BENNY
[b.] March 15, 1943, Roanoke, VA; [p.] T. B. Firestone (father); [m.] Carole, September 26, 1992; [ch.] Benny Jr., Beth, John, Amy; [ed.] B.A. Degree in Economics, Roanoke College; [occ.] Realtor.

FISHER, KATHRYN M.
[pen.] Kathryn Fisher; [b.] November 9, 1930; High Point, NC; [m.] Arthur M. Fisher (Deceased) [ch.] Nelda Manna; [ed.] Some college courses, including Art, Writing and Accounting; [occ.] Retired; [memb.] First Presbyterian Church of Kernersville; [oth. writ.] Many poems and some songs, some poems published in religious publications, two songs sung in church services and community performances; [pers.] Faith in God and a sense of humor can carry you through life with a smile on your face.; [a.] Kernersville, NC

FISLER, REBECCA
[b.] October 22, 1977; Jamestown, NY; [p.] Bestie Karen Fisler; [ed.] High School—King Philip H.S., Graduated in '96; [a.] Plainville, MA

FITZGERALD II, GARRY
[b.] March 15, 1967; Washington, DC; [p.] Garrett and Diane Fitzgerald; [ed.] A.A. Degree in Business Mgmnt. From Howard County Community College (1997), St. Vincent Pallohi (1987), Laurel, MD; [occ.] Supervisor at UPS, part-time real-estate investor; [memb.] Road-Runners Club of America (R.R.C.A.); [oth. writ.] "Inspired By A Woman" published in A Prism of Thoughts; [pers.] Writing is a personal expression of one's innermost self.; [a.] Laurel, MD

FLEMING, SANDRA
[b.] April 22; Chippewa Falls, WI; [p.] Ray and Marty Masopust; [m.] Mike; April 22, 1974; [ch.] Michelle and Jon; [ed.] St. Joseph H.S; [memb.] International Society of Poets; [hon.] Editor's Choice Award; [oth. writ.] Take my Hand, Three Little Words, Fantasy Dream, God's Plan, An Artist Eye, Heart Wouldn't Lie, being recorded by Emerald Records in Nashville; [pers.] Would love to have my own book of poems and have more of my work recorded.; [a.] Madison, MS

FOWLER, NIKKI
[b.] March 15, 1982; Tecumseh, MI; [p.] Tami Knierim and Phil Fowler Jr; [ed.] High School Student; [pers.] "In my writings I love to express my own personal feelings, and thoughts through good days and bad for others to read." [a.] Palmyra, MI

FOX, NICOLE R.
[pen.] Fox; [b.] April 24, 1978; Dayton, OH; [p.] Georgia and Darriel Fox; [ch.] Satin Jane Fox; [pers.] I may not be known, but I will be. My Book is coming to you soon and it's coming from the heart, so, please dear forget me not; [a.] London, OH

FREEMAN, CHRISTIE
[b.] August 24, 1979; Henderson, TX; [p.] Joe and Louise Freeman; [ed.] Beckville High School; [hon.] United States National Honor Student Award, Who's Who Among American High School Students, Superintendent's List; [oth.writ.] Wrote poem for my senior class motto; [pers.] My writings are used to glorify Jesus Christ and hopefully lead others to Him.; [a.] Beckville, TX

FREEMAN, LUCILLE
[pen.] Lucille Freeman; [b.] October 15, 1922; Burmingham, ALA; [p.] Tom and Emma Orr; [m.] Raleigh Freeman; October 18, 1953; [ch.] Rallyne Freeman; [ed.] High School Education, 2 years Business College and finished Key Punching Schools of Automation Institute of America; [a.] Warrensville Hights, OH

FULMER, DANIELLE
[pen.] Dani; [b.] December 12, 1984; Oklahoma City; [p.] Mike and Abbi Fulmer; [ed.] I'm in the 7th grade. I enjoy reading class and math. I'm a good student, with lots of friends.; [hon.] I've won other contests with other writings. I've won story writing contests, too.; [oth.writ.] I enjoy writing stories. I also write goofy poems. They are my favorite. I write them for fun. I love reading and writing scary books.; [pers.] Writing is my way of letting my feelings out. I hope to become a writer when I grow up, or an actress. I love to play sports—Hockey! If you ever want to let your feelings out, write them down.; [a.] Greenwood, MO

GALLEGOS, FRANCINE
[b.] July 31, 1981; Denver, CO; [p.] Alfonso and Donna Gallegos; [pers.] I only write what is in my heart.; [a.] Colorado Springs, CO

GARDNER, JAMES L.
[b.] February 21, 1939; Alexandria, VA; [m.] Miyako Kimori; [ch.] 2; [ed.] BA—Univ. of Colorado, MA—University of Hawaii, MLS—Brigham Young University; [occ.] Librarian; [hon.] Phi Beta Kappa; [oth. writ.] Ark of Time, Zen Buddhism, a classified bibliography, Japan Access, bibliographies of various articles and poems in journals in English, Japanese and German.; [a.] Salt Lake City, UT

GARDNER, MELISSA
[pen.] Melissa Gardner; [b.] April 28, 1983; Santa Maria, CA; [p.] Terry and Cindy Gardner; [ed.] Benjamin Foxen, Righetti High School; [occ.] Student; [memb.] American Quarter Horse Association, FFA, 4-H, California Gymkana Association; [hon.] Honor Roll, Citizenship Merit Roll; [oth. writ.] Two poems published by Anthology of Poetry by Young Americans; [pers.] Poetry is one of my great talents. The two people who have influenced me the most are Michelle Boyd, my teacher, and William Shakespeare—a wonderful poet.; [a.] Santa Maria, CA

GATES, J.
[pen.] Josie; [b.] May 19; [oth.writ.] Wait for the book; [pers.] Find me if you want to talk to me. I am the journey you have always hesitated to take.; [a.] Chicago, IL

GAZA, IRENE M.
[b.] Honolulu; [p.] Mosho and Hatsumi Gaza; [ch.] Deborah Tasato-Kodama, Allyson Mellone, Keith M.Y. Tasato, Dayle David Y. Tasato; [ed.] Our Lady of Loretto High School, Los Angeles, CA, University of Hawaii—West Oahu Campus, Pearl City, HI; [occ.] Outrigger Hotels and Resorts, Account Clerk III; [memb.] Honolulu Academy of Arts, University of Hawaii, West Oahu Alumni Association; [hon.] Editor's Choice Awards for "Sunshine Through Jalousies" and "My Son, Dayle"; [oth.writ] The Broken Toys, Life's Analogy, The Tall Pine, Hidden Agenda, Man of Contradiction, A Dawn To Purpose, The Puppet, Miss-Understanding, The Bus Ride, This Island In My Land, Spring, A New Beginning, Prose: Myself—My World, Cans of Money; [pers.] Everyone should be given every opportunity to achieve their goals, to attain a quality of life they would want for themselves, including the handicapped.; [a.] Honolulu, HI

GENNARDO, PETER
[pen.] "CHAZ"; [b.] May 29, 1963; [p.] Maria L. & Francis J. Gennardo; [ch.] Godfather of Joseph Carmine Barra; [ed.] Bachelor of Arts in Psychology, Adelphi University, School of Arts and Sciences, May 1986; [occ.] Program Supervisor—The Evening/Weekend Psycho-Social Program, Utilization Review Authority; [memb.] Chapter Advisor—Kappa Theta/Tau Kappa Epsilon, Honorary Membership—Kappa Theta /Tau Kappa Epsilon, M.C.S.A. Basketball Coach—3 Junior Division Championships (1991-1993); [hon.] Sportmanship Award (1977), Suffolk Lutheran Basketball Champions (1980), Aggie Spirit Award (S.U.N.Y. Farmingdale), Most Active Senior Award (Adelphi Univ., 1986), Student Life Award (Adelphi Univ., 1986), Leadership Recognition Award (Adelphi Univ., 1986), Outstanding Service (Adelphi Univ., 1988), Hoop It Up Championship (Long Island, NY, 1990); [oth. writ.] "Angry Clowns," published in River of Dreams, The National Library of Poetry, 1994; [a.] Centereach, NY

GHIOTTO, RONALD
[b.] October 2, 1951; Chicago; [p.] Josephine Ghiotto; [ch.] Son: Santino R. Ghiotto; [ed.] Fenger High; [occ.] Roofer; [oth. writ.] Personal poems to friends and those I have met on my journey thru life.; [pers.] I hope that one day everyone will see each other in only one way—as human beings.; [a.] Merrillville, IN

GIBBONS, DONDREW C.
[b.] July 21, 1973; Barbados; [p.] Bridget Harewood, Julius Roett; [ed.] Weaver High, Eastern CT State University, UCONN School of Social Work; [occ.] Student (Masters UCONN School of Social Work); [pers.] Life is too short to focus on the trivial things within it. Open your eyes and realize what really matters.; [a.] Hartford, CT

GIBBS, CONSTANIE
[pen.] Constanie Gibbs; [b.] May 16, 1954; New Richmond, WI; [p.] Don and Georgia Anchka; [m.] Jim Gibbs; September 28, 1979; [ch.] Nicholas, Elizabeth and Adrienne; [ed.] High School, some college; [occ.] Telegraph Herald, Promotion Director; [memb.] Dubuque Museum of Art, Dubuque Country Historical Society; [hon.] International Newspaper Marketing Association; [oth. writ.] A Treasure Portfolio to be published in fall, 1997; [a.] Dubuque, IA

GIBSON, LISA GAYLE
[b.] January 15, 1963; Fresno, CA; [p.] Mike Ogle and Jo Ogle; [m.] Ned Anderson Gibson; January 14, 1984; [ch.] Stefani and Ryan; [occ.] Carefinder Assist; [oth. writ.] "My Darling One," published by Nat'l Library of Poetry, many poems; [pers.] I write what is in my heart. As a child of God, mother, wife, lover, daughter, sister and friend, I have many cherished relationships. I have a lot to write about. My heart is full.; [a.] Fresno, CA

GLASER, DAVID
[b.] September 29, 1919; Brooklyn, NY; [a.] Wantagh, NY.

GONZALES, ALIDA J.
[b.] September 13, 1971; Bronx, NY; [m.] Pedro Gonzales; April 16, 1994; [ch.] Mya Janei and Nadja Janise; [ed.] Graduated St. Raymond's Academy; [occ.] (housewife) CEO of Family Operations; [pers.] If you're going to come, come correct.; [a.] Bronx, NY

GOODWIN, LYNN M.
[b.] August 30, 1971; Iowa; [p.] "Ty" Tisinger and Dyan Fell; [m.] Tim R. Goodwin Sr; January 7, 1995; [ch.] 1 Timothy R. Goodwin Jr; [ed.] H.S. GED—Seneca Valley High School, Germantown, MD—1989; [occ.] Business Owner: "Goodwin Housekeepers"; [hon.] Many sports awards through the years! Swimming mostly, but soccer and volleyball too. Unfortunately no writing awards; [oth. writ.] Lots of scribbles but no published work . . . until now.; [pers.] Always write what you feel. Forget punctuation, spelling and tense . . . Just let it all flow; and you will be happy with the results every time.; [a.] Washington, IA

GRACE, ASHLEY NICOLE
[pen.] Ash Baby Bear; [b.] March 26, 1988; Hayward, CA; [p.] Kimberly K. Johnson Grace, Timothy J. Kimbark (Stepfather); [ed.] I'm going into 4th grade, and I am 9 years old. I go to Marshall Elementary School, Castro Valley, CA.; [occ.] 3rd Grade School Student; [memb.] 94.9 K-San Club Member #2574430, and proud to be the great, great, great granddaughter of Belle Starr and being part Native American Indian.; [hon.] Student of the Week (April 14th-18th 1997), Most Advanced Progress Achievment in Reading (June 12, 1997), Mrs. Morrell's 3rd grade Class Room #14; [oth.writ.] My Dazzling Unicorn, Short Story Book writen—3rd grade, Mrs. Morrell's class; Marshall Elementary School, Castro Valley, CA; [pers.] Dedicated to my Mom, (Kimba) Because I love you, always, and forever! XOXO Ash.; [a.] San Leandro, CA

GRAESER, R0N
[b.] March 12, 1924; College Point, NY; [p.] Edward L. Graeser; January 20, 1951; [ch.] Ronald D., Ellen J., Beverly R; [ed.] Bayside High, New York University (1 + yrs); [occ.] Retired from Brookhaven National Laboratory, Technical Specialist; [memb.] 11th Airborne Division Assoc., 82nd Airborne Division Assoc., Contributing Editor: Airborne Quarterly Magazine; [oth. writ.] Poem published in Northern Ireland Newspaper—poems published in Airborne Quarterly Magazine;

[pers.] Influenced by William Shakespeare and Greek Mythology; [a.] Ctr. Moriches, NY

GRAHAM, BRANDY
[pen.] Puppy; [b.] December 12, 1976; Fort Jackson; [p.] Ernest Wohnig, Debra Wohnig; [m.] Daren Graham; August 3, 1996; [occ.] Babysitter; [a.] Pomaria, SC

GRAHAM, EUNICE
[b.] 1913; Sarepta, MS; [p.] B.O. and Elsie Freeman; [m.] Adrian O. Graham; May 9, 1936; [ch.] Charles, Ann; [ed.] Masters Degree, Special Education Degree; [occ.] Retired; [pers.] The words in this poem seemd to flow softly in a way that seemed to be spiritually inspired.; [a.] Amarillo, TX

GRANDBERRY, LES
[b.] Chicago, IL; [oth.writ.] A Smile, I Can, Can You Love, "A Thousand Year 1 Day", Whisperlesss Feeling, Someone Special, Vows, The Unspoken; [pers.] I do not write for the glory of men nor do I write for the praise of men. I write for happiness, spiritual enlightenment that "Jesus" has put in my heart. He said, "Don't worry about what you may say, because in that given hour it will be I speaking through you."; [a.] Harvey, IL

GRAY, DAN
[b.] February 19, 1987; [p.] Gerald and Pennie Gray; [ed.] Hilliard Elementary 5th grade; [occ.] Student; [memb.] Student Council; [pers.] Likes to write poems about history, sports, also likes to write humorous poems.; [a.] Westlake, OH

GREEN, JEFFERY
[pen.] Tes; [b.] February 27, 1962; Phila, PA; [m.] Valerie; [ch.] J'lise; [occ.] Children's Counselor; [pers.] All things in life dedicated to three, Valerie, J'lise, and Me; [a.] Phoenix, AZ

GREEN, MARCUS D.
[pen.] Abysmal; [b.] June 11, 81; Jackson, MS; [p.] Georgia M. Gree; [ed.] Flint Southeastern Academy School; [occ.] Crossroads Village Employee as Interpreter Craftsman I; [memb.] Young Explorers Club; [hon.] Michigan State University extension certificate of recognition; [oth.writ.] My own collection of poems; [pers.] I basically write what I feel sometimes and go deep within the style that I use.; [a.] Flint, MI

GRIFFITHS, JOHN S.
[pen.] John "The Food Guy"; [b.] May 28, 1955; Port Arthur, TX; [occ.] Thomas Jefferson Sr. High, Thomas Edisour. High and Lamar University; [oth.writ.] "My Poor Old Car"; [pers.] All credit of inspiration I owe to a very special friend in my life by the name of Lori "The Artist, Poet and Tennis Player of Southeast, Texas and Scattle, WA"; [a.] Port Arthur, TX

GRODSKI, ARLENE
[b.] April 19, 1976; Southampton, NY; [p.] Edward and Thirza Grodsiu; [pers.] This came from my heart, soul, body and mind. This is dedicated to the most precious person in my heart . . . Abner Vega Jr.; [a.] Lakeworth, FL

GRUWELL, BRADLEY O'NEIL
[b.] July 16, 1960; Madison Co., IA; [ed.] Quit early and got GED and then the Air Force; [occ.] Self-made artist, philosopher, inventor, visionary; [memb.] I am a child of God, and a member of the Human Race; [hon.] Several Air Force ribbons and medals; [oth. writ.] "Modestly unspoken, wise men cannot teach the ignorant, for they haste in all their ways."; [pers.] Let my hands be your eyes, my ears be your sight, my heart be your love, God's true and gracious light. One and all, reach out in any way you can. It's our purpose.; [a.] Iowa City, IA

GUERRERO, RENE J.
[pen.] R. Manuel; [b.] January 9, 1966; Dallas, TX; [p.] Joe Philip Guerrero and Gloria Gray; [ed.]

Jesuit Arts Magnet at Booker T. Washington, Dallas, Music Major at NTSU, Denton, Photography/Graphic Design, El Centro Community College, Dallas; [occ.] Digital Imagist/Designer (Mistral Design Group, Dallas TX); [oth. writ.] Songwriting for Dallas Swing Singer Hunter Sullivan, currently working on first novel (fiction), due June '98; [pers.] I strive to convey the eternal hunger of modern man for knowledge, affection, power, and enlightenment in a Progressive Christian Voice, Cynically Optimistic, in Praise of the Fallibility of Human Nature and the Constant Desires to obtain immortality.; [a.] Dallas, TX

GUILFOYLE, SR. THEOPHANE
[b.] February 1, 1904; NY, NY; [p.] John and Mary Guilfoyle; [ed.] BS in Secondary Education College of St. Mary of the Springs, Columbus, Ohio; [occ.] Retired; [memb.] Alumni of Ohio Dominican College; [hon.] Previous published poem, "A Memorable Flight"; [a.] Columbus, OH

GUY, DARLENE JOYCE
[b.] September 26, 1944; Oakland; [p.] Arthur Clive, Martha Marie McKee [m.] Lemuel Jester "Butch" Guy; December 21, 1963 [ch.] Steven, Ronald, Frank, James; [ed.] Verdugo Hills High School, Santa Ana, Orange Coast, Riverside City Colleges; [memb.] Lifetime Member of International Society of Poets, Church of Latter Day Saints; [occ.] Member Hybrid Miero Circuit Staff, G.M. Hughes Electronics 25 years; [hon.] 2 Editor's Choice Awards (1996), and in 1994 judged best 3% poems published in 6 anthologies in 4 years. Presently having first book published "Written by The Window," second book, at the end of '97, "With Pen in Hand," to be published in early 1998, "The Buds Blossoms and Thorns of Love." Numerous chap books in process; [oth. writ.] I have written 135 poems this year. So far compiling into books. Emily Dickenson wrote 1800 poems in her short 56 years of life. At 52, I am still under 1000 so I am using her as my goal post and example. Wish me luck.; [pers.] "May my words open windows and you let sunshine in. Showing your life's feelings are normal and natural they are nobody's sins." "May you find joy in your reading and voice for your feelings as I share with you my written song."; [a.] Riverside, CA

HABITO, LOLITA P.
[pen.] Lolita Ramos Poriwasdoro Habito; [p.] Nicanor and Brigida Pornasdoro; [m.] Fernando Habito; December 23, 1975; [ch.] Maybelyn and Noel Habito; [ed.] Bachelor of Science in Education, Community Development, Office and Computer Skills; [occ.] Studying, Verifying the reasons why the human Spirit breaks; [memb.] FAAN 1; [oth. writ.] Booklet on prayer entitled "A More Secured World"; [pers.] Blessed are we if within our lifetime we were able to understand that doing good to others is pleasing to God when it is done not because of the law, honor, prestige, command or fear of punishment, but because of our love, concern or compassion. And more blessed we are when we translate our love, understanding and knowledge into actions.; [a.] Waukegan, IL

HAGEN, ANDREW
[b.] July 27, 1984; River Falls, WI; [p.] Todd A. Hagen, Michelle J. Pepper; [ed.] Glenwood City Jr. High School; [oth. writ.] Currently working on various poems and stories.; [a.] Glenwood City, WI

HALSTEAD, BERNARD C.
[b.] July 9, 1909; Charleston, WV; [m.] Lottie Hastead; November 15, 1941; [ch.] Lloyd Edward, Lewis Whyne; [ed.] Ninth Grade, Lincoln Junior High School, Charleston, W.V; [occ.] Caregiver to invalid wife; [memb.] Scott Depot Christ Fellowship, Scott Depot, WV; [oth. writ.] Presently writing a psychic autobiography titled The Alger Syndrome; [pers.] Adversity can build character if you let it.; [a.] Winfield, WV

HAMILTON, LAWRENCE E.
[b.] November 9, 1936; Yoncalla, OR; [p.] Thomas E., Maude Hamilton; [m.] Marjorie J. Hamilton; June 13, 1964; [ed.] Douglas High School, Winston, Oregon, 1956, B.S, Engineer Technology, 1972, Washington University, St. Louis, MO; [occ.] Professional Engineer, Retired, US Army Corps of Engineers; [memb.] Jeffco Challengers and Capital T, Toastmasters Clubs; [hon.] Distinguished Toastmaster, the highest communication and leadership award conferred by Toastmasters International; [pers.] In order to enjoy poetry to the fullest extent, it should be heard, not just read. Poetry is fun.; [a.] St. Louis, MO

HAMILTON, RACHEL LEE
[b.] January 16, 1986; Martinsburg, WV; [p.] Donna Painter, Terry Hamilton; [ed.] Boonsboro Middle School; [hon.] Principals Citizenship Award, President's Education Awards Program; [a.] Knoxville, MD

HAMLET, SHAWN
[pen.] Shawn Hamlet; [b.] April 16, 1981; Trinidad; [p.] Cynthia H. Rivers; [ed.] Junior in high school right now; [hon.] Won 2nd place in the 1997 Pal Illustrated poetry contest; [oth. writ.] Other little poems and stories; [pers.] Every human being has the ability to do good. Every human being has the ability to be ignorant. There is a fine line between the two . . . choose wisely; [a.] New York, NY

HANCOCK, PAT C.
[pen.] Pat C. Hancock; [b.] May 17, 1933; Pilot Point, TX; [p.] Sam and Edna Crawford; [ch.] Joe, Jerry, Sherri, Cindy, Jim, Melyn; [ed.] RB Cousins Elementary, Meria Jr. High, Meria High School, AAS in Childhood (Child care and Development) Licensed Vocational Nurse, Automated Accounting Secretary; [occ.] Medical out-patient Clinic Clerk; [oth. writ.] Other poetry, short stories in the 1st person from life experience, Greeting Cards, a poem set to music; [pers.] I began writing poetry in the 1970's to vent my frustrations. My early writings were done about my family experiences. I believe that God has guided my thoughts and creativity.; [a.] Tyler, TX

HANNA, RICHARD
[b.] August 17, 1937; Bath, ME; [occ] Retired; [oth. writ.] "A Bettor's Dream," "Patriot(ic) Lament," idea borrowed from Ogden Nash's "A Poet's Laments," "Relatively Speaking"; [pers.] I write these for self-satisfaction, also hoping to please the people I write about or anyone who wishes to read them and comment about them. I doubt very much that their overall quality is publishing material.

HANSON, GARY W.
[b.] June 18, 1955; Elgin, IL; [p.] Gerald W. and Elizabeth M. Hanson; [m.] Lisa Ann; December 26, 1981; [ch.] Christian G. and Megan E; [ed.] Elgin High School, Elgin Community College Elgin, Illinois; [occ.] Tool and Die Maker for U.S. CAN-Elgin; [memb.] Phi Beta Kappa Honor Fraternity; [pers.] "Family Tree" was inspired by my genealogy research and consideration for my family, living and deceased. My love for literature and verse was developed by dedicated educators in my youth and nurtured by life and love for my creator, wife and children.; [a.] Belvidere IL

HARDEN JR., ROBERT L.
[b.] November 17, 1969; Cambridge, MA; [p.] Robert L. Harden, Christine D. Harden; [ed.] Minoteman High (88), Newburg College (90), University of Massachusetts, Amherst (95), Untited States Army (93); [occ.] Assistant Food and Beverage Manager, Wyndham Garden Hotel, Alburquerque, NM; [hon.] Presidential Scholarship (Newburg College), Liberation of Kuwait Award, 3 Army Achievement Medals, Good Conduct Medal, Cum Laude (Newburg College), National Dean's List; [pers.] When all of human kind realizes that

we are all connected, as a people and as a part of the planet, that is when war, hate, and greed end and awakening begins.; [a.] Watertown, MA

HARDY, LAUREL ANN
[b.] August 16, 1964; Brooklyn, New York; [ed.] B.S.N. and M.A in Nursing; [occ.] Registered Nurse R.W; [a.] Flushing, NY

HARMER, BEN
[b.] September 9, 1975; Tacoma, WA; [p.] S. Dean and Jo-Ann Harmer; [m.] Laura Astle Harmer; June 13, 1997; [ed.] Radford High School, LDS, 2-Year Mission to Berlin, Germany, Brigham Young University; [memb.] Church of Jesus Christ of Latter-Day Saints; [hon.] Eagle Scout; [pers.] Many thanks to be my beautiful bride, Laura. I love her very much.; [a.] Sandy, UT

HARRISON, KAREN S.
[b.] August 1950; Benkelman, NE; [p.] Beldon and Betty Jenik; [m.] Harry P. Harrison; March 16, 1969; [ch.] Son: Jared R. Harrison; [ed.] Douglas County High School, Castle Rock, CO; [occ.] Secretary, Cheylin USD 103; [pers.] My first writing in memory of a very special neighbor and friend.; [a.] McDonald, KS

HARTMAN, BECKY
[b.] July 21, 1982; Minneapolis; [p.] Bonnie Hartman; [ed.] North Star Elementary School, Pillsbury Elementary School, Northeast Middle School, Edison High School; [occ.] High School, Student; [memb.] "YM" and "Teen" Magazines; [hon.] Student of the Week and Student of the Month twice in elementary school, D.A.R.E. Award in fifth grade; [oth. writ.] I've entered a poetry contest before, (present), not sure if I won yet. The poems were published, as far as I know.; [pers.] I like to write poems and songs whenever I think of a rhyme, usually when I listen to music. I like to share my life and feelings in writing.; [a.] Minneapolis, MN

HASELL, JULIA L.
[a.] Charleston, SC

HASKETT, SUSAN MILLIGAN
[b.] December 28, 1937; Waveland, IN; [p.] Harry and Dorothy Milligan; [m.] William J. Haskett; March 16, 1967; [ch.] William B. Haskett; [ed.] Hanover College, Hanover, IN; [occ.] School Social Worker; [pers.] This poem was inspired by my mother-in-law, Meredith R. Haskett, who has written many fine poems. It is dedicated to her.; [a.] Plainfield, IN

HATHAWAY, KEVIN T.
[b.] December 23, 1970; Copake, NY; [p.] Dexter and Nancy Hathaway; [ed.] Taconic Hills High Johnson and Wales University SUNY at Plattsburgh; [occ.] Hotel Manager; [pers.] My poetry is influenced by my childhood experiences. I would like to thank Mrs. Heisey, my high school English teacher for giving me the courage and knowledge to write my first poem.; [a.] Plattsburgh, NY

HAUPTLY, MICHAEL
[b.] February 21, 1973; Reclony PA; [occ.] Electrician; [oth. writ.] None Published; [pers.] I write mostly about the darker side of everyday life. About cheery things like loneliness, insanity and death. But on the shadows of my work there is always hope.; [a.] Mt. Penn, PA

HAWKINS, GABRIELLE
[b.] October 18, 1980; Amarillo, TX; [p.] Della Armstrong; [pers.] Inspiration for this poem: Paige, Brad, and the poetic beauty of Poppy Z. Brite.; [a.] Amarillo, TX

HEALD, CHARLES
[pen.] C. Alan Heald; [b.] June 21, 1955; Midland, TX; [p.] K.C. and Joan Heald; [ch.] Jennifer Heald; [ed.] B.S. Geology—University of Texas, 1980;

[occ.] Managing Representative Excel Communications; [memb.] Galveston Historical Society, American Association of Petroleum Geologists; [oth. writ.] Currently working on a book to be entitled "The Path of Logical Healing." Other recent poetry, "The River," unpublished; [pers.] I have been strongly influenced, touched, by the work of David Whyte. For me poetry is an expression of my soul, an expression that has just begun to come forth, to live.; [a.] Houston, TX

HENSON, EVELYN RENA HARRIS
[pen.] Rena; [b.] January 21, 1963; B'ham. Al; [p.] Donald C. and Linda F. Harris; [ch.] Angel Marie and Allana Renae; [memb.] Trinity Baptist Church; [hon.] Editors Choice Award, The National Library of Poetry; [oth.writ.] 'It Takes Me' published in the anthology The Colors of Thought by The National Library of Poetry; [pers.] Why worry when you can pray? Trust in the Lord with all faith and belief.; [a.] Adamsville, AL

HERNANDEZ, GABRIEL
[b.] May 16, 1952; Brooklyn, NY; [p.] Claudio and Irma Hernandez; [m.] Julia Angel Hernandez; February 14, 1989; [ch.] La Tonya and Gabriella and Deiserae, Iris and Walter; [ed.] Associate in Art from Dutchen Community College, Bachelor of Science degree from State University of NY, Empire State College; [memb.] NAACP; [hon.] Genessee Community College Dean's List, Certificates recurred for Industrial Carpentry, honor for Gymnastics leadership; [oth. writ.] "Amigo I Am," "Brown Sugar," "Testimony to Death," "Friendship Anew"; [pers.] My word is my bond.; [a.] Brooklyn, NY

HIGGENBOTTOM, HAYDEN
[b.] September 17, 1923; Silver Point, TN; [p.] Wesley and Prilla Higgenbottom; [m.] Etta Frances Higgenbottom; September 27, 1947; [ch.] Fred, Robert, Richard; [ed.] B.S.—Middle Tennessee State, University graduate work at Tennessee Tech. University; [occ.] Retired School Teacher; [memb.] First Baptist Church, Sparta, TN, Tenn. Retired Teachers Assn. American Legion AARP; [hon.] Sigma Club—Middle Tenn. State University, Dean's List—Middle Tenn. State Univ., Honorable Discharge—US Navy—World War II; [pers.] I taught school for thirty-six years. There is a special place in my heart for young people.; [a.] Sparta, TN

HIXSON, PHYLICIA R.
[b.] January 10, 1986; Greensburg, PA; [p.] Terry L. and Dolores A. Hixson; [ed.] Full-time student going into sixth grade; [memb.] USAG (Gymnastics); [pers.] I am excited that this poem, being the first that I have written, is eligible to win and award.; [a.] Hunter; PA

HOFF, IRA W.
[b.] September 14, 1916; Rexford, KS; [p.] (Pliny Brewster and Ethel Roberts) Hoff; [m.] Margaret Hickson Hoff; March 22, 1938; [ch.] Diana, Barbara, Margaret; [ed.] Arapahoe Grade and High School, AB and AM, Science and Math, Colorado State College of Education, Ph.D., Walden University Ed. Adm.; [occ.] Retired; [hon.] None worth mentioning; [oth. writ.] Several (more than 50) poems on various topics, Wyoming PTA, the first 50 years other poems, some philosophical, some religious, some, educational.; [a.] Grand Junction, CO

HONSE, CORINA
[b.] September 30, 1982; Pottsville, PA; [p.] Cathy Honse and Chris Honse; [ed.] Central Columbia Middle School, Completed 8 yrs; [hon.] Math, English, Science, S.S., Citizenship, Helping Accelerated Reader, and Honor Roll for 8 yrs; [oth. writ.] Do You Ever Wonder? You Little Girl, "She," and Daddy, I Love You; [pers.] I wrote this poem for my father Christopher Lee Honse who died on April 6, 1997 in Fontana, California. "I miss and love you Daddy."; [a.] Bloomsburg, PA

HORN, MARY N.J.
[pen.] Mom; [b.] May 23, 1927; Evansville, IN; [p.] William and Lollie Mullen; [ch.] Tom, John, Tim, Steve, Patty; [ed.] Bosse High; [occ.] Retired; [pers.] I wrote "Angel of Mine" during thoughts of my life, that's limited time with Cancer.; [a.] Evansville, IN

HORTON, CHERYL T.
[b.] January 29, 1929; Bemidji, MN; [p.] Tim and Constance Bjella; [m.] Dale V. Horton (Deceased) in 1961; December 22, 1949; [ch.] Roxanne, Rhonda, Reldine, Dale Jr; [ed.] Bachelor of Science from Bemidji State University Bemidji, MN 56601 in 1949; [occ.] Retired; [memb.] A.A.V.W. Retired Teacher's Association; [oth. writ.] Appeared in a newspaper; [pers.] I try to express human frailties, virtues, social injustice, social triumph and the power of the pen. Sinclair Lewis has influenced me.; [a.] Fremont, NE

HUBBARD, DANIELLE ANTOINETTE
[pen.] Danielle Antoinette Hubbard; [b.] December 4, 1974; Bethlehem, PA; [p.] Paulette Terrell and Anthony Hubbard; [ed.] Cosumnes River College—Received A.A. Degree, California State Univ. of Sacramento—English major, working towards a B.A.; [occ.] Insurance Authorization and billing Specialist for a Home Health Agency; [pers.] Deep down there lives a voice inside of me. It tells me I am meant to be a writer. It is my passion and my peace. It is my escape and my joy. May we all strive to listen to the voice with each of us and find truth, happiness and fulfillment in carrying forth its message.; [a.] Sacramento, CA

HUDSON, JUDITH
[pen.] Patsy; [b.] June 20; Kingston Jam; [occ.] Freelance writer and poet; [hon.] Writers Scholarship; [oth. writ.] Several poems have been publish abroad and have appeared in anthologies with some of the world greatest poets.; [pers.] All my poems are aimed at mankind's heart, hoping to me they too change.; [a.] Miami, FL

HUDSON, LOIS
[pen.] Lois Hudson; [b.] June 26, 1934; New York, NY; [m.] Hal S. Hudson; [ch.] 2 Children, 2 Grandchildren; [ed.] University of Michigan, Texas Women's University. 1956—Bachelor of Music, 1981—Master of Occupational Therapy; [occ.] Occupational Therapist—work with special children; [memb.] American Occupational Therapy Association; [hon.] Freshman at University of Michigan, Ann Arbor, MI, Hopwood Award (1952). Pi Theta Epsilon Honor Society at Texas Women's University; [oth. writ.] Poem published in Michigan Alumnus Quarterly Review (1953); [pers.] I have returned to writing poetry after many years.; [a.] Houston, TX

HUDSON, LORI B.
[b.] November 16, 1968; Milwaukee, WI; [p.] Ron and Sandra Gelhar; [m.] Thomas James Hudson; April 8, 1995; [ch.] Cassi Marie; [ed.] Kettle Moraine High School; [occ.] Floral Manager; [oth. writ.] Four poems published in high school publication, "Echoes," one poem published in A View From Afar; [pers.] Always be good. In the end, good always wins.; [a.] Reidsville, NC.

HUHN, GINMARIE RODONDI
[b.] May 8, 1945; San Mateo, CA; [p.] Arthur and Parina Rodondi; [m.] Larry Huhn; June 4, 1966; [ch.] Carolyn, David, Kristen, Tracie, Michael; [ed.] University of San Francisco, Columbus State Community College; [occ.] Paralegal at Mediation Center for Alternative Dispute Resolution, MPLS, MN; [memb.] MN Paralegal Association, National Federation of Paralegal Assoc. Inc., Feminists for Life of America; [hon.] Graduated Summa Cum Laude from Columbus State Community College, Vice President of Student Organization for Legal

Assistants at Columbus State C.C., Phi Theta Kappa; [oth. writ.] Published articles for specialty newspaper; [pers.] I believe a dream can become a reality and a goal can become a success. I have been inspired by woman who have achieved their greatest literary and academic successes during their middle years. I believe that my best work is yet to be accomplished.; [a.] Eden Prairie, MN

HUIGEN, AMANDA
[b.] October 13, 1980; St. Ignatious, MT; [p.] Hendrik and Nancy Huigen; [ed.] Junior at Bozeman MT Senior High; [occ.] Intern for Gallation Co. Historical Society; [memb.] PETA—People for the Ethical Treatment of Animals, Model United Nations Drama Club, School Mascot; [hon.] Ribbon and trophies in 4-H Club, Honor Roll at school, Certificate of Appreciation for work at the Museum of the Rockies; [oth. writ.] Numerous poems and stories published in the school paper; [pers.] I am the sister of Phillip, Angie, Sonny, Starla, Edward, Robin, Hank; Aunt of Board Chance and they have been he inspiration of my writing.; [a.] Bozeman, MT

HULET, NICOLE
[b.] May 10, 1963 Sherman, TX; [p.] Nadyne Hulet; [ed.] Computer Learning Center, Cert. '90 Irvine Valley College as '96/Valedictorian Arizona State University BSE in Progress; [occ.] Computer Consultant; [memb.] National Assoc. of Female Executives, Phi Theta Kappa Alumni; [hon.] Phi Theta Kappa Int'l Honor Society, National Dean's List, 2 yrs, Who's Who of American Women; [oth. writ.] Poetry Guild—Semi finalist '97, sculpture and poetry display at Da Gallery, California '96; [a.] Chandler, AZ

HUSSONG, DELORES A.
[b.] April 25, 1947; Joplin, MO; [p.] Roy and Bernice Hussong; [ed.] Golena High School, MO Southern State College, Pittsburg State University for Masters degree and Administration; [occ.] Teacher/Director of Federal Programs for Galena, KS Schools; [memb.] Alpha Delta Kappa, Galena Christian Church; [hon.] Who's Who Among America's Teachers, 1994; [a.] Galena, KS

INGRAM, MICHELLE
[b.] April 13. 1973; Chicago, IL; [p.] Holman and Lynnette Ingram; [ed.] Kenwood Academy (high school) University of Illinois at Chicago (graduate); starting graduate work in August 1997 at UIC; [occ.] Office clerk and graduate student; [a.] Chicago, IL

IZZO, JENNIFER
[b.] March 25, 1997; Somerville, NJ; [p.] Nancy and Peter Izzo; [occ.] Going to High School; [hon.] Numerous Awards [pers.] When the power of love exceeds the love of power, the world will know peace.; [a.] Asbury, NJ

JACKSON, KAROL LYNN
[b.] June 23, 1970; Town of Ramapo, NY; [p.] Carolyn Johnson and Raif Johnson (Deceased); [m.] Al Jackson; April 15, 1989; [ch.] Al Jerome Jackson Jr.; [ed.] Vigor High School, Prichard, AL, Pikes Peak Community College, Colorado Springs, CO; [occ.] Data Entry Clerk, WABB Radio Station, Mobile, AL; [memb.] Phi Theta Kappa Honor Society, Member of Phillips Temple AOH Church of God, US Veteran; [pers.] I have personally come to realize that there is no problem too hard for God, and so I try to encourage in my writing that he is the answer to every problem no matter how large or small.; [a.] Prichard, AL

JAUGE, TORGER
[pen.] Stark Raving; [b.] January 13, 1979; Spokane, WA; [ed.] High School—however, didn't learn much there; [oth. writ.] Just other poems and short stories I doodle down in my notebooks and keep hidden in my room; [pers.] Life isn't always about being happy as much as it is facing its unpleasantries and overcoming them. I probably wouldn't even have entered if it was not for a wonderful woman in my life. I love you, "Kitten.";
[a.] Havre, MT

JAYARAMAN, VINODINI
[pen.] Vinodini Jayaraman; [b.] May 7, 1959; India; [p.] Meera and K.C. Sankara Narayanan; [m.] K. Jayaraman; July 31, 1983; [ch.] Sanjeev and Sreedhar; [ed.] Master's Degree in International Studies from Jawaharlal Nehru University, New Delhi, India; [occ.] Homemaker and Artist; [hon.] Selected as one among three women painters from KERALA and honored by the Indian Council of Cultural Affairs in 1985, Received award from W.K. NO Gallery Ten, Art and Antiques auction held at Memphis TN in Nov, 1993; [oth. writ] I write poetry about the stories of my paintings, which I believe is a kind of my 'pictorial diary.'; [pers.] After 38 years of happiness, joys and sorrows, the only lesson I've learned is that this too shall pass away.; [a.] Memphis, TN

JENNETT, SHIRLEY L.
[b.] January 14, 1933; Sandpoint, ID; [p.] Alvin and Gwendolyn Gehrke; [m.] Joseph E. Jennett, Deceased; February 15, 1970; [ch.] Pamela J., David L., Michael J., Lisa D.; [ed.] Central Valley High School; [occ.] Human Resource Manager (Retired); [oth. writ.] One poem published in a military base paper, also some church bulletins. One poem, "A Beloved Friend," published in '96 National Library of Poetry anthology. One also selected for '97 Best Poems of 1997—"Memories"; [pers.] I've always enjoyed reading and collecting poetry. I began writing myself when my husband was in Viet Nam. It was an outlet and expression of loneliness and of my deep faith in God.; [a.] Veradale, WA

JEZIOR, BARBARA
[pen.] Barb; [b.] November 9, 1966; Cleveland, OH; [p.] Wayne Giles and Dorothy Giles; [m.] Jeff Jezior; August 16, 1993; [ch.] Kristy, Stephany and Holly; [ed.] I went to North High School in Akron OH, Graduated June 1985; [occ.] I work for WalMart, DC 6022. I have worked there for 3 yrs; [oth. writ.] This is my first poem I have written and entered into a contest.; [pers.] This poem was written for my husband. The reason I wrote it was because we work different shifts and I miss him very much.; [a.] Greencastle, IN

JOHANSON, FRITZ E.
[pens.] Fritz E. Johanson; [b.] July 7, 1917; Sweden; [p.] Oscar F. Johanson, Elin (Strand); [m.] T. Majken (Olson) Johanson; September 26, 1942; [ed.] WPI B.S. in ME—WPI Eve Grand School, Harvard Univ, Adv. Mgt. Program; [occ.] Retired; [memb.] Masons, WPI Tech Old Timerszion Lutheran Church, Holden Sen. Soc., Norton Alumni Soc. Club, Vasa Order of Amer: Worcester Country Club; [hon.] Service WPI H.F. Taylor Distinguished Award (1935), 2nd Prize Nat. Oratorical Conf., Aucusfana, IL, Mass. Registered Prof. Enc.; [oth. writ.] 1965 Russian Mach. Tool Industry, Published "Industry"—Mass, Poem "Zion," and 75th Anniv. WPI Class of '40 Historian Anniv. Reports; [pers.] Motivated by children, animals, birds, sports nature and experiences while traveling extensively throughout the world.; [a.] Holden, MA

JOHNS II, HARRY
[b.] December 29, 1934; Klaynesboro, PA; [ch.] Ginger, Ron, Brady, Tina, Harry III, Joel, Jeanine, Charlene, Karen, Kelley; [occ.] Retired; [pers.] I look at the world through poetry. Reality fogs the real beauty of our world.; [a.] Klaynesboro, PA

JOHNSEN, JOSHUA
[pen.] Joshua Johnsen; [b.] October 23, 1982; St. Louis, MO; [p.] Gregory and Elizabeth Johnsen; [ed.] Ritenour Elementary School Fort Zumwalt Middle School; [occ.] Student; [memb.] Fort Zumwalt High School Ice Hockey Club Made Honor Roll every quarter of middle school; [hon.] 1st place in drawing contest for the cover of a reading magazine; [pers.] You always pass failure on the way to success.; [a.] O'Fallon, MO

JOHNSON, ASHLEY
[b.] January 24, 1985; Colorado Spring; [p.] Robert Johnson, Sandra Johnson; [ed.] Eagleview Middle School, Colorado Springs, CO; [pers.] Writing is a great way to let your emotions and imagination run free.; [a.] Colorado Springs, CO

JOHNSON, CAROLYN M.
[b.] August 23, 1925; Ashland, VA; [p.] Mr. and Mrs. H.B. Magill; [ch.] Mike Walters, Curt Walters, Doww; [ed.] St. George High School; [occ.] Retired nurse; [pers.] Reading before I could walk. Poetry was always my favorite. Late husband said I had a head full of useless knowledge. He was wrong.; [a.] St. George, SC

JOHNSON, DEBORAH
[b.] December 30, 1952; St. Louis MO; [p.] Richard and Jamir Brown; [m.] John E. Johnson; [ch.] Dion Annette Brown; [ed.] Soldam High School; [occ.] Teacher Assistant; [memb.] Kennerly Temple C.O.G.I.C Bishop R.J. Ward (pastor); [pers.] I thank God for all things, my husband Minister John E. Johnson and sister, Louise Brown, and mother, Mable Reynolds, and Sis, D. Ward; [a.] St. Louis, MO

JOHNSON, REBECCA
[pen.] Jade Paralis; [b.] June 1, 1969; Dos Palos; [p.] Chloe Ann, Williard Eugene Parsons; [ed.] Roseville High, Sierra College Sunrise, Christian School; [occ.] Self employment, Housekeeper—Janitorial; [memb.] Big Sisters Assoc., Sacramento Valley Volunteers—doing work for the elderly; [hon.] Various Awards for Poetry Recital; [oth. writ.] Persona; short stories children's books poetry of all sorts; [pers.] I can open myself up on paper. I flow free. I only hope I can give something to this creation. I always bear in mind the children.; [a.] Dos Palos, CA

JONES JR., CLARENCE W.
[pen.] Casper; [b.] August 17, 1961; Southampton County; [p.] Lizzie Jones, Walter Jones; [m.] Barbara W. Jones; April 21, 1990; [ed.] Southampton High, Paul D. Community; [occ.] Semi Operatory Air Brush Painter; [memb.] New Life Choir, God Kingdom; [hon.] 5 Physical Fitness Awards, T-shirt Business Award, God's Son Award; [pers.] Guided by the Holy Spirit I write to unfold my innermost feelings to the reader to sometimes set him or her free from emotional or physical bondage.; [a.] Smithfield, VA

JULMIS, JACELAINE
[b.] June 29, 1980; Haiti; [p.] Francois Julmis, Harceline J.; [ed.] High School Miami Central Sr. High 1781 NW, 95th Streets Miami, FL 33147; [occ.] Babysitting, and High School occupation; [oth. writ.] I started to write poems in my English class some of them are: "Too Late!" "Meaning Of Love." I wrote several other poems to the D. County Youth Fair, also.; [pers.] I'm very pleased to be a part of this program and to continue to assist others to get involved. I'm writing poems to share the positive thoughts with others.; [a.] Miami, FL

KAFEL, MARY SUE
[b.] September 22, 1941; Atlanta, GA; [p.] Jay and Juanita Briscoe; [ed.] B.S. Ed, Univ. GA '63, Diploma, Computer Programming, Dekalb Tech, Atlanta GA; [occ.] Computer Programmer; [memb.] Alpha Omicron Pi Sorority, UGA Sigma Delta Chi, Dekalb Tech; [hon.] Who's Who in American Junior College, 1984 Dean's List, Dekalb

Tech; [pers.] Hobbies: Artist, Designer. I draw my inspiration for my poetry from my beloved Lord.; [a.] Marietta, GA

KAITBENSKI, JOSEPHINE
[b.] September 23, 1947; Sciacca, Sicily; [m.] Stanley; [ch.] 2 sons, and one grandson; [ed.] Revere High School Mansfield Beauty Academy Quinsigamond College Sheffield School of Interior Design; [memb.] Harrington Hospital Auxiliary, Executive Board-Director, Nominating Committee; [hon.] Past President of The Harrington Hospital Auxiliary; [pers.] When things go wrong, I always look for the possible good that could come out of a situation, or perhaps some lesson to be learned.; [a.] Sturbridge, MA

KAPLAN, GLORIA WILSON
[pen.] Gloria Sadler; [b.] July 30, 1917; Detroit, MI; [p.] Lottie and Dadd Rosen; [m.] Morris Kaplan MD; October 11, 1992; [ch.] Barbara Hans and Andrea Nathanson; [ed.] Los Angeles High School, Chaunard College of Art, Tyler College—Temple University UC La Saddlehach College of Art; [occ.] Poet, Sculptor; [memb.] San Diego Museum of Art Continuing Education, Rancho Bernardo, Friends of the Rancho Bernardo Library; [hon.] I have had a number of exhibits of my paintings and sculpture. Some group exhibits at the Palm Springs Museum and a few single exhibits; [oth. writ.] Never published; [pers.] I am very excited about the coming twenty first century. If I make it, I'll be 83. I have been involved in the art field for six decades I really enjoy writing poetry.; [a.] San Diego, CA

KASPER, TIFFANY
[pen.] Crow, TLK, Legs; [b.] November 27, 1981; Kalamazoo, MI; [p.] Geri and Mick Kasper; [ed.] I'm still in High School (10th grade); [oth. writ.] (unpublished works follow), Alone Death, Time, True Love, The Ocean, Restless, Dreams, Confused by Love, War, Love is Like a Rose, Wind, Fear, Love is Like a Tree. Plus many without titles; [pers.] Not all my poems rhyme but I believe they still prove points. I love writing and I know that it is a good way to express feelings.; [a.] Grand Junction, MI

KAVANAGH, KEVIN
[pen.] Kevin Kavanagh; [b.] March , 1958; Buffalo, NY; [p.] Joseph and Ann Kavanagh; [ch.] Kelly Ann Kavanagh; [ed.] West Seneca East Sr. High; [occ.] Certified welder/fitter, heat transfer technology division, American Precisions Industries; [memb.] Wyoming County Sky Divers, International Society of Poets, International Association of Machinists and Aerospace Workers; [hon.] 100 parachute jumps completed June 4, 1988; 1st place—accuracy parachute competition (1982). Editor's Choice Award ('96). Nomination—International Poetry Hall of Fame ('97), Special Thanks to Mart and Fran Gorman; [oth. writ.] Wooden Structures, Distant Travellers, Monuments of Time. All published with the National Library of Poetry; [pers.] I'm thankful to be an instrument in the orchestra of God's great symphony of life. Painting with words on the Canvas of the Human imaginations. Hope is my message that fuels today's efforts for living a better tomorrows.; [a.] Springville, NY

KAYE, LI ANN
[b.] March 12, 1989; Honolulu, Hawaii; [p.] Martin and Lily Kaye; [occ.] 3rd Grade Student Kamiloiki School, Honolulu; [pers.] "My Kaleidoscope" was my first poem. I hope to write many more.; [a.] Honolulu, HI

KEELEY, FELICITY NOEL
[b.] December 25, 1986; Boynton Beach, FL; [p.] Jacquelyn Keeley; [ed.] The North Broward School, Grandview Preparatory School; [occ.] Student; [memb.] Star Dancers, U.S. Chess Federation, National Geographic Society; [hon.]

Straight "A" Honor Roll, 3rd Runner-Up "Miss Jr. Pre-Teen, Ft. Lauderdale," 1st Runner up "Miss Photogenic Jr. Pre-teen," Safety Patrol Honors, 3rd Place in Science Fair; [pers.] I hope all young students study hard and strive for their goals and dedicate all their positive efforts to the benefit of others.; [a.] Boca Raton, FL

KEELING, JOHN FRUM
[b.] February 12, 1938; Dover, AR; [occ.] Writer-Courier; [memb.] Ician International Fellowship; [oth. writ.] "The Key To Heaven's Gate" "How to Get to Heaven Alive," Email: 1stbooks@1stbooks.com (down-load); [pers.] ICIAN is a fellowship. Believe in the teachings of Jesus. Live the Golden Rule. See heaven here on earth. Earth is life; life is God.; [a.] Russellville, AR

KELLY, D'AN
[pen.] D'An Monet; [b.] May 23, 1963; Sacto, CA; [ed.] Hiram W. Johnson Sr. High, Roe State Junior College; Oklahoma City, OK; [occ.] Secretary with the U.S. Government; [oth.writ.] Several dozens of unpublished poems and writings of which await some notoriety.; [pers.] Trust God!; [a.] Sacramento, CA

KENNEDY, MARGUERITE D.
[b.] January 7, 1919; Hellerton, PA; [m.] Robert H. Kennedy; [ch.] One daughter and two sons; [ed.] College; [pers.] My "entrance fee" has been paid into Heaven, by Jesus' death on the cross, so I have pardon peace, strength for each day and bright Hope for "Tomorrow."; [a.] Honey Brook, PA

KHAKSARI, MANSOOR
[b.] August 26, 1943; Abadan; [p.] Vali and Hajigh; March 26, 1980; [ch.] Two daughters; [ed.] Master of Science in Economy; [occ.] Accountant; [memb.] Iranian Writers' Association; [oth. writ.] The Story of Blood, Nightly Sparks, With The Trees of Love's Knowledge, Elegy of Journey, Poet's Land, Los Angelinos; [pers.] As a young boy, I familiarized myself with literature through studying major Persian and world literary scholars like Ferdoosi, Homer, Dante, Roomi, Hafez and T.S. Elliot, Nima Yoosheed, in search of freedom and justice, I found a strong voice in my soul through poetry.; [a.] Playa del Rey, CA

KIM, SHANNON BURNETT
[b.] September 4, 1962; Portsmouth, VA; [p.] John W. and Rebecca M. Burnett; [m.] David; December 27, 1992; [ed.] B.A. in English, Honors, Minor in Political Science, 1983-1986, University of Kentucky, Juris Doctorate, 1989-1991, College of Law, University of SC; [occ.] Attorney; [memb.] SC Bar Association, American Bar Association Federation, SC Dressage Association; [hon.] Rotary Scholarship, Alternate Rhodes Scholar, Ralston Scholastic Achievement Scholarship, Numerous house riding (Dressage) honors at local level; [oth. writ.] Thesis on state of women in workplace published in 1987 in St, Louis, Miss., College Publications, newspapers; [a.] Winnsboro, SC

KING, MARTINA L.
[pen.] M. L. King; [b.] February 28, 1948; Poughkeepsie, NY; [p.] Eugene Crew and Binnia Simpson Crew; [ch.] Noelle; [ed.] Bay State Community College, Boston, MA; [occ.] Underwriter, Charter One Bank, FSB, Cleng, OH; [pers.] Words, as a body, evoke emotion, cause joy, pain, rend and heal. They are that most powerful force that exposes our hearts and souls. They are the mirrors of mankind.; [a.] Cleveland, OH

KIRKMAN, JAN T.
[b.] May 8, 1930; Kurtistown, HI; [p.] Kiyoshi Ura; [m.] Don Kirkman; June 15, 1952; [ch.] Two sons; [ed.] High School, Business College, (2 yrs.), Oakland City College (AA degree), and a Semester at Long Beach State (American Lit.); [occ.] Retired 1993 from the State of California Unemployment and Employment Services; [oth. writ.] Memo-

ries of my grandfather are in the process of being published in August, 1997; [a.] La Palma, CA

KLEMYK, ROBERT JAMES
[b.] Robert Klemyk and Beverly Klemyk; [ed.] Marketing Manager; [memb.] University Center Club at Florida State University (Founding Member); [hon.] Cum Laude and Dean's List Student as well as Who's Who of College and University Students member 1992; [pers.] I draw on my study of Celtic, Ancient, Medieval, 18th Century Western history and the pursuit of pleasure to guide my pen.; [a.] Newington, CT

KNAPPER, RALPH
[b.] July 2, 1916; Cleveland, OH; [p.] Joseph and Lillian Knapper; [m.] Grace Lee Greer Knapper; October 7, 1944; [ch.] Janylee Knapper; [ed.] GED—1966, Correspondence Course on Investigation; [occ.] Retired—security, Pantex Plant; [memb.] United Methodist Men, Golden Spread Emmans Community, Certified Lay Speaker—United Methodist Church; [hon.] Texas Commission on Law Enforcement Officers Standards and Education Recognition, many for safe work from Pantex; [oth. writ.] Poem and Hymn Garden of Gethsemane; [pers.] I wrote the poem (or rhyme) "Heavenly Home" out of clear blue. These came to me along with tunes from God. As a lay speaker, I have written a number of sermons.; [a.] Amarillo, TX

KOGLE, ANGELA
[pen.] Angy; [b.] March 21, 1976; Denver; [p.] Therese Harris-Leady, Bob Cominiello; [m.] Matthew Kogle; November 3, 1995; [ch.] Cerra Lynn Kogle; [occ.] Custom Service Representative for Norwest Bank; [memb.] Latin Honor Society, Norwest Diversity Corner; [oth. writ.] "Devil's Lust," "Dreams" and several other privately published poems; [a.] Thorton, CO

KOVAC, FRANK K.
[b.] June 16, 1965; Cleveland, Ohio; [ed.] John Cabboll University, Bachelor's of Science (physics 1989); [hon.] Math and Physics awards in both high school and college; [oth. writ.] Several published poems, economics essay; [pers.] Poetry reflects the loner needs we conceal by way of all other contact.; [a.] Lattewood, OH

KREIDER, CYNTHIA A.
[b.] August 6, 1955; Lancaster, PA; [p.] Clayton, Rosemary Breneman; [m.] Divorced twice; [ch.] 1 Son, Ryan Lee Flosser; [ed.] Penn Minor High, Millersville, PA, Graduated 1973, Willow St. Votech, Willow St, PA (1970-1973); [occ.] Secretary/ Scottb bookkeeper/ Receptionist at Specialized Auto Care Tune Up; [memb.] Adorers of the Blood of Christ, Pampered Chef, United Methodist Church of Conesoga; [hon.] 1973—VICA Cosmetology 1st Place, Extemporaneous Speaking, 1st Place, Gob Interview 1st Place, Certification in Touch for Health—Holistic Medicine Certification thru M.U.; [oth. writ.] Many pieces of work lying around the house—none published; [pers.] God says we should use our talent given by him to pass the word of his love, writing and painting and photography are my talents and I am thankful for what raw talent I have. Education is the ticket and your heart will support the ride. I try to put my heart and soul in all I do.; [a.] Conestoga, PA

KRISTENSSON, ANNA KARIN
[b.] Sweden; [occ.] Actress and Photographer; [a.] Santa Monica, CA

LACK, LILLY
[pen.] Lillian Newell; [b.] January 27, 1975; Dexter, MO; [p.] Brenda Fisher, Phillip Newell; [m.] John Bennie Lack III; August 12, 1994; [ch.] John Bennie Lack IV; [ed.] Campbell High School; [oth. writ.] Several unpublished poems; [pers.] I believe everything you want in life is worth going for, just

make sure it's what you really want before you get it! This is dedicated to Norman Tinnon and Charles Woodson.; [a.] Campbell, MO

LACKMAN, ANNA
[b.] February 16, 1919; Clinton, MO; [p.] Bruno and Brooksie Albin; [m.] Paul Lackan (now deceased); December 3, 1946; [ch.] Jane, Laura, Eva; [ed.] High School two years Junior College; [occ.] Retired; [oth. writ.] One Step Ahead, The USS American Sails, Retirement Day, When Home Ties Are Severed, Happy Birthday, In Memory; [pers.] I have tried to pass on my inner feelings to others, and to help others as they have encourage me.; [a.] Hitterdal, MN

LACY, NIKKI WARQUINYA
[b.] April 14, 1979; Dallas, TX; [p.] Ray and Warjeania Madden; [ed.] Lawa Magne High Spelman College; [occ.] Retailing at Sears in Townest Mall, Dallas, TX; [memb.] National Honor Society. Dallas "100" Fellows Urban League PALS (Peer Assistance Leadership), UVJ (Universal Voices of Joy Gospel Choir), HOSTS (Helping One Student To Succeed), Speech Club Student Council Senator; [hon.] 1st in UIL Poetry Division (94-95), 2nd in UIL Poetry Division (96-97). Superintendent Scholar (94-95). Who's Who (94-95). Who's Who (96-97). Laureate Award (96-97). A Honor Roll Award (96-97), Links, AKA, TTLA Scholarship Finalist (96-97); [pers.] My writings are the pictures I perceive from the world. My thoughts should capture people universally, acquiring their hearts, minds and souls. My writings are part of my influence towards traveling on the pathway from the virtual to the real.; [a.] Dallas, TX

LAMBERT, MEGAN M.
[b.] July 28, 1993; Portland, ME; [p.] Donna M. Garron and Mike Lambert; [occ.] Student; [hon.] Student of the month. Student Counsel; [a.] Lyman, ME

LANGHAM, BARBARA A.
[b.] June 29, 1946; Staten Island, NY; [p.] Chester and Martha Bradbury; [m.] Perry L. Langham; July 6, 1996; [ch.] Brian Crook, Shannon Prince, Colleen Crook; [ed.] Blessed Sacrament Elementary, St. Joseph Hill Academy High School, Eastern School for Physician's Aides—Medical Technology, Western School of Feng Shui; [occ.] Technician—American SIDS Institute, Nutritional Specialist—Cell Tech. Feng Shui Practitioner; [pers.] I want to be remembered for making a difference in the lives of the people that I contact in any way.; [a.] Conyers, GA

LANHAM JR., MOSES C.
[b.] July 30, 1961; Monroe, MI; [p.] Moses C. Lanham and Ruby J. Lanham; [m.] Felicia J. (Bair) Lanham; May 31, 1986; [ch.] Moses C. "Trey" Lanham, IL; [ed.] Monroe High School Monroe County Community College; [occ.] Assistant Manager, Office Max, Inc; [memb.] Hutt River Province, Lakeside Missionary Baptist Church—(Offices Held: Deacon, Treasurer, Asst. Superintendent); [oth. writ.] Over 50, not yet published; [pers.] In my writings, I try to reflect actual feelings, thoughts and/or experiences of myself in hope that it may inspire others.; [a.] Monroe, MI

LATHEROW, TAMISAN LYNN
[pen.] Tamisan; [b.] November 7, 1981; Clearwater, FL; [p.] Richard Latherow, Trinda Latherow; [ed.] Class of 2000, Tarpon Springs Senior High School; [occ.] Presently Student; [memb.] East Bay World Tae Kwon Do Academy, Youth Alive Christian Club, St. Ignatius Youth, First United Methodist Youth; [hon.] T.S.H.S. Honor Roll, TKD Brown Belt; [oth. writ.] Various Short Stories/Poems, Movie Critique for St. Petersburg Times; [pers.] Live life to the fullest and you will find not only true love, but that you have given a gift to future generations as well.; [a.] Tarpon Springs, FL

LAUSON, ANN
[pen.] Ann Lauson; [b.] August 22, 1920; Baltimore, MD; [p.] Deceased—Frances and Arthur Altvater; [m.] A. Randolf Lauson; August 22, 1941; [ch.] Randy, Steve, Bonnie; [ed.] Franklin High, Baltimore City College, UW-GB, UW-Manitowoc; [occ.] Retired, (Previous) Owner and Pres. of Lullaby Shop, Manitowoc, WI 20 yrs; [memb.] Deacon—Presbyterian Church, Manitowoc, WI, Currently Cypress Lake Presbyterian Church, Ft. Myers, FL; [hon.] Ribbons for artwork; [pers.] The poetry and artwork I do comes from the heart and most have been done for family and friends.; [a.] Ft. Myers, FL

LEACH, GILLIAN
[b.] Oxford, England; [p.] George Hembury and Janet Hembury; [occ.] Writer, Artist; [pers.] My greatest reward for my through efforts, will be see that I can enrich another fellow man my work.; [a.] Phelan, CA

LEBLANC, ROBYN
[b.] December 8, 1985; Pasadena, CA; [p.] Marc and Elaine Le Blanc; [ed.] Entering 6th Grade; [occ.] Student; [hon.] Reading Award February 15, 1993; Excellent Author Award January 15, 1993. The Sky's The Limit Reading Award—February 8, 1995, 5 Principal's Honor Roll 4.0 Grade Average, President's Education Award—June 11, 1997, Accelerated Reader—96/97; [oth. writ.] (Poem) Angel Child, (Poem) Dreaming, (Poem) Guns; [pers.] I truly am a dreamer. One day I hope to play pro basketball in the WNBA. This dream is reflected in my poems and stories, and it inspired me to write more in school.; [a.] Altadena, CA

LEE, ERIC
[pen.] Elancelot or Elzaphan; [b.] June 29, 1971; Duluth, MN; [p.] Patricia Gilmore; [ed.] Henry Sibley High Class of '89; [occ.] Order processor at Best Buy Distribution Center; [oth. writ.] Personal poems written for friends, family and special acquaintances; [pers.] "Everyone is special in the creator's eyes, so I've written poems to reflect what perhaps God may see for each of those unique individual persons.; [a.] Bloomington, MN

LEONARD, APRIL M.
[pen.] November 28, 1984; Atlanta, GA; [p.] Gloria Leonard-Mother; [ed.] Fickett Elementary School, Ralph, Bunche Middle School; [occ.] Student—promoted to 7th grade; [memb.] Northwest Georgia Girl Scout Cadette Troup #797, Junior Beta Club, GRS Baptist Church; [hon.] Principal's List, First Place Language Arts Festival 1997; [oth.writ.] Several poems—one published in Anthology for Young Americans and one published for 1996 Olympics which was used as a night card to go on the bed pillows at hotels where guests stayed; [pers.] I love to write poems and short stories. I also like to practice reciting them with expression. I write what expression. If I don't feel it, I can't write it.; [a.] Atlanta, GA

LESSO, GERALDINE
[pen.] Gerri Anderson; [b.] July 14, 1946; Jacksonville, FL; [p.] William Anderson, Bessie Anderson; [m.] Divorced; [ch.] Dale, Gene, Lori, Jaclyn, Reese, Dawn; [ed.] Paxon Sr. High, FCCJ, Jacksonville, FL., Certified for Managing Day Care North Campus, Certified Home Health Aide North Campus; [occ.] Home Health Aide; [memb.] Home Garden Baptist Church; [hon.] Jacksonville Journal, YWCA, Championship Spelling Certificate; [oth. writ.] Several poems, songs and children's stories, unpublished, for my family; [pers.] I have always enjoyed books of poetry, poems by Edgar Allen Poe. My writings vary from humorous to serious and spiritual, as I feel a need to balance these in our daily lives. I love writing stories for my Grandchildren to enjoy long after I am gone.; [a.] Jacksonville, FL

LEVERSON, MARILYN BEALE
[b.] February 17, 1955; Pittsburgh. PA; [p.] Gertrude and Robert Beale; [m.] Ralph Leverson; September 11, 1982; [ch.] Erin K. Brian D., Sean M. Leverson; [ed.] Taylor Allderdice High School, Ohio State University; [occ.] Director, Occupational Therapy, Mercy Hospital and Medical Ctr (Chicago, IL); [memb.] Illinois Occupational Therapy Association, American Occupational Therapy Association; [hon.] Featured in the Sept. 1995 Edition of Ebony Magazine. The Article was entitled "Children and Careers: The Best of Both Worlds"; [pers.] I have been blessed to have parents who inspired me to discover the best within myself. It is they who have set the standard for parenting which I attempt to achieve.; [a.] Chicago, IL

LIBUTTI, GERARD M.
[b.] July 2, 1960; Huntington NY. [ed.] Associate degree in Psychology and Sociology—Educated in Music for 15 years (trumpet) received certificate in Culinary Arts 1984; [occ.] Head chef of a Sports Bar; [oth. writ.] A collection of over 100 poems, a series of children's short stories, currently working on two screen plays; [a.] Huntington, NY

LIMA, MARGARET SOUSA
[pen.] Maggie; [b.] November 10, 1983; Providence, RI; [p.] Jose Lima, Margarida R. Sousa; [ed.] Sacred Heart School East Providence, RI (grades 1-8); [occ.] Student at St. Mary's Academy Bay View, Riverside, RI; [hon.] Essays and other contests for the Providence Journal; [a.] East Providence, RI

LONG, ALLEGRA
[b.] April 21, 1986; Santa Monica, CA; [p.] Dr. James and Mrs. Darlene Long; [ed.] 5th Grade at Carlthorp School; [occ.] Student; [hon.] Winner of Math Olympiad, highest Spanish Grade point value for two years in a row, top honors, in National Word Masters' competition, and honor roll; [oth. writ.] I love to write about cats. This is my first poem to be published. I not only write poems, but all genres including newsletters, short stories, and essays.; [pers.] I strive to prove what Leonardo Di Vinci said was true: "The smallest feline is a masterpiece.".; [a.] Los Angeles, CA

LORANT, ANNETTE
[pen.] Annette Lorant; [b.] April 1, 1961; Boulogne/Billacount, France; [p.] Andre Lorant Marie Markus; [ed.] High School diploma in Paris, France "Licence" degree in Fine Arts at Paris I; [occ.] Actress, make-up artist; [oth. writ.] Poems—this is my first published one. This is the first time I looked into being published.; [pers.] Finding the colors of emotions and being able to put them in words is a great satisfaction, to transmit it to others is even a greater one.; [a.] Studio City, CA

LOVEDAY, PAM HARPER
[b.] March 24, 1952; Copperhill, TN; [p.] James and Patricia Harper; [m.] Ronnie Loveday; August 26, 1969; [ch.] Heather and Ronda; [ed.] Sevier County High School, Walter's State Community College; [occ.] Home school Teacher; [pers.] My poems come from life's experiences. Spencer, Hope, Ashley, Kelsey and Mackenna give great joy to this life.; [a.] Sevierville, TN

LOWELL, LAURETTA JANE
[b.] 1946; Gunnison, CO; [p.] Howard Milton Lowell, Linnia; [m.] Dale; [ed.] 2 years associate in General Science degree from Pike's Peak Community College (Colo. Spgs.) Junior at Mesa State College, Grand Junction Majority in English; [occ.] Homemaker, I make leather wallets, purses, belts; [hon.] Presently a finalist in the Quality Cup Award presented for efforts to help mentally handicapped individuals; [oth. writ.] Selected Poems of a Religious Nature, included in numerous anthologies; [pers.] "Since I am finding out how hard it is to change the world, I do well to live in it.".; [a.] Delta, CO

LUKENS, ELSIE MAE
[pen.] Elsie Mae Olofsson Lukens; [b.] February 10, 1920; Grand Rapids, MN; [p.] Malkolm and Alma Olson; [m.] Paul Clement Lukens; August 30, 1956; [ch.] Deborah and Victoria; [ed.] Itasca Community College, Grand Rapids, MN, Duluth Branch, University of Minnesota, BS. Degree—Teachers College, Columbia University, MA, degree, Post-Graduate study in eleven colleges and universities; [occ.] Organist, Choir Director—Presbyterian Church—Taft, CA. Pianist and professional accompanist; [memb.] Delta Kappa Gamma, American Guild of Organists, American Legion Auxiliary, Young Audiences of America, Bakersfield Philatelic Club; [hon.] (Scandinavian and Coros Collector's Club) Two scholarships—U. of MN and DKG—in piano; [pers.] I strive to give God thanks for my talents.; [a.] Taft, CA

LUM, GRETCHEN YATES
[b.] June 10, 1945; Honolulu, HI; [p.] Mr. and Mrs. F.G. Yates; [m.] Philip Wayne Lum; May 30, 1967; [ch.] Jadine Lum; [ed.] BFA, CA College Arts and Crafts 1970; [occ.] Fine Jewelry Sales/Artist/Poet; [memb.] International Society of Poets, Volunteer: Sidha Yoga, Whitney Museum of American Art (New York), Aldrich Museum of Contemporary Art (Connecticut), member and volunteer; [hon.] 1996 Who's Who in America, 1995 Best Poems of 1995, National Library of Poetry 1995, Editor's Choice 1993; [oth. writ.] Standing on Tip Toes, (1991), recording—The Sound of Poetry (1993), Visions (1994), (anthology) Whispers in the Wind, Best Poets; [pers.] Discovery is at the root of all my poetry, as is inner contemplation and self-realization.; [a.] Brentwood, CA

MACARTNEY, COPY R.
[b.] April 11, 1982; Santa Clara, CA; [p.] Jill Cody and Robert Macartney; [ed.] Sophomore, Las Altos High School, Los Altos, CA; [occ.] Student; [hon.] 1995-96 Outstanding Student, Egan Jr. High School Los Altos, CA; [oth. writ.] "Papa Who Wakes Up In The Dark," "Experience"; [pers.] Poetry is the frontier of our mind—space is the frontier of our future.; [a.] Los Altos, CA

MACLEOD JR., NORMAN LAUCHLIN
[b.] March 14, 1914; New York City; [p.] Anna M. Osborne, Norman L. MacLeod; [m.] Christine H. MacLeod; 1950; [ch.] Roderick Dorn MacLeod, Norman Derek MacLeod (also have two grandsons) [ed.] Engelwood, New Jersey, High School, Columbia University, A.B., 1935, Southwestern Baptist Theol. Seminary, Fort Worth, Texas—Th. M., 1945; [occ.] Retired; [memb.] "Clan MacLeod Society USA, Inc.," "Sons in Retirement"; [oth. writ.] Religious book, entitled: "He Called Himself the Son of Man." Copyrighted by me, 1993, Published by Old Rugged Cross Press, Roswell, GA; [pers.] Have strong Christian Evangelical beliefs, including faith in Jesus, and that we all should be studying the Bible more thoroughly, regarding it as the accurate, in-detail message from God to us. (A special note about the writing of this poem: Being challenged to write a short poem, I found myself mentally hearing what I call a "melody of flow of words"—a very "broken" melody, but nothing would come out. Finally, after 24 hours, I suddenly sat down and in a few minutes dashed it off, almost exactly as it now appears, with but two very minor changes.); [a.] Walnut Creek, CA

MAGEE, SHAMIKA
[pen.] Mika; [b.] November 15, 1982; El Paso, TX; [p.] Cowart and Martha Magee; [ed.] Ninth grade (9th); [pers.] I love to write love short stories.; [a.] Hinesville, GA

MANGUM, SUE O.
[b.] June 19, 1937; Blenheim, SC; [p.] Johnny and Beulah Owens; [ch.] Susan, Andrea, Douglas, Julie; [ed.] Wingate College, Coker College; [occ.] Administrative Assistant and Self-Employed Tax Return Preparer; [memb.] SC Council on Child Abuse and Neglect, Licensed Caregiver—Board of Disabilities, Pee Dee Coalition Against Domestic Violence Chapter Board; [oth. writ.] My intent is to honor God through my writing.; [a.] Pageland, SC

MARCHMAN, KELLI
[b.] August 25, 1981; Milledgeville; [p.] Linda and James Marchman; [ed.] Kindergarten, Middle, at Brentwood High, Washington County High; [occ.] Student; [hon.] Editor's Choice Award—At Day's End; [oth. writ.] Memories, published in At Days End, 2 school literary journals; [pers.] I have written over 30 poems and a book. This is my second poem published. If anyone out there could publish or help me publish my book of poems I'd be very grateful.; [a.] Wanthen, GA

MARRERO, JACQUELINE
[pen.] Chris E. Alegre, Henry Alegre; [b.] March 23, 1973; Brooklyn, NY; [p.] Victor Marrero, Nancy Miranda; [ed.] Pablo Avila H.S. Kingsborough Community College, Long Island University, Hunter College; [occ.] Home Health Aide, Patient Care, Brooklyn, NY; [hon.] Art, Associate in Applied Science, Recognition for Self Sufficiency; [oth. writ.] I've written various songs, using my lyrics for many styles of music; [pers.] Tell that special person how you feel, if not by words of mouth, then do it in writing. What you know can't be taken from you. Show your love and care by being there.; [a.] Brooklyn, NY

MARTIN, CATHY RAE
[b.] May 30, 1957; Grand Haven, MI; [p.] Clifford Erdmann, Hazel Erdmann; [m.] David William Martin; October 27, 1979; [a.] Grand Ledge, MI

MARTIN, KRISTY
[b.] May 19, 1982; Okeene, OK; [p.] Ernie and Beverly Martin; [ed.] 9th grade Canton High School, Canton, OK; [occ.] Student; [memb.] Future Homemakers of America, Technology Students of America; [hon.] Principal's Honor Roll, Who's Who Among American High School Students, Treasurer/Reporter of Freshman Class; [a.] Canton, OK

MARTINEZ, BOB G.
[b.] June 7, 1949; New Mexico; [p.] Mrs. Mary Jane Martinez; [m.] Annette E. Martinez; February 10, 1973; [ch.] Lita (20); [ed.] High School graduate from Denver's North in '68; [occ.] Security Guard at Denver Merchandise Mart; [memb.] Distinguished Member of ISP-NLP, Columbine Poets of Colorado, Mile High Poetry Society, Best Little Can on a Mexican (1976); [hon.] Plethora of Editor's Choice Awards among many publications; [oth. writ.] My Time To Rhyme: Personal Journal from 1949 to 1994. Sidetracks: compilation of my poems; [pers.] Commit your thoughts to the Lord and your words will flow out of you like The Ever-Flowing Stream.; [a.] Denver, CO

MATROS, LARISA
[pen.] Larisa Matros; [b.] June 30, 1938; Odessa, Ukraine; [p.] Grigory and Eva Akselrod; [m.] Yurii Matros; July 25, 1960; [ch.] Master in Law, State University Odessa, 1963, Philosophy PhD State University Novosibirsk (Russia) 1972; [occ.] Freelance Writer, Researcher; [memb.] P.E.N. International Pushrinists Association, Lifetime Deputy Governor, American Biographiea Institute Research Association, Cambridge (England) International Biographiea Association Lifetime Fellow; [hon.] Award of Excellence at 23rd International Congress of Art and Communications, San Francisco, 1996, American Biographical Institute's World Lifetime Achievement Award, 1996, Listed in Marguis Who's Who In The World; [oth. writ.] Author about 100 publications (include two books about problem of mankind), articles, short stories, literary reviews, poems, essays, now I am close to finish a novel.; [pers.] I strive to reflect my nation about contradictions of mankind, life and human personality in all my writing. However, poetry is the best form for the concentrated expression of knowledge and emotions.; [a.] Chesterfield, MO

MATTIX SR., SAM
[pen.] Sam; [b.] June 2, 1931; Crockett Texas; [p.] Mr. and Mrs. Houston Mattix; [m.] Mrs. Bessie Marie Mattix; August 7, 1993—wife of four years; [ch.] Four—Sam Jr., Carolyn, Lashon, Texas; [ed.] Carver Jr. High School, Kountze, TX, San Jacinto College, Houston, TX, Graduated May 22, 1969 in the field of Roofing and Waterproofing; [occ.] Roofer—retired now from Roofers Local Union Number 116; [memb.] Greater Outreach Missionary Baptist Church—Deacon there; [hon.] Two Editor's Choice Awards from the National Library of Poetry, 1 Brotherhood award from church, 1 Certificate from the American Federation of Labor in Roofing and Waterproofing, May 22, 1969. Equipment operation and maintenance, June 1974, Houston, TX; [oth. writ.] Four songs, two books unpublished, lots of poems; [pers.] I, Sam H. Mattix Sr., thank God, who is the head of my life, my wife, my children and the many friends and all the people who take time out to read my poem.; [a.] Houston, TX

MCCARTHY, SUSAN
[b.] January 16, 1949; Long Island, NY; [m.] Bruce McCarthy; May 17, 1969; [ch.] Kelly Elizabeth, Eric Scott; [ed.] High School-Miami Norland Sr. High, Real Estate Classes and Classes of various interest at CFU; [occ.] Sales; [oth. writ.] I have had one other poem published. I am writing poems and a children story at this time.; [pers.] I would like to leave of hope. And joy and a thirst for discovering poetry.; [a.] Denver, CO

MCCLAIN, MARGARET
[pen.] Margaret McClain; [b.] February 24, 1935; Olive Branch, MS; [p.] John B. Barbour, Evelyn Barbour; [m.] Jimmy L. McClain; June 16, 1958; [ch.] Tina, Janet, Darrell, Clark; [ed.] Graduate of Olive Branch High School; [occ.] Homemaker, part-time Bookkeeper for All Speed Elect. Motors [memb.] Church of Christ, Franklin County Arts Guild (Inactive At The Moment.), Franklin County, TN; [hon.] No special awards, but have been actively involved in several art exhibits locally at: 100 Oaks Castle Board of Education, Franklin County Library, also art donations, to Channel 8 art auction in Nashville, TN; [oth. writ.] Several poems and writings in my Personal Collection, but nothing published. I'm excited at the idea of having a published work. I appreciate being chosen as a semifinalist in your contest with all of the adversity in the world.; [pers.] I have chosen to reflect the Lightest side of Life in most of my writings, and to capture the beauty of nature (flowers, landscapes, birds) in my Art.; [a.] Winchester, TN

MCDONALD, MICHAEL
[b.] July 9, 1969; Texas; [p.] Ron McDonald; December 3, 1993; [ch.] Jarred and Michelle; [ed.] Albuquerque Job Corp; [occ.] Security; [oth. writ.] Several Poems; [pers.] I believe that poetry is not only the way the spirit conceives the world but the way the world acknowledges its own spirit.; [a.] Hurst, TX

MCGARRAHAN, KEVIN
[b.] October 7, 1964; Port Arthur, TX; [p.] Paul McGarrahan, Lucille Strickland; [ch.] (1) son: Kevin Ian McGarrahan; [ed.] Graduated from Por† Neches-Groves High School, Port Neches, TX; [occ.] Construction, Millwright/Pipefitter; [memb.] First Baptist Church Of Groves; [pers.] I hope to turn other poems I have written into songs. I hope to go into the studio to record the songs soon. It will include "Broken Wings.".; [a.] Beaumont, TX

MCINROE, VIVIAN ELLIOTT
[b.] June 10, 1912; Moran, TX; [p.] J.A. and Cornelia Elliott; [m.] T.O. McInroe (Deceased); [ed.] College Med. Tech; [occ.] Retired Med. Tech; [memb.] Church Affiliation; [oth. writ.] Numerous Poems; [pers.] Love and Respect of Individual Personal Trait; [a.] Hurst, TX

MCLAUGHLIN, LOIS
[b.] September 20, 1932; Wilkes-Barre, Pa; [p.] James L. McLaughlin, Cassie Sergent McLaughlin; [m.] Divorced; [ch.] Cathryn Ellen, Patricia Ann, Anastasia Janette; [ed.] James M. Coughlin High School, Olaf Trygvasson School of Music, Fayetteville Community College, Methodist College Community Music Course; [occ.] Retired; [memb.] AAMT, AAMA, National Honor Society; [hon.] Editorial Key (Coughlin High School), National Honor Society, Journalism Awards (High School), Certificates of Merit (Art Competitions); [oth. writ.] Poems Published in national anthology, editorials published in H.S. Journal; [pers.] I try to write from personal experience. I favor the Persian poets. Interested in genealogy and presently researching my family origins.; [a.] Wilkes-Barre, PA

MCLOUD, MILDRED HYATT
[b.] August 24, 1927; GA; [p.] Ora Louvorn, L.L. Hyatt; [m.] Donald R. McLoud; February 22, 1947; [ch.] Five Children; [ed.] Graduated Martha Berry—January 22, 1945, Murray Business Schools—1954, Polk College of Real Estate Licensed, FL, 10 yrs.; [memb.] SC Teachers Assn., Sub Teacher. Ret., Red Cross Emergency Service Worker, Church Groups; [hon.] Berry Golden Guard, Int'l Society of Poets, Int'l Poetry Hall of Fame; [oth. writ.] Nat'l Library of Poetry anthologies: Frost at Midnight, Morning Song, Best of '97, Dance Upon The Shore, Web Site for works; [pers.] Best said in Web poems "Never Give Up The Ship" and "Uniquely You."; [a.] Killdeer, ND

MCMASTER, LUCY
[b.] May 26, 1925; Winnsboro, SC; [p.] Wilburn and Josephine Lewis; [m.] Quay W. McMaster; August 31, 1963; [ch.] Richard H. Thomas and James Myer, Thomas (deceased) sons lot my first marriage; [ed.] Green High School-Winnsboro, SC and Winthrop College, Rock Hill SC; [occ.] Housewife; [oth. writ.] Many rhymes over the years to family friends and about my inner thoughts, all of which will soon end up in a book—compliments of a friend.; [pers.] "To Thine own self be true."; [a.] Winnsboro, SC

MCMILLEN, SUZANNE
[b.] Warren, OH; [m.] Gene Fallon, March 17, 1992; [ch.] Son, Chad C. McMillen; [ed.] Associate Director: Television Workshop, Inc, and Center for Communication Arts, (Proprietary Schools), Cleveland, OH, Motivational Speaker, Universal Studios of FL, Dale Carnegie Foundation, Valencia Community College, Orlando, FL; [occ.] Adjunct Professor, Embry-Riddle Aeronautical University; [memb.] International Society of Poets, North Shore Animal League; [oth. writ.] Editor's Choice Award, Life is Good; [pers.] If there's one message to share with others, it is to remind individuals of God's omni-present love for humankind. One's character is the reality in the unfolding of God's open doorway to enlightenment and truth. Man's reality is: Choice.; [a.] Mukiteo, WA

MCNELLEN, JOSHUA CHRISTIAN
[b.] April 1, 1979; San Diego, CA; [p.] Megan R. O'Rourke and Scott D. McNellen; [ed.] Mt. Carmel High School (1997) will begin fall sem. and CSU San Marcos as Education Major; [occ.] Line Cook, Dalomar College Cafeteria; [pers.] I wrote this piece in my Senior English class in High School at Mt. Carmel. Thanks to Mrs. L-T, Jennifer C., and of course my Mom. I love you.; [a.] San Diego, CA

MEADE, LILLIAN M.
[pen.] Lil; [b.] September 10, 1952; Newport News, VA; [p.] John H. Boyd, Lillian Mae Woodard; [m.] David A. Meade, Sr.; July 27, 1969; [ch.] Almettia, Karen, Patricia, David III, Alena, Jeremiah, Jessica, Matthew; [ed.] GED 1989, Attended Thomas Nelson Community College Seeking Associate Degree in Business; [occ.] Food service worker, cashier, shift manager; [pers.] I use personal experiences to write my poems. I give God all the glory and honor for His inspiration and leadership in my life.; [a.] Hampton, VA

MEARS, JEANNE K.
[b.] August 10, 1962; Nassawadox, VA; [oth. writ.] A few unpublished poems, such as "Golden Gates of Heaven" and "Run to the Hills"; [a.] Eastville, VA

MESSINA, RAYMOND J.
[pen.] Raymond Messina; [b.] August 4, 1938; Brooklyn, NY; [p.] Agostino and Josephine Messina; [m.] Rosallie Messina; April 12, 1970; [ch.] Bachelor of Industrial Engineering, Juris Doctor, New York Law School, June, 1964; [occ.] Attorney-at-law; [memb.] The Hastings Center, New York Academy of Sciences, American Society of International Law, Earthwatch, New York County Lawyers' Associations, The Asia Society; [hon.] Selected to participate in the certificate Program in Bioethics and the Medical Humanities sponsored by Columbia University, College of Physicians and Surgeons and Montefiore Medical Center; [oth. writ.] Cage the Little Bird, Witness to a Miracle, The Boy Child, Sunbeams, The Hardhats, A Face Tells a Story, Holding Onto Freshness, Options Unlimited/Options Restricted, The Delay Essays, Aggression, Expression of Identity, The Baby, It's Possible, Fantasies; [pers.] If there is anything that I have learned over the years, it is that everything and everybody counts in this world, which brings to mind the line in the song by Nana Mouskouri, which states: "I have come to understand that every hair is numbered like very grain of sand."; [a.] New York City, NY

MIDWOOD, NANCY M.
[b.] January 31, 1929; Buston, MA; [p.] Prof. William H. McAdams and Jennie Estelle Dubbs [m.] Kenneth E. Brown; June 17, 1949, Divorced; Arnold J. Midwood, 1980, Widowed, 1990; [ch.] Christopher, Jennifer, Michael, Jeffrey Brown; [ed.] Newton High School, 1946, Mount Holyoke College; Wellesley College B.A., 1973, Boston College, Med. 1975, with Distinction; [occ.] Retired Teacher; [memb.] Hospice of Palm Beach County, South Guild, Board of Directors; [hon.] 1973 Phi Beta Kappa, Wellesley College.

MILLER, KIMBERLY
[pen.] Kim Timbrook Miller; [b.] March 11, 1964; Royal Oak, MI; [p.] Donald Timbrook, Nancy Timbrook; [m.] Kenny Miller; May 27, 1995; [ch.] Codee Alexandra, Kala Lee, Lexi Ann; [ed.] West Iron County High, Bay de Noc Community College, Professional Career Development Institute; [occ.] Interior Decorator and Flooring Store Owner, Precision Flooring and Decorating; Iron River, MI; [memb.] Upper Peninsula Writers, Bible Truths Group; [hon.] Several poems published in local papers; [oth. writ.] Currently working on a Sci-Fi book; [pers.] I tend to write from personal experience more than anything and always attempt positivity and truthfulness.; [a.] Iron River, MI

MILLER, LINDA DAWN
[pen.] Dawn Miller; [b.] August 22, 1949; K.C., MO; [p.] Mother—Deceased, Father—Maimon Miller; [m.] Divorced; [ch.] Kerry J. Sullivan; [ed.] Ruskin High School of K.C., MO; [occ.] Cash Flow Manager; [memb.] Colonial Church of Prairie Village, KS, Member of the Board of Outreach Ministry; [oth. writ.] First published writing; [pers.] I was reborn and held in 1996. Thanks to God's blessing I started writing. I simply I'm trying to tell my life's experiences to help someone else along the way.; [a.] Kansas City, MO

MILLER, NEIL J.
[b.] December, 1996; Boston, MA; [p.] George Miller, Erlene Hayes; [ch.] Terrence Richardson and Janelle Reddic; [occ.] Currently incarcerated; [oth. writ.] 142 other poems (some sent out and awaiting answers), 2 short stories and working on 3rd; [pers.] I hope to become a decent writer of articles and short stories as well as poetry. And I hope, also, to touch people the way other writers and poets touched me.

MILLER, STEPHEN GEORGE
[pen.] George McClure, William Young; [m.] (Divorced) Susan Mary Pugsley; 1986; [ed.] B.A. Univ. Arizona, 1978, B.A. Univ. North Carolina, 1985; M.C.S. Texas A and M Univ. 1988; [occ.] Touring Singer/Musician and Recording Artist, part-time Professor, Writer; [memb.] American Mensa, Ltd., BMI (Broadcast Music, Inc.), Harry Fox Agency (NMPI), American Federation of Musicians (AFM), National Parks and Conservation Association; [hon.] TNN (Nashville Network) "Country News" appearance Sept. 1994. Nashville Banner article, July 1994. "The Thing Called Love" (Paramount—acted as extra), Fall 1992. Sunny Summer Blues album released Fall 1992. (With six SGMiller songs.); [oth. writ.] "Double-Sided Mirror," publ. 1990, Rainbow Wind, Sabre publ., Variation on Theme, publ. 1980, Chapel Hill, NC. Published song-writer ("Alien Love," "Ballad of O.J. Simpson," etc.).; [a.] Nashville, TN

MITCHELL, CLARITA
[pen.] Patsy; [b.] September 8, 1963; Antigua, WI; [p.] Joachim and Clarence Mitchell; [m.] Sgt. Leo Phillip; December 7, 1987; [ch.] Alexandria E. Phillip; [ed.] St. Croix Central High School, Fayetteville Technical College, Dekalb College; [occ.] Framing Gallery (Framing Expensive and Inexpensive Art; [hon.] Lay Catechist at St. Joseph Catholic Church, Awards for most Volunteer Parents at Cumberland Road Elementary School; [pers.] I was influenced by my daughter Alexandria, who always wants me to write short stories about her fish "Bubbles."; [a.] Fayetteville, NC

MITCHELL, PAUL
[pen.] Blue; [b.] July 17, 1970; Trinidad; [p.] Mr. and Mrs. Hellen Mitchell; [ch.] Lexus Mitchell; [ed.] Two years at B.C.C.; [occ.] Nurse Aid; [memb.] Local 1199, "Health and Medical Association at New York; [oth. writ.] Framed on the walls of several hospitals in the Tri-State area; [pers.] This poem came out of the love that I have for my lady baby.; [a.] Beacon, NY

MITCHELL, WALTER
[pen.] W.L. Mitchell, T. Mitchell Guy; [b.] July 1, 1952; Mesa, AZ; [p.] Willie Mitchell and Willie Frank Mitchell; [m.] Divorced; May 30, 1985; [ch.] Miss Ashley Race Mitchell; [ed.] B.S. Liberal Arts—Sociology A.S.U. 1974, Masters of Arts Education (MAE) '83, ANNG—Another John Nelson Graduate; [occ.] Disability Retirement from Teaching 1993; [memb.] Various teacher-related organizations from Yuma, AZ ('75-'78) to Phoenix, AZ ('78-'80) to Flags Taffi ('80-'82), Las Vegas, NV, ('82-'89), Hawaii Public Schools ('92-'93), Phoenix Union H.S. ('89-'93); [hon.] Several poems published in various poetry books over the past 10 years. Poetry keeps me in touch with myself and others.; [oth. writ.] To my daughter and of course, more and more poetry under T. Mitchell, Walter L. Mitchell but I like T. Mitchell Guy the Best.; [pers.] I strive to write for no one else except me but, if I catch someone else's ear or touch their soul, my writing has close what is needed; [a.] Austin, TX

MITCHELL SR., THOMAS E.
[pen.] "Tombo"; [b.] April 25, 1927; Cadiz, KY; [p.] Tandy and Beulah A. Mitchell; [m.] Lucy Dyer Mitchell; May 10, 1952; [ch.] Thomas E. Jr. and Jacque D; [ed.] High School—Louisville Male High, Louisville,KY, Class of 1946 1/2; [occ.] Retired; [memb.] Church Hoosier Hills Bluegrass Association; [oth. writ.] A few columns for small local papers and wrote and edited a bluegrass assoc. paper that no longer exists.; [pers.] I am much better known by my nickname "Tombo" than any other, and use it full-time unless on checks or legal papers.; [a.] Fairdale, KY

MOATS, PATRICK A.
[pen.] The Praying Traveler; [b.] January 5, 1958; Norfolk, NE; [p.] Myron L., Nylotis G. (Overhue) Moats; [ch.] Jessica Lynn; [ed.] Norfolk Nebraska Public Senior High, N.E. Tech. Comm. College (C.E.T.A 1975), Norfolk Nebraska Central Comm. College, Hasting, NE, some Bible study courses; [occ.] Driver/Foreman of Transportation for Pole Maintenance Company, Columbus, NE; [memb.] Seventh Day Adventist Church, Columbus, NE, Distinguished member of the International Society of Poets, National Arbor Day Foundation, Nebraska City, NE; [hon.] Elected into "The International Poetry Hall of Fame" on Monday, Dec. 30th, 1996, "Editor's Choice Awards" from "The National Library of Poetry." Having my poems published by "The National Library Of Poetry"; [oth. writ.] A few letters to the editors and ads published in local area newspapers, anonymous letters and cards of encouragement to various people to brighten their days.; [pers.] To be of service to others is one of many great blessings in life given by Lord Jesus Christ for the asking.; [a.] Norfolk, NE

MONEY, WILLIAM MATTHEW
[pen.] Matt Money; [b.] June 4, 1980; Louisville, KY; [p.] Bill Money, Rhonald Karnes; [ed.] Senior at Jeffersonville High School; [occ.] Lifeguard; [memb.] American Chung Do Kwan, Tae Kwondo Association, YMCA; [hon.] Young Authors' Award; [oth. writ.] No published works, but have several poems written; [pers.] Those who struggle to move on will move on, but those who are determined will gain all of a what was put into their future.; [a.] Jeffersonville, IN

MOORHOUSE, HERBERT I.
[pen.] Waffles The Clown Chief"; [b.] March 10, 1915; Lake Geneva, WA; [p.] Mr. and Mrs. William Ed Moorhouse; [m.] Mrs. Patnia Moorhouse; January 26, 1951; [ch.] Teresa, Loretta, Karha, Karen, Lawrence; [ed.] All have College education; BA—Journalism, Art tano girls, sociology, BA, and one Technology, TV; [occ.] Retired; [memb.] Cousin Otto's Clown Alley #22 Ltd, Clowns of America, American Legion; [hon.] Not so much an honor but a Bachelor of Arts in English, GI Bill, graduating in 1950, starting grad. school, library science—no degree; [oth. writ.] "Re" Thavers vows of kernels of corn! Listing similar in Essence of a Dream, 1997; [pers.] I wish to write for the achievements of mankind, especially humorous achievements.; [a.] Lake Geneva, WI

MORRIS, LORNA
[b.] November 29, 1958; Houston, TX; [p.] Henry S. Fields/Ermateen L. Fields; [m.] Mark E. Morris, D.O.; April 9, 1983; [ch.] Stephen Mark Morris; [ed.] Phyllis Wheatley Sr. High, Hermann Hospital School of Vocational Nursing, University of Houston.; [occ.] Homemaker, Church School Teacher—Mt. Calvary Baptist Church; [memb.] New Macedonia Baptist Church of Houston, TX. Rev. James E. Morris, Sr. Pastoral Minister. Mt. Calvary Baptist Church of Fort Worth, TX. Rev. E.C. Reynolds, Pastor.; [hon.] Who's Who Among American High School Students, Most Progressive Church School Class 1997—"Sisters In Christ" of Mt. Calvary Baptist Church of Fort Worth, TX; [oth. writ.] Poems and short stories (unpublished) and songs; [pers.] My writings are culminations of real life error, either experienced or witnessed. I desire to express truths in such away that even a child can comprehend.; [a.] Fort Worth, TX

MOSCATO SR., GARY J.
[b.] August 16, 1937; Turlock, CA; [p.] James A, Helen E; [m.] Carilyn; October 1985; [ed.] San Mateo High, Diablo Valley College, US Army/U.S. Air Force; [occ.] Senior Mechanic; [pers.] Study Western History The American Indian and Civil War; [a.] Pacheco, CA

MOTT, CELESTE
[b.] August 8, 1976; [p.] Ellen and Neil Nuzman; [m.] Brian K. Mott; October 13, 1994; [a.] Okinawa, Japan

MOWATT, HOLLI
[pen.] Holli Mowatt; [b.] January 20, 1979; Port Jervis; [p.] Ed and Kathy Mowatt; [ed.] High School Graduate, Attending College in September; [occ.] Student; [hon.] 2 times NCA All-American Cheer Leader; [pers.] Carpe Diem; [a.] Port Jervis, NY

MUELLER, AMANDA J.
[pen.] Mandy; [b.] August 11, 1987; Desert, Sam; [p.] Rusty and Karen Mueller; [ed.] 4th grade of J.O. Combs Elementary School in Queen Creek, AZ; [hon.] Honor Roll all for quarters; [pers.] Answer inquiries about how the poem came about.; [a.] Queen Creek, AZ

MULLICAN, ROSS
[b.] May 26, 1982; South Lyon, MI; [p.] Cheryl Wagner, Floyd Seal; [ed.] Currently attending Deerfield Academy as a Sophomore; [occ.] Student; [memb.] Atlanta Athletic Club; [oth. writ.] Currently writing a poetry book. Published in "The Outlook"; [pers.] I use poetry to express my emotions. The hardest thing in life is to express what you are feeling at a given time.; [a.] Alpharetta, GA

MURPHY, MICHELLE J.
[pen.] Shelley Isobel; [b.] December 1, 1962; Poughkeepsie, NY; [m.] Robert M. Murphy; May 2, 1992; [occ.] Housewife, mother of Poetry. The "furry four" and poet; [memb.] The International Society of Poets; [oth. writ.] I have had several other poems published by the National Library of Poetry; [pers.] Stardust Serenade (Abby) is an 8 + yr. old white Shetland sheepdog who has been shifted through 7 homes before ours. She is a darling, precious little lamb, which make this poem so special.; [a.] Stanfordville, NY

MURRAY, ROBYN L.
[b.] July 27, 1961; Teaneck, NJ; [p.] Melva, Cortland Murray; [ed.] Bachelor of Science in Nursing from William Paterson College in Wayne, NJ; [occ.] Critical Care Nurse; [memb.] National League for Nurses. International Society of Poets, Distinguished Member; [hon.] Army Spirit of Nursing Award, PCCC, 1995, Alumni Representative on Board of Trustees, Passaic County College; [oth.writ.] I write song lyrics, short stories and poems; [pers.] Birds who cry when trying to sing know the pain of freedom. Singing songs to those in chains . . . People should hear and listen.; [a.] Paterson, NJ

MYER, KATHRYN R.
[b.] April 11, 1917; Suttern, NY; [p.] Mabel and John Ritchie [m.] Dr. Edwards H. Myer Jr; November 16, 1940; [ch.] Edward H. Myer III, Meri Kathryn Peed; [ed.] Paterson General Hospital, R.N.—Paterson, NJ, Good Samaritan Hospital—Suttern, NY; [occ.] Retired; [memb.] Retired; [hon.] Short Stories published in local newspaper in youth; [a.] Charlotte, NC

MYERS, CLARISSA R.
[pen.] Clarissa R. Myers; [b.] January 29, 1911; South Bend, IN; [p.] Madden, Leander and Winifred; [m.] Harold L. Myers; May 1, 1946; [ch.] Son Bruce A. Myers; [ed.] Perley School—South Bend, IN (1-4), Plymouth Washington School (5-8), Plymouth High School (9-12); [occ.] Retired from ASCS (Farm Program) on disability (1965); [memb.] 1st United Methodist Church, Plymouth, IN; [hon.] I was Valedictorian of my graduating class from Plymouth High School, Plymouth, IN in May 1929; [oth. writ.] Many poems; [a.] Plymouth, IN

NARRAGON, JACQUILINE A.
[pen.] Jackie A. Narragon; [b.] January 24, 1936; San Francisco CA; [p.] Wilton R. Wooliever, Frances Wooliever; [m.] Dale C. Narragon; June 18, 1955; [ch.] Maureen Groff, Mike Narragon, Jim Narragon, Barbara Hobbs, Ray Narragon, Robert Narragon, Marlene Hinderleider, Tom Narragon; [ed.] Taft High, Taft College, De Anza College; [occ.] Homemaker; [memb.] St. Lucy's Church, Y.L.I. AMRA; [hon.] C.S.F. Pius Award, Morgan Center Service Award, Eucharistic Minister for the Sick, Volunteer for disabled; [oth. writ.] Short story for Astec Newsletter, 1983. Articles for local Newspaper; [pers.] My family has been the inspiration for my writing. They've taught me that each person has a unique quality that is worth expressing in words.; [a.] San Jose, CA

NEACE, KRISTI
[b.] January 20, 1970; Granite City, IL; [p.] Russell and Audrey Kitchen; [m.] Richard Neace; July 9, 1988; [ch.] Christopher, Cameron and Meghan; [ed.] Jackson High School, Metro Business College, and East Central College; [occ.] Homemaker/ student; [a.] Union, MO

NELSEN, NORMAN R.
[b.] December 13, 1936; Staten Island, NY; [p.] Benhard R. and Gladys M. Nelsen; [m.] Divorced; [ch.] Ronald K. Nelsen (deceased), Katherine E. Nelsen; [ed.] Princeton University, AS International Affairs 1958, Yale University Graduate School 1960 (61); [occ.] Retired International Marketing Executive/Consultant; [memb.] USS Yorktown Ass'n Trustee, Somerset Hills Historical Society International Society of Poets (Distinguished Member); [hon.] Phi Beta Kappa, Princeton, Magma Cum Laude, Nine Editor's Choice Awards 1997, Six in 1996, one in 1995 from The National Library of Poetry; [oth. writ.] (1) "Revival" in Sea of Treasures. (2) "Critters Who Aren't Quitters" in Spirit Of The Age. (3) "On Castle Rock Road" in Where Dawn Lingers. (4) "A Risky Mission" in Across The Universe. (5) "Loonacy" in Best Poems Of The '90's. (6) "The Tree Tao" in Portraits Of Life. (7) "Mass Murder in a Cathedral Town" in Daybreak on the Land. (8) "Water and Wind: The Word and The Spirit" in Colors of Thought. (9) "Poetic Justice" in Of Moonlight and Wishes. (10) "At Appomattox Court House" in Into The Unknown. (11) "A Bellyful of Wisdom" in Silence of Yesterday. (12) "The Circle of Salvation" in Etches of Time. (13) "Provident in Paradise" in The Isle of View. (14) "Fresh Growth" in Through A Looking Glass. (15) "Monkey See, Monkey Do" in Best Poems of '97. (16) "Recycling" in A Lasting Mirage. (17) "We All Melt Differently" in Dance Upon The Shore. (18) "It's Soon Spring" in With Flute Drum and Pen. (19) "Transitions" in A Whispering Silence. (20) "Tears of The Nation" in Journey Between Stars. (20) "Out of Season" in Journey Between Stars.; [pers.] Often I write of the Unity and Diversity of what God has created and continues to create.; [a.] Basking Ridge, NJ

NELSON, KRISTINA B.
[b.] March 30, 1967; Winnipeg, Canada; [p.] Carl R. Nelson, Professor Colleen H. Nelson, Author Ornithologist; [ed.] Vincent Massey Collegiate;

Some university, the American Musical and Dramatic Academy, NYC; [occ.] Personal Trainer, Competitive Athlete; [memb.] Save the Children; [oth. writ.] I have a book of poetry and am currently working on a novel. This is my first published work; [pers.] On every letter or note I send, I write, "Keep smiling. It makes the world a brighter place."; [a.] Beverly Hills, CA

NETHERTON, SHEILA NAOMI
[pers.] Janie; [b.] August 18, 1954; Blount, CO; [p.] Mr. and Mrs. John Bodine; [ch.] Kendle, Angela; [ed.] 1 year New World College Degree—Cosmetologist, Gadsden State; [occ.] Stylist at Cost Cutters "Oneonta"; [hon.] Outstanding Jr., Outstanding Sr. at New World, Made the Dean's List, Many awards in Cosmetology; [pers.] I know if you work hard enough you can do anything (God is the one that behind me.).; [a.] Altodna, AL

NEWMAN, JOHN W.
[pen.] "Johnny Dakota"; [b.] April 2, 1936; [p.] John and Edna Newman; [m.] Karon Lea Solomon; February 2, 1995; [ed.] GED U.S. Army Europe 1995. Graduated Ironworker's Apprentice Ship School 1958, Also WA.State Real Estate Liscense 1993; [occ.] Retired Journeyman, Ironworker and Welder; [memb.] Congregation Sharrie Torah. Portland, OR. B.M.I. I.S.A. Portland Songwriters Assn. Portland, Oregon; [hon.] Top ten award, NCA Recording Co. Nashville, TN. Certificate of merit, talent and companies, Boston, MA."Little Angels" on song and C.P. to be production, Richmond, VA. 1997; [oth. writ.] "Poems To Touch Your Heart," a book of poetry, distributed by Pacific Pipeline, Kent, WA, major west coast book distributor in major book stores, Borders, Barnes and Noble and Walden Books, and may independents.; [pers.] "Be prepared for lots of rejection; just kick the dust from your sandals and continue on to the next publisher or music producer." Keep on writing.; [a.] Yuma, AZ

NEWTON, MARIANNE
[b.] December 4, 1943; Evergreen Park, IL; [p.] Ken and Margaret Ann Settel Myer; [m.] John Robert Newton; August 5, 1989; [ch.] Mark Alvin Nelson, Robert Newton; [ed.] Carl Sandbury High School, Northern Illinois University (B.S. in Ed) National—Louis University (M-Ed.); [occ.] Elementary School Teacher, Beacon Hill School, Chicago Heights; [oth. writ.] Newton M., Nash D., Ruffin L. (1996). A Whole Language Trilogy: The Covered Bridge Connection, In G. Burnaford, J. Fischer, D. Hobson (Eds), Teachers Doing Research, Practical Possibilities (pp. 82-90) Mahwah, NJ: Lawrence Earlbaum Associates Publishers; [pers.] "Choices" was written especially for my second grade students in celebration of Black History Month in February.; [a.] Richton Park, IL

NEWTSON, LEE
[b.] July 2, 1942; Chicago, IL; [p.] Bert and Mabel Newtson; [m.] Betty Ann Newtson; November 14, 1982; [ch.] Steve and Tracy Pekala; [ed.] Kaneland High School, Maple Park, IL. Some college courses attended; [occ.] Quotation Coordinator, Aurora Brg. Co., Ind. and Aerospace Accts., Aurora, IL; [memb.] St. David's Episcopal Church, Aurora, IL, Life Member American Legion, Elburn, IL. Longtime member Aurora and St. Charles, IL. Legion of Moose; [hon.] "Editor's Choice Award"—National Library of Poetry (1996), "International Poet of Merit"—International Society of Poets (1996), Elected to International Poetry Hall Of Fame (1997); [oth. writ.] Poem, "Caring and Sharing," in book Carvings In Stone, Best Poems of the 90's—"Our Lady Down On The Farm." "My Brother of the Heart," "Generosity Above Reproach," poems for and about friends and loved ones, also speeches.; [pers.] I was lucky to be influenced by the real life ABC's (The Aston, Bunce, and Conley Families). Payton Family, who instilled love through caring and sharing.; [a.] Elgin, IL

NGUYEN, ALFONSE T.
[pen.] Yvette Springfield; [b.] May 3, 1944; H.N. Vietnam; [p.] D. and G. Nguyen; [p.] Thiennga T. Pham; October 22, 1983 Stras. France; [ch.] Andrew Linh V. Nguyen and Stephen Bao Q. Nguyen; [ed.] Pol-War. College/DL.U.O. Saigon/VN. Teacher, Vinh-Son-Liem H.S. R.S. VN Army/Navy O. Several poems and articles published in local magazines. [pers.] My writing is trying to reflect the nature and human beauty in the sense of perpetual and long lasting.; [a.] Minneapolis, MN

NOLES, JENNIFER
[pen.] Jennifer Robyn Noles; [b.] August 5, 1976; Columbus, OH; [p.] Dave Noles, Tim and Karen McCartney; [ed.] High School Diploma and Associates Degree; [occ.] Legal Assistant; [hon.] President's List (honor roll in College); [oth. writ.] I've been reading and writing poetry since the age of 13.; [pers.] My poems reflect emotions that I've felt or observed in others. My writing style is a mixture of all my favorite poets.; [a.] Uniontown, OH

NORDE, KATHY VAN
[b.] July 26, 1950; New Brunswick, NJ; [p.] Rick and Edna Rowley; [m.] Bruce Van Norde; June 19, 1968; [ch.] Four sons: Ricky, Eric, Jason, Kirk; [ed.] Long Branch Elementary, Brick Township High; [occ.] Geriatric Nursing Assistant, Foster-Mom to orphaned baby animals; [oth. writ.] "Not Born To Hate"; [pers.] Nothing in this world is more important than family. I'd like to thank mine for always being there for me. A special thank you to all my friends.; [a.] Long Branch, NJ

OLIANA, JESUS E.
[pen.] J. E. Oliana; [b.] July 12, 1951; New York, NY; [p.] Christopher and Martha; [ed.] George Washington High School; [occ.] I lost my job, I suffer from Epilepsy. My boss dismissed me.; [hon.] For writing, I have won many Trophies for Chess, including 1st Place in a city-wide competition, back in 1978, Second Place in a state-wide contest in 1979; [oth. writ.] Some time ago, I had a show on public access television, "Poetry," a half-hour in which I used to read/recite poems from my book "Gems Of Poetry" (unpublished). I also write poetry in Spanish; [pers.] I speak, read and write in six (6) different languages (English, Spanish, French, Italian, Greek and Some German). However, I only write my poetry in English and Spanish.; [a.] New York, NY

OROZCO, JUAN
[b.] July 23, 1979; Salinas, CA; [p.] Tomas Orozco, Maria Orozco; [ed.] Gonzales High School University of San Diego; [occ.] Student; [memb.] California Scholarship Federation—(Seal Bearer, life member); [hon.] National Football Foundation and Hall of Fame Scholar Athlete, Bank of America Plaque winner—Social Science; [oth. writ.] Several poems not yet in publication; [pers.] When you believe you have accomplished everything possible, it is then that you become complacent and no longer accomplish anything in life.; [a.] Soledad, CA

OSBORN, LINDA S.
[b.] February 9; Sterling, IL; [p.] Elaine Knox; [m.] Paul Osborn; May 8, 1990; [ch.] Jacob, Hilary, Hayley; [occ.] Student, future teacher; [hon.] President's List; [oth. writ.] Awards for non-fiction from local writer's competition and from local community college; [pers.] Thanks to my family for smiling at the right moment.; [a.] Sterling, IL

OTT, LARRY C.
[pen.] Rambo; [b.] May 22, 1953; Marshfield, WI; [p.] Ken Ott, Rose Ott; [m.] Divorced; [ch.] Daniel Lee, Brandon Edward; [ed.] Lincoln High, MSTC; [occ.] Supervisor, Consolidated Papers; [hon.] Having one of my writings selected by the National Library of Poetry; [oth. writ.] Many of which now

appear on family's and friend's walls and some that remain in their hearts.; [pers.] Very strong influence to express myself; inspired by my parents. I feel we all have an inner desire to be something other than what we have become.; [a.] Wisc. Rapids, WI

OTTANI, CORDELIA
[pen.] Delia; [b.] February 23, 1959; Casablanca Morocco; [p.] Elsie and Raoul Gaouette; [m.] Anthony Ottani; May 25, 1986; [ch.] Christiane, Tiffany, Glenn; [ed.] Last Grade Completed, West Field State Two Years; [occ.] Mother, I also do Treework with my husband part-time; [hon.] I have received trophies for dancing, but this was many years ago; [oth. writ.] I have written many poems over my 38 years, but I have never submitted any until now; [pers.] The ladder of life, like a rocky terrain, is fattered with sunshine snow sleet, and rain.; [a.] Chicopee, MA

OUELLETTE, JACQUELINE
[b.] September 6, 1958; Hartford; [m.] Leo Ouellette; April 22, 1989; [ch.] Nicole Ouellette; [occ.] Claim Assistant.

OWENS, L. BRIAN
[pen.] L. Brian Owens; [b.] October 20, 1971; Rome, GA; [p.] Larry and Sandra Owens; [m.] Sheri L. Owens; December 30, 1995; [ed.] Cedartown High School, Covington Theological Seminary, Moody Bible Institute; [occ.] Credit Manager, Sears Credit; [oth. writ.] Various reflections, devotions, and sermons from both the Hebrew and Christian scriptures; [pers.] Life can only be understood backwards, but it must be lived forwards.; [a.[Louisville, KY

PADRON, BABETTE
[b.] June 10, 1981; Amarillo, TX; [p.] Estella Cohn; [ed.] Caprock High School; [occ.] Student at Caprock; [pers.] Two statements that have helped me in my writing. "There has not been any great talent without an element of madness." —Seneca. "Be patient and tough, someday this pain will be useful to you." —Ovid.; [a.] Amarillo, TX

PARKER, REBECCA D.
[b.] November 30, 1982; Wilmington, NC; [p.] Paul and Beverly Parker; [ed.] G.E. Massey Elementary School, Lincolnton and Middle School, Entering the Ninth grade at Lincolnton High School; [memb.] Salem Baptist Church Youth Group, Lincolnton High School Marching Band; [oth. writ.] "Someone Feels The Same," published in the Anthology of Poetry by Young Americans; [a.] Lincolnton, NC

PARTEE, TRINA
[b.] October 8, 1971; Memphis, TN; [ch.] Lacressa, Kelvette and Rshema; [oth. writ.] I, Trina, dedicate "What's Up Above?" to my 3 girls, Lacressa, Kelvette and Rshema. I also dedicate this poem to the readers to those who seek for love. Love is the heart and soul.; [a.] Memphis, TN

PATTERSON, KAROLYN MARIE
[pen.] Toni Arthur; [b.] May 20, 1978; Los Angeles; [p.] William and Jo Anne Patterson; [ed.] Graduated from high school at age 15, Currently attending Southern California Conservatory of Music with plans to go Berkeley College of Music; [occ.] Musician, Singer, Songwriter; [oth. writ.] Have written over 100 poems and over 200 songs. Also currently working on my autobiography; [pers.] I hope to have most of my poetry published someday, as well as the two autobiographies I've been working on. I've been greatly influenced by Maya Angelou and Arthur Rimbaud.; [a.] Valencia, CA

PATTON, WILLIAM G.
[pen.] Billy Bob, Bill, Pat; [b.] November 8, 1954; Birmingham, AL; [p.] Lillie and Andrew Edwards; [m.] Leona Watts Patton; October 25, 1973; [ch.]

(God's Children)—Roshonda and Samarhari; [ed.] Headed Toward a BA in BA GED with numerous college credits toward a degree in Business Admin; [occ.] Executive Secretary USARJ/9th TAACOM-Camp Zama, Japan; [memb.] 32 Shriner, Retired Military after (20) Twenty Years of Service to my country; [hon.] An Abundance of Awards during my military career. 13 Army Achievement Certificates, 3 Army Commendation Certs./ Medals and 1 Meritorious Service Medal, 6 Good Conduct Certificates, Human Relations Instructor—A Letter of Commendation for Bravery; [oth. writ.] Numerous Poems and Songs. In the process now of producing my first (CD) Gospel; [pers.] The way I see it, life will carry us along or it will drop us off and continue to move. Whether we want to be in this game of life is up to us. My wife and I are here temporarily, Heaven is our home; [a.] Camp Zama, Japan

PEPITONE, KRISTIN
[b.] January 1, 1981; Englewood, NJ; [p.] Debbie Lougnney; [ed.] Dumont High School, Currently Junior (grade II) as of 1997-1998 year; [occ.] Babysitter, office person at Tenafly Swim Club; [hon.] Honor Roll; [pers.] In my opinion, family is the most valued gift in life, so treasure the moments you have with the ones you love most.; [a.] Dumont, NJ

PERMENTER, ROBERT J.
[b.] June 30, 1981; Long Beach, CA; [p.] Nea and Robert Permenter; [ed.] I have been home-schooled for eight years. I am now in tenth grade; [oth. writ.] I had my first poem published in a local magazine entitled, "Play" when I was eight years old; [pers.] I have played the saxophone for 4 years. I also enjoy film making and acting.; [a.] Davenport, FL

PERRIELLO, DINA M.
[b.] August 25, 1970; Dunburf, CT; [p.] Jo-Ann Perriello/Saverio Perriello; [ch.] Gretel (my Dachshund Daughter); [occ.] Reader's Digest Association Production Assistant; [pers.] The spirit of writing begins with experience.; [a.] Mt. Vernon, NY

PHELAN, MERRIE CHRISTMAS
[b.] December 19, 1955; Flint, MI; [p.] Ray Palmer, MaryLou Carter Palmer; [m.] Kevin J. Phelan; May 23, 1981; [ch.] Timothy Nicholas, Benjamin Joseph; [ed.] Columbia High, Arapahoe Community College; [occ.] Furniture Sales Consultant; [memb.] Light of the World Music Ministry. The Low Downs (sing 50's, 60's and 70's music); [a.] Littleton, CO

PHILLIPS, MYRTLE B.
[b.] September, 1913; Barbados, West Indies; [p.] Charles and Nina Bourne; [m.] Royce E. Phillips (deceased); August 1941; [ch.] Constance E., Sorrentino and Ronald E. Phillips; [occ.] Retired; [memb.] Distinguished Member, International Society of Poets; [hon.] Editor's Choice Award, National Library of Poetry; [pers.] The poetry anthology is a wonderful book and I am proud to be part of it. I especially appreciate it because I am a shut-in. It feels like I have made many friends through the shared experience of your publication.; [a.] Arlington, VA

PICCINNI, A.
[pen.] A. Piccinni; [b.] Italy; [p.] Mr. and Mrs. M. Geannove; [m.] Deceased; May 15, 1949; [ch.] My only son killed at age of 31; [ed.] Kindergarten/ Wilton Jr. High School and graduated also Jane Adam's Trade School and went to work about 51 years; [occ.] Flea Mkt's time a time, also help the homeless and feed birds 4-17 years; [hon.] An award from many, many years ago; [oth. writ.] Marriage, My Only son, Old Age; [pers.] I love life and was very sick in 1989 and God himself brought me back to reality and I am strong and a survivor. Thanks to Jesus.; [a.] Bronx, NY

PICKETT, ALECIA R.
[b.] June 22, 1979; Butte, MT; [p.] Karen and Lynn Palmer and Allen and Dori Pickett; [ed.] Student at Western Montana College Pursuing a degree in Athletic Training; [occ.] Student, Dillion, MT; [memb.] 4-H; [hon.] High School Setter and Server for Volleyball, Letter in track and volleyball Drummond student of the week; [pers.] My poems come from real emotions and real problems of you guessed it, guys.; [a.] Drummond, MY

PISKOROWSKI, AMY
[b.] August 23, 1979; Indianapolis, IN; [p.] Pamela and Jerome Piskoworski; [ed.] High School Graduate - Avon High School; [occ.] Student at Purdue University—Civil Engineering; [oth. writ.] Nothing else published.; [a.] Danville, IN

PLUMER, PATRICIA
[pen.] Rachel Montgomery; [b.] February 21, 1980; Elkton, MD; [p.] George and Jillian Plumer; [ed.] Currently Senior at Oxford Area High School, PA; [memb.] One of Jehovah's Witnesses; [hon.] Every marking period am on the High honors or honor roll. 1st place award in a Science Fair. During elementary school I won several drawing contests.; [oth. writ.] Other than having poems published in the school newspaper, this contest is the extent of my works published to date. But I write short stories and poetry constantly.; [pers.] I am seventeen years old and have transverse myelitis, which is a spinal disfunction disease, since the age of five. My poetry is usually dark, but with a hopeful ending, which reflects my feelings about coping with my disability and other people's reactions to a disable person.; [a.] Lewisville, PA

PRICE, MARY T.
[pen.] Mary T. Price; [b.] February 13, 1917; St. Louis, MO; [m.] William S. Price, Jr. deceased; [m.] December 25, 1947; [ed.] Private Girls School, Military training, business college Temple Junior College. Member of armed forces; [occ.] Retired. Enjoying travel. Looking forward to publishing a book; [memb.] Former Soroptomist; [hon.] 7 Medals U.S. Army; [oth. writ.] Published experts of books Sayeda! Poetry, news articles in Washington, D.C. and so on; [pers.] Having lived in foreign countries for years, there is still a nugget of information there.; [a.] Washington, DC

PULLENS, TYLER MARCEL
[pen.] Ty, "T", and "T-boy"; [b.] November 15, 1987; Loma Linda, CA; [p.] Rory and Juanita Pullens; [ed.] Honor student at Grace Lutheran School in Denver, CO, Currently in the 4th grade; [occ.] Student; [memb.] Manager for a social club called the "Panthers" since the first grade, Denver Public Library systems; [hon.] Student of the Month, Academic Honor Roll, Oratorical Contest Winner for Temperance Poem and Jingle, 1st Place Field Day Winner, 1st place Science Fair Winner; [oth. writ.] I keep a daily journal, write regularly to Mayor Wellington Webb of Denver, CO and President Clinton, pen pal writing.; [pers.] I want to show through my writings the beauty and wonder of life. Poetry expresses things that nothing else could.; [a.] Antioch, TN

PURCELL, MARCUS L.
[b.] March 5, 1979; Alexandria, VA; [p.] Elmer Purcell, Tamara Purcell; [ed.] James B. Dudley High School, University of North Carolina at Greensboro; [occ.] Cashier/Stocker, Winn Dixie, Greensboro, NC; [memb.] National Beta Club; [hon.] A/B honor roll (9, 10, 11, 12); [pers.] I write about things that come from my heart, and of experiences in my life.; [a.] Greensboro, NC

QUIRK, ALLAN MICHAEL
[b.] October 27, 1942; Brooklyn, NY; [p.] Henry and Frances Kelly both deceased; [m.] Divorced; [ch.] Debra Jean; [ed.l] 2 years college; [occ.] Semi-retired, due to a severe injury sustained in an auto accident; [oth. writ.] None at present but I am taking Humor Writing classes at NYU; [pers.] I wish the hyperocitis would end before this Great Nation of our does.; [a.] New York City, NY

RAFIH, DEBRA CLARKE
[b.] November 4, 1970; Guyana, SA; [p.] Monica and Franklin Clarke; [m.] Ahmed Fahd Rafih; November 2, 1992; [ed.] BS in Applied Psychology from School of Education and New York University; [occ.] Youth Entrepreneurship Program Coordinator and Union Settlement Association; [memb.] Sister CEO Club, NY Women's Foundation, New York University Applied Psychology Club, NY/NJ Sisters and Allies, The Asia Society, NY Metropolitan Opera; [hon.] Dean's List 1993-97, Major's Award for Community Service, B'nai B'rith Award for Community Service, African Teacher's Association Award for Writing; [oth. writ.] Other poetry published by the New York University Women's Studies Journal Fall 1996/ Spring 1997, Playtime's Science News letter Educational Equity Concepts 1993-96; [pers.] In order to affect change, we must first empower the individual to believe that change is possible. We will then be able to build community one person at a time.; [a.] New York, NY

RAGSDALE, JERRY D.
[b.] January 1, 1944; Marten, TN; [p.] William and Minnie Ragsdale; [m.] Judith Kay Ragsdale; March 16; [ch.] 4 Boys—Joel, Samuel, David, Jacob; [ed.] Degs: Computer Science, Mathematics, electronics, Engineering; [occ.] Maintenance Tech., 3rd Shift (my quietest time); [oth. writ.] Manuscripts: Father Speaks, Gifts, Sex and Love, The Doorkeeper; [pers.] Fatherless and motherless at age six. My voice was heard and he answered me. Out of the stillness came the still, small voice, "I will be your Father." At every prayer I still hear an audible voice.; [a.] Lisle, IL

RALOFF, JODY
[b.] January 18, 1965; Adrian, MI; [p.] Daid Raloff, July 28, 1984; [ch.] Sara Eden and Hannah Ashley; [ed.] Adrian High School; [occ.] Mother and Homemaker; [memb.] National Downs Syndrome Society; [oth. writ.] One other poem about Down's Syndrome that was published in a local newspaper ad for "October's National Down's Syndrome Awareness Month"; [pers.] Our daughter, Hannah was born with Down's Syndrome. As a mother it is my goal to educate people about Down's Syndrome and to convey through my poetry just how special these children are. Our daughter's determination to learn and her heart-melting smile inspire me in my writing.; [a.] Coldwater, MI

RALPH, M.D. TENNESSEE
[pen.] Tennessee Ralph; [b.] June 19, 1931 Caruthersville, MO; [p.] B.W. and Nell Ralph (Both Deceased); [m.] Mildred M. (Spires) Ralph; August 9, 1977; [ch.] Dennis, Mike, Janice, Ronnie, Kristi, and 5 stepchildren; [ed.] Byars-Hall High, Vovington, TN, and Erskine College (A.B. '57), Due West, SC, plus the "School Of Mistakes" in everyday life. I wrote poem, "Lie and Lay," on September 24, 1953 for my English teacher at Erskine College; [occ.] Car Salesman; [memb.] Salem Baptist Church, Anderson, SC, and Hejaz Shrine Temple, Greenville, SC; [hon.] I made "Plugger Golfer of the Year" at my local club, "Rolling(s)" course, because I found more balls than I lost. Also because I'm always picking up every piece of paper and trash that is in my path.; [oth. writ.] I write songs about nearly anything that comes along. Some Titles are: "Sixteen Women In A Limousine"; "My 3-D Woman"; "The Equal Rights Blues"; "In All My Dreams"; "The Rat Race"; "It's a Going-Out-of-Business Sale"; "Where The Radar Is"; "Bottom Of The Ladder"; "Where The Fuzz Wuz"; "The Great Silver Bridge"; "In Name Only"; "The Organ Donor Blues"; and many more.; [pers.] "I've never written a poem or song

unless it was about an event relating in some way to my own life," so "My songs are no happier, no more sad, or funnier, than the events in my life that cause me to write them."; [a.] Gray Court, SC

RAMIREZ, LOUIS PHILLIPS
[pen.] L.P; [b.] November 16, 1957; Salinas, CA; [p.] Louis and Grace Ramirez; [m.] Lydia Ramirez; June 22, 1997 (2nd marriage); [ch.] 3 girls and stepchildren—3 girls and 1 boy; [ed.] HS, 2 years Community College; [occ.] Vice President of a Personal Staffing services; [oth. writ.] Numerous Country Gospel songs and various poems. Currently writing an autobiography about my life and ministry in God's church; [pers.] I am here in this life only for a brief stay. There are lessons to learn in order for me to return home. If I can touch another soul through my writings it will all be worth the while.; [a.] Hillsboro, OR

RAY, BRENDA
[b.] October 18, 1946; New York, NY; [p.] Garland Rogers, Ruth Rogers; [m.] Tom Ray; June 29, 1995; [ch.] Ariel Martin; [ed.] Thomas Jefferson High, City College of New York; [occ.] Writer; [hon] National Academy of Television Arts and Sciences Award for Contributions to the Emmy Award Winning Program "Columbo"; [oth. writ.] Published magazine articles; published greeting card verse for Freedom Greeting Cards; [pers.] If I can never be in all the universe, then let me send a message in writing.; [a.] Burbank, CA

READER, MELISSA ANNE
[b.] July 6, 1979; Jacksonville, FL; [p.] Pat and Elaine Doyle; [m.] Michael Edward Reader; January 4, 1997; [ed.] New Testament Christian School, North Florida Community College; [occ.] Owner of Madison Service Company; [memb.] New Testament Christian Center; [pers.] I write about my husband, because the Lord has given me the talent and the love for writing so that it will always edify Jesus Christ for others to see his undying love for us all.; [a.] Lee, FL

REGIS, SHANNON L.
[b.] March 26, 1972; Olean, NY; [p.] Roy Regis and Dorothy Regis; [ch.] iSummer Regis; [ed.] Western Penna School for the Deaf, Rochester Institute iof Technology; [occ.] Writing songs; [hon.] International creating arts ifestival 2nd place 1987, sigma sigma sigma and singing in sign language iwith songs and poems I wrote at local churches; [oth.writ.] Currently am iwriting songs and hoping to be an American first deaf country singer and isings my songs along with a hearing vocialist singer, to become a success!; i[pers.] I've been writing poems and songs since I was little. And last year iafter recieving Jesus Christ, I opened my eyes and I know God gave me this italent!; [a.] Smethport, PA

REICHARDT, HELEN C.
[b.] October 29, 1915; Hawarden, IA; [p.] Glady and Clifford Heald; [m.] Edward A. Reichardt; March 5, 1935; [ch.] 3 boys, 3 girls; [ed.] High School; [oth. writ.] Clown, Dear God Do Be Aware— Just more man.

REVERE, MICHAEL
[pen.] Michael Rigsby Revere; [b.] July 26, 1951; East Point, GA; [ed.] currently attending Southwestern Community College, Syla, NC; [occ.] Writer, Roofer, Rock Drummer; [memb.] Phi Theta Kappa Honor Society; [hon.] National Dean's List, 1996-97; [oth. writ.] Spirit Happy, 1974, Loom Press, The Milky Way Poems, 1976, Carolina Wren Press; Shotgun Vision, 1977, by Design Publishers; [pers.] I try to love and accept people as they are and to be content with the simple blessings of life.; [a.] Cullownee, NC

RHODEN, REBECCA
[pen.] Rebecca Rhoden; [b.] May 4, 1942; Springfield, MO; [p.] Walter E. Parker and Lois M.

Parker; [m.] Kenneth W. "Kay" Rhoden, deceased; December 29, 1968; [ch.] Lisa Annette Rhoden And Gregory Alan Rhoden; [ed.] B.S. Ed. Southwest Missouri State University; [occ.] Insurance Executive; [memb.] Baptist Church, Kansas City Chiefs Arrowhead Club; [hon.] Have received awards for writing as a student; [oth. writ.] Several poems published by the National Library of Poetry—"Kevin's Stance, "Ode To Little Granny 'B'," "Tortured Heart," "Winter Solstice of our Love." Currently working on short story for screen play; [pers.] Record your memories and thoughts in writing either through poetry, short stories, screen plays or music to enjoy yourself and for others as a tribute to yourself and others.; [a.] Springfield, MO

RICHARDSON, BETTY
[pen.] Elizabeth Richardson; [b.] November 5, 1934; [ed.] MA—Archetypal Art Therapy, MA—Art Education, BA—English, BA—Art, Minor—Music Ed; [occ.] Writer, Artist, Metaphysical Poet, Lyricist, retreat and workshop leader; [memb.] Association for Transpersonal Psychology; Michael Teachings Mystery School; Clearsong Workshops; [hon.] Dean's List, University of NM, University of WI, Alverno College; [oth. writ.] Upcoming book on creativity; [pers.] I strive to reveal the Divine Feminine as the Creative Source in all of us. I am inspired by Stephen Mitchell's translation of the Too Te Ching, and the prose of Laura Esquivel.; [a.] Albuquerque, NM

RIDDELL, BLAIR ÁINE
[pen.] Blair Áine Riddell; [b.] February 4, 1987; Fort Worth, TX; [p.] James Alexander Riddle (father), Dierdre North Riddell (mother), Blake Alexander Riddell (brother); [ed.] I am entering fourth grade at Fort Worth Academy Elementary School.; [occ.] I am a student.; [memb.] St. Andrew's Catholic Church, Shady Oaks Swim Team and Dive Team, Fort World Horseshoe Club; [hon.] Poems and Stories Award, Reading Awards, Kindness Award, Friendship Award, Swimming and Diving Awards; [oth. writ.] I will be published in the 1997 edition of The Anthology of Poetry by Young Americans; [pers.] Reading and writing are a joy for me. It is something I can do for the rest of my life.; [a.] Fort Worth, TX

RIDDLE, BRIDGETTE B.
[b.] February 3, 1967; St. Louis, MO; [m.] Anthony T. Riddle; August 10, 1991; [ch.] Brandi S. Riddle; [ed.] Graduated from O'Fallon Technical Center 1985; [occ.] Seamstress; [hon.] Appreciation Award for Participation and active member of the Children's Guild, "The Mustard Seeds," Honorary Awards for active participation in the "Adventist Thespian Society"; [a.] St. Louis, MO

RITTER, LISA
[b.] October 13, 1961; Oak Ridge TN; [p.] Allan S. and Dutchie Casteel; [m.] James (Doug) Ritter; December 12, 1988; [ch.] Shawney, Ben, Jim, Shana, and Grandson Alec; [ed.] College M.O.A.; [occ.] Secretary at Methodist Medical Center of Oak Ridge; [memb.] Humane Society, Disabled American Vets; [hon.] Quality Care Award; [oth. writ.] "Letting Go," "Heart Fragments," "Falling in Love," "Memories," "Life's Long Road," "Buffy"; [pers.] My mom has been a great influence in my life. It was her push that got me to try to get a poem published. Thank you, Mom. I love you.; [a.] Oak Ridge TN

ROACH, JOHN W.
[b.] October 19, 1917 Tompson Fall, MT; [p.] Moses Roach; [m.] Dona Belle Pallett; February 14, 1952; [ch.] John Jr., David and Edith; [ed.] Polytech College of Engineering Draftsman, 1941 Stockton College, 1952, AA.; [occ.] Retired—Sheetmetal Worker, Loftsman, Fire Fighter; [memb.] First Baptist Church Sonora; [oth. writ.] 1994, '95, '96, '97—National Library of Poetry,

local paper; [pers.] I strive to show the goodness of God and His care for us, also the beauty of our world under any circumstances.; [a.] Sonora, CA

ROBINSON, KENNETH L.
[pen.] Kenneth L. Robinson; [b.] July 18, 1926; Wichita, KS; [p.] Frank and Della Robinson; [occ.] Retired from Cessna Aircraft, Wichita, KS; [memb.] Lifetime Member of Disabled Americans; [hon.] Service-connected Awards, Bronze Star, Purple Heart, Victory Medal Europe, 4 Battle Stars; [oth. writ.] Poem published in Veteran Voice Magazine—for vets: "This Is My Kansas"; [pers.] These poems that I have written are from a person who had no interest poetry while in school.; [a.] Haysville, KS

ROCKHILL, MARTHA
[b.] July 13, 1934; Texarkana, TX; [p.] Aaron Anderson and Lillie Helms; [m.] Robert Rockhill; February 27, 1957; [ch.] Six; [ed.] High School; [occ.] Dietary Department. The Woodlands Health Center Waterburg, CT.; [oth. writ.] Nothing published; [pers.] I write poems when something comes to me.; [a.] Wolcott, CT

RODKEY, MARGARET L.
[b.] July 7, 1928; Flinton, PA; [p.] Ross and Adaline Hockenberry; [m.] Theodore G. Rodkey; July 31, 1958; [ch.] Dianna, Jean, Jane, Judy, Cindy, Teddy, Eddie; [ed.] 10th grade high school; [occ.] Housewife, working with the elderly; [memb.] International Society of Poets (lifetime member); [hon.] I have received 2 award plaques from the International Society of Poets. I have received several Editor's Choice Awards from the National Library of Poetry; [oth. writ.] I have been chosen twice to go to Washington, DC to recite my poems. I received 2 award plaques from the International Society of Poets; [pers.] I was born in Flinton, PA. I was brought up by United Brothers Church. I had several books published. I personally thank Howard Ely for giving me coverage.; [a.] Altoona, PA

ROE, MIKE
[b.] August 30, 984; Long Beach; [p.] Randy B. Leslyn Roe; [ed.] 8th Grade; [occ.] Student; [pers.] Reading is worthwhile and it is more worthwhile to learn how to read.; [a.] Antelope, CA

ROGERS, STEPHANIE
[b.] May 8, 1997; [p.] Glenn and Shirley Rogers; [ed.] Northwest High School Tarrant County Junior College; [hon.] Who's Who Among American High School Students 1993-1997, Honor Roll; [pers.] By expressing my thoughts through poetry, I feel I am expanding my knowledge of the world.; [a.] Justin, TX

ROSEN, FRANCINE
[b.] June 10, 1963; Jamaica Hosp; [p.] Nicholas and Jean Dell Eracio; [m.] Theodore S. Rosen; November 3, 1985; [ch.] Stephanie and Amanda Jean; [oth. writ.] Never Alone, His Love, Another Day, Today, Tomorrow and Always, Upon A Tree, Walking With Jesus; [pers.] I am grateful to be able to express such emotion when writing. My poems reflect genuine feelings found in my heart, soul. I hope others not only find them pleasing to read but also relative to one's own being.; [a.] Massapequa, NY

ROTHCHILD, DAVID
[pen.] Bernard Strockbine; [b.] February 9, 1981; Bayshore, NY; [p.] Sid Rothchild, Therese Rothchild; [ed.] Manchester High School Bailey Bridge Middle School; [occ.] Busboy, Dishwasher, and Assistant Chef at Surfrider Restaurant; [memb.] Manchester JROTC, JROTC Honor Guard; [hon.] 2 years Honor Roll, 1 year Perfect Attendance, Eagle Scout; [oth. writ.] Poems and essays for school projects; [pers.] I just sit down and write. If something comes into my mind I write it down. If I don't like it—oh well.; [a.] Midlothian, VA

RUARK, LESTER L.
[b.] January 16, 1940, Peoria, IL; [p.] Marie V. and Lester G. Ruark; [m.] Maria M. Schales; April 10, 1961; [ch.] Evelyn E., Robert A., Richard A.; [ed.] Manwal H.S. Park College; [occ.] Condominium Manager Palm Club West I, West Palm Beach, FL.; [memb.] National Notary Association, Palm Beach Community Managers Association.; [hon.] Magna Cum Laude; [oth. writ.] Other poems published local and national.; [pers.] God was guiding my hand when I wrote my poems. They reflect my love, emotions, and devotions to my wife, my family, and to God.; [a.] Lake Worth, FL

RUE, MICHAEL
[pen.] Mick Street, Mark Malone, Marc Marcuson, Mitch Michaels; [b.] January 12, 1973; [occ.] Entertainment, Entrepreneur; [oth. writ.] Not yet published: Mick Street Mysteries, The Malone Chronicles, Dream Anthologies, Of Muts And Morphs, Various Songs and Poems; [pers.] My objective is to entertain.

RUFF, STEPHANIE
[b.] August 22, 1983; Wichita, KS; [p.] Robert Ruff, Teri D. Ruff; [ed.] Harris Elementary, Gilbert Jr. High; [memb.] Girl Scouts, Pink Sunset Barbie Club; [hon.] Girl Scout Leadership Award and Outstanding English Student; [pers.] I would like to thank my English teacher, Mrs. Glenn, for inspiring me to write.; [a.] Gilbert, AZ

RUIZ, JR., VEDA
[pen.] Sullivah Biddle; [b.] March 28, 1978; San Antonio, TX; [p.] Veda Ruiz, Sr. (Deceased), Glo Ruiz; [ed.] Harrison High (graduated), Valdosta State University; [occ.] Full-time Student; [memb.] The Planetary Society, Nufon; [hon.] Dean's List; [pers.] I would like to thank my mother who has always stood behind me in whatever I pursued. Finally to James and Matt, thanks for being my best friends.; [a.] Kennesaw, GA

RUSSELL, DANIELLE
[b.] Adrian, MI; [occ.] Consulting Engineer; [hon.] Most Promising Poet, Siena Heights College; [a.] Benicia, CA

RUTKOWSKI, NANCY BARTELS
[pen.] Cherrie; [p.] January 30, 1946; Newark; [p.] Edith and John Bartels; [m.] Mark F. Kowalsky; October 21, 1962; [ed.] Jonathan Dayton, Reginal High Middlesex College, Anat and Phy—Bryman School Dental Assistant; [occ.] Recreation Assistant; [memb.] ASME Union; [hon.] Editor's Choice Award 1996-1997; [oth. writ.] Holiday Blessings in Poem and More

SALAS, ARNADO
[b.] August 20, 1960; La Habana, Cuba; [oth. writ.] "Un Sitio en el Corazon" ("A Place in the Heart"), a short novel that includes several poems about love and family; [pers.] Poetry is a reflection of facts.; [a.] Miami, FL

SAMUELS, ZANDRA
[b.] June 25, 1964; Jamaica, WI; [p.] Aston Samuels, Ethlyn Thomas; [ch.] Kia Royster; [ed.] Kingsborough Community College, Brooklyn College; [occ.] Nursing Assistant; [memb.] Brooklyn Tabernacle Church; [pers.] Each man is an island independent of the Ocean, but one with the ocean. We must work together to gain together.; [a.] Brooklyn, NY

SANTOS, CARMEOLINDA PEREIRA
[pen.] Carmen Pereisan; [b.] May 30, 1955; Brasilia - Brazil; [p.] Francisco F. Costa/Eva P. Santos; [ed.] Educational Center High, Brasilia's University; [occ.] Nurse and Self-employed; [hon.] Gold Medal at the VII Contest of Poetry in Brasilia - by Brasilia, Magazine; Gold Medal in the 2nd Contest of Poetry - by Journal de Brasilia FM - Brasilia - Brazil; [oth. writ.] Poems published in the Brasilia Magazine and in the Poetry anthology at 2nd Contest of Poetry by Journal de Brasilia, FM. Brasilia - Brazil; [pers.] I write everything that comes from my life, now, like a wind, serene and calm, and then, like a whirlwind of torments. It is my life emotion by emotion.; [a.] New York, NY

SATIJA, RACHANA
[pen.] Rach, Rachi; [b.] July 23, 1976; Camden, NJ; [p.] Kanwar and Chander Satija; [ed.] Shawnee High School in Medford, NJ, Rutgers University in New Brunswick, NJ; [occ.] Student; [pers.] I just write what I feel. My poetry is the gateway to my emotions and my life as a whole.; [a.] Tabernacle, NJ

SAVIANO, ERIKA LYNN
[b.] August 3, 1980; Providence, RI; [p.] Vincent Saviano, Elizabeth Saviano; [ed.] Mt. Hope High School Senior; [occ.] Student; [hon.] National Honor Society, Captain Varsity Soccer and Softball, 1st team and 3rd team All-Division soccer, 1st team All-Division softball; [oth. writ.] Personal poetry that has not yet been published; [pers.] I write from the heart about the heart.; [a.] Bristol, RI

SAXTON, PAMELA
[pen.] Pam Saxton; [b.] August 9, 1967; Atlanta, GA; [p.] Jim and Margaret Bridges; [m.] Terrence Saxton; April 18, 1987; [ch.] 2 (Chris and Aaron); [ed.] C.L. Harper High; Dekalb College; Georgia State University; [memb.] Infant Mortality and Teen Pregnancy Committees; [hon.] Dean's List 1995, Dekalb College. Oral Interpretation Awards in High School; [a.] Lithonia, GA

SCHLERETH, SHARON E.
[pen.] Sharon E. Schlereth; [b.] February 23, 1948; Upland, Ca; [p.] Mary and Jim Mayfield; [m.] Steven A. Schlereth; November 12, 1977; [ch.] Thomas and Jennifer; [ed.] Graduated San Gabriel H.S., some Jr. College; [occ.] Alameda County Emergency Ambulance Dispatcher, Self Employed Calif. Notary Public and Finger Print Services; [memb.] National Notary Assoc. Member; [oth. writ.] Personal growth and insight poems and essays in the Sharon Schlereth "ME" Book; [pers.] My life is dedicated to spreading love, compassion, understanding and respect.; [a.] Hayward, CA

SCHMIEL, JOHN
[b.] February 23, 1953; Queens, NY; [p.] F. John Schmiel M. Hedwig Schmiel; [ed.] St. John's Preparatory High School, St. Matthias Grammar School, City College of New York; [occ.] Unemployed; [pers.] I hope in my poetry to give value to my religion—Nichiren Daishonin's true Buddhism—or the chanting of Nam-Myolo-Renge-Kyo. I also hope to have career as a film critic (I have seen over 1000 films), and as a film-maker as well as a poet.; [a.] Linden Hurst, NY

SCHNEIDER, KELLY JEAN
[b.] March 1, 1983; Kenosha, WI; [p.] Father: Gregory A. Schneider, Mother: Connie R. Massie; [ed.] Lance Jr. High School—Kenosha Jr. High School Student—8th grade; [a.] Kenosha, WI

SCHWARTZ, CAROL ANN
[b.] December 16, 1960; Cincinnati; [p.] Mr. and Mrs. Stanley R. Gershuny; [m.] Michael D. Schwartz; June 23, 1985; [ch.] Matthew, Allison and Elana; [ed.] University of Cincinnati, Bachelor's in Business Administration, majored in Marketing and Management, minor in Economics, Xavier University Master's in Business Administration, Majored in Finance, National Association of Realtors, GRI Designation; [occ.] Executive Vice President with the Morris Investment Company, Commercial Property Management; [memb.] Hadassah, Yaweh Day School PTA, NCJW, League of Women Voters, Cincinnati Board of Realtors, OAR, NAR, Adath Israel Synagogue, Adath Israel Sisterhood, Cincinnati Business and Professional Women etc; [hon.] Who's Who Among Women in Business, Cincinnati FWI, State of Ohio FWI, Leadership Award Hadassah Cincinnati, Ya'al Group, Who's Who in Executives and Business; [oth. writ.] This is the first piece that I have ever submitted to be published.; [pers.] Life is too short. We need to be more giving and thankful.; [a.] Cincinnati, OH

SCOTT, GAYNELL DAY
[b.] April 10, 1960; Chicago, IL; [p.] Ethel Day Sr. June Day; [m.] Michael D. Robinson; June 21; [ch.] Ronnell Stephenson; [ed.] Charles P. Steinmetz High, Loyola University; [occ.] Educator, Board of Education, Chicago, IL; [pers.] Always keep God in your presence. Respect all human beings. Live life with morals and values. Accept change, constantly grow. Live to love.; [a.] Chicago, IL

SEMAN, BERNA
[b.] January 31, 1979; New York; [p.] Ahmet Semen and Seher Seman; [ed.] Graduated from Susan E. Wagner High School in June 1997; [a.] Staten Island, NY

SEYMOUR, KEVIN FLOYD
[pen.] Kevin F. Seymour; [b.] December 8, 1965; Orange City, CA; [p.] Leslie and Ann Seymour; [ch.] 1 Boy Elijah; [ed.] High School; [occ.] Musician; [oth. writ.] Numerous Private Writings; [pers.] A step in can always be the positive direction you seek.; [a.] Orange, CA

SHARRON, HELEN B.
[b.] Poland; [p.] Bryna and Jacob Sheinrope; 1960; [ed.] High School Education; [occ.] Retired; [memb.] Red Cross, Hadassah, Educational Alliance, Local SNIUR Center; [hon.] Never bother to keep them; [oth. writ.] If into someone's inner goal you would care to share, then come and gather near my chair and before the tears begin to flow sit and listen to this tale of woe.; [pers.] "Too bad that wisdom comes to late in life." We need it most when we are young; [a.] New York, NY

SHAW, ELIZABETH PERKINS
[pen.] Elizabeth R.P. Shaw; [b.] March 25, 1919; Wash. DC; [p.] Col. James W. Riley, Eugenie W.R. Riley; [m.] 1st—Cdr. Van O. Perkins KIA '44, 2nd—R. Adm. J.C. Shaw (deceased); [m.] 1940, 2nd 1946; [ch.] 1 Perkins, 3 Shaws; [ed.] World wide and varied emphasis in history of art, apprentice sculptor, History and geography; [occ.] Writing, Teaching and Art; [memb.] Art Students League, Writers' Union, Asiatic Squadron Asso., Gold Star Wives of America, and others charitable and political, Itsus; [hon.] Honorary A.A. from Bennetti College (1996 and 1997), "Best Poets" volume; [oth. writ.] Historical Bio of 4 people, poems of various subjects published in newspapers, and short political on social articles; [pers.] My poetry is eclectic—social commentary, romantic, epic—written in many styles—blank verse, lyric, even doggerel—whatever suits the subject.; [a.] Alstead, NH

SHAW, SARAH
[b.] August 29, 1923; Lake Geneva, WI; [p.] Ruth and Shorty Kirk; [m.] Bob; March 22, 1942; [ch.] Gary, Laurel, Elaine; [ed.] High School and 1 yr. college. Life itself is greatest source of knowledge and growth and education.; [occ.] Retired-Volunteer. Live in log cabin on a 200-acre farm; [memb.] Jerome Unit of Methodist Church Albion, UNIW team; [oth. writ.] Many poems and programs for my church, my family and my friends. I now have 4 other poems in Nat'l Library of Poetry Books.; [pers.] I write because I must! A desire to express my love for God and for people in my life compels me to write letters and poetry.; [a.] Jerome, MI

SHEARER, ESTHER K.
[b.] August 17, 1916; Winnipeg, Canada; [occ.] As an 80-year-old I plan to retire before long; [oth. writ.] Some; [pers.] Volunteerism needs its own vocabulary. I hope I've inspired others where I left off.; [a.] Austin, TX

SHELDEN, MARGE
[b.] August 2, 1925; Marlete, MI; [p.] Merle and Norman Landon; [m.] Deceased; [ch.] Katherine, Elizabeth and Frances; [ed.] Marlette High School (MI), Attended Michigan State University in East Lansing, MI; [occ.] Retired consultant, Community Volunteer; [memb.] Ganges United Church, Lake Michigan Store Assn., Vice Pres., Saugatuck/Douglas Historical Society, Pier Cove Ravine Trust Assn., Vice-Pres, Christian Neighbors, Inc., Douglas, MI; [hon.] V.P. National Assn. of Women in Chambers of Commerce, Exec. Director, National Athena Award Foundation (national recognition program for women), Lansing Regional Chamber of (MI) Civic Award, Mulliken Dist. Library (MI), President's Award, 1993 Athena Award Recipient presented by Athena Foundation. Owner/Operator Shelden Insurance Agency, 36 years; [oth. writ.] Poems published in Lansing State Journal (MI), Senior Times (Holland) and in various professional business newsletters. Published Family Poem Book of 150 pages; [pers.] I have two personal mottos: "Confront the issue." and "You must do the thing you think you cannot do." I have mentored and encouraged many young women in business to believe in themselves and their ideas.; [a.] Fennville, MI

SHELTON, LEWIS R.
[pen.] Randy Ran-del; [b.] May 16, 1956; Reidsville, NC; [p.] Lewis D. and Edna M. Shelton; [m.] Beverly W. Shelton; September 2, 1989; [ed.] Wentworth High School; [occ.] Sub-Contractor/Carpenter; [memb.] North American Fishing Club; [hon.] Certificate of Merit "Small Business", Certificate of Achievement "Growth for the Church"; [oth. writ.] Wrote, published 4 songs, write for myself and other artists; [pers.] As musician, singer, songwriter I strive to be professional in my writing.; [a.] Reidsville, NC

SIGLEY, VIRGINIA
[b.] July 9, 1953; Philippines; [p.] Mamerto Eriful, Petra Eriful; [m.] Paul Di Sigley; May 16, 1982; [ch.] Christopher; [ed.] Batanes National High School, Philippines, The National Teachers College Philippines; [occ.] Teacher, Faith Christian School, Collingswood, NJ; [mem.] Christ Community Church Choir; [oth. writ.] Several poems unpublished; [pers.] In my poetry, I try to reflect my sensitive nature and my appreciation of my surroundings.; [a.] Lindenwold, NJ

SILVERMAN, EMILY
[pen.] Emily Silverman; [b.] June 23, 1987; [p.] Michael and Donna Silverman; [ed.] JCC and Beth Am Day School; [occ.] Student; [hon.] Writings accepted into the Youth Fair, Writers Luncheon at my school; [oth. writ.] "Peace," "Anna," and the "Mysterious Factory"; [pers.] I am only 10 years old, and I enjoy writing books. My teachers noticed my talent in kindergarten. I've written many poems and stories, since I am eager to be an author when I grow up. This contest has influenced me even more.; [a.] Miami, FL

SLAYTON, GLORY DENISE
[pen.] "Glo"; [b.] September 28, 1954; Florence, AB; [p.] John Harven and Jessie Mary Warren; [m.] Delbert Slayton Sr.; June 22, 1974; [ch.] Delbert Jr, Derrick, Eric, Erika; [ed.] Completed 12th Grade; [occ.] Housewife/Mother; [pers.] "Just as a mirror reflects the face, poetry reflects the heart." With loving appreciation to my husband (Delbert Sr.) for believing in the reflections of my heart.; [a.] Detroit, MI

SMALL, TERESA MARIE
[b.] April 23, 1974; Machias, ME; [p.] Yvonne Marie Ney and Stillman Small; [m.] Engaged to Jason Lee Leavitt; [ed.] Machias Memorial High School, ME, Hermond High School, ME; [occ.] Musician, Food Services; [hon.] Having the most supportive, loyal and loving, future husband in the entire world—all to myself! I love you Jason Lee Leavitt! You're the best.; [oth. writ.] Several, a few other poems, and many thoughts; [pers.] Time you now have less! To my Dad, Mom, brother, aunts, uncles, friends, Grandfather, cousin and new extended family—the only distance between us is mileage! I love and miss you all.; [a.] Windsor, CT

SMITH, ABBEY
[b.] July 3, 1984; Milwaukee; [p.] Wayne Smith and Kathleen Smith; [ed.] Entering 8th grade in September 1997 at St. Paul's Church; [pers.] I have always dreamed of becoming an author and now, because of this poem, I am.; [a.] Greenfield, WI

SMITH, BRANDIE
[b.] August 28, 1981; Brownsville, TN; [p.] David and Rena Smith; [ed.] Haywood High School (Junior); [occ.] Student; [memb.] Christians in Action, Teen Advisors, Haywood High School Delta Team, Chamber Choir, AQHA, Bible Club; [oth. writ.] Poems for personal enjoyment.; [pers.] I write about emotions that come from deep within a heart.; [a.] Somerville, TN

SMITH, ROBIN ANN
[b.] February 26, 1961; Bedford, IN; [p.] Orville and Phyllis Strunk; [m.] Blair C. Smith; December 31, 1981; [ch.] Nathan and Angela; [ed.] Owen Valley High School, Western Business College; [occ.] Administrative Asst., City of Gresham, Gresham, OR; [oth. writ.] Two essays for the Daughters of the American Revolution (D.A.R.), and personal collections of poems; [pers.] Dedicated to my mother and father for all of their love and encouragement throughout my life.; [a.] Gresham, OR

SMITH, SAMUEL S.
[b.] May 18, 1938; Putnam Station, NY; [p.] Grant and Evelyn Smith; [m.] Fern Smith; August 21, 1958; [ch.] Julie Smith Shook and John C. Smith; [occ.] Self-employed; [a.] Putnam Station, NY

SNYDER JR., JOSEPH
[pen.] Jojo; [b.] January 17, 1983; Jacksonville, FL; [p.] Benny and Beverly Brown; [ed.] 9th Grade at Robert E. Lee, Sr. High School; [hon.] 4th runner-up in the essay contest for "Operation Turn-Around" Youth and Crime in America; [a.] Jacksonville, FL

SORG, JUSTIN
[b.] November 14, 1981; Wichita, KS; [p.] Jake and Mary Sorg; [ed.] Currently I'm going into the 10th grade; [occ.] Student; [pers.] I've always found writing to be the best way to convey those feelings best left unspoken. When reality is frustrating, cold, or boring I create one that's not.; [a.] Wichita, KS

STEEL, ALEXIS RENEE
[b.] July 24, 1970; Jamaica, WI; [p.] Fred and Jean Steel; [m.] (Boyfriend) Christopher Sory, whose love continually inspires me!; [ed.] Kwantlen College, I.C.C., Institute of Children's Literature, Vancouver Film School; [occ.] Film Actress/Professional Stunt Artist, Song/Scriptwriter; [memb.] Screen Actors' Guild, American Teacher Cadets, I.S.P., "Feed The Children," Christian World Mission; [hon.] Nat'l. Honor Society Literary Award—1997, Inspirational Teacher Cadet of 1995 Award, S.A.G., Editor's Choice Award 1994; [oth. writ.] "Measure Of Time"—Colors Of Thought (1996—Nat'l Library of Poetry), "Bulls-Eye!" (1995—Focus Magazine), "When Daddy Comes Home" (1992—I.C.L.), various articles/poems for local newspaper, magazines and film scripts; [pers.] My poetry explores common thread in human emotion, to bond every searching soul closer together in the magical, universal tapestry of unconditional love. My spiritual inspiration stems solely from my higher power and heavenly captain of my heart.; [a.] Orlando, FL

STEEPY, RUTH E.
[b.] October 2, 1928; Trenton, NJ; [p.] Mr. and Mrs Clifford S. Smith [m.] Calvin R. Steepy (deceased); June 4th 1949; [ch.] Linda Lizette and Mark Calvin; [ed.] Grammar School, Jr. High, Trenton Central High, Industrial Art School and night classes; [occ.] Retired in 1992 because of heart problems. Worked for an Ins. Co. 15 years; [memb.] President of PTA and Police Wives' Assoc. Girl Scout leader, neighborhood chairman, Bible School teacher. Taught free Art lessons to children and became a teacher of Craft store; [hon.] Received Editor's Choice Award in 1996 for the poem "The Light of Love." I was nominated by Elizabeth Barnes as Best Poet of the Year 1997; [oth. writ.] First poem, won the Editor's Choice Award ("The Light of Love") published in The Rippling Waters—1996, "It's Clear" was published in The Best Poems of 1997, "The Seed of Love" was published in Poetic Voices of America (1997), "Painted Picture" will be in the book Beyond the Horizon; [pers.] Flowing stream. I love poetry, painting and gardening and I hope that when I leave this world, that I can be content, in knowing that the time spent here was very wisely spent.; [a.] Morrisville, PA

STEWART, EILEEN P.
[b.] September 19, 1963; Baltimore, MD; [p.] Malcolm and Patricia Stewart; [ed.] BSCS Univ. Of MD; [occ.] Systems Administrator; [memb.] American Quarter Horse Assoc, United States Team Penning Assoc, Texas Regional Team Penning Assoc, National Cutting Assoc; [hon.] 1982 Student Government Award, 1983 Student Government Award; [a.] Hutto, TX

STEWART, OLIVIA STONE
[b.] December 7, 1983; West Palm Beach, FL; [p.] Robert and Ivonne Stewart; [ed.] Westward Elementary K–1st, Allamanda Elem. 2nd–5th, Howell L., Watkins 6th, I now attend Alexander W. Drefoos, Jr. School of the Arts; [pers.] I write my poems because it makes me feel happy to know that I can do something. My poems reflect what mood I am in and how I feel at that very moment. It makes me feel happy to know my poem is being published and people are going to read it.; [a.] Palm Beach Gardens, FL

STINSON, MISTY A.
[b.] December 26, 1968; Charlotte, NC; [p.] Del Newhouse, Lynn Richardson; [m.] David L. Stinson; January; [ch.] Taylor Stinson and Devin Stinson; [ed.] Independence High School; [occ.] Teller, Piedmont Aviation, Credit Union, Charlotte, NC; [oth. writ.] Poem, "My Mother," published in Anthology Book "Between the Raindrops" in 1996; [pers.] Cherish every moment, for the seconds slip through your fingers leaving only memories.; [a.] Charlotte, NC

STONE, CHRISTINA
[b.] August 28, 1970; Army Base, MD; [m.] Larry Weise; Since 1991; [ch.] Alex and Justin; [ed.] PhD from the school of hard knocks with a specialty in coping strategies, High School, Bank Teller training grad., Professional development, Modeling; [occ.] Student/Writer; [memb.] Lumbee Nation—American Indian Tribal Membership, International Method Model Training School Membership—lifetime, North Shore Animal League Contributer; [oth. writ.] I'm currently studying and gathering the means with which to type out my first book.; [a.] Madera, CA

SWALLOWS, JANICE FAYE
[pen.] Jan; [b.] September 9, 1953; Cleveland, TN; [p.] Charles and Helen Swallows; [ch.] Anthony and Gabriel Gowell; [ed.] High School, some college, Hypnotherapist, Cosmetologist, Business; [occ.] Photo Studio, Swallows Studies and Hypnotherapist; [memb.] Cosmetologist Member

and Certified Hypnotherapist; [hon.] I have received many awards in my life. The only honor to me is the love my family gives to me.; [oth. writ.] (None published) Book in work. And many poems and songs written for friends and family and a few bonds.; [pers.] Take love as it comes because that is what life is made of. Min by Mom.; [a.] Murf, TN

TANTON, KATHY
[b.] October 24, 1953; Rochester, NY; [m.] Divorced; [ch.] Paul; [ed.] ASS Degree in Legal Assisting at Phoenix College; [occ.] Freelance Legal Assistant, Bookkeeper; [memb.] L.A.M.P. (Legal Assistant of Metropolitan Phoenix); [hon.] I was valedictorian for the 1994 graduating class of Phoenix College; [oth. writ.] I have had a few of my other poems published. One is about my dad, the others are about friendship.; [pers.] I find poetry to be a great way to express my thoughts and feelings.; [a.] Phoenix, AZ

TAYLOR, ALEXIS MICHELLE
[b.] May 30, 1982; Peoria, IL; [p.] Doris J. Taylor; [ed.] Sophomore in high school; [occ.] Student at Sand Creek High School in Colorado Springs; [hon.] Honor student; [pers.] Poetry is a wonderful way to express your feelings and I'm glad I can use it creatively.; [a.] Colorado Springs, CO

TAYLOR, BRITTNEY MARIE
[b.] May 31, 1988; Kirkwood, MO; [p.] David L. Taylor Jr, Deborah L. Taylor, sister—Brandi Lee Taylor; [ed.] Meramac Heights Elementary; [memb.] First Baptist Church, Arnold, MO; [hon.] Mastadon Art and Science Fair, Principal's Award 95, 96 and 97; [pers.] I wrote this poem for my Grandpa after he was killed in a car accident. I miss him and I love him globs.; [a.] Fenton, MO

THELAKKATT, XAVIER
[b.] March 9, 1954; Cochin, India; [p.] Anne And Varkey Thelakkatt; [ed.] MA in English literature from MG University, Keraler, India Currently a student of MA in Theology at St. Thomas University, St. Paul, MN; [occ.] Catholic Priest; [memb.] Presbyterate of the Catholic Archdiocese of ERNAKULAM in India, Staff member of St. John Vianney Seminary, St. Paul, MN; [oth. writ.] Short articles of general interest and letters to the Editor in Newspapers in India and U.S.A.; [pers.] It is my convictions that compel me to write either in prose or in poetry.; [a.] St. Paul, MN

THOMAS, EVA M.
[pen.] Mary Smith; [b.] February 4, 1932; Jonesboro, AR; [p.] Rev. and Mrs. W.J. Thomas; [m.] John Vernon Smith; September 12, 1955; [ch.] Four; [ed.] Master of Arts, University of Denver, BA—Language and Literature, BA—Philosophy and Psych.; [occ.] Minister of God "The Church of the Living Stones"; [memb.] Church of the Living Stones Ministry, Alpha Kappa Alpha Sorority, College—P.S. College; [hon.] I won a four year scholarship to college in 1949. I was the Valedictorian of my high school class. Received highest honor in my class.; [oth. writ.] The poem that I entered into your contest is from a book that I published in 1981: "The Miracle Of Love"; [pers.] I am a "Born-Again" Christian. I am also a licensed and an ordained Minister. My second book in process of being published is: "Regeneration: I Am Born Again."; [a.] Denver, CO

THOMAS, PAULINE
[pen.] Pauline Thomas; [b.] August 18, 1937; [m.] Richard L. Thomas; June 3, 1956; [ch.] Jodee and Karmen; [ed.] H.S. Graduate; [pers.] I write only for my personal enjoyment about life, family and my innermost thoughts and feelings.; [a.] Collins, IA

THOMPSON, CHERI
[b.] September 15, 1972, Festus, MO; [p.] Paul and JoAnn Thompson; [ch.] Kayla and Kyle Thomp-

son; [ed.] Crystal City High School; [occ.] Part-time Model; [pers.] This poem I dedicate to Ira, for who is so deeply embedded in my heart, I could never let go.; [a.] Festus, MO

THOMPSON, JOAN
[b.] Kingston, Jamaica; [p.] Percy Thompson, Mavis Thompson; [ed.] Prospect Hall College Computer Business Administration, Miami-Dade Community College—Associate in Arts, Florida International University Bachelor of Science in Social Work, Master of Social Work; [occ.] Social Worker; [hon.] Who's Who Among Students In American Junior Colleges, The National Dean's List (1988-1989, 1989-1990, 1990-1991; [pers.] Helping humanity keep in touch with reality both through written and spoken words.; [a.] Miramar, FL

TILLMANNS, MARIA DAVENZA
[pen.] Maria daVenza Tillmanns; [b.] April 1, 1955; New York City; [ed.] PhD Candidate Univ. of Illinois at Urbana, Champaign; [occ.] Writing my dissertation or philosophical counseling; [memb.] The American Society for Philosophy, Counseling and Psycho Therapy; [oth. writ.] "Essay on Philosophical Counseling" eds, Ran Lahar and Maria daVenza Tillamanns; [pers.] Life is to maintain the freedom given at birth.; [a.] Champaign, IL

TIMS, MILDRED H.
[b.] July 24, 1016; Pipestone, MN; [p.] Robert E. and Anna G. McGaw; [m.] Tony C. Tims; June 11, 1939; [ch.] Helen Louise, John Marshall, Linda Lorraine; [ed.] Mankato State Teachers College, AA; [memb.] American Association of Retired Persons, Caroline County Chapter #915; Car. Co. Representative Payee Program Advisory Board and Volunteer; S.A.L.T. (Seniors and Lawmen Together) Board and Volunteer; [hon.] Maryland Senior Citizens Hall of Fame, 1995; [oth. writ.] Editor, AARP Chapter Newsletter, 1996, 1997; [pers.] As I pass only once along life's way, I try to help my fellow man whenever I can.; [a.] Denton, MD

TONEY, DELVERY C.
[pen.] Virginia Toney; [b.] March 13, 1961; Williamsburg, VA; [p.] Tommie Jones and Virginia A. Jones; [m.] Engleburg D. Toney; June 22, 1990; [a.] Celeburne, TX

TORRES, AMANDA JOELLE
[b.] April 11, 1988; Oakland, CA; [p.] Danny and Heidy Torres; [ed.] 4th grade—Bay Elementary San Lorenzo, CA; [occ.] Student; [memb.] Girl Scouts; [pers.] I am grateful to my Grandma Brinda and my family for their belief in me. I want to write and illustrate children's books, hoping to touch their hearts and imagination as I've been touched by other authors.; [a.] Oakland, CA

TORRES, VERONICA
[b.] July 14, 1983; Bronx, NY; [p.] Luz E. Torres, Efrain Torres; [ed.] CES35X—Roberto Clemente, CIS1660—Jane Addams High School; [memb.] National Junior Honor Society, Roberto Clemente Orchestra, Student Government; [hon.] Borough President's Award, U.S. Presidents Award—Reading, Principal's Honor Roll; [a.] Bronx, NY

TOWNSEND, WYATT C.
[pen.] Wyatt; [b.] August, 30, 1983; Oklahoma City; [p.] Linda and Brad Townsend; [ed.] Presently in 8th Grade; [occ.] Student; [memb.] National Honor Society, Holy Spirit Roman Catholic Church; [hon.] Masonic Award, Superintendent's Honor Roll, Outstanding English Achievement; [oth. writ.] 1 short story and 3 poems; [pers.] Heart contains deepest, most unforgettable thoughts, soul contains thoughts from your own world. You lose either one, you lose yourself.; [a.] Yukon, OK

TRANTHAM, ALTHEA
[pen.] "Queen" New Wave Productions; [b.] October 20, 51; Washington, DC; [p.] Elmo Peete (mother deceased); [ch.] Kenny J. and Keith W. Peete; [ed.] Dunbar High, U.D.C. College; [occ.] Computer Specialist Help Desk—Trouble-Shooting; [oth. writ.] Solo Artist, Prolific Lyric Song-Writer, have over 200 pieces of copyrighted material consisting of love songs, raps, ballads, gospels. Currently writing country. I am quite versatile writer, Screen Tested for Screen Test U.S.A; [pers.] Staying well focused, concentrated and positive. Knowing within myself that I will soon attain my goals. Never forgetting where I came from. Whoever helps me along my way, in return I give back. Thanking God for my many talents.; [a.] Clinton, MD

TRAYLOR, MARCEE YVETTE
[b.] August 19, 1981; Atlanta, GA; [p.] Carolyn Harris and Willie Haynes; [ed.] Still in high school Arondale High School—going to 11th grade; [hon.] Honor roll in elementary school and in high school, also; [oth. writ.] None. 1st writing "Black Girl"; [pers.] I just want to say that this is the first poem I ever wrote in my life and I never thought I would make a semi-finalist and I'm happy for myself.; [a.] Decatur, GA

TRAYNOR, LONNA
[b.] Louisville, KY; [occ.] Secretary; [oth. writ.] Several poems published in other books; [a.] Madison, TN

TUINSTRA, TRESA
[b.] December 19, 1973; Rochester, MN; [p.] Brad and Kay Swarthout; [m.] Paul Tuinstra; August 2, 1993; [ch.] Meggan Tuinstra; [ed.] High School Pine Island High; [occ.] Waitress; [oth. writ.] Several poems published in local newspaper, song that was sung at high school graduation by the high school choir; [pers.] Writing poetry is my favorite hobby. I have been influenced by happenings in my life, the people I love and the world around me.; [a.] Rochester, MN

TYSON, JUDY
[b.] J. Tyson; [b.] January 4, 1950; Denver, CO; [ed.] BFA from the University of Tennessee (Knoxville, TN); [occ.] Second Degree Practitioner in the Usui System of Reiki Natural Healing, Artist; [memb.] Tennessee Artist's Association, Unitarian Universalist Church; [pers.] Writing poetry is a pleasurable venture for me. I am merely to tap into the inherent kind and peaceful state of mankind.; [a.] Maryville, TN

UGLOW, THERESA L.
[b.] December 26, 1942, Gilroy, CA; [p.] Frank Mesa, Bessie; [m.] Marion Gay Lord Uglow, August 26, 1963; [ch.] Wayne, Shelley, Cecil; [ed.] Campbell High 1960, City College/San Jose, CA; [occ.] Retired; [memb.] Member of North Valley Christian Fellowship/San Jose, CA; [hon.] Graduate of June Terry's Modeling School/United States Power, Squadron/Boating, Movie extra in "The Misfits"; [oth. writ.] None published, song "You're The Biggest Hurt Of All"—Patent #EU 128779, short stories, poems/none published; [pers.] God is the power and love, that gives me any talent I have. For his Glory I dedicate my work. To my Grandmother, Rayleen Kevin Brandon Spencer.; [a.] San Jose, GA

UPDYKE, JENNIFER
[b.] January 30, 1981; Monterey, CA; [p.] Mrs. and Mr. Thomas E,. Updyke; [ed.] Carmel High School Student. Year 2000 graduate; [occ.] Contemplating the meaning of love; [memb.] Carmel High School band and dance; [pers.] Through writing, I am able to allow my feelings to exit my conscience. Inspired by those who have influenced me to move on to the next level.; [a.] Carmel, CA

UZANAS, BEVERLY CASEY
[p.] John P. and Alwilda Casey; [m.] Philip A. Uzanas; [ch.] Elizabeth, Melinda, Kimberly, William, Laura; [ed.] Cathedral High, Colby Sawyer College, NH; [occ.] Artist, amateur poet, short-story writer, craftsperson (art objects and jewelry from the ocean); [memb.] Mystic Art Assoc., Mystic CT; [hon.] Shown in many Connecticut shows—sold paintings and ocean-related art and jewelry; [pers.] My short stories are a result of what I see in many everyday happenings, peppered with humor. My poems come to my mind during periods of quiet meditation. Insight into a new way of perceiving is shown. My poems are cathartic; I hope to touch many hearts through my poetry.; [a.] Groton, CT

VALTIERRA, FERNANDO
[pen.] Richard Raul Cruz; [b.] October 12, 1969; Chicago; [p.] Elias Valtierra, Fransica V. Mora; [m.] Cruzcita Z. Valtierra; Talking about it; [ch.] Julian M.V., Fernando, A.V.; [ed.] Curie High School. Did not graduate, studying to get my G.E.D. Basically I schooled myself through my adult years.; [occ.] Machine Operator, taking a big responsibility manufacturing-truck springs; [hon.] Baseball trophies as a youth, Some Blue Ribbon Awards from grammar school. Recent awards, Mathematics Training Awards from Chicago Public Awards; [oth. writ.] In process of writing a book called Never Is Now. I am also writing many poems in a poem book which I have called Escaping The World With Two, determined poems to hit titled. "A Flower, A Guinea Pig," "A Wounded Bird I Hurt"; [pers.] Striding to make up for the years I let slip through my fingertips. Putting of my talent as a teenager, and with all the bad and good experiences in life. I am finally letting my talent "escape and touch many heart."; [a.] Chicago, IL

VANDETTA, KIMBERLY J.
[pen.] Kimberly Vandetta; [b.] December 9, 1964; Fairmont, WV; [p.] N. Robert and Diane A. Satterfield; [m.] Carlo "Sonny" A. Vandetta; May 16, 1987; [ch.] Christopher A. Vandetta; [ed.] BS—Allied Health Administration Associate—Medical Laboratory Technology; [occ.] Medical Technologist II; [memb.] American Society of Clinical Pathologists (ASOP), Mothers Against Drunk Drivers (MADD), Safety Committee, Quality Control Officer; [hon.] Quill and Scroll Honorary, Science Honorary, Keywanettes, Mat Maid, DECA, Dean's List; [oth. writ.] Times West-Virginian—In Memoriam, East Fairmont High—Orion (1981-1983), Fairmont State College—Poetry Newspaper; [pers.] I have been inspired by my Catholic faith in many of my poems. Family and friends have been a great influence for me and in my writings. I enjoy reading anything by Shakespeare and the early romantic poets.; [a.] Fairmont, WV

VAZIN, G.R.
[pen.] Ray Vazin; [b.] March 29, 1940; Kerman; [p.] M. and M. Vazin; [m.] Virginia; October 19, 1963; [ch.] Donna, Debra, Scott and Dara; [ed.] M.S. Seronputicol Engineer; [occ.] Retired engineer, stock market speculator, writing poetry and letters; [memb.] LOPA; [hon.] Aviation Safety; [oth. writ.] Technical-safety-related books and operating procedures; [pers.] If the first amendment is the supreme law of the land, let us communicate and make all understand. By poetry, essays, verse and song, so every human in this world can get along.; [a.] Westminster, CA

VAZQUEZ, JENNIE
[pen.] Jenvaz; [b.] December 21, 1939; New York, NY; [p.] Alvara and Juan Garcia; [m.] Geraldo Vazquez; July 31, 1971; [ch.] Victor, Venus, David (Dec'd); [ed.] Julia Richardman HS, New York City Mercy College, BS Dobbs Ferry, N.Y. L.I.U. Masters, Dobbs Ferry Campus, NY; [occ.] E.S.L. Teacher; [memb.] Hispanics for Political Action—Peekskill Chairperson, Continental Cablevision Talk Show "Que Pasa En Peekskill," Host, Peekskill Community Action Program Member of Board of Directors; Peekskill Area Health Center Member of Board of Directors, Dept. of Social Services Member of the Board of Directors; [hon.] Certificates Awarded for Community Services, Peekskill Area Health Center, Mercy College, Peekskill Campus Student Recruiter - Service Award, The Westchester County Hispanic Advisory Board Member of the Board of Directors - appointed certificate; [pers.] It is more blessed to give then to receive.; [a.] Peekskill, NY

VELNICH, ANGELA MARIE
[b.] February 22, 1977; Abington, PA; [ed.] Council Rock High, University of Pittsburgh; [occ.] Perpetual Student; [memb.] NCTE; [pers.] Personal growth that occurs by searching for peacefulness is the key to survival in this world. My past and future educators are my daily inspiration.; [a.] Deer Park, NY

VIANNA, MANUEL F.
[b.] April 28, 1959; Lisbon, Portugal; [p.] Joao and Angelita; [m.] Katia; August 1, 1984; [ed.] BSC—Engineering, Federal University of Rio De Janeiro, MBA—Harvard Business School; [occ.] Management Consultant; [a.] Boston, MA

VICTOR, MANZOOR
[b.] October 14, 1932; Chwharkana, Pakistan; [p.] Barkat Victor, Daisy Victor; [m.] Shanti Victor; February 12, 1962; [ch.] Lubna, Edwin and Aftab; [ed.] MSC (Maths) Karachi Univ. Pakistan Senior; [occ.] Actuarial Analyst, CNA Ins. Co., Chicago; [hon.] Music Award from Local Church for writing Christian Lyrics; [oth. writ.] Write songs and poems on a continuous basis for my church and at work for Baby Showers Weddings, Anniversaries; [pers.] I believe that every human being is in this world to create in form of writing Expressions of Love and to Shine.; [a.] Arlington Heights, IL

VIEIRA, JOSEPHINE
[pen.] Bushie; [b.] September 3, 1957; Newark, NJ; [p.] Joseph and Rose Caputo; [m.] Thomas P. Vieira; January 9, 1987; [ch.] George, Lisa, Victoria; [ed.] Keypunch Specialist; [a.] West Orange, NJ

VIGIL, MARIO
[b.] May 30, 1983; Alamosa, CO; [p.] Tony and Ruth Vigil; [occ.] Student beginning 9th grade 1997 school year; [hon.] Reading Penmanship (most improved in grade 2), The Pilgrimage for Vocations (walked 100 miles with church groups). Lived in Taos County, NM all my life (14 yrs. of age).; [pers.] "Never Stop Trying"; [a.] Arroyo Seco; NM

VILLAFUERTE, BRIANA DELL
[b.] September 20, 1983; [p.] Mary Lou and Randy Villafuerte; [ed.] Our Lady of Lourdes Grade School (K-8) and Marian High beginning fall of 1997; [occ.] Student; [hon.] High School Scholarship, honor roll; [pers.] Poetry helps me express my feelings at any stage in my life, good or bad.; [a.] Omaha, NE

VOLLMUTH, FREDERICK A.
[b.] February 17, 1910; New York, NY; [p.] Louisa and Adam; [m.] Arlynne; February 21, 1987; [ch.] Loretta and Frederick H; [occ.] Retired 1973; [memb.] Coral Ridge Yacht Club, Florida Grand Opera Ft. Lauderdale Philharmonic Society, Freedoms Foundation of Valley Forge, Ft. L. Chapter; [hon.] Pompano Beach Chamber of Commerce, Super Citizen Award, Pompano Beach Chamber of Commerce Second Wind Award; [pers.] A friend to mankind.; [a.] Ft. Lauderdale, FL

W0OD, GLENN M.
[b.] August 30, 1925; Menahga, MN; [p.] Max G. Wood, Alma (Lalli) Wood; [m.] Eleanor M. Murray; September, 15, 1951; [ch.] Daniel, Thomas, Roger; [ed.] Illinois Inst. of Tech. BSME, Massachusetts Inst. of Tech. MSME; Rensselaer Polytechnic Inst. Mengr. Science; [occ.] Retired Mechanical Engineer; [memb.] American Society of Mechanical Engineers (ASME), World Wildlife Fund, Nature Conservancy, Sierra Club, The National Arbor Day Foundation; [hon.] Fellow of American Society of Engineers (AMSME), Pi Tau Sigma (Honorary Mechanical Engineering Fraternity); [oth. writ.] Authored and co-authored several technical papers, many of which were published in the transactions of ASME; [pers.] I have an abiding love of nature and am vitally concerned with environmental issues.; [a.] East Hampton, CT

WALKER, RODNEY T.
[b.] June 10, 1953; Philadelphia, PA; [p.] Mr. Obediah and Mrs. Mary Walker; [occ.] Hotel Security; [hon.] Honorable Discharge From U.S. Navy Various Awards for Security Performance is in the Line of Duty; [oth. writ.] "I Am There," "Nothing So Soft"; [pers.] I just want to share with the world the beauty of poetry.; [a.] Philadelphia, PA

WALTON, DONALD
[pen.] Dona L. Walton; [b.] February 5, 1938; Toledo, OH; [p.] Helen and James Thompson; [m.] Divorced; [ch.] Karen, Jon, Donald; [ed.] Graduate of Libbey High School; [occ.] Therapeutic Program Worker; [oth. writ.] "The Vision" in A Lasting Mirage; [pers.] "Through God all things are possible."; [a.] Maumee, OH

WALTON, NICK
[b.] June 13, 1979; Codar Rapids; [p.] Mike and Lisa Walton; [ed.] Washington High School; [occ.] Part Salesman at Antozono; [oth. writ.] Other poems, such as "Hello"; [pers.] I like people, except if they are racist.; [a.] Codar Rapids, IA

WARFIELD, ANNE MARIE
[b.] June 14, 1951; Fort Bragg, NC; [p.] Anna, Kenneth L. Billings; [ch.] Christopher T. Mann, Alexander B. Warfield; [ed.] AA Degree Major Dietetic Tech. Community College Of Balt., BS Degree—Major in Home Econ. from Morgan State University, Glen Burnie Senior High; [occ.] Federal Civil Service Employee; [memb.] Vietnam Veterans' Memorial Fund; [pers.] Expect nothing from life, and you'll always be surprised. Expect something, and you'll be disappointed. My Dad was my greatest inspiration.; [a.] Brunswick, GA

WASSERMAN, MARTIN M.
[b.] October 12, 1980; Milwaukee, WI; [p.] Laurie Moeckles, Lew Wasserman; [ed.] Milwaukee Jewish Day School Nicolet High School; [occ.] Joyous Student; [memb.] B'nai Brith Youth Organization. Chapter Vice-President, Regional Bridge the Gap Chairman; [hon.] First Prize in 1st Award Milwaukee, Jewish Community Holocaust Youth Essay Contest, 1995, Dean's at NHS; [oth. writ.] "Autumn's End" published in Tracing Shadows, dozens of poems, Women and Other Enigmas, a novel entitled Nora, a play entitled Caedes Prima Noci; [pers.] As my poems reflect, I believe that life is a gift, and we should indeed "Seize the Day." Also, King Solomon AZA 24:44 is the best damn chapter in the world.; [a.] Glendale, WI

WEANT, GARY ALAN
[b.] August 10, 1950; [p.] Harvey and Margaret Weant; [m.] Linda Morgan Weant; July 2, 1972; [ch.] Rebekah Marie, Jonathan Alan; [ed.] Lenoir, Rhyne College (AB degree in mathematics) South Rowan High School, Lutheran Theological Southern, Seminary (M.Div. Degree) Graduate studies at Lutheran Theological Southern seminary (STM Degree); [occ.] Lutheran Pastor, Evangelical Lutheran Church in America; [memb.] 1997-Assisted the Dallas Area Lutheran Churches to resettle a nine member Hmong/Laotian refugee family. 1977-78—Member of the N.C. Synod Task Force on

ministry with the handicapped. 1977-81—Member of the N.C. Synod Educational Ministry Resource Team. 1979—Assisted the Dallas area Lutheran Churches resettle and eight-member Viet Namese/ Laotian Family. 1978-84—Member of the Professional Preparations Committee of the NC Synod; [hon.] 1967—Recipient of the Sr. Rowan Sr. High Scholarship Award. 1967—Recipient of the Sr. Rowan Sr. High Citizenship Award. President of the South Rowan Sr. High National Honor Society, Co-editor of the Yearbook, Member of the Science Club, Junior Classical League and annual staff photographer. Voted most likely to succeed. 1976 recipient of the Lutheran Theological Southern Seminary/ American Bible Society Award for excellence in the public reading and exposition of the Scriptures. 1993—One of five recipients of the 1993 "Family Advocate of the Year Award Presented by the Gaston County Commission on the Family and Gaston County Commissioners; [oth. writ.] 1979-80 Chairman of the Religious Inventory Task Force in Gaston County. Co-author of A Study of Religion in Gaston County, which is local follow-up to some of the studies of religion in Gaston County by Liston Pope in Millhands and Preachers and by Earl, Shriver, and Knudsen in Spindles and Spires. Fall 1983 Coordinator for the Listing to the People Conference held at Lutheridge by the NC Synod and DMNA in preparation for the development of the 1984 LCA Social Statement, Peace and Politics. 1994-1995—Co-convener of The Theological Work Group and co-editor of an eighteen month research document entitled: Seeking Common Ground for the Good of All: A Biblical and Theological Critique of Issues Regarding Public Education In A Pluralistic Democracy; [pers.] The Prayer by Reinhold Niebuhr: God grant me the serenity to accept the things I cannot change, the courage to change the things I can, and the wisdom to distinguish the one from the other.; [a.] Dallas, NC

WEANT, LINDA MORGAN
[b.] May 3, 1950; [p] Roy and Willie Morgan; [m.] Gary Alan Weant; July 2, 1972; [ch.] Rebekah Marie, Jonathan Alan; [ed.] West Rowan High School - Mt. Ulla, NC., Lenoir-Rhyne College, Hickory, NC; [occ.] GED Instructor Gaston College; [memb.] Philadelphia Lutheran Church; [hon.] Chi Beta Phi Scientific Fraternity; [pers.] I wrote this poem for devotions for NC Women of the ELCA concerning child abuse.; [a.] Dallas, NC

WEBER, MELISSA
[pen.] J. Weber; [b.] December 18, 1985; Bay Shore; [p.] Robert and Janet Weber; [ed.] Canaan Lake Elementary; [memb.] Library Club; [hon.] Nyssma Clarinet, Chorus, Band, School Safety Art Club, Show choir; [oth. writ.] What Is Love, What Is Blue; [a.] Patchogue, NY

WHITFORD, KATHRYNE
[pen.] Kathryne Whitford; [b.] November 5, 1948; Los Angeles; [p.] I. Elwin and Barbara Merrill; [m.] David B. Whitford, Jr; September 1, 1973; [ch.] Kevin, Andrew, Jeffrey, Jessica and Jennifer; [ed.] A.A. Cosmetology BA—English, Minor Music and History from Brigham Young University; [occ.] High School English/ESL Teacher at Ramona H.S. in Riverside, CA; [memb.] Delta Kappa Gama; [oth. writ.] I've written many poem a few short plays and stories I have published poems in HS year books and local newspapers; [pers.] As a recovering cancer patient life has taken on a much deeper meaning to me. I love to observe the wonders of life and its challenges.; [a.] Riverside, CA

WHITWORTH JR., JOHN WAYNE
[pen.] 777; [b.] June 8, 1960; Anchorage, AK; [p.] John and Carolyn Whitworth; [ed.] Black Mtn., NC Rehab., Grandpa's Clevenger's Railroad Corn Cramerton, NC, [occ.] Jack of all trades; [hon.] Beta and Skeeting 96 out of 100; [oth. writ.] Have others, but do not enter, because not top notch.; [pers.] I give all my talent to the one above.; [a.] Kings Mtn., NC

WILKINSON, HELEN LOUISE OREM
[pen.] Maggie; [b.] January 26, 1941; Baltimore, MD; [p.] Doris E. Orem and James R. Orem Sr; [m.] Jon A. Wilkinson; November 7, 1981; [ed.] Betsy Ross Elementary, Gwynn's Fall's Junior High; [occ.] Housewife, Daycare Provider; [hon.] Many blue ribbons for first place for cooking and baking contests; [oth. writ.] I don't care for fiction, I like true things. I've always had a great imagination, and have been able to sit down with paper and pen and come up with some things, but this is the first contest I've entered.; [pers.] I always tell people: Saying nothing sometimes says a lot. I believe that's a true meaning of "silence is golden."; [a.] Annapolis, MD

WILLIAMS, CURTIS
[pen.] Curtis Williams; [b.] February 5, 1935; Tarboro NC; [p.] Deceased; [m.] Alice Williams; 1957 Wife passed 1985/remarried 1990; [ch.] Son—Curtis B. Williams; [ed.] Graduated from H.S. from Tarboro NC 1954, I wrote poems and lyrics in school and sang in the Choir; [occ.] Salesman for Modell's Sporting Goods Department. I worked for Macy's for 37 yrs. until the company went bankrupt. I was writing poems even then and lyrics for songs; [memb.] I was a member of the 25 yrs. Club when I was with Macy's and the Ambassador Club; [hon.] I also received documents from the clubs; [oth. writ.] I think everyone should write poems to express their feelings. I enjoyed to see others react to my poems.; [pers.] I have always enjoyed writing poems and writing lyrics for songs. I'm also a gospel singer and made a tape.; [a.] Irvington NJ

WILLIAMS, DOROTHY OBRIEN
[pen.] Dorothy O'Brien Williams; [b.] May 14, 1972; Fort Worth, TX; [p.] Thomas O'Brien and Jane Pryor O'Brien; [m.] Divorced; [ch.] Michael William, Cathy Williams Wilson; [ed.] High School Graduate R.L. Paschal High School 1944; [occ.] Retired; [oth. writ.] Children's Stories; [pers.] My relationship with others follows the golden rule. Additionally, in day to day living, it is my feeling . . . If it is right in your heart, your mind will follow.; [a.] Fort Worth, TX

WILLIAMS, KIMBERLY
[b.] March 15, 1981; Indiana; [p.] Linda Harnick and Samuel Williams; [m.] Fiance—Jason Eden; [ch.] Expecting—September 20, 1997; [ed.] American Correspondence School; [memb.] 4-H 7 years; [hon.] Three first place in creative writing—Vanderburg County Fair 4-H and Four Second place creative writing on poetry, short stories, and essay.; [pers.] It is easier for me to write down my feelings. My poetry is the way I express myself.; [a.] Evansville, IN

WILLIAMS, STEVEN R.
[b.] May 17, 1959; Lockney, TX; [p.] Dean and Jonell Williams; [ch.] Amanda Marie and Stephanie Anne; [ed.] BS Electronic Engineering; [occ.] Program Manager; [hon.] Dean's Honor List at New Mexico State University; [oth. writ.] Several writings have published by The National Library of Poetry "Having You Near," "Thoughts Of You," "Need You," "Worth Waiting For," other writings have not yet been published; [pers.] "Ever Since That Wonderful Day" is dedicated to Sharon Myzell. I'm very glad that our paths crossed on that wonderful. Sharon is someone worth waiting for. Hope someday we'll be together.; [a.] Summerville, SC

WILLIAMSON SR., ANTHONY E.
[b.] January 6, 1957; Kansas City, MO; [p.] Fannie Mae Brown, Albert Frank Williamson Sr; [m.] May 7, 1977, Separated April, 1981; [ch.] Lakissia Renee Davison, LaTasha Diane Williamson; [ed.] Graduated High School 1975, K.C., MO; [occ.] Production Technician; [hon.] None, except a Certificate from English Class 1973; [pers.] Peace actually is natural. Pain isn't such a bad thing. Its purpose is to alert you before you do serious damage to what God has created—Life and all of the

accessories, such as Spirits, Soul, Mind, Body. Everything is or can be effected or attested by pain.; [a.] Oceanside, CA

WILSON, SAMANTHA
[pen.] Sam; [b.] April 7, 1987; Fullerton, CA; [p.] Jim and Wendy Wilson; [ed.] 5th Grade Gate Student; [occ.] Student; [memb.] Leadership Club at Seneca Elementary Member of the Universalist Unitarian Church; [hon.] Science Fair—Honorable Mention, Honor Roll; [pers.] Try to do your best, knowledge is an important key to life!; [a.] Moreno Valley, CA

WILSON, SANDRA
[b.] March 22, 1956; MI; [p.] Paul Rockwell and Ethel Lurd; [m.] Tim L. Wilson; [ch.] 3 Children; [occ.] Nursing Assistant; [oth. writ.] One poem published in "Great Poems of the Western Word Vol. II"; [pers.] I write mostly about family and friends, most of the time something deep from my heart, and usually personal. My family and friends are wonderful, but my grandson Joshua is magical.; [a.] Niles, ME

WITT (SPROUL), AGNES ANN
[pen.] Agnes Sproul; [b.] October 8, 1941; Detroit, MI; [p.] Robert John Sproul, Elizabeth Detvay; [ch.] 5 daughters: Sheila, Elizabeth, Teresa, Jill, Maria; [ed.] Lee M. Thurston High School, Redford Twp. Michigan—Class of "60"; [occ.] Clerk Typist—Med. Rec. Heritage Hosp., Taylor, MI; [hon.] July 1996—"Star of Heritage Hospital" (awarded for outstanding job performance with patients and co-workers); [oth. writ.] "Touched by an Angel," "Visions In The Clouds," "When My Work Is Done," "What Is Justice?," "Looking Forward"; [pers.] I am inspired by life itself, and only by God's Grace can I express my feelings.; [a.] Lincoln Park, MI

WOJCUICH, LINDA KAY
[pen.] Linda Coffey; [b.] October 30, 1963; Galveston, TX; [p.] Virginia Alsobrook, Robert Coffey; [m.] Robert Wojcuich; July 8, 1994; [ch.] John Robert; [ed.] BA Communications University of Texas at Arlington; [occ.] Graduate Student in Communication and Information Systems at Robert Morris College; [memb.] Friends of the NAACP; [pers.] Take risks and look of the humor and beauty in everyone situation.; [a.] New Brighton, PA

WOLTJER, MATTHEW
[b.] June 5, 1977; St. Paul, MN; [p.] Dennis and Cindy Woltjer; [ed.] Forest Lake High School, Covenant Bible College, AB Canada; [memb.] US Chess Federation; [oth. writ.] Personal collection of free verse poems and various short stories; [pers.] I wrote "White Knight" for my dear friend Jessica Zaytsoff, because she is an inspiration to me.; [a.] Scandia, MN

WOOD, ELISABETH
[b.] November 18, 1982; Tulsa, OK; [p.] Fred Wood, Judy Wood; [ed.] Will be a Freshman in High School beginning August, 1997. Attended Central Middle School in Edmond; [occ.] Student; [pers.] Elisabeth lived in Zambia, Africa for 5 years at a mission school. She went back this summer for a visit and is considering being a missionary when she finishes school.; [a.] Edmond, OK

WOOD, JEANNE
[b.] November 13, MO; [m.] Howard; [ch.] Barry and Ronne, grandchildren: Ryan, Keegan, Tikisha; [ed.] College; [hon.] Honorary Service Award for working with children and the community. Awards for writing poetry; [oth. writ.] 2 children's books titled The Last Leaf and Not My Skin! Several published poems. Now working on a novel. Have also written short stories and songs.; [pers.] Not to dwell on your troubles, but to use them as stepping stones for growth.; [a.] Sunnyvale, CA

WOOD, RYAN
[b.] October 2, 1988; Arlington, TX; [p.] Ron and Regina Wood; [ed.] Third Grade; [hon.] Honor student, received awards for art and attendance. Favorite subject is math, collects comic books, baseball cards likes to read, play piano. Sports awards include soccer, roller hockey, bicycle racing, running. Has an older sister and brother and the best parents in the world. "Quotes Ryan"; [pers.] I already have my life planed out—I'm going to become a professional soccer player and a lawyer and I'm not going to smoke or take drugs.

WRIGHT, CHRISTIAN
[b.] April 8, 1972; Jamestown, TN; [p.] Roger and Barbara York; [m.] Darrell Wright; June 1, 1992; [ch.] Cassie, Amelia, and Catherine; [occ.] Mother and Homemaker; [a.] Jamestown, TN

YAMADA, EMI CAMILLA
[pen.] Camilla; [b.] September 5, 1980; Gadsden; [p.] Mother deceased Father Aki Yamada; [ed.] Junior in High School; [a.] Rome, GA

YEARWOOD, STEPHEN ALLISTAIR
[pen.] Iyawo; [b.] May 6, 1948; Trinidad; [p.] Mrs. Alnoresy Vanory Casey; [ed.] St. Johns High, Guyana, South America; [occ.] Refrigeration Technician; [memb.] Member of the International Society of Poets; [hon.] Editor's Choice Award presented by The National Library of Poetry, 1947; [oth. writ.] As listed: "Come See My Ways," "Or So It Seem," "Give Respect," "One For The Read"; [pers.] Hope is that beacon that guides crafts to safety on stormy nights. The elements of life intrigue me.; [a.] Brooklyn, NY

YI, CHRISTINA
[b.] May 1, 1985; Glendale, CA; [ed.] Currently attending Huntington Middle School in San Marino, CA; [pers.] I let my heart and feelings write my poems. If you do so, your work becomes part of your soul.

YOUELLS, ANNA
[b.] November 29, 1987; Towson, MD; [p.] Stephanie and Patrick Youells; [ed.] 4th Grade—Villa Cresta Elementary School; [occ.] Student; [memb.] Girl Scouts; [hon.] Good Student Awards; [pers.] Anna enjoys reading, writing and school. She is a member of Scouts as well as ice skating and roller skating groups where she takes lessons. She also performs in skating shows.; [a.] Parkville, MD

YOUNG, JUNE
[b.] June 15, 1943; Knoxville, TN; [p.] Robert and Violet Venator; [m.] Pat Young Jr; February 8, 1985; [ch.] Gerald, Diana and Robert; [ed.] Gibbs High, Knoxville, TN, Long Beach City College; [occ.] Retired Eligibility Worker Los Angeles County Department of Public Social Services, "DPSS"; [hon.] Letter of commendation from Los Angeles County in 1984; [oth. writ.] "Fairytale Love" 1972, "Perfect World" 1972, "The Day After Christmas" 1976, "Drinkers Delight" 1989, a few of my favorites, none have ever been published; [pers.] Favorite poets: Kipling, and Longfellow. I am inspired by people and events.; [a.] Apple Valley, CA

YOUNG-HODGES, SHIRLEY
[pen.] Joie Lee Hodges; [b.] January 1, 1948; St. Louis, MO; [p.] James Hoskin and Lodie Mae; [m.] Donald Hodges; March 29, 1996; [ed.] Southern IL. University Spelman College, School of Practical Nursing, Dist 189 East St. Louis Sr. High School; [occ.] Medical Sec., Event Planner and Staffing Coordinator; [pers.] In a poet's heart flows a never-ending stream of wisdom and beauty.; [a.] Marietta, GA

ZAPPA, KAREN E.
[pen.] K. Case; [b.] July 7, 1963; Detroit, MI; [p.] Robert and Mary Case; [m.] Paul Zappa; December 7, 1990; [ch.] Robert Jarvis; [ed.] Macomb Community College; [occ.] Registered Nurse; [memb.] St. John Lutheran Church; [hon.] Dean's List; [pers.] My writing is strongly influenced by believing in and by following the Golden Rule of life.; [a.] Sterling Hts., MI

ZIZKA, ROSE J.
[pen.] Rose J. Zizka; [b.] December 14, 1908; Cleveland, OH; [p.] Rudolf and Julia Zizka; [ed.] Grammar and Business Col. in a Parochial School; [occ.] Retired; [pers.] This is my first attempt at writing anything.; [a.] Cleveland, OH

INDEX
OF POETS

Index

A

Aaron 158
Abbot, Carolyn T. 16
Abramovitz, Blake 213
Abramowitz, Faith L. 54
Abrams, Emily 208
Abron, Pauline E. 69
Adams, Cassandra 91
Adams, Charlene 136
Adams, John 60
Adams, Lisa L. 208
Adams, Nicholas 111
Adamson-McMullen, Tammy 39
Adkins, Marilyn S. 125
Adkins, Shaneon 180
Adkinson, Sharee 141
Akins, Brittany 91
Alarie, Bonnie 113
Alberg, Jennifer 98
Alexander, Merilyn 25
Alger, Keith E. 175
Allen, Amanda A. 48
Allison, Phyllis Gail 160
Allnutt, Betty 57
Allsup, Mary M. 213
Almodova, Wanda Atkins 63
Anderson, Angie Lea 123
Anderson, Anita Gill 186
Anderson, Eliza J. 11
Anderson, Keith 155
Andoniello, Michelle 30
Andrews, Gregory 53
Ankhesenamen, Shelly 119
Anthony, Samara 61
Antrim, Bruce Charles 6
Aponte, Awilda 120
Archivilla, Merlin 62
Arebelo, Candace 197
Arjune, Holly 129
Armas, Rony 131
Armbrust, Dale Charles 222
Arnell, Lucille Land 118
Arnold, Michael Stephen 36
Arredondo, Martha L. 168
Arrigo, Frank A. 164
Arrington, Tasya Michellena 31
Arritola, George 94
Ashbaugh, Sara 96
Askew, Maxine 209
Atkinson, Jennifer 109
Atlas, Harold 152
Aukerman, Robert B. 65
Austin, Marika H. 25
Avery, Jessica 34
Avery, Tierre 105
Axton, Florence G. 21
Ayer, Dorothy F. 80

B

Babcock, Cathy 14
BaccHus, Peter T. 117
Baecher-Lowery, Beverly D. 170
Baillargeon, Jessica 43
Bak, Autumn Eve 211
Baker, Donna 61
Baker, Glenn M. 114
Baker, Julie A. 179
Baker, Marolyn E. 52
Baker, Paul 143
Baker, Peggy 104
Baker, Sabra 136
Bakun, Alvin Jan 169
Balcom, Cindy 187
Baldo, Virgilia 38
Baldwin, Betty 91
Baldwin, Chris 185
Baldwin, Edward T. 210
Balestrieri, Maria 36
Balla, Joyce 85
Ballard, Pearl 187
Balmer, Jessica 159
Balogh, Barbara 106
Balogh, Diana 158
Bandy, Winnell Wade 193
Banks, Britonya D. 126
Banks, Carl 218
Banks, Shawn 183
Baran, Kim 73
Barger, Shannon Denise 163
Barile, Bonnie D. 93
Barmes, Edward R. 209
Barnard, James Taylor 44
Barnes, Barbara J. Brown 207
Barnhart, Laurie G. 107
Barone, Michael J. 120
Barreiro, Joseph 53
Barron, Sheila 208
Barry, Anna M. 97
Basirico, Jeanette M. 152
Bass, Joann 51
Bass, Mary 122
Bassett, Caroline 6
Battle, Alberta Tylia Dorethea 151
Baugh, Lauren Michele 136
Bauza, David 140
Bay, Ruth 60
Bayard, Yseult 4
Beam, Howard 138
Beard, Annie D. 21
Beard, Joseph A. 111
Beck, Diane 152
Beck, Stephanie 63
Becker, Arielle Lee 93
Beier, Heather A. 104
Bell, Cynthia 131
Bell, Jennifer 156
Bell, Nancy Ann 167
Bello, Clare M. 146
Benavente, Rose A. 18
Benedict, Kathyrine 23
Beneux, Carol 66
Bennet, Rachel 58
Bennion, Heidi 119
Benson, Kizzy 154
Benson, Michelle 58
Berardo, Timothy 199
Berbes, Stephen 197
Berg, Desiree M. 207
Berg, Eddie 64
Bergeron, Andrew 112
Berkshire, Patricia A. 72
Berkson, Lee 5
Bernard, Patricia 216
Berrios, Mario Efrain 50
Beschoner, Judy 65
Best, Andre C. 183
Best, Victoria 66
Bettenhauser, Nikki 152
Bichel, Grethe 19
Biermann, Sarah 121
Bieszki, Patricia 142
Bihlear, Joey E. 33
Billadeau, Diana M. 104
Bilon, Dr. Ouide 164
Binder, Christina 140
Binder, Joseph 61
Bingham, Debra J. 70
Bingham, Matt 126
Bird, Ellen 82
Bischof, Marisa 129
Bishop, E. Alan 89
Bishop, Harold 190
Bitson, Angela 195
Bitson, Gary 30
Black, Aaron 222
Black, Alexis 63
Blackburn, Christy 103
Blake, Sidney 6
Bland, Ashley Lauren 206
Blazak, Bonnie 183
Bleck, Ryan B. 143
Blinebury, Beth 14
Blumberg, Charles 90
Boadu, Margaret 141
Boatwright, Anna 207
Bocchetti, Paul M. 206
Boggs, Matthew R. 166
Boisvert, Joseph J. R. 69
Bollnow, Pamela 214
Bonnes, Amanda 158
Boom, Julie 210
Boothe, David 170
Borton, Cassandra 154
Boschert, Marie 207
Boshears, Kim 24
Boss, Evelyn 136
Bost, Walter L. 78
Bosworth, William 35
Bourcier, Danny 35
Bourgoise, Michael L. 77
Bowden, Estelle 123
Bowden, Maggie Estelle 117
Bowen, Marie 95
Bowers, Ellen 58, 9
Bowler, Roland T. IV 112
Bowser, Christopher G. 200
Bowser, Donna M. 116
Boyington, Chris 51
Boyle, Huey 186
Boyle, Patricia 214
Boynton, Denise S. 192
Brackeen, George 215
Bradford, Timothy Scott 210
Bradley, Anne 222
Bradley, Sharon E. 118
Brady, Dee 19
Brand, Nellie M. 15
Brando, Robert 127
Branham, Donald 213
Brashear, Lori Joan 55
Bratton, Mary 101
Braun, Ruth J. 24
Breakfield, Kathleen Johnson 197
Brevard, Sara Elaine 95
Brewer, James D. Jr. 129
Briggs, Harry B. 180
Briggs, Travis 100
Brightbill, Melissa 205
Brill, Michael H. 179
Brink, Lillian 20
Brinkman, Dee Dee 25
Bristow, Connie 175
Brock, Dan 73
Brockish, Shelley 108
Brogan, Allen E. 22
Brokopp, Sherri Kay 83
Brolsma, Sheila 14
Brooke, Nicole 98
Brower, Jamie L. 106
Brown, Chastity 191
Brown, Debra 212
Brown, John A. 38
Brown, Lanre A. 11
Brown, Nicole 97
Brown, Terri Sue 205
Browne, Harriet 158
Brownlie, Todd A. 69
Bruce, E. Warren 128
Bruner, Rob 123
Brunn, Mindy 34
Bruno, Gabrielle 159
Brusse, Monique 130
Bryson, Ollie 64
Bubb, Kariann 147
Buchanan, Robert A. 109
Buck, Rose A. 24
Buckland, Geneva 154
Bucklew, Rose 27
Buckshee, Dr. Natahsa 181
Bullard, Scott 159
Bulow, Lori 45
Burd, Gina 217
Burdine, Rochelle 158
Burke, Charlotte 22
Burnett, Charlie 8
Burwell, Barbara 12
Buscaglia, Marti 13
Bush, Carol Ann 102
Buzaki, Nell Ann 86
Byrne, McKenna 88
Byrum, Barney L. 206

C

Caballero, Gloria 50
Calamuci, Daniel 11
Calder, Jean VS 66
Cales, Ella M. 160
Caley, Shilo 112
Calise, Michelle 96
Callahan, Rosemary 50
Callaway, Stephen C. 113
Cameron, Deborah 40
Camp, David L. 151
Camp, James F. 199
Campbell, Clair G. 151
Canada, Sheila 147
Cannella, Michelle 192
Cappadona, Stephanie 63
Cardwell, Vivian A. 48
Carlo, Evelyn F. 205
Carney, Marguerite L. 72
Caron, Estelle 184
Carr, Doris Denton 17
Carroll, Joseph 163
Carroll, Pamela C. 210
Carter, Damien 200
Carter, Deborah L. 187
Carter, Ross 96
Carter, Tammy 220
Carter, Tom 29
Carvalho, Joseph 100
Case, Colleen W. 66
Case, E. R. 40
Case, Michael D. 55
Casey, Daniel 204
Cash, Ramona 81

Casterlow-Bey, Gary 191
Castillo, Pamela 88
Castillo, Roze 214
Cavaciuti, Frank 217
Cavanaugh, Nancy L. 195
Cecilio, Rachel 115
Celesnik, John J. 168
Cephas, Shatonda 86
Chaffin, Michelle 99
Chancellor, Robert 3
Chandler, Lillie Mae 146
Chapman, Virginia L. 221
Charles, Captain Sir 150
Chattaway, Irene Carol 185
Chattman, Vanessa M. 147
Chavez, Olga 84
Chidester, George A. 6
child of the storms, a 199
Childs, Wilbur J. 60, 3
Chiodo, Audrey 169
Chmielak, Albert S. 155
Choudhury, Kalyani 104
Chowdhury, Aparna 67
Christell-Sandri, Lisa 168
Christopher, Margaret 177
Ciesicki, Tiffany 209
Cintron, Edwin M. 211
Cioffi, Elaine M. 170
Cirincione, Suzanne M. 119
Claffy, Forrest 192
Clark, Jeffrey Scott 138
Clark, Michael F. 93
Clark, Misty Jane 134
Clark, Robbie 175
Clark, Vicki Ann 219
Clearfield, Jamie 92
Cleary, Krystal L. 187
Clemans, David 216
Clements, Ben 122
Clifford, Kerrie 179
Cline, Crystal 208
Clisso, Brittany 219
Clough, Paul 198
Cluff, John Hank 211
Clyde, Donald 165
Cochran, Melody T. 148
Cody 202
Cody, Charles M. 155
Cohen, Morton 22
Cohn, Kristine 56
Cohn, Muriel 179
Colacicco, Patricia Marie 109
Cole, Benny L. 210
Cole, Mary 40
Coleman, Brian 194
Collins, Ellouise 121
Conger, Rachel 128
Connolly, Holly C. 30
Connolly, Robert J. 153
Connor, Marianne 7
Connors, Jeff 34
Cook, Anna L. 154
Cordero, Josephine 15
Cordrey, Jamie M. 142
Cornelius, Allan Dietz 211
Coronel, Susanna 62
Cortese, Anne 193
Costello, Diana 87
Couch, Russ 5
Coulter, Katie 99
Courson, Heather Renee 93
Coville, Renee A. 7
Cowan, Jeremy 192

Cox, Karen R. 116
Coy, Doris Tobias 118
Crawley, Amanda H. 137
Crippen, Keely A. 71
Crosbie, Mark A. 48
Cross, Angela 78
Cross, Paul L. 33
Crowel, Linda 133
Cruchet, Myra Istne 144
Crudup, Mary C. 10
Crue, Bronwen Mary Elizabeth 218
Cruickshank, Robin 93
Crum, Richard 79
Crupper, Jenny O. 105
Cruz, Alex 85
Cruz, Valerie 73
Cummings, Dave 111
Cummings, Shannon 119
Cunningham, Jeannette 175
Cupper, Cassie 32
Currier, Andrea Jane 132
Cyrus, Ruthy 65
Czarnecki, Jenny 57

D

Daddona, Charlotte R. 71
Dakota, Johnny 49
Daley, Cassie 93
Daniels, Pat L. 122
Danko, Brian 85
d'Arcy, Robbin A. 43
Darrah, Lonna D. 139
Daru, Valerie 80
Dauk, Adrienne Lorraine 190
Davidson, Carl W. 59
Davis, Amanda Lynne 151
Davis, Anthony L. 201
Davis, Gary E. 177
Davis, Joseph Patrick 185
Davis, Karen L. 72
Davis, Larry Curtiss 60
Davis, Michael Owen 212
Davis, Sandy 42
Davis, Shirley Moroney 41
Davis, William R. 60
Davit, Richie Lee 187
Davitian, William 129
De Angelo, Jane 86
De Casas, Veronica 104
De Leon, Raymond A. 73
Deahl, Ciarran 158
Dearing, Robert 184
Dearman, Michael Dean 207
DeBonis, Freda 112
Decker, Mark 12
Dedeaux, Patricia D. 216
Delany, George 103
Delgado, Elba I. 52
DelGrosso, Elaine V. 215
Delia 143
DeLotell, Ray 75
DeMichele, Christine 209
Demmer, Clara 18
Dempsey, Frances 219
Dempsey, Patricia 173
Demshock, Alexandra 207
DeNiro, Frank J. 89
Derrickson, Howard 110
DeVané, Paul F. 130
Devereau, Barbara 73
Devlin, Caitlin 208
D'Heilly, Douglas J. 40
Diallo, Ibrahima 76

Diaz, Phillip 94
Dickerson, Danielle 75
Dickerson, Pamela 209
Dickey, Shelly 87
Dinkins, Teresa 30
Dodge, Cathy 73
Doherty, Deborah E. 120
Dolan, Melissa 101
Donahue, Kim 180
Donahue, Lynne 147
Donaldson, Ted 3
Donner, Isaac C. 24
Donohue, Linda 177
Donovan, Kimberly Ann 130
Dooley, Alex 28
Doran, Jennifer 170
Doshi, Nirav 208
Dotson, Lorri 214
Dowd, Stephanie 193
Downing, Mary Pat 207
Draves, Jimmy J. 174
Dreier, Eliza 202
Drinkard, Dianna 64
Droz, Selina 161
Dubs, Amber 213
Duca, Patrizia 183
Ducote, Matthew J. 116
Duenkel, T. Johanna 209
Dufur, LaDonna 98
Duggal, J.S. 48
DuMond, J.R. 43
duncan, denise 15
Dunkel, Brian Jerome 163
Dunkel, Frank D. 108
Duran, John 165
Dusseault, Alyson 160
Dutcher, Dan 167
Dyer, Kelly W. 71
Dykstra, Erica 160

E

Ead, Michelle 108
Easley, Alonzo D., Sr. 219
Eason, Kimberly Ann 64
Easter, Heidi 194
Eaton, Andrea Marie 157
Eckerle, Philip A. 61
Eckerson, Cecilia 198
Economou, Anargyros E. 88
Edwards, H.W. 113
Effinger, Kelly 185
Egan, Margaret 120
Eisenberg, Elizabeth 210
El Sayed, Laura 168
ELancelot 46
Elder, Stephen 5
Elliott, Jeff 220
Ellis, Robert 49
Elsenberg, Michelle Mostovy 200
Emery, Diane 128
Endicott, Brenda 216
Endress, Aliece Marie 111
Engravalle, Pamella Jean 175
Ennis, John Wellington 9
Entriolo, Mary Rose 76
Enzman, Jenni 210
Erickson, Heather 109
Ernest, Stephanie R. 159
Erney, Dalia 151
Erwin, Dale Michael 132
Espada, Haniff 48
Ewing, John 134

F

Fairbairn, Desmond 7
Fairbanks, R.J. 161
Faison, Patricia Ann 181
Falzone, David 114
Farfan, Edith 90
Faye, Lillian 118
Feasel, Ron 94
Feldman, Mark Evan 200
Feliciano, Noelle 117
Felknor, Kathy L. 184
Felton, Helen K. 193
Ferguson, Nancy L. 143
Fernandez, G. Ross 92
Ferrari, Melissa M. 15
Ferreira, Roger C. 159
Fesi, Elisabeth 102
Few, Lindsey D. Jr. 97
Feyer, Rose 42
Fields, Amber 41, 6
Fields-Kretzer, Marilyn 126
Fiester, Dana Y. 212
Finholm, Faith 66
Finnerty, Edythe Ledee 193
Finney, Norma V. 66
Firestone, Benny 89
Firsdon, Craig 43
Fisher, Jade 88
Fisher, Kathryn M. 205
Fisler, Becky 111
FitzGerald, Garry II 70
Flaherty, Suzanne 99
Fleming, Sandra 62
Flynn, Sandra J. 168
Foran, Megan Michael 216
Fortier, Debbie 218
Fortune, Thomas M. 45
Foster, Ona 73
Fowler, Nikki 112
Fox, Nicole 137
Francese, Keith Anthony 108
Franz, Eugene F. 191
Frasco, Marian 121
Frazer, Ella May 27
Frederick 189
Free, Christopher 205
Freeman, Christie 126
Freeman, Lucille Orr 169
Freilino, Florence E. 210
Friedman, Susan J. 19
Frisby, Shannon 185
Fugate, Murray Jr 112
Fuller, Barbara 119
Fuller, Valencia O. 159
Fulmer, Danielle 212
Funes, Jose L. 28
Fung, Cora K.S. 141
Fung, Dora Low 20

G

Gabbard, Janet L. 36
Gagne, Amy 86
Gail, Denise 125
Gaines, Wilma 120
Gajda, Melissa 109
Gall, Robert 177
Gallegos, Francine 40
Ganguly, Amitava 121
Ganninger, Brian 24
Garcia, Glenna 123
Garcia, Therese Feser 90
Gardner, James L. 221

Gardner, Melissa 216
Gargiulo, Maria 206
Garrett, Becky 182
Garrett, Roberta 113
Garrison, Rosemary 128
Gartside, Noelle 37
Gaston, Dorris Burks 116
Gates, J. 109
Gauthier, Martha Helene 68
Gaza, Irene M. 65
Geist, Nancy 66
Gemeinhardt, Judith M. 219
Gennardo, Peter 64
Gennerman, Christian David 69
Genson, Larry A. 108
Gerhard, J R 165
Germany, Charita L. 146
Gerstman, Maria K. 62
Ghiotto, Ronald L. 109
Giannini, Michael J. 220
Gibbons, Dondrew C. 203
Gibbs, Constance 216
Gibson, Lisa G. 70
Gilbert, Patricia Wylie 23
Gilkerson, Vanessa 167
Gilligan, Angela R. 47
Gillit, Daniel Jared 50
Giron, Maria Sostenita 163
Glaser, David 61
Glasz, Francheska 38
Glazebrook, Janet Limbert 213
Glesner, Jeremy 80
Globig, Cheryl A. 180
Glogowski, Theresa 60
Glover, Grace M. 27
Godinez, Ira 110
Goetz, John Arthur 157
Goldemberg, Rose Leiman 186
Gomez, Donald 29
Gomez, Sylvia 49
Gonzales, Alida J. 28
Gonzalez, Oscar R. II 172
Good, Linda 45
Goodwin, Lynn 115
Gore, Sarah 205
Gouley, Anna 214
Gracie, Sarah A. 25
Grady, Rory 118
Graeser, Ron 75
Graham, Brandy M. 100
Graham, David 149
Graham, Eunice 199
Graham, Letha I. 167
Gramkow, Angela 219
Granberg, Catherine 118
Grandberry, Les 202
Grant, Seth 55
Grau, Jean E. 16, 3
Gravenstein, Megan 82
Gray, Cherylann 28
Gray, Clint 165
Gray, Daniel 101
Gray, Laura P. 145
Gray, Nessie 57
Grech, MaryRose 85
Green, Jeffery N. 221
Green, Kate 129
Green, Marcus D. 148
Green, Nina 82
Green, Nona 183
Greenfield, James G. 19
Greenhill, William 56
Greenidge, Phyllis 188

Gregory, Lee Ryan 100
Griffin, Sharon J. 128
Griffiths, Drew 5
Griffiths, John S. 174
Griffiths, Kimberly 212
Grimste, Jason 10
Grochala, Jeni 68
Grodski, Arlene L. 81
Grone, Lindy 213
Gruss, Amy L. 224
Gruwell, Bradley O. 156
Guerrero, J. René 8
Guerrero, Shirley Nesom 203
Guido, Concetta M. 212
Guilfoyle, Sister Theophane 171
Gulbrandsen, Lois C. 94
Gusdon, John P. Jr. 114
Guthrie, George W. 223
Guy, Darlene Joyce 46
Guyan, Loretta 206

H

Haack, Michelle 204
Habito, Lolita Pornasdoro 223
Hadden, Holly 166
Hagen, Andrew 38
Haigh, Harry 3
Haithcox, Kelly D. 55
Hall, Allen L. 197
Hall, Christine 72
Hall, Diane L. 60
Hall, Jeff 173
Hall, Lazette 64
Haller, Melody Nicolle 223
Halstead, Bernard C. 116
Hamilton, Lawrence E. 42
Hamilton, Rachel 206
Hamlet, Shawn 102
Hancock, Pat C. 90
Handel, Jane Harlow 207
Haney, Joe 216
Hanna, Richard R. 120
Hansen, Melinda L. 207
Hanson, Gary W. 176
Harberts, Marilyn 18
Harden, Robert L. Jr 198
Hardy, Carolyn V. 96
Hardy, Laurel Ann 163
Harmer, Ben 129
Harold, Margaret V. 21
Harrington, April 152
Harrington, Mildred Ardys 143
Harris, Edna 171
Harris, Margaret R. 141
Harris, Robyn 144
Harrison, Karen S. 144
Harshman, Michelle 211
Hart, Virginia 141
Hartman, Becky 156
Hartsell, Robin A. 159
Harven, Al 107
Harwood, Jane R. 15
Harwood, Travis 77
Hasell, Julia 215
Haskett, Susan Milligan 33
Hatfield, Neil 204
Hathaway, Chris 190
Hathaway, Kevin T. 119
Hauptly, Michael G. 74
Hauser, David G. 215
Haverman, Konni 106
Hawkins, Gabrielle 217

Hayner, Richard Brian 14
Haynie, Marie B. 218
Hazelton, Crystal 159
Headley, Henderson T. 124
Heald, C. Alan 127
Heath, Paula J. 17
Hedlund, Daniel 193
Heintz, Elizabeth A. 31
Heintze, Deonna 188
Heisey, Mark 13
Henderson, Brenda Joan 29
Henson, Rena 72
Herber, Amy 128
Hernandez, Felicity 76
Hernandez, Frank 104
Hernandez, Gabriel 101
Herrington, Chard 88
Hickman, Michelle 216
Higgenbottom, Hayden W. 94
Higgins, Allison 121
Hilbert, Phillip 40
Hill, Kecia A. 54
Hills, Jamie 137
Hinkle, Michael 34
Hinojosa, John 186
Hinrichs, Julie 162
Hinrichsen, Jaime 204
Hinrichsen, Merry Miller 199
Hinson, Stenna Michelle 164
Hixson, Phylicia 169
Hodge, Carrie 65
Hodge, Naia S. M. 98
Hodges, Courtney 161
Hodges, Jessy 217
Hoff, Ira W. 33
Hogue, Jamie L. 157
Hohn, Patricia 110
Holder, Janie 123
Holder, Nola Grace 26
Holen, Judith 111
Hollenbeck, Brian 121
Hollingsworth, Traci L. 165
Hollopeter, Beth 138
Holt, Sheila S. 89
Holter, Patti 215
Honse, Corina 158
Hooks, Virginia 152
Hoover, Dana 50
Horn, Mary N. 118
Horton, Brian 162
Horton, Cheryl T. 39
Hoskins, Harold 80
House, Anthony C. 69
Hoysgaard, John 21
Hubbard, Danielle 169
Hudson, Judith P. 45
Hudson, Lois 214
Hudson, Lori Beth 27
Hudson-Moore, Phenia M. 126
Huffman, Marilyn 87
Huigen, Amanda 142
Hulet, Nicole 73
Humpal, Doris M. 203
Hunkele, Gregory 84
Hunt, Shannon 162
Hunter, H. H. 17
Hunter, John 186
Huntsberry, Ida 110
Hurst, Renda 193
Hurt, Alledria Ebony 77
Huschka, Rita 34
Hussong, Delores A. 88
Hutchinson, Marinette 125

Hyde, David L. 61
Hyde, Lauren 110

I

Iacovangelo, Teresa J. 63
Iannone, Catalina 180
Igoe, Michael 13
Ingoglio, Melinda 111
Ingram, Michelle 160
Inman, Carrie 26
Ippolito, Ryan 149
Irwin, Susan 213
Isaacs, Gordon 218
Izzo, Jennifer 185

J

Jaben, Korey 51
Jackson, E. D. 5
Jackson, Karol L. 146
Jackson, N. Rose 134
Jackson, Renée 163
Jackson, Tawanna 39
Jacob, Jasmine 81
Jacobson, Janet 108
James, Cassidy 171
James, Frederick Leon 114
James, H. Stewart 12
James, Timothy J. 65
Jank, Sandra Dawson 136
Jankowski, Mark L. 44
Jarrell, Donna 123
Jarrett, Laura 47, 9
Jayaraman, Vinodini 113
Jennett, Shirley L. 68
Jennings, Devan 132
Jensen, Garrett 93
Jessup, Michelle 48
Jezior, Barbara 144
Johanson, Fritz E. 213
Johns, Harry II 218
Johnsen, Joshua 159
Johnson, Ashley 216
Johnson, Bob 66
Johnson, Carolyn M. 204
Johnson, Christine E. 148
Johnson, Deborah 139
Johnson, Derek L. 181
Johnson, Frances M. 188
Johnson, Horace M. 176
Johnson, James W. 67
Johnson, Louise N. 138
Johnson, Ralph B. 18
Johnson, Rebecca Parsons 178
Jones, Clarence W. Jr. 80
Jones, Connie 217
Jones, Grasshopper 209
Jones, Lawrence F. 129
Jones, Luann 198
Jones, Lynette R. 101
Jones, Renee 204
Jordan, Lisa 116
Joseph, Annette 121
Joseph, Denise 158
Joyner, Heatherlynn 211
Joyner, Kim G. 170
Julmis, Jocelaine 172
Jump, Michele W. 97

K

Kadota, Holly Mock 61
Kafel, Mary Sue 204

Kafka, Lisa A. 166
Kai, Cyrus 63
Kaitbenski, Josephine 210
Kalbaugh, Mary Morris 161
Kalinowski, Judith A. 4
Kammler, Jen 87
Kanaby, Nicole 92
Kaplan, Gloria Wilson 110
Kaplan, Helen 154
Kaptain, Kelly 78
Karrick, Russell Edward 173
Karunamurthy, Aroon 12
Kasper, Tiffany Lyn 205
Kassouf, Michael J. 29
Kavanagh, Kevin 53
Kawasaki, Jennifer 77
Kaye, Li-Ann 87
Keeffe, Van Der Aa 11
Keeley, Felicity 111
Keeley, Mary Ann T. 92
Keeling, John Frum 118
Keeth, Tamra Dickenson 168
Keller, Elizabeth 96
Keller, Mary Lou 55
Kellogg, Michelle 89
Kelly, D'An 190
Kelly, Sean 167
Kelsch, Abigail 213
Kelton, Angela C. 162
Kemmerlin, Courtney 153
Kennard, Sarah 95
Kennedy, Marguerite D. 37
Kerting, Erin 222
Kesser, Kristen 192
Kessler, Amanda 115
Key, Elstress 95
Khaksar, Mansoor 194
Kiddy, Kristen 14
Kilgore, Joe 209
Kim, Shannon Burnett 126
Kimber, Sandra E. 75
King, Carey 116
King, Fatimah 149
King, Ina W. 203
King, M. L. 31
Kirchhoffer, Casey 170
Kirkman, Jan T. 74
Kirst E A, Ralph F. 51
Kirt, Georgiann 47
Kissinger, Jill Christine 139
Kleiber, Marshall 75
Klemyk, Robert J. 71
Kline, Marshall 52
Kline, Matt 158
Knaiz, Eugene 205
Knapper, Ralph O. 91
Knickerbocker, Rose A. 122
Knudson, Denise K. 100
Knupp, Frances 19
Koback, Patricia M. 92
Koehler, Stephen Robert 10
Kogle, Angela P. 94
Koltz, Kathleen 220
Korosec, Alicia 195
Kosovych, Adriana 173
Kovac, Frank K. 18
Kraus, Lynn C. 113
Krause, Andrea 139
Kreider, Cynthia A. 180
Kreutzer, Jennifer 147
Krishnaswamy, R. 170
Kristensson, Anna Karin 41
Krolikoski, Virginia J. 153

Kubin, Cheryl Louden 146
Kucheruck, Beth 76
Kulla, Joan Ann 44
Kumbla, Rekha 148
Kuntz, Wynona 21
Kwong, Elaine 26
Kyrke, Ann Venables 6

L

Labberton, Kinsey 171
Lack, Lillian 162
Lackman, Anna Lee 114
Lacy, Nikki 156
Lahner, Gary 115
Laieta, James P. Jr. 38
Lalama, Carmina 110
Lamb, Ann 196
Lambert, Megan 96
Langen, Charles M. 165
Langham, Barbara 95
Lanham, Moses C. Jr. 211
Larkin, George 59
Larkin, Glen 78
Larkin, Jessica 206
Lasiter, Daniel E. 42
Lassiter, Ashley 53
Lathan, Ernestine Hamtion 95
Latherow, Tamisan 114
Laurens, Alma B. 169
Lauson, Ann 118
Laut, Norma 187
LaVelle, Sandra Lee 56
Laws, LaKiesha N. 196
Lea, Leandra 160
Leach, Gillian 165
Leach, Phyllis A. 13
League, Susan 162
LeBlanc, Robyn 125
LeClaire, James 32
LeClear, Randi 195
Lee, Donald J. 206
Lee, Joyce E. 30
Lee, Karen 72
Lee, Valynn 28
Lee, Venus 168
Lefkoe, Michael 24
Lehnardt, Christine 152
Lemasters, Christal 112
Leonard, Amanda 218
Leonard, April M. 173
Lesso, Geraldine 115
Leverson, Marilyn Beale 51
Levine, Jessica 175
Levinson, Jacki Lynn 172
Lewis, Gary 109
Lewis, Nadine 27
Lewis, Richard Clyde 187
Libutti, Gerard M. 56
Light, Ashley 167
Lillie, Angelica 206
Lima, Margaret S. 84
Lineberry, Doris Sue 36
Liter, Barbara 214
Liverett, Kelly D. 171
Lloyd, J. Frederick 69
Loken, Janna A. 181
Long, Allegra 167
Long, Elizabeth J. 49
Looney, Amee 161
Lopez, Michael Anthony 110
Lorant, Annette 164
Losk, Michael H. 94

Lota, Tammy 114
Lottes, D. 9
Love, Julia L. 207
Love, Melissa M. Creek 177
Loveday, Elaine 67
Loveday, Pam 160
Loveuc, Bonnie 66
Lowell, Lauretta Jane 70
Lowther, Johnathon 68
Lu, Gain G. 221
Lucken, Kerri M. 150
Luinski, Bonnie 130
Lukens, Elsie Mae 102
Lum, Gretchen Yates 215
Lundt, Cara 155
Lundy, Fred M. 62
Lundy, Theresa 208
Luther, Amanda 171
Lyon, Christopher 97
Lyons, Marilyn 184

M

MacAfee, Mary Ann 103
Macartney, Cody 49
Macek, Marian 77
MacLeod, Norman L. Jr. 106
Madding, Billie R. 71
Magditch, Denise 144
Magee, Shamika 105
Magno, Coleen Robbie M. 114
Mahannah, Esther 105
Malaske, Joyce 157
Maley, Craig 189
Malone, Carole 205
Manges, Gloria 89
Manginello, Monica A. 58
Mangum, Sue O. 46
Maples, Melanie 206
Marchewka, Kate 68
Marchman, Kelli 35
Marcinak, Kathryn 44
Markus, Chris 177
Marr, Judith M. 184
Marrero, Jacqueline 32
Marsh, Leah 65
Marshall, Alice 65
Marshall, Ethel 23
Martell, Barbara Ann 82
Martell, Stephanie Lynn 133
Martin, Cathy Rae 166
Martin, Christina 18
Martin, Christopher M. 165
Martin, D. A. 89
Martin, Dana 83
Martin, Julie 212
Martin, Kristy 184
Martin, Leonard A. 167
Martin, Oliver Hugh Jr. 203
Martin, Rose 67
Martinez, Bob G. 20
Martini, Forest 165
Martinson, Jody A. 9
Maselli, Kim 137
Mason, Betty D. 16
Massaglia, Denise A. 15
Massey, Alma Jean 26
Masters, David 224
Mathis, Jean K. 182
Matin, Asna A. 29
Matiska, Amy L. 202
Matros, Larisa 176
Mattix, Sam H. Sr. 124

Mauldin, Jon 130
Maurizzio, Tim 211
May, Tommy 218
Maylath, Christine E. 57
Mayle, Sherman L. III 103
McCarthy, Susan 74
McClain, Margaret Barbour 170
McCollin, Paul 173
McCoy, David A. 79
McCreery, Kimberly 117
McDonald, Brian 207
McDonald, Linann 220
McDonald, Michael 170
McDowell, Sarah 158
McGann, Christe Marie 214
McGarrahan, Kevin 70
McGee, Sarah 161
McGeorge, Tony 95
McGill, Helen Felice 34
McGinnis, Deborah A. 202
McGraw, Hesse 7
McGuire, Willette Caudle 17
McInroe, Vivian 218
McIntosh, John Mark 179
Mclaughlin, Colleen 92
McLaughlin, Lois 82
McLean, Megan C. 180
McLean, Monica 131
McLennan, Cecelia A. 91
McLoud, Mildred Hyatt 26
McMaster, Lucy 117
McMillen, David 8
McMillen, Maggie 131
McMillen, Suzanne 35
McMurray, Robert H. Jr. 182
McNellen, Joshua 166
McQuillan, William P. II 102
McRea, Maggie L. 204
McRoberts, Shauna 135
Meade, Lillian M. 209
Mears, Jeanne K. 138
Meeks-King, Peggy J. 39
Megge, J. 217
Melaney, William 189
Merrill, Dreana 35
Messina, Raymond 109
Metcalfe, Elizabeth 200
Metzger, Betty 136
Meyer, Randy C. 134
Meyers, Robert L. 138
Michalopoulos, Aris 175
Michaud, Mike 178
Midwood, Nancy M. 22
Miko, Rebecca 150
Miles, Michael 146
Miller, Anita Kay 172
Miller, Dawn 173
Miller, Donald T. 168
Miller, Doris R. S. 194
Miller, Hayley Lynn 159
Miller, Joyce W. 107
Miller, Kim Timbrook 215
Miller, Mary Ann 92
Miller, Neil J. 166
Miller, S. George 108
Miller, Twyla C. 201
Miller, William 31
Minute, Michele 196
Mitchell, Clarita 181
Mitchell, Paul 123
Mitchell, Peg 25
Mitchell, Thomas "Tombo" 84
Mitchell, Walter L. 73

Moats, Patrick A. 21
Modak, Roseann 120
Modugno, Shannon L. 74
Moe, Aaron 140
Mollo, Dorothy 63
Molnar, Edith B. 65
Monat, Joan 67
Money, Matt 210
Monroe, Barbara 195
Moody, Heath 189
Moorhead, Robert K. 17
Moorhouse, Herbert 25
Morales, Jason 28
Morris, Lorna L. 221
Morrison, Jonathan 86
Moscato, Gary J., Sr. 215
Mossholder, Louise 185
Mote, Barbara 44
Mothorn, Justus John Caleb 157
Mott, Celeste 206
Moulton, Anita 68
Mowatt, Holli 223
Mueller, Amanda 166
Mueller, Jamie 77
Mueller, Melinda 188
Mulka, Nuray 32
Mullican, Ross 71
Muñoz, Michael Daniel 209
Murphy, Brandon 71
Murphy, Martin L. 82
Murphy, Michelle J. 25
Murphy, Victor C. 11
Murray, Justin M. 41
Murray, Robyn 62
Murrey, B. J. 165
Myer, Kathryn R. 31
Myers, Christine 142
Myers, Clarissa R. 119

N

Nagle, Gay Phyllis 78
Narragon, Jacqueline 217
Natividad, Nida Ines R. 163
Neace, Kristi 164
Neary, Ryan P. 81
Nelsen, Norman R. 150
Nelson, Kristina B. 164
Nelson, Reid Lewis 166
Nelson, Sandra E. 31
Netherton, Sheila 140
Newberry, Barbara 135
Newman, Edie 61
Newman, Marsha 81
Newswanger, Heather 160
Newton, Marianne 149
Newtson, Lee 153
Ng, Willie C. Sr. 221
Nguyen, Alfonse T. 169
Nichols, Nancy R. 66
Nichols, Nicki 79
Nicholson, Edward A. 47
Nicholson, James B. 117
Nickleson, Bonnie Ryan 111
Nicole, Ashley 164
Nied, Lou 32
Nielson, Alyce M. 15
Noday, Sharyl 202
Nodl, Edna Marie 78
Noe, Susan 197
Noles, Jennifer R. 44
Norling, Aubrey Rose 213
Norman, Louise 35

Norris, Jennifer L. 132
Nunes, Laura 209
Nunn, Willena T. 131

O

O'Connell, Jared 194
Ocwieja, Irene L. 202
O'Dalaigh, Rosey 205
Ogden, Mike D. 28
Ograbisz, Sarah 203
O'Leary, Jennifer 54
Oliana, Jesus F. 83
Oliver, Earl D. 202
Olson, Jennifer 37
O'Meara, Melonie 135
O'Neal, Lillian M. 178
Orozco, Juan 134
Orr, Leonard 217
Osborn, Linda 115
Otoshi, Yoshiyuki 19
Ott, Larry C. 83
Ott, Nancy B. 47
Ouellette, Jacqueline 151
Overton, Laura B. 23
Owens, L. Brian 93

P

Padilla, Carol 164
Padron, Babette 216
Palffy, Laurie 182
Panetto, Lucas 35
Pannell, Shirley M. 17
Panter, Eric 178
Pape, Amanda 117
Pariseau, Judy 139
Parker, Jeffrey 56
Parker, Joel B. 27
Parker, Rebecca Dawn 33
Partee, Trina 117
Pascale, Moira 13
Pascucci, Keeley 113
Passey, Michelle 207
Pasternak, David 166
Patchen, Jennifer 188
Patchin, Albert 23
Patrick, John Hanssen 16
Patterson, Jenna 99
Patterson, Karolyn 52
Patton, William 197
Payan-Prizio, Patricia 53
Payne, Trudy 211
Pearce, Amber 202
Pedro, Kathleen 139
Peel, Jerry L. 185
Pehrson, Shirley 206
Pendleton, Lucinda 99
Peoples, Marlene 106
Pepitone, Kristin 130
Pepple, Alexander 4
Pereisan, Carmen 131
Perez, Hector 216
Perkins, Norman C. 135
Perkus, Marion 26
Permenter, Robby 180
Perriello, Dina M. 46
Perrigan, Terri 162
Perritano, Thomas 162
Perrucci, Michelle 191
Perry, Tasha 161
Pertile, Jonathan 121
Peterson, John 80
Peterson, Michelle 212

Peterson, Sheryl L. 70
Petty, Laurie 168
Peyser, Liz 13
Pfankuchen, Carol 62
Pfitzenmeyer, Frank 26
Phelan, Loraine A. 43
Phelan, Merrie Christmas 214
Phillip, Melba 83
Phillips, Lois E. 196
Phillips, Myrtle B. 175
Piccinni, Angela 62
Pickett, Alecia R. 184
Pierson, Sally 67
Pieszchala, Terry Lee 20
Pilkinton, Teresa 136
Piowaty, Tara 121
Pirtle, Eric J. 166
Piskorowski, Amy 72
Plazak, Molly 79
Pliskin, Laura 202
Plumer, Patricia E. 190
Pole, John Graham 11
Polley, Lisa 117
Polnicki, Sherry 155
Poole, Tina M. 27
Poole, W. Edward Jr. 37
Popovich, Marguerite 14
Post, Jessica 145
Potter, Stephanie 156
Potts, Maureen M. 145
Poush, Nikki 77
Powell, James Edward, III 177
Powell, Jolynn 169
Powell, LaTonya JanNell 213
Powell, Tabitha 98
Powers, April L. 201
Price, Amanda 9
Price, Mary T. 215
Price, Mary T. 216
Price, Rodney 186
Pritty, Lillian Gip 112
Prosser, Veronica 114
Provenzano, Michael 72
Pullens, Tyler Mareel 219
Purcell, Craig 59
Purcell, Marcus 104

Q

Qasir, Therese "Leitch" 31
Quintiliani, Shirley Jones 100
Quirk, Allan Michael 105

R

Rafih, Debra Clarke 127
Rager, Madeline Jean 72
Ragsdale, Jerry 134
Rake, Wade Nathan 190
Raley, Monica Marie 204
Raloff, Jody 33
Ralph, M. D. Tennessee 195
Ramachandran, Deepa 56
Ramirez, Louis P. 128
Rand, Jason Scott 201
Rapaport, Dr. Wendy Satin 168
Rash, Andrew J. 215
Raving, Stark 166
Ray, Brenda 219
Ray, Cassandra 201
Ray, Robert 68
Raynes, Trula 85
Rea, Stephen 72
Reader, Melissa 211

Recalde, Fernando 28
Reed, John P. 147
Reeder, Betsy 84
Reese, Tommye 119
Regis, Shannon 222
Regular, Sheron 198
Reichardt, Helen C. 207
Reid, Jessica 120
Reis, Brian 203
Reisinger, Willie 222
Reist, Lisa Marie 217
Repsher, Adrienne 72
Rettberg, Dorothy 39
Revere, Michael 164
Rhoden, Rebecca 61
Richard, Michael 185
Richards, Patricia N. 179
Richardson, Catherine 189
Richardson, David O. 208
Richardson, Elizabeth 6
Richter, Kenneth R. 86
Riddell, Blair Áine 29
Riddle, Bridgette B. 44
Riddle, Matthew John 73
Riedel, Lynn 154
Riegel, Brian 202
Rife, Rachel 156
Riggio, Daniel C. 182
Riley, Beverley 63
Rinkel, Margaret 3
Riola, Sara Hewitt 60
Ritter, Lisa 138
Roach, John W. 70
Robert 10
Robertson, Jean A. B. 105
Robichaux, Jackie 97
Robinson, James 158
Robinson, Kenneth L. 181
Robinson, Robert 220
Rockhill, Martha 45
Rocle, Jacqueline Elizabeth 41
Rodkey, Margaret L. 14
Rodondi-Huhn, Ginmarie 127
Rodriguez, Crystal 201
Rodriguez, Virginia I. 85
Roe, Mike 151
Roeder, Alan 133
Roettger, Kelli N. 84
Rogers, Stephanie 186
Rollin, Marty 16
Romeo, Sara 64
Rook, Rob 62
Roop, Franklin 136
Rosen, Francine 68
Rosenblatt, Arlene 188
Rossi, Raymond E. 8
Rossiter, Mark 178
Roth, Barbara 152
Rothchild, David 159
Rowe, David Johnson 42
Roy, Anne 212
Ruark, Lester L. 190
Rue, Michael 83
Ruedy, Catherine 223
Ruff, Stephanie 95
Ruggieri, Susan 112
Ruiz, Veda Jr. 107
Rupert, Antonio 64
Rushing, Shirley 150
Russell, Danielle Marie 51
Rutkowski, Nancy 71
Ryan, Marlene A. 88
Rynd, Mark 140

S

Sadler, Norman J. 22
Salas, Arnaldo 206
Saldana, Jason A. 221
Salmons, Brittany 178
Salvador, Victor S. 141
Sampedro, Monique 86
Samuels, Zandra 144
Samuelson, Elizabeth 204
Sanchez, Miriam 64
Sanders, Abbey C. 124
Santiago, Kamylle 122
Sardelli, Shannon M. 207
Satija, Rachana 125
Sauerbry, Glen L. 110
Saurer, Rosemary 210
Saviano, Erika 113
Saxton, Pamela 133
Sayles, Jenny Jann 137
Saylor, R. L. 154
Sbarbaro, Pepper 4
Scalzi, Jennifer 98
Scarafoni, T. A. 57
Schafer, Matthew 66
Schettino, Allyson 191
Schlager, Maria 172
Schlang, Arlene 70
Schlayer, Robby 4
Schlereth, Sharon 92
Schmidt, Patricia 37
Schmiel, John 181
Schnapf, Miriam Rembold 183
Schneck, Randy L. 83
Schneider, Amy R. 40
Schneider, Kelly 103
Schneller, David 121
Scholl, Shirley 22
Schrecongost, Ellen 79
Schreiber, Scot 57
Schroeder, Jennifer 68
Schulz, Patty M. 145
Schwartz, Carol Ann 48
Schwartzman, Debbie 141
Scott, Gaynell 174
Scott, Kelli 218
Scott, Michael-Lyn 81
Scotto, Ann 196
Seadeek, Esther Ferrell 63
Sears, Christina 208
Seaton, Olivia N. 8
Seay, Brian K. 187
Sectish, Michael Guy 174
Selinger, Leah 80
Seman, Berna 156
Seraphine, Peter 32
Seremet, Christine 150
Serna, Ernest 47
Sewell, Elwanda R. 58
Seymour, Kevin F. 203
Shah, Sohil M. 43
Shamon, Jimmie Abraham Jr. 23
Shanks, Marianne 78
Shansky, Sara 57
Sharkey, Christopher B. 223
Sharron, Helen 104
Shaw, B. N. 208
Shaw, Elizabeth R. P. 61
Shaw, Melissa L. 30
Shaw, Sarah L. 53
Shearer, Esther 166
Shelden, Marge 69
Shelley, Randall Jr. 111

Shellman, Gena 111
Shelton, Jennifer 164
Shelton, LeeAnn 164
Shelton, Lewis R. 195
Shelton, Ruth 73
Shollenberger, Amy 162
Shorb, Michelle 122
Shreckengost, Melissa 168
Shubert, Jennifer 94
Siegel, Ceceil 151
Sigley, Virginia E. 30
Silverman, Emily 90
Silvey, Sarah Davie 163
Simek, Helen 45
Simon, Diane R. 62
Simones, Alicia 160
Simper, Manderie 21
Simpkins, Chalotte 71
Sims, Tobie Leigh 19
Singh, Shawn 45
Skelton, Eunice 167
Skillman, Brian 161
Skinner, Jackie 157
Skipper, Mary Ann 113
Slayton, Glory D. 153
Slyfield, Ruth 46
Small, Teresa Marie 111
Smart, Donna L. 217
Smith, Abbey 198
Smith, Brandie L. 127
Smith, Douglas R. 182
Smith, Fannie B. 64
Smith, Francis S. 9
Smith, Jeffrey S. 114
Smith, Jennifer 107
Smith, Julie 105
Smith, Nathan 174
Smith, Robin Ann Strunk 205
Smith, Samuel S. 191
Smith, Sarah 165
Smith, Tia 62
Snow, Dr. Alan Albert 220
Snyder, Joseph F. Jr. 127
Snyder, Rose E. 22
Sobel, David 8
Sobel, Moshe 128
Soltes, Eileen 161
Sorg, Justin 102
Sorrell, Tammy L. 109
Sorter, Evelyn M. 208
Sourk, Grant 81
Spackey, Frances 99
Spataro, Julie 130
Speer, Tera 174
Spence, Mark 110
Spencer, Linda Segui 86
Spencer, Steve 170
Sperske, June M. 164
Spinney, Erin Lee Snow 52
Spitnale, Casey 91
Spitnale, Lindsey 181
Spivey, Edwin P. 60
Springer, Tracie 166
St. Jean, Melinda 189
Stack, Catherine M. 161
Stadler, Tom 121
Staerkel, Matthan S. 106
Staley-Trull, Thomas 10
Staniszewski, Jill 131
Stanley, John 63
Steel, Alexis Renee 146
Steepy, Ruth E. 22
Stein, Susan G. 215

Steinmeyer, Robert Charles 51
Sterba, Libby 125
Stevens, Ashley 145
Stevens, Doris J. 123
Stewart, Eileen 74
Stewart, Olivia 181
Stiles, Stephanie J. 138
Still, Brad 69
Stinson, Misty 204
Stivala, Imelda Loreto 119
Stone, Christina L. 119
Stone, Emily 10
Stosberg, Tom 64
Strader, Brian J. 43
Strauser, Delores 55
Street, Megan 197
Strong, Charles A. 39
Stutzman, Amber 194
Suarez, Joseph 120
Sullivan, Sharon 106
Sulzer, Danielle 65
Sum, Diana 34
Suwyn, Janice A. 160
Swallows, Janice 213
Swinney, Harry E. 186
Sylva, Dale Ann 36

T

Taber, Debbie 67
Taft, Adrian 37
Talasek, Tarah 147
Tam, Erin 82
Tanton, Kathy Anne 204
Taurence, Mark A. 132
Taylor, Alexis M. 142
Taylor, Betty Jean 54
Taylor, Brittney 37
Taylor, Heather 116
Taylor, Holly 214
Taylor, Tabitha 70
Terlecki, G. M. 58
Thanickal, John 20
Thate, Karlie 162
Thelakkatt, Xavier 189
Therrien, Erica J. 69
Thom, Arthur E. 71
Thomas, Corrie 161
Thomas, Edward L. 223
Thomas, Eva M. 203
Thomas, Pauline 142
Thompson, Cheri 63
Thompson, Chris R. 116
Thompson, Coni 222
Thompson, Felicia 197
Thompson, Joan 179
Thompson, Lisa 67
Thomson, Martha 87
Thordarson, William 169
Tierney, Dan 105
Tijerina, Elenora 118
Tillmanns, Maria daVenza 73
Tims, Mildred H. 160
Tocci, Louis T. 60
Tompkins, Miranda 160
Toney, Virginia 178
Topping, Amber 91
Torelli, Christine A. 79
Torres, Amanda 163
Torres, Jesus BenHur R. 109
Torres, Veronica 68
Tootell, Jack 7
Townsend, David A. 4

Townsend, Wyatt 145
Trantham, Althea 149
Trantham, Rebecca J. 41
Traylor, Marcee 76
Traynor, Lonna 24
Trivedi, Shamita 31
Trosky, Shaun 179
Troxclair, Chandra 65
Trujillo, Matthew 162
Tse, Marie Audene 33
Tsertos, Nicolle 115
Tucker, Jason E. 144
Tudor, George Mason 192
Tuinstra, Tresa 115
Turman, Mary Ann 139
Turman, Shenise Marie 43
Turner, Edward D. 13
Tuttle, Rhonda J. 67
Twomey, Colleen A. 211
Tymony, Robert 176
Tyson, Judy 134

U

Uglow, Theresa K. 47
Updyke, Jennifer 98
Upham, Melissa Sorensen 158
Uris, Auren 17
Usher, Sarah O. 198
Uy, Jayme M. 113
Uzanas, Beverly Casey 36

V

Valtierra, Fernando 155
Van Norde, Kathy 169
Vandagriff, Oliver Kim 90
Vanderhoof, Vickie L. 17
Vandetta, Kimberly J. 71
VanHyfte, Crystal R. 155
Vazin, Ray 50
Vázquez, Jennie 159
Veach, Ralph J. 163
Velnich, Angela 203
Verderber, Karen 113
Verone, Rosann 85
Vianna, Manuel F. 115
Victor, Manzoor 96
Vieira, Josephine 135
Vigil, Mario 168
Villafuerte, Briana Dell 116
Villesvik, Karen 5
Villines, Corey 161
Vincent, Lorraine Walker 46
Vogel, Shannon 107
von Paffen, Louise R. 170
Vucinich, Cary 82

W

Waddle, Catherine 7
Wade, Kristen 149
Wagner, Ashley 109
Walker, Dan 120
Walker, Rodney T. 184
Walker, Willie 24
Wall, Ursula M. 40
Wallis, Olivia 182
Walsh, Herb 20
Walston, Maryann 218
Walters, Eric 171
Walton, Dona 69
Walton, Nick 23
Ward, Brigitte Moore 219

Warfield, Anne Marie 205
Wasserman, Martin M. 52
Watson, Craig 3
Watson, Dawn Jolin Shireman 74
Wattel, Jeanne-Helene 140
Watts, Stephen D. 200
Weant, Linda 180
Weant, Rev. Gary 172
Weber, Melissa 210
Weeks, Marta S. 159
Weems, Mary E. 148
Weggum, Per 177
Weible, Robert 64
Weideman, August 203
Weilnau, Duane E. 119
Weise, Scott 208
Weisenburger, Katie 34
Weller, Stephanie 56
Wells, Kaley 160
West, Kathleen E. 167
West, Narice 167
West, Sharon 100, 220
Wetherby, Jeanne 124
Wethey, Edward E. 137
Wheatcroft, Anita 205
Wheaton, Scott E. 72
Wheeler, John A. Jr. 70
Wheeler, Tammy 163
White, Christy 159
White, Jewel 68
White, Joshua Seth 131
White, Lela Gayles 112
White, Timothy R. 90
Whitford, Kathryne 126
Whitson, Danelle 107
Whitten, Cathy 132
Whitworth, John Wayne, Jr. 91
Wick, Natasha N. 133
Wicker, Ashlie 62
Wickham, Patti Paz 124
Wiesinger, Janice C. 132
Wigington, Sheila 38
Wilbur, Sarah 69
Wiley, Dr. Larry A. 29
Wiley, June 21
Wilkin, Jennifer 33
Wilkinson, Maggie 217
Willard, Sandra K. 114
Williams, Brenda 220
Williams, Charlotte M. 53
Williams, Curtis 127
Williams, Dorothy O'Brien 115
Williams, Jennifer 75
Williams, Kimberly 117
Williams, Lynn 176
Williams, O. Avaris B. 155
Williams, Steven R. 61
Williamson, Anthony E., Sr. 100
Williamson, Chris 152
Willihnganz, Kaitlin 58
Willing, Stephanie 145
Willis, Tonya 59
Wilson, Deborah 137
Wilson, Michael 133
Wilson, Michelle 165
Wilson, Pauline 119
Wilson, Samantha 119
Wilson, Sandra L. 192
Wilson, Sean 181
Winfrey, Victoria J. 209
Wingenbach, Melinda 124
Wingo, Ellen 120
Winkel, Jessie D. 81

Winters, Stacey D. 148
Winters, Tammy 118
Witt, Agnes 101
Wnuk, Emma Marie 168
Wojcuich, Linda Coffey 36
Wold, Amber 188
Wolf, Marcus 42
Wolfinger, Sophia 143
Woltjer, Matthew 212
Wood, Alexis 27
Wood, Elisabeth 199
Wood, Glenn M. 135
Wood, Jeanne 16
Wood, Ryan 196
Woodard, Karen Parrish 49
Woods, Richard Sr. 37
Word, Allison 53
Worline, Kristina 116
Wormley, J. Bernice 219
Wright, Christian 212
Wright, Justin Eriel Herring 171
Wyland, Carrie 205
Wynn, Christen 68

Y

Yamada, Camilla 153
Yanni, Mary 156
Yarborough, Kathryn 143
Yavich, Dina 124
Yearwood, Stephen Allistair 66
Yenner, Francine 26
Yergey, Marilyn E. 153
Yi, Christina 176
Yomes, Patricia Ellabelle Mae 103
Youells, Anna 169
Young, Brandi 79
Young, June E. 178
Young, Melinda E. 118
Young-Hodges, Shirley 176

Z

Zadrowski, Mikki 167
Zahradnick, Robert F. 115
Zappa, Karen E., RN 46
Zarabi, Sherry 76
Zarzyczny, Phyllis 157
Zeanah, Robert C. 140
Zebarth, Sonya 189
Zehmisch, Tara 75
Zimmerman, Sophia 5
Zizka, Rose 168
Zolan, Ness 215
Zuccaro, Lucinda Brant 2